PUBLIC CHOICE CONCEPTS AND APPLICATIONS IN LAW

∎ ∎ ∎

By

Maxwell L. Stearns
Professor of Law and Marbury Research Professor
University of Maryland School of Law

Todd J. Zywicki
George Mason University Foundation Professor of Law
George Mason University School of Law

AMERICAN CASEBOOK SERIES®

WEST®
A Thomson Reuters business

Mat #40556308

American Casebook Series is a trademark registered in the U.S. Patent and Trademark Office.

© 2009 Thomson Reuters

    610 Opperman Drive
    St. Paul, MN 55123
    1–800–313–9378

Printed in the United States of America

ISBN: 978–0–314–17722–3

To Vered, Shira, Keren and Eric

MS

To Kim and Claire

TZ

*

FOREWORD

In this book, Max Stearns and Todd Zywicki show how public choice theory can illuminate our understanding of legal issues. Although the book is designed for classroom use, it also provides an invaluable resource for scholars through its synthesis of the current state-of-the-art. All of those who work in the field owe the authors a debt of gratitude for this comprehensive and lucid overview.

A brief description of public choice may help to put their accomplishment in context. Public choice applies the tools of economists to the problems of political science. But there is a difference in emphasis. Economics is often a narrative of collective success, at least in terms of total social welfare. Economists see markets as successful institutions with problems, not pathology-prone institutions that can sometimes be nudged into producing good results. By contrast, public choice theory is typically a story of political pathologies and struggles to overcome them. In politics, unlike markets, theorists do not see an invisible hand that converts individual choices into desirable societal outcomes. Indeed, it is the role of government to act precisely when the invisible hand has failed.

The absence of an invisible hand in politics means that political decisions must be made collectively, and this simple fact creates two problems. The first problem, which is explored in depth in Chapter 2 of the book, is that it is costly and time-consuming to contribute to group decisions. It is frequently easier for small groups of people with high stakes to make this investment than it is for large groups of people with diffuse interests. The result is that special interests may prevail over the broader public welfare.

The second difficulty in collective action, which is the subject of Chapter 3, is the inherent messiness involved in combining individual preferences into a group decision. Over fifty years ago, Kenneth Arrow proved that no voting method can aggregate individual preferences in a minimally reasonable way (including, for example, that there be no single person who can dictate the group outcome). The most common manifestation of this inherent limitation on group decision making is Condorcet's paradox, where the group may prefer option a to option b and option b to option c, but then prefer option c to option a.

The earliest work in public choice tended to focus on how the inherent problems of collective action deflect policy from maximizing social welfare. One way of describing the evolution of the field is to say that these inherent problems are now often seen as the background conditions of politics, significant mostly because of the institutions and behaviors that are necessary to overcome them and create effective democratic governance. In this mode,

Stearns and Zywicki not only pinpoint distortions in collective decision-making but ingeniously explore a variety of corrective measures.

Why is this research on governance relevant to law? The reason is that law is a collective enterprise, involving Constitutions adopted by whole societies (and designed to govern future collective actions), statutes adopted by legislatures, and judicial rulings by multimember courts. All of these group decision-making processes involve the very challenges that public choice theory studies.

Thus, public choice theory can provide new insights on difficult legal issues. Stearns and Zywicki demonstrate these insights repeatedly, in connection with legal issues ranging from the constitutionality of state taxes to the use of eminent domain to assist private developers, and from theories of statutory interpretation to perplexing issues in the application of precedent. Public choice unquestionably has something to add to our understanding of these issues.

This does not mean that public choice provides definitive answers. "Often," as Stearns and Zywicki say, "public choice analysis will complement intuitions drawn from other disciplines, and other times it will encourage us to reconsider these intuitions. But any complete analysis will inevitably depend upon a combination of analytical approaches." Yet even without being definitive, ideas drawn from public choice can add a new and often unexpected perspective on crucial issues.

Public Choice Concepts and Applications in Law is amply deserving of careful study and a wide audience among legal scholars. It is a great pleasure to have this opportunity to introduce this groundbreaking book to readers.

DAN FARBER
Berkeley
July 17, 2009

PREFACE

Public choice theory, a discipline that marries the tools of economics with the subject of political science, has emerged a dominant force in modern legal scholarship and jurisprudential analysis. While key term searches provide only a rough proxy for the importance of any methodological approach to law, it is nonetheless notable that at the time of this writing, the Westlaw JLR database finds approximately 8400 citations for the term "public choice," 4000 for the term "rent seeking," 2800 for "social choice," and over 3200 for "prisoners' dilemma" (or "prisoner's dilemma").

Of course the frequency of citation understates the profound impact public choice theory has had on the law in recent decades. Superficial references to any external discipline or analytical concept, for example, might not reveal that something more foundational is happening concerning the role that such a discipline or any specific concept has played—or is continuing to play—in influencing modern thinking about important questions of law and public policy. In this instance, the importance of public choice transcends citation counts.

Public choice theory has emerged an essential part of the modern legal scholarship landscape because it provides a means of closing the gap between the normative prescriptions associated with the traditional economic analysis of law, on the one hand, and the observed realities of legal practice and doctrine, which so often resist wide ranging calls for reform, on the other. Public choice is not merely an antidote, or complement, to the neoclassical law and economics scholarly tradition. Instead, public choice presents its own independent set of tools that provide the means for restoring a positive analysis of, and appreciation for, some of the most confounding features of law and public policy.

For this reason, it might not be surprising that many prominent legal scholars have increasingly relied upon public choice tools to study law and lawmaking institutions. These scholars have produced an impressive array of books. Without wishing to exclude other excellent contributions to this field, many of which we discuss in this volume, the following partial list helps both to situate this book and to demonstrate its unique qualities even as compared with these major scholarly contributions. The following books have greatly influenced our thinking as we developed this book:

Douglas G. Baird; Robert H. Gertner & Randal C. Picker, *Game Theory and the Law* (1994)

Robert Cooter, *The Strategic Constitution* (2000)

Daniel A. Farber & Philip P. Frickey, *Law and Public Choice: A Critical Introduction* (1991)

Daniel Farber & Anne Joseph O'Connell eds., *Elgar Handbook in Public Choice and Public Law* (Forthcoming 2009)

Jerry L. Mashaw, *Greed, Chaos, and Governance: Using Public Choice to Improve Public Law* (1997)

Dennis C. Mueller, *Public Choice III* (2003)(along with the earlier editions)

Dennis C. Mueller, ed., *Perspectives on Public Choice: A Handbook* (1997)

Each of these books—and others that we discuss in this volume—are important to students, and scholars, who seek to broaden their understanding of the implications of public choice for legal doctrine and lawmaking institutions. And yet, none fill the need served by this book. In this single volume, accompanied by an active and ongoing webpage, we introduce students in law, along with interested students in other disciplines, to the essential tools of public choice analysis and to the implications of these tools for lawmaking institutions and legal doctrines. Our approach combines positive and normative analyses. It also offers systematic comparisons of a public choice approach to carefully selected topics across the vast landscape of public and private law to approaches from other disciplines, including most notably traditional tools of legal analysis and law and economics.

Most legal scholars today acknowledge the central role that economic analysis plays within law school curricula, in legal scholarship, and in the concrete setting of adjudication across fields too numerous to mention. For this reason, virtually every law school in the United States, and many law schools throughout the world, offer courses or seminars on law and economics. Even skeptics of law and economics increasingly acknowledge the importance of addressing claims by scholars influenced by an economics methodology in their work. While such scholarship offers the basis for an important external critique that challenges the premises of law and economics, public choice analysis offers a critique of the economic analysis of law from within. Using an economic analysis as the camera, public choice adds a wide angle lens, thus broadening the scope of inquiry to include not only the effect of regulation on markets, but also the effect of group behavior on wide ranging institutions, including legislatures, executives (and agencies), and courts. This broader perspective carries profound implications for law and public policy that sometimes complement and sometimes run in tension with perspectives drawn from other disciplines.

Public choice is not an adjunct to law and economics. The disciplines are better thought of as analytical cousins, and both of us have successfully taught this course to students who have had no prior exposure to economic analysis of law (or indeed to economics), to Ph.D. economists, and to a wide range of students in between. We have also taught this subject to American law students and to students abroad. While we draw heavily on applications from within the United States, the methodological approach transcends any specific set of institutions.

Legal scholars and economists have long recognized that public policy recommendations are only as meaningful as the ability of institutional actors to implement them consistently with intended objectives. While it was once common to claim that a market failure demanded regulatory intervention, sophisticated policymakers now appreciate that they must first inquire whether governmental intervention is likely to improve or exacerbate the problem under review. Answering that question demands a careful understanding of the relevant institutions.

Perhaps for that very reason, it is not surprising that an impressive cohort of Nobel Prize winning economists have played a foundational role in the study of public choice and its implications for law and public policy:[1] Kenneth Arrow (1972), James M. Buchanan (1986), George Stigler (1982), Gary Becker (1992), and Douglass C. North (1993). Still other Nobel laureates, whose primary contributions lie elsewhere, have nonetheless improved our understanding of how public choice informs public policy: F.A. Hayek (1974), Milton Friedman (1976), Ronald Coase (1991), William Vickrey (1996), Amartya Sen (1998), Vernon Smith (2002), and Thomas Schelling (2005). It is a privilege to imagine that with this volume, and through courses designed around it, we will introduce a new generation of law students to contributions of these and other great thinkers whose works remain central to appreciating foundational aspects of law, public policy, and lawmaking institutions.

The implications of public choice theory cut across broad areas of a standard law school curriculum running the gamut literally from A to Z: Administrative Law, Bankruptcy Law, Choice of Law, Constitutional Law (both Governance and Individual Rights), Corporate Law, Criminal Procedure, Evidence, Federal Courts, Jurisprudence, Legislation, Local Government and Finance, Tax Law and Policy, and Zoning Law. And yet, despite its broad implications, exposure to public choice in law school curricula presently remains haphazard and unsystematic, driven by the peculiarities of particular subject areas, the predilections of the professor, and the pedagogical preferences of casebook editors.

We believe that providing a systematic introduction to public choice theory that uses methodological tools to inform a range of legal subjects— rather than relying upon specific legal subjects to pick up occasional methodological tools—best serves the interests of law students and those in other disciplines who seek to broaden their understanding of the implications of this emerging field. Certainly this has been our experience in over seventeen years of teaching public choice to law students. We have also learned that a more comprehensive approach is essential to avoiding the risk of superficial invocation of concepts—rent seeking and the prisoners' dilemma come to mind—as catch-all phrases designed to encourage a particular result without careful consideration of the broader implications of these and other public choice tools for the policy under consideration.

Throughout the book, we rigorously distinguish the positive and normative implications of public choice theory for the questions we present. In fact,

---

1. For a complete listing of recipients of the Bank of Sweden Prize in Economic Sciences in Memory of Alfred Nobel 2008–1969, more commonly referred to as the Nobel Prize in Economics, see http://nobelprizes.com/nobel/economics/economics.html (last visited July 26, 2009). The year identifies when each listed recipient obtained the Nobel Prize.

we deliberately juxtapose competing perspectives by scholars who despite applying common public choice tools come to opposing conclusions as to the implication of those tools for any given policy question. One of the underlying themes of this book is teaching students not only what specific scholars have said, but also how to actively engage in independent qualitative assessments of (often conflicting) scholarly claims.

This book also exposes students to the essential concepts of constructing economic models and hypothesis testing. Much of law school education, by necessity, involves training students in how to construct of arguments to justify particular outcomes. After all, lawyers represent clients, and clients appear on both sides of any given dispute. We believe nonetheless that legal education benefits from complementing this important pedagogical technique with one that encourages the development of higher order theories that can be tested against observed realities. Throughout the book, we not only present the various theories of public choice, but also wide ranging empirical works of economists, political scientists, historians, and law professors that are designed to test hypotheses drawn from public choice theory and to explore the theory's promise and to test its limitations.

While public choice often is dismissed as being unduly "cynical" or "pessimistic" about the promise of governmental action, we could not disagree more strongly. Indeed, we think that the value of public choice is in providing a *realistic*, and often *restorative*, understanding of collective action and institutions. Public choice helps to restore confidence by demonstrating the inherent limits with any institution and the remarkable adaptation of actual lawmaking institutions in overcoming many (although certainly not all) of the problems that many scholars have too quickly determined to be intractable. As with economics generally, if there is value in the methodology of public choice, that value derives from its ability to help us better understand complex phenomena and institutions that we observe in the real world. By and large we believe that public choice in its various forms provides the basis for developing meaningful constructs respecting both the promise and limits of collective action and respecting the institutions that transform collective inputs into public policy. More importantly, we believe that public choice demonstrates that converting good ideas into sound policies requires an extensive understanding of the incentives of those who produce policy and of citizens who hold governmental officials in the public trust. Public choice helps to illuminate the ways in which specific institutional actors—flesh-and-blood legislators, judges, and bureaucrats—interact, and how differing institutions operate individually and in combination.

This book is divided into three parts, the first two of which are contained in this volume. Part I introduces the basic analytical tools of public choice. Chapter 1 provides an introduction to economic reasoning and its implications for law and institutions, with a specific focus on rationality, free riders and holdouts, opportunity cost, various concepts of efficiency, and basic microeconomic theory (including an Appendix that serves as a primer on price theory). Chapter 2 introduces interest group theory and explores the role of groups in affecting institutional processes in legislatures, courts, and agencies. Chapter

3 introduces social choice theory and demonstrates how various institutions process individual or constituent preferences into collective outcomes, and explores how institutional rationality affects decisions to assign lawmaking tasks to specific organs of government. Chapter 4 introduces elementary game theory and presents a set of cooperative and non-cooperative games that help to inform how incentives motivate desirable (or inhibit undesirable) behavior. Together, these four chapters provide the basic tools of public choice. Throughout these chapters (and the book as a whole) we altogether avoid mathematical presentations in favor of clear expositional analyses tied to concrete illustrations at every analytical step.

Part II turns to a systematic analysis of the four most important collective decision making institutions for the study of law: the Legislature (Chapter 5), the Executive Branch and Administrative Agencies (Chapter 6), the Judiciary (Chapter 7), and Constitutions (Chapter 8). These chapters present wide-ranging approaches to each institution under review and explore these institutions from the combined perspectives introduced in part I. This part also explores the role of institutional complementarity in affecting outcomes and in improving the seemingly intractable problems that social choice reveals any single institution would confront if operating alone. Each chapter, including those in part I, concludes with (or embeds) illustrations based upon actual cases or other primary source materials. These materials allow students, with their professors, to test the various theories in concrete doctrinal or public policy settings. Each chapter is also interspersed with questions, some of which admit of correct (or at least more plausible) answers, and others of which are specifically designed to foster open-ended classroom discussion.

Part III, which can be found at our on-line website, which accompanies this bound volume, provides a series of applications of public choice to various subject areas of law.[2] These include such areas as the antitrust, commerce clause, corporate and bankruptcy law, environmental law, equal protection, the non-delegation doctrine, standing, and others. The materials in Part III can be used as optional course teaching materials or as basic research tools. We plan to update the selection in this part of the book as public choice scholarship develops in new areas of law. We will also include instructional materials in the form of a Teacher's Manual and sample syllabi. And with permission, we will post successful research papers that students have produced in our classes and that other instructors send us for this purpose.

The bound volume (containing Parts I and II) serves as the basis for a complete course on public choice and the law for those who elect to use it that way. Depending on the instructor's preferred pace of coverage, each chapter (or subparts of each chapter) can be used for one or two weeks in a seminar or course. If taught at the pace of one chapter per week, the topical materials in Part III can fill out the remaining weeks of the semester (or quarter). One benefit of this approach is that the instructor can select specific topics of particular interest to him or her and to his or her students. This book, or

---

2. Instructions on how to obtain access to the Part III materials appear at the end of the Preface.

portions of it, is also designed for use as a supplement to other courses for which a public choice analysis can add a meaningful dimension. Such courses include, but are not limited to, Administrative Law, Jurisprudence, Law and Economics, and Legislation.

Readers of this book will quickly learn that the real value of public choice is in expanding the power of students of law (and of related disciplines) to consider *how* to think about legal questions, rather than in suggesting any particular set of outcomes. Oftentimes public choice, and especially scholars who rely on the combined set of tools under that broad umbrella, do not speak with a single voice; in fact, such scholars frequently disagree about the implications of public choice for outcomes as sharply as legal scholars more generally. The more critical point, however, is that those lawyers equipped with these tools will be more effective advocates, and more informed policy makers, than those who are not.

Because we focus on the practical implications of public choice, we set aside certain questions that assume central importance in a course on public choice theory taught to graduate students in economics or political science. In particular, we do not instruct how to develop formal mathematical models or how to comprise large number data bases for empirical testing, although we will refer to studies relying upon such methods where appropriate.

Public choice has been described as an umbrella discipline beneath which stand two complementary disciplines: interest group theory and social choice theory. In this book, we also include elementary game theory (and price theory) as those tools help to inform the public choice analyses of law and lawmaking institutions. In addition, public choice theory has historically developed with reference to three geographically, and conceptually, distinct schools of thought: the Chicago School, the Virginia School, and the Rochester School,[3] and graduate curricula were largely influenced by which school or schools most influenced the professor's preferred approach or methodology (and quite often, where he or she trained).

Each of these schools boasts major contributions to the discipline of public choice and to how public choice informs our understanding of law. The Chicago School has produced leading works by George Stigler, Gary Becker, and others, and has focused in large part on the role of interest groups in affecting the nature and efficacy of regulatory policy. The Virginia School, which boasts as contributions *The Calculus of Consent* by James Buchanan and Gordon Tullock, and works by Robert Tollison, Nicolaus Tideman, and others, has largely focused on specific features of institutional design as they affect the formulation of law and public policy. The Rochester School, associated most notably with the impressive body of work by William Riker, has tended to focus on how the dynamics of decision-making processes affect outcomes within legislatures and other institutions. Major contributors to social choice include Kenneth Arrow, Duncan Black, and William Vickrey, whose works have greatly influenced our thinking in developing this book.

---

3. For an overview of each of these schools, *see* MAXWELL L. STEARNS, *Preface, in* PUBLIC CHOICE AND PUBLIC LAW: READINGS AND COMMENTARY (1997) and Charles Rowley, *Introduction, in* PUBLIC CHOICE THEORY (Charles K. Rowley ed., 1993).

Any discussion of public choice must also include two major contributors who, for a time, were colleagues at the University of Maryland Department of Economics. Two leading works by Mancur Olson, *The Logic of Collective Action* (1971), and *The Rise and Decline of Nations: Economic Growth, Stagflation and Social Rigidities* (1982), even in the years following his passing, continue to serve as part of the essential lexicon of public choice. And of course, Dennis Mueller, now Emeritus Professor of Economics at the University of Vienna, has produced, among other works, three numbered editions of his invaluable encyclopedic work, appropriate titled *Public Choice*, with the result for many of us of rendering his name practically synonymous with the discipline.

Although it would be mistaken to say that the "schools" of public choice are merely geographic reference points or historical markers, by and large most scholars tend to borrow across them as is helpful in analyzing specific problems under review. Similarly, the once distinct fields of interest group theory, social choice theory, and game theory (and even price theory) now generally form the basis for combined, and more dynamic, modeling of myriad institutions and rules. This book deliberately forges a fluid approach in integrating the most useful tools and techniques from all these schools and disciplines based on their ability to illuminate legal institutions and policy questions. We are confident that as you, or your students, delve into these materials, you too will share our enthusiasm for this developing field.

Acknowledgements

For both of us, this book represents the culmination of longstanding research projects. Our thinking was undoubtedly influenced not only by comments given on this manuscript, or individual chapters, but also by comments on the separate works we each produced throughout our careers. While it is not possible to acknowledge everyone who ever commented on our prior scholarship, we sincerely thank everyone who has taken the time to make us better scholars by reading, commenting on, and criticizing our earlier works. With respect to this specific project, we owe many thanks. Among those who read and commented on earlier drafts of various parts of the book were Steven Brams, Kelly Casey, Eric Claeys, Eric Crampton, Lee Epstein, Mark Graber, Nathan Jones, Martin Kraus, Saul Levmore, Joseph Oppenheimer, Eric Rasmusen, Bill Reynolds, Nathan Sales, Gilles Serra, Daniel Sokol, Ilya Somin, Sam Vermont, and Joshua Wright. We would especially like to thank Saul Levmore of the University of Chicago Law School and Don Boudreaux of George Mason University, who taught draft chapters in manuscript form. We also thank Ryan Pfeifer and Louis Higgins at West for helpful feedback and for their constant support, Aaron Cabbage for his assistance in helping to develop the webpage, and Jan Pluff and Kathleen Vandergon for converting our manuscript into book form.

Special thanks are in order to two former Deans, and the present Dean, at George Mason University School of Law. When Max first joined the George Mason Law School faculty in 1992, Henry Manne asked him to develop a course in public choice. At that time, there was no suitable book for course length treatment for law students. This inspired what eventually became the first set of materials designed for student use in public choice and the law, Maxwell L. Stearns, *Public Choice and Public Law: Readings and Commentary* (1997). We thank Anderson Publishing Company for its generosity in releasing its copyright to allow us to adapt portions of that volume for inclusion in this book and on our webpage. This book supersedes, updates, and broadens that earlier book, retaining those features that have served students well and discarding others that have proved less successful over time. Those familiar with the earlier volume will see that this book is truly an original work, both in style, scope, and substance. In addition, Maxwell L. Stearns, *Constitutional Process: A Social Choice Analysis of Supreme Court Decision Making* (paperback ed. 2002) substantially contributed to the development of materials especially informing chapters 3 and 7. We also appreciate the permission that the University of Michigan Press has granted to allow us to adapt relevant portions of that earlier work to benefit this volume. Unlike either of these earlier works, this book is a collaborative effort that has undoubtedly benefitted from the differing expertise and perspectives of its two authors.

Shortly after Todd joined the faculty at the George Mason University School of Law in 2001, Dean Mark Grady and then-Associate Dean (and current Dean) Dan Polsby, granted our request to team teach public choice. That class started us on the path culminating in this book. While these materials were in draft, we have continued to enjoy teaching jointly on a more limited basis by guest lecturing in each other's seminars at the George Mason University School of Law and the University of Maryland School of Law (where Max now teaches) respectively. (And just to show that we do take rationality to heart, depending on where you are, there is always a good chance one of us might be quite willing to come give a guest lecture in your class!)

Max Stearns would like to thank the Dean Emeritus Karen Rothenberg and Dean Phoebe Haddon of the University of Maryland School of Law for their past and ongoing support. My recently renewed Marbury Research Professorship, a three-year rotating research professorship, has afforded me critical time to work on the early writing stages of this manuscript. I would like to thank the following for their research assistance (both at the University of Maryland and George Mason University): Colleen Clary, Brandon Draper, Christine Kymm, Meaghan McCann, Joseph Meyers, David Myers, Ed O'Shea, Heather Pruger, Brian Woodbury and Jason Zappasodi. I owe a special acknowledgement to Professor Glen O. Robinson, of the University of Virginia School of Law, to whom I asked the following question during my second year of law school: If the President is smart about it, wouldn't he be more likely to use the item veto to direct legislative policy than to get rid of special interest (or pork barrel) legislation? The ensuing conversation led to an independent study during which Professor Robinson for the first time introduced me to a body of literature called public choice. This not only resulted in my first article using these tools, and a related separate article by Professor Robinson (both discussed in chapter 8), but also set me on a long path exploring the implications of public choice in all its dimensions for law and public policy.

I also want to thank all of the students to whom I have taught public choice since I began teaching in 1992. Their input has provided me with great insight (and hopefully accumulated wisdom) in seeing what does and does not work and in appreciating just how important this subject is for those students who elect to include it in their training. I have taught public choice to students at George Mason University School of Law, the University of Florida School of Law, the University of Maryland School of Law, the University of Michigan School of Law, Tel Aviv University Buchmann Faculty of Law (Tel Aviv, Israel), and Brisbane University School of Law (Brisbane, Australia). I thank Dan Farber and Anne O'Connell for inviting me to contribute the introductory chapter on social choice to the *Elgar Handbook on Public Choice*, and the several contributors to that volume who have generously shared their drafts in progress with Todd and me as we prepared this book.

I am especially indebted to the phenomenal library support staff at the University of Maryland School of Law, which is truly second to none. Sue McCarty deserves special mention for her never ending generosity and her willingness to share her depth of expertise in writing and in producing published work of the highest quality during virtually every stage of production. The quality of the book is substantially improved as a result of her constant dedication and hard work, which extends beyond the specific items for which she is listed below. Sue McCarty and Alice Johnson read the manuscript for citation form and for substantive cite checking. Janet Sinder provided support in finding too many obscure sources to count. Jeffrey Elliott provided diligent and patient work on permissions requests that Sue McCarty organized and arranged for final publication. I am indebted to LuAnn Marshall, who patiently and painstakingly created exemplary graphics and tables throughout the volume and to Paul Bohman (of the George Mason University School of Law), who provided great assistance in developing the artful graphics that appear in chapters 6 and 8. Ed O'Shea, a recent GMU law graduate, provided tremendous assistance on discrete research related to various chapters, including especially chapter 6. Brian Woodbury, also a recent GMU law graduate, provided special assistance in cite checking and formatting chapter 4. Together, Ed O'Shea and Brian Woodbury developed the remarkably thorough Table of Authorities. Richard Shafer produced an outstanding subject matter index.

I thank my parents, Herb and Audrey Stearns, who instilled a constant curiosity about the world that has provided the foundation for a lifelong love of learning. Most of all, I thank my wife, Vered, and my three children, Shira, Keren, and Eric, without whose patience, love, and affection this book would not have been possible, and for so often reminding me that the most valuable things in life might not always seem rational.

In addition to those who Max thanked for their contributions to this volume, Todd Zywicki would like to thank Dean Dan Polsby of George Mason University School of Law who encouraged this project throughout. I would also like to thank my professors at the Clemson University Department of Economics who exposed me to public choice theory as part of my Masters' Degree program, including Bill Dougan, David Laband, Bobby McCormick, Roger Meiners, Robert Staaf, and Bruce Yandle. Roger Meiners served as my Masters' Thesis advisor on a public choice analysis of the Seventeenth Amendment and Bruce Yandle encouraged me to pursue public choice analysis of environmental law and regulation.

I also benefited from being first a student in and later a lecturer at the annual Public Choice Outreach Seminar sponsored by the George Mason University Public Choice Center and from invitations to lecture in the Institute for Justice's Summer Seminar for Law Students and Institute for Humane Studies summer programs. Special thanks to Donald Boudreaux, Chip Mellor, and Marty Zupan for the invitations that made those opportunities possible. I would also like to especially thank the Searle Foundation for its generosity in sponsoring me as a Searle Fellow at George Mason University School of Law during the Fall 2008 semester, which permitted time to work on this project. I am indebted to the Hoover Institution, where I was a W. Glenn Campbell and Rita Ricardo–Campbell National Fellow and the Arch W. Shaw National Fellow during the 2008–09 year for a congenial stay during which some work on the book was completed. I am also indebted to the George Mason University School of Law and the Law and Economics Center at George Mason University School of Law for financial support. I would like to thank my students in my public choice class both at George Mason and at Georgetown Law School. Most importantly, I would like to thank Kim and Claire, for their patience, love, and support during the several years this project was being completed, and my parents, Henry and Jo Ann Zywicki, to whom I owe the greatest debt of all.

MAXWELL L. STEARNS
Professor of Law and
Marbury Research Professor
University of Maryland
School of Law
Baltimore, Maryland

TODD ZYWICKI
George Mason University
Foundation Professor of Law
George Mason University
School of Law
Arlington, Virginia

Instructions Regarding Part III Materials

Students purchasing these materials for classroom instruction will obtain supplemental materials through their courses. Other purchasers may obtain access by sending an email request that includes your name, email address, and, if appropriate, your institutional affiliation to publicchoiceconcepts@gmail.com.

Copyright Acknowledgements

The authors thankfully acknowledge permission to reprint materials from the following works:

Michael Abramowicz & Maxwell L. Stearns, *Beyond Counting Votes: The Political Economy of* Bush v. Gore, 54 VAND. L. REV. 1849 (2001). Copyright 2001 by Vanderbilt Law Review. Reproduced with permission of Vanderbilt Law Review from VANDERBILT LAW REVIEW, Michael Abramowicz and Maxwell L. Stearns, Vol. 54, No. 5, © 2001; permission conveyed through Copyright Clearance Center, Inc.

Bruce A. Ackerman, *Beyond* Carolene Products, 98 HARV. L. REV. 713 (1985). Copyright 1985 by Harvard Law Review Association. Reproduced with permission of Harvard Law Review Association from HARVARD LAW REVIEW, Bruce A. Ackerman, Vol. 98, No. 4, © 1985; permission conveyed through Copyright Clearance Center, Inc.

Ian Ayres, *Playing Games with the Law*, 42 STAN. L. REV. 1291 (1990). Copyright 1989 by Stanford Law Review. Reproduced with permission of Stanford Law Review from STANFORD LAW REVIEW, Ian Ayres, Vol. 42, No. 5, © 1990; permission conveyed through Copyright Clearance Center, Inc.

DOUGLAS G. BAIRD, ROBERT H. GERTNER, & RANDAL C. PICKER, GAME THEORY AND THE LAW (1994). Reprinted by permission of the publisher from GAME THEORY AND THE LAW by Douglas G. Baird, Robert H. Gertner and Randal C. Picker, pp. 21, 37, 313, Cambridge, Mass.: Harvard University Press, Copyright © 1994 by the President and Fellows of Harvard College.

WILLIAM J. BAUMOL & ALAN S. BLINDER, ECONOMICS: PRINCIPLES AND POLICY 217 (10th ed. 2006). From Baumol/Blinder ECONOMICS, 10E. © 2006 South–Western, a part of Cengage Learning, Inc. Reproduced by permission. www.cengage.com/permissions.

JAMES M. BUCHANAN & GORDON TULLOCK, THE CALCULUS OF CONSENT: LOGICAL FOUNDATIONS OF CONSTITUTIONAL DEMOCRACY (1962). Reprinted by permission. Copyright © by the University of Michigan Press 1962.

Steven P. Croley, *Theories of Regulation: Incorporating the Administrative Process*, 98 COLUM. L. REV. 1 (1998). Copyright 1998 by Columbia Law Review

MAX STEARNS, PUBLIC CHOICE AND PUBLIC LAW: READINGS AND COMMENTARY (1997). Copyright 1997 by Matthew Bender & Company. Reproduced with permission of Matthew Bender & Company from PUBLIC CHOICE AND PUBLIC LAW: READINGS AND COMMENTARY, Maxwell L. Stearns © 1997; permission conveyed through Copyright Clearance Center, Inc.

Matthew Stevenson, *Legislative Allocation of Delegated Power: Uncertainty, Risk, and the Choice Between Agencies and Courts*, 119 HARV. L. REV. 1035 (2006). Copyright 2006 by Harvard Law Review Association. Reproduced with permission of Harvard Law Review Association from HARVARD LAW REVIEW, Matthew Stevenson, Vol. 119, No. 4, © 2006; permission conveyed through Copyright Clearance Center, Inc.

James Q. Wilson, *The Politics of Regulation, in* THE POLITICS OF REGULATION 357 (1980). Copyright 1980 by James Q Wilson. Reproduced with permission of James Q Wilson from THE POLITICS OF REGULATION, James Q. Wilson, © 1980; permission conveyed through Copyright Clearance Center, Inc.

Ralph K. Winter, Jr., *Economic Regulation vs. Competition: Ralph Nader and Creeping Capitalism*, 82 YALE L.J. 890 (1973). Copyright 1973 by Yale Law Journal Company, Inc. Reproduced with permission of Yale Law Journal Company, Inc. from YALE LAW JOURNAL, Ralph K. Winter, Jr., Vol. 82, No. 5, © 1973; permission conveyed through Copyright Clearance Center, Inc.

Donald Wittman, *Candidate Motivation: A Synthesis of Alternative Theories*, 77 AM. POL. SCI. REV. 142 (1983). Copyright 1983 by the American Political Science Association. Reprinted with the permission of the Cambridge University Press.

Todd J. Zywicki, *The Rise and Fall of Efficiency in the Common Law: A Supply–Side Analysis*, 97 NW. U. L. REV. 1551 (2003). Reprinted by special permission of Northwestern University School of Law, *Northwestern University Law Review*.

*

Summary of Contents

TABLE OF CONTENTS

*

TABLE OF AUTHORITIES

The principal cases are in bold type. Cases cited or discussed in the text are in roman type. References are to pages. Cases cited in principal cases and within other quoted materials are not included.

CASES

FEDERAL STATUTES

STATE STATUTES

OTHER OFFICIAL MATERIALS

OTHER SOURCES

ARTICLES, BOOKS AND OTHER COMMENTARY

PUBLIC CHOICE CONCEPTS AND APPLICATIONS IN LAW

*

CHAPTER 1

INTRODUCTION TO THE ECONOMIC ANALYSIS OF COLLECTIVE DECISION MAKING

■ ■ ■

Introduction

Public choice applies the methodology of economics to the subject matter of political science. In recent decades, scholars writing in such disciplines as political science, economics, and law have expanded the scope of public choice to study the closely related subject areas of law and the legal process. Extending public choice to study law and lawmaking institutions is natural. The institutional focus of political science bears striking similarities to the institutional focus of law including especially public law. And yet, the public choice methodology is notably different from the doctrinal approach that legal scholars generally employ. Quite often the two disciplines suggest different implications for the same legal doctrine or policy. Perhaps more notably, public choice sometimes also suggests different implications concerning questions of legal policy, respecting both public and private law, than does its analytical cousin, law and economics.

The study of law and economics, which began in the middle part of the twentieth century, gained substantial traction within large segments of the legal academy beginning in the 1980s.[1] Law and economics has since developed into an established and widely respected approach to the study of legal policy.[2] Early scholars writing in the field applied principles of economic reasoning, with a heavy emphasis on neoclassical price theory and its concomitant emphasis on microeconomic efficiency, to study substantive common law rules. While economic analysis had long been associated with antitrust law, it soon became notable for providing "positive," or descriptive, accounts of longstanding doctrines of contract, tort, and

---

1. Among the reasons was the influence, and controversy, provoked by the first edition of Richard Posner's famous treatise, RICHARD A. POSNER, ECONOMIC ANALYSIS OF LAW (1973), a book now in its seventh edition.

2. *See* Bryant G. Garth, *Strategic Research in Law and Society*, 18 FLA. ST. U. L. REV. 57, 59 (1990) ("[L]aw and economics represents the one example of a social science that has successfully found a place at the core of the legal arguments made in courts, administrative agencies, and other legal settings.").

property, that when viewed strictly through the analytical frameworks set out in judicial opinions often appeared imprecise or even internally inconsistent.[3] More recently, scholars have broadened the focus of law and economics to offer valuable insights into wide ranging bodies of both public and private law, including, for example, civil procedure, tax, and even family law.[4]

The differing analytical approaches of law and economics and public choice can roughly be described as follows. Law and economics directly shines the light of economics onto legal doctrines, while public choice instead passes economic analysis through an intermediate institutional filter before illuminating legal doctrines. Some readers might be surprised that these two complementary methodologies are capable of generating substantially divergent implications for the same questions of legal policy. Providing a brief illustration that draws upon an actual Supreme Court case will help to draw out the comparison between these two economic methodologies,[5] and to contrast both with the more traditional, and familiar, doctrinal perspective. In the remainder of this chapter we will explore several foundational assumptions and analytical tools that the two economic methodologies share in common as a prelude to developing the specific public choice tools in the chapters that follow.

I.   THREE ANALYTICAL PERSPECTIVES ON THE DOCTRINE OF EXPORT TAXATION[6]

We begin with a simplified presentation of an actual Supreme Court case, *Commonwealth Edison Co. v. Montana*.[7] The *Commonwealth Edison* case draws upon the dormant Commerce Clause doctrine, an important and hopefully familiar doctrine from American constitutional law.

In the 1970s, it was estimated that Montana held about 25% of the nation's coal reserves and over 50% of the nation's low-sulfur coal reserves. During this period, oil and gasoline prices were rising rapidly. The Montana legislature enacted a 30% severance tax on coal with knowledge that about 90% of that coal was regularly shipped out of state. Because low-sulfur coal was an alternative to increasingly costly gas and oil, the Montana legislators anticipated that even the costly severance tax would not substantially reduce the quantity of coal that consumers purchased for

---

3. RICHARD A. POSNER, ECONOMIC ANALYSIS OF LAW § 2.2, 24–26 (7th ed. 2007) (describing origins of positive and normative economic analyses of law).

4. *See generally id.* (presenting chapters that apply economic analysis of law to these and other disciplines).

5. The example that follows will draw upon tools of both interest group theory and game theory, both of which we place under the broad umbrella of public choice. *See infra* chapter 2 (introducing interest group theory), and *infra* chapter 4 (introducing game theory).

6. Portions of this discussion will draw upon Maxwell L. Stearns, *A Beautiful Mend: A Game Theoretical Analysis of the Dormant Commerce Clause Doctrine*, 45 WM. & MARY L. REV. 1 (2003); *see also* Saul Levmore, *Interstate Exploitation and Judicial Intervention*, 69 VA. L. REV. 563 (1983).

7. 453 U.S. 609 (1981). We will present a more comprehensive analysis of this case and of the Commerce Clause in a chapter in Part III (on the webpage).

out-of-state shipment. In fact, the severance tax did not substantially reduce coal consumption in or out of state and, as anticipated, through out-of-state purchases, the tax funded approximately 20% of the state's tax revenues. Commonwealth Edison, a company that purchased large quantities of coal from Montana for out-of-state shipment, claimed that the severance tax violated the dormant Commerce Clause doctrine.

A. DOCTRINAL ANALYSIS

Let us first consider a brief, and somewhat simplified, doctrinal analysis of *Commonwealth Edison*. The analysis necessarily begins with the text of the Commerce Clause itself, set out in Article I, § 8 of the Constitution. The Commerce Clause states: "The Congress shall have Power ... To regulate Commerce with foreign Nations, and among the several States, and with the Indian Tribes."[8] The Commerce Clause challenge presented several questions, some of which had been resolved in prior Supreme Court cases, which applied to this case through the doctrine of stare decisis or precedent, and others of which were of first impression, meaning that they had yet to be resolved.

To determine the constitutionality of the severance tax based upon the Commerce Clause challenge, the Supreme Court had to answer the following questions: (1) Does the Commerce Clause go beyond delegating regulatory power to Congress, as a strict reading of the text might suggest, and also empower courts to invalidate state legislation that undermines a unified national market in the absence of a federal statute? (yes, based upon long-standing Commerce Clause precedents) (2) Given that the Commerce Clause operates in a dormant capacity, and given that the challenged Montana tax, although neutral in wording—all purchasers had to pay the tax—was designed with the knowledge that it would primarily burden out-of-state purchasers while benefiting Montana taxpayers, should the Court apply strict dormant Commerce Clause scrutiny, rather than the substantially more relaxed balancing test? (no, because the case involves a neutral tax, the balancing test applies) (3) Applying the balancing test, does the neutrally apportioned severance tax survive despite its anticipated disproportionate impact on out-of-state purchasers? (yes, under the balancing test, the Court focuses primarily on fair apportionment without closely evaluating the true incidence of the tax).

To summarize, in *Commonwealth Edison*, the Supreme Court determined that the primary issue was whether the tax discriminated against out-of-state coal purchasers. Because it did not, the Court rejected the application of strict scrutiny under the Commerce Clause and instead applied a balancing test. Under that test, the Court rejected the argument that the tax was not "fairly apportioned." While the anticipated burden on out-of-state consumers might have suggested unfair apportionment, the Court instead used the case to establish that under the balancing test, it

---

8. U.S. Const. art. I, § 8.

would not analyze the difficult questions that arise when a particular neutral tax produces a disproportionate burden on one group of taxpayers as compared with another, even when the difference is that the disadvantaged group is out of state.

B. A LAW AND ECONOMICS ANALYSIS

Let us now consider an alternative analysis that draws upon the analytical tools associated with law and economics.[9] The severance tax challenged in *Commonwealth Edison* was applied during a period in which the demand for coal was "inelastic," meaning that the demand was largely insensitive to changes in price.[10] Imposing the severance tax, therefore, was not likely to dramatically reduce the amount of coal purchased. As a result, the tax had the anticipated effect of transferring wealth (the tax proceeds) from out-of-state purchasers to benefit in-state taxpayers in the form of lower tax obligations.

To properly evaluate the tax, it is important to consider the primary disciplining mechanism that promotes the proper, or "efficient,"[11] allocation of "public goods."[12] The efficient provision of such goods requires that the anticipated beneficiaries are financially responsible for their procurement through taxation. Sustaining the Montana severance tax threatened to undermine the efficiency of public goods provision in Montana and in other states that might enact similar laws. It did so by encouraging those states to devise methods through which to export substantial portions of their tax obligations onto out-of-state consumers who thus pay for, but do not benefit from, state-provided goods and services. Thus, the law and economics analysis reveals a problematic implication of *Commonwealth Edison*. The case threatens to promote inefficient incentives regarding the provision of public goods. And it does so in apparent tension with a central objective of the dormant Commerce Clause doctrine, namely, facilitating a unified national market.

C. PUBLIC CHOICE ANALYSIS

Finally, let us consider an alternative analysis of *Commonwealth Edison* from the perspective of public choice.[13] The public choice analysis begins with an assessment of the political dynamics that gave rise to the challenged severance tax on coal. The Montana state legislators under-

---

9. For a thoughtful analysis consistent with this discussion, see Levmore, *supra* note 6.

10. For a more detailed discussion of elasticity, see PAUL A. SAMUELSON & WILLIAM D. NORDHAUS, ECONOMICS 64–68 (16th ed. 1998). *See also infra* pp. 30–31.

11. For a discussion of two competing definitions of efficiency, Pareto superior and Kaldor Hicks, see *infra* p. 16.

12. Public goods are characterized by two features: (1) value is not diminished by consumption; and (2) once the goods are provided, noncontributors cannot be effectively excluded from receiving the benefits of those goods. *See* Paul A. Samuelson, *The Pure Theory of Public Expenditure*, 36 REV. ECON. & STAT. 386–89 (1954).

13. For a discussion consistent with this analysis, see Stearns, *supra* note 6.

stood that under the Supreme Court's dormant Commerce Clause doctrine, facially discriminatory taxes are subject to strict Commerce Clause scrutiny, a test that is generally fatal to the challenged law. To avoid this result, the Montana legislators crafted the severance tax on coal in neutral terms. This ensured that the tax applied equally, based upon the quantity of coal purchased, to both in- and out-of-state purchasers. Adopting the neutral tax allowed the Montana legislature to benefit from a more relaxed standard of scrutiny associated with a balancing test even though those enacting the tax were well aware that the actual burden, or "incidence,"[14] of the tax would fall most heavily on out-of-state purchasers.

While the severance tax thus threatened to promote a seemingly inefficient incentive to provide government goods and services funded by those who would not receive the benefits, public choice analysis suggests two countervailing institutional considerations. These considerations lend support to the Court's decision to apply a lower standard than strict dormant Commerce Clause scrutiny, with the effect of sustaining the severance tax. First, if the Supreme Court were to strike down the challenged severance tax based upon considerations of fairness to out-of-state coal purchasers (protecting them from funding public goods provided to Montana residents), the precedent would create seemingly intractable burdens on future courts presented with challenged tax policies that impose differential burdens on taxpayers, but that do so in less stark terms than those characterized by *Commonwealth Edison*. Determining the acceptable incidence of tax burdens on particular payers is not conducive to clear, articulable judicial standards. For that reason, questions of tax fairness are generally left to political processes to resolve. Second, like coal generally, low-sulfur coal is a natural resource that is randomly distributed among states. While allowing Montana to impose its severance tax on coal undoubtedly burdens out-of-state purchasers, it is unlikely to provide residents in burdened states with a meaningful opportunity to reciprocate by passing tax laws that singularly target residents in Montana. Sustaining the Montana severance tax produces, in effect, a single wealth transfer from out-of-state purchasers to Montana citizens, but does so without threatening to generate reciprocal laws that undermine the objective of national political union among states that lies at the core of the dormant Commerce Clause doctrine.

The preceding discussion was not intended to conclusively resolve the issues presented in *Commonwealth Edison* or to demonstrate the rightness (or wrongness) of the holding. Instead, the discussion highlights important differences between and among three approaches used to address an important constitutional doctrine. In this example, the law and economics analysis provides an important normative basis for challenging

---

14. The incidence of a tax is not necessarily where the tax is imposed in the first instance, but rather is a function of the ability of those nominally paying the tax to pass on the tax to end consumers by raising prices. For a discussion of incidence analysis, see SAMUELSON & NORDHAUS, *supra* note 10, at 73 ("By incidence we mean the ultimate economic impact or burden of a tax." (emphasis removed)).

the doctrine that the Supreme Court developed in *Commonwealth Edison* involving export taxation. In contrast, the public choice analysis suggests an alternative account that helps to restore the doctrinal distinction between discriminatory laws subject to strict dormant Commerce Clause scrutiny and neutral tax policies with differential effects that are instead subject to a more relaxed balancing test.

This is the first of many illustrations of the differing perspectives offered by doctrinal analysis, law and economics, and public choice, as applied to a wide range of topics in both public and private law. In some cases, the normative approaches of law and economics and public choice will coincide, while in others, public choice will help to explain apparent ongoing tensions between insights drawn from efficiency analysis and seemingly stubborn or resistant doctrine.

While the discussion thus far has focused on the divergent implications of public choice and law and economics as applied to an actual Supreme Court doctrine, the two disciplines share an important common methodological foundation. The remainder of this chapter, which considers the economic analysis of collective decision-making, develops several common threads that help to tie these disciplines together. For students who have a background in economic theory, much of what follows will be a refresher. For those students for whom this course represents their first entrée into economic reasoning, what follows can best be conceived as a helpful primer on several foundational economic principles that will be further developed throughout this book.

In developing and applying the specific tools associated with public choice, the chapters that follow will flesh out the concepts introduced below. We begin with several foundational assumptions, or "axioms," which public choice scholars generally assume (but do not always state) in their work.

II. AXIOMS OF ECONOMIC ANALYSIS

Like economists generally, public choice scholars construct models that are intended to capture or describe important defining characteristics of a broad range of complex phenomena observable in the real world. One of the most important aspects of the methodology of economics is appreciating that the models are not intended to capture the underlying complex reality; instead, they allow scholars to construct a manageable image of that reality. In this course, we will present numerous public choice models that are intended to help explain law-making institutions, judicial practices or norms, and legal doctrines. It is important up front to observe that these models are not intended to exclude analyses or insights growing out of other disciplines that study the same phenomena. Often the public choice analysis will complement intuitions drawn from other disciplines, and other times it will encourage us to reconsider those intuitions. But any complete analysis will inevitably depend upon a combination of analytical approaches.

The public choice approach, like that of economics generally, is deliberately reductionist. While it seeks to capture essential features of studied phenomena, in doing so it deliberately excludes other aspects of the same phenomena. As with all models, the goal is not to capture the innumerable subtleties associated with the complex world. Instead, it is to distill the essence of the phenomena under review into an image that allows the scholar to develop and test various hypotheses.[15]

We will now introduce some basic assumptions that are relevant to understanding public choice theory and economics more generally, including several analytical techniques that scholars use to generate testable public choice hypotheses. At the end of the chapter, we will present three brief public choice applications that demonstrate the potential range of public choice in explaining various aspects of collective decision making. Following the chapter is an appendix that provides a more detailed introduction to several price theoretical concepts. We begin with a critical, and often misunderstood, foundation of all economic analysis, namely the assumption of individual rationality.

A. THE ASSUMPTION OF INDIVIDUAL RATIONALITY

Human beings are infinitely diverse and complex creatures who manifest a dizzying array of instincts, passions, and behaviors. Humans are variously impulsive or cautious, analytic or careless, selfish or altruistic, hardworking or lazy, ambitious or content, heroic or cowardly, and compassionate or cruel. Not only do different people hold wide-ranging traits, but individuals also possess a peculiar combination of sometimes inconsistent traits. Individuals often exhibit conflicting or erratic behaviors, and even behaviors that seem ill-suited to furthering objectives that they sincerely express a desire to pursue.[16] All of this might appear to pose an insurmountable obstacle to scholars who seek to construct analytical models that rest upon some set of underlying generalizations concerning how individuals behave as a means of testing hypotheses about how changes in institutions or rules are likely to influence or modify human behavior.

Economists and public choice scholars avoid setting out strong assumptions concerning individual human desires or motivations. Instead, they rest their models on the seemingly simple assumption of individual

---

15. *See* Milton Friedman, *The Methodology of Positive Economics, in* ESSAYS IN POSITIVE ECONOMICS 3–43 (1953). For a debate on whether public choice scholarship has lived up to its expectation of developing testable hypotheses capable of falsification, see *infra* chapter 2 (discussing DONALD P. GREEN & IAN SHAPIRO, PATHOLOGIES OF RATIONAL CHOICE (1994), and THE RATIONAL CHOICE CONTROVERSY: ECONOMIC MODELS OF POLITICS RECONSIDERED (Jeffrey Friedman ed., 1996)).

16. For a useful discussion that ascribes certain documented manifestations of behavior that appear in tension with the economist's understanding of rationality to cognitive processes that evolved at a time far removed from modern developed market structures, see Owen D. Jones, *Time–Shifted Rationality and the Law of Law's Leverage: Behavioral Economics Meets Behavioral Biology*, 95 NW. U. L. REV. 1141 (2001).

"rationality." Individual rationality posits that whatever divergent preferences an individual might hold, she is presumed to engage in the cost-effective pursuit of her desired objectives. Along with economists generally, public choice scholars take individual motivations as assumed or given. For example, one can be as rational in the pursuit of starting or growing a firm as in building or contributing to a charity.

The economic understanding of rationality is thus quite different from *homo economicus.* Critics of economic analysis often presume that the theory rests upon the understanding that individual conduct is invariably narrowly self-interested. In fact, this is a caricature of the economist's assumption of rationality. Individuals may be motivated by any number of inspirations. While this can, and often will, include the desire to maximize income or profit, it also includes competing concerns, for example, supporting family and friends; gaining intellectual stimulation; increasing leisure; or exhibiting commitments to religion, charity, or a community. Economists assume that *whatever* ends an individual seeks, he or she will do so "rationally." This simple assertion about individual rationality distinguishes an economic or public choice approach to the study of human behavior from those associated with such related disciplines as psychology, philosophy, or sociology.

Economists further assume that while individuals are widely divergent, rationality renders certain attributes of human nature constant. This point is perhaps best illustrated by way of comparison. Consider, for example, the approach to human behavior associated with "republican" philosophy.[17] Such an approach assumes that however selfish individuals may be when they are operating within the private economic sphere, they are expected to relinquish personal motivations in favor of the "public good" when entering the public or political sphere. An influential modern variant, "civic republicanism" contends that ideology or public spiritedness, rather than rational self interest, is necessary to explain certain political behaviors, including for example why people vote. Scholars embracing this perspective contend that because most voters understand that their votes will almost certainly not control the outcome of an election, economic or public choice models are hard pressed to explain voting or to do so other than in a circular manner.[18]

Similarly, some legal scholars contend that ordinary and constitutional politics are distinguished based upon the level of public spiritedness among those participating in the process. Thus, for example, Bruce Ackerman has contended that while self-interested behavior characterizes the rough and tumble of "ordinary politics," those developing constitutions tend to engage in a higher level of public spiritedness that includes

---

17. To avoid confusion, we are discussing small "r" republicanism, which describes a political philosophy, often associated with JEAN JACQUES ROUSSEAU, THE SOCIAL CONTRACT (Penguin Classics Reprint ed., 1968) (1762), rather than large "R" Republicanism, which instead describes a political party associated with an ideology or bundle of ideologies.

18. For a more detailed discussion of voting, see *infra* pp. 21–26.

focusing on the good of the larger populace.[19] In contrast, consider the views of Nobel Laureate James Buchanan, working in the public choice tradition.[20] Buchanan, like Ackerman, predicts that choices and behavior will differ in the context of constitutional decision making. But Buchanan argues that this differing behavior will result from the different nature of the rules and institutions implicated by constitutional decision making. Because of the different natures of constitutions versus statutes, Buchanan argues, constitutions tend to be written at a higher level of abstraction and neutrality. As a result of this difference in generality, it is more difficult for individuals to predict where they will be in a post-constitutional regime than it is to predict how specific pieces of legislation, enacted within an existing constitutional regime, might affect them. Constitutional choice problems are thus analogous to the "veil of ignorance" thought experiment advanced by philosopher John Rawls.[21] Buchanan predicts that individuals will behave differently in a constitutional choice setting versus a legislative setting because of the institutional choices they confront, not because of a change in their preferences.

Other well known scholarly traditions, dating to Karl Marx,[22] assume that individual preferences are a product of group or class associations. Marxian economic analysis is premised upon the idea that the ruling class will seek to further its interest at the expense of the working class. In more modern times, legal scholars associated with critical legal studies, critical race theory, and certain strands of feminist scholarship,[23] have built on this insight to criticize legal policies that benefit perceived elites or to advance policies that help those perceived as marginalized or otherwise disadvantaged.

In contrast, economists influenced by a neoclassical perspective question whether individuals, behaving rationally, will further interests inuring to the benefit of a group they are associated with when doing so operates to their individual detriment. For an interesting, and controversial, example, consider the following economic analysis of racial discrimination among private firms. Nobel prize-winning economist Gary Becker has suggested that in competitive labor markets, firms that seek to indulge racial prejudices in the process of hiring or promotions will incur a cost that puts them at a competitive disadvantage relative to firms that do not. Over time, the racist firms will thus be forced either to change their policies, regardless of personal views concerning matters of race, or risk falling out of the market.[24] One noted criticism of the Becker model is that

---

19. *See, e.g.,* BRUCE ACKERMAN, WE THE PEOPLE 1: FOUNDATIONS (1991).

20. *See* JAMES M. BUCHANAN, THE LIMITS OF LIBERTY (1975); JAMES M. BUCHANAN & GORDON TULLOCK, THE CALCULUS OF CONSENT: LOGICAL FOUNDATIONS OF CONSTITUTIONAL DEMOCRACY (1962).

21. JOHN RAWLS, A THEORY OF JUSTICE § 24, at 118 (rev. ed. 1999).

22. *See, e.g.,* KARL MARX & FRIEDRICH ENGELS, THE COMMUNIST MANIFESTO (W.W. Norton ed. 1988) (1848).

23. For a helpful introduction to this literature, see MARK KELMAN, A GUIDE TO CRITICAL LEGAL STUDIES (1987). *See also* LESLIE BENDER & DAAN BRAVEMAN, POWER, PRIVILEGE AND LAW: A CIVIL RIGHTS READER (1995).

24. *See generally* GARY S. BECKER, THE ECONOMICS OF DISCRIMINATION (2d ed. 1971).

it responds to the problem of racism by suggesting that as a theoretical matter, it should not exist.[25]

In considering the merits of Professor Becker's theory, consider once again the nature of economic analysis. Through deliberately reductionist models of interactive human behavior, the theory allows economists to construct models capable of empirical testing. Can you think of any tests that one might develop to falsify or reaffirm Professor Becker's theory that, holding all else constant, private market competition should be expected to drive racially discriminatory firms out of the market? Given that racism does exist in numerous institutional settings, can Becker's model be extended to explain the circumstances in which it can arise and persist?

More generally, economists are skeptical of claims that individual rationality, and thus behavior, changes simply as a function of the context in which such behavior takes place. Economists are inclined, for example, to question whether citizens who engage in self-interested private pursuits 364 days a year will shed this predilection on the Tuesday after the first Monday in November (Election Day) thus casting their ballots in a manner that in otherwise uncharacteristic fashion seeks to advance a larger notion of public good. Similarly, economists are inclined to question whether a greater degree of public spiritedness better characterizes constitutional politics than ordinary politics. While economists doubt that context or group affiliation alone changes rational motivations, economists believe that institutional incentives can and do shape human behavior.

B.   INSTITUTIONS MATTER

Public choice theorists question whether individuals change their personal *motivations* as they move from one sphere of activity to the next. They agree, however, that individual *behavior* often changes as individuals move from one institutional environment to the next. An individual member of Congress, for example, who is motivated to procure special interest legislation for her district or to further partisan concerns associated with her party is unlikely to abandon these goals simply because she is called upon to address a set of questions that are labeled constitutional, rather than ordinary, politics. For example, her motivations are likely to remain constant when voting on a prospective judicial nominee, a proposed constitutional amendment, or a decision whether to impeach the President or some other officer. But the constancy of human nature does not imply constancy of individual behavior. Quite the contrary.

Economics is predicated on the assumption that individuals respond rationally to changes in incentives.[26] If the price of oranges rises relative

---

25.   *See, e.g.*, Robert E. Suggs, *Poisoning the Well: Law & Economics and Racial Inequality*, 57 HASTINGS L.J. 255 (2005).

26.   To be clear, "rationally" does not mean "perfectly." *Cf.* Jones, *supra* note 16, at 1166–67 (explaining the error of assuming that evolutionary processes transform the human mind into a perfectly calculating utility maximization machine).

to the price of grapefruits, then holding all else constant (for example assuming that the same land is hospitable to both crops and that the demand functions for both crops are otherwise similar), economists would predict that citrus farmers will, along the relevant margin, increase their production of oranges relative to grapefruits, and conversely, that consumers will purchase fewer oranges and more grapefruits. Changes in relative prices change individual incentives.

While price often affects behavior, so too do incentives created within institutions. A fundamental tenet of public choice is that *institutions matter*. By this, economists understand that institutions internalize mechanisms that reward or punish particular behaviors and that individuals, behaving rationally, modify their behavior in response to the resulting institutional incentives.

This of course raises the question: What is an institution? Nobel prize-winning economist Douglass North has defined "institutions" as follows: "[T]he humanly devised constraints that structure human interaction. They are made up of formal constraints (e.g., rules, laws, constitutions), informal constraints (e.g., norms of behavior, conventions, self-imposed codes of conduct), and their enforcement characteristics. Together, they define the incentive structure of societies and specifically economies."[27]

As an example of the importance of institutions in motivating individual behavior, consider the relative difference in "independence" that judges have in various institutional settings. In the United States, federal judges have a high degree of independence. Article III judges are appointed for life rather than elected for a term of years and serve during "good behavior." This has been interpreted to permit removal only for corruption or malfeasance, rather than for the substantive content, or popularity, of their rulings or written opinions. In contrast, many states have various forms of elected judiciaries. In some states, judicial candidates run for office in standard partisan elections.

Imagine two otherwise identical candidates for judgeships, one of whom is appointed to a federal court and the other of whom is elected to a state court for a term of years. Notwithstanding their similar ideologies and common philosophy concerning the proper judicial role, it is reasonable to predict that each will behave differently based upon the incentives associated with the two differing institutional settings.[28] Few would deny that federal judges care about how their rulings and opinions are received.[29] We can predict, however, that in contrast with state judges who

---

27. Douglass C. North, *Economic Performance Through Time*, 84 AM. ECON. REV. 359, 360 (1994).

28. For now we set aside the problem that once the institutional arrangements are put in place, these different judicial institutions attract potential judges who no longer share common approaches to the methodology of judging.

29. Or as Finley Peter Dunne's Mr. Dooley famously put it: "NO matter whether th' constitution follows th' flag or not, th' supreme coort follows th' iliction returns." FINLEY PETER DUNNE, MR. DOOLEY ON THE CHOICE OF LAW 52 (Edward J. Bander comp., 1963) (1901).

face reelection pressure, Article III judges are less likely to respond directly to the pressures of popular opinion and are more likely to adhere to their preexisting judicial philosophy, including, perhaps, indulging their personal ideological views even if those views are unpopular with the general public.

As is often the case, this important question of legal policy does not admit of a right or wrong answer. A careful analysis based upon economic principles, however, can help to unmask important—if unstated—assumptions that enter into the relevant policy choice. In this instance, the analysis, which reveals likely divergent incentives among judges appointed for life versus judges elected for a term of years, reflects assumptions concerning who the principals are to whom we wish the judges to direct their responsive behavior. Elected judiciaries, responsive to the political pressures of current constituencies, implicitly view judges as agents of voting constituencies. In contrast, independent judiciaries, those relatively isolated from popular political pressures, implicitly view judges as agents of those who enacted the laws that they are now called upon to interpret. Of course if judges or other actors were perfect agents for their respective principals there would be no need to build incentives within institutions that minimize potential divergences between the goals of the principal and the actions of the agent. It is thus not human nature, but rather the different incentives created by the different institutions, that lead to different predictions about judicial behavior.[30]

C. AGENCY COSTS

The divergence between the goals of a group of voters or other decision makers and the actions of those they elect or otherwise choose to represent their interests is referred to as "agency costs." Agents, whether they are legislators or judges, are not blank slates. A fundamental tenet of public choice holds that agents are not neutral conduits through which principals further their goals. Instead, the agents themselves possess preferences and motivations that sometimes coincide with, and other times diverge from, those of their principals. James Madison highlighted the problem of agency costs in creating Congress in a famous passage from the *Federalist No. 51*:

> If men were angels, no government would be necessary. If angels were to govern men, neither external nor internal controls on government would be necessary. In framing a government which is to be administered by men over men, the great difficulty lies in this: you must first enable the government to control the governed; and in the next place oblige it to control itself.[31]

Madison was discussing the problem of agency costs in the context of the legislature. But the problem of agency costs also arises in selecting any

---

30. We will revisit the question of the possible motivations and preferences of judges *infra* Chapter 7.

31. THE FEDERALIST No. 51, at 322 (James Madison) (Clinton Rossiter ed., 1961).

governmental official, whether the Executive, bureaucrats, or judges. As the preceding discussion shows, in the judicial context, the problem is complicated because before we can identify appropriate measures to reduce agency costs, we must confront the logically antecedent question, who is the principal?

Public choice alone does not provide an answer as to the optimal degree of judicial independence in a constitutional system. And, as our divergent systems of judicial selection between the federal government and the states, and among states themselves, demonstrate, this is not a question that necessarily admits of a single correct answer. Public choice can, however, assist in identifying the tradeoffs between accountability, independence, and agency costs, in designing institutions that will improve the probability of obtaining a preferred balance among these concerns. In addition, public choice analysis can help to unmask implicit assumptions concerning the role of judges and whose interests, or which principals, they are expected to serve.

D. METHODOLOGICAL INDIVIDUALISM

Like economics generally, public choice rests on the premise of methodological individualism.[32] A careful assessment of any institution demands that one first understand how that institution affects the incentives of the individuals comprising or affected by it. James Buchanan and Gordon Tullock, two leading public choice theorists, expressed this intuition as follows: "Collective action is viewed as the action of individuals when they choose to accomplish purposes collectively rather than individually, and the government is seen as nothing more than the set of processes, the machine, which allows such collective action to take place."[33] And as Kenneth Shepsle, another leading public choice scholar, famously put it: "Congress is a 'They,' not an 'It.' "[34]

Methodological individualism lies at the foundation of economic analysis, underpinning all models of human interaction and behavior. To illustrate, consider a commodity cartel, such as a cartel for oil production. Considered as a *collective*, the cartel members have a strong incentive to reduce aggregate output, with pro rata allocations among individual producers, in an effort to set the price at the same level that a monopolist would who controlled the entire market. And yet, it is well understood that this result is likely to be unstable. The resulting instability arises as a direct consequence of the divergent motivations of the cartel as a whole, on the one hand, and its individual members, on the other. Assuming pro

---

32. Methodological individualism has been an important working assumption within other social sciences since at least the beginning of the twentieth century, including the work of Max Weber, Friedrich von Hayek, and Karl Popper. Joseph Heath, *Methodological Individualism*, *in* The Stanford Encyclopedia of Philosophy (Edward N. Zalta ed., Spring 2009), http://plato.stanford. edu/archives/spr2009/entries/methodological-individualism/.

33. *See* Buchanan & Tullock, *supra* note 20, at 13.

34. Kenneth Shepsle, *Congress Is a "They," Not an "It": Legislative Intent as an Oxymoron*, 12 Int'l Rev. L. & Econ. 239 (1992).

rata cuts based, for example, on preexisting market share or some other formula (perhaps an average over the prior three years), each *individual* cartel member, behaving rationally, has an incentive to "cheat." Specifically, each member is motivated to sell just a bit more than the allocated cartel share at a price just below the level dictated by the cartel. Each individual member of the cartel hopes to get away with modest cheating while also hoping that the remaining cartel members adhere to their quotas, thus sustaining the overall favorable pricing structure. For the cartel as a whole, however, the problem gets much worse. Each cartel member shares the same incentive to benefit from the artificially inflated cartel price, by selling more than the allocated share. Over time, therefore, the cartel output and pricing scheme tends to erode, with the effect of moving both the output and price back toward the pre-cartel, competitive level.

Although each of the cartel members would have been better off had all adhered strictly to the allotted quota than by participating in a regime in which all members cheat on their quota, thus driving the price back down to the competitive levels, the difficulty is that the ultimate production decisions are made individually. Admonishing members to cooperate will not ensure that they do so. The individual firm's goal of maximizing profits does not disappear simply because the firms have collectively identified themselves as a cartel.

E. FREE RIDING AND FORCED RIDING

Collective choice institutions likewise give rise to problems of "free" and "forced" riding, key concepts that underlie public choice theory. Free riding occurs when an individual is able to gain some of the benefit of the provision of a collective good without being required to pay the marginal cost associated with its provision. Free riding occurs most commonly in connection with the provision of public goods.[35] Consider, for example, national defense. Once an army is formed, all Americans benefit from its existence in that the army cannot decide to protect my home from invasion, but not my neighbor's. Thus, if I pay taxes to support an army, my neighbor benefits as well, even if he makes no similar financial contribution. As a result, my neighbor has the opportunity and incentive to "free ride" on my willingness to provide the public good by declining to contribute his fair share. Each individual (including myself) has the same incentive to free ride, however. As a result, if left to voluntary individual contribution, rational self-interest will tend toward an *underproduction* of public goods. Although the group as a whole would be better off if everyone contributed to the provision of the public good, each individual's personal incentive deviates from this collective goal.

In other collective choice situations, similar dynamics might lead to "forced riding," the mirror image of free riding. Forced riding occurs

---

35. *See supra* note 12 (defining public goods).

when an individual is forced by other members of the group (such as under a majority voting regime) to contribute to the provision of a public good beyond the personal benefit he receives from it.[36] At the extreme, an individual might gain negative utility from the provision of a given public good; for instance, a pacifist may actually feel herself to be made worse off by the provision of national defense. As a less extreme example, consider those who do not enjoy opera but whose taxes subsidize opera productions or those who do not enjoy sports but whose taxes subsidize the construction of a new baseball stadium. Even assuming that a majority fully supports these expenditures, those receiving the benefit of the publicly procured goods do not bear the full cost. This suggests forced riding, which results in an *overproduction* of such collective goods relative to those public goods where members of the majority coalition are not able to force others to subsidize the satisfaction of their preferences. Does the forced riding concept offer insight into *Commonwealth Edison v. Montana*? If so, which of the three analyses used to describe that case does it tend to support?

F. STRUCTURING APPROPRIATE MICRO–FOUNDATIONS

As the twin concepts of free riding and forced riding demonstrate, in seeking to promote the ability of institutions to generate preferred outcomes, it is essential first to provide appropriate "micro-foundations" for individual actions. Effective group performance is impossible unless the institutions motivate individuals to act in a manner that advances the objectives at the appropriate levels the collective body was designed to accomplish.

Let us return to the problem of the cartel. Assume once again that the objective is to reduce output in an effort to raise price.[37] An obvious way to align the incentives of the individuals with those of the group of producers is to combine the productive capacities into a single firm. At that point, the individual running the now single firm has an incentive to reduce output and raise price, even though the same individual, as one of several members of a cartel, would instead have an incentive to cheat from an imposed quota intended to achieve the same overall result.

G. POLITICS AS AN EXCHANGE MODEL

Disaggregating collective action via the assumption of methodological individualism not only helps to explain the formation and structure of

---

36. For a similar analytical problem, consider cases of forced subsidization of livestock and agricultural marketing programs, which are challenged by contributors who do not perceive a proportional benefit of the collective advertising. *See, e.g.*, Johanns v. Livestock Mktg. Ass'n, 544 U.S. 550 (2005) (rejecting First Amendment challenge to program that forced subsidization of government advertising and distinguishing cases that struck down similar non-government advertising programs).

37. Such an objective is obviously detrimental to consumers who would prefer the benefits of a competitive regime, which increases output and lowers price.

private institutions, but also it transforms the traditional understanding of politics. In contrast with the conventional understanding of politics as a search for the "public interest," public choice helps to reframe collective action as an exchange model. We will present the exchange model in more detail in chapter 2. For now, it is sufficient to note that within this analysis, those who demand government-provided goods and services— voters, interest groups, and lobbyists—offer their support to those elected officials who, in exchange, agree to provide them. Unlike private market exchange, however, the costs and benefits of lawmaking "transactions" affect persons who do not necessarily participate in the bargain. As the *Commonwealth Edison* case illustrates, the contributions of those who receive particular services might not match those who contribute—and indeed who might be forced to contribute—to the provision of those services.

H. PARETO OPTIMALITY VERSUS KALDOR HICKS EFFICIENCY AND THE HOLDOUT PROBLEM[38]

In theory, even without adhering to a unanimous consent rule as a precondition to collective action, it is possible to ensure outcomes that benefit all persons affected by the decisions of the group. If a proposed change in law is welfare maximizing, those benefiting by the action (the "winners") could compensate those harmed by the action (the "losers") and still come out ahead. The winners would thus be made better off, even after paying compensation to the losers, and the losers would be no worse off once they had been fully compensated for any losses. If such compensation took place, the result would satisfy the most stringent definition of economic efficiency. A change from the status quo to an alternative state is *Pareto superior* if it improves the position of at least one participant without making anyone else worse off. *Pareto optimality* demands that all potential Pareto superior moves have already taken place. When this occurs, any further changes from the status quo would instead effect a wealth transfer between or among participants, with the result that at least one party to the exchange would be made worse off.[39]

---

38. For general discussions of these definitions of efficiency, see Allan M. Feldman, *Kaldor–Hicks Compensation*, *in* 2 THE NEW PALGRAVE DICTIONARY OF ECONOMICS AND THE LAW 417–21 (Peter Newman ed., 1998); Allan M. Feldman, *Pareto Optimality*, *in* 3 THE NEW PALGRAVE DICTIONARY OF ECONOMICS AND THE LAW, *supra*, at 5–9.

39. The importance of the Pareto principle in formulating law and public policy has long been the subject of academic debate. *See, e.g.*, Daniel A. Farber, *The Problematics of the Pareto Principle* (bepress Legal Series Working Paper No. 698, 2005), *available at* http://law.bepress.com/cgi/viewcontent.cgi?article=3513 & context=expresso (demonstrating theoretical and practical limitations in applying Pareto principle in legal policymaking); Marc Fleurbaey, Bertil Tungodden & Howard F. Chang, *Any Non-welfarist Method of Policy Assessment Violates the Pareto Principle: A Comment*, 111 J. POL. ECON. 1382, 1383 (2003) (using social welfare function analysis to critique Kaplow and Shavell's assertion that "welfarism and the Pareto indifference condition are equivalent"); Louis Kaplow & Steven Shavell, *Any Non-welfarist Method of Policy Assessment Violates the Pareto Principle*, 109 J. POL. ECON. 281 (2001) (arguing that policy making should be based solely on Pareto criterion, the claimed equivalent to welfarism); Guido Calabresi, *The Pointlessness of Pareto: Carrying Coase Further*, 100 YALE L.J. 1211 (1991) (maintaining that

In private markets, at least assuming no negative externalities,[40] meaning that persons not party to the transaction are not adversely affected, *Pareto superior* exchanges routinely occur. When an individual purchases a latte for $3, the buyer presumably values the coffee more than the money, and the vendor values the money more than the coffee. In contrast, when the government provides goods and services, it uses its coercive power of taxation to fund its programs. When this occurs, not everyone benefits and those who do benefit might not do so to the same degree. Thus, the benefits such programs confer might only loosely match the specific contributions that particular taxpayers provide. In theory, those who benefit could pay off those who are disadvantaged, and the result would satisfy the condition of *Pareto superiority*. Because those previously disadvantaged and now compensated would no longer be worse off, while those who are advantaged would continue to be (albeit with a reduction equal to the amount of compensation to the losers), the program would improve the plight of the winners without causing others harm. The practical difficulties with such a regime, however, are generally thought to make actual compensation implausible.

Under an alternative definition of efficiency, *Kaldor Hicks*, a change from the status quo is efficient when the potential for such compensation exists even though the actual compensation does not occur. The intuition is that because the winners' welfare has improved by more than the losers' welfare has suffered (hence the possibility of compensation), the overall result is welfare enhancing. This more relaxed standard for efficiency, while acknowledging the unavoidable nature of winners and losers in the procurement of publicly provided goods or services, provides an important normative foundation for the provision of many public programs that cannot satisfy the more stringent Pareto criterion.

In the collective choice setting, from an economic perspective, the best evidence of whether a given collectively chosen policy maximizes social welfare would be the unanimous consent of all members of the relevant community to the action. The unanimity benchmark for collective choice, therefore, appears functionally identical to the *Pareto superiority* criterion for market transactions.[41] A unanimity rule for collective choice, however, creates the difficulty that even a single person could prevent the proposed law from passing. A single person might oppose based upon the merits of the proposed change or in a strategic effort to use veto power to demand some other benefit as a precondition to tendering support. In the context of individual market transactions (such as for purchasing a cup of coffee), the problem of the strategic *holdout* does not arise, as an individual lacks the power to impose costs on anyone other than herself. In a collective choice setting, however, the need for consent among all relevant parties

---

Pareto criterion has limited normative implications because logically, all Pareto improvements should already have taken place).

40. For a discussion of externalities, see *infra* part II.I.

41. James M. Buchanan, *The Coase Theorem and the Theory of the State*, 13 NAT. RESOURCES J. 579 (1973).

can be very expensive and thus give rise to serious problems of strategic hold-outs.

As a result, although a rule requiring the unanimous assent of those governed as a precondition to coercive governmental action might prevent imposing costs on those who do not benefit from such action, both as a theoretical and as a practical matter, the unanimity norm is impossible to implement. Thus, in judging the merits of a given collective choice institution, it becomes necessary to adopt an alternative to *Pareto* superiority, or its analogue, unanimous consent, such as *Kaldor Hicks* efficiency, and to accept a majority or supermajority decision-making rule.

I. THE PROBLEM OF EXTERNALITIES AND THE COASE THEOREM

In well-functioning markets, with well-defined and freely transferable property rights, the rational actions of individuals will not only tend to raise each person's utility, but will also promote societal welfare. Where, however, property rights are poorly defined, or individuals can pass part of their costs of production on to others, one can no longer assume that individual actions combine to raise social welfare. For instance, a farmer might be able to raise and sell pigs to consumers under mutually beneficial terms. And yet, pig farming also gives rise to odors and pollution that are likely to annoy and harm the farmer's neighbors. If the farmer is not required to compensate his neighbors for the harms created by pig farming, the farmer and his purchasers will not bear the full cost of the activity of raising pigs. At this point, it is no longer possible to infer an increase in social welfare from the transactions that improved the welfare of the farmer and his purchasers.[42]

This problem, known as *negative externalities*,[43] has long been a major focus of neoclassical economic theory. The influential economist Arthur Cecil Pigou believed that a major challenge facing market economies was ensuring that firms absorb the full costs of their own productive activities, and thus that regulation served to minimize potential negative externalities.

Nobel Prize-winning economist Ronald Coase was highly critical of Pigou's project of devising mechanisms through which to limit externalities. Instead, Coase posited that a principal objective of the legal system is to limit barriers to private market transactions because such transactions help to move resources to their most highly valued uses. If transactions cost barriers are minimized or removed, any problems associated with negative externalities could then be handled exclusively through private market transactions. Most surprisingly, Coase contended that this benign

---

42. Activities that have externalities are clearly not *Pareto* optimal and may or may not be *Kaldor Hicks* efficient. Do you see why?

43. There are also *positive* externalities, as for example, when a developer enters a blighted part of a city and introduces new shopping, employment, and entertainment opportunities with the effect of improving the overall quality of life for those residing there.

result obtained regardless of whether the legal system nominally protected the firm producing, or the firm suffering, the negative externality. Coase published this result in a famous essay, *The Problem of Social Cost*,[44] which is most well known for setting out the now famous Coase Theorem.

The Coase Theorem is at once counterintuitive, controversial, and widely misunderstood. The theorem posits that in a world with zero transactions costs and perfect information, resources will flow to their most highly valued uses without regard to liability rules.[45] This seemingly basic insight has generated a vast scholarship that has revealed both the theorem's complexity and its significance in evaluating institutions.

One immediate difficulty that Coase confronted was that many critics understood the theorem to imply that transactions costs *are* low, and that as a result, resource allocation *is* generally efficient and welfare enhancing. Of course there are countless illustrations in the real world of inefficient resource allocations and of costly barriers to welfare-enhancing private market exchange.

What Coase intended, however, was quite the opposite. Coase posited two preconditions that render liability rules irrelevant to efficient allocation of resources: zero transactions costs and perfect information. Certainly in the real world, there is little reason to assume that transacting is costless. Transactions costs include travel, documentation, and communication. They also include opportunity cost, defined as the time and energy taken from other potentially profitable activities. And perhaps most significantly, although he specified perfect information as a separate condition, the cost of gathering the necessary information with which to enter into transactions is certainly among the greatest cost impediments to contracting.

To illustrate how Coase's stylized world, one with zero transactions costs and with perfect information, yields optimal outcomes without regard to liability rules (meaning without regard to whether there is a "right" to cause or to be free of a negative externality), consider the following hypothetical.[46] Imagine a laundry and a factory that pollutes into a river to the laundry's detriment.[47] The factory is worth $11,000; but by polluting, it reduces the laundry's value from $40,000 to $24,000. Further assume that for the laundry to realize its potential value of $40,000, the factory must cease all pollution, which would require the factory to shut down.

The Coase Theorem posits that in a world with zero transactions costs and perfect information, this efficient result will be achieved—the factory

---

44. R.H. Coase, *The Problem of Social Cost*, 3 J.L. & Econ. 1 (1960).

45. *See id.* As demonstrated *infra*, chapter 3, the term Coase Theorem might be a misnomer because under certain conditions associated with empty core bargaining, even when the theorem's articulated assumptions are satisfied, the predicted efficient resource allocation is not guaranteed.

46. We will later develop this hypothetical to present a limitation of the Coase Theorem in the context of empty core bargaining.

47. This is adapted from Varouj A. Aivazian & Jeffrey L. Callen, *The Coase Theorem and the Empty Core*, 24 J.L. & Econ. 175 (1981). *See also* Stearns, *supra* note 6, at 103–04.

will close and the laundry will operate—regardless of which of the two businesses owns the property right to pollute or to enjoin the pollution. Assume first that the factory owns the right to pollute. The laundry will pay up to $16,000—the difference in its value with and without the factory polluting—to purchase that right from the factory. Because the factory is worth only $11,000 even with the right to pollute, it has a rational incentive to sell its right to pollute, thus allowing the laundry to purchase the right to enjoin the pollution. Conversely, if the laundry owns the right to enjoin the factory's pollution, the factory will not be able to purchase the pollution right from the laundry. The factory values that right at $11,000, $5000 less than the laundry values its contrary right to prevent the pollution. The example illustrates that if the owner of the laundry values the right to pollute more highly than does the owner of the factory, then regardless of who bears the property right to pollute—or conversely is the beneficiary of the liability rule when the factory pollutes—in a world with zero transactions costs and perfect information, the laundry will ultimately obtain that right.

A critical assumption in the analysis is that the numbers in the example capture all relevant costs. If there are hidden costs, psychological or otherwise, and if such costs are of sufficient magnitude to inhibit the deal, then the result will break down and the efficiency-promoting transaction will not occur, leaving the property right wherever the legal system happened to place it. If that right happened to rest with the laundry, then the efficient result is fortuitously achieved, but if it rested instead with the factory, then the transactions costs would suffice to prevent the efficient flow of resources, costing society up to the $5000 premium value that the laundry places on the property right.[48]

The preceding discussion introduced several important aspects of economic reasoning.[49] This is an important starting point that will help you in appreciating the many public choice, social choice, and game theoretical concepts introduced throughout this book. We will now briefly consider three case studies that will help you in developing public choice insights in the chapters that follow.

III. THREE CASE STUDIES[50]

The following case studies are intended to encourage you to think about the power of economic reasoning to tackle foundational questions about our political and legal processes. For each case study, you will continue to be able to revise your analysis as you acquire new frames of

---

48. Can you identify circumstances in which, even with low transactions costs, the Coasian result is unlikely to arise? If so, could you characterize the implicit impediment to the efficient outcome as a transaction cost? What does the preceding question suggest about the nature of transactions costs as that term is employed in the Coase theorem?

49. We present a more detailed introduction to price theory in the appendix following this chapter.

50. Portions of the discussion that follow are adapted from MAXWELL L. STEARNS, PUBLIC CHOICE AND PUBLIC LAW: READINGS AND COMMENTARY 64–72 (1997).

reference throughout this book. For now, evaluate each case study based upon the general intuitions developed in the preceding discussion.

A. IS VOTING IRRATIONAL?

Public choice applies economic principles, including those developed thus far, to politics and political processes. One foundational aspect of the political process, namely voting, however, is widely viewed as paradoxical especially when viewed from an economic perspective. The "paradox of voting" is that while virtually no informed voter expects her vote to control the outcome of an election and while voting is a costly activity, in every election, a considerable percentage of the population votes. The obvious costs of voting in terms of time and inconvenience are exacerbated when one also considers the cost of becoming sufficiently informed to cast a ballot for a desired candidate or group of candidates. As a result, some scholars claim that the act of voting defies "rationality" as that term is understood within economic analysis. One argument used to "rescue" voting from the claim that it is an irrational activity returns us to the definition of rationality itself. Rationality does not mean narrow self interest. Instead, individuals may rationally vote because they derive any number of non-pecuniary benefits, or an overall sense of satisfaction, from doing so. Consider the following rejoinder by Professors Daniel Farber and Philip Frickey:

> Attempts have been made to reconcile voter behavior with the economic model by postulating a "taste" for voting. This explanation is tautological—anything people do can be "justified" by saying they have a taste for doing it.[51]

Professors Farber and Frickey go on to ask: "Why is it so difficult to admit that people vote out of political commitment, not personal satisfaction?"[52]

In contrast, Professors Michael DeBow and Dwight Lee have argued that voting is rational if one views it as a "consumption" activity. Indeed, they argue that the apparent paradox of voting may even serve to *increase* the consumption value, or enjoyment, of voting.[53] If individuals are confident that their votes will not control outcomes, then they might feel free to vote based upon their conscience, without regard to how the ultimate outcome might affect them personally. Knowledge of the paradox of voting might therefore be liberating in that it enables voters to make decisions based upon matters of principle, rather than pocketbooks.

Others have argued that if voters understand that their votes "do not count" this might make them increasingly irresponsible, allowing expres-

---

51. Daniel A. Farber & Philip P. Frickey, *The Jurisprudence of Public Choice*, 65 TEX. L. REV. 873, 894 n.129 (1987).

52. Daniel A. Farber & Philip P. Frickey, *Integrating Public Choice and Public Law: A Reply to DeBow and Lee*, 66 TEX. L. REV. 1013, 1017 (1988).

53. Michael E. DeBow & Dwight R. Lee, *Understanding (and Misunderstanding) Public Choice: A Response to Farber and Frickey*, 66 TEX. L. REV. 993 (1988).

sions of pure preference on a particular issue without coupling that preference with an expectation of producing any result.[54] Similarly, it has been argued that when certain issues, for example abortion, are constitutionalized and thus removed from ordinary political processes, the result might be to produce more extreme and polarized public views, as votes cast become symbolic, rather than regulatory, acts. The limited influence of an individual's vote on any given issue might give rise to this sort of irresponsible voting on a range of public policy issues, from immigration to national defense to spending.

Professors Farber and Frickey have responded to this line of argument by claiming that if people derive the ultimate satisfaction from voting *because* they expect their votes not to count, then they could derive *even more* satisfaction by locking themselves up in an empty house and shouting support for their favorite candidates.[55] Obviously few people engage in this sort of senseless activity, but many people vote. If you conclude that although people have a taste for voting, they generally do not have a taste for senseless wastes of time, consider whether this merely restates the apparent tautology that Farber and Frickey have identified. If people actually did lock themselves in a room and shout support for candidates, we would have to maintain that because participants apparently derive some consumption value from this activity, they do not regard it as a senseless waste of time.

1. An Expressive Theory of Voting

One explanation for why people vote is that they gain value from "expressive voting," meaning that voting allows citizens to express their views on important matters of public policy.[56] People might vote rather than merely shout in an empty house because they view voting as a more effective vehicle for expression. For example, voting results are tallied and widely reported in the media. In this view, the utility from voting comes from the act of voting itself and from the opportunity for expression that voting enables, rather than strictly from any expected payoff respecting the effect that any individual vote is likely to have on the outcome of the election. Thus, the act of voting might be similar to writing letters to the editor expressing views on political issues or engaging in peaceful political demonstrations. In each case, the effect of each individual in affecting the preferred policy outcome might be minuscule, and yet, if an individual gains utility from expressing herself in one manner rather than another, it is fully consistent with the rationality postulate. The "expressive theory" of voting is often referred to as a *noninstrumental* theory of individual

---

54. Geoffrey Brennan & James Buchanan, *Voter Choice: Evaluating Political Alternatives*, 28 AM. BEHAV. SCIENTIST 185 (1984).

55. *See* Farber & Frickey, *supra* note 52, at 1017.

56. GEOFFREY BRENNAN & LOREN LOMASKY, DEMOCRACY AND DECISION: THE PURE THEORY OF ELECTORAL PREFERENCE (1993).

motivation because the act of voting is an end in itself, rather than a means to the end of affecting the outcome of an election.

2. A Cost Function of Voting

If the cost of voting rises, holding all else constant, people are less likely to vote. If people vote out of "political commitment" rather than personal satisfaction, this tends to suggest that economic considerations, such as the cost of voting, should be largely irrelevant to the decision whether to vote. If individuals vote for consumption or expressive purposes, however, then this would suggest that the individual willingness to vote (the demand for voting) should decline as the price of voting rises. Available evidence suggests that this is generally, although not invariably, true.[57] For instance, where jury pools are drawn from voter registration rolls, voter registration and participation rates are lower. Jury duty is a substantially more costly activity than merely voting, thus when the activities are linked, jury duty increases the cost of voting. If, in contrast, voting behavior was animated by a pure sense of civic commitment, then one would predict that the increased risk (or prospect) of jury duty (another form of civic commitment) should have no impact, or perhaps should have a positive impact, on the likelihood of registering to vote. Similarly, it has been argued that introducing the secret ballot reduced voter participation because secret voting eliminated a benefit to those who sought to bribe prospective voters, namely removing the ability to verify that commitments were honored. While eliminating this benefit might have reduced voter turnout, it surely improved the quality and representativeness of elections! Finally, factors such as bad weather, difficulty of registration requirements, and distance to the polling place generally lead to reduced levels of voting, although the effect might not be uniform across demographic groups.

3. Possibilities of Strategic Electoral Voting

There is some evidence that under specific conditions, individuals vote in a manner that might be described as strategic.[58] For instance, in primary elections, many voters base their votes in significant part on the apparent electoral viability of the available candidates, rather than on which of those candidates is closest to their ideal point,[59] meaning the point along a continuous liberal to conservative issue spectrum that most closely corresponds to a voter's ideological preference.[60] In addition, some studies suggest that voter turnout is higher in elections that are expected

---

57. Partners of the following discussion are based upon DENNIS C. MUELLER, PUBLIC CHOICE III, at 321–22 (2003).

58. *See generally* Timothy J. Feddersen, *Rational Choice Theory and the Paradox of Not Voting*, J. ECON. PERSP., Winter 2004, at 99 (reviewing literature).

59. For a discussion of potential strategic voting in the 1988 Presidential primaries, see Paul R. Abramson et al., *"Sophisticated" Voting in the 1988 Presidential Primaries*, 86 AM. POL. SCI. REV. 55 (1992).

60. For a helpful discussion, see Roger D. Congleton, *The Median Voter Model, in* THE ENCYCLOPEDIA OF PUBLIC CHOICE 382 (Charles K. Rowley & Friedrich Schneider eds., 2004). For a more detailed analysis of spatial reasoning in public choice modeling, see *infra* chapter 3.

to be close.[61] If so, is this also an example of strategic voting? Can you identify electoral contexts in which the possibility of strategic voting is instead likely to be limited? If so, what are the factors that limit strategic voting?

4. Group–Based Model of Vote Mobilization[62]

Some commentators have suggested a non-instrumental theory of voting in which certain socioeconomic groups inculcate voting as a positive value. Examples of such groups include especially the well-educated and wealthy, and identifiable subgroups of voters, such as union members. In this model, voting might be analogized to cheering at a sporting event. At the margin, each fan in an 80,000 seat stadium adds little to the noise made in support of the team, even though each individual incurs a cost (such as a sore throat) from cheering (or booing). Nonetheless, fans do cheer for their team out of a sense of shared group solidarity. Similarly, citizens are trained through education and social norms to think—perhaps erroneously—that their votes make a difference in an instrumental sense. Indeed, some have suggested that democracy is dependent upon this form of misinformation. If so, does this also suggest that ultimately voting rests upon some tautological understanding of taste?

5. Voting as a Game of Cat and Mouse[63]

Now consider the first of two purely instrumental voting models. Imagine a world in which everyone was familiar with the voters' paradox. In theory, we might predict that no one would vote. If that were the result, however, even a single individual (let us call her an "initial voter") who chose to vote—equipped with the understanding that the rest of the populace was rationally apathetic—could control the outcome of the election. Of course there is no reason to assume that the initial voter's preferences will reflect the preferences of the population as a whole. As a result, some of those who previously declined to vote might now decide to vote simply to prevent an idiosyncratic individual from controlling the outcome (let us call these people "responsive voters"). But once the responsive voters turn out, this reduces the incentives of the initial voter to cast her ballot. And without the threat that the initial voter poses, the responsive voters lose their incentive to vote. This creates opportunities for a new set of initial voters to control the election. Now the responsive voters choose to cast their ballots, driving the new set of initial voters away. And on and on it goes.

Some studies suggest that this non-cooperative game can explain why every election produces at least some voters.[64] The same studies suggest, however, that with a high degree of uncertainty concerning the behavior of other participants, rational voters will only vote if they derive some

---

61. *See* MUELLER, *supra* note 57, at 315.

62. *See id.* at 326–28; Feddersen, *supra* note 58, at 99–112.

63. MUELLER, *supra* note 57, at 303–32.

64. *See id.* at 306–07.

utility from the act of voting itself, without regard to the impact of their votes. At that point, are we back to an explanation based upon the taste for voting?

Consider, however, whether a cat and mouse game can be reframed to modify the end of voting itself. Perhaps it is rational to vote even if voters understand that the act of voting will not control outcomes in particular elections. Studies have suggested a high correlation between wealth and education on the one hand and voting on the other.[65] This might appear anomalous in that well-educated and wealthy persons are more likely to be aware of the voters' paradox than less educated and poor persons. But if educated persons know that it is "irrational" to vote, or more precisely that their individual acts of voting do not control outcomes, then they might intuit that this insight will dissuade many citizens from voting. As a consequence, they might also reason that if they do vote, their votes are likely to be afforded a disproportionate weight relative to their numbers given the disincentive of others to vote. This analysis ties into the game of cat and mouse. Even though these voters know that they are unlikely to be the marginal voters, they also know that by voting they are able to send a powerful signal to those who might try to become marginal voters in the future. In other words, the so-called paradox of voting may be premised upon an overly stringent view of the voter's instrumental calculus. The paradox is premised on excluding any potential payoffs *other than* the prospect of influencing the outcome of a given election as the marginal voter.

Thus viewed, those most likely to vote do not anticipate being the marginal voter; instead they vote to invest in a signal. The signal conveys that regardless of where the voting margin lies, this core group of eligible voters will predictably vote. Those who consistently vote, e.g., in non-Presidential elections and regardless of weather conditions, signal to other voters that because they will vote no matter what, there is no point trying to play the game of cat and mouse with them. Moreover, signal strength directly correlates with the number of votes even though no single vote is predictably decisive.

This phenomenon might also provide another instrumental benefit to voting; within the relevant social groups to which such voters belong, the failure to vote is viewed negatively because it weakens the political signal for the group as a whole. The opposite is also true. Within the relevant social group, the act of voting is rewarded while the failure to do so—at least without a good excuse—may be frowned upon. Thus viewed, consistent voters create a form of political capital that is independent of the election-specific instrumentality of voting. In the event a core group of regular voters is unable to vote in a particular election, they need not worry because they will already have generated sufficient voting capital that others in the political process will likely behave *as if* most members of the core group had voted.

---

65. *See id.* at 327.

6. The Voter as Minimax–Regret Strategist[66]

Let us now consider an alternative instrumental voting model. Assume that potential voters register a weak preference as between the two dominant candidates and that they ignore the probabilities of success of those candidates. Assume that a third, fringe candidate, perhaps one affiliated with either the Ku Klux Klan or a neo-Nazi group, enters the race. In this situation, mainstream voters turn out in large numbers because they fear that the fringe candidate might win. The strategy is named minimax regret because the voters are not seeking to optimize ideal outcomes, but rather to minimize the probability of an outcome that leads to a maximum regret.

Perhaps surprisingly, those who turn out to vote for this reason tend to vote for their first choice candidate even if the second choice candidate stands a better chance of defeating the least favored candidate. Such voters appear to discount the low probability that the fringe candidate will win and the somewhat higher probability that their second choice candidate is more likely to prevent this least favored result from potentially emerging. Consider, for example, the possibility that a voter prefers candidate A to candidate B to candidate C, and that candidate C has drawn support away from candidate A. Candidate B may be the most effective challenger to the voter's feared candidate C. If the voter were behaving in a strictly instrumental fashion, she would vote for B, but the relevant studies suggest that if she votes at all, she will likely vote for A.

Perhaps the voter's rationale can be expressed as follows: "Because my vote is almost certainly not going to control the outcome, at the very least I can send a strong signal *against* candidate C; but if that's the purpose of my vote, I may as well vote for my most favored candidate." Does this further support the intuition that even in the minimax regret context, voters cast ballots because they derive a consumption benefit from doing so?

Final questions: Using the economist's understanding of individual rationality, do you think it is rational to vote? If you said yes, how would you express your intuition? If you said no, what significance does your conclusion have for the ability to use models premised upon the economist's understanding of rationality to explain other aspects of political processes? These are questions that you might wish to revisit as you further explore the tools of public choice theory throughout the course.

B. IS LEGISLATIVE LOGROLLING GOOD OR BAD?

In chapter 2, we develop models that treat political processes as an exchange network, similar in some respects to a private market but with important qualifications. One of the most important qualifications is that unlike private market exchange, which generally depends upon the unani-

---

66. *See id.* at 307–08.

mous assent of parties to transactions and which therefore is presumably welfare enhancing, or *Pareto superior*, lawmaking occurs through various majority, and sometimes supermajority, rules. As a result, even if the resulting laws are Kaldor Hicks efficient, implying that the law is welfare enhancing overall, winners and losers nonetheless remain.

Legislative processes do not, however, simply involve a series of votes cast on proposed legislation. Instead, they involve a complex framework that includes voting based upon merit, strategic voting or vote trading, and reciprocal commitments made over extended periods of time. Here we consider the peculiar dynamic of vote trading, also known as logrolling.

Logrolling is often thought to be anathema to the "public good" and sound legislative decision-making processes because it permits private interests to attach unrelated, usually narrowly focused private benefits to larger public-regarding legislation. As such, it is often thought that legislative processes should be adapted to prevent or to minimize the power of special interests to attach private legislation (such as "pork barrel" projects) to general-interest bills. Such proposals can take any number of forms, including perhaps most notably the item veto and germaneness rules. On the other hand, if politics actually is an exchange process, then there might be nothing intrinsically wrong with logrolling. Instead, laws that further the public interest will often have unequal distributive effects. Even though welfare is generally enhanced, it is inevitable that certain people will be disadvantaged even by the most benign laws.

Logrolling might simply be a form of side payment from the social surplus created by the adoption of the law to compensate the "losers." Just as compensatory side payments are sometimes involved in Pareto-improving exchanges—consider possible private arrangements to compensate third parties who suffer negative externalities—so too such payments might arise through political processes.

Alternatively, logrolling might be viewed as a means through which interest groups extort perks through the political process in exchange for allowing legislation to pass. In politics, as in football, it is generally easier to block than pass. Those empowered for various reasons to prevent the passage of desired legislation might use logrolling simply as a means to get preferred legislative benefits even though the larger legislation does not impose unique costs on them.

Can you think of circumstances in which logrolling is more likely to impose significant costs than benefits? In what circumstances is it likely to promote the passage of desirable legislation? Do you think that logrolling is likely to be a force for good or harm in Congress? If you wished to test this question empirically, how could you falsify either of these competing claims? Can you identify practices in Congress or elsewhere that affirmatively limit logrolling? What distinguishes institutions that prohibit or at least discourage opportunities for logrolling from those that encourage or at least condone logrolling? Can the question whether logrolling is good or bad be resolved outside of a particular institutional context? Why or why not? Bear these questions in mind especially as you read chapter 3.

C. IS LEGISLATIVE INTENT AN OXYMORON?

The preceding discussion highlights another important difference between private and public lawmaking markets. Unlike in private markets, decisions in public markets are made collectively. One of the major tasks of law, and one reason for the considerable overlap between public choice and public law, is the need to interpret statutes that are vague or imprecise as applied to new factual contexts presented in real cases.[67]

Consider for example how the problem of logrolling, discussed above, affects legislative meaning. If legislation is the product of collective decision making, and if decision making is not only a function of the legislators' views of the merits of the proposed bills, but also the product of strategic voting behavior related to matters extraneous to the bill, is it possible to construe meaning beyond the literal text of a statute? Does this help to justify arguments, advanced for example by Justice Antonin Scalia and Judge Frank Easterbrook,[68] against judicial reliance upon legislative history when applying statutes in cases? In answering that question, should it matter that even when courts err in construing statutes, Congress rarely "corrects" such constructions by amending the laws? Does the practical inability of Congress to revisit statutes counsel in favor of a more liberal rule concerning legislative history or other related materials? To what extent do the answers to these questions depend upon how sanguine one is about the overall legislative process? Please bear these questions in mind especially as you read chapter 5.

D. CONCLUSION

The questions presented throughout this chapter will remain important throughout the course. As you acquire new skills, you might change your thinking about the relationships between markets and lawmaking institutions, and between and among various lawmaking bodies. One important aspect of a course in public choice is to question baselines against which one assesses public policy and to develop new techniques with which to evaluate proposed changes in public policy, whichever baselines one happens to select. In the next chapter, we introduce the tools of interest group theory, and in chapter 3, we further build upon these skills by introducing the unique problems of collective decision making associated with social choice. In the appendix that follows, we offer a brief primer on price theory, which will be of value in these and later chapters.

---

67. This problem is exacerbated by another aspect of rationality, introduced in chapter 3, namely the problem of social choice and collective intransitivity of preference.

68. ANTONIN SCALIA, A MATTER OF INTERPRETATION: FEDERAL COURTS AND THE LAW (1998); Frank H. Easterbrook, *Some Tasks in Understanding Law Through the Lens of Public Choice*, 12 INT'L REV. L. & ECON. 284 (1992); Frank H. Easterbrook *Statutes' Domains*, 50 U. CHI. L. REV. 533 (1983).

Appendix: Elements of Price Theory[69]

To evaluate the claim that private markets are generally more prone to promoting Pareto-improving outcomes than political markets, it is important to understand the essential features of how private markets work. Understanding price theory is helpful not only in explaining private market functioning, but also in providing an essential foundation for many important concepts that arise in public choice. Public choice uses many terms that derive from price theory, and those with a foundation in price theory thus have an advantage in appreciating the deeper connections across these two economic methodologies.

Any economic analysis, whether grounded in neoclassical economics, public choice theory, or game theory, requires a basic foundation in the theory of pricing mechanisms. While political markets, the subject of public choice theory, are not price driven, public choice analysis nonetheless builds upon important theoretical foundations from price theory. This includes an understanding of how price operates within both competitive and noncompetitive markets. The analysis once again begins with the premise of individual rationality.

Supply, Demand, and Marginal Revenue

While economics itself offers no insight into what any individual will consider a "good," rationality does assume that more of any given good is generally preferred to less. This implies that as the price of a given good declines, an individual valuing that good will tend to demand more of it. This is true whether the good is purely private, for example, a piece of jewelry, or is instead collectively provided, for example, police officers or schoolteachers. Economists generally depict this intuition graphically, with the amount demanded of a good increasing as a function of price. Thus as the price of a good declines, holding all else constant, individuals and the market as a whole will demand more of the good.

The supply function operates on the opposite premise. Holding all else constant, the higher the price that one can command for a good, the more he or she will invest in procuring that good and offering it to the market. In this very simplified presentation of the market, an equilibrium, or stable outcome, occurs where the two curves meet, and this point identifies the market-clearing price and quantity. This is depicted in Figure 1:1.

---

69. Portions of the presentation that follows are based upon STEARNS, *supra* note 50, at 110–26.

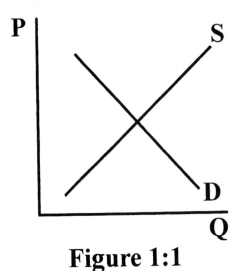

Figure 1:1

A. *Elasticity of Demand and Supply*

The preceding discussion presented the demand curve as a downward sloping function of price and the supply curve as an upward sloping function of price. Within economic analysis, the extent to which the respective curves slope downward or upward proves important in a variety of contexts, including several that relate to law and public policy. The concept of *elasticity* specifically focuses on the relationship between how an incremental change in price will affect the amount demanded (or supplied) of a given good. When demand for a good is inelastic, that means that even a potentially significant increase in price will not have a substantial effect on the quantity of the good demanded. Conversely, when the demand for a good is *elastic*, that means just the opposite; even a small increase in the price will have a large impact on the quantity of the good demanded.

In Figure 1:2, below, we present two demand curves. While both curves are downward sloping (as was the case with the demand curve in Figure 1:1), the first curve, which is *inelastic*, is closer to vertical, and the second, elastic curve, is closer to horizontal. If you begin at any price and quantity along the first curve and move up along the vertical axis, representing price, you will see a relatively small effect on the quantity demanded. If you do the same for the second curve, however, you will see a relatively more dramatic effect on the quantity demanded.

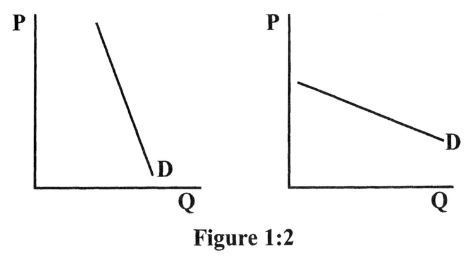

Figure 1:2

The same set of intuitions affect the supply of goods. Thus in Figure 1:3 below, we depict an inelastic (closer to vertical) supply curve in which changes in price do not affect a substantial increase in production. We then present an elastic (closer to horizontal) supply curve in which an increase in price affects a substantial increase in production. As the next discussion shows, it is possible in a single market for elasticities to vary depending on whether we are describing a single producer of goods or the aggregation of producers for the entire market.

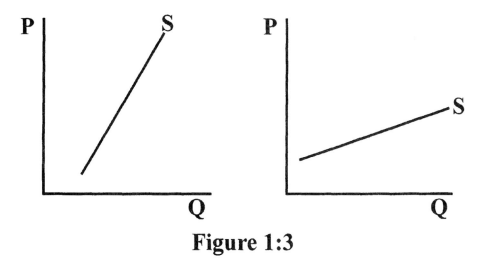

Figure 1:3

B. *Competitive versus NonCompetitive Markets*

Economists distinguish two paradigmatic market situations, competitive and noncompetitive, or monopolistic, markets. Within competitive markets, individual firms are unable to control the market-clearing, or equilibrium, price. The price is determined at the point where supply and demand (Dm) intersect for the market as a whole. Pure competition means that no single firm is large enough to affect the price for the overall market. For each individual firm, therefore, the price is effectively fixed, meaning that the demand curve (Di) is flat (or elastic). If the firm elected to sell at a price one cent below the prevailing market price, it could in theory sell an infinite amount of that good. Conversely, if it priced the good one cent above the prevailing market price, no one would buy it. Thus, within competitive markets, individual firms are *price takers*. As Figure 1:4 suggests, firms operating in competitive markets will sell as much as it is cost effective for them to sell at the prevailing market price over which they have no control.

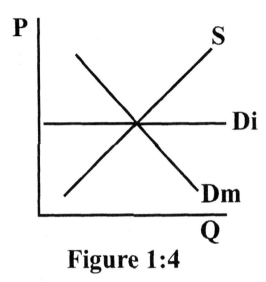

Figure 1:4

While we will next consider a market in which the seller is a monopolist, it is important to recognize that most markets operate somewhere between the two analytical poles representing pure competition and pure monopoly. Most often, firms operate within markets in which the sellers possess a limited, not absolute, degree of market power. Market power implies that the firm is not a price taker. Firms with complete market power, known as monopolists, assume the same position as the aggregate set of firms in a competitive market environment. Just as the entire set of firms faces a downward sloping, instead of a flat demand curve, so too does the monopolist. Most importantly, because the monopolist confronts the demand for the entire market, it is able to affect price by controlling the quantity of goods produced and sold.

Professors William Baumol and Alan Blinder have explained the circumstances giving rise to monopoly power as follows: "There are two basic reasons why a monopoly may exist: barriers to entry, such as legal restrictions and patents, and cost advantages of superior technology or large-scale operations that lead to natural monopoly."[70] The authors add

---

70. WILLIAM J. BAUMOL & ALAN S. BLINDER, ECONOMICS: PRINCIPLES AND POLICY 217 (10th ed. 2006).

that "It is generally considered undesirable to break up a large firm whose costs are low because of scale economies. But barriers to entry are usually considered to be against the public interest except where they are believed to have offsetting advantages, as in the case of patents."[71]

In chapter 2, we will introduce the concept of rent seeking, the process through which firms impose barriers to entry. For now, we will focus on natural monopoly. Baumol and Blinder explain the conditions that give rise to natural monopoly as follows:

> In some industries, economies of large-scale production or economies of scope (from simultaneous production of a large number of related items, such as car motors and bodies, truck parts, and so on) are so extreme that the industry's output can be produced at far lower cost by a single firm than by a number of smaller firms. In such cases, we say there is a natural monopoly. Once a firm becomes large enough relative to the size of the market for its product, its natural cost advantage may well drive the competition out of business whether or not anyone in the relatively large firm has evil intentions.
>
> A monopoly need not be a large firm if the market is small enough. *What matters is the size of a single firm relative to the total market demand for the product.*[72]

A defining characteristic of a natural monopoly firm is *declining average cost*. This means that the cost of production for each unit becomes lower the larger the scale of the operation in which those units are produced.

When production is characterized by declining average cost, a single monopolistic firm will drive smaller competing firms out of the market because smaller firms cannot match the natural monopolist's low average cost. This is most likely to arise with utilities, for example, gas or electric, that require distribution networks operating on a vast scale to function and that once constructed can offer services at a lower average cost than potential market entrants. The major concern with natural monopolies is that once competing firms are driven out (or once potential competitors realize that entry into the market is futile), the remaining firm, behaving rationally, will reduce its output and raise its price to the monopoly level. This is the traditional justification for regulating utilities.

More typically, several producers exist in a given market and each has some degree of market power based upon brand name recognition and *product differentiation*.[73] Coca Cola can raise its price relative to Pepsi, and those who are brand loyal will not immediately switch. If Coca Cola tripled its price relative to Pepsi, however, all but the most loyal fans would develop a taste for Pepsi or another alternative. Because individual

---

71. *Id.*

72. *Id.* at 216 (italics in original).

73. Baumol and Blinder explain that the "rigid requirements make pure monopoly a rarity in the real world," *id.* at 214, but that "like perfect competition, pure monopoly is a market form that is easier to analyze." *Id.* at 214–15.

firms with market power face downward sloping, rather than flat, demand curves, they are price setters rather than price takers.

Figure 1:5 illustrates the supply and demand configuration for a firm operating in a noncompetitive market:

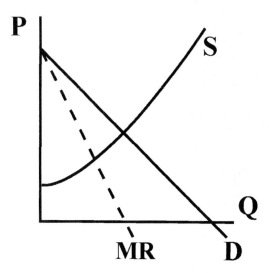

Figure 1:5

The demand curve facing a firm in a noncompetitive market, like that for the market as a whole, slopes downward. Most notably, the monopolist confronts a *marginal revenue curve* (MR) that lies below the demand curve. The model assumes that that the seller is not able to engage in *price discrimination*, which would allow her to vary price according to the buyer's willingness to pay. As a result, for each additional unit sold, the firm must lower the price not only for *that* unit, but for all units sold to that point. The marginal revenue curve captures this intuition and reflects the gain associated with each additional unit of sale less the reduced price for all units sold up to that point.

The monopolist is, of course, concerned with maximizing profit, not revenue. To do so, it sells up to the point where marginal revenue equals supply, which is also marginal cost. At that point, the seller will sell quantity Qm, setting price at Pm, as shown in Figure 1:6. Because the marginal cost for any additional unit sold exceeds the marginal revenue associated with the sale of that next unit, the firm stops producing at that point. Any further output would generate net losses to the firm because in order to sell each additional unit, the firm would have to lower the price for that unit along with that for all additional units sold.

Discussion questions: Can you identify any circumstances in which a firm with market power is capable of engaging in price discrimination? Does the answer depend upon how one defines the relevant product? Is a designer outfit offered on sale several months after it is introduced the same "product" as when it first entered the market? Is the same meal offered at half price as an "early bird special" an act of price discrimination, or is it two different products, priced accordingly? Should the legal system be concerned with these examples of differential pricing? If such pricing schemes were banned, who would benefit and who would lose?

C. *Profits and Rents*

Monopolistic pricing produces societal welfare losses that the preceding analysis helps to identify. To understand the difficulties that monopolistic pricing can produce, we must introduce three concepts: *monopoly profit*, sometimes referred to as *economic profit*; *Ricardian competitive rents*; and *monopoly rents*.

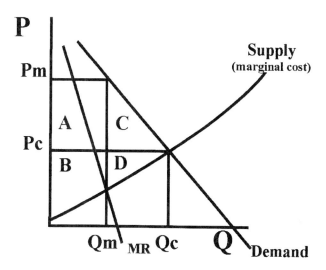

Figure 1:6

From the perspective of consumers, the ideal result would be for the monopolist to sell a quantity represented as *Qc* and to set price at *Pc*. Assume that through regulation, a firm with market power is forced to set price where marginal cost, or supply, equals demand. At that point, the price and quantity are the same as those arising under competitive conditions. Under competitive conditions, the triangle labeled *C* represents the consumer surplus, namely the additional amount that consumers would be willing to pay to secure the additional output from *Qm* to *Qc*. The regions *B* and *D* represent Ricardian competitive rents, namely the ordinary profit that would accrue to a firm selling under competitive conditions. Because the marginal cost, or supply, curve is upward sloping, and lies below the competitive price, regions *B* and *D* demonstrate the potentially different profit levels at firms operating in a competitive environment.[74] Without such regulation, the firm instead sets output at Qm and price at Pm. At this point, monopoly profits are represented in regions A plus B, where the monopoly price lies above the supply curve.

Monopoly profits do not, however, represent the gains to the firm from moving from competitive to monopoly pricing. In moving from Qc and Pc to Qm and Pm, the firm has given up its Ricardian competitive rents. To calculate the difference between profits under competitive and noncompetitive pricing strategies, referred to as monopoly rents, we need to subtract B plus D (the Ricardian competitive rents) from A plus B (the monopoly profit). Note that $(A + B) - (B + D) = A - D$. Thus, $A - D$ represents the gains from moving from a competitive to noncompetitive market, or the monopoly rents. At the same time, C plus D, representing the foregone consumer and producer surpluses, respectively, constitute the deadweight societal loss associated with monopoly pricing.

Discussion questions and comments: Are there any circumstances in which prohibiting monopoly rents might undermine consumer welfare? Consider the following argument. Some markets are characterized by very large start up costs. Firms willingly incur such costs in anticipation of potential monopoly rents that they will generate, at least in the short to moderate term, which offset that upfront investment. A rule that prohibits monopoly rents potentially inhibits the requisite start up costs that result in the provision of valuable goods and services to the market. Is this argument persuasive? Does this explain the general rule that individual firms with market power are free to earn monopoly profit, but not free to engage in collaborative practices with other firms to earn monopoly profit?[75] What countervailing arguments counsel in favor of limiting the ability of firms to earn monopoly rents?

D. Opportunity Cost, Ordinary Profit, and Economic Profit

The preceding analysis helps explain one of the most important concepts in economics, namely *opportunity cost*.[76] Opportunity cost recog-

---

74. Ricardian competitive rents capture the intuition that even in competitive conditions, some firms will receive greater profits than others, namely those who can produce at lower cost. Thus, for example, even in competitive markets for oranges and grapefruits, we would expect, all else being equal, those farms with particularly good soil conditions to receive higher Ricardian competitive rents than farms with poor soil conditions as a result of the differing cost of production. For a helpful discussion of various forms of rent, see Armen A. Alchian, *Rent, in* 4 THE NEW PALGRAVE: A DICTIONARY OF ECONOMICS 141–42 (John Eatwell et al. eds., 1998).

75. For an article that explores this theme, see David S. Evans & Keith N. Hylton, *The Lawful Acquisition and Exercise of Monopoly Power and Its Implications for the Objectives of Antitrust,* 4 COMPETITION POL'Y INT'L 203 (2008).

76. For a helpful introduction to opportunity cost, see RICHARD A. IPPOLITO, ECONOMICS FOR LAWYERS 120–24 (2005).

nizes that the real cost of activities is not limited to out of pocket expenses, but also includes the foregone opportunity associated with the next best use of one's time or resources.

Understanding opportunity cost is essential in distinguishing *economic profit* from *ordinary profit*. Economists often distinguish between competitive environments in which firms earn zero profit and noncompetitive environments in which firms earn economic profit. Obviously no firm will stay in business that earns zero profit in an accounting sense. But economists do not use zero profit in that manner. Instead, by zero profit, economists mean ordinary profit, which is equivalent to the generally expected rate of return in the economy. When the return on a particular activity is no better than alternative market opportunities for an entrepreneur's time or resources, then she is earning the generally expected rate of return, meaning zero profit. If there are no market opportunities that present better expected rates of return, then the opportunity cost of remaining in the present activity is low.

In contrast, if another opportunity presents itself that allows a substantially higher rate of return, then the opportunity cost for the present activity has risen, and holding all else constant, rational actors will leave their present (ordinary profit) activity for the alternative (economic profit) activity. As more resources flow toward the activity earning economic profit, the return on that activity will predictably decline toward the normal rate of profit. At that point, the opportunity cost of that activity becomes closer to that of the originating activity.

E.   The Production Possibility Frontier

The production possibility frontier, depicted in figure 7, represents the potential economic output for an individual, firm, or nation, as between two commodities.

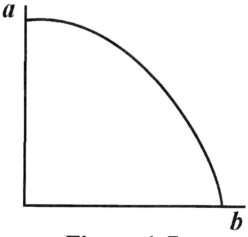

Figure 1:7

Assume that an individual is capable of producing two forms of output, a and b, but that in doing so, for each commodity the person experiences decreasing marginal productivity. In other words, producing the first unit of b would require this person to forego relatively little of a, and producing each additional unit of b would require this person to forego producing a somewhat larger quantity of a. The opposite also holds; as the person produces additional increments of a, she is required to forego producing larger and larger increments of b. This relationship is captured in the convex *production possibility frontier* (PPF). The PPF can be viewed as an individual's supply potential as between x and y. The PPF can also depict the potential production of an individual, firm, or nation. On a larger scale, industries maximize their economic output when they produce at the most highly valued point along their production possibility frontier.

F. Production Schedules, Indifference Curves, and Budget Constraints

To determine the maximum value of an individual's *production schedule*, we need to introduce two related concepts: *indifference curves* and *budget constraints*. In contrast with the PPF, which is convex, *indifference curves*, which depict an individual's relative valuation as between two commodities, are concave. This reflects the decreasing marginal utility associated with additional acquired (whether produced or purchased) increments of a relative to b, and the reverse, decreasing marginal utility for additional acquired increments of b relative to a. Because the indifference curve plots only *relative* valuation as between two goods, rather than how many of those goods a person can afford, each individual has an infinite number of indifference curves for any potential choice between two commodities or between any given commodity and money, which stands in for a potential basket of all competing commodities.

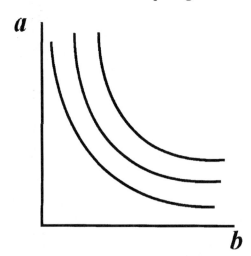

Figure 1:8

Each indifference curve lies just slightly farther from the vertex (where *a* and *b* meet) than the one beneath it. Of course depending upon one's resources, based either on production or purchasing capability, some of those curves are more relevant than others. By way of illustration, an indifference curve respecting the relative valuation of between 1000 to 10,000 perfect two-carat diamonds versus 1000 to 10,000 prime acres of real estate is not of particular concern to someone who can only afford a one carat diamond and a half acre of land. In addition, we are not limited solely to our own production in allocating our decisions as between two commodities.

The mechanism of market exchange allows persons to specialize and to improve the value of their outputs. Unlike Robinson Crusoe, whose choice between foraging and building a shelter is strictly limited by how he allocates his own labor, within markets, individuals can produce more of a particular good that they are quite good at producing and then sell those goods on the market. Monetizing one's productive resources in this manner dramatically improves efficiency and thus overall societal welfare.

Through exchange, we can convert our optimal production into money that forms a *budget constraint* for commodities that someone else produces. Budget constraints, which represent how much of *a* and *b* a person can afford, can be depicted as a straight downward sloping line from a point along the *a*-axis to a point along the *b*-axis. Figure 1:9 depicts a budget constraint for two goods, where the *a* and *b* axes represent sandwiches respectively.

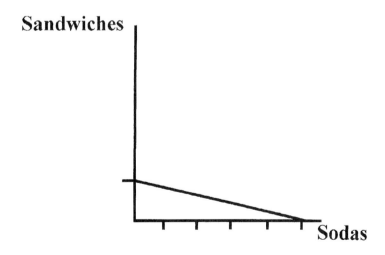

Figure 1:9

The slope of the curve reflects the relative value of these two commodities. In this example, it is assumed that sandwiches cost five times more than cans of soda. Although the slope of the curve is constant, the location of the curve—how far it lies from the vertex—varies as a function of the person's wealth. Individual utility is maximized when she has reached a point along her highest available (meaning the farthest from the vertex) indifference curve.

To be on the highest indifference curve with respect to two commodities, a person must produce or purchase to the point where an indifference curve is tangent to (meaning it touches but does not overlap), the budget constraint or PPF. This is illustrated with a budget constraint respecting two commodities, a and b, and the potential set of relevant indifference curves in Figure 10.

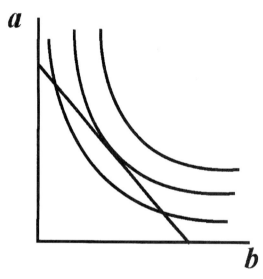

Figure 1:10

If, instead, the indifference curve overlaps with her budget constraint or PPF, she could reallocate either production or purchasing decisions to move onto a higher indifference curve, thus deriving greater utility.

While this brief overview of several price theoretical concepts will be helpful for the materials that follow, it is not intended as a substitute for more in depth course length treatment. Several of these concepts will be developed more fully throughout this course.

CHAPTER 2

INTEREST GROUP THEORY AND RENT-SEEKING

■ ■ ■

INTRODUCTION

In order to aid the American steel industry in March 2002, President George W. Bush imposed tariffs on imported steel that ranged from eight to thirty percent,[1] depending on the type of steel.[2] The tariffs aided the steel industry by dramatically increasing the market price of steel in the United States. At the same time, however, this price increase was passed on to producers who relied upon steel inputs, including, for example, automobile manufacturers, producers of machinery, and the construction industry. The resulting price increases were substantial. One study estimates that over 200,000 jobs were lost in the United States in steel-using industries in the first year of the tariff alone, a number that exceeds the total employment in the entire United States steel industry.[3] In contrast, the same study estimates that the tariffs saved fewer than 10,000 jobs within the steel industry at a cost of between $450,000–$584,000 per job. Some manufacturers were able to pass along part of the raised cost of steel inputs to end users in the form of higher prices. This strategy was most effective in those industries for which demand for goods was relatively

---

1. *See* Proclamation No. 7529, 3 C.F.R. 15 (2003) ("To Facilitate Positive Adjustment to Competition from Imports of Certain Steel Products"). The action was taken by President Bush pursuant to Article 2.1 of the World Trade Organization (WTO) Agreement on Safeguards (1994), *available at* http://www.wto.org/english/docs_e/legal_e/25-safeg.pdf (setting forth the rules for application of safeguard measures pursuant to Article XIX of the General Agreement on Tariffs and Trade (Apr. 15, 1994), *available at* http://www.wto.org/english/docs_e/legal_e/gatt47_02_e. htm#articleXIX [hereinafter GATT 1994]), which permits a country to impose "Emergency Safeguards" if "serious injury" could result to domestic producers as a result of unfair trade practices such as the improper dumping of goods. *See* WORLD TRADE ORGANIZATION, TRADING INTO THE FUTURE 29–32 (2d ed. 2001), *available at* http://www.wto.org/english/res_e/doload_e/tif.pdf. The procedures for implementing safeguards are codified in U.S. law at 19 U.S.C. § 2253 (2006).

2. For an informative discussion of the steel tariffs, see Robert Read, *The Political Economy of Trade Protection: The Determinants and Welfare Impact of the 2002 US Emergency Steel Safeguard Measures*, 28 WORLD ECON. 1119 (2005). The steel tariffs were lifted twenty-one months later in December 2003 following an adverse ruling by the WTO that the tariff violated the GATT 1994. *Id.* at 1132–33.

3. Joseph Francois & Laura M. Baughman, The Unintended Consequences of U.S. Steel Import Tariffs: A Quantification of the Impact During 2002, at 12 (Feb. 4, 2003), *available at* http://www.citac.info/about/issues/remedy/2002_Job_Study.pdf.

inelastic,[4] including, for example, in the markets for certain automobiles, motor vehicle parts, machine goods, and construction inputs. Nonetheless, some analysts have determined that the net effect of the tariffs, including the increased cost of consumer goods and jobs lost within manufacturing industries relying upon steel inputs, was substantially greater than the benefits in terms of jobs retained or gained within the steel industry itself.

In *Federalist No. 10*, James Madison famously expressed fear that transient majorities, or "factions," would form with the power to deploy the machinery of government to their advantage. Madison posited that one of the principal missions of constitutionalism is to divide and control the government to make more difficult the possibility that factional violence would form and operate the machinery of government to the detriment of the electorate. While Madison's thesis represents a major contribution to contemporary American political theory, the example of the steel tariff raises the possibility that as a description of how the United States system of governance actually operates, the theory might be incomplete.[5]

Building upon the tools from chapter 1, and introducing several new ones, this chapter will begin the process of constructing simple models designed to explain important features of the political process. Although we will emphasize familiar processes within the United States, several of the insights that we develop can be generalized to alternative political systems. The analysis will explore the conditions under which majoritarian or minoritarian factions, meaning interest group coalitions that produce majority alliances or influential minority interest groups, are likely to thrive within the U.S., or other, political processes; how those processes are structured to limit or to harness such interests; and what the implications of such processes are for the procurement of various forms of public and quasi-private legislative goods. We begin by introducing the essential tools from interest group theory. After doing so, we will discuss actual cases that raise important questions concerning the relationship between processes through which legislation is procured and the proper role of courts in evaluating resulting legislation.

We begin by inquiring how the steel industry was able to succeed in acquiring a protective tariff even though, whether weighed in terms of the number of people, the number of firms, or the value of economic activity, it appears that the aggregate economic losses well exceeded the resulting gains to the steel industry.[6] For those who might assume that governmen-

---

4. For a discussion of price elasticities, see chapter 1, appendix.

5. It is also often believed that the President will be less responsive to special interests than a typical member of Congress will be because the President has the incentive to consider the interests of the entire country and thus internalizes all of the costs of inefficient policies. *See* Peter H. Aranson, Ernest Gellhorn, & Glen O. Robinson, *A Theory of Legislative Delegation*, 68 CORNELL L. REV. 1, 41 (1982). Yet the steel tariff was imposed by the President interpreting GATT and was only repealed after an adverse ruling by the World Trade Organization. What might explain the President's behavior in this case? For a discussion, see Read, *supra* note 2, at 1126–27, 1133–34.

6. For an analysis that establishes that these various measures reveal that losses exceeded gains, see Read, *supra* note 2, at 1129–31.

tal processes generally conduce to the "public interest," the steel tariff at a minimum appears to be an important cautionary tale. The story becomes even more significant, however, if it somehow reveals a fundamental limitation of the public interest view of legislative procurement of public goods and services.

I. PUBLIC AND PRIVATE INTEREST MODELS OF GOVERNMENT

We begin with the "public interest model" of government regulation, which dominated throughout much of the twentieth century. This view came into prominence with the rise of the industrialized era. Both within the media and popular culture, there was a strong perceived need for the government to provide benign intervention to combat the increasingly horrific working conditions associated with early industrialization. For one prominent example, consider Upton Sinclair's famous 1906 novel, *The Jungle*, which, in widely exposing the unsafe and unsanitary conditions associated with the meat packing industry at the turn of the twentieth century, provided a strong impetus for the creation of the Food and Drug Administration.[7]

The development of economic science provided a strong theoretical foundation for relying upon the government to correct widely perceived imperfections within market processes that generated "market failures." Regulatory advocates recognized that self interest did not invariably align with the public good and believed that proper government intervention was necessary to ensure that markets produced socially optimal, or at least preferred, results.

The analysis once again returns us to the works of the economists, Arthur Cecil Pigou and Ronald Coase.[8] Pigou claimed that where property rights were imperfectly defined, property owners acting in their self interest were motivated to engage in profitable economic activities even when those activities generated substantial "negative externalities" such as pollution. Because owners of polluting firms did not internalize the full social cost of production, Pigou claimed, the quest for profit thrust a wedge between the level of output chosen by a self-interested private actor and the socially optimal level of the activity. The resulting market failure implied that left to its own devices, the market (or more accurately individuals within the market) tended to produce too many goods for which all costs were not internalized, with the effect of passing on real costs to others who did not benefit from their economic activities. Pigou

---

7. UPTON SINCLAIR, THE JUNGLE (1906). For alternative accounts, see Marc T. Law & Gary D. Libecap, *The Determinants of Progressive Era Reform: The Pure Food and Drugs Act of 1906, in* CORRUPTION AND REFORM: LESSONS FROM AMERICA'S ECONOMIC HISTORY 319 (Edward L. Glaeser & Claudia Goldin eds., 2006) (noting influence of producer groups); Gary D. Libecap, *The Rise of the Chicago Packers and the Origins of Meat Inspection and Antitrust*, 30 ECON. INQUIRY 242 (1992).

8. *See supra* chapter 1, at section II.I (discussing Pigou and Coase).

proposed resolving this difficulty by, among other means, imposing a tax that resulted in the full internalization of the costs of economic activity.

The public interest model of government that corresponds with Pigouvian regulation rests on an important premise. It assumes that the government can identify various deficiencies in private market orderings, with the negative externality of pollution as one important example, and then create an appropriate legal response that will encourage private actors to account for the divergence between private costs and total costs. By better aligning private and social costs of economic activities, Pigouvian regulation would promote socially beneficial outcomes.

Pigou's argument has been subject to two lines of critique, the first offered by Nobel Prize-winning economist Ronald Coase. Coase challenged the assumption that government is capable of collecting and using all of the information needed to identify and correct such market failures. Public choice provides the basis for the second critique. The government, even if theoretically capable of operating as a Pigouvian central planner, is unlikely to actually do so in practice. Thus, while the public interest model of government rests upon identified market failures as compared with a theoretically perfectly functioning market that aligns private and social costs, public choice identifies the failings of an idealized view of regulation in which the government can effortlessly (and costlessly) correct market failures. Public choice is not concerned with theoretically ideal institutions, whether markets, legislatures, or other institutions.[9] Rather, it is concerned with identifying the relative strengths and weaknesses of real world institutions as a means of making more meaningful assessments concerning when particular responsibilities for decision making are better channeled toward one institution or another.

Not long after the rise of industrialization, political scientists began to critically assess the public interest understanding of benign government processes. One famous illustration, E.E. Schattschneider's study of the 1930 Smoot–Hawley Tariff,[10] demonstrates some of the conceptual difficulties that reemerged in the steel tariffs.[11] The Smoot–Hawley Tariff differs from the recent Steel Tariffs in that it resulted from a federal statute rather than from an executive proclamation. Through a series of logrolls, Congress managed to endorse a combination of prohibitive tariffs that benefited various industries, but that did so at tremendous cost to the national economy. Schattschneider's analysis, which rests on a pluralist understanding of politics,[12] views Congress as a neutral conduit that

---

9. *See* Harold Demsetz, *Information and Efficiency: Another Viewpoint*, 12 J.L. & ECON. 1 (1969) (describing the nirvana fallacy that "pervades much public policy economics"); *see also infra* chapter 3, at section I.F.2.

10. Tariff Act of 1930, Pub. L. No. 71–361, 46 Stat. 590 (codified as amended at 19 U.S.C. §§ 1202–1681b (2006)).

11. E.E. SCHATTSCHNEIDER, POLITICS, PRESSURES AND THE TARIFF (photo. reprint 1963) (1935).

12. Pluralist theory, a precursor to the modern theory of public choice, viewed the legislature as a conduit through which special interest groups accomplished their own legislative outcomes. *See* EARL LATHAM, THE GROUP BASIS OF POLITICS 35 (1952) (positing that "[the] legislature referees the group struggle, ratifies the victories of the successful coalitions and records the terms of

rubber-stamped an industry-negotiated pact, one primarily reached outside formal political processes. Modern public choice analysis builds upon pluralism but recognizes the importance of modeling the interest of legislators themselves in interacting with various other forces, including constituencies, lobbyists, and actors within other branches of government. The public interest view of government stands in stark contrast with this pluralist understanding, and also with its more modern counterpart, the modern theory of public choice.

As the steel tariff example and the discussion of the Smoot–Hawley Act demonstrate, the public interest model imperfectly describes the workings of actual political processes. At a minimum, these examples might illustrate the possibility that political actors, and Congress as an institution, sometimes depart from the "public interest" in favor of producing outcomes that benefit special interest groups. Public choice theorists claim that interest group influence on legislative outcomes is commonplace, with the effect of producing narrow tax exemptions, protective tariffs, industry subsidies, and competitive restrictions (also known as barriers to entry). While Madison expressed the concern that governmental processes would allow majoritarian factions to benefit at the expense of the public, revisiting the microfoundations of collective decision making allows us to appreciate how well-organized minority interest groups frequently prevail even in Madison's complex constitutional scheme that was specifically designed to improve legislative accountability and limit the vice of factional violence.

A. RENTS, QUASI–RENTS, AND RENT SEEKING

We can now more fully appreciate the concept of economic rents, introduced in the appendix to chapter 1. Recall that an economic rent arises when an economic activity, for example labor, earns a return that exceeds the opportunity cost of the income-producing asset. Monopolists earn economic rents by imposing restrictions on outputs with the effect of commanding a price paid for the resulting goods or services that is higher than that dictated in a competitive market. Restrictions on the ability of potential competitors to supply the same or similar goods results in "economic rents" for those who capture the market. Those exempt from competition are thus able to supply their goods at a price that exceeds the opportunity cost, or next best use, of the various factors of production. A firm with market power, exemplified by a monopolist, can extract economic rents by restricting supply and thereby raising prices.[13] The monopolist

---

surrenders, compromises, and conquests in the form of statutes."); THEODORE J. LOWI, THE POLITICS OF DISORDER xviii–xix (1971) (positing that "[the] basis of pluralism and quiescence is the organized group and group interactions, with political man holding the whole together through delegation and negotiation."); Maxwell L. Stearns, *The Public Choice Case Against the Item Veto,* 49 WASH. & LEE L. REV. 385, 400 n.94 (1992) (collecting authorities on pluralism). A major difference between pluralism and the modern theory of public choice and is that the latter accounts for the independent role of political actors, based upon their personal motivations, in affecting institutional outcomes. Stearns, *supra.*

13. For a more detailed discussion, see chapter 1, appendix.

receives rents equal to the difference between the level of profit available under conditions of monopoly and that available under competitive conditions. The following graphic illustrates the monopolistic pricing strategy and the resulting economic rents:[14]

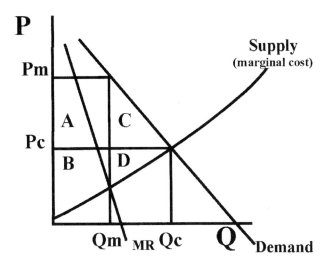

Figure 2:1

Figure 2:1 illustrates the social welfare loss of monopoly. The triangular areas C and D represent the resulting social "deadweight loss." These triangles represent foregone mutually beneficial, and thus wealth producing, exchanges that would have been conducted absent the monopolistic pricing strategy. Area C represents the foregone consumer surplus and area D represents the foregone producer surplus. These "deadweight loss triangles" are often referred to as "Harberger triangles," named after the economist Arnold Harberger, who was the first to formalize the analysis and to measure the resulting social loss resulting from monopolistic practices, including those resulting from government policies such as price regulations and government taxes.[15] A principal normative justification for antitrust law, for instance, is to "recoup" these deadweight losses for the economy by preventing a monopolist from restricting supply and thereby raising prices.

As previously shown, areas $A - D$, equivalent to the monopolistic rent minus the foregone producer surplus in Figure 2:1, represents the "economic rent," which is largely a wealth transfer from consumers to producers as the result of monopolistic pricing strategy. That strategy allows a reduction in output and an increase in price. Another way of

---

14. *See supra* p. 35, Fig. 1:6.

15. *See* James R. Hines, Jr., *Three Sides of Harberger Triangles*, J. ECON. PERSP., Spring 1999, at 167.

generating economic rents is through the enactment of regulations that have the same effect of restricting competition and allowing producers to raise prices above competitive levels. Consider the steel tariff. Steel tariffs raise the price of imported steel relative to domestic steel. But they also allow producers of domestic steel to increase their prices to the level of imported steel even though domestic producers do not pay the tax. With respect to imported steel, the tariff proceeds are paid directly to the federal government. With respect to domestic producers, however, the price increases are a direct wealth transfer from consumers to producers of steel.

The distribution of economic rents among the various stakeholders in the benefiting firms, primarily shareholders and employees, depends on how these groups negotiate. In general, however, we can predict some "sharing" of rents between employees and owners of the firm,[16] depending in large part on the relative bargaining power of the different groups. For instance, unionized employees might be in a stronger position to bargain for a greater share of rents than nonunionized employees. The fact that rents typically are shared between owners and employees suggests that employees will generally be willing to provide political support for protectionist or other beneficial regulation.[17]

While monopolistic pricing generates rents like those resulting from protectionist regulatory policies, public choice helps to explain why as a general matter the latter source of rents is likely to be more durable. When markets create opportunities for monopolistic pricing, the rent opportunity attracts new entrants that tend to compete away those rents. For example, markets produce opportunities for monopolistic pricing when start-up investments are sufficiently high that the average cost of the goods in question declines as a result of economies of scale. Declining average cost makes it difficult for potential competitors to enter the market, as a single firm tends to drive out competition at least in the short to moderate term.[18]

Familiar paradigms include electrical utilities, mail systems, and airplane and automobile manufacturers, each of which is characterized by extraordinarily high start-up costs. In most circumstances, however, even these industries eventually invite new entrants and thus competition.

---

16. *See* Sandra E. Black & Philip E. Strahan, *The Division of Spoils: Rent–Sharing and Discrimination in a Regulated Industry*, 91 AM. ECON. REV. 814 (2001) (finding that regulation of competition in banking industry resulted in rent-sharing with banking employees); *see also* Marcello Estevão & Stacey Tevlin, *Do Firms Share their Success with Workers? The Response of Wages to Product Market Conditions*, 70 ECONOMICA 597 (2003); Pedro S. Martins, *Rent Sharing Before and After the Wage Bill* (IZA discussion paper No. 1376, 2004), *available at* http://papers. ssrn.com/sol3/papers.cfm?abstract_id=614441.

17. For instance, the United Steelworkers of America were vigorous political supporters of the decision to impose steel tariffs. *See* Read, *supra* note 2, at 1125–26. The United Auto Workers also provided strong support for federal bailout proposals of the automobile industry in 2008. Matthew Doland & John D. Stoll, *UAW Faces Prospect of More Concessions*, WALL ST. J., Nov. 17, 2008, at A4 (noting that "the UAW is standing shoulder-to-shoulder with the [auto] companies in an intense public campaign to plead for a federal bailout").

18. *See supra* chapter 1, at note 73 (citing WILLIAM J. BAUMOL & ALAN S. BLINDER, ECONOMICS: PRINCIPLES AND POLICY 217 (10th ed. 2006)).

Federal Express competes with the United States Postal Service, oil distributors compete with natural gas, and while the market remains concentrated, several manufacturers compete in the production of automobiles and airplanes. But one need not resort to this sort of large scale industry to illustrate the proposition of market power. While large scale natural monopoly is uncommon, conditions that characterize natural monopoly such as declining average cost for the relevant range of outputs, arise within many start-up industries. In nearly every industry, for at least some period of time, high start up costs give rise to economies of scale and declining average costs. Over time, however, the perceived opportunities for the resulting quasi-rents—rents that result from temporary market conditions that allow prices above the opportunity cost for the relevant factors of production[19]—encourage others to incur the necessary initial start-up costs to offer competing market products.[20]

Government-conferred rents in contrast are usually created by erecting barriers to entry, such as restrictive licensing or permit regimes. Thus, the process of eroding rents through entry of market competitors is stifled. Governmentally created rents are also more permanent for a second reason. While monopolistic activity is subject to prosecution under antitrust laws, regulatory schemes with anticompetitive effects are exempt from such laws.[21]

II. THE ECONOMIC THEORY OF REGULATION[22]

Given the durability of legislatively conferred rents, it is important to consider the circumstances under which legislators, behaving rationally, are likely to confer such rents and the nature of the rents that industry groups, behaving rationally, are likely to seek. In two famous articles, written in the 1970s, George Stigler and Sam Peltzman addressed these questions. In *The Theory of Economic Regulation*,[23] George Stigler chal-

---

19. Fred McChesney defines "rent" as, "[R]eturns to the owner of an asset in excess of the level of returns necessary for him to continue using the asset in its current employment. Thus, a rent is any return above what the owner would earn in the asset's next-best alternative use." FRED S. MCCHESNEY, MONEY FOR NOTHING: POLITICIANS, RENT EXTRACTION, AND POLITICAL EXTORTION 10 (1997). As McChesney notes, economists have never agreed on a precise conventional definition of "rent," especially in contrast to the term "quasi-rent," which refers to *temporary* returns on assets above opportunity cost. *Id.*; *see* Armen A. Alchian, *Rent*, *in* 4 THE NEW PALGRAVE: A DICTIONARY OF ECONOMICS 141–42 (John Eatwell et al. eds., 1998). Unless otherwise specified, in this book, we will follow the general convention of public choice economics and use the term "rent" to refer to returns above the asset's opportunity cost, regardless of whether temporary or permanent.

20. Another vehicle for the production of quasi-rents is product differentiation, which provides a vehicle even within markets generally characterized by competition for varying degrees of market power as a result of increased inelasticity of demand for the differentiated good.

21. *See* Parker v. Brown, 317 U.S. 341 (1943); *see also* Report of the State Action Task Force, Federal Trade Commission Office of Policy Planning (2003), *available at* http://www.ftc.gov/os/2003/09/stateactionreport.pdf.

22. Portions of the discussions that follow are adapted from MAXWELL L. STEARNS, PUBLIC CHOICE AND PUBLIC LAW: READINGS AND COMMENTARY 120–21 (1997).

23. George J. Stigler, *The Theory of Economic Regulation*, 2 BELL J. ECON. & MGMT. SCI. 3 (1971).

lenged the intuition that most regulation is imposed upon industries to benefit the public and instead posited that much regulation is affirmatively acquired by industries to secure monopolistic rents. Stigler questioned why, for example, the oil industry, in which the supply is relatively elastic (meaning that output is sensitive to changes in price), lobbied for import quotas rather than for import tariffs or direct cash grants. If the regulation had been aimed at protecting domestic production capabilities for national defense purposes, as industry interests generally claimed, tariffs could have achieved that with all costs paid into the national treasury rather than to industry participants. Direct cash grants or subsidies also would have produced the stated objective of ensuring a domestic oil supply at a substantially lower cost to consumers than import quotas.

Quotas, unlike tariffs, by definition limit market supply and thereby prevent entry from dissipating rents. Stigler posited that the industry preference for quotas reflected the desire of producers, operating in a market typified by elastic supply, to prevent potential market entrants from sharing the benefits of regulation. He further demonstrated that state licensure requirements often serve the same purpose of inhibiting market entry and securing monopolistic rents for the industry acquiring the regulation.

Stigler considered when legislators, behaving rationally, are likely to provide regulatory benefits sought by industries. His analysis suggests that well organized and small groups (especially those without significant opposition), those best able to confer regulatory benefits upon their members, are most likely to engage in effective rent seeking, meaning affirmative lobbying efforts to secure beneficial legal protections against competition, while large and diffuse groups are not.[24] Behaving rationally, legislators are likely to be responsive to these sorts of constituent pressures, which help to further prospects for reelection.

In explaining the significance of Stigler's insight, Sam Peltzman stated:[25]

> In one sense, Stigler's work provides a theoretical foundation for [a] "producer protection" view [of regulation]. . . . Stigler seems to have realized that the earlier "consumer protection" model comes perilously close to treating regulation as a free good. In that model the existence of market failure is sufficient to generate a demand for regulation, though there is no mention of the mechanism that makes that demand effective. . . . Since the good, regulation, is not in fact free and demand for it is not automatically synthesized, Stigler sees the task of a positive economics of regulation as specifying the arguments underlying the supply and demand for regulation.[26]

---

24. These themes are systematically explored in MANCUR OLSON, THE LOGIC OF COLLECTIVE ACTION: PUBLIC GOODS AND THE THEORY OF GROUPS (1965).

25. Sam Peltzman, *Toward a More General Theory of Regulation*, 19 J.L. & ECON. 211 (1976).

26. *Id.* at 212.

Peltzman refined Stigler's model to link regulatory output not only to the size and organization of the lobbying group, but also to the votes gained and lost in response to the implemented regulation. Peltzman explained:

> In sum, Stigler is asserting a law of diminishing returns to group size in politics: beyond some point it becomes counterproductive to dilute the per capita transfer. Since the total transfer is endogenous, there is a corollary that diminishing returns apply to the transfer as well, due both to the opposition provoked by the transfer and to the demand this opposition exerts on resources to quiet it.[27]

By focusing on votes rather than group size, Peltzman was able to incorporate a factor into his model that was only a detail in Stigler's original formulation: "[T]he costs of using the political process limit not only the size of the dominant group but also their gains."[28] In the resulting model, regulation results not merely from a bidding process in which optimally formed industry groups win, but also it arises as a result of a more subtle and complex process through which the suppliers of regulation, namely the legislators, weigh the gains derived from the prospective transfer against the costs borne in terms of lost votes.

In a comment on these articles, Gary Becker posited that competitive political forces might serve to reduce the relative size of those deadweight societal losses that result from industry regulation. Thus, whether quotas, tariffs, or subsidies predominate in a particular industry is likely a function of which is the most cost effective, and thus efficient, form of wealth transfer, meaning a transfer that creates the smallest deadweight loss. For Becker, this insight explains the choice of regulatory form in terms other than the common belief that "voters are systematically fooled about the effects of policies like quotas and tariffs that have persisted for a long time."[29]

One issue that will be addressed throughout this course is whether the economic theory of regulation supports heightened judicial scrutiny as a means to minimize legislatively procured rents. Many scholars whose works we discuss later in this book have proposed imposing judicial barriers to enforcing the products of legislative rent seeking. At least since the New Deal, however, the Supreme Court has not gone along. One potential silver lining, suggested by Becker, is that if we are willing to accept the fact that at least some regulation is a form of wealth transfer, rather than a vehicle for promoting the public good, we need not worry terribly much about the form that the regulation takes. The public choice equivalent of Adam Smith's invisible hand will move wealth transfers to their most cost effective form.

---

27.   *Id.* at 213.

28.   *Id.*

29.   Gary Becker, *Comment*, 19 J.L. & ECON. 245, 246 (1976). To be clear, Becker is not addressing the normative merit of the redistributive policy, but only the extent to which the choice among available policies generating a wealth transfer affects the size of the resulting deadweight loss.

A. ATTORNEY LICENSING

Based upon this analysis, consider the age-old regime of professional attorney licensure. By requiring membership in a state bar, the licensure regime effectively limits the supply of lawyers in each jurisdiction. From a public interest perspective, licensing of professional services can be justified on the basis that consumers might find it difficult to determine the quality of these services. But by restricting supply, the bar also allows lawyers to raise their prices above what the prevalent market price for legal services would be in the absence of the licensure regime, with the effect of facilitating rents for those admitted to practice law.

In setting admissions standards to the bar, lawyers might be tempted to take into account (perhaps subconsciously) their financial self-interest in restricting the supply of lawyers, thus increasing their own salaries in addition to pursuing the more benign goal of protecting consumers against incompetent lawyers. This temptation is especially strong given that the bar is a self-regulatory regime, meaning that members of the bar, working through their state supreme courts, set the standards for the entry of new lawyers into the profession.[30]

This unusual, non-legislative process adds to the difficulties of consumers organizing to oppose consumer welfare-reducing rules adopted by the bar.[31] One estimate concludes that licensing of attorneys in the United States raises entry level salaries for lawyers by more than $10,000, resulting in "a total transfer from consumers to lawyers of 19% of lawyers' wages and a total welfare loss of over $3 billion."[32] Moreover, it appears that the difficulty of the bar exam is set not to guarantee a certain minimum level of competency to practice law, as would be consistent with the public interest theory of the bar. Instead, the bar failure rate is correlated with the number of test-takers, suggesting that the exam is more difficult to pass as the number of applicants to the bar rises, regardless of the applicants' merits.[33] A purely cynical view of this regime might suggest that while law students lament the need to study for and pass the bar exam, it is lawyers themselves, rather than prospective clients, who most benefit from the licensure regime.

The supply restriction may have distributional consequences with the bar as well. For instance, to the extent that the requirements of the bar exam are set higher than necessary to protect the public, this may have a

---

30. James C. Cooper, Paul A. Pautler & Todd J. Zywicki, *Theory and Practice of Competition Advocacy at the FTC*, 72 ANTITRUST L.J. 1091, 1101–02 (2005); *see also* Einer R. Elhauge, *The Scope of Antitrust Process*, 104 HARV. L. REV. 667 (1991).

31. *See* Cooper, Pautler & Zywicki, *supra* note 30, at 1101–02.

32. Mario Pagliero, What Is the Objective of Professional Licensing? Evidence from the US Market for Lawyers 1 (Mar. 11, 2005), http://www.fep.up.pt/conferences/earie2005/cd_rom/SessionÏI/II.G/Pagliero.pdf.

33. Mario Pagliero, *The Impact of Potential Labor Supply on Licensing Exam Difficulty in the US Market for Lawyers* (Carlo Alberto Working Paper No. 53, July 2007), *available at* http://www.carloalberto.org/files/no.53.pdf.

disproportionately negative effect on the admission of minority lawyers to the practice of law.[34] One need not embrace an extreme view of the role of the bar in advancing the interests of its own members to appreciate that while this regime does benefit consumers of legal services by ensuring a higher degree of professionalism, greater accountability, and more uniform standards, it also provides substantial benefits to lawyers in the form of reduced competition and correspondingly higher fees.

In addition, this combined set of benefits is not costless. The net result might be to price legal services above what some persons in need of such services might be able to afford.[35] One indication of the resulting social welfare loss is the growing market for services that lawyers traditionally provided through alternative and lower cost means. Some such services do not even require the assistance of any professional, for example computer software that makes it easier for consumers to write a will or to file for bankruptcy.

As a result of the licensure regime, lawyers need not fear entry of unlicensed lawyers undercutting their prices. Not surprisingly, however, lawyers might well be motivated to lobby against the provision of services by unlicensed individuals that at one time required, but are now exempt from, provision by licensed practitioners of law.[36] In addition, through various regulations prohibiting the "Unauthorized Practice of Law," governments promise to prosecute and punish those who provide legal services without being properly licensed.

The practice of law can be analogized to a regulated monopoly in which lawyers earn economic rents for their services. As shown in the discussion that follows, economic theory predicts that at least some of these rents should be "dissipated." What are some of the ways in which the economic rents of the practice of law are dissipated? Why does law school in the United States take three years to complete and cost so much?

B. STEEL TARIFFS AND RENT SEEKING REVISITED: THE ELUSIVE WELFARE LOSS TRIANGLE

In light of the preceding analysis, let us also reconsider the case of the steel tariffs. Assume that a protectionist tariff on steel imports will benefit the steel industry by a total of $10 million. Further assume that there is

---

34. George B. Shepherd, *No African–American Lawyers Allowed: The Inefficient Racism of the ABA's Accreditation of Law Schools*, 53 J. Legal Educ. 103 (2003).

35. Even within the regulated legal profession there is a variety of quality of lawyers and a variety of fee arrangements and rates. Lawyers who charge high rates for high-expertise services today likely would be unaffected by open entry, as the primary source of their pricing power is their unique expertise. Lower-rate lawyers providing less-sophisticated services, however, likely would see greater competition and lower wages.

36. *See* Cooper, Pautler & Zywicki, *supra* note 30, at 1101–02. For instance, the bars in some states have attempted to expand the definition of the "practice of law" to apply to many services that can be competently performed by non-lawyers, such as title companies, at much lower cost. Requiring lawyers to perform these ministerial services is estimated to add several hundred dollars to the price of a home closing with no discernible benefit to consumers. *See* Letter from R. Hewitt Pate, Acting Ass't Att'y Gen., Timothy J. Muris, Chairman of the FTC, et al., to the Standing Comm. on the Unauthorized Practice of Law of the State Bar of Georgia (Mar. 20, 2003), *available at* http://www.ftc.gov/be/v030007.htm.

only one manufacturer of steel or a sufficiently low number that the producers are able to coordinate outputs to affect price. In theory, the steel industry would be willing to pay up to $10 million in campaign contributions and other forms of lobbying expenditures in an effort to have the steel tariff enacted. If no other costs were involved, including most notably the opportunity cost of alternative uses of firm assets, the steel industry would be willing to pay as much as $9,999,999 to secure the resulting $1 quasi-rent, or "profit" above normal returns.

With some simplifying assumptions, we can now illustrate not only the potential burdens that the tariffs impose on intermediate producers and ultimate consumers of steel products, but also explain why the pressure in favor of the tariff is likely stronger and more persistent than pressure in opposition.[37] Consider the tariff from the perspective of the myriad consumers of steel. These include intermediate consumers who use steel as inputs in production of direct consumer products or as indirect inputs into other production processes and who under certain conditions can pass at least some of the costs on to those who purchase their products. While it is not necessary to set out numbers, we can explain the essential intuition that the tariff results in imposing considerable costs, perhaps greater costs than gains, without generating sufficient opposition to prevent its enactment.

Numerous industries use steel as one of the factors of production. These include, for example, construction, and manufacturers of automobiles and industrial machines.[38] Each of these sets of producers, and each producer individually, has varying degrees of market power, based for example upon product differentiation, brand recognition, and goodwill. In general, market power does not arise as a consequence of some form of industry monopoly, but rather as a result of some combination of these other factors. Purchasers are not indifferent, for example, between which cars or appliances they buy, or even which they buy within a specific price range. Some consumers strongly prefer Toyota, while others strongly prefer Honda. And within any given brand, some strongly prefer sedans, sports cars, minivans, SUVs, or hybrids in any of these categories. While consumers hold strong preferences, and will pay more for their favored products, few if any consumers are entirely unconcerned about price. Thus, despite brand loyalty, a consumer who generally prefers to drive a Toyota Camry might strongly consider a Honda Accord, if the price or the

---

37. In a later discussion of the Wilson–Hayes model, we will place this analysis in the larger context of legislation that variously benefits or burdens broad to narrow constituencies. *See infra* note 84 and accompanying text.

38. In fact, it is estimated that there are approximately 193,000 steel-using firms in the United States, of which about ninety-eight percent are small businesses with fewer than 500 employees. Read, *supra* note 2, at 1131.

features resulting from a particular promotion are substantially more attractive.

While some factors of production are fungible, consumer products usually are not. Depending upon a producer's degree of market power, it will be more or less able to pass on increased costs to end consumers through higher prices. If we assume that steel is not a good that admits of ready substitutes as a factor of production (at least in the short run), then the demand for steel is relatively inelastic. This means that intermediate purchasers will absorb, at least as an initial matter, most of the burdens of the tariffs through costs that the producers of steel pass on to them: in this example approximately ten million dollars. In turn, they will tack part of that additional cost onto their own products in the form of higher prices. How much they will successfully pass on, versus how much they will absorb in the form of lost profits, is a function of their relative market power over the goods they produce and sell. While incidence analysis, which studies the ability of various industries to pass on costs, would be required to determine where the ultimate burdens of the tariffs fall, our immediate purpose is instead to evaluate the likely impact of interest groups on the creation of the steel tariff. To simplify the analysis, assume that the intermediate producers are able to pass on most or all of the additional costs to the hundreds of thousands of purchasers of products in which steel is a major factor each year.

If there are 100,000 such purchases in a given year, likely a very low estimate, then the average added cost per consumer is approximately $100. If the costs are passed on over several years, the figure will be substantially lower. And of course to the extent that the producers themselves bear part of the cost through lost profits, the cost to consumers is further reduced. Of course prices fluctuate based upon numerous factors, and few consumers will focus on the precise cost of each individual factor when making a major purchasing decision. But for simplicity, let us assume that they do or that the information concerning the precise impact of the tariff on the products they purchase is freely available, or perhaps even stated on the invoice.

Consider whether from the perspective of 100,000 purchasers of steel products *each year*, it is rational to invest in opposing the steel tariff. One might imagine that as with the producers, it is rational for each consumer to invest up to the full value of the passed on cost, here $100, in opposing the tariff. And yet, consumers face additional obstacles to effective lobbying. A core insight from interest group theory is that when the size of the affected group is large and diffuse it is unlikely that such opposition will effectively mobilize.

C. FREE RIDING AND THE LOGIC OF COLLECTIVE ACTION

In *The Logic of Collective Action*, public choice theorist Mancur Olson argued that when groups are small and well organized, as appears to be the case with steel manufacturers, they are well positioned to lobby in favor of beneficial legislative procurements.[39] In contrast, when groups are large and diffuse, as is the case with the consumers of products for which steel is a major factor of production, they are poorly positioned to lobby for or against such procurements.

While numerous problems can inhibit effective lobbying, the most important for our immediate purposes returns us to the phenomenon of "free riding."[40] Each individual consumer will rationally decline to invest in opposition to the extent that successful lobbying efforts benefit consumers of such products generally. Each person or firm hopes that other similarly situated consumers will lobby in his or her place. Of course, the incentive to free ride is universal, and so it is rational for the group as a whole to decline to make the necessary investment in opposition to the procurement of the tariff. And this is so even though the aggregate benefit of the lobbying might well exceed even the financial benefits the tariff affords the steel industry.

1. Information Costs, Rational Ignorance, and the Timing of Payoffs

The preceding analysis assumes that consumers freely obtain information about particular factors of production for the goods they purchase. That assumption is certainly ambitious. Information is extremely costly to obtain. Complex consumer goods have a sufficiently large number of inputs that it would be impractical for most consumers to educate themselves concerning the precise costs of any individual factor, such as the price of steel, and how that cost affects the overall price of the good. Economists have dubbed this problem "rational ignorance."[41] Given the cost of acquiring information, the likelihood that the information could be used productively, and the obvious difficulties of free riding, relatively few consumers will be rationally motivated to invest in researching regulatory processes that benefit specific industry constituencies at their expense. To what extent might rational ignorance, combined with free riding, help to explain the political dynamics of the steel tariffs?

Finally, the prior discussion assumed that both the benefits to the steel producers and the cost to consumers of the steel tariffs was borne at a single time, or within a single year. That is almost certainly not the case. The steel producers did not immediately realize the full $10 million estimated value of the tariffs, and consumers did not bear the entire burden at one time, or even within a single year. Instead, the benefits to the producers and the costs to consumers were spread over many years,

---

39. *See* OLSON, *supra* note 24, at 53–65.

40. *See supra* chapter 1, section II.E.

41. Rational ignorance means that individuals will decline to invest in obtaining information where the marginal costs of gathering that information exceed the expected marginal benefits. For a general discussion, see Morris P. Fiorina, *Voting Behavior, in* PERSPECTIVES ON PUBLIC CHOICE 391, 396 (Dennis C. Mueller ed., 1997) (citing ANTHONY DOWNS, AN ECONOMIC THEORY OF DEMOCRACY 238–59 (1957)); *see also* JAMES M. BUCHANAN, PUBLIC FINANCE IN DEMOCRATIC PROCESSES: FISCAL INSTITUTIONS AND INDIVIDUAL CHOICE 7–9 (1967).

and most likely even decades, in the form of more highly priced goods and services affected by the price of steel.[42]

The same is true for virtually all legislatively conferred rents, including those associated with professional attorney licensure. In each case, the value of the barrier to competition (from foreign producers in the case of steel, and from unlicensed practitioners in the case of attorneys) is spread over a sufficiently long period of years that the burden such a regime poses for any individual consumer is substantially further reduced. For end consumers, the effect, predictably, is to exacerbate both the free rider and rational ignorance problems.

More recently, theorists have debated whether rational ignorance produces random or systemic effects in inhibiting such potentially welfare-enhancing policies as free trade. In *The Myth of Democratic Failure*,[43] Donald Wittman argues that although voters are likely to be rationally ignorant, this alone should not produce flawed political outcomes if voter errors are not systematically biased and thus are randomly distributed over policy options. Economist Bryan Caplan instead claims that because voter preferences are subsidized through political processes as a result of the forced-rider problem, their ability to indulge welfare-reducing policy preferences might systematically and adversely skew public policy over a range of issues.[44]

2.   Group Size Revisited

The effects described above might well be different for small and organized groups. An affected interest group will have a considerable motivation to factor in the potential financial benefit of a conferred quasi-rent. While this requires such groups to calculate the *discounted present value* of the expected stream of economic benefits to be generated over the life of the regulation in question, this is essential to assessing the potential value of the proposed regulation and to evaluating how much it is worth investing in lobbying. The interest group will have to discount the stream of benefits in light of the (1) time-value of money ($1 million ten years from now is worth far less today than $1 million next year), and (2) the probability that the law might be repealed in any given year as actually

---

42. This analysis, however, would not hold for a firm seeking to acquire a company that benefits from a tariff. *See* PAUL A. SAMUELSON & WILLIAM D. NORDHAUS, ECONOMICS 700–02 (16th ed. 1998) (explaining effect of a tariff). For the firm seeking to be acquired, the present value is a function of the additional predicted income stream, discounted to present value, associated with the tariff. *Id.* at 252–54 (explaining general formula for present value). As a result, the steel tariffs would represent a one-time capital gain to the acquired firm, but no gain to the acquiring firm. *See* RICHARD A. BREALEY & STEWART C. MYERS, PRINCIPLES OF CORPORATE FINANCE 41–43 (6th ed. 2000) (defining an asset that pays a fixed sum for a specified time as an annuity and describing its valuation.)

43. DONALD A. WITTMAN, THE MYTH OF DEMOCRATIC FAILURE: WHY POLITICAL INSTITUTIONS ARE EFFICIENT (1995).

44. BRYAN CAPLAN, THE MYTH OF THE RATIONAL VOTER: WHY DEMOCRACIES CHOOSE BAD POLICIES (2007). While Caplan labels this phenomenon "rational irrationality," his usage of those terms might depart from standard economic convention as used throughout this book. For our purposes, the more important point, however, is whether Wittman or Caplan is more likely to be correct in viewing rational ignorance as having systemic or nonsystemic effects on public policy.

occurred within less than two years in the case of the steel tariffs following a World Trade Oganization (WTO) ruling.[45] Whatever the discount times probability yields, it remains rational for the benefiting group to invest up to that amount to secure the present value of the stream of rents. This calculation informs cost-effective, or rational, rent-seeking activity.

D.   THE GEOMETRY OF RENT SEEKING[46]

To understand the economic significance of such legislation, it will be helpful to reconsider the market power paradigm:[47]

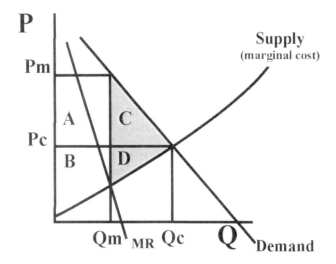

Figure 2:2

The shaded area in Figure 2:2, depicting forgone consumer and producer surpluses, represents a societal deadweight loss. If the firm produced to the point where the supply (or marginal cost) curve intersects the demand curve, societal welfare would improve as more of the relevant goods are produced and sold at a lower price. The monopoly rents, A—D, that arise in noncompetitive markets provide industries with incentives to attempt to secure market power through the political process. As Professor Charles K. Rowley has observed: "[D]uring the 1960s ... economists [tended to] dismiss the welfare cost of tariffs and monopolies as unimportant in view of the minute values associated with the Marshallian deadweight loss triangles of lost consumers' surplus associated with their existence."[48]

---

45.   *See supra* note 2, and cites therein.

46.   Portions of the discussion to follow are based upon STEARNS, *supra* note 22, at 120–25.

47.   *See supra* chapter 1, appendix.

48.   Charles K. Rowley, *Introduction, in* PUBLIC CHOICE THEORY I: HOMO ECONOMICUS IN THE MARKET PLACE, at xxiv (Charles K. Rowley ed., 1993).

In a famous paper, *The Welfare Costs of Tariffs, Monopolies, and Theft*,[49] Gordon Tullock challenged the intuition that deadweight loss triangles imposed a relatively small cost on society by demonstrating additional costs to monopoly power, and in particular monopoly power created and protected through the process of regulation.[50] In what Rowley describes as "arguably [The Virginia School's] single most important contribution to public choice,"[51] Tullock posited that the deadweight loss represented by foregone consumer and producer surpluses do not represent the full costs of rent seeking. Instead, he argued that the full value of monopoly rents might be dissipated in the very process of rent seeking.[52] Given the value of monopoly power, we would expect interest groups, behaving rationally, to expend significant resources in attempting to secure legislatively conferred rents. The resulting costs constitute a further deadweight societal loss that might well offset the value to the acquiring firm of the resulting monopoly rents.

Figure 2:2 helps to illustrate Tullock's essential insight.[53] As previously noted, the areas $C + D$ (foregone consumer and producer surplus respectively) are the deadweight cost of monopoly, or "Harberger Triangles." The area A was recognized as a simple wealth transfer from consumers to producers that takes the form of a monopoly "rent." Tullock observes, however, that producers would be willing to expend the full value of the monopoly rent, here depicted as the rectangular area A minus the foregone producer surplus D, to secure the monopoly rent. This process of expending some of the economic rents in pursuit of acquisition of the expected value of those rents is a process known as "rent dissipation."[54] The full social cost of rent-seeking can be estimated as the sum of the Harberger deadweight loss triangles (areas $C + D$) *plus* the so-called Tullock rectangle (area A). In equilibrium the analysis suggests that all rents will be fully dissipated. Generating accurate estimates of the social welfare losses that result from rent-seeking activity has proven elusive, but as Tullock maintains, including the cost of rent seeking itself increases the likelihood that these losses will be substantial.[55]

---

49. Gordon Tullock, *The Welfare Costs of Tariffs, Monopolies, and Theft*, 5 W. Econ. J. 224 (1967).

50. *Id.* at 226, 232; *see also* Richard A. Posner, *The Social Costs of Monopoly and Regulation*, 83 J. Pol. Econ. 807 (1975).

51. Rowley, *supra* note 48, at xxiv.

52. Tullock, *supra* note 49, at 226, 232.

53. In Tullock's original formulation, he presented a flat supply curve that did not account for area C plus D, which represents forgone Ricardian Competitive Rents. The presentation in the text presents the analysis based upon an upward sloping supply curve to render the analysis consistent with the presentation in the chapter 1, appendix.

54. Note that the phenomenon is not limited to political rent-seeking. For instance, the acquisition of a patent right provides the patent holder with a monopoly rent during the enforcement period. The opportunity to collect these monopoly rents will tend to encourage overinvestment in research designed to produce a patented product relative to one that is not patentable. As an example, it is often observed that there might be a "patent race" to invent a new drug before a competitor does so, leading to heightened investment in attempting to be the first to patent the drug and thereby win the "prize" of a legal monopoly for the period of the patent.

55. *See* Robert D. Tollison, *Rent Seeking*, *in* Perspectives on Public Choice, *supra* note 41, at 506, 512–14 (summarizing studies).

Rent-seeking expenditures reduce social wealth in a number of ways, including diverting resources from productive activity toward lobbying for purely redistributive transfers.[56] These costs include the efforts and expenditures of those seeking monopoly rents, such as hired lobbyists and managerial time, all of which could instead be deployed to productive economic activities. Public choice theorists posit that as rent-seeking becomes more lucrative, politicians and regulators will increase their efforts to secure positions that provide them with the power to confer rents. Just as firms will rationally invest in rent seeking, so too legislators will invest time and other resources in securing positions that empower them to respond to rent-seeking efforts. Ambitious legislators will tend to concentrate on those regulatory areas more likely to be the subject of rent-seeking activity, such as appropriations committees, as compared with committees that although equally important from a public interest per-spective, lack such opportunities. The incentive to rent seek distorts activities of other economic actors by diverting attention from socially productive activities. Consider whether top legal talent is more fruitfully deployed, for example, in drafting commercial contracts or other activities that increase social wealth or in facilitating or directly lobbying on behalf of industry.

1. The Rise and Decline of Nations[57]

In his influential book, *The Rise and Decline of Nations*,[58] Mancur Olson took the preceding analysis a significant step further. Olson linked the tendency of interest group influence—or rent seeking—over time to the decline in the rate of economic growth in Western democracies after World War II.[59] Olson demonstrated that those countries whose economic and political infrastructures were harmed most severely during World War II—Germany, Italy, and Japan—sustained the strongest economic develop-ment over the next twenty-five years, while those whose economic and political infrastructures remained intact—Australia, New Zealand, the United Kingdom, and the United States—performed most poorly during the same period.

While it might appear counterintuitive that the military victors in World War II would prove the subsequent losers and vice versa, the result makes more sense when we reconsider it from the combined perspectives of rent seeking and opportunity costs. At any given time there are two different ways for a producer to earn money in an economy. They can either produce new goods in the competitive market, or they can engage in rent-seeking activity. When a nation's political infrastructure is gutted, firms behaving rationally will make a different calculation concerning the

---

56. *See* James M. Buchanan, *Rent Seeking and Profit Seeking, in* TOWARD A THEORY OF THE RENT-SEEKING SOCIETY 3 (James M. Buchanan, Robert D. Tollison, & Gordon Tullock eds., 1980).

57. Portions of the discussion that follows are based upon STEARNS, *supra* note 22, at 121–23.

58. MANCUR OLSON, THE RISE AND DECLINE OF NATIONS: ECONOMIC GROWTH, STAGFLATION, AND SOCIAL RIGIDITIES (1982).

59. *Id.* at 74–117.

extent to which they deploy resources across these two activities. Not only are rent-seeking opportunities likely to be scarcer in a regime with a compromised political infrastructure, but also the ability of the government to issue the necessary commitments (or bonds) that confer regulatory protections that will remain in place is diminished. Conversely, politically conferred rents are likely to be more durable in more stable regimes. And because the present discounted value of those rents will be higher as a result of more durable bonds, rational firms will be increasingly willing to make the necessary investments to secure those rents in stable regimes with well-established political infrastructures.

Olson's analysis suggests that substantially reducing rent-seeking behavior requires radical, rather than narrow or incremental, institutional reform. Olson demonstrated that rent seeking not only imposes significant economic costs that can pull the production possibility frontier inward,[60] but also, it can inhibit ordinary economic growth that otherwise would push the frontier outward over time.[61] In light of the significant societal loss that rent seeking represents, public choice theorist Dennis Mueller has posited that: "The task of reform is to design institutions that allow and encourage those forms of competition that create rents by creating additional consumer and citizen surpluses, and discourage competition designed to gain and retain existing rents."[62] Still others have posited that even if we can devise such institutional reforms, their adoption will simply relocate—but not eliminate—rent seeking. Thus, William H. Riker and Steven J. Brams explain:

> Of course, when vote trading is banished from the legislature, political compromise goes on someplace else politically antecedent to the legislature. Thus in state legislatures and city councils with disciplined parties, it is in the majority caucus or in the mind of the boss that the compromise takes place. In England, the Cabinet serves as one place of compromise and very probably something like vote trading goes on there. Since the Cabinet situation is unstructured in comparison with the Parliamentary situation, however, it is probably hard to identify the trades and compromises that do occur.[63]

Recall that the production possibility frontier, reproduced from chapter 1 below,[64] represents the potential economic output for an individual, firm, or nation, as between two commodities.

---

60. *See* chapter 1, appendix.

61. *See* DENNIS C. MUELLER, PUBLIC CHOICE III 555 (2003).

62. DENNIS C. MUELLER, PUBLIC CHOICE II 245 (1989).

63. William H. Riker & Steven J. Brams, *The Paradox of Vote Trading*, 67 AM. POL. SCI. REV. 1235, 1238 (1973).

64. *See supra* chapter 1, at III.F.

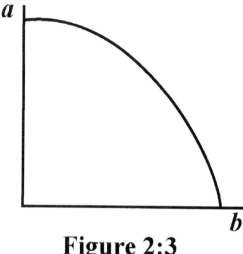

Figure 2:3

An individual is capable of producing two forms of output, *a* and *b*, such that for each commodity the person experiences decreasing marginal productivity. Producing the first unit of *b* would require this person to forego relatively little in her production of *a*, and producing each additional unit of *b* would require this person to forego producing a somewhat larger quantity of *a*. Conversely, producing additional increments of *a* requires relinquishing larger and larger increments of *b*.

The production possibility frontier can be used not only to depict the production potential for an individual or firm, but also on a larger scale, to depict the maximal output of an industry, state, or nation. Industries maximize their economic output when they produce at the most highly valued point along their production possibility frontier. Olson's analysis of the post World War II economies of the former Allied and Axis powers not only reflects diminished opportunities for rent seeking, but also might reflect more profitable private market opportunities in nations whose economic and political infrastructures had been destroyed. There was great pent-up postwar demand for new goods in those economies destroyed by the war and great economic opportunities for private sector development. In contrast, for those nations that suffered less infrastructure damage, in the aftermath of a booming wartime economy, one that had succeeded in pulling the affected nations out of the Great Depression,[65] industries were likely already producing at or near their production possibility frontiers. If so, the potential profits that such industries were capable of generating from rent seeking were as high or higher than the potential profits such industries were capable of generating from the next best available investment activity. Mueller captures this insight as follows:

---

65. J.R. Vernon, *World War II Fiscal Policies and the End of the Great Depression*, 54 J. ECON. HIST. 850, 850 (1994) ("What ended the Great Depression? In the traditional view, the answer is World War II, a conclusion that appears in the works of numerous economist and historians.").

To temper the resistance of [interest] groups to the losses they would experience by eliminating those programs that facilitate rent seeking, even greater gains must be offered. Perhaps this observation explains why it is sometimes politically easier to eliminate or reduce a large group of restrictions on trade than just a few. The deregulation movement in the United States [in the 1980s during the Reagan Administration appeared to have been successful] because it attacked regulations in many industries. To come fully to grips with the rent-seeking problem, one must think in terms of radical reforms; funda-mental redefinitions of property rights.[66]

If Olson is correct, then his analysis would require us to weigh the benefit of societal and institutional stability against the cost of rent seeking. The calculus is especially daunting given that to the extent institutional reform is successful, meaning that it is a stable solution to prior rent-seeking activity, we might once again expect to see rent seeking rearing its ugly head.

E. HOLDOUTS, TAKINGS, AND THE COMPARISON BETWEEN PUBLIC CHOICE AND LAW AND ECONOMICS REVISITED

The concepts of rent seeking and rent dissipation have significant implications for the economic analysis of law. Consider, for example, Richard Posner's analysis of the Fifth Amendment's requirement of "Just Compensation" for property taken for public use under the Eminent Domain Clause.[67]

Posner postulates that the purpose of the Eminent Domain Clause is to prevent welfare-reducing takings of private property. The basic econom-ic logic of the Eminent Domain power is to permit the government to overcome "holdout" problems in order to assemble contiguous parcels of land in order to build public works, such as roads, schools, and public buildings. Holdouts are the flip side of free riders. Both involve problems of collective action; while free riding focuses on the supply side, in the willingness of group members to affirmatively support group interests, holdouts focus on the demand side, on the disinclination of individuals to sell to an interested buyer seeking to transform assembled parcels into a substantially more highly valued use.

A classic theoretical holdout illustration involves the efforts of a developer, for example Disney Corporation, to acquire a sufficiently large tract of land to build a theme park, in this instance Disney World in Orlando, Florida. If Disney simply announced its intent, and then offered the fair market value to relevant property owners, would those owners

---

66.   MUELLER, *supra* note 62, at 245 (citing James M. Buchanan, *Reform in the Rent–Seeking Society*, *in* TOWARD A THEORY OF THE RENT-SEEKING SOCIETY, *supra* note 56, at 359).

67.   U.S. CONST. amend. V ("nor shall private property be taken for public use, without just compensation"). The Takings Clause applies to state and local governments through the Four-teenth Amendment Due Process Clause.

sell? Certainly not. Some might, but more savvy owners would "hold out" in the hope that Disney would acquire a sufficiently large number of properties that it would desperately need the remaining property to facilitate the development. At this point, Disney and the final holdout, or group of holdouts, stand in the relation of a *bilateral monopoly*.[68] In this example, the most highly valued use of the property involves the sale to a single buyer, Disney, and Disney needs to acquire the property from a very specific seller or group of sellers. Assume that without the property, Disney cannot build the park, but with the full group of contiguous parcels it can, thus producing a value of $100 million. The final holdout might try to extract a "rent" up to the full value of the $100 million, say $99,999,999. Disney will try to minimize its payout (above the previous fair market value of say, $200,000). The resulting negotiating range— between $200,000 and $100 million—is huge, and in a bilateral monopoly, unlike in a competitive market regime, there is no obvious or stable equilibrium outcome. Instead, the ultimate sale will result in the purchaser and the holdout allocating the enormous gains from the ultimate sale. In fact, Disney solved the holdout problem in Orlando through reliance upon several "straw" purchasers, meaning separate individuals who acquired the properties without disclosing that they were making those purchasers for a common entity, namely Disney Corporation.[69]

1. A Law and Economics Analysis of Takings

Consider the extent to which the holdout problem explains the inclusion of the requirement of just compensation in the Fifth Amendment Eminent Domain Clause. Under standard law and economics analysis, the constitutional requirement of "Just Compensation" is presumed a necessary means of forcing the government to pay the market price for the property that is taken. If the price that has to be paid for the land exceeds the value that the government places upon it, then the government will forego taking the property because it will not be willing to pay more for the land than it is worth. Conversely, if the government values the land more highly than the fair market value, it can effect the taking, compensate the owner, and still improve societal welfare. In this analysis, the just compensation requirement ensures that the government will take property only when it actually places a higher value on its proposed use of the land than does the landowner.[70]

---

68. A bilateral monopoly is a relationship involving a monopolistic seller and a monopsonistic buyer. A monopsonist is a buyer with market power over purchases such that it has price-setting power, comparable to that of a monopolistic seller, based upon how much of the good in question it elects to purchase. SAMUELSON & NORDHAUS, *supra* note 42, at 238 (explaining bilateral monopoly in the union/labor market context).

69. For an informative discussion of reliance upon straw purchasers, including those involved in the Disney acquisition of property in Orlando, Florida, see Daniel B. Kelly, *The "Public Use" Requirement in Eminent Domain Law: A Rationale Based on Secret Purchases and Private Influence*, 92 CORNELL L. REV. 1 (2006).

70. This assumes that the government fully internalizes the costs in engaging in these sorts of projects. Given the problem of agency costs, as described in chapter 1, however, it may be that the incentives of those individuals who make the actual decisions are not fully aligned with that of "the government" as a whole.

Richard Posner claims that this traditional law and economics justification is incomplete.[71] Assume that as compared with the government, the landowner places a higher value on her property. Posner maintains that under standard economic assumptions,[72] a welfare-reducing taking still will not occur even in the absence of a requirement of just compensation. Posner observes that a property owner who is about to have his or her land seized will not acquiesce in the taking, but will instead expend resources, including hiring lawyers or lobbyists, to fight it. Indeed, based upon the preceding analysis, we could predict that the property owner would rationally invest up to the total value he or she places on the property to avoid the welfare-reducing taking. Alternatively, the property owner would be willing to simply pay off the government to let the property owner retain the land, rather than to have the government acquire it and deploy it to a lower valued use. In contrast, if, as compared with the homeowner, the government places a higher value on the property, the landowner will not rationally invest sufficient resources in attempting to block the welfare-enhancing taking. Thus, Posner concludes, the outcome should be the same whether or not just compensation is expected.[73]

2. An Alternative Public Choice Analysis of Takings

While Posner's analysis reveals the limits of the standard account of the Just Compensation Clause, public choice also demonstrates the limits of this alternative law and economics analysis.[74] As a matter of standard economic analysis, Posner appears correct in asserting that eliminating the requirement of just compensation would not increase the risk of social welfare reducing takings. But this analysis focuses solely on the deadweight loss resulting from a potentially inefficient government taking. Relying on public choice theory, Todd Zywicki has suggested an alternative analysis grounded in public choice that provides a positive justification for requiring just compensation in the context of eminent domain. As Zywicki observes, Posner's analysis fails to account for the social cost of this regime, which includes the additional expenses Tullock associates with rent seeking (or rent extraction).[75] These include the very expenses that Posner properly identifies as ameliorating the risk of inefficient takings, such as expenditures on lawyer's fees and political efforts. These are real resources expended solely for the purpose of blocking the transfer that results in moving land from a more highly valued to a less highly valued use. So although such lobbying activities reduce the risk of realizing the deadweight loss (the lost "triangle"), it substantially increases the

---

71. RICHARD A. POSNER, ECONOMIC ANALYSIS OF LAW § 3.7, at 56 (7th ed. 2007).

72. The analysis assumes no transactions costs.

73. In effect, Posner's argument is an application of the Coase Theorem. Do you see why?

74. *See* Todd J. Zywicki, Rent Seeking: What It Is, Why It Matters (working paper) (on file with author.)

75. Richard Posner has acknowledged this caveat to his argument. *See* RICHARD A. POSNER, ECONOMIC ANALYSIS OF LAW § 3.7, at 59 n.6 (6th ed. 2003) (citing Zywicki, *supra* note 74).

amount of social wealth that is dissipated to prevent this loss from occurring (the lost "rectangle").

The just compensation requirement requires a wealth transfer from the government to an individual to compensate him for the taking. In Zywicki's analysis, rather than encouraging socially wasteful expenditures on lawyers and political activity, the just compensation requirement puts the value of the land in the hands of the property owner and not those of the property owner's lawyers. There may still be some litigation over the proper value to assign to the property, but this will substantially narrow the range of conflict and disagreement, and hence the range of expenditures for rent-seeking or rent avoidance by the parties. In contrast, eliminating the requirement of just compensation would facilitate a rent-seeking game with the potential for substantial social cost, thereby replacing what is otherwise a relatively low-cost wealth transfer.

F. RENT–SEEKING IN EQUILIBRIUM: THE CASE OF CAMPAIGN FINANCE REFORM

A corollary of Mancur Olson's analysis of rent seeking and economic growth following World War II suggests that behaving rationally, economic actors will allocate resources until the marginal value of private market production and of rent-seeking expenditures are equal. Thus, if the economic returns to rent-seeking increase over time, public choice predicts that interest groups will invest increasingly greater resources pursuing rent-seeking activities.

Consider the important and controversial question of why campaign expenditures on political activity have historically risen over time. In a provocative article, John R. Lott, Jr.[76] posits "a simple explanation" that campaign expenditures are increasing because the government is getting bigger. The explanation is straightforward: "the more transfers the government has to offer, the more resources people will spend to obtain them."[77] And "[a]s government has more favors to grant, the effort spent to obtain those favors should increase."[78] As the size of government grows, the government, by definition, will have greater ability to transfer wealth. Even public goods such as national defense and highway construction will have important private goods elements susceptible to rent-seeking activity. In other words, if the government has the power to enact laws or regulations that can substantially benefit certain firms or industries (such as a narrowly tailored tax break or a congressional "earmark"), then there will be potential beneficiaries who will rationally invest in rent-seeking in an effort to capture those benefits. Similarly, if the government has the power to enact laws or regulations that can impose substantial costs on particular firms (such as a tax increase or

---

76. John R. Lott, Jr., *A Simple Explanation for Why Campaign Expenditures Are Increasing: The Government Is Getting Bigger*, 43 J.L. & ECON. 359 (2000).

77. *Id.* at 363.

78. *Id.*

strict regulation), those firms will rationally invest in rent-seeking to prevent the imposition of the cost. Controlling for other possible factors that might have increased the costs of campaigns during that time (such as increases in the costs of television advertising), Lott concludes that the near 180% increase in federal campaign spending and 136% per capita real expense increases for House and Senate races from 1976 through 1994 resulted primarily from the increased opportunities that the growing federal and state governments presented for rent seeking.

Lott concludes that the conventional approach of addressing increasing campaign expenditures by imposing spending or contribution caps is misguided. Although spending caps might reduce the direct monetary expenses of campaigns, they are not likely to alter the total social cost of political campaigns, and, ironically, might even increase social costs by forcing them into less cost-effective forms, including in-kind contributions, rather than direct payments to a candidate. The changed form of contribution, however, does not mean that the overall portion of societal wealth devoted to supporting campaigns has diminished.

Lott further observes that the forms that these contributions can take is nearly infinite and that the corresponding range of governmental transfers is quite broad. Lott states: "If the hypothesis presented here is correct, increased abilities to transfer wealth in any form (for example, regulations or expropriation of property) should lead to increased campaign expenditures."[79] Lott claims that his empirical results, which use government expenditures as a proxy for an increased ability to transfer wealth, support his hypothesis. Lott asserts therefore that the present policy debate misses the critical insight that the difficulties associated with excessive campaign spending cannot be solved by limiting donations. This would simply change the form of payments. Attempts to reduce campaign contributions, for example the McCain–Feingold Campaign Finance Act, which attempts to regulate the form, timing, and substance of political activity,[80] focus primarily on the symptoms rather than the causes of growing campaign finance.

Based upon this analysis, is it surprising that soon after the McCain–Feingold Campaign Finance Act was enacted, it was determined that there were problematic "loopholes," such as the activities of private so-called 527 groups[81] that engaged in political activity outside the reach of the McCain–Feingold Act? If the "loophole" for 527 groups were closed, would that be likely to eliminate the amount of social resources expended on political campaigns? Why or why not?

G. THE PROBLEM OF RENT EXTRACTION

Professor Fred McChesney has demonstrated that through the phenomenon of "rent extraction," legislators can generate the equivalent of the social-welfare loss associated with rent seeking even absent a specific

---

79. *Id.* at 364.

80. Bipartisan Campaign Reform Act of 2002, Pub. L. No. 107–155, 116 Stat. 81 (codified as amended in scattered sections of 2 U.S.C.).

81. 26 U.S.C. § 527 (2006).

effort by an interest group to direct resources toward securing legislatively produced rents. Assume that a law is enacted that promises a stream of benefits over the next ten years at an expected value of $1 million per year, such as a protectionist licensing scheme. Further assume that six years after the law was initially passed, a member of Congress on the relevant committee that oversees this program announces that she is considering initiating proceedings to have the law repealed.

At this point, if the law remains effective, then the interest group will still receive four more years of economic rents at $1 million per year. How do you predict that an interest group would respond to the proposed legislative action? Interest group theory suggests that behaving rationally, the interest group would be willing to invest up to the present discounted value of the $4 million income stream with the program in place to avoid its repeal. Fred McChesney refers to this scheme as rent extraction or rent "extortion," which he likens to a sort of political blackmail. The politician essentially coerces various forms of contributions or support in exchange for not affirmatively harming the interest group either by taking away an existing benefit or imposing a new cost.[82]

Alternatively, even if there is no quasi-private benefit to protect, the same legislator could approach industry leaders with the threat to impose a costly new regulation. For example, a member of Congress on the committee that oversees the Medicare Program could approach leading pharmaceuticals makers proposing reimbursement caps that are substantially lower than those currently under Medicare. The pharmaceutical industry might respond by offering various forms of political support in exchange for leaving the present higher reimbursement caps in place. In this analysis, it is even possible that the legislator could succeed in rent extraction even if she had no intention of imposing the lower reimbursement caps, provided that her threat appears credible to the pharmaceutical industry leaders.[83]

III. TOWARD A GENERAL MODEL OF REGULATION

Building on the tools set out in this chapter, we will now introduce a matrix that helps to identify the conditions under which the legislature is likely to provide various forms of legislation, including quasi-private goods or public goods, and also under which it is likely to delegate to administrative agencies. While the analysis is necessarily simplified—most legislation will not fit neatly into a single category—it is nonetheless a starting point in assessing the dynamics of legislative processes, procurement, and compromise.

---

82. McChesney, *supra* note 19, at 124.

83. For McChesney's empirical support, see *id.* at 45–68 (chapter 3). A politician's credibility will turn on his or her willingness to occasionally act upon such threats. It does not matter if the interest group already "paid" for the law at the outset, as those investments are now sunk costs.

A.   THE WILSON–HAYES MATRIX[84]

Two public choice theorists, James Q. Wilson and Michael T. Hayes, have used these insights to create a model of four legislative categories designed to predict which supply and demand configurations will tend to produce too much public action as well as which ones produce too little.[85] For simplicity, Wilson and Hayes divide the benefits associated with legislation into general benefits to the public at large, for example, defense, and narrow or special interest benefits, for example, an industrial subsidy or tariff. Similarly, Wilson and Hayes divide the costs associated with legislation into those that are distributed widely, for example, the former federal fifty-five mile-per-hour speed limit, and those that are distributed narrowly, for example, rent control or socialized medicine. While the costs and benefits of most legislation fall between these extremes, these categories, which are depicted in Table 2:1,[86] are useful in setting up the analytical paradigm.

Table 2:1. The Four Box Static Model

	Widely Distributed Benefits	Narrowly Conferred Benefits
Widely Distributed Costs	*Legislative Characteristics:* This desired category of legislation tends to be undersupplied as constituents express too little pressure in support; alternatively when pressure is brought on both sides, legislatures sometimes delegate to avoid the resulting conflict. *Illustrations:* Desired legislative responses to various environmental crises, e.g., waste management or global warming; and national fiscal management, e.g., social security reform.	*Legislative Characteristics:* Because small organized groups exert pressure disproportionately to numbers in political processes, legislatures tend to oversupply special interest legislation. *Illustrations:* Tariffs, industry subsidies.
Narrowly Conferred Costs	*Legislative Characteristics:* Given the fear that factional violence (Madison Federalist No. 10), or interest group politicking (the modern equivalent), will disadvantage unpopular minorities, congressional processes include numerous features that tend to enlarge successful coalitions above minimum winning size. *Illustrations:* Rent control, national health care reform.	*Legislative Characteristics:* Because intense interests directly conflict, legislators prefer to delegate to agencies, hoping to shift blame for resulting failures while claiming credit for resulting successes; legislators can also benefit from simply threatening regulatory delegation and can benefit from monitoring agencies. *Illustrations:* The National Labor Relations Board.

---

84. Portions of the following discussion are based upon Stearns, *supra* note 12, at 402–11.

85. *See generally* JAMES Q. WILSON, POLITICAL ORGANIZATIONS 332–37 (1973); MICHAEL T. HAYES, LOBBYISTS AND LEGISLATORS: A THEORY OF POLITICAL MARKETS (1981). While Wilson first posited these four categories, Hayes, relying upon the works of several public choice theorists, substantially developed the original model.

86. Stearns, *supra* note 12, at 407.

The difficulty with categorizing legislation between the extremes of conferring narrowly distributed and widely distributed benefits or between imposing narrowly distributed and widely distributed costs is exacerbated by the tendency of interest groups to characterize government policy in favorable terms. Thus, it is strategically beneficial for special interest groups to characterize special interest goods, for example, a particular defense contract, as benefiting the general public, for example, by claiming that it will help the national defense. Professor Glen O. Robinson has offered a useful definition that helps to respond to this problem:

> We can roughly define "public goods" as those in which there is some symmetry in the distribution of benefits and costs (within some near-term time period), whereas "private goods" are those where distribution of benefits and costs is asymmetrical; benefits are concentrated in a particular geographic region or special group, whereas costs are distributed more broadly over the general population.[87]

The traditional, or public interest, view of Congress is that legislators follow their mandate to collectively supply goods benefiting the general public and bargain only as to detail. The irony highlighted by public choice theory is that individual members of society are least likely to lobby for such goods. Because no one can be excluded from the benefits of such classic public goods as a police force or national defense, individuals will free ride in their efforts to lobby for such legislative procurements, waiting for others to do so on their behalf. Because everyone engages in this behavior, the model predicts that goods providing benefits to the general public tend to be undersupplied. While everyone benefits from them, no one is willing to incur the necessary costs to procure them.

Alternatively, there is a stronger incentive to lobby for goods that provide narrow and direct benefits to identifiable groups. The free rider phenomenon is not eliminated altogether, but it is reduced to the extent that individuals can be excluded from the group benefiting from the legislation. The problem here is analogous to that of "cheaters" in a cartel.[88] To avoid having potential beneficiaries of narrow benefit legislation "cheat" by not contributing to lobbying efforts, special interest lobbyists will try, where possible, to make the legislative benefits divisible and excludable.

The problem with lobbying incentives is the same with respect to the costs of collectively supplied goods as it is with respect to the benefits. For public goods with widely distributed costs, one would expect minimal lobbying in opposition, just as one would expect minimal lobbying in support of goods conferring widely distributed benefits. Similarly, for goods imposing costs on a narrow group, one would expect greater

---

87. Glen O. Robinson, *Public Choice Speculations on the Item Veto*, 74 VA. L. REV. 403, 408–09 (1988).

88. *See supra* chapter 1, at section II.D.

lobbying in opposition, subject to the same free-rider or "cheating" problem that occurs with goods that confer narrow benefits. In sum, lobbying efforts in favor of or in opposition to legislation will increase in proportion to the degree to which benefits are narrowly conferred or costs are narrowly imposed.

The same factors driving the demand for legislation are at work in driving the supply. Just as constituents will press more vigorously for legislation conferring narrow and excludable benefits, legislators will supply legislation more readily when they can credibly claim credit with their constituents for having procured the legislative benefit.[89] An individual Congressman is aware that constituents will be dubious of claims that he or she was single-handedly responsible for a major legislative success. The Congressman also knows that constituents will be more willing to give credit for narrow and discrete legislative procurements aiding their district. In addition, one theorist claims that Congressmen expect their constituents to remember votes against their interests longer than votes in their favor.[90] This creates an obvious dilemma for legislators faced with some constituents who would benefit by proposed legislation at a price borne by other constituents. Congressmen can avoid this problem by exercising a third option beyond supplying or not supplying legislation. Specifically, Congressmen also can delegate decision-making responsibility to agencies or courts.

Congressmen can be expected to exercise this third option in instances in which one constituent group benefits directly at the expense of another, whether the costs and benefits of the legislation are widely or narrowly distributed. Legislators can use delegation as a means to let both sides claim victory in the legislative process, while blaming the agency at some future date for imposing the legislative cost. Frequently, regulation results in the interest groups "capturing" the agency such that the ensuing regulation is closer to the model of legislation under the old pluralist theory typified in E.E. Schattschneider's study of the Smoot–Hawley Act.[91] In essence, the interest groups win at the expense of the general public.

As shown in table 2:1, Wilson and Hayes combine these demand and supply configurations to create four legislative categories. While the distributed benefits/distributed costs category is the category of legislation that Congress was traditionally expected to provide, public choice theorists posit that, in fact, it is the one most likely to be undersupplied. Because this legislative category involves a conflicting demand pattern in which all

---

89. *See generally* DAVID R. MAYHEW, CONGRESS: THE ELECTORAL CONNECTION 52–54 (2d ed. 1974). Mayhew explains that because individual Congressmen cannot convincingly take credit for grandiose legislation, and because constituents are aware of immediate legislative procurements, Congressmen seek legislation that provides "particularized benefits" to their constituents. Particularized benefits must be given to an identifiable group and on an *ad hoc* basis so that a Congressman can have an identifiable role in their procurement.

90. *See* MORRIS P. FIORINA, REPRESENTATIVES, ROLL CALLS, AND CONSTITUENCIES 38–39 (1974) (explaining influence on Congressmen of "the ungrateful electorate").

91. *See supra* notes 11–12 and accompanying text (defining pluralism and collecting authorities).

constituents receive a slight benefit and incur a slight cost, and because lobbying efforts are not likely to be intense on either side, legislators will respond with inaction, or with symbolic action in the form of delegation. One method Congressmen can use to increase the likelihood that a proposed bill in this category will secure enough votes for passage is to agree to attach to the bill legislation from another category in which the incentive for lobbying is stronger. This explains not only how non-germane riders come into being, but also why the Wilson–Hayes matrix is arguably most important for its dynamic implications for legislative bargaining.

The distributed benefits/concentrated costs category is characterized by weak lobbying in support of legislation and strong lobbying in opposition, and is thus conflictual. One example involves proposals to nationalize the provision of health care services. Because everyone at some point requires medical services, the benefits of such a regime medicine would be distributed widely. The costs, in contrast, would be more narrowly contained, falling, at least in the near-term, on those providing medical services. Not surprisingly, the American Medical Association (AMA) has had a long history of lobbying, with considerable success, against proposals to nationalize health care in the United States.[92]

Legislators faced with this conflicting demand configuration are likely either to do nothing or to delegate. The United States system of lawmaking contains numerous protections against the formation of majoritarian factions, including such constitutional protections as bicameralism, presentment, and constitutional judicial review. In addition, numerous internal practices, including complex committee structures and calendaring rules, make the passage of legislation more difficult, and thus make majoritarian interest group politics more costly and thus less likely. These and other institutional protections or impediments to the passage of legislation are especially important in this context. In fact, one could argue that these protections, referred to as "negative legislative checkpoints," or "veto gates"[93] are in place to slow down or to stop legislation that benefits the public at large at a cost borne largely or entirely by a narrow interest group.

B. MINIMUM WINNING COALITIONS AND NEGATIVE LEGISLATIVE CHECKPOINTS

In effect, these negative legislative checkpoints or veto gates serve to increase the size of coalitions necessary to succeed in passing legislation.[94] William Riker, who developed the theory of "minimum winning coali-

---

92. Proposals on this issue were a major focus of debate both during the Democratic primaries and in the general election leading up to the current Obama Administration. *See* Ceci Connolly, *Support for Health Reform Is Growing: But Deep Rifts Remain over How to Pay for Coverage,* WASH. POST, Mar. 29, 2009, at A1 (describing proposal endorsed by a coalition of health industry organizations, including the AMA, which rules out nationalized health care and suggests an alternate system of government-supported insurance).

93. *See* Stearns, *supra* note 12, at 410 (defining "negative legislative checkpoints"); McNoll-gast, *Legislative Intent: The Use of Positive Political Theory,* LAW & CONTEMP. PROBS., Spring 1944, at 3, 7 (defining "veto gates"). The following discussion uses these terms interchangeably.

tions," reasoned that, in theory, the most stable coalition in a legislative body will be comprised of one more than fifty percent. A larger coalition can benefit its membership by excluding others from the generalized benefits until a simple majority is achieved.[95] Riker's theory is most easily understood as the public choice analogue to Madison's theory of factions. In essence, these congressional processes and the constitutional impediments to the rapid formation of successful majority factions reduce the possibility that a simple majority will be a successful coalition.[96]

Protection against minimum winning coalitions is especially important in the distributed benefit/concentrated cost category. It is in this category that the interests of distinct minority groups are in the greatest danger of being thwarted by the legislative process. The benefits of negative checkpoints as a device to prevent minimum winning coalitions from prevailing are even more pronounced in comparison with state and municipal legislatures that lack them to the same degree as Congress.[97] Although the American Medical Association has historically been successful in lobbying against proposals to fundamentally redistribute access to health care (such as through nationalizing medical access), landlords, for example, have in many instances been less successful in opposing rent control in cities throughout the United States, such as New York City. While the interests of the two groups, medical doctors opposed to nationalized health care and landlords opposed to rent control, bear important similarities, the difference in legislative results might reflect the absence of such constitutional and structural impediments to the passage of legislation at the state or local level, as compared with their presence in Congress.

The concentrated benefits/distributed costs paradigm is characterized by strong demand for legislation and weak lobbying in opposition. When this occurs, public choice theory predicts enactment of legislation favorable to the active lobbying group. The most important legislative byprod-

---

94. *See generally* WILLIAM H. RIKER, THE THEORY OF POLITICAL COALITIONS 32–46 (1962).

95. Riker's theory includes specific limitations. *See id.* at 32 ("In person, zero-sum games, where side-payments are permitted, where players are rational, and where they have perfect information, only minimum winning coalitions occur.").

96. *See* Harold H. Bruff, *Legislative Formality, Administrative Rationality*, 63 TEX. L. REV. 207, 219–20 (1984) (explaining that devices such as House Rules Committee agenda controls and threat of presidential veto serve to increase size of winning coalitions); RIKER, *supra* note 94, at 89–101 (observing that historically, successful coalitions are larger than minimum winning size); PETER H. ARANSON, AMERICAN GOVERNMENT: STRATEGY AND CHOICE 367 (1981) ("To pass, bills usually require more than simple majorities, because unconvinced lawmakers can use any number of lethal and dilatory strategies for defeating, or delaying, or substantially modifying them.").

97. *See* ARANSON, *supra* note 96, at 65 (asserting that according to available evidence, winning coalitions in state legislatures, as opposed to in Congress, become increasingly stable as they approach minimum winning size).

uct of this category is the rider, often one that is not germane to the overall substance of the underlying legislation to which it is attached. The skewed lobbying incentives in this category result in the legislative process of logrolling, with the effect of broadly conferring quasi-private goods as a means of achieving legislative compromise. Logrolling is the process by which legislators trade votes for each others' concentrated benefit/distributed cost items in exchange for their own. The predicted result is a proliferation of pork barrel appropriations, the sum total of which may leave everyone worse off than had no legislation been passed at all. Not surprisingly, perhaps, the logrolling problem is exacerbated in large part by the very veto gates designed to protect special interests from general benefit legislation enacted at their expense. The same legislators empowered to slow down or stop bills encroaching on the rights of particular interest groups also can use their power to coerce items conferring narrow benefits on other special interest groups.

The final category, concentrated costs/concentrated benefits, like the first configuration, is conflictual. But unlike with the first configuration, lobbying efforts here are intense on both sides. This is a classic situation in which legislators will opt out by delegating their authority to either an agency or to courts. Examples include the National Labor Relations Act,[98] establishing the National Labor Relations Board, and the Labor Management Relations Act,[99] vesting federal district courts with authority to resolve disputes over labor-management contracts. Delegation allows legislators to claim credit for creating legislative benefits while blaming the agency or courts for imposing the costs.

While rent seeking is often associated with the procurement of quasi-private goods through the legislative process, it is important to recognize that public goods often generate rent-seeking behavior and thus result in rent dissipation. Part of the problem is definitional. While "national defense" is generally characterized as a public good, the government does not provide national defense generically. Instead, it selects particular tanks, planes, or ships to buy, companies to contract with, and localities in which to place various bases. Embedded in the provision of the public good of national defense, therefore, are many decisions that have the potential to substantially enrich particular industries, firms, or communities, especially those in districts of influential politicians. Large defense contractors actively lobby and contribute to political campaigns in the hopes that their firms will be selected for lucrative defense contracts. For the same reasons that the Wilson–Hayes model predicts a tendency to oversupply quasi-private goods, it also tends to suggest that once the decision to supply a public good is made (such as national defense) there will be a strong tendency toward "privatizing" substantial aspects of the public goods provision.

---

98.   29 U.S.C. § 153 (2006).

99.   29 U.S.C. § 185 (2006).

The Wilson–Hayes model has implications for several public policy proposals. While we will reconsider these issues throughout the book, for now consider whether the tendency to favor special interest over general interest legislation provides support for such proposals as the item veto, single subject amendments, or the balanced budget amendment. Does the same tendency favor greater judicial scrutiny of legislation, especially special interest legislation? To what extent do these questions require one first to assess the proper baseline for evaluating the proper extent of interest group influence on the political process?[100]

C. BAPTISTS AND BOOTLEGGERS

One insight that emerges from the foregoing analysis is that for interest groups and lobbyists to successfully work political processes, they cannot be entirely selective in choosing with whom to negotiate. The frequent observation that politics makes strange bedfellows has found a theoretical analogue in public choice. Consider Bruce Yandle's "Baptists and Bootleggers" model of regulation.[101] In Yandle's analysis, regulations can emerge out of the confluence of the narrow economic self-interest of groups working together with more public-spirited parties. Yandle offers the example of so-called Sunday Blue Laws which have long existed in many states (especially in the southern United States, but also in Massachusetts), forbidding the sale of alcoholic beverages on Sundays.

Yandle observes that two very different groups, indeed groups that one would not expect to associate with each other, might agree to offer strong support for such regulation. First, there were those who he refers to as the "Baptists," morally motivated teetotalers who support these laws out of a sense of moral and religious conviction concerning the social benefits of temperance. Yandle observes, however, that there is a second group who might support these laws for less charitable or altruistic motives, the so-called Bootleggers, producers of illegal "moon-shine whiskey," who essentially had a monopoly on the sale of liquor one day a week. While one might have assumed that "Baptists" and "Bootleggers" are ideological opponents—as indeed they generally are—on this one issue the two groups share a strong common interest, albeit for nearly opposite reasons.

Similarly, prior to its demise, the notorious Enron Corporation was a staunch supporter of the Kyoto Treaty on Global Climate Change, primarily because Enron was heavily invested in alternative energy sources. Although one would expect Enron and various environmentalist groups to typically oppose one another on issues of environmental regulation and policy, the Kyoto Treaty benefited Enron because it raised the costs of

---

100. *Cf.* Einer R. Elhauge, *Does Interest Group Theory Justify More Intrusive Judicial Review?*, 101 YALE L.J. 31 (1991).

101. BRUCE YANDLE, THE POLITICAL LIMITS OF ENVIRONMENTAL REGULATION: TRACKING THE UNICORN 23–28 (1989).

using traditional fuels and thus increased the cost effectiveness—and thus the demand for—the novel alternatives in which Enron was invested.[102]

IV. IMPLICATIONS OF INTEREST GROUP THEORY FOR THE STUDY OF LAW

Interest group theory raises profound questions for the study of law. These include foundational questions that concern many of the Supreme Court's most famous and familiar constitutional decisions. In this section, we reexamine a few such cases from the perspective of public choice. We invite you to consider the extent to which, if any, insights from interest group theory affect the manner in which you now view the underlying issues that these cases present. In addition, consider more generally whether the analysis informs your understanding of the proper role that judges play, or should play, within our constitutional system of governance when construing constitutional challenges of the sort presented in the cases described below. In the final section, we will then introduce more broadly two important normative critiques of public choice that will further encourage reconsideration of these and other issues presented throughout this course.

A. LOCHNER v. NEW YORK

In *Lochner v. New York*,[103] the Supreme Court, with Justice Peckham writing, confronted a constitutional challenge under the Fourteenth Amendment Due Process Clause to a New York statute known as the Labor Law of New York, which prohibited bakers from working more than sixty hours per week, and more than ten hours per day. The case arose at the intersection of the relatively broad understanding concerning the scope of state police powers and a substantive reading of the Due Process Clause to protect certain economic liberties, including the right to contract. The specific question the case raised was whether in the exercise of the state's police powers, the state could effectively prohibit private contracting in this employment setting. Thus, Justice Peckham framed the inquiry as follows:

> If the contract be one which the State, in the legitimate exercise of its police power, has the right to prohibit, it is not prevented from prohibiting it by the Fourteenth Amendment. Contracts in violation of a statute, either of the Federal or state government, or a contract to let one's property for immoral purposes, or to do any other unlawful act, could obtain no protection from the Federal Constitution, as coming under the liberty of person or of free contract. Therefore, when the State, by its legislature, in the assumed exercise

---

102. *See* Bruce Yandle & Stuart Buck, *Bootleggers, Baptists, and the Global Warming Battle*, 26 HARV. ENVTL. L. REV. 177 (2002) (applying Yandle's theory of Baptists and bootleggers to explain the political support for the Kyoto Protocol).

103. 198 U.S. 45 (1905).

of its police powers, has passed an act which seriously limits the right
to labor or the right of contract in regard to their means of livelihood
between persons who are *sui juris* (both employer and employé), it
becomes of great importance to determine which shall prevail—the
right of the individual to labor for such time as he may choose, or the
right of the State to prevent the individual from laboring, or from
entering into any contract to labor, beyond a certain time prescribed
by the State.[104]

While the state defended the regulation, claiming that regulating the
hours of bakers was necessary to promote the general health and safety,
as well as that of the bakers themselves, Justice Peckham found the
argument attenuated:

> The mere assertion that the subject relates though but in a remote
> degree to the public health, does not necessarily render the enactment
> valid. . . .
>
> 　　. . . .
>
> . . . There must be more than the mere fact of the possible
> existence of some small amount of unhealthiness to warrant legisla-
> tive interference with liberty. It is unfortunately true that labor, even
> in any department, may possibly carry with it the seeds of unhealthi-
> ness. But are we all, on that account, at the mercy of legislative
> majorities? A printer, a tinsmith, a locksmith, a carpenter, a cabinet-
> maker, a dry goods clerk, a bank's, a lawyer's or a physician's clerk,
> or a clerk in almost any kind of business, would all come under the
> power of the legislature, on this assumption. No trade, no occupation,
> no mode of earning one's living, could escape this all-pervading power,
> and the acts of the legislature in limiting the hours of labor in all
> employments would be valid, although such limitation might seriously
> cripple the ability of the laborer to support himself and his family.[105]

Justice Peckham then specifically addressed whether bakers were in
need of unique legislative protection, as urged by the state:

> [We] think that such a law as this, although passed in the assumed
> exercise of the police power, and as relating to the public health, or
> the health of the employés named, is not within that power, and is
> invalid. The act is not, within any fair meaning of the term, a health
> law, but is an illegal interference with the rights of individuals, both
> employers and employés, to make contracts regarding labor upon such
> terms as they may think best, or which they may agree upon with the
> other parties to such contracts. Statutes of the nature of that under
> review, limiting the hours in which grown and intelligent men may
> labor to earn their living, are mere meddlesome interferences with the
> rights of the individual, and they are not saved from condemnation by
> the claim that they are passed in the exercise of the police power and

---

104. *Id.* at 53–54.

105. *Id.* at 57, 59.

upon the subject of the health of the individual whose rights are interfered with, unless there be some fair ground, reasonable in and of itself, to say that there is material danger to the public health or to the health of the employés, if the hours of labor are not curtailed.

. . . .

... Adding to [a legitimate series of bakery inspection requirements] a prohibition to enter into any contract of labor in a bakery for more than a certain number of hours a week, is, in our judgment, so wholly beside the matter of a proper, reasonable and fair provision, as to run counter to that liberty of person and of free contract provided for in the Federal Constitution.[106]

Justice Peckham concluded that "Under such circumstances the freedom of master and employé to contract with each other in relation to their employment, and in defining the same, cannot be prohibited or interfered with, without violating the Federal Constitution."[107]

In his dissenting opinion, Justice Harlan challenged both the premises of Peckham's analysis and the Court's application on its own terms. Justice Harlan began by discussing the Supreme Court's role in assessing the proper scope of the state's exercise of police powers:

It is plain that this statute was enacted in order to protect the physical well-being of those who work in bakery and confectionery establishments. It may be that the statute had its origin, in part, in the belief that employers and employees in such establishments were not upon an equal footing, and that the necessities of the latter often compelled them to submit to such exactions as unduly taxed their strength. Be this as it may, the statute must be taken as expressing the belief of the people of New York that, as a general rule, and in the case of the average man, labor in excess of sixty hours during a week in such establishments may endanger the health of those who thus labor. Whether or not this be wise legislation it is not the province of the court to inquire. Under our systems of government the courts are not concerned with the wisdom or policy of legislation.[108]

... What the precise facts are it may be difficult to say. It is enough for the determination of this case, and it is enough for this court to know, that the question is one about which there is room for debate and for an honest difference of opinion. There are many reasons of a weighty, substantial character, based upon the experience of mankind, in support of the theory that, all things considered, more than ten hours' steady work each day, from week to week, in a bakery or confectionery establishment, may endanger the health, and shorten the lives of the workmen, thereby diminishing their physical and

---

106. *Id.* at 61–62.

107. *Id.* at 64.

108. *Id.* at 69 (Harlan, J., dissenting).

mental capacity to serve the State, and to provide for those dependent upon them.

> If such reasons exist that ought to be the end of this case, for the State is not amenable to the judiciary, in respect of its legislative enactments, unless such enactments are plainly, palpably, beyond all question, inconsistent with the Constitution of the United States. We are not to presume that the State of New York has acted in bad faith. Nor can we assume that its legislature acted without due deliberation, or that it did not determine this question upon the fullest attainable information, and for the common good.[109]

In arguing that the law should be upheld as a proper exercise of the state's police powers, Justice Harlan relied upon several studies discussing the safety conditions for bakers:

> Professor Hirt in his treatise on the "Diseases of the Workers" has said: "The labor of the bakers is among the hardest and most laborious imaginable, because it has to be performed under conditions injurious to the health of those engaged in it. It is hard, very hard work, not only because it requires a great deal of physical exertion in an overheated workshop and during unreasonably long hours, but more so because of the erratic demands of the public, compelling the baker to perform the greater part of his work at night, thus depriving him of an opportunity to enjoy the necessary rest and sleep, a fact which is highly injurious to his health." Another writer says: "The constant inhaling of flour dust causes inflammation of the lungs and of the bronchial tubes. The eyes also suffer through this dust, which is responsible for the many cases of running eyes among the bakers. The long hours of toil to which all bakers are subjected produce rheumatism, cramps and swollen legs. The intense heat in the work-shops induces the workers to resort to cooling drinks, which together with their habit of exposing the greater part of their bodies to the change in the atmosphere, is another source of a number of diseases of various organs." . . . The average age of a baker is below that of other workmen, they seldom live over their fiftieth year, most of them dying between the ages of forty and fifty.[110]

Finally, consider the following passage from Justice Oliver Wendell Holmes's dissenting opinion:

> This case is decided upon an economic theory which a large part of the country does not entertain. If it were a question whether I agreed with that theory, I should desire to study it further and long before making up my mind. But I do not conceive that to be my duty, because I strongly believe that my agreement or disagreement has nothing to do with the right of a majority to embody their opinions in law. . . . The Fourteenth Amendment does not enact Mr. Herbert Spencer's Social Statics. . . . [A] constitution is not intended to em-

---

109. *Id.* at 72–73.

110. *Id.* at 70–71.

body a particular economic theory, whether of paternalism and the organic relation of the citizen to the State or of *laissez faire*.[111]

Does public choice provide a means of assessing the various opinions in *Lochner*? One possible answer is that the case turns strictly on a matter of the substantive interpretation of the Fourteenth Amendment Due Process Clause. While that view might help to explain Chief Justice Holmes's dissent, it does not explain the extent to which Justices Peckham, for the majority, and Harlan, in dissent, relied heavily on their own understandings of both the factual nature of the baking profession and their understandings of the wisdom, or lack thereof, of the legislative processes that resulted in the challenged law.

Do the analyses that Justices Peckham and Harlan offer turn on assumptions concerning the effectiveness of the political process in New York in reflecting the popular will or wisdom of legislative policy? Does the majority's analysis rest upon a notion of political market failure? If so, what is that intuition based upon? Does Harlan's discussion of the studies concerning the safety of the baking industry overcome such claims? Why or why not? In another passage, the majority asserts: "It is impossible for us to shut our eyes to the fact that many of the laws of this character, while passed under what is claimed to be the police power for the purpose of protecting the public health or welfare, are, in reality, passed from other motives."[112] What does this mean? What does Justice Harlan mean when he asserts, "It is plain that this statute was enacted in order to protect the physical well-being of those who work in bakery and confectionery establishments," and that "We are not to presume that the State of New York has acted in bad faith."[113] Does Harlan believe that legislators are invariably sincere in their motives? Should it matter if public choice theory, or available empirical evidence, demonstrates this assumption to be false, or at least suspect?

Professor Bernard Siegan provides an interest-group analysis of the statute under review in *Lochner*.[114] Siegan questions the dissent's assumption that the motivation for the law, as was claimed, was to protect the physical and economic well-being of the bakers. For example, he observes that the bakers' pay might be reduced along with the reduction in hours, making it more difficult for the bakers to support themselves and their families. In addition, he suggests that the law might not be the product of a benign motivation to protect bakers from the potential health risks associated with long hours, but rather to protect bakers working at larger industrial bakeries that already complied with the various safety and hours regulations reflected in the New York law, at the expense of smaller, often immigrant-owned bakeries, that did not. Siegan explains:

---

111. *Id.* at 75 (Holmes, J., dissenting).

112. *Id.* at 64 (majority opinion).

113. *Id.* at 69, 73 (Harlan, J., dissenting).

114. BERNARD H. SIEGAN, ECONOMIC LIBERTIES AND THE CONSTITUTION 113–20 (1980).

In New York, as elsewhere, the baking industry was split between sizable bakeries whose plants had been specifically built or fully converted for such purposes, and small bakeries, operating out of limited, often subterranean quarters not originally intended for such use.... The New York trend was also toward bigger operations....

Contemporary articles in the *New York Times* reported that sanitary, health, and working conditions in the small bakeries were far below those in the large ones....

Working hours were [also] much longer in the small bakeries than in the large ones, and the maximum hours provision hit employers and employees of the former much more.... [W]orkers in some small bakeries ... remained on the business premises (if not actually on the job) from twelve to as many as twenty-two hours a working day. The workday in the larger firms ... met or was close to the statutory maximum of ten hours.

... [The] restrictions on working hours meant higher labor costs for the small bakers, who, due to competition from the corporate bakers, were limited in the amount they could pass on in the form of higher prices. A number of the small bakers would have to terminate their businesses.

The effect on the larger bakeries would be far less adverse. They were much closer to the hour standard, and unlike the small bakeries, they might sustain a modest increase in costs if they had to hire more workers. However, extra production costs would be offset by the lessened competition from the small bakeries, which would lead to higher prices.[115]

Also consider Professor David Bernstein's complementary analysis,[116] which posits that larger corporate bakeries also had unionized work forces, whereas smaller, immigrant-owned bakeries did not:

The larger New York bakeries tended to be unionized, and were staffed by bakers of Anglo–Irish and (primarily) German descent; the latter group came to dominate the Bakery and Confectionery Workers' International Union.... The smaller bakeries employed a hodgepodge of ethnic groups, primarily French, Germans, Italians, and Jews, usually segregated by bakery and generally working for employers of the same ethnic group. Employees of smaller bakeries were generally not unionized, especially among the non-Germans.

By the mid–1890s, bakers in large bakeries rarely worked more than ten hours per day, sixty hours per week. However, these bakers were concerned that their improved situation was endangered by competition from small, old-fashioned bakeries, especially those that employed Italian, French, and Jewish immigrants. These old-fash-

---

115. *Id.* at 116–18.

116. *See* David E. Bernstein, Lochner v. New York: *A Centennial Retrospective*, 83 WASH. U. L.Q. 1469 (2005).

ioned bakeries were often located in the basement of tenement buildings to take advantage of cheap rents and floors sturdy enough to withstand the weight of heavy baking ovens. Unlike the more modern "factory" bakeries, which operated in shifts, the basement bakeries often demanded that workers be on call twenty-four hours a day, with the bakers sleeping in or near the bakery during down times. Workers in such bakeries often worked far more than ten hours per day.

Union bakers believed that competition from basement bakery workers drove down their wages.[117]

Professor Bernstein sees the eventual law as the outcome of a coalition that included reformers concerned about public health and the bakers' union, which wanted to put small basement bakeries that generally failed to meet the new sanitary standards, out of business. Bernstein claims that the bakers' union, which was well-organized at the time, as opposed to the baking industry, which was less well organized, provided the impetus behind the law. Eventually, the bakery owners became better organized and decided to fund Mr. Lochner's challenge to the maximum hours provisions of the Labor Law of New York in part because they believed that those provisions were only being enforced against nonunion bakeries. While Bernstein claims that large corporate bakeries were supporters of the provisions of the law that gave them a comparative advantage in the market over smaller rivals, he also observes that a coalition of organized labor and public health reformers procured the challenged labor law.[118]

How, if at all, do the analyses by Professors Siegan and Bernstein affect your thinking about the relative merits of the various *Lochner* opinions? Assuming that these commentators are correct that the New York law was largely motivated by the desire of larger, unionized bakeries to limit competition by smaller bakeries, does this provide a normative justification for striking the law down? How, if at all, might this analysis change if, as Bernstein contends, the challenged law arose from a Baptist and Bootleggers coalition that was at least partly motivated by concerns for public health and safety? Does the federal judiciary have the institutional competence to make appropriate assessments concerning the political forces that support or oppose a given piece of legislation? Should the answer to the prior question affect the how the Supreme Court analyzes cases like *Lochner*? Why or why not? Does the analysis suggest that conventional presentations that pit the interests of "management" against the interests of "labor" fail to recognize that often the relevant competition giving rise to protectionist laws is labor against labor or management against management? If so, should this affect the judicial approach to cases like *Lochner*?

---

117. *Id.* at 1476–77 (footnotes omitted).

118. *See* DAVID E. BERNSTEIN, REHABILITATING LOCHNER (forthcoming).

B. WEST COAST HOTEL v. PARRISH

In the landmark case *West Coast Hotel Co. v. Parrish*,[119] which overturned *Adkins v. Children's Hospital*,[120] the Supreme Court sustained a minimum wage law for women.[121] This case is widely understood to represent the end of the *Lochner* era. The Court not only signaled the end of the era of economic substantive due process in its holding, but also in its broad assertion: "What is this freedom? The Constitution does not speak of freedom of contract. It speaks of liberty and prohibits the deprivation of liberty without due process of law."[122]

Ultimately, the choice between the *Lochner* regime, which allows the federal judiciary to check market regulations that interfere with private contracting, and the *Parrish* regime, which permits legislatures, both state and federal, to regulate markets in a manner that thwarts at least some mutually agreeable transactions, comes down to institutional competence. The *Lochner* regime presumes market transactions to be beneficial because mutually entered into, while the *Parrish* regime presumes legislative limits on the market to be permissible because legislative processes are assumed to represent majoritarian preferences. Building upon an insight from chapter 1, the *Pareto* superiority criterion, we can construct a simple analysis that reveals the inevitability of this ultimate choice, either to prefer market transactions or democratic decisions, in at least some sets of circumstances.

Market transactions are presumed to be welfare enhancing because they are entered into with the mutual consent of the contracting parties. The participants would not engage in the exchange if at least one participant (and probably both participants) did not expect to be made better off as a result. But logrolling also involves the mutual consent of those who agree to the relevant vote trades. Ironically, however, a regime that steadfastly honors mutually agreeable legislative trades, for example *Parrish*, creates the possibility and perhaps the actuality of legislation that inhibits certain forms of private market contracting, for example, contracts to work below the minimum wage or above the maximum number of hours. Conversely, a regime that steadfastly honors mutually agreeable private market exchange, for example *Lochner*, creates the possibility and perhaps the actuality of preventing legislation that is the product of mutually agreeable exchange in the form of logrolls among legislators, producing such laws as minimum wages or maximum hours. In a constitutional system, it is inevitable that at some point, the judiciary will be forced to confront this choice because there is no set of mechanisms that can invariably protect both sets of mutually agreeable exchanges.

---

119. 300 U.S. 379 (1937).

120. 261 U.S. 525 (1923).

121. 300 U.S. at 398–99.

122. *Id.* at 391.

One could avoid this seeming dilemma by claiming that private transactions that do not produce externalities are *Pareto* superior, while legislative logrolling invariably affects parties other than the members of the legislature, and thus they invariably produce externalities and cannot be assumed *Pareto* superior. The difficulty, however, is that ultimately this is an argument of definition. Consider the argument that market transactions (other than those with externalities) do not harm anyone and are thus *Pareto* superior. Economists making this argument are focusing solely on externalities among other private market actors, for example in the case of pollution. But by insistently honoring private market exchanges such as contracts below specified minimum wages, economists disregard potential harm to other actors, those in an altogether different institution, namely legislators who wish to enact minimum wage laws. Only by defining such actors as outside the scope of the model can one claim that private market transactions should be vindicated against contrary laws on the grounds that they uniquely satisfy the *Pareto* principle.

Of course the same is true with respect to those who seek to protect legislative compromise. It would also be a mistake to claim that such laws are invariably desirable because legislators have agreed to enact them. This calculus fails to consider the potential negative effects within the private market. Those who hold strong *laissez faire* views will be inclined to dismiss the significance of the concern about thwarting laws they deem socially detrimental, and those who are more skeptical of private markets and who are favorably inclined toward market regulation will hold a contrary view. The point here is not to demonstrate that either set of views is right or wrong. Rather it is to demonstrate that one cannot guarantee both sets of concerns simultaneously; there is a necessary choice, or at least the potential for a choice, that tests the outer limits of concerns for protecting the market and concerns for protecting democratic decision making. The history of the doctrine of economic substantive due process suggests that the Supreme Court has changed its mind over time with respect to this fundamental issue.

C.   UNITED STATES v. CAROLENE PRODUCTS

Consider next the famous case *United States v. Carolene Products Co.*,[123] a case that was decided one year following *West Coast Hotel Co. v. Parrish.*[124] *Carolene Products* is notable not only because it provides a theoretical justification for low-level scrutiny of economic regulation, in this case a challenge to a prohibition against lower cost "filled milk," but also because in its famous footnote 4, it offers an express and influential theory concerning those defects in political processes that might provide a normative justification for applying strict scrutiny to certain forms of legislation.

123.   304 U.S. 144 (1938).
124.   300 U.S. 379 (1937).

In *Carolene Products*, Justice Stone, writing for a majority, sustained the Filled Milk Act, a federal statute that "prohibit[ed] the shipment in interstate commerce of skimmed milk compounded with any fat or oil other than milk fat, so as to resemble milk or cream,"[125] as an adulterated product deemed injurious to the public health, against a challenge based upon the Fifth Amendment Due Process Clause and the Commerce Clause. The Court relied upon an earlier case, *Hebe Co. v. Shaw*,[126] for the proposition that "a state law which forbids the manufacture and sale of a product assumed to be wholesome and nutritive, made of condensed skimmed milk, compounded with coconut oil, is not forbidden by the Fourteenth Amendment."[127] The Court did not rest solely on precedent, however, asserting:

> [A]ffirmative evidence also sustains the statute. In twenty years evidence has steadily accumulated of the danger to the public health from the general consumption of foods which have been stripped of elements essential to the maintenance of health. The Filled Milk Act was adopted by Congress after committee hearings, in the course of which eminent scientists and health experts testified. An extensive investigation was made of the commerce in milk compounds in which vegetable oils have been substituted for natural milk fat, and of the effect upon the public health of the use of such compounds as a food substitute for milk.... [T]he House Committee on Agriculture ... and the Senate Committee on Agriculture and Forestry ... concluded ... that the use of filled milk as a substitute for pure milk is generally injurious to health and facilitates fraud on the public.[128]

While the Court relied upon such legislative findings and the underlying testimony, it further noted that such findings were not necessary to sustain the Act. The Court continued:

> Even in the absence of such aids the existence of facts supporting the legislative judgment is to be presumed, for regulatory legislation affecting ordinary commercial transactions is not to be pronounced unconstitutional unless in the light of the facts made known or generally assumed it is of such a character as to preclude the assumption that it rests upon some rational basis within the knowledge and experience of the legislators.[129]

In the famous footnote 4 that followed this passage, Justice Stone, joined by a plurality of four, stated:

> There may be narrower scope for operation of the presumption of constitutionality when legislation appears on its face to be within a specific prohibition of the Constitution, such as those of the first ten

---

125. *Carolene Prods.*, 304 U.S. at 145–46.

126. 248 U.S. 297 (1919).

127. *Carolene Prods.*, 304 U.S. at 148.

128. *Id.* at 148–49 (citations omitted).

129. *Id.* at 152.

amendments, which are deemed equally specific when held to be embraced within the Fourteenth.

It is unnecessary to consider now whether legislation which restricts those political processes which can ordinarily be expected to bring about repeal of undesirable legislation, is to be subjected to more exacting judicial scrutiny under the general prohibitions of the Fourteenth Amendment than are most other types of legislation....

. . . .

Nor need we enquire whether similar considerations enter into the review of statutes directed at particular religious, or national, or racial minorities. [P]rejudice against discrete and insular minorities may be a special condition, which tends seriously to curtail the operation of those political processes ordinarily to be relied upon to protect minorities, and which may call for a correspondingly more searching judicial inquiry.[130]

The Court's argument in footnote 4 that the majoritarian political process generally protects individuals, but that "discrete and insular" minorities, such as racial or religious minorities, may be entitled to special protection by the judiciary, underlies John Hart Ely's well known book, *Democracy and Distrust*.[131] In this analysis, the true vice of factions is in failing to protect groups that systematically are disadvantaged, in part due to numbers and in part due to organizational abilities, within traditional political processes. As a result, Ely maintains, heightened scrutiny of laws that adversely affect specified racial minorities and women are normatively justified by perceived failures in political markets.

Consider the response by Professor Bruce Ackerman.[132] Following Mancur Olson, Ackerman contends that while the size of minority groups might be a weakness, their insularity might be a strength, at least when compared with other noninsular groups. Thus, Ackerman states:

> Other things being equal, "discreteness and insularity" will normally be a source of enormous bargaining advantage, not disadvantage, for a group engaged in pluralist American politics. Except for special cases, the concerns that underlie *Carolene* should lead judges to protect groups that possess the opposite characteristics from the ones *Carolene* emphasizes—groups that are "anonymous and diffuse" rather than "discrete and insular." It is these groups that both political science and American history indicate are systematically disadvantaged in a pluralist democracy.[133]

---

130. *Id.* at 152–53 n.4 (citations omitted).

131. JOHN HART ELY, DEMOCRACY AND DISTRUST: A THEORY OF JUDICIAL REVIEW (1980).

132. Bruce A. Ackerman, *Beyond* Carolene Products, 98 HARV. L. REV. 713 (1985).

133. *Id.* at 723–24.

Are there reasons to suspect that those groups that have traditionally benefited from the Court's treatment of *Carolene Products* footnote 4, namely African Americans, might lack some of the benefits that Ackerman ascribes to discrete and insular minorities? If so, what are those factors? Is it possible that Ackerman's analysis commits a category mistake, meaning that it equates as "discrete and insular" minorities two separate groups in the Wilson–Hayes framework:[134] those minorities who seek protections from laws benefiting majority groups at their expense (the lower left) and special interest groups seeking quasi-private legislation at the expense of a diffuse electorate (the upper right)? If so, which box is the target of Ackerman's analysis, and which box is the target of footnote 4?

Professor Geoffrey P. Miller has offered a critical account of the *Carolene Products* opinion, in which he claims that the result was to prevent access to a low cost product for those consumers most in need.[135]

> Filled milk was a technological innovation in the canned milk industry, an industry that was itself a response to the technological difficulties of bringing fluid milk to markets. The problem of dairy marketing has always been the perishability of fluid milk.... The early decades of the twentieth century saw rapid development of transportation, refrigeration, and pasteurization, facilitating the creation of home delivery systems of bottled milk. Even so, there remained a demand for fluid milk that resisted spoilage. Many homes, especially in poorer areas, did not have refrigerators; and it was useful for all households to have some extra fluid milk on hand for emergencies. Canned milk filled these needs.[136]

Given his conclusion that filled milk was a wholesome and economical milk product, Miller rejects the court's public interest justifications for the law as being "patently bogus," instead attributing the law to the influence of the dairy industry. Filled milk, which was made with skim milk and vegetable oil, sold for a much lower price than whole milk, which was enriched with butterfat. Much of the profit for dairy farmers and large milk distributors (such as Borden) came from sales of fluid and condensed whole milk. Moreover, increased consumption of filled milk threatened to divert millions of pounds of butter into the market, thereby "driving down the price of that commodity."[137] Finally, in 1923 the federal Filled Milk Act was enacted, which prohibited the shipment in interstate commerce of filled milk, and by 1937, thirty-one states had also banned the manufac-

---

134. *See supra* table 2:4 (The Four Box Static Model).

135. Geoffrey P. Miller, *The True Story of* Carolene Products, 1987 SUP. CT. REV. 397.

136. *Id.* at 400.

137. *Id.* at 404.

ture or sale of filled milk, three states had enacted effectively similar legislation, and three states had imposed conditions and regulations on the manufacture and sale of filled milk. "The effect of the federal statute, coupled with prohibitory state legislation," Miller observes, "was to drive most producers out of business."[138] Miller concludes:

> The battle over filled milk seems well-described by interest group theory. The most plausible inference is that the statute was enacted at the behest of a coalition of groups intent on advancing their own economic welfare at the expense of less powerful groups. An impressionistic view of the events surrounding the statute's enactment supports this inference: the sponsors were from big dairy states, while the chief opponents were from cotton states.[139]

Miller also conducted an empirical analysis that generally supported his conclusions. He observes:

> In the *Carolene Products* footnote, Justice Stone suggested that special protections were needed for "discrete and insular minorities" because such groups would not be adequately served by the political process. The statement, if meant as a general observation about American politics, is obviously misplaced. Public choice theory demonstrates that, in general, "discrete and insular minorities" are exactly the groups that are likely to obtain disproportionately large benefits from the political process.
>
> The insights of public choice theory are amply demonstrated by the battle over filled milk, where one discrete minority—the nation's dairy farmers and their allies—obtained legislation harmful to consumers and the public at large. To be sure, the legislation discriminated against another discrete minority—the filled milk industry—but this fact simply reflects the complexity of the dairy industry. Filled milk producers, if they had not been trumped by a politically more powerful group, might themselves have been able to obtain special legislative favors to the detriment of the public interest.[140]

Does this analysis affect your thinking about the deferential approach that the *Carolene Products* Court took to the statute under review? About its less deferential approach in cases involving discrete and insular minorities? Miller posits:

> The political theory underlying the *Carolene Products* footnote, now a half-century old, needs to be updated. The results of that process may call in question the Supreme Court's policy of blind deference to

---

138. *Id.* at 410.

139. *Id.* at 423.

140. *Id.* at 428 (footnote omitted).

legislation favoring special industrial interests. Is it time to re-examine the wisdom of "see-no-evil, hear-no-evil" as the prevailing philosophy in economic regulation cases?[141]

To what extent is the Supreme Court's deferential standard of review in *Carolene* based on its embedded assumptions about how the legislative process operates? Does the Court provide any justification for its assumptions? Is the filled milk industry the sort of "discrete and insular" minority that the Supreme Court had in mind in *Carolene Products* footnote 4? Is it possible that Professor Miller has also committed a category mistake that the Wilson–Hayes analysis helps to identify?[142] Should the Court carefully scrutinize both economic regulation and legislation affecting discrete and insular minorities? What might the costs of such a regime be? To what extent if any are your answers informed by public choice?

V. NORMATIVE CRITIQUES OF INTEREST GROUP THEORY AND INTEREST GROUP THEORY BASED LEGAL SCHOLARSHIP

In this section, we consider two normative critics of interest group theory and of legal scholarship relying upon interest group theory. We begin with Professor Einer Elhauge's article, *Does Interest Group Theory Justify More Intrusive Judicial Review?*[143] The author answers the title question in the negative. The article presents two central arguments, the first of which is of particular importance to this chapter. We then consider the critique by Professors Donald Green and Ian Shapiro, set out in their book, *Pathologies of Rational Choice Theory.*[144]

A. THE PROBLEM OF BASELINES[145]

Elhauge's analysis responds to claims by an impressive cadre of legal scholars who have relied upon public choice to identify claimed defects in political processes and to rely upon those identified defects to advocate less judicial deference to legislative outcomes.[146] Elhauge advances two arguments that together represent a broadside attack on the literature relying on interest-group theory to advocate changes in judicial interpretation of statutes:

---

141. *Id.*

142. *See supra* note 134, and accompanying text.

143. Elhauge, *supra* note 100, at 31.

144. DONALD P. GREEN & IAN SHAPIRO, PATHOLOGIES OF RATIONAL CHOICE THEORY: A CRITIQUE OF APPLICATIONS IN POLITICAL SCIENCE (1994).

145. Portions of the discussions that follow are adapted from STEARNS, *supra* note 22, at 246–53.

146. Elhauge includes the following, and reviews many of their articles in his analysis: Erwin Chemerinsky, Frank Easterbrook, Richard Epstein, William Eskridge, Jonathan Macey, Jerry Mashaw, Gary Minda, William Page, Martin Shapiro, Bernard Siegan, Cass Sunstein, and John Wiley. Elhauge, *supra* note 100, at 33.

First, any defects in the political process identified by interest group theory depend on implicit normative baselines and thus do not stand independent of substantive conclusions about the merits of particular political outcomes. Accordingly, expansions of judicial review cannot meaningfully be limited by requiring threshold findings of excessive interest group influence. Further, the use of interest group theory to condemn the political process reflects normative views that are contestable and may not reflect the views of the polity.

Second, even if interest group theory succeeds in demonstrating defects in the political process, that would not justify the leap to the conclusion that more intrusive judicial review would improve lawmaking. The litigation process cannot be treated as exogenous to interest group theory because that process is also subject to forms of interest group influence that would be exacerbated if judicial review became more intrusive. More generally, when one makes the necessary comparative assessment, interest group theory does not establish (as it must to justify more intrusive judicial review) that the litigation process is, overall, less defective than the political process.[147]

In essence, Elhauge's major critique of normative legal scholarship that relies upon interest group theory is that it invariably presumes, usually without acknowledgement, that having identified tendencies toward some degree of interest group influence in the political processes, that input is *excessive*. The problem is that it is never clear what the proper level of interest group input actually is, and thus the critical question—*excessive as compared with what?*—is not asked.

Elhauge further adds that the difficulty with such scholarship is that by identifying a given level of interest group influence, and claiming it disproportionate, the reader risks assuming a different baseline concerning interest group influence than would be the case absent the interference of interest group theory. Elhauge explains:

> More generally, ... interest group theory can be seriously misleading unless one recognizes and identifies the nature of the implicit normative baseline. Unawareness that an implicit baseline exists can mislead one into believing that value-neutral defects in the political process justify expanding judicial review. Unawareness of the content of that implicit baseline can mislead one into applying normative standards different from the standards one would otherwise apply.[148]

In the remainder of Elhauge's article, he proceeds to evaluate a large number of potential normative baselines that one could use interest group theory to advance. While he views all of the potential baselines as contestable, his larger point is that once a baseline is selected, one can apply it directly to a proposed policy change without the intermediate step of considering the policy in question through the lens of public choice.

---

147. Elhauge, *supra* note 10. *Id.* at 34.

148. *Id.* at 49.

At one level, Elhauge's analysis is almost certainly correct. As with economic analysis generally, interest group theory is a set of positive tools.[149] Proper economic analysis uses models to suggest the likely implications of a proposed policy change—and also to suggest means of testing a given thesis—but it cannot of its own force evaluate the merits of those implications. Such conclusions lie outside the scope of the economic models and necessarily rest, as Elhauge phrases it, on implicit normative baselines. This suggests that those reading normative scholarship resting upon public choice (we might say based upon any theory) must be careful to not only to assess the care with which the public choice analysis (or whatever relevant analysis) is undertaken, but also to look carefully for unexpressed normative baselines capable of biasing the resulting analysis.

The second part of Elhauge's analysis, which involves baseline assessment, suggests that virtually any baseline is contestable. This raises an important set of concerns as well. How does one select a baseline or set of baselines with which to evaluate proposals that are made in the name of public choice? If public choice demonstrates tendencies of political processes to favor one set of inputs over another, or one interest group over another, how does one select a baseline to inform the judiciary as to how best to proceed in assessing the resulting laws? Does the possibility that large bakeries or labor unions motivated the challenged law in *Lochner* or that large dairy producers influenced the filled milk ban in *Carolene Products* change the analysis? Would such findings counsel different results than would be the case if we instead accepted the premise that in both cases, the legislatures' goals were truly to protect bakers and consumers of baked goods and consumers of dairy products, respectively? Also, how are we to assess whether, as Elhauge also suggests, courts are also susceptible of interest group influence, thus calling into question their ability to check against interest group driven laws, assuming that the operative baseline suggests such influence to be excessive? Is there a coherent methodology, perhaps but not necessarily including one drawn from economics, for selecting among baselines? Should we assume that one baseline or set of baselines invariably applies? Might different baselines apply to different institutions? If so, how would one make such an assessment? Please bear these questions in mind as you read the materials in chapter 3.

B. THE PROBLEM OF TESTABILITY

In 1994, Professors Donald Green and Ian Shapiro wrote *Pathologies of Rational Choice Theory*.[150] This book presented a major attack on public choice that unlike the Elhauge analysis rested primarily on method-

---

149. And it is worth noting that Professor Elhauge carefully distinguishes the positive use of public choice from the normative legal scholarship that relies upon public choice insights to advocate changes in the proper scope or level of judicial review. *See id.* at 48.

150. GREEN & SHAPIRO, *supra* note 144.

ological grounds. The authors' analysis, which generated a strong response from public choice scholars,[151] rested on two principal bases. The primary difficulty, the authors claim, is that there has been a lack of empirical support for some of the strongest rational choice claims.[152] For example, the authors posit that "Focusing centrally on [the works by such leading theorists as Kenneth Arrow, Anthony Downs, and William Riker], we claim that to date few theoretical insights derived from rational choice theory have been subjected to serious empirical scrutiny and survived."[153] In addition, the authors claim, public choice theorists have been willing to rest upon relatively thin evidence, but well-developed theoretical models, to advance ambitious normative proposals. The authors observe: "Too often prescriptive conclusions ... are floated on empirically dubious rational choice hypotheses, as when Riker and Weingast argue that the susceptibility of majority rule to manipulation justifies robust court-enforced constitutional constraints on what legislatures may legitimately do, as was undertaken by the U.S. Supreme Court during the *Lochner* era."[154]

There is no denying the importance of resting proposed policy changes on sound empirical testing and falsifiable theses. As you go through this course, consider the extent to which, if any, those advancing proposals to change existing practices offer sufficient empirical support or purely theoretical justifications. Also consider the extent to which public choice, broadly defined to include social choice and game theory, is helpful in providing positive explanations for existing, and sometimes counterintuitive, practices that conventional legal analysis has proved ill-equipped to explain. To what extent does providing a more robust positive theory serve as a form of empirical testing of rational choice models designed to explain underlying phenomena? Consider also whether this benefit of public choice responds to Elhauge's analysis claiming no need to engage in the intermediate step of developing economic models to assess questions of law and public policy? When evaluating proposals to maintain the status quo or to accept a proposed change, how does one select a proper normative baseline? These are questions that we will revisit in the next chapter, which introduces the problem of social choice.

---

151. *See Symposium on Pathologies of Rational Choice*, 9 CRITICAL REV. 25 (1995) (including as symposium contributors: Jeffrey Friedman, Robert P. Abelson, Dennis Chong, Daniel Diermeier, John Ferejohn, Debra Satz, Morris P. Fiorina, Stanley Kelley, Jr., Robert E. Lane, Susanne Lohmann, James Bernard Murphy, Peter C. Ordeshook, Norman Schofield, Kenneth A. Shepsle, and Michael Taylor).

152. For a presentation claiming that since the Green and Shapiro book was published, a large literature has developed within public choice offering testable hypotheses, see Tonja Jacobi, *The Judiciary, in* ELGAR HANDBOOK IN PUBLIC CHOICE AND PUBLIC LAW (Daniel A. Farber & Anne Joseph O'Connell eds., forthcoming 2009).

153. GREEN & SHAPIRO, *supra* note 145, at 9.

154. *Id.* at 11 (citing William H. Riker & Barry R. Weingast, *Constitutional Regulation of Legislative Choice: The Political Consequences of Judicial Deference to Legislatures*, 74 VA. L. REV. 373, 378 (1988)).

CHAPTER 3

AN INTRODUCTION TO SOCIAL CHOICE[1]

■ ■ ■

Introduction

The study of social choice grows out of a deceptively simple insight. While economic theory assumes as a condition of rationality that individuals hold transitive preference orderings (A preferred to B preferred to C implies A preferred to C), social choice reveals that the assumption of transitivity cannot be extended to groups of three or more individuals selecting among three or more options through a method of unlimited majority rule. This stunningly simple insight—that the preferences of group members sometimes cycle over options such that $ApBpCpA$, where p means preferred to by simple majority rule—enjoys an impressive historical pedigree that dates back to two French philosophers writing contemporaneously with the founding and constitutional framing periods in the United States.[2] Since the 1950s, social choice has generated a rich literature that boasts a prominent Nobel Prize in Economics for Arrow's Impossibility Theorem, or simply Arrow's Theorem, awarded to economist Kenneth Arrow in 1972.[3] Social choice now also forms the basis of a growing legal literature that studies the nature and competence of institutions, including elections, legislatures, courts, and agencies or bureaus.

Before proceeding, let us consider the relationship between interest group theory (the subject of chapter 2) and social choice. Both disciplines study institutions. Unlike interest group theory, however, which disaggregates institutions and studies the micro-level incentives of institutional constituencies or members, social choice takes member preferences as a given. Social choice then considers how institutions process member preferences (or inputs) into collective decisions (or outputs). The study of these processes often proves essential in understanding institutional policy formation and implementation. The essential insight of social choice is that how well institutions perform in their policy or law making role is not

---

1. Portions of this chapter are adapted from MAXWELL L. STEARNS, CONSTITUTIONAL PROCESS: A SOCIAL CHOICE ANALYSIS OF SUPREME COURT DECISION MAKING 41–94 (chapter 2) (paperback ed. 2002), Maxwell L. Stearns, *The Misguided Renaissance of Social Choice*, 103 YALE L.J. 1219 (1994) [herein after *Misguided Renaissance*], and Maxwell L. Stearns, *An Introduction to Social Choice*, *in* ELGAR HANDBOOK IN PUBLIC CHOICE AND PUBLIC LAW (Daniel Farber & Anne Joseph O'Connell eds., forthcoming 2009) [herein after *Introduction*], *manuscript available at* http://digitalcommons.law.umaryland.edu/fac_pubs/702/.

2. For a brief discussion of this history, see Stearns, *Misguided Renaissance, supra* note 1, at 1221–28.

3. *See id.* at 1224.

a simple function of the preferences that constituents hold, but also of the quality of the processes through which institutions transform member preferences into group outputs. Social choice is the study of how group decision making affects these important processes.

This chapter proceeds as follows. Section I introduces several foundational social choice concepts. These include majority rule, the median voter theorem, cycling, the Condorcet criterion, path dependence, agenda setting, minimum winning coalitions, and Arrow's Theorem. This part also provides a summary of proposals advanced by legal scholars relying on social choice theory. Section II adds another layer to social choice analysis that helps to place these and other normative proposals for institutional reform within a broader context. The analysis explains the important role of institutional complementarity in improving the quality and rationality of institutional outputs. The analysis also helps to recast social choice—and in particular Arrow's Theorem—as a set of positive tools that can be used in comparative institutional assessment. In this part, we introduce several related concepts including the fallacy of composition, the isolation fallacy, the nirvana fallacy, empty core bargaining games, and structure-induced equilibria. This section also introduces a study of parliamentary rules that shows how social choice helps to explain institutional adaptation as a means of improving the quality of institutional decision-making processes and outputs. The study also provides a basis for identifying a set of normative baselines, all growing out of economic reasoning, that potentially operate in tension with traditional understandings of efficiency. Combining these baselines proves essential in comparative institutional analysis. Section III reintroduces the Arrow's Theorem criteria and provides a preliminary comparative assessment of the most important institutions in the formation of public law and policy.[4] After a brief conclusion in section IV, section V provides two illustrations of the underlying concepts related to the issue of bankruptcy. In two appendices to this chapter,[5] we introduce important additional social choice concepts for those interested in further exploring some of this chapter's underlying themes.

I. THE PROBLEM OF SOCIAL CHOICE

A. FOUNDATIONS: MAJORITY VERSUS PLURALITY RULE

An obvious starting point in the study of group decision making is majority rule. At first blush, majority rule appears to be a simple concept.

---

4. The second part of this book, and in particular chapters 5 through 7, provides a more detailed comparative institutional account based upon the full range of tools introduced in part I.

5. These appendices are available on the course webpage. *Appendix A: Peaks, Dimensionality, and Symmetry*, offers a more technical, yet non-mathematical, presentation that helps to identify the conditions that give rise to cyclical and noncyclical group preferences. *Appendix B: A Study of Voting Rules*, introduces several proposed rules (including some that have been implemented in identified contexts) designed to overcome the analytical difficulties that social choice reveals concerning collective decision making. These rules include Borda Counts, Coombs Voting, Hare Voting (or Single Transferable Voting), Copeland Voting, Plurality Voting, and Approval Voting. This appendix defines each rule, highlights its respective strengths and weaknesses, and assesses its relative Condorcet efficiency—meaning its probability of securing a Condorcet winner when one is available—as compared with the remaining voting alternatives, under specific conditions. The materials in *Appendix B* are also described in Stearns, *Introduction, supra* note 1.

In making a cake for five children, if three prefer chocolate to vanilla, while two prefer vanilla to chocolate, assuming the cake will have only one flavor, chocolate it is![6] In practical operation, however, majority rule is anything but simple. Depending upon the context, majority rule is often difficult, and sometimes impossible, to justify. One obvious problem is identifying strength of preference. Suppose that one of the two children who prefer vanilla is severely allergic to cocoa, the main ingredient in chocolate. In this context, most would (we hope) concede that majority rule is no longer appropriate. What if, instead, the same child merely holds an intense dislike of chocolate? Is majority rule still inappropriate? If so, what should replace it? Perhaps we might ask the children how strongly they feel about their choice of flavors. How might you expect them to respond? Can you think of a mechanism that would discourage the children from exaggerating their preferences? Is the risk of exaggeration in articulating the strength of preferences limited to children? Why or why not?

For now we will set the problem of intensity of preference aside, and focus on another limitation of majority rule. What happens when no option has first choice majority support? When this occurs, decision makers need to consider alternative voting protocols. One obvious alternative is plurality voting. Plurality voting chooses as the winner that option that receives the most votes, whether or not that option secures majority support. With only two options and an odd number of voters, majority rule and plurality rule coincide, but with three or more options, plurality rule can identify a winner even when majority rule does not. In the absence of a first choice majority winner, is the plurality choice always defensible? Why or why not? Can you identify circumstances in which the socially superior choice receives *fewer* votes than the plurality choice? Is it possible that selecting the plurality option might in some circumstances violate foundational principles of majority rule?[7]

To answer these questions, we need to consider another voting alternative, one that returns once again to the concept of rationality. This time, however, we focus on a dimension not captured in cost-effective pursuit of desired objectives. In social choice, rationality simply means assuming that individuals hold transitive preference orderings. Transitivi-

---

6. For a formalization of the special properties of majority rule, consider May's Theorem, which holds that "D is determined only by the values of D_i, and is independent of how they are assigned. Any permutation of these ballots leaves D unchanged." DENNIS C. MUELLER, PUBLIC CHOICE III 134 (2003) (describing May's Theorem, which holds that only simple majority rule satisfies the conditions of decisiveness, anonymity, neutrality, and positive responsiveness).

7. Writing in 1770, Jean–Charles de Borda provided an early analysis demonstrating that plurality rule sometimes fails to capture the will of the voters. *See* Robert J. Weber, *Approval Voting*, J. ECON. PERSP, Winter 1995, at 39 (discussing Jean–Charles de Borda, *Mémoires sur les Élections au Scrutin*, *in* HISTOIRE DE L'ACADEMIE ROYAL DES SCIENCES (1781)).

ty holds that if *A* is preferred to *B* and if *B* is preferred to *C*, then *A* is preferred to *C*. The median voter theorem, described below, helps to illustrate this proposition.

B. THE MEDIAN VOTER THEOREM

The median voter theorem is the analytical starting point for a great deal of public and social choice analysis.[8] We begin with the basic model. We will later relax some of the simplifying assumptions to bring the model closer to actual institutions.[9]

Assume a one-stage election in which the policy positions of the candidates and the preferences of the voters can be expressed along a single dimensional scale. This scale represents extreme liberal to extreme conservative views of public policy over the relevant set of issues. Each voter has a preferred position along this ideological continuum, known as an "ideal point," and prefers whichever candidate expresses a set of policy positions that places him or her closest to that ideal point. Assume that the electorate has ninety voters with preferences evenly clustered in nine groups of ten. Each group occupies a specific ideological increment that represents a degree of liberalism or conservatism spread along the single dimensional scale.

Imagine an election between two candidates. Candidate *R*, who is a conservative Republican, occupies position 9, the most conservative position along the spectrum. Candidate *D*, who is a liberal Democrat, occupies position 1, the most liberal position along the spectrum. The median voter theorem posits that if these two candidates are primarily motivated to be elected (or once in office reelected), behaving rationally, they will eventually modify, or water down, their extreme policy positions until they converge at or near the ideal point of the median voter or voters, represented at position 5.[10] Figure 3:1 depicts this result.

---

8. While Duncan Black initially introduced the model, Duncan Black, *On the Rationale of Group Decision-making*, 56 J. POL. ECON. 23 (1948), Anthony Downs popularized it in AN ECONOMIC THEORY OF DEMOCRACY (1957). For an informative review of the literature, see Roger D. Congleton, *The Median Voter Model, in* THE ENCYCLOPEDIA OF PUBLIC CHOICE 382 (Charles K. Rowley & Friedrich Schneider eds., 2004).

9. In the next subsection, for example, we relax the assumption of a single dimensional issue spectrum to introduce the concept of cycling, a topic also explored in greater analytical detail in *Appendix A: Peaks, Dimensionality, and Symmetry*. In chapter 6, we introduce two-staged elections, and in chapter 7, we extend the model to explain the Supreme Court's narrowest grounds rule and the rule's limitations.

10. In the context of spatial competition in markets, Harold Hotelling achieved a similar result, predicting that two shops competing along a single street would rationally converge at the midpoint of the street, thwarting the socially superior outcome of placement at distances 25% and 75% along the street. This preferred result would allow all consumers to travel no more than a quarter of the street to get to a shop, while the predicted result requires some to travel halfway along the street. Harold Hotelling, *Stability in Competition*, 39 ECON. J. 41 (1929).

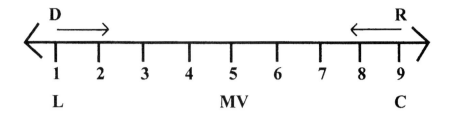

Key: L = Liberal
      C = Conservative
      MV = Median Voter
      D = Liberal (Democratic) Candidate
      R = Conservative (Republican) Candidate

Figure 3:1

The median voter theorem posits that as each candidate seeks to maximize support, he or she will gravitate toward the median electoral position in an effort to capture larger and larger segments of the electorate. The model assumes full electoral participation and that each voter's primary objective is to secure electoral victory for the candidate who is closest to his or her ideal point.[11] Based upon these assumptions, provided that there is some policy distance between R and D (with R to the right of D) after the candidates' general convergence toward the median voter, the voters will not punish the candidate who remains closest to their ideal points by declining to vote or by voting for the other side's preferred candidate. Otherwise, a voter would be voting for a candidate farther from his or her ideal point, with the effect of moving policy opposite the preferred direction.

The median voter theorem predicts that the stable, or Nash equilibrium,[12] outcome for the two candidates converges at or near the median voter, in this example, position 5 on the nine point scale. While this model rests upon strong and admittedly unrealistic simplifying assumptions, it is important to explore its internal logic before relaxing the assumptions to better reflect actual voting contexts. In the most literal application of this model, the two candidates would converge upon the same policy position at 5, leaving the candidates with identical platforms and the voters with no meaningful policy choice. Of course in any large number electorate, it is unlikely that there is a single identifiable median voter.[13] Imagine for

---

11. In fact, the assumption of full electoral participation is a necessary consequence of the assumption that voters seek to move policy toward their ideal point. Can you explain this result?

12. For a discussion of the Nash equilibrium concept, see *infra* 170, chapter 4, Introduction.

13. As we will see, however, this does not mean that there are not median voters in other contexts. For a discussion of actual median voters in the Supreme Court, see *infra* chapter 7. *See also* Stearns, *supra* note 1, at 97–156.

example that in their move toward the median, candidates R and D retain a slight difference in platforms, with the result that D now occupies position 4, while R now occupies position 6. Each candidate is now one increment to the left and right respectively of the true median (position 5) in the direction of his or her electoral base.

Now imagine that the voters divide into three broad constituencies, liberals (A), moderates (B), and conservatives (C), each occupying a range of three points along the nine-point ideological spectrum. Thus, A occupies positions 1 through 3; B occupies positions 4 through 6; and C occupies positions 7 through 9. Given that none of these constituencies possess a majority of voters, how will the election affect the ultimate set of adopted policies? While the voters' ideal points are important, we must further consider how voters rank the package of policy positions, ABC.

The median voter theorem is premised upon the assumption that all voters behave rationally and that they express that rationality consistently with their internally transitive preference orderings. The model assumes that voters whose ideal points occupy the ends of the political spectrum (A or C), will as a second choice prefer the policy position closest to their ideal point (B) and will least prefer the position farthest from their ideal points (C or A).[14] As a result, the liberal voters rank their preferences ABC and the conservative voters rank their preferences CBA. The second and third choices of the moderate voters do not matter. Whether they rank their preferences BAC or BCA, if all voters vote sincerely, in a regime of direct comparisons over the three options, a majority (conservatives and moderates) prefers B to A and another majority (liberals and moderates) prefers B to C.[15] The choice between A and C is irrelevant because whichever option prevails would lose to B in a direct contest.

In this example we still do not know which of our two candidates, R or D, would win the election. Based upon the model itself, the answer would likely turn on whether a majority of the voters aligned at position five have ideal points closer to position 4 (D's position) or position 6 (R's position). Of course in the real world the ultimate choice would turn on myriad factors that belie this simplified single dimensional model.

Despite this concern, the underlying intuition of the median voter theorem has potential applications in concrete lawmaking contexts, such as decision making in the Supreme Court.[16] Consider for example, the following stylized presentation of the 1992 Supreme Court decision, *Planned Parenthood of Southeastern Pennsylvania v. Casey*.[17] In that case, the Supreme Court confronted a constitutional challenge to a Pennsylvania statute that imposed a series of restrictions on the right to abort

---

14. Indeed, if they do not, this implies that the assumption of a single dimensional political spectrum is mistaken. For a more detailed analysis, see *APPENDIX A: PEAKS, DIMENSIONS, AND SYMMETRY supra* note 5.

15. For a discussion linking this analysis to the Condorcet criterion, see *infra* at pp. 102–105.

16. For a more detailed analysis that links the following analysis to the narrowest grounds rule, see *infra* chapter 7, section I.C.1.B. *See also* Stearns, *supra* note 1, at 129–38.

17. 505 U.S. 833 (1992).

announced in *Roe v. Wade*.[18] Assume that the Court divides into three camps, which for simplicity we will refer to as Liberal (*L*), Moderate (*M*), and Conservative (*C*). Further assume that the Liberals prefer to maintain the original *Roe* holding and that based upon *Roe*, they wish to strike down all of the restrictive provisions of the challenged abortion laws on constitutional grounds. The Conservatives would prefer to overrule *Roe* outright, thus rejecting any constitutional right to abort and to sustain all of the challenged provisions. Finally, while the Moderates would not necessarily endorse *Roe* as a sound ruling on first principles, they conclude based on stare decisis that some version of a right to abort should remain, albeit not in the stronger form that the Liberals prefer. The Moderates proceed to redefine *Roe* in a manner that preserves the essential right to abort but that gives states somewhat broader regulatory power over abortion. Applying the new standard, the Moderates sustain all but one challenged abortion regulation, which demands that women seeking an abortion first notify their spouses.

Table 3:1. *Casey* through the Lens of *Marks*

(L) Blackmun and Stevens (concurring)	(M) O'Connor, Kennedy and Souter (plurality)	(C) Rehnquist, Scalia, White, and Thomas (dissenting)
Strike down all restrictive provisions based upon either *stare decisis* or analysis of merits of original *Roe* decision.	Strike down only spousal notification provision, based upon *stare decisis* revision of *Roe*.	Uphold all provisions based upon critical analysis of merits of original *Roe* decision.
Broad abortion right ←——————————————→Narrow abortion right		

Table 3:1[19] captures the three positions in *Casey* along a single dimensional scale, this time representing a liberal position (*L*) providing a broad abortion right, a moderate position (*M*) seeking to modify but retain *Roe,* and a conservative position (*C*) declining to provide an abortion right and seeking to overrule *Roe*. In this example, there are two votes for *L*, three votes for *M*, and four votes for *C*, but the specific numbers do not matter provided any two-group combination has sufficient votes to produce a majority. Since the three positions can be cast along this single dimensional scale, we can further assume that if asked to rank all three options, the Liberals will choose *LMC*, the Conservatives will choose *CML*. The second and third ordinal rankings of the Moderate camp (*MCL* or *MLC*) are irrelevant. Either way, position *M* emerges the dominant outcome, where dominant means that no other outcome contains the requisite majority support among the potential coalitions to displace it.

The median voter theorem reveals an implicit decisional rule in the absence of a first choice majority candidate that is at odds with plurality

---

18.   410 U.S. 113 (1973).

19.   STEARNS, *supra* note 1, at 129 tbl.3.6 (*Casey* through the lens of *Marks*).

rule. The median voter theorem suggests that when preferences align along a single dimensional scale, and when there is no first choice majority candidate, voters will be willing to continue supporting candidates slightly in their ideological direction even as the candidates converge upon the median position. While the median voter outcome has the potential to coincide with the plurality outcome, it need not always do so.

Let us now consider an example in which outcomes predicted by the median voter theorem and plurality rule diverge. Imagine an electoral distribution in which fewer voters occupy the median position B than either of the extreme positions A or C.[20] Assume that the liberals (A) hold 40% of the electorate, the moderates (B) hold 25% of the electorate, and the conservatives (C) hold 35% of the electorate. Figure 3:3 depicts this distribution of voters above the incremental policy positions one through nine:

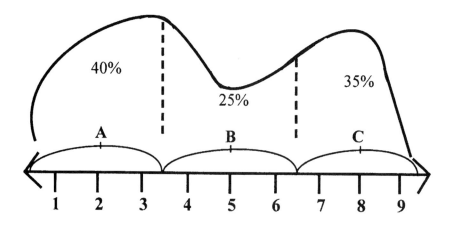

Figure 3:2

Assume as in the prior voting example that the policy positions divide into rough ideological clusters A, B, and C, and that the voters occupying each position can rank order their choices over the remaining positions. In Figure 3:2, while the median voter occupies position four rather than position five, that position remains moderate at B. And yet, option A obtains a plurality of 40% of the votes as compared with option B's 25% and option C's 35%. Under plurality rule, option A would prevail. Applying the analysis from the earlier discussion, however, in which we assume that those occupying the extreme positions A and C rank position B as a second choice, it might appear that the median outcome, B, is the better choice.[21]

---

20. The same analysis would apply if the median position received the second largest number of votes.

21. As explained below, *see infra* pp. 101–05, option B is the Condorcet winner, named for the French philosopher who described this result in 1785. *See also* Stearns, *Misguided Renaissance, supra* note 1, at 1221.

Given the preferences, which platform, *A* or *B*, is the optimal social choice? Why? As previously noted, in the actual *Casey* opinion, option *L* received two votes, option *M* received three votes, and option *C* received four votes. Which rule, plurality voting or the median voter theorem, is more suitable in that setting?[22] Which voting rule, plurality or median voter, is generally preferred? Is it possible that each is preferred in some contexts, while disfavored in others? If so, what might those contexts be? To answer these questions, we must once again revisit the concept of rationality. The analysis that follows will demonstrate that the median voter theorem depicts a special case of preferences in the absence of a first-choice majority candidate. Identifying the circumstances that are or are not conducive to generating a dominant median outcome is important in developing a social choice analysis of institutions and rules.

C.   RATIONALITY REVISITED: CYCLICAL AND NON–CYCLICAL PREFERENCES

We begin, once more, with a deceptively simple insight that underlies the social choice understanding of rationality. Imagine that three persons are choosing among three options *A*, *B*, and *C*. The options can represent virtually anything, including policy positions for political candidates, the amount of federal bailout money for the automobile industry, or even something as trivial as the flavor of a cake. Once again, we generally assume that *A* preferred to *B* preferred to *C* implies *A* preferred to *C*. In selecting ice cream flavors, for example, if Alice likes mint more than chocolate, and chocolate more than vanilla, we would infer that she also likes mint more than vanilla. This does not, of course, mean that Alice is forever barred from selecting vanilla when mint is available, as very well might occur if Alice has had mint ice cream several nights in a row.[23] But if asked whether she likes mint more than vanilla, most would think it odd if Alice instead picked vanilla.

Social choice theory reveals that this simple assumption respecting individual rationality, namely that persons generally hold transitive preference orderings, does not universally hold for groups seeking to transform individually rational (or transitive) preferences into collective outcomes. Stated differently, the median voter theorem, which illustrates how, in the absence of a majority candidate, group preferences along a single dimensional continuum tend to converge on the median position, rests on a special set of assumptions about group preferences. As a result, the median voter model fails to capture all of the important dynamics of social choice.

---

22. Keep this question in mind as you read the discussion of the narrowest grounds doctrine, *infra* chapter 7, section I.C.1.B, *see also infra* note 141, and accompanying text.

23. It also does not mean that at some future time, Alice might not change her mind and acquire a taste for a flavor that she once disliked, thus transforming her preferences. But once this occurs, we would once again presume that she holds her now updated preferences in a similar transitive fashion.

To keep the analysis simple, let us assume that three persons (represented as P1, P2, and P3), are choosing among three options, or alternatively that each person represents a constituency such that any two-group combination contains sufficient votes to form a majority.[24] Assume that after the members disclose their first choices over options *ABC*, they discover that none holds the same preference and thus there is no first choice majority winner. After the participants discover the absence of a first choice winner, they each candidly disclose their ordinal preference rankings from most-to-least preferred, as follows:

P1: *ABC*

P2: *BCA*

P3: *CAB*

Since there is no first choice majority candidate, the members take a series of pairwise votes, meaning votes between two available options, in the hope of selecting a winner. Assume further that each member votes sincerely, meaning consistently with the above rankings in each direct comparison.

As between options *A* and *B*, *A* wins, with P1 and P3 defeating P2. As between options *A* against *C*, *C* wins, with P2 and P3 defeating P1. Thus far, the regime of pairwise voting has revealed that *C* is preferred to *A* and *A* is preferred to *B*. Notice that if an individual held these preferences, as does P3, we would infer that she also prefer *C* to *B*. And yet, social choice reveals that when the group aggregates the preferences of all three persons in a regime of unlimited binary comparisons, the group as a whole achieves a different result than the one P3 would achieve acting alone. With these preference orderings, the group as a whole prefers *B* to *C*, with P1 and P2 defeating P3. The final pairwise contest thus reveals an intransitivity, or cycle, over options *ABC*, such that *CpApBpC*.

This example illustrates the voting paradox, also called the Condorcet paradox after a French philosopher who described it in an essay in 1785.[25] Simply put, the paradox is that transitivity, assumed to be a basic tenet of individual rationality, cannot be assumed for groups of three or more individuals selecting among three or more options. Assume that each member satisfies the condition of transitivity, such that consistent with the above-listed preferences, P1 prefers *A* to *C*, P2 prefers *B* to *A*, and P3 prefers *C* to *B*. When we take the options pairwise by majority vote, the result is nonetheless an intransitivity, or cycle, for the group as a whole.

In addition to writing about the paradox, Condorcet proposed an important, if partial, solution to the problem concerning how to transform individual preferences that lack a first choice majority outcome into a normatively defensible outcome for the group as a whole. As we will see, Condorcet's proposed voting rule rests substantially on, and anticipates,

---

24. Notice that this held true with the final example in the median voter theorem discussion in which liberals held 40%, moderates held 25%, and conservatives held 35% of the electorate. *See supra* p. 100.

25. *See* Stearns, *Misguided Renaissance, supra* note 1, at 1221.

the intuition that underlies the median voter theorem.[26] Condorcet proposed that when an available option would defeat the remaining options in direct pairwise comparisons, an option now referred to as the Condorcet winner, that option should be selected.

To illustrate, consider once more three persons selecting among options ABC, except this time with the following slightly modified preferences: P1: ABC; P2: BCA; and P3: CBA. Other than switching P3's second and third ordinal ranking (as between B and A), the remaining preferences are unchanged. As before, each person holds a different first choice and thus there is no first choice majority candidate. Now apply Condorcet's proposed method. As between A and B, B wins, with P2 and P3 defeating P1; and as between B and C, B wins, with P1 and P2 defeating P3. The choice between A and C is irrelevant (C wins, with P1 losing) because option B, the Condorcet winner, defeats each of the remaining alternatives in direct comparisons. Institutions or rules that ensure that available Condorcet winners prevail are said to satisfy the Condorcet criterion.

The Condorcet criterion is an important benchmark for evaluating the decision-making competence of institutions. That is because, as demonstrated in the median voter theorem, the criterion is closely linked to the concept of majority rule and one person, one vote. As Professor William Riker observed, "when an alternative opposed by a majority wins, quite clearly the votes of some people are not being counted the same as other people's votes."[27] Consider, once again, the discussion of an electorate in which a plurality of 40% most prefer the liberal platform, A; 25% most prefer the moderate platform, B; and 35% most prefer the conservative platform, C. While plurality rule would select a liberal platform, this outcome would suppress a majority (moderates and conservatives) who prefer the moderate platform to the liberal platform, just as a conservative platform would suppress a majority (liberals and moderates) who prefer the moderate platform to the conservative platform. Because the liberals and conservatives each rank the moderate platform B, which obtains only 25% of the vote, as their second choice (with preferences ABC and CBA respectively), that option nonetheless defeats options A and C, with 40% and 35% of the vote respectively, in direct comparisons. And for that reason, consistent with the median voter theorem, selecting option B is more consistent with majority rule than is selecting plurality option A.

Returning to the presentation of *Casey* in Table 3:1,[28] we can apply this intuition to a Supreme Court decision. By specifying the membership in each of the three camps in *Casey*—liberal, moderate, and conservative—we can see once more a potential divergence between outcomes dictated by

---

26. Indeed, the preferences set out below track those depicted in the opening illustration *supra* p. 99, in which liberals preferred *ABC*, conservatives preferred *CBA*, and the moderates preferred either *BAC* or *BCA*.

27. WILLIAM H. RIKER, LIBERALISM AGAINST POPULISM: A CONFRONTATION BETWEEN THE THEORY OF DEMOCRACY AND THE THEORY OF SOCIAL CHOICE 100 (1982).

28. *See supra* pp. 98–99 (presenting stylized discussion of *Casey*).

the competing logic of the Condorcet criterion and plurality rule. As previously noted, two justices, Blackmun and Stevens, embraced the liberal position, voting to strike down all of the restrictive Pennsylvania abortion provisions. Three justices, O'Connor, Kennedy, and Souter, embraced the moderate position, voting to sustain all provisions except the spousal notification provision. And four justices, Rehnquist, Scalia, White, and Thomas, embraced the conservative position, voting to sustain all challenged abortion provisions. While a majority of five justices (the liberals and the moderates) voted to strike down the spousal notification provision, in a regime of plurality rule, the conservative dissenters, with the largest coalition of four justices, would instead control, thus sustaining the spousal notification provision along with the remaining challenged provisions.[29] By contrast, applying the Condorcet criterion, the coalition expressing the median position along the spectrum of how far abortion rights extend expresses the holding, with the result of striking down the spousal notification provision (with the liberal and moderate justices controlling) but sustaining the remaining provisions (with the moderate and conservative justices controlling).

Despite the Condorcet criterion's normative appeal, as a result of two important limitations, some important institutions have rules that thwart the Condorcet criterion. For example, while *Casey* illustrates how the Condorcet criterion applies in the Supreme Court, we will see other Supreme Court decision-making rules that thwart the Condorcet criterion and its commitment to majority rule in favor of other normative considerations.[30] The Condorcet criterion suffers from two weaknesses. First, as we have already seen, depending upon the preferences of the group members, there might not always be a Condorcet winner. When there is no Condorcet winner, rules that meet the Condorcet criterion and thus allow separate majority votes over all available pairwise comparisons produce an intransitivity or cycle. Second, as we saw in the simple example involving the choice of vanilla or chocolate cake where one child was allergic to cocoa, majority rule fails to account for the differing levels of interest that participants have in the outcome due to the disparate intensities with which they hold their preferences. The Condorcet criterion is grounded in majority rule, meaning one person, one vote, regardless of individual stakes in the outcome and, as such, it too fails to account for intensity of preference.

To illustrate, imagine a decision concerning how much money to allocate for a park renovation, with three proposals: low, moderate, and

---

29. The discussion in the text simplifies the form of the opinions in the actual case by avoiding partial concurrences and partial dissents. Omitting this detail does not change the analysis. The discussion further assumes sincere voting, implying that a change in the voting regime will not change the position each justice takes on the merits of each challenged provision. For a discussion of how a change in voting protocols threatens to compromise this assumption, see STEARNS, *supra* note 1, at 117–22. *See also* Maxwell L. Stearns, *How Outcome Voting Promotes Principled Issue Identification: A Reply to Professor John Rogers and Others*, 49 VAND. L. REV. 1045 (1996).

30. *See infra* chapter 7, (presenting outcome voting and stare decisis as non-Condorcet rules).

high. Each proposal is of comparable quality and the differences are due to the scope and ambition of the proposed renovation. Assume that there are three city council members, each holding a different first choice and each agreeing that the only issue is the scope of the project. We might imagine convergence toward the moderate expenditure, with those preferring the low and high expenditures ranking the moderate position as a second choice and the opposite extreme expenditure as a third choice. In this example, the moderate outcome emerges a Condorcet winner. Imagine, however, that only the high expenditure will include access ramps to the various activities for children suffering certain physical limitations, including reliance upon wheel chairs. Assume that while the members whose first choices are the low and moderate expenditures would prefer to save resources for some other public works project, they are not as strongly opposed to the larger expenditure as the one member whose constituency includes parents of physically impaired children hoping to enjoy the newly renovated park is in favor of the expenditure. In this case, while the moderate Condorcet result operates more consistently with majority rule, when we account for intensities of preference it is possible that the socially preferred outcome is the high expenditure and the most ambitious renovation. While the Condorcet criterion is important, it remains only one of several potentially competing benchmarks to be used in evaluating collective decision-making processes.

As this example (along with the earlier ice cream cake example) illustrates, the Condorcet criterion generalizes the principle of majority rule outside the limited context in which group preferences include a first choice majority candidate. As such, the Condorcet criterion carries with it the same strengths (including operating consistently with democratic norms) and weaknesses (including failing to account for preference intensities) as simple majority rule.

D. CYCLING, PATH DEPENDENCE, AND AGENDA SETTING

As previously explained, one limitation of voting rules that satisfy the Condorcet criterion is the risk of cycling. A cycle implies that for any possible outcome, another is preferred in a regime of direct pairwise comparisons by simple majority rule. Because this result holds for all possible outcomes, when members hold such preferences, rules that satisfy the Condorcet criterion fail to guarantee a stable outcome. We can think of rules that satisfy the Condorcet criterion as having the characteristic feature of unlimited majority veto. Pairwise comparisons remain available until there no longer exists a majority whose preferences would be thwarted by the proposed outcome. As we have seen, however, when group preferences cycle, this is not possible because some majority always prefers another outcome. To illustrate, reconsider the first set of preferences above: P1: *ABC*; P2: *BCA*; and P3: *CAB*. Even assuming that each participant's preferences are internally rational (transitive), a regime of unlimited pairwise voting yields an intransitivity for the group as a whole. Thus, the group prefers A to B (with P2 losing) and B to C (with P3 losing), but C to A (with P1 losing), or $ApBpCpA$. Given unlimited majority veto, the cycle starts anew and as a consequence no outcome is stable.

Although groups possessing such preferences cannot select a winner without thwarting the preferences of a majority in one potential pairwise comparison, we do not intend to suggest that groups characterized by such preferences forever remain in the throes of cycling. Rather, assuming the group does not opt for inaction, thus "choosing" the status quo, the cycle is somehow embedded in whichever outcome the group ultimately selects. To explain why, we must identify a characteristic feature of rules that satisfy the Condorcet criterion. Such rules allow the same number of pairwise contests as available alternatives (in this instance, three pairwise votes over three alternatives). In contrast, when decision rules limit the number of such pairwise contests relative to available options and when member preferences cycle, provided the members vote sincerely, the substantive outcome will turn on the order, or path, in which options are voted. To be sure, such path-dependent outcomes can be stable. They might even be predictable, for example, if we have a clear sense of the preferences of the person who controls the agenda, referred to as the "agenda setter", and if participants are somehow prevented from voting strategically. At the same time, however, path-dependent outcomes thwart the preferences of at least one majority who would have preferred an alternative outcome in a suppressed binary, or pairwise, comparison.

To illustrate we return once more to the example with cycling preferences (*ABC, BCA, CAB*). If we permit only two votes over the three options, and if we assume that members vote sincerely, then we will induce a path toward a determinate result. If we begin with A versus B (A wins) followed by C versus A (C wins), the path leads to C. Only by bringing back option B, which was defeated in the first round, and pitting it against option C do we formally reveal the cycle. If we knew the ordinally ranked preferences in advance of voting, we could intuit that option C thwarted the majority preferences of P1 and P2, who form a majority preferring option B to option C. Once again, although path dependence leads to a stable outcome, with full disclosure or the subsequent discovery of suppressed preferences, we can discover an embedded cycle. Of course participants will not always possess or have the means to acquire such information. As a result, non-Condorcet rules have the potential to produce path-dependent results that give the appearance of having majority support. After all, the outcome ultimately selected follows a series of separate majority votes. The voting process might therefore lend normative legitimacy to the eventual outcome even if that outcome thwarts the preferences of a majority that would have favored an alternative in a direct pairwise comparison.

Path dependence is the flip side of agenda setting. Assuming that the members vote sincerely according to their ordinal preferences, then when preferences are intransitive, a rule that only allows two votes over the three options will allow the agenda setter to control the outcome. By positioning the votes such that the option that would defeat her first choice is itself defeated in the first round of voting, the agenda setter can produce a voting path that leads directly to her first choice.[31] Not surprisingly, therefore, in devising rule making procedures, an important consideration is controlling the power of the person who sets the voting path.

To what extent are judicial or legislative outcomes likely to be path dependent? Can you identify an institution that grants agenda setting power to one or more participants? If so, can you identify mechanisms that limit such agenda-setting power? Do you recall having been disadvantaged or benefited by agenda setting? If you were disadvantaged, can you identify strategies that might have facilitated a better result?

E.   A BRIEF COMMENT ON ARROW'S THEOREM

While we provide a more detailed introduction to Arrow's Impossibility Theorem (or simply "Arrow's Theorem") later in this chapter,[32] for the discussion that follows, a brief summary will be helpful. Arrow's Theorem generalizes the voting paradox.[33] In effect, the theorem proves that any decision-making rule designed to "solve" the potential impasse resulting from cyclical preferences necessarily violates some other important norm associated with fair, or democratic, decision making. Kenneth Arrow posited a group of conditions, which in a simplified version of the proof William Vickrey reduced to four,[34] and proved that no institution can simultaneously satisfy those conditions while also guaranteeing the ability to translate the individual preferences of members into rational, or transitive, orderings.[35] At its most basic level, Arrow's Theorem exposes an inevitable tension confronting collective decision-making bodies between the desire to ensure rational (transitive) outcomes and the objective of adhering to a set of fair or democratic norms.

Before briefly describing these fairness conditions, it is worth noting their somewhat technical quality. In Arrow's proof, he set out his condi-

---

31. We have already seen the path leading to *C*. If, instead, the agenda setter most prefers option *A*, she would first present *B* versus *C* (*B* wins), then *B* versus *A* (*A* wins). Option *C*, the sole option that would defeat *A* in a direct pairwise contest, was defeated in the first round. And if the agenda setter most preferred option *B*, she would first present *C* versus *A* (*C* wins), and then present *C* versus *B* (*B* wins). Option *A*, the sole option that would defeat option *B* in a pairwise contest, was defeated in the first round.

32. *Infra* section V.

33. *See* RIKER, *supra* note 28, at 116.

34. STEARNS, *supra* note 1, at 81, 344–45 n.91. *See also* William Vickrey, *Utility, Strategy, and Social Decision Rules*, 74 Q.J. ECON. 507 (1960), *reprinted in* WILLIAM VICKREY, PUBLIC ECONOMICS 29 (Richard Arnott et al. eds., 1994).

35. For a discussion of the relationships between the criteria described in this chapter, based upon William Vickrey's simplified proof, and the original Arrow's Theorem criteria, see STEARNS, *supra* note 1, at 344–45 n.91, 346–47 n.104, 337 n.22, 347–48 n.112.

tions with mathematical precision. What follows is a verbal summary adapted from William Vickrey's simplified proof. Even these descriptions are easier to understand with specific applications, which we will provide when we present a more detailed overview of the theorem later in the chapter. Our immediate purpose is more limited. By introducing Arrow's fairness conditions, we hope to convey that the problem of cycling (or rationality) is but one dimension in an inevitably complex set of tradeoffs that Arrow's Theorem reveals for the study of institutions and rules.

Arrow's fairness conditions can be expressed as follows: (1) *range*: the collective decision-making rule must select its outcome in a manner that is consistent with the members' selection from among all conceivable ordinal rankings over three available alternatives; (2) *independence of irrelevant alternatives*: in choosing between paired alternatives, participants are assumed to decide solely based upon the merits of those options and without regard to how they would rank options that might be introduced later; (3) *unanimity*: if a change from the status quo to an alternate state will improve the position of at least a single participant without harming anyone else, the decision-making body must so move; and (4) *nondictatorship*: the group cannot consistently vindicate the preferences of a group member against the contrary will of the group as a whole.[36]

We will not revisit these technical terms until the end of the chapter. Throughout this chapter, however, we will apply several concepts to describe institutions that we later translate into the framework of Arrow's Theorem. This preliminary introduction is helpful in revealing potentially inevitable tradeoffs that institutions confront when formulating decision-making rules. Avoiding cycling, on the one hand, or promoting majority rule, on the other, represents only one potential tradeoff between normative values in conflict. Others include, for example, the desire to ensure that decision makers sincerely express their preferences, or that institutions allow members to register cardinal utility rather than mere ordinal preferences. Arrow's Theorem helps to expose the possibility of unavoidable conflicts among independently valuable normative criteria used to analyze institutions and rules.

The inability of any single institution to satisfy all of these conditions while ensuring rational or transitive outputs raises one obvious and important question: Which normative concerns should any given rulemaking system seek to protect? Remember that Ralph Waldo Emerson deemed "a foolish consistency . . . the hobgoblin of little minds."[37] Similarly, we might imagine that rationality, which demands consistency in the form of insisting upon adherence to transitivity of collective preferences as a precondition to generating outcomes, is less important than it first appears. If so, perhaps we can sacrifice rationality as the price of satisfying the various fairness conditions.

---

36. STEARNS, *supra* note 1, at 84–94.

37. RALPH WALDO EMERSON, *Self–Reliance, in* ESSAYS: FIRST SERIES 37 (Everyman's Library ed. 1906) (1841) ("A foolish consistency is the hobgoblin of little minds, adored by little statesmen and philosophers and divines.").

Let us now revisit this chapter's opening question: Why is rationality at least potentially important, and how should it be traded off against other fairness considerations grounded in democratic norms? One reason for the importance of rationality is that institutions that do not demand rationality cannot ensure stable, or at least socially significant, outputs. That is not to suggest that stability of outputs (or that ensuring socially significant outputs in the sense of ensuring that available Condorcet winners prevail) is vital to all institutions, but it certainly is important to some. As we have previously observed, path-dependent outcomes are potentially stable, but such outcomes embed thwarted majorities. If such majority preferences were disclosed through the formal decision-making process, then the institution would discover that for any proffered outcome, a majority prefers yet another. If the institution required a collective decision without regard to collective preferences and to the possibility of cycling, the resulting endless veto power of potentially thwarted majorities might threaten that obligation. The resulting process might further threaten the legitimacy, and thus the willingness to accept, any outcome eventually selected. In effect, institutions that facilitate path-dependent outcomes elevate the concern for ensuring outputs that give the appearance of legitimacy, even if they also embed cyclical preferences, over at least one of Arrow's fairness conditions. Do you see why this result is inevitable?

Because Arrow's Theorem proves that no institution can simultaneously ensure transitive outputs and satisfy the specified fairness conditions, it exposes inevitable tradeoffs between the need for certain and stable outcomes, on the one hand, and rule-making features designed to ensure fair collective processes, on the other. One critical implication of Arrow's Theorem, for example, is in exposing an inevitable tradeoff between rules that ensure transitive outputs and rules that prevent minorities from exerting power disproportionate to their numbers.[38] If unlimited majority veto has the potential to block outcomes as a result of underlying cycling preferences, at some point it is possible that the only method by which to allow an institution to ensure stable outputs is to vest ultimate decision-making power in a minority. A set of rules designed to avoid the danger of indecision resulting from cycling, for example, might instead produce a regime that allows an individual or group to set (or manipulate) the agenda for the decision-making body as a whole. In effect, collective decision-making difficulties implicate not just the paradox of voting, meaning the possibility that collective preferences might cycle, but also implicate more broadly the tradeoff between rationality and the fairness conditions that Arrow's Theorem demonstrates are at least theoretically in tension.

---

38. To be clear, we do not mean to suggest that outcomes cannot favor numerical minorities, racial or otherwise, without violating Arrow's fairness criteria. Quite the contrary, an institution meeting some combination of Arrow's fairness plus rationality conditions is potentially capable of furthering any normative policy whether involving antidiscrimination, affirmative action, or something else entirely.

F. IMPLICATIONS FOR INSTITUTIONAL REFORM: NEGATIVE LEGISLATIVE CHECKPOINTS AND THE THEORY OF MINIMUM WINNING COALITIONS

Given the abstract nature of Arrow's Theorem, it will be helpful to introduce some specific proposals for institutional reform that legal scholars have relied upon the theorem to advance. Several of the proposals that follow rest upon the proponents, assumptions about the relative institutional competence of appellate courts and legislatures. These assumptions are linked not only to Arrow's Theorem and the theoretical possibility of cycling, but also to well developed institutional features that arose at least partly in response to the difficulty of aggregating collective preferences. As a result, this subsection considers both these institutional practices and the proposals themselves, which help to lay a foundation for later analyses of courts and legislatures, including especially Congress and the Supreme Court, based upon the tools of social choice.

1. Congressional Practices That Affect Transformation of Preferences into Outputs

One group of legal scholars has questioned whether the inevitable tendency of institutions to cycle undermines the general presumption of judicial deference to legislative policymaking.[39] Whether or not cycling is understood to mean a perpetual state of indecision—as each proffered alternative is defeated in favor of another, which is again defeated in the same manner, a process that is repeated *ad infinitum*—Congressional roadblocks to the passage of legislation, also known as "negative legislative checkpoints," or "veto gates"[40] certainly raise the cost of securing proposed legislation. James Madison's theory of factions, grounded in the earlier work of David Hume, gives these legislative practices an historical pedigree and perhaps constitutional legitimacy. Given Madison's premise set out most clearly in *The Federalist No. 10*, that rapidly forming majoritarian factions should be feared,[41] such devices as bicameralism, presentment, various elaborate committee structures, calendaring rules, and even the filibuster might have the benefit of broadening coalitions needed to pass legislation. These practices therefore have an important theoretical foundation in the theory of minimum winning coalitions.[42]

Recall that Professor William H. Riker posited that, with some helpful simplifying assumptions concerning legislative bargaining, coalitions become increasingly stable as they approach minimum winning size, meaning a simple majority.[43] This theory provides a helpful public choice

---

39. For an introduction to this literature, see Stearns, *Misguided Renaissance, supra* note 1, at 1225–27.

40. For a discussion of these terms, *see supra* p. 72, note 93, and cites therein.

41. *See* THE FEDERALIST No. 10 (James Madison).

42. *See supra* chapter 2, section III.A.

43. Riker's theory provides that "[i]n *n*-person, zero sum games, where side-payments are permitted, where players are rational, and where they have perfect information, only minimum

analogue to the Madison–Hume theory of factions. Riker posited that supermajorities tend to break down in favor of simple majority coalitions because the smaller the successful coalition, the larger each member's *pro rata* share of the resulting gains. Consider a legislature with nine members in which the successful coalition shares a benefit equal to one hundred. An overweighted coalition of seven would provide each member a *pro rata* benefit of just over fourteen (one hundred divided by seven), while a simple majority coalition of five would provide each member a larger pro rata benefit of twenty (one hundred divided by five). Thus, absent any structural impediments, coalitions larger than a bare majority tend to decompose into coalitions of a bare majority. A principal concern raised by both Riker and Madison is that absent barriers to simple majority coalitions, legislative processes might routinely redistribute wealth or other benefits from broad constituencies to successful narrow-majority coalitions.

While negative legislative checkpoints afford defenses to factional legislation by demanding larger coalitions, they also produce a paradox. By vesting minority groups with blocking or veto power over majoritarian legislation, these legislative roadblocks also provide opportunities for various forms of strategic behavior, including demanding rents as a precondition to supporting (or declining to thwart) the often critical path that shapes the substance of enacted legislation. While these practices, which arise in part to overcome the difficulties that confront legislatures aggregating collective preferences, including preferences that cycle, into outputs, thus serve to legitimate legislative outcomes, they also contribute to normative criticisms of Congress as an institution capable of rationally aggregating collective preferences. In turn, they have also contributed to proposals seeking to expand the lawmaking role of courts in interpreting, or limiting the reach, of statutes.

2. Social Choice Implications for Institutional Competence as Between Congress and the Judiciary

Based on the claimed defects that social choice reveals for legislative decision-making, prominent legal scholars have challenged legal doctrines that express deference to legislative policy making. One group of scholars, including William Eskridge, Lynn Stout, and Jonathan Macey, has challenged the assumption underlying rational basis scrutiny that absent an identified constitutional violation, federal courts ought to assume that legislatures have rationally processed the preferences of their members and constituents.[44] Instead, based upon social choice insights demonstrating the difficulties with collective preference aggregation, these scholars

---

winning coalitions occur." WILLIAM H. RIKER, THE THEORY OF POLITICAL COALITIONS 32 (1962). *See also supra* chapter 2, section III.B.

44. *See, e.g.,* William N. Eskridge, Jr., *Politics Without Romance: Implications of Public Choice Theory for Statutory Interpretation*, 74 VA. L. REV. 275, 279 (1988); Jonathan R. Macey, *Promoting Public–Regarding Legislation Through Statutory Interpretation: An Interest Group Model*, 86 COLUM. L. REV. 223, 261–66 (1986); Lynn A. Stout, *Strict Scrutiny and Social Choice: An Economic Inquiry into Fundamental Rights and Suspect Classifications*, 80 GEO. L.J. 1787, 1799, 1823 (1992).

maintain that judges should engage in more liberal construction of statutes and broader constitutional judicial review to further the divergent objectives that each scholar regards as consistent with the public good.

Other scholars, most notably Daniel Farber and Philip Frickey, have cautioned against using social choice as a means of enhancing judicial power, claiming instead that to the extent that social choice calls legislative decision making into question, the methodology supports institutional reform within Congress itself as a means of addressing the problem of cycling, as opposed to transferring decision-making authority elsewhere, including most notably courts.[45] Farber and Frickey argue that social choice analysis belies purely pluralist conceptions of legislation. As a result of legislative features that have developed in part as a response to potential cycling, they posit that unbridled pluralism is conducive to zero-sum pluralist politicking, the modern day equivalent to what Madison called factional violence. These scholars further contend that social choice theory proves consistent with their preferred small "r" republican vision of politics, which tends to favor broad electoral participation. Whether focusing upon judicial or legislative reform, these scholars are part of neo-republican scholarly tradition within the legal academy that is concerned with ensuring that institutions properly represent broad constituencies and protect their preferences against the often hard-boiled realities of American politics.

Evaluating these and other such proposals for institutional reform, whether targeted to courts or legislatures, requires a comparative analysis of the affected institutions. Arrow's Theorem will prove helpful in undertaking such an analysis in a manner that avoids the pervasive "nirvana fallacy."[46] Scholars commit the nirvana fallacy when they identify a defect in a given institution and then, based upon the perceived defect, propose fixing the problem by shifting decisional responsibility somewhere else. The fallacy is in failing to consider whether the alternative institution for which decisional authority is proposed would be better or worse than the original institution at performing the assigned task in a manner that avoids the initial institutional difficulty.

Other commentators have focused on the implications of social choice for decision making in collegial courts. Because appellate courts generally, and the Supreme Court in particular, are collective decision-making bodies, to the extent that social choice reveals potential defects in the legislative process, so too it reveals defects in the judicial process.[47] Responding to such arguments, Professors Farber and Frickey have suggested that if the problem of cycling applies to both legislatures and the

---

45. *See generally* DANIEL A. FARBER & PHILIP P. FRICKEY, LAW AND PUBLIC CHOICE: A CRITICAL INTRODUCTION (1991); Daniel A. Farber & Philip P. Frickey, *Legislative Intent and Public Choice*, 74 VA. L. REV. 423 (1988).

46. For a famous discussion of the nirvana fallacy, see Harold Demsetz, *Information and Efficiency: Another Viewpoint*, 12 J.L. & ECON. 1 (1969).

47. *See, e.g.*, Frank H. Easterbrook, *Ways of Criticizing the Court*, 95 HARV. L. REV. 802, 818–31 (1982); *see also* Einer R. Elhauge, *Does Interest Group Theory Justify More Intrusive Judicial Review?*, 101 YALE L.J. 31, 101–08 (1991).

judiciary, then as a tool of analysis, social choice leaves us at an impasse. The authors explain:

> In a sense, the ... thesis [that cycling plagues both courts and legislatures] proves too much. If chaos and incoherence are the inevitable outcomes of majority voting, then appellate courts (which invariably have multiple members and majority voting rules) and even the 1787 Constitutional Convention are equally bankrupt. As a result, the ... thesis is bereft of any implications for public law, since it tells us to be equally suspicious of *all* sources of law. If we accept the thesis as to legislatures, we are left with nowhere to turn.[48]

While we will not evaluate each of these proposals in this chapter,[49] in the discussion that follows, we combine the nirvana fallacy with two additional analytical fallacies: the fallacy of composition and the isolation fallacy. Together, these tools provide a basis for using social choice to better appreciate several existing institutional norms and functions. Indeed, we will argue that social choice helps to provide a strong normative foundation for some of the more enigmatic features of constitutional lawmaking. In the next section, we consider two additional fallacies that help to explore the power of social choice in assessing the competence of various forms of institutional decision making.

II.   INSTITUTIONS RECONSIDERED: THE FALLACY OF COMPOSITION, THE ISOLATION FALLACY AND THE PROBLEM OF TIMING

To illustrate the fallacy of composition, we introduce two hypotheticals. The first is inspired by Shakespeare's *The Tragedy of King Lear*,[50] and the second is based upon a 1992 Supreme Court case, *New York v. United States*.[51] The analysis demonstrates that collective decision-making bodies can improve the quality of their outputs when they operate together *even if* each institution is separately prone to the problem of cycling.

A.   THE FALLACY OF COMPOSITION

The fallacy of composition is the assumption that if phenomenon X produces result Y, more of phenomenon X will produce more of result Y. For a simple illustration, imagine a proposed housing development in which the basic model house is brick. An individual purchaser could make her house distinctive by instead selecting a stone façade. But now imagine that every purchaser shares this intuition and thus seeks to render his or her home distinctive in the same manner. After several home buyers make

---

48.   FARBER & FRICKEY, *supra* note 45, at 55.

49.   For a more detailed critique, see Stearns, *Misguided Renaissance, supra* note 1.

50.   WILLIAM SHAKESPEARE, THE TRAGEDY OF KING LEAR. For an earlier presentation of this example, see STEARNS, *supra* note 1, at 54–58.

51.   505 U.S. 144 (1992).

this decision, it is no longer the case that a stone façade renders a home distinctive. Indeed, if so many purchasers followed this strategy that most homes had a stone façade, a home buyer could make her home distinctive by instead opting instead for brick. Of course, the same problem would arise if everyone mimicked that strategy.

Similarly, an individual homeowner could make her house safer against burglary by installing an alarm. While sophisticated burglars can get past most alarms, holding all else constant,[52] alarms divert would-be burglars in favor of homes that lack alarms and can be broken into with less effort and at lower risk. Of course, if most or all homeowners in the housing complex install an alarm, this diversionary benefit is dramatically reduced. While it remains true that each alarmed home is slightly more difficult to burgle, the larger benefit of encouraging would-be burglars to thieve elsewhere is substantially reduced. In both examples, phenomenon X (a stone façade or a house alarm) produced result Y (distinction or a reduced risk of burglary relative to neighboring homes) *only if* a relatively small number of actors followed the distinguishing strategy. Otherwise, if most or all homeowners followed the same strategy, the benefits of distinction are substantially reduced and perhaps eliminated.

B. IMPLICATIONS FOR COLLECTIVE DECISION MAKING

We now return to the context that motivated our discussion, namely the problem of cycling in collective decision-making institutions. Professors Farber and Frickey aptly expressed the concern: If the problems revealed in Arrow's theorem are a universal feature of collective decision-making bodies, then the theory of social choice might leave us "nowhere to turn."[53] After all, while each institution is susceptible of cycling, the theorem might imply that there is no institution capable of the much needed rescue.

In fact, however, when we apply the fallacy of composition in this context, we instead see that even two collective decision-making bodies that independently cycle can reduce cycling by operating together. The critical point is that, even when two institutions cycle, they do not necessarily cycle in response to the same underlying phenomena. As a result of the different triggers to institutional cycling, it is possible that although phenomenon X (an institution processing member preferences) produces result Y (producing occasional cycling), more of phenomena X (multiple institutions processing member preferences) can avoid or reduce result Y (inhibiting cycling).

In some respects, this is old news. The United States Constitution, after all, establishes two lawmaking bodies, Congress and the Supreme

---

52. This includes assuming that the presence of an alarm does not signal higher value of contents in the home to steal.

53. *See* FARBER & FRICKEY, *supra* note 45, at 55.

Court. These bodies were never intended to operate in complete isolation, one from the other. And as we will see, several Supreme Court doctrines allocate decisional responsibility between these two branches in a manner that promotes their collective rationality.[54]

The important question, then, is which factual predicates cause cycling in one lawmaking institution while inhibiting it in the other. The most important difference in these factual predicates is a function of timing. Specifically, institutions are more likely to cycle when faced with the prospect of allocating the benefits of an unanticipated windfall or gain or the burdens of an unanticipated or capital loss.[55] Conversely, institutions are less likely to cycle when issuing outcomes that apply generally and prospectively, and thus before the circumstances arise capable of generating such a windfall or loss. To demonstrate the general nature of this proposition, we offer two illustrations. In the first, private actors are prone to cycling and the legislature breaks the impasse. In the second, the legislature itself is prone to cycling, thus inviting a judicial response to break the impasse. The critical point is that there is nothing inherent about the legislature that causes, or that avoids, cycling. Rather, any multimember institution can cycle on its own or limit cycling elsewhere. The particular result in each instance depends upon the nature of each institution's interaction with the factual predicates that motivate (or inhibit) cycling.

C. THE PROBLEM OF THE EMPTY CORE AMONG PRIVATE ACTORS

The next two examples rely upon a game theoretical concept known as the empty core. While we introduce game theory more formally in chapter 4, the social choice phenomenon of cycling is closely related to this game theoretical concept. Empty core games are generally used to describe cycling among private actors, while cycling is generally used to describe the behavior of lawmaking institutions.

The first hypothetical will take as its inspiration William Shakespeare's *The Tragedy of King Lear*.[56] In the original story, an aging Lear vainly disinherits his youngest and most beloved daughter, Cordelia, because unlike her sisters, Goneril and Regan, Cordelia was unwilling to express her love for him in unconditional terms as a precondition to taking her share of the kingdom. Cordelia claimed that while she loved him dearly as a father, her foremost love would be for her yet unchosen husband. As the story unfolds, we learn the devastating consequences of both Cordelia's disinheritance and the premature conveyance to Lear's remaining daughters.

---

54. *See infra* chapter 7.

55. *See* Stearns, *Misguided Renaissance*, *supra* note 1, at 1242 (positing that negotiations concerning how to allocate capital gains or losses are prone to generating cycling).

56. WILLIAM SHAKESPEARE, THE TRAGEDY OF KING LEAR.

Our adaptation involves a more modern yet similarly dysfunctional family. Professor Lear, an eccentric mathematics professor who has recently won $30 million in the lottery, has long been estranged from his three daughters who are also estranged from each other. Because the daughters have not had any contact with Lear since their mother died ten years ago, they are unaware that he won the lottery five years earlier. To simplify the presentation, assume that the full lottery proceeds were distributed as a single lump sum with no discounting. Upon winning the lottery, Lear did not change his reclusive lifestyle. Instead, he placed the full proceeds of the lottery into a trust fund, with the objective of passing the money to his daughters if certain conditions were met. Five years after winning, Lear was diagnosed with a fatal disease and told that he had only six months to live. After he was informed of his diagnosis, Lear saw an opportunity to construct a controlled high stakes social choice experiment with real players.

Lear immediately contacted the administrator of the trust and had the trust's terms modified as follows. If the terms governing the distribution of the corpus of Lear's trust for the lottery winnings were satisfied by the time of his death, the full proceeds of the trust would then be distributed in accordance with the terms of his daughters' assented-to division of the trust assets. Failing that, the corpus of the trust would instead pass into the residuum of Lear's will, from which it would be used to endow the new Lear Institute, a research center devoted to studying applied social choice and game theory.

The relevant provisions of the trust require that the full proceeds are to be distributed based upon the consent of any two of Lear's three daughters, provided that the following two conditions are met. The first is that the allocations must be agreed upon by two of the three daughters by no later than 5:00 p.m. for ten days prior to Lear's death and remain unchallenged for ten consecutive days. The first plan that meets this ten day rule without being superseded by another plan will be regarded as final. Second, after the final plan is submitted, any daughter, whether or not a signer of the final distribution plan, will forfeit her entire share in the event that she seeks to alter the final distribution by any means other than forming a superseding coalition. This includes filing an action in a court of law or equity. The trust further provides that the daughters can employ any rules that they wish to achieve a distribution, provided it is accomplished privately and without violating any criminal laws. Upon being in receipt of the basis for final distribution that satisfies the trust terms, the trust administrator is to immediately notify Lear of the terms of the final distribution. Otherwise, the full corpus of the trust shall pass to the residuum of Lear's will.

Before considering how the daughters might respond, a few general comments about the hypothetical will be helpful. Under the terms of the trust, the daughters are expected to agree to an outcome governing the distribution of what will be an extremely valuable windfall. Of course one daughter can try to supersede any proposed solution with an alternative provided that she forms a new coalition and files in time to meet the ten-day requirement before Lear's death. In addition, while the daughters are permitted to employ any background rules they wish, they will suffer a complete forfeiture if they try to have those rules legally enforced. Under the terms of the trust, a minimum of two out of the three daughters must agree upon, and submit in writing, the terms of the final distribution for the requisite ten-day period. Thus, no single daughter can disrupt this plan unless she forms a superior coalition that files a superseding plan subject to the same rule. Finally, while the daughters are aware that Lear is terminally ill, no one knows precisely when he will die and thus each later-filed plan increases the risk that his death will cut short the necessary ten-day filing period to satisfy the will.

Now consider the options confronting the daughters. One obvious solution exists: Each daughter could take $10 million and the three now wealthier sisters could go on with their lives. Based upon this intuition, Professors Farber and Frickey have posited that in such cycling games, simple and obvious fairness (or value) solutions, like equal division, prove practical and potentially stable.[57] Indeed, this solution might also be a Schelling Point.[58]

Before evaluating whether the value solution proves a stable outcome, consider the pathology that underlies our hypothetical. This hypothetical is a classic illustration of an "empty core" game, a game that is functionally equivalent to the Condorcet paradox. The empty core implies that for any existing coalition, there exists an alternative "superior" coalition that can improve the payoffs for both the excluded party and a defector. Because this holds true for any potential coalition, no coalition is stable. In contrast, a game has a core, thus producing a stable solution, when, for a coalition or set of coalitions, there is no alternative superior coalition that will improve the plight of an excluded party and a defector. Because our game has an empty core, for any proposed solution there exists an alternative favored by a newly formed coalition, thus generating a cycle.

To simplify, assume a pool of $30, where each dollar represents $1 million. Further assume that Goneril and Regan begin by submitting a plan for each to take $15 each. Cordelia can now break up that coalition within the allotted ten-day period by offering Regan $20 and agreeing to take only $10. Goneril, the excluded party, can now break up the new (Cordelia, Regan) coalition within the ten-day period by offering Cordelia $20, and herself taking $10. And now Regan, the excluded party, can

---

57. The authors state:

> [T]his solution is a sort of equilibrium. It is true that any player could offer an amendment that would beat th[e] [equal division] outcome—but what would be the point of doing so and thereby setting off a round of endless cycling? In a sense, the existence of massive cycling provides the basis for a new form of equilibrium adopted precisely to avoid the cycles.

Farber & Frickey, *supra* note 45, at 434. As the following discussion demonstrates, despite the normative appeal of equal division, it is less clear that it constitutes an equilibrium.

58. *See* THOMAS C. SCHELLING, THE STRATEGY OF CONFLICT 57 (1960) (introducing the concept of "focal point[s] for each person's expectation of what the other expects him to expect to be expected to do," which was later named after Schelling). The problem in the example in the text is that the sisters cannot bind themselves to the Schelling Point of equal division.

break up the (Goneril, Cordelia) coalition within ten days by offering Goneril $20 and herself taking $10. Of course, now Cordelia, the excluded party, can start the ball rolling again, thus breaking up the second (Goneril, Regan) coalition, this time by offering Regan $20 and agreeing to take only $10. The coalitions have now come full circle, with (Goneril, Regan), split $15/$15, replaced by (Regan, Cordelia), split $20/$10, replaced by (Cordelia, Goneril), split $20/$10, replaced by (Goneril, Regan), split $20/$10. And yet, the final listed coalition is no more stable than it was in the initial round.

It might appear that the whole problem would be solved if, as previously suggested, the three sisters simply agreed to submit a written plan calling for the fairness solution of equal division. But this too is unstable. After the $10/$10/$10 plan is submitted, Goneril can approach Regan, offering to cut Cordelia from the coalition and proposing an alternative (Goneril, Regan) coalition with a $15/$15 split. That, of course, was the starting point in the prior example, which was not a stable solution.

We can only speculate, of course, what the final outcome would be and whether the daughters would reach a satisfactory resolution lasting ten days without a later filing before their father's death or whether as a result of efforts by the excluded sister to improve her payoff by forming a new coalition the daughters would ultimately force the trust corpus into the residuum of their father's will and take nothing. It is also important to observe that even if they succeeded in forming a successful coalition that meets the requirements under Lear's will, say the fairness solution that Farber and Frickey propose, that result would necessarily embed a thwarted majority that would have received higher payoffs had a superior coalition supplanted that result in favor of a preferred alternative.

The point, however, is not to predict the actual outcome. And it is sufficient for our purposes that there is a substantial risk that cycling will prevent a final timely disposition of assets or will embed an outcome disfavored by an alternative controlling majority. Instead, our purpose is to explain why, in some circumstances, lawmaking institutions have a comparative advantage over private decision makers in avoiding certain pitfalls that plague collective decision making. And yet, under alternative conditions, law making bodies themselves are prone to the very cycling problem that in other contexts they are able to solve. As the next variation on the Lear hypothetical demonstrates, institutional comparative advantage is a function of timing. Empty core bargaining problems arise when parties negotiate after the facts arise that produce an unanticipated windfall or loss.

Let us now modify the hypothetical to allow the sisters to enforce any interim agreements that they reach without sacrificing any of the resulting gains that come through legal enforcement. In this revised hypothetical, Lear's trust does not prevent the sisters from invoking judicial enforcement of a standard expectancy damages rule for breach of contract.[59] This rule imposes liability upon the breaching party and restores the victim of the breach to the position she would have been in had the breaching party fully performed.[60] While it is not possible to predict which coalition might initially form that would then give rise to a contract action following a breach, we can safely predict that if any coalition does form, this basic contract rule will restore stability in favor of the initial result.

To illustrate how a regime of enforceable contracts changes the analysis, assume that Goneril and Regan submit the original plan for each to receive $15. Cordelia offers Regan to form a superior coalition, in which Regan receives $20 and Cordelia receives $10. In contrast with the initial hypothetical, behaving rationally based upon the payoffs, Regan will decline. If Regan enters into the superior coalition with Cordelia, she will gain $5 (receiving $20 rather than $15), but will risk forfeiting $15 to Goneril in compensatory damages, thus placing her in an inferior position relative to honoring the original bargain. The principle can be generalized. Once any coalition has formed, an expectancy damages rule will ensure that any gains to the defector from forming a superior coalition with the initially excluded daughter will be depleted by the compensatory damages award.[61]

The contract damages rule might appear to avoid any possibility of cycling, but this is an oversimplification. This seeming solution has the potential to simply shift the threat of a cycle back to pre-contractual negotiations. While any coalition that actually formed would be stable with such a rule in place, at the preliminary negotiating stage, the very same empty core problem has the potential to rear its ugly head. Preliminary coalitions can, in theory, form and reform, prior to any formal agreements that, once breached, would give rise to a contract damages action. Does this observation help to explain why contract law demands the formation of an actual contract rather than an interim agreement during negotiations as a precondition to an action for breach of contract?[62] While the expectancy damages rule can avoid a cycle once an actual agreement is formed, as the next variation on the Lear hypothetical will demonstrate, this is not the only solution to the problem of cycling in the context of intestacy.

59. For ease of exposition, we assume immediate judicial enforcement.

60. *See* JOSEPH M. PERILLO, CALAMARI & PERILLO ON CONTRACTS § 14–4, at 564–67 (5th ed. 2003). Alternatively, the revised regime would potentially allow a sister to invalidate or enjoin any superseding coalition, thus increasing the likelihood that a submitted plan would satisfy the ten-day submission requirement prior to Lear's death.

61. For a somewhat more complex presentation that explores the empty core bargaining game and its relationship to the Coase theorem, see Varouj A. Aivazian & Jeffrey L. Callen, *The Coase Theorem and the Empty Core*, 24 J.L. & ECON. 175 (1981). *See also* R.H. Coase, *The Coase Theorem and the Empty Core: A Comment*, 24 J.L. & ECON. 183 (1981). For a general discussion of this illustration and Coase's response, see Stearns, *Misguided Renaissance, supra* note 1, at 1234–40.

62. For a provocative alternative proposal, see Omri Ben–Shahar, *Contracts Without Consent: Exploring a New Basis for Contractual Liability*, 152 U. PA. L. REV. 1829 (2004) (suggesting a basis for contractual liability in the absence of mutual assent taking the form of formal acceptance).

A legislature can induce stability among private actors facing an unanticipated windfall or loss not only by enacting a rule that facilitates a potential contractual solution, but alternatively by creating a rule that takes the form of a property right. In this example, assume that Lear dies intestate. As we have already established, the sisters, if left to their own devices, have the potential to cycle over the various alternative allocation schemes. This problem is solved, however, in the laws of virtually every state under which the sisters take in equal shares.[63]

To see why the legislature can devise this simple and compelling solution when the sisters seem unable to do so, consider the different incentives that confront the private market actors versus the law-making body in this example. While the sisters are motivated by the desire to maximize their individual payout once the windfall is announced, the legislature is instead motivated to announce rules that apply generally and prospectively. If successful, the rule will mirror what the parties would have agreed to prior to the announcement of the windfall gain. But after such a windfall is announced, the sisters no longer find themselves in the same *ex ante* frame of reference that helps to avoid unattractive strategic behavior. In this game, the legislature is well suited to replicate the more beneficial *ex ante* perspective on their behalf and, for that reason, can develop a solution that limits cycling when operating in combination with the sisters as private market actors.

This analysis provides a response to the earlier suggestion that because all institutions are theoretically prone to cycling, social choice leaves us "nowhere to turn."[64] The answer lies in the fallacy of composition. If the separate institutions prone to cycling, here the private market actors seeking to allocate a large windfall and the legislature seeking to devise an off-the-rack rule, cycle in response to different factual phenomena, by operating together they are able to reduce, and perhaps even avoid, cycling.

The same analysis applies with respect to the expectancy damages rule. Once again, assuming that the legislators have no stake in the outcome of any particular set of coalitions that form among siblings trying to negotiate in the absence of a will, the obvious facilitating rule places the improperly excluded party who was victim of a breach in a position to sue and thus to be restored to where she would have been but for the breach. This rule will restore a stable outcome, albeit one that thwarts an available superior coalition, regardless of which coalition initially forms. To be clear, while each of these rules—equal division among siblings absent a will or expectancy damages in the event that a contract is

---

63. *See* WILLIAM M. MCGOVERN JR. & SHELDON F. KURTZ, WILLS, TRUSTS AND ESTATES: INCLUDING TAXATION AND FUTURE INTERESTS § 2.2, at 52–54 (3d ed. 2004). In the event that this off-the-rack, or one-size-fits-all, rule turns out not to fit for particular parents, those parents, again in virtually all states, are free to supersede it by the express terms of their will. Other rules such as primogeniture, with or without a sex preference, for example the common historical practice of preferring the first male child, would also solve the empty core problem, suggesting the importance of additional criteria, beyond cycle breaking, for the selection of optimal rules.

64. *See* FARBER & FRICKEY, *supra* note 47, at 55.

breached to one sister's detriment—ensures a stable outcome, neither avoids an embedded set of preferences that can be characterized in terms of a cycle. The outcome remains stable because the legal rule ensures that there is no basis for supplanting the off-the-rack outcome (following the property rule) or that the cost of displacing an agreed-upon outcome exceeds any resulting gain (following the contract rule).

Does this mean that all lawmaking bodies, or all legislatures, are uniquely capable of devising benign *ex ante* solutions? As the next hypothetical will demonstrate, legislatures can also fall prey to the adverse consequences of relative timing, and thus can cycle, sometimes provoking a judicial response.

D. LEGISLATIVE CYCLING: LOCATION OF TOXIC–WASTE DISPOSAL FACILITY

The next hypothetical is based upon the 1992 Supreme Court decision, *New York v. United States*.[65] This example illustrates the conditions under which a state legislature, which in the prior illustration was able to devise a stable solution to an empty core bargaining game among private actors, can itself fall prey to the problem of empty core bargaining or cycling. The *New York* Court struck down the take-title provisions of the Low–Level Radioactive Waste Policy Amendments of 1985. These amendments were enacted after a series of unsuccessful regulatory initiatives designed to ensure adequate facilities for storing low-level radioactive waste. The amendments solved this problem by imposing sufficient sanctions such that the individual states would be motivated either to become self-sufficient or to join in a pact with other states that collectively would be self-sufficient.

Under the terms of the amendments, states that failed within a specified time frame to join a successful regional waste-disposal pact with other states or to become self-sufficient by creating their own in-state waste disposal facilities were required to take title to low-level radioactive waste or to compensate producers for any resulting liability. While the amendments produced a series of three compliance incentives that were intended to ensure self-sufficiency on the part of states by the end of 1992, Justice O'Connor, writing for the *New York* Court, determined that only the take-title provisions exceeded Congress's powers under the Commerce Clause, or alternatively, under the Tenth Amendment.

The case facts revealed that by December 31, 1992, the compliance deadline under the 1985 amendments, only New York had failed to either join a regional pact or to create an in-state disposal facility for low-level radioactive waste. New York then filed suit to challenge the take-title provisions as exceeding the permissible scope of Congress's regulatory powers under the Commerce Clause. The facts further revealed that while New York had initially decided to join a regional pact, it later opted

---

65. 505 U.S. 144 (1992).

instead to create an in-state disposal facility. The New York State Assembly eventually rejected each of five proposed sites, with the result that New York was the only noncompliant state and thus the only state subject to the onerous take-title provisions.

Consistent with the preceding analysis, the following simplified rendition of the *New York* facts demonstrates how the state legislature is prone to cycling following new federal regulatory requirements. Imagine that instead of five proposed sites there are three, *ABC*. Consider the incentives among the legislators representing those districts or for any three groups of legislators such that any two form a majority. The general problem of course is that no legislator wants the facility in her own district, a phenomenon that environmentalists refer to as Not In My Back Yard, or simply NIMBY. Assume that *AB* form a majority, voting to place the facility in *C*. *C* can offer *A* a sufficient legislative perk to form a superior *CA* coalition, with the result of instead voting to place the facility in *B*. *B* can now propose a similar deal to *C* if *C* defects in favor of a superior *BC* coalition, voting to place the facility in *A*. Now *A* can make a similar promise to *B*, reforming the now superior *AB* coalition, and once again voting to place the facility in *C*. At this point the coalitions have come full circle, *AB*, *BC*, *CA*, *AB*, with the facility voted to be placed in *C*, *B*, *A*, *C*. Of course no outcome is stable because this game, like the Lear game, has an empty core.

The question then is why the state legislature is itself prone to cycling in this example when in the prior example involving the allocation of assets in the absence of a will, the state legislature succeeded in eliminating the sisters' cycling problem. When faced with the issue of how to allocate the proceeds of a large and unanticipated windfall, the sisters were not concerned with devising the best or most equitable public policy respecting the division of assets among siblings in the absence of a will. Instead, each sister was concerned with engaging in whatever strategy maximized her personal gain. In the absence of a core, these combined strategies produced a cycle. In contrast, the legislators, when developing a prospective regime governing rules of heredity in the absence of a will, sought to devise a fair and general solution. That is a characteristic feature of off-the-rack rules, whether taking the form of contractual rules (the expectancy damages rule) or property rights (the equal division rule). While the legislators were therefore able to devise an *ex ante* solution to this bargaining problem, the sisters were instead motivated by the desire for *ex post* gain. The legislators, unlike the sisters, were able to behave as if the relevant facts giving rise to a potential cycle had not yet occurred. Even though the legislators are prone to cycling when they are confronted with a legislative capital loss (allocating the burdens of a newly imposed regulation that requires locating a waste facility), they are able to inhibit cycling among private actors when constructing a general and prospective off-the-rack rule. This beneficial result occurs *even though* both private market actors and legislators are sometimes prone to the problem of cycling.

E. WHY SO MUCH STABILITY? CONNECTING INTEREST GROUP THEORY AND THE PROBLEM OF CYCLING

In a famous essay posing this question, Professor Gordon Tullock questioned the practical significance of cycling in the face of generally stable institutional outcomes.[66] Tullock observed that, while the literature on legislative cycling is extensive, observed legislative cycling is practically nonexistent. Tullock proposed that the solution to the apparent gulf between theoretical prediction of frequent legislative cycles and empirical observation of stable legislative outcomes results from logrolling, or vote trading. Tullock maintained that logrolling promotes stable legislative outcomes by allowing legislators to register cardinal values, rather than mere ordinal rankings, when selecting among alternatives.

In an important series of articles, Professors Kenneth Shepsle and Barry Weingast questioned logrolling as a general explanation of the absence of observed cycling, demonstrating that when participants lack different intensities of preference, logrolling itself conduces to cycling.[67] In effect, with equal intensities, vote-trading mechanisms manifest the underlying cycle in a different form. Shepsle and Weingast argue instead that a variety of institutional structures in Congress, including committees, calendaring rules, the filibuster, and bicameralism—devices that include what we have previously referred to as negative legislative checkpoints or veto gates—induce stability by raising the cost of identifying and commodifying potential cyclical preferences. In effect, these combined mechanisms raise the costs of working bills through the legislature and in doing so reduce the likelihood that thwarted majority preferences will be revealed, thus inhibiting potential cycles.

This account provides an important conceptual link between interest group theory and social choice theory by offering a positive account for the emergence of lawmaking structures without which the possibility of exposing cyclical preferences would be enhanced. At the same time, because of the tendency of interest groups to exploit these very devices, they are also important subject matter for interest group theory. Thus, even if we can explain the emergence of institutional features in legislatures that diminish cycling, the question remains what the normative implications of such structures are for legislative outcomes.

In response to an argument by Professors Farber and Frickey that questioned the practical importance to legislatures of the theoretical literature on cycling,[68] Professor Shepsle addressed the normative signifi-

---

66. Gordon Tullock, *Why So Much Stability?*, 37 PUB. CHOICE 189 (1981).

67. Kenneth A. Shepsle & Barry R. Weingast, *Structure–Induced Equilibrium and Legislative Choice*, 37 PUB. CHOICE 503 (1981) [hereinafter *Structure–Induced Equilibrium*]; Kenneth A. Shepsle & Barry R. Weingast, *The Institutional Foundations of Committee Power*, 81 AM. POL. SCI. REV. 85 (1987); *see also* DENNIS MUELLER, PUBLIC CHOICE III, at 104–08 (1989).

68. Professors Farber and Frickey have also relied upon such concepts as the Yolk, Covered Set, and Strong Point to explain why we do not observe cycling in legislatures. Although formally

cance of cycle-breaking rules for legislative outcomes in considering the apparent paradox of legislative stability in light of the theoretical plausibility of cycling, Farber and Frickey, state: "Arrow's Paradox is both fascinating and illuminating, but it may have little direct relevance to legislative practice."[69] Now consider Professor Shepsle's response:

> The authors are confused by the fact that even in voting processes victimized by the Arrow result, we are sometimes able to identify equilibria. These equilibria, however, are strongly affected by the underlying incoherence of majority preferences and, because of this, lack a compelling normative justification. Arrow's theorem does not necessarily entail constant flux and indeterminacy; rather, it implies that the manner in which majority cycling is resolved is arbitrary or otherwise morally indefensible.[70]

In effect, Shepsle suggests that Farber and Frickey have focused on the wrong question. Farber and Frickey observe the absence of cycling and infer that cycling must therefore not be a significant real world concern. But Shepsle notes that the absence of observed cycling outcomes does not imply an absence of cycling preferences. Instead, Shepsle maintains, the failure to observe cycling suggests the presence of institutional structures within legislatures that promote stable outcomes by raising the cost of disclosing preferences that reflect voting cycles. These institutions do so by raising the cost of acting on preferences that reflect voting cycles. Thus, even if cyclical preferences are common, Congress can produce stable outcomes—outcomes that Shepsle and Weingast refer to as "structure-induced equilibria"[71]—by effectively suppressing (or embedding) cycling preferences. Shepsle claims that the real problem is not legislative instability resulting from cycling, but rather the potential arbitrariness of the results that cycle-suppressing rules potentially generate. While these rules can produce stable outcomes, the outcomes nonetheless embed a set of underlying cyclical preferences. For Shepsle, this implies that the ultimate set of chosen outcomes, regardless of their stability, might well

---

modeled differently, each concept rests on the intuition that legislative cycling is avoided in favor of a stable center of gravity that represents a set of outcomes capable of defeating *most* alternatives in direct comparisons. FARBER & FRICKEY, *supra* note 45, at 54 ("The 'sense of the legislature' or the legislative center of gravity corresponds to the solution sets (yolk, strong point, uncovered set or whatever) of recent formal models."). By definition, the set of options that satisfies this criterion does not defeat *all* alternatives in direct comparisons. As a result, depending upon the stakes involved and the intensity with which a potentially thwarted majority prefers an alternative to an option falling, for example, within the yolk, this concept appears not to provide a complete account for the failure of observed legislative cycling. The authors have also suggested that the desire to avoid cycling itself can prevent cycling. Farber & Frickey, *supra* note 45, at 434 (positing that "the existence of massive cycling provides the basis for a new form of equilibrium adopted precisely to avoid the cycles"). For this thesis to succeed, the participants must value avoiding cycling sufficiently to change the nominal payoffs in a manner no longer characterized by a cycle. If they do not, then the cycle persists; but if they do, the problem of cycling is avoided by assuming that the payoffs that conduce to cycling no longer exist.

69. Daniel A. Farber & Philip P. Frickey, *The Jurisprudence of Public Choice*, 65 TEX. L. REV. 873, 904 (1987).

70. Kenneth A. Shepsle, *Congress Is a "They," Not an "It": Legislative Intent as Oxymoron*, 12 INT'L REV. L. & ECON. 239, 242 n.6 (1992).

71. *See* Shepsle & Weingast, *supra* note 67.

lack an adequate normative justification when compared with potentially foregone legislative outcomes.[72] Stated differently, because the outcomes generated by cycle-breaking rules might thwart majority preferences for an alternative outcome, Shepsle suggests that there is no compelling normative justification for crediting the actual outcome more than various theoretical outcomes that the legislature might have produced.

To evaluate the moral significance of structure-induced equilibrium outcomes, we must distinguish what Shepsle labels the normative *justification* for such outcomes from what we will instead label the normative *legitimacy* of such outcomes.[73] Legitimacy refers to societal acceptance of outcomes based upon the quality of the processes that generated them.[74] In contrast, justification, as Professor Shepsle uses the term, refers to a merits-based comparison, based upon legislative preferences, between the selected outcome and foregone alternatives.[75] A similar analysis can be applied to courts. For instance, a group might unanimously agree with a rule that courts should follow precedent in subsequent cases even if the practice leads to occasionally unsatisfactory results. The general rule— follow precedent in materially indistinguishable cases—would legitimate even some disfavored outcomes because the precedent regime is grounded in a larger or more generally set legal principle.[76]

Because structure-induced equilibrating rules make it difficult to distinguish socially significant outcomes (in the sense of being Condorcet winners) from those that are the arbitrary product of voting rules (and thus no more meritorious than rejected outcomes), Shepsle suggests that actual outcomes should be regarded as normatively suspect.[77] But if the distinction between legitimacy and justification is valid, it challenges Shepsle's sweeping judgment about the normative merits of legislative outcomes affected by structure-induced cycle breaking practices. Even if a particular legislative outcome lacks independent merit in comparison with a foregone alternative, the overall set outcomes might be legitimated by acceptance of the process that produces a larger set of agreed upon outcomes.

---

72. *See* Shepsle, *supra* note 70, at 241–42.

73. Professor Stearns initially developed this argument in STEARNS, *supra* note 1, at 41–94.

74. Thus, the 8 OXFORD ENGLISH DICTIONARY 811 (2d ed. 1989), defines *legitimate* as "Comfortable to law or rule; sanctioned or authorized by law or right; lawful; proper," and further describes its etymology as follows: "[T]he word expresses a status which has been conferred or ratified by some authority. . . ."

75. Professor Riker suggests the same comparison when he discusses potential outcomes based upon the presence, or absence, of agenda manipulation. Professor Riker observes that:

The[] consequences [of social choice] are either that power is concentrated in society or that any system of voting can be manipulated to produce outcomes advantageous to the manipulators or at least different from outcomes in the absence of manipulation.

RIKER, *supra* note 27, at 137.

76. For a discussion demonstrating that the regime of precedent breaks cycles that manifest over groups of cases, see *infra* chapter 7, I.D.2.

77. For similar analyses to that offered by Shepsle in the legislative context, see RIKER, *supra* note 27, at 192–95, and in the judicial context, see Frank Easterbrook, *Statutes' Domains*, 50 U. CHI. L. REV. 533, 547–48 (1983).

To summarize, the pervasiveness of theoretical cycling among all collective decision-making bodies does not imply that social choice undermines institutional competence across the board. Rather, it suggests the need to consider the differences between or among institutions and how institutions operate in combination to ameliorate each other's deficiencies. In addition, within institutions, procedures that raise the cost of identifying preferred alternatives to a proposed outcome can also inhibit cycling. While structure-induced equilibrating rules might render outcomes path dependent (with the result that other potential outcomes are preferred by thwarted majorities), those outcomes might nonetheless be considered legitimate if the participants regard the processes that generated those outcomes as fair.

F. A PRELIMINARY COMPARISON BETWEEN LEGISLATURES AND APPELLATE COURTS

Even with structure-induced equilibrating rules in place, with respect to legislative matters for which the stakes—either as a matter of policy or based upon monetary values at stake—are sufficiently high, legislators might be able to identify intransitivities through informal means. We do not mean to imply that legislators will identify cycles as such. Instead, with respect to important matters, legislators can discover information from which they can infer that a majority prefers an alternative to a proposed or selected outcome. When this occurs, legislators might intuit the absence of a normative justification for moving forward with an option that changes the legal landscape but that appears to lack adequate support. As a result, they might simply choose not to act, thus allowing the status quo to continue.

In contrast with this combination of formal and informal mechanisms that allow legislative bodies to discover and to decline to act when faced with intransitive preferences, appellate courts are institutionally obligated to issue a collective decision, i.e., decide the case properly before them, regardless of whether a Condorcet winning option exists. Later in this book, we will see that even if judicial preferences are prone to cycling in a given case or over a group of cases, the Supreme Court is nonetheless generally obligated to resolve the cases, even though doing so will inevitably thwart the preferences of a majority of its members in some respect.[78]

In addition to having the option of inaction, legislatures possess one other important means of avoiding the difficulties of cyclical preferences that appellate courts lack. While appellate court judges are generally understood, or certainly expected, not to trade votes both across issues within cases and across case outcomes,[79] legislators routinely vote trade or

---

78. For a more detailed analysis, see STEARNS, *supra* note 1. *See also infra* chapter 7, section I.C and I.D.2.

79. This is not to suggest, of course, that judges never engage in strategic behavior in their efforts to promote desired policy objectives in a given case. *See generally* LEE EPSTEIN & JACK KNIGHT, THE CHOICES JUSTICES MAKE (1998). As explained herein *infra* p. 142–51, such behavior is

logroll both within and across bills. As Professors Shepsle and Weingast have observed, when the decision makers' intensities of preference are uniform, vote trading can reintroduce cycling.[80] Most often, however, legislation produces relative winners and losers and thus intensities of preference vary considerably.

To see how vote trading can improve results when preferences are not uniform, let us consider a hypothetical designed by Professor William Eskridge to illustrate the limits of legislative competence:

> Assume that Legislator *A* controls the agenda, so that Decision 1 is the last to pair up, winning against Decision 3. In addition, assume that the social benefit of Decision 1 is 100 (55% of which accrues to District *A* and 45% to District *B*) and that the social benefit of Decision 3 is 120 (shared equally by the three Districts). Obviously, from the collective point of view, the best decision is Decision 3 . . ., yet a coalition of *A* and *B* will vote for Decision 1. This is not only unfair to *C* (which gets no benefit even though it pays taxes), but is collectively wasteful as well (to the tune of 20).[81]

This result arises because the legislators vote solely in accordance with their immediate ordinal assessments over options. The effect, as Eskridge observes, is to produce a social welfare loss to *C*'s detriment. Could vote trading avoid this undesirable outcome? If the same legislators are planning on future interactions, we might instead imagine that legislators *A* and *B* would recognize the potential for gains from trade. In this instance, excluding *C* from the coalition produces a welfare loss, meaning to the group in its entirety, of 20. If *A* is willing to forego a payoff of 15 (55 from Decision 1 minus 40 from Decision 3) and if *B* is willing to forego a payoff of 5 (45 minus 40), thus foregoing their combined benefit of 20, the entire group, *ABC*, gains an additional payoff of 20. This result constitutes a substantial welfare enhancement. In this case *C* receives the immediate benefit (increasing the payoff from 0 to 40).[82] Provided that *C* is willing to promise a future payoff to *A* and *B* in an amount between the 20 they gave up from foregoing Decision 1 and the total of 40 that *C* has now gained as a result of Decision 3, Decision 3 becomes the likely result in this example because it makes *C* better off and leaves *A* and *B* no worse off. Given Professor Eskridge's assumptions, Decision 3 yields no social welfare loss. This preferred result arises because vote trading allows the members to set cardinal utilities over options. The same intuition explains how vote trading can avoid a cycle.

---

generally limited to compromise along a unidimensional issue continuum within a case, almost invariably toward the median, rather than across issues within a case or across cases. For a competing normative account, see ROBERT D. COOTER, THE STRATEGIC CONSTITUTION 205–09 (2000) (proposing that broader judicial commodification of preferences through vote trading might be welfare enhancing).

80. Shepsle & Weingast, *Structure–Induced Equilibrium, supra* note 67, at 506–07.

81. Eskridge, *supra* note 44, at 284.

82. By this we mean that the first 20 (15 from *A* and 5 from *B*) are redistributions to *C*. But *C* receives a total payoff of 40, 20 of which is due to a welfare enhancement, or increase in societal wealth, resulting from making the better policy choice.

While ordinally ranked preferences can yield cyclical outcomes in a regime of unlimited majority rule over binary comparisons, in many real world instances such theoretical cycles prove inconsequential. Assume that three legislators possess the paradigmatic cyclical preferences (1: *ABC*; 2: *BCA*; and 3: *CAB*) and that following a regime of path-induced voting, the likely result, benefiting legislators 2 and 3, is to produce result *C*. Despite the participants' ordinal rankings, it is quite possible that legislators 2 and 3 care less about the choice among options than does legislator 1, who winds up with her last choice. If so, legislator 2 or 3 might be willing to support an alternative outcome favoring legislator 1 in exchange for that legislator's future reciprocal accommodation. Thus, as Gordon Tullock posited, with different intensities of preference, vote trading can eliminate cycles.[83]

Even thwarting available Condorcet winners might sometimes be preferable to acting on such options, and logrolling also allows this to occur. This follows from the limitation that the Condorcet criterion does not account for intensity of preferences. Imagine that the legislators hold the following preferences yielding *B* as the Condorcet winner: 1: *ABC*; 2: *BCA*; 3: *CBA*. While legislator 1 ranks option *B* second, it is possible that she significantly prefers option *A*, while legislators 2 and 3 do not care very much about this particular legislative issue. If so, legislators 2 and 3 might be willing to subordinate their ordinal ranking over these options to produce a more beneficial result for legislator 1 in exchange for a reciprocal future commitment.

Now compare the mechanism of private market exchange. As shown in the Lear hypothetical, private market actors can cycle over options. This is most apt to occur when markets are "thin." By thin, we mean that the markets disallow robust competition that attaches meaningful prices, or cardinal values, to options. In "thick" markets, meaning markets characterized by robust competition, the price mechanism allows commodification of preferences, which restores cardinal values, with the effect of rendering many theoretical cycles inconsequential.[84]

While there is no doubt that the practices discussed above have the potential to frustrate majority preferences, consider whether the processes themselves are nonetheless meritorious. As the nirvana fallacy implies, when evaluating a given institutional practice, we must assess not only the immediate outcome or set of outcomes that provoked a given instance of dissatisfaction, but also whether the institution functions better overall with or without that practice in place. In addition, to rely upon social choice to justify a shift in decision-making responsibility from one organ of government to another—say from a legislature to a court—we must undertake the following comparative analysis. We must first identify each institution's Arrovian deficiency based upon its combined internal rules

---

83. *See* Tullock, *supra* note 66, at 190.

84. For an interesting hypothetical that illustrates this proposition with a three-way empty core bargaining game and that illustrates the difficulty that such games pose for the Coase theorem, see *supra* note 61, and cites therein.

and structures. We must then determine which institution, warts and all, is better suited to the task in question. As the next subsection demonstrates, it is also important to consider the combined impact of cumulative rules that affect any given institution's rationality.

G. EXPANDING THE BREADTH OF NORMATIVE ECONOMIC CRITERIA: A SOCIAL CHOICE ANALYSIS OF PARLIAMENTARY RULES

In his study of parliamentary rules, Professor Saul Levmore has suggested that the staging of rules improves the overall rationality and fairness of legislative outputs.[85] In addition to explaining how legislative bodies make decisions, Levmore's analysis expands the breadth of normative criteria for evaluating institutions and thus it contributes to a broader comparison of markets, legislatures, courts, and agencies.

Levmore studied a large number of sets of parliamentary rules written in the mid-nineteenth century, including Robert's Rules of Order, and determined that when Condorcet-winning options are likely to be available, the selected decision-making rules generally satisfy the Condorcet criterion.[86] By contrast, when it is more likely that the various options before the legislature lack a Condorcet winner, parliamentary rules tend to vary significantly. Levmore proposed that while the drafters of these rules were almost certainly unaware of the Condorcet paradox, meaning that group preferences sometimes cycle when aggregated by a regime of endless majority rule, participants in various legislative assemblies pushed the rules in a manner consistent with the pattern he observed as a result of confronting "avoidable dissatisfaction." Avoidable dissatisfaction arises when the rules produce a non-Condorcet winner despite the availability of a Condorcet winner. When this occurred, Levmore posited, the thwarted majority coalition likely pressured those controlling the proceedings to replace the existing rule with one more likely to generate satisfactory outcomes. The following hypothetical five-member assembly helps to illustrate Levmore's analysis. Assume each member holds the following ordinal rankings over five alternatives, ABCDE.[87]

P1: *ABCDE*

P2: *ABCED*

P3: *CBDEA*

P4: *CBEAD*

P5: *EDBCA*

A careful analysis reveals that although option *B* is no one's first choice, it is a Condorcet winner. Imagine that the voting rule is plurality

---

85. *See generally* Saul Levmore, *Parliamentary Law, Majority Decision Making, and the Voting Paradox*, 75 Va. L. Rev. 971 (1989).

86. *See generally id.*

87. This discussion is adapted from Stearns, *Misguided Renaissance, supra* note 1, at 1254.

with a runoff, such that each member votes her first choice and, absent a majority winner, the two top candidates run off against each other. In this regime, option B will be suppressed in the first round of voting. There is no first choice majority candidate and as between the two top first choice candidates, A and C (each getting two votes), C prevails, with P1 and P2 losing.

Now assume that this result emerged with respect to a high stakes legislative matter. After the meeting, P1, P2, and P5 discuss the outcome and with little effort discover that together they form a majority preferring B to C. With somewhat greater effort, involving the remaining members of the assembly, they might learn that B defeats each remaining alternative in a direct pairwise contest. Even without that step, they could reason that consistent with majority rule, C should not have prevailed over B. At the next meeting, these members might express their dissatisfaction with the earlier proceedings and propose replacing the problematic plurality and runoff regime with an alternative voting protocol that better respects majority preferences.

If the new voting regime also thwarts the Condorcet criterion, this process is likely to repeat itself. Through continuous tinkering with the rules, frustrated majorities will eventually seize upon a rule that satisfies the Condorcet criterion, for example motion-and-amendment voting.[88] At that point, by resolving the problem of avoidable dissatisfaction the assembly will have settled on a stable rule although, as shown below, other difficulties might emerge. Assuming no change in preferences and the newly adopted voting regime, if P3 moves to adopt option C, P1 can then move instead to substitute option B. The motion to amend will get majority support (P1, P2, and P5), and because option B is a Condorcet winner any other motion to amend (seeking to supersede B with A, D, or E) would fail. The resulting motion to approve option B would pass, and motion-and-amendment voting would emerge as the stable voting rule.

This simple story is noteworthy in two critical respects. First, it demonstrates the importance of an economic benchmark potentially in tension with efficiency against which to evaluate the competence of parliamentary decision-making rules. While the Condorcet criterion and efficiency do not invariably conflict, there are circumstances where they might. While option B in the prior example is a Condorcet winner, it might nonetheless be an inefficient public policy choice. For example, that

---

88. An important clarification: For this regime to succeed, the motion-and-amendment voting procedure must permit at least as many binary comparisons as options. Unlimited motion and amendment voting will necessarily satisfy this criterion, but even a less liberal regime will succeed provided that it permits at least as many binary comparisons as options. If instead the regime prevents reconsideration of an option defeated in one round of voting and if that option would defeat the ultimately successful option, then the restrictive regime prevents participants from knowing whether the selected outcome is socially significant, in the sense of being a Condorcet winner, or is instead the arbitrary product of a voting path. For an informative discussion in the context of Congressional voting procedures, see William H. Riker, *The Paradox of Voting and Congressional Rules for Voting on Amendments*, 52 AM. POL. SCI. REV. 349, 355–56 (1958) (identifying restrictions on permissible amendments relative to options that prevent members of Congress from determining if outcomes are Condorcet winners).

option might set a minimum wage so high that an industrious class of minimally skilled workers is rendered unemployable or place a ceiling on rents so low that landlords are thereby discouraged from maintaining properties in sound repair or are encouraged to convert them for sale as condominiums, thus thwarting an otherwise profitable rental market. Second, the example explains an evolutionary process toward rules satisfying the Condorcet criterion that does not in any way depend upon familiarity with the Condorcet paradox or social choice. Rather, through a simple process of adaptation, rules that continue to serve their intended purposes remain in place, while those that do not are abandoned and replaced.

The analysis does not imply that the process of testing and replacing rules is random. As with all economic actors, legislators think carefully about the difficulties that confront them and about how to devise solutions. Sometimes they seize upon the best result quickly; other times they stumble along the way. To the extent that individuals consciously adopt beneficial strategies that affect the evolution of institutions and rules, they quicken the pace of beneficial adaptation. The pace of adaptation, however, is inessential to the underlying evolutionary process.[89]

1. Dimensionality and Symmetry: The Foundations of Cycling

In some instances, there will be no Condorcet winner, and thus not all dissatisfaction is avoidable. One foundational insight of social choice is that as options increase, the likelihood of a Condorcet winner decreases.[90] As more options are introduced, so too are arguments for preferring among them.[91] Introducing more options therefore also increases the number of analytical dimensions along which to assess those options normatively. Identifying a Condorcet winner presupposes the presence of a single analytical dimension that enables choices to be ranked along a common normative scale. Increasing the dimensions along which participants assess options reduces the likelihood that participants will grade the options along a common normative scale as required to identify a Condor-

---

89. *See* Armen A. Alchian, *Uncertainty, Evolution, and Economic Theory,* 58 J. POL. ECON. 211 (1950). Thus, for example, whether or not the first person to try vertical integration had in mind solving a potential long term bilateral negotiating problem, or, instead, was simply a power monger, to the extent that the strategy worked to avoid difficult bilateral negotiating problems among the affected actors, it was destined to survive. Future economic actors facing such problems, again whether or not they held even a rudimentary intuition consistent with what we now appreciate as the economic theory of the firm, might opt to mimic the initial entrepreneur's strategy for no other reason than that he is doing better than they are under otherwise similar conditions. For a seminal discussion of the theory of the firm, see R.H. Coase, *The Nature of the Firm: Origin,* 4 J.L. ECON. & ORG. 3 (1988).

90. William V. Gehrlein, *Condorcet's Paradox,* 15 THEORY & DECISION 161, 192 (1983) ("The results suggest that the probability of the no-winner form of Condorcet's paradox increases as the number of dimensions in the attribute space increases. The probability also tends to increase as the number of candidates increases."); Bradford Jones et al., *Condorcet Winners and the Paradox of Voting: Probability Calculations for Weak Preference Orders,* 89 AM. POL. SCI. REV. 137, 138 (1995) ("As is apparent, Condorcet winners become less likely as (1) the number of alternatives increases and (2) the number of individuals increases.").

91. For a more detailed analysis, see *Appendix A: Peaks, Dimensionality, and Symmetry* supra note 5 (explaining role of unipeakedness and multipeakedness, single and multiple dimensions, and symmetry and asymmetry in affecting stable or cyclical preferences).

cet winner. Absent such a common scale of measurement, therefore, the probability that a Condorcet winning option exists declines. Increasing the number of options available, therefore, increases the probability of cycling.

In considering the relationship between options and cycling, it is important to consider two aspects of the term dimensionality. The choice among options can involve more than a single dimension in the sense of formal questions or issues to be considered in making a decision. A choice implicating more than a single dimension in the limited sense of issues for consideration does not necessarily imply that preferences will cycle. Revisiting the earlier analysis of *Planned Parenthood of Southeastern Pennsylvania v. Casey*[92] illustrates this idea.

In *Casey*, some Justices assessed the case according to their preferred substantive rule on the claimed right to abortion, while others assessed the case based solely on the separate issue of the stare decisis effect of *Roe v. Wade*,[93] and thus without regard to the underlying merit of the claimed constitutional right to abortion. Despite these two potential issue framings, it was easy to recast the various opinions in *Casey* along a single normative dimension involving whether to grant a relatively broad or relatively narrow right to abortion. The *Casey* opinions are thus susceptible to measurement along a unidimensional scale because those who preferred a strong form of the abortion right also preferred a strict application of stare decisis, while those who preferred a weak form of the abortion right also preferred a weak application (or a rejection of) stare decisis. As a result, the preferences of those Justices on opposite ends of the *Casey* Court—the liberals and the conservatives respectively—were "symmetrical." Symmetry means that opposite resolutions of the dispositive case issues—(1) is there a fundamental right to abortion?, and (2) does *Roe v.* Wade control *Casey* as a matter of stare decisis?—also led the liberal and conservative Justices to opposite resolutions respecting the judgment for the case as a whole. In this analysis, while *Casey* involved two issue dimensions, the meaningful dimension of choice "flattened" such that the overall group of opinions in the case could be cast according to the strength or weakness that the Justices attached to the abortion right claimed.

In other cases, however, judicial preferences are asymmetrical, revealing a true problem of dimensionality.[94] In those cases, asymmetry arises because unlike in *Casey,* the camps of Justices who resolve the dispositive case issues in opposite fashion nonetheless prefer the same case judgment, while the Justices writing in dissent resolve one issue in favor of each opposing camp yet prefer the opposite judgment. These cases thus reveal an analytical impasse concerning whether the various judicial camps care more about the resolution of one or more of the underlying case issues or

---

92. 505 U.S. 833 (1992). *See supra* pp. 98–99 (discussing *Casey*).

93. 410 U.S. 113 (1973).

94. *See infra* chapter 7, section I.C.1.A (demonstrating multidimensionality and asymmetry in Kassel v. Consol. Freightways Corp., 450 U.S. 662 (1981), and Arizona v. Fulminante, 499 U.S. 279 (1991)).

the case as a whole. This tension and this form of dimensionality does not arise in *Casey* because within each camp, whether the Justices view the case from the perspective of the dispositive issues or the case outcome as a whole, the analysis leads the Justices to the same outcome.

Whether we are dealing with a legislative or judicial context, the analytical point is the same. As institutional actors introduce more options, they simultaneously increases the risk that those called upon to assess the options will reveal a deeper problem of dimensionality, meaning disagreement in a manner that thwarts a common normative scale for analysis. When this occurs, there is a heightened probability of asymmetry and thus that group preferences will cycle.

2.   Return to Parliamentary Rules

As applied to parliamentary rules, a legislative body is likely to have a large number of options, for example, when selecting an annual budget or when choosing among dates for an election or other event. Even seemingly similar options can add dimensionality and thus increase the likelihood of cycling. If there are only a few dates, then decision makers are more likely to base their preferences on their perspectives along a common normative dimension, for example, the desire for an early or late adjournment. Similarly, if there are few proposed budgetary allocations, voters are more likely to assess their choices along the common dimension of how much to allocate to the project in question. With such preferences, and assuming sincere voting, there is a natural pull toward a median position. But as options increase, some voters will base preferences on criteria that are out of keeping with such a single dimensional scale, and will instead factor in such concerns as avoiding meeting on particular holidays or on certain days of the week, or how this choice will affect other parts of the calendar. In the budgetary context, some will evaluate choices not only on the amount spent, but also on a combination of factors that includes other opportunities for spending funds, the quality associated with each level of expenditure, or even the symbolism associated with allocating larger or smaller amounts to a given public project.

Because increasing options reduces the likelihood of a Condorcet winner, it also increases the likelihood of thwarted majority preferences. When preferences cycle, any given option thwarts some majority that would prefer another outcome. For this reason, Levmore posits that dissatisfied majorities are once again likely to force tinkering with the rules.[95] This time, however, the resulting dissatisfaction is unavoidable and further tinkering will not push the rules toward a stable alternative. Instead, as Levmore explains, there is likely to be substantial variation across different sets of parliamentary rules, a result supported by his survey.

---

95. Levmore, *supra* note 85, at 1024 ("[W]ell-informed and clever chairpersons can manipulate motion-and-amendment voting by recognizing favored members first so that their motions need not survive a great many votes.").

Within an important subset of these varied parliamentary rules, Levmore discovered an apparent common thread. As previously discussed, voting rules that do not satisfy the Condorcet criterion generally ground outcomes in the order in which votes are taken. As a consequence, whoever is afforded the authority to set the voting agenda will possess disproportionate power. In contrast, when a decision-making body employs a rule that satisfies the Condorcet criterion and when a Condorcet winner is available, assuming sincere voting, a dominant outcome emerges without regard to the order in which votes are taken. All rules that satisfy the Condorcet criterion produce a Condorcet winner when one is available. By contrast, rules that defy the Condorcet criterion vary in the results that they produce whether or not there is an available Condorcet winner. Rules that do not meet the Condorcet criterion also vary in their susceptibility to agenda manipulation, for example, by a committee chair.[96]

When options are unlikely to include a Condorcet winner, the legislature might elect to modify the motion-and-amendment procedure to prevent reconsideration of previously defeated options. In contrast with the unlimited motion-and-amendment procedure, which ensures a Condorcet winner when one is available, but which cycles absent a Condorcet winner, this regime produces an outcome whether or not there is a Condorcet winner. Recall that without at least the same number of pairwise contests as options, it is not possible to determine whether the outcome is a Condorcet winner or is instead the arbitrary product of a voting path. By prohibiting reconsideration of defeated alternatives, this voting regime ensures an outcome, but risks preventing the requisite number of binary comparisons to determine that outcome's social significance, or merit, in comparison with foregone alternatives.

Based upon this intuition, Professor Riker criticized a rule employed in both houses of Congress permitting only "four amending motions to a bill or resolution."[97] Riker contended that the rule had the potential to mask voting cycles and thus to produce outcomes he deemed arbitrary. While Riker is certainly correct that, with more than five options, this voting rule has the potential to mask a cycle by preventing the requisite number of binary comparisons relative to options, his observation nonetheless presents two difficulties. First, as Riker recognized, if the legislative preferences cycle, expanding the number of permissible amendments will reveal the cycle, but will not provide a means of ensuring a stable outcome over alternatives.[98] Second, even a formal limit on the number of

---

96. For a classic illustration of agenda manipulation, see Michael E. Levine & Charles R. Plott, *Agenda Influence and Its Implications*, 63 VA. L. REV. 561, 572 (1977) (describing manipulated voting scheme in context of flying club to acquire authors preferred fleet of aircraft and confirmation of results in lab experiments).

97. Riker, *supra* note 88, at 354.

98. Recognizing this problem, Riker observed:

Even if both houses were to provide this method of discover[ing potentially cyclical preferences], they would still need a procedure for resolving the intransitivities discovered....

... But, as Arrow has shown, an intransitivity, once in existence, cannot be eliminated simply by juggling the techniques of counting.

Id. at 364.

permissible votes relative to options might not prevent legislators from discovering cyclical preferences through various informal mechanisms, especially if the stakes are sufficiently high. As in other business settings, important legislative matters are often resolved well in advance of formal meetings, the purpose of which is often to ratify results that by the time of the meeting are a *fait accompli*. This is certainly likely to characterize at least some congressional negotiations over high stakes matters. Indeed, perhaps ironically, some of the very equilibrating rules previously discussed that formally break cycles might function as venues for the informal discovery of cycling preferences or Condorcet winners, and thus as loci at which to negotiate around potentially problematic voting paths. If so, the practical effect of these institutional practices is to create focal points at which to potentially broaden the number of iterations that occur informally despite the formal number of binary comparisons that the voting rules allow.

While these arguments provide a partial response to Riker's concerns about path dependence that arise when opportunities to amend are limited, there is little doubt that prohibiting reconsideration of defeated alternatives affords committee chairs tremendous power over the critical voting path. Chairs determine, for example, who gets the floor and, very often, the order in which issues are raised. As Levmore explains, motion-and-amendment voting favors early motions because after an original motion is proposed, members can propose amendments to that motion, and amendments to that amendment (termed an amendment in the second degree) and to that amendment (amendments in the third degree) and so on. Voting begins at the outer edge, thus pitting the highest ordinal amendments against each other, the victor against the next highest ordinal amendment, until the successful amendment is directly voted against the original motion. In contrast with later amendments that must survive a series of successive rounds to be voted against the original motion, the original motion itself need only survive a single round, against the final surviving amendment, before it (or the amendment that replaces it) is voted up or down.

Because motion-and-amendment voting favors early motions, Levmore posits that the regime affords committee chairs substantial agenda-setting power. It does so by allowing chairs to favor early proponents and then to order amendments so that problematic options raised in the form of later amendments can be eliminated in early rounds of voting.[99] Levmore concludes, therefore, that while motion-and-amendment voting works well when there are few options to consider (because it locates Condorcet winners thus eliminating avoidable dissatisfaction), it is likely to produce dissatisfaction as larger numbers of options become available. At that point, the regime invites the threat of strategic agenda setting.

---

99. *See supra* note 95.

This insight provides the basis for Levmore's next step in analyzing the development of parliamentary rules. Levmore suggests that when there are likely to be several potential options, a good defensive strategy against agenda setting is a switch to succession voting. While motion-and-amendment favors early motions, succession voting favors relatively late motions.[100] In this regime, motions are voted upon in the order in which they are raised until a motion secures the requisite majority to pass. In addition, under this regime defeated options cannot be reconsidered. Thus, the regime ensures a result even when preferences cycle. Because it is more difficult for the chair to control the order in which motions will be advanced than to sequence options already presented, it is generally more difficult to manipulate succession voting than motion-and-amendment voting.

Once again, however, succession voting, which violates the Condorcet criterion, threatens occasional avoidable dissatisfaction, for example, when there are relatively few options available. Levmore thus observes one more evolutionary step involving, for example, the selection among either dates or budgetary allocations. Structuring votes over such options raises important social choice implications. As we have already seen, increasing options on such issues can produce more than a single dimension and thus introduce the risk of cycling. And yet, options pertaining to such options as dates or budgetary allocations are often conducive to a natural sequencing, including most obviously early-to-late or low-to-high (or the reverse). Although not without exception, such issues are often likely to include a Condorcet winning option representing the median choice among participants on a single dimensional scale. One way to increase the likelihood of choosing an available Condorcet winner is to base the order of consideration on an underlying logical sequence. This can take the form of an incremental voting rule, for example, working from the top down or the bottom up. Importantly, when the logical sequencing structure rests along a single dimensional scale, the voting protocol will yield the same outcome—the Condorcet winner—regardless of the end of the spectrum (high or low, early or late) at which voting begins.

Professor Levmore summarized the evolutionary process affecting parliamentary rules as follows:

> The codes can be regarded as evolving along the lines of, or as having adopted, the following reasoning: (1) employ the motion-and-amendment process when there are few alternatives because it promises to find any Condorcet choice without encouraging unavoidable dissatisfaction; (2) when there are numerous alternatives likely to be proposed, facilitate a switch to succession voting because a Condorcet winner is quite unlikely and the switch will make it difficult for the

---

100. *See* Levmore, *supra* note 85, at 1024–25. Levmore explains that "In contrast [with motion and amendment voting], succession voting often favors later—but not too late—entries into the fray, but since it is difficult for the chair to judge the quantity of alternatives yet to be proposed, it is difficult to position one's favorite correctly." *Id.* at 1025. The danger of being too late is that under this voting rule, the first motion to secure a majority wins. As a result, a relatively late successful option will foreclose options not yet introduced.

chair to manipulate the order of recognition to unfairly influence the outcome; and (3) when succession voting exposes unavoidable dissatisfaction, tinker with the order in which proposals are considered.[101]

Despite the explanatory power of this social choice account of parliamentary rules, Levmore found the departure from motion-and-amendment voting in favor of a plurality voting rule for the selection of committee chairs paradoxical given the relatively low cost of repeated votes within legislative assemblies.[102] A characteristic of rules that satisfy the Condorcet criterion helps to resolve this seeming anomaly.

Recall that when preferences over options cycle, rules meeting the Condorcet criterion would threaten an impasse. When choosing whether and how to resolve *issues*, legislatures often avoid issuing formal institutional decisions, whether as a result of cycling or following a deliberate collective decision to prefer the *status quo* to any proposed change. By contrast, when choosing among *people* to fill positions, inertia is generally not an option, even when preferences cycle, because electing committee chairs and the like is essential to conducting any business. As Levmore's study reveals, when legislatures choose among people, rules thus gravitate away from the Condorcet criterion.[103]

Can you think of other voting contexts that favor a non-Condorcet rule? If so, what is it about the institutional context that demands an outcome even when preferences cycle? Might such rules differ in a legislative versus judicial context? Why or why not?[104]

H. A COMMENT ON BASELINES

As the preceding analysis demonstrates, social choice reveals several normative dimensions for assessing the quality of institutional outputs and the processes that institutions employ to generate those outputs. While these baselines grow out of economic analysis, they extend beyond both the traditional concerns for promoting microeconomic efficiency and the Condorcet criterion. The discussion throughout this chapter exposes no fewer than the following five baselines:

---

101. *Id.* at 1026–27.

102. Levmore offers two tentative explanations for this seeming anomaly. First, some rules that employ paired comparisons, for example, round-robin voting, would undermine perceptions of fairness by allowing one candidate to wait out all other votes and run only in the final election. *Id.* at 1018–21. Second, single round plurality election, or a plurality with a runoff, reduces transactions costs relative to the more costly round-robin regime. *Id.* at 1017. Finally, Levmore observes that "[i]t is interesting, but not terribly helpful, to note that plurality voting often concerns a choice among *individuals* while motion-and-amendment voting often involves decision-making with regard to *issues*." *Id.* at 1013 n.122.

103. *See id.* at 1013 n.122. Consider also Levmore's comparison of two non-Condorcet rules in this context, plurality voting, and round-robin voting. Levmore suggests that as between the two, plurality voting appears fairer in this context because round-robin voting allows some to wait out multiple rounds, while forcing others to undertake numerous direct comparisons in the interim. *Id.* at 1020–22 & nn.137–38.

104. We will revisit these questions in chapters 5 (the legislature) and 7 (the judiciary). *See also* STEARNS, *supra* note 1 (using social choice to distinguish legislative and judicial voting processes).

1) Respecting the democratic norm of majority rule (the Condorcet criterion),

2) Ensuring that a collective decision is made whether or not preferences cycle (rationality),

3) Controlling or limiting agenda manipulation (promoting fairness),

4) Encouraging principled rather than strategic decision making (ensuring merit-based decisions),

5) Allowing commodification of preferences when individuals hold different intensities of interest in particular outcomes (improving social welfare).

Broadening economic analysis to include these and perhaps other baselines promotes a substantially richer analysis than applying any single baseline. What is missing is a framework for assessing the tradeoffs that these or other criteria produce in the design of collective decision-making institutions.

In effect, the analysis throughout this chapter has thus far been directed at understanding potential institutional *objectives*. What are the goals that society holds for any given institution under review? The next section, which provides a more detailed introduction to Arrow's Theorem, is instead directed at the question of institutional *capacity*. What does social choice tell us about the ability of particular institutions to satisfy society's objectives and at what cost in terms of core democratic values or institutional rationality?

III. ARROW'S THEOREM

Arrow's Theorem proves that all institutions contain some inherent weakness or set of weaknesses, at least as compared with what Arrow defined as a minimally acceptable set of benchmarks for assessing institutional competence. Whether the identified weaknesses of any given institution are a reason for serious concern, or simply the price of doing business, turns in large part on the specific functions we expect our institutions to perform. As you read the discussion that follows, consider how Arrow's various normative criteria help to inform our understanding of the quality of institutions as well as the choice among institutions for various functions in a constitutional democracy.

A. A CLOSER LOOK AT ARROW'S THEOREM

Kenneth Arrow set out to create a set of governing rules to be used by a planning authority that would simultaneously satisfy a fundamental tenet of rationality, namely the ability to ensure that the authority's collective decisions satisfy the minimal criterion of transitivity, and several seemingly noncontroversial assumptions about fair collective decision-making processes.[105] Although then unaware of the work of the Marquis de Condorcet, Arrow ultimately demonstrated that any effort to fix the problem of collective indeterminacy or irrationality that results from the problem of cycling will necessarily violate at least one important condition that people would commonly, or at least intuitively, associate with fair collective decision making. Arrow's Theorem has therefore aptly been characterized as a generalization of the Condorcet paradox.[106] Arrow proved that no collective decision-making body can simultaneously satisfy four seemingly noncontroversial assumptions about fair collective decision making and guarantee the ability to produce collective results that satisfy the basic condition of transitivity. Thus, while Condorcet demonstrated that the general assumption of individual rationality cannot be extended to groups, Arrow demonstrated that devices designed to cure collective irrationality will undermine collective fairness in some fundamental way.

Before explaining the four conditions that Arrow presumed essential to fair collective decision making, a few comments on methodology will be helpful. While the term "fairness" is admittedly general, Arrow defined each fairness condition with mathematical precision in his axiomatic proof, and defended each condition on credible normative grounds. That is not to suggest that every fairness condition is equally important or that all fairness conditions have been universally accepted for their normative validity, at least in all contexts. For now it is sufficient to note that individually and collectively, the various fairness conditions are sometimes at odds with both traditional economic understandings of efficiency and rationality, as defined to mean ensuring the power to translate internally consistent member preferences into transitive orderings for the group as a whole.

In an important respect, the whole of Arrow's Theorem is greater than the sum of its parts. Even if we were to flatly reject either the normative validity of Arrow's understanding of collective rationality or one or more of his claimed fairness conditions,[107] this would not undermine the power of the theorem as a positive tool in establishing bench-

---

105. For a discussion of Arrow's initial results and how Arrow corrected an error in his first proof, see STEARNS, *supra* note 1, at 344–45 n.91. With one modification, see STEARNS, *supra* note 1, at 336–37 n.104 (explaining history of range criterion in works by Arrow and Vickrey, and as presented by Mueller, and how the more stringent definition presented in the text conforms to the alternative presentations), following MUELLER, *supra* note 69, we are employing the definitions from William Vickrey's more accessible proof, *see* Vickrey, *supra* note 34, at 508–09, in lieu of those set out in Arrow's revised proof. For an explanation, including a comparison to Arrow's original and revised proofs, see STEARNS, *supra* note 1, at 344–45 n.91, 346–47 n.104, 347–48 n.112.

106. *See* RIKER, *supra* note 27, at 116.

107. Professor William Riker, for example, strongly questioned the validity of independence of irrelevant alternatives. *See id.* at 130. Professors Richard Pildes and Elizabeth Anderson have questioned the validity of collective rationality or transitivity. *See* Richard H. Pildes & Elizabeth S. Anderson, *Slinging Arrows at Democracy: Social Choice Theory, Value Pluralism, and Democratic Politics*, 90 COLUM. L. REV. 2121, 2146–58, 2192 (1990). For a response to these arguments, see Stearns, *Misguided Renaissance, supra* note 1, at 1249–50 (discussing independence) and 1251–52 nn.114 & 115 (discussing rationality), and STEARNS, *supra* note 1, at 41–94.

marks for a meaningful comparison of institutions and rules. That seeming counterintuition is closely linked to the "nirvana fallacy." Recall that scholars commit the nirvana fallacy when they identify a defect in a given institution or rule and then propose either shifting decisional authority elsewhere, or devising a different governing rule, without having first assessed whether the proposed alternative would improve or exacerbate the problem that it is offered to cure. This intuition was most notably captured in Voltaire's observation that "the perfect is the enemy of the good."[108] Surprisingly perhaps, in undertaking comparative institutional analysis, it is more difficult to ascertain what is good than it is to define what is perfect. Arrow did not set out to define a perfect institution, but rather an adequate one that honored what he regarded as basic conditions of rationality and fairness. Even so, Arrow proved the impossibility of achieving his seemingly modest objectives. In doing so, Arrow provided a credible combined set of normative benchmarks for meaningful comparative institutional analysis. Whether or not Arrow's Theorem defines the "perfect," what we will now frame as Arrow's Corollary defines what is "good enough," or more to the point, what is "good enough for our purposes."

Arrow's Theorem proves that no single collective decision-making body can simultaneously satisfy four simple conditions of fairness: *range* (the outcome must be consistent with the members' selection among any conceivable ordering over three options), *unanimity* (the *Pareto* criterion, but with a twist), *independence of irrelevant alternatives* (in choosing among options presented, the decision makers are to decide based solely upon the merits and without regard to how they would rank options that might later be introduced), and *nondictatorship* (the decision-making rule cannot systematically honor the preferences of an individual against the contrary preferences of the group as a whole), while ensuring the ability to produce collective results that are rational (transitive).[109] We will provide more detailed definitions of each of these terms below and connect the definitions with several of the previously described examples.

We turn now to a necessary corollary to Arrow's Theorem:[110] Because *no* collective decision-making body can ensure compliance with all five stated criteria (the four fairness conditions plus collective rationality), any collective decision-making body that functions, meaning simply that it issues collective decisions, has necessarily sacrificed at least one (and possibly more than one) of those five criteria. This corollary implies that adherence to all of the five criteria is not essential to the functioning of all institutions. Moreover, conditions that are essential to the functioning of some institutions are easily sacrificed, and might even prove detrimental,

---

108. Voltaire, *La Bégueule: Conte Moral* (1772) ("Le mieux est l'ennemi du bien."), *available at* http://www.archive.org/details/labgueulecontem00voltgoog.

109. *See supra* note 105, and cites therein (describing Arrow's Theorem criteria).

110. *See* STEARNS, *supra* note 1, at 82–83 (describing Arrow's Corollary and its implications for constitutional process).

to the functioning of others. This argument rests on the following normative assertion: As a society, we do not reject all of our collective decision-
making bodies—including markets, state legislatures and Congress, state
and federal appellate courts, and agencies—as inherently irrational or
unfair even though we are sometimes dissatisfied with the particular
results that each of these institutions produce.[111] This implies that there
is a standard for evaluating our collective decision-making institutions,
which, although rendering them below the unattainable goal that Arrow's
Theorem establishes, nonetheless renders them generally acceptable, or
good enough.

By prescribing the unattainable, the combined Arrow's Theorem
criteria provide a set of objective standards with which to assess institutions, knowing that each separate institution will necessarily come up
short in some respect. As previously noted, however, Arrow's proof says
nothing about which of the particular criteria are most (or least) important in any given institutional setting. It is for that reason that Arrow's
Theorem speaks to institutional *capacity*, but not to institutional *objectives*. If we use Arrow's Theorem as the benchmark in making such
comparative institutional assessments, however, we can determine the
nature of each institution's *different* capacities and, notably, each institution's deficiencies. Based upon identified deficiencies, we can then assess
whether the existing allocation of decisional authority is less bad than the
alternative allocations that would result from the various proposals for
institutional reform. In addition, by applying the same analysis to rules
within institutions, we can, once again, evaluate proposed changes to
those rules to see if they are likely to improve or worsen whatever
problems in institutional functioning the proponents seek to cure.

Comparative institutional analysis implicates the fallacy of composition *and* the closely related isolation fallacy. One important method of
improving institutional fairness and rationality, including, for example, in
Congress and the Supreme Court, is through the combined operation of
more than one institution in a manner that allows each to help compensate for the other's identified deficiencies. Evaluating an institution as if it
were operating in isolation undervalues the quality of institutions operating in combination that exhibit differing strengths and weaknesses that
can be analyzed with social choice theory. One important example involves
the evolution of initial Supreme Court rules away from the Condorcet
criterion (for example, outcome voting and stare decisis) and the evolution
of Congressional rules and practices toward the Condorcet criterion (for
example, motion-and-amendment voting and informal practices that allow
the discovery of thwarted majority preferences under limited motion-and-
amendment or other voting protocols).

This is not to suggest that the Supreme Court generally misses
available Condorcet winners,[112] or that Congress invariably finds them.

---

111. *See id.* at 83.

112. For a discussion of how the narrowest grounds rule operates to locate available
Condorcet winners even when there is no majority first choice opinion, see *id.* at 124–39
(discussing narrowest grounds doctrine) and *infra* chapter 7, section I.C.1.B.

Instead, the analysis shows that the starting point for the rules in each institution reflect their general obligations to either resolve matters properly before them or their power to remain inert when confronted with proposals lacking sufficient support to justify a collective decision that displaces the status quo. These starting rules, however, often combine with companion rules that improve each institution's outputs. In the Supreme Court, for example, the companion narrowest grounds rule reduces the risk of missing Condorcet winners even though the non-Condorcet outcome-voting rule ensures that the institution satisfies its obligation to resolve cases properly before it.[113] And in Congress, as we have already seen, structure-induced equilibrating rules raise the cost of locating intransitive preferences notwithstanding that institution's power to pass on proposed legislation without formal action.[114] Simply put, the starting point in the development of these rules is substantially informed by the different institutional responsibilities that arise in the event that member preferences are prone to cycling.

B. A MORE DETAILED APPLICATION

We will now set out a more detailed analysis of Arrow's Theorem that ties together several of the concepts developed in this chapter and that provides a basis for future applications of social choice to specific institutions and rules. In Vickrey's simplified proof,[115] Arrow's Theorem establishes that no single institution can simultaneously satisfy four conditions of fairness and ensure collective rationality. We now provide a detailed definition of each of the fairness criteria and link these definitions to the earlier discussion.

Range (and the *Condorcet criterion*): Range requires that when a group is selecting among three options, the outcome be the universal product of a rule that permits all members to rank all three options in any order.[116] This admittedly cryptic sounding condition—one that ensures adherence to the Condorcet criterion—becomes intuitive when we consider an application. For three options *ABC*, there are six potential sets of ordinal rankings. While we can easily list all six (*ABC, ACB, BAC, BCA, CAB, CBA*), mathematically, this is intuitively expressed as three factorial. This means that for the first choice ranking, the decision maker can select among all three options, *ABC*; for the second choice ranking, having already selected one option, the decision maker can select among the remaining two, *AB, AC,* or *BC*. And for the final choice ranking, the decision maker has no choice. Having already selected two of the three options only one remains. Three factorial, or the product of these three choice sets (3x2x1), equals six.

---

113. *See infra* at chapter 7, section I.C.4.

114. *See infra* at chapter 7, section I.C.4.

115. *See* Vickrey, *supra* note 34, at 509–11.

116. For a more detailed discussion of the history of this criterion, see Stearns, *supra* note 1, at 336–37 n.104.

Range has two components, one governing the participants' freedom of choice in ranking options and the other governing the nature of the rule used to combine these rank orderings into a group outcome. Adhering to range requires that each decision maker be permitted to select from any of those potential six combinations of ordinal rankings so that none is off-limits. Range also requires that the decision-making rule select an outcome that honors, and thus that operates consistently with, each member's selection from the various sets of ordinal rankings.

When broken down into these constituent parts, the range criterion appears intuitive. If participants are not permitted to rank all options in the order of their choosing (thus barring selection from all combined ordinal rankings over options), then whoever decides which combined rankings are off-limits can exert disproportionate power relative to the other participants over the ultimate decision. It is for that reason that adhering to range furthers democratic norms. We have already seen some examples. Recall that in a group with non-Condorcet-winning preferences (P1: *ABC*, P2: *BCA*, P3: *CAB*), a regime that permits unlimited pairwise voting will disclose a cycle, such that *ApBpCpA*. If, instead, range is restricted so that the ranking *CAB* is off limits, then out of the six potential ordinal rankings (*ABC*, *ACB*, *BAC*, *BCA*, *CAB*, *CBA*), P3 might select *CBA*, the only remaining option that ranks *C* first. If the remaining preferences are unaffected, then *B* would emerge the winner as against *A* and *C*, even though with the true ordinal rankings disclosed, *A* defeats *B*. If given the power, P2 might exclude ranking *CAB* because doing so is likely to produce a voting path leading to his preferred outcome, *B*, although it does so at the expense of P3 who ranks *C* first and *B* last. Notice that in this example, excluding *CAB* effectively prevents option *A* from winning even though that is the only option capable of defeating *B*.

In two important institutional contexts, the range criterion is relaxed as a means of ensuring collective outcomes even when members hold preferences that cycle. As we have already seen, in selecting committee chairs, parliamentary rules avoid motion-and-amendment procedures in favor of plurality voting. This non-Condorcet rule effectively violates range by disallowing the necessary final pairwise comparison to disclose that when all relevant binary comparisons are considered, the members' preferences cycle. In effect, some members are prevented by vote orders from expressing preferences for all candidates in any order of their choosing, thus relaxing range. To paraphrase George Orwell, when range is relaxed some person's votes are more equal than others.[117]

Appellate courts also relax range to meet their collective obligation to resolve properly docketed cases even when judicial preferences cycle. The Supreme Court's collective obligation to produce a judgment in a case that is properly before it, for example, prevents the Court from employing a

---

117. GEORGE ORWELL, ANIMAL FARM 88 (Alfred A. Knopf 1993) (1946) ("All animals are equal, but some animals are more equal than others.").

case decision rule that satisfies the Condorcet criterion.[118] A regime of unlimited pairwise comparisons by majority rule, for example, has the potential to produce a collective impasse. This does not mean, of course, that the Supreme Court must *always* produce a judgment, as, for example, when it determines that *certiorari* has been granted improvidently or when a case is remanded in light of a recently issued governing case. But even then it must affirmatively select a method of disposition taking the form of collective action. In addition, the Court is not obligated to resolve issues in the manner preferred by the litigants. More broadly, appellate courts generally lack the degree of agenda control that the Supreme Court exercises through its power of certiorari. Even in the Supreme Court, however, each decision-making juncture—from deciding whether to decide a case, to deciding whether a case is justiciable, to deciding the merits of a case—requires some formal, if *de minimis*, collective institutional decision. In the event that judicial preferences cycled, a regime that adhered to range would instead threaten an impasse. As we will demonstrate in more detail in the chapter on the judiciary,[119] the rule requiring an odd number of Supreme Court justices to vote on the judgment almost always ensures an outcome in the case even though the justices might hold preferences over the combination of possible rationales that when aggregated reveal a cycle.

In contrast, as we have seen, various legislative practices allow Congress to remain inert when members discover preferences that cycle. While range thus marks an important distinction between rules employed in appellate courts and legislatures, including the Supreme Court and Congress, this does not mean that legislative preferences endlessly cycle. In Congress, the combination of structure-induced equilibrating rules and logrolling, which allows members to register intensities of preference, generate equilibrium results.[120] Even with these combined institutional arrangements, Congressional rules prove more resilient in satisfying the Condorcet criterion than do those in the Supreme Court. Through informal means, members of Congress have the capacity to locate Condorcet winners even when formal rules appear to limit all necessary binary comparisons over options. When stakes are sufficiently high, members of Congress can negotiate outside formal voting and thus reveal preferences that encourage inaction or discourage adverse voting paths. In contrast with the Supreme Court, which is generally obligated to issue judgments in cases properly before it, Congress has no parallel obligation to even vote as an institution on each bill that is proposed. Instead, Congress allows countless legislative proposals never to become bills and the vast majority of bills that are proposed simply to die.

In addition, Congressional practices sometimes improve the quality of outputs by avoiding the Condorcet criterion in favor of other norms.

---

118. Once again, we will also see that companion rules emerge that allow the Court, once it has formally decided a case, to increase the likelihood that among the opinions offered, the one that expresses the holding is a Condorcet winner.

119. *See infra* chapter 7.

120. *See* Maxwell L. Stearns, *The Public Choice Case Against the Item Veto,* 49 Wash. & Lee L. Rev. 385, 397–98 (1992). Such devices include elaborate committee structures, bicameralism, filibusters, and formal limits on the number of permissible amendments for pending legislation. *See supra* at chapter 2, section III.A.

Remember that the Condorcet criterion does not account for intensities of preference. In a group with the following ordinal preferences, P1: *ABC*; P2: *BCA*; and P3: *CBA*, while *B* is the Condorcet winner, it might also be an inferior social alternative to another option, for example *C*. If, for example, P1 is nearly indifferent among all options, she might happily forego voting for *B* in a contest with *C*, thus allowing *C* to prevail, in exchange for the support of P2, who least prefers option *A*, in some other matter. Thus, through the commodification of preferences, legislators sometimes produce results that, while thwarting the Condorcet criterion, are nonetheless beneficial for all participants to the exchange.[121]

Unanimity and *Independence of Irrelevant Alternatives*: Unanimity is defined as follows: "If an individual preference is unopposed by any contrary preference of any other individual, this preference is preserved in the social ordering."[122] While unanimity is equivalent to the efficiency criterion of *Pareto superiority*, introduced in chapter 2, the different contexts in which these terms apply have the potential to invite some confusion. Within the study of private markets, a move from the status quo to an alternative state is defined as *Pareto superior* if it benefits at least one participant without harming others. An outcome is *Pareto optimal* if no further *Pareto superior* moves are available, meaning that all potential welfare-improving moves have already taken place. At this point, any further changes from the existing allocation of resources will necessarily have distributional consequences, benefiting some at the expense of others.

Welfare economists generally regard private markets as uniquely suited to producing wealth by facilitating *Pareto superior* transactions. When an individual purchases food from a supermarket, the buyer values the food more than the money and the supermarket values the money more than the food; if not, the transaction would not take place. If we set aside such problems as initial wealth endowments and externalities, and assume away illegal or coercive tactics such as fraud or duress, then it is a fair supposition that market transactions are the product of unanimous consent. Because people voluntarily engage in market exchange, it is also fair to assume that they do so with the intent to improve their position. Private market exchanges are thus likely to improve the utility of at least one, and probably both, of the affected parties to the resulting exchange.[123] Otherwise they would not have bothered.[124]

The difficulty with applying the *Pareto* criterion in the context of lawmaking is that mutually assented-to trades in legislatures, or *logroll-*

---

121. Of course this does not mean it is helpful to society. *See infra* pp. 145–50 (discussing tension between unanimity in legislatures and markets).

122. DENNIS C. MUELLER, PUBLIC CHOICE II, at 385 (1989). For a discussion of the origin of this condition, see STEARNS, *Misguided Renaissance*, *supra* note 1, at 88–92, 347–49 nn.112–130.

123. Exchange is one of two mechanisms for wealth creation; the other, of course, is production.

124. Thus, price theory is conceptually an adjunct to the theory of social choice, rather than the other way around. *See* James M. Buchanan, *Social Choice, Democracy and Free Markets*, 62 J. POL. ECON. 114 (1954).

ing, has the potential to inhibit wealth producing private market exchange. As Oliver Wendell Holmes famously observed, "[r]egulation means the prohibition of something."[125] Regardless of the wisdom of the underlying regulatory policy, legislation that restricts private market transactions elevates legislative unanimity over private market unanimity. For most regulatory policies to succeed, they must inhibit at least some potential *Pareto superior* private market transactions. Conversely, constitutional doctrines that invalidate such regulation elevate private market unanimity (or *Pareto superiority)* over legislative unanimity.[126]

Does this analysis help to explain the tradeoffs discussed in chapter 2 in the doctrinal transformation from *Lochner v. New York*,[127] decided in 1905, to *West Coast Hotel Co. v. Parrish*,[128] decided in 1937? Is the social choice analysis of these doctrines consistent or in tension with the implications of interest group theory? Why?

An extensive public choice literature posits that legislative processes at both the federal and state levels are systematically biased in favor of regulatory policies that tend to undermine private market efficiency.[129] Recall that in his article, *Does Interest Group Theory Justify More Intrusive Judicial Review?*, Einer Elhauge posited that interest group theory itself cannot answer whether interest group involvement in legislative processes is excessive because one must first apply a normative baseline concerning the proper extent of interest group influence.[130] Does social choice theory do better in the sense of providing the basis for comparing among alternative normative baselines? Why or why not?

Independence of Irrelevant Alternatives: To fully appreciate unanimity, we must now introduce another Arrovian fairness condition, namely *Independence of Irrelevant Alternatives*. The criterion is defined as follows: "The social choice between any two alternatives must depend only on the orderings of individuals over these two alternatives, and not on their ordering over other alternatives."[131] Independence thus requires that each

---

125.   Hammer v. Dagenhart, 247 U.S. 251, 277 (1918) (Holmes, J., dissenting).

126.   To be clear, legislative decision making usually requires approval by majority rule, and not unanimous legislative consent. The unanimity criterion, however, does not apply at the level of final legislative approval, but rather at the level of individual exchanges that occur during the process of logrolling. For this reason, private market transactions actually proceed with a lower level of social consensus than legislative transactions. When two private market actors unanimously transact business, barring any legal prohibitions to the deal, the exchange proceeds. There is no need for additional consent by other market participants. In contrast, when two legislators engage in a logroll through their unanimous consent, that exchange acquires no force unless and until it is ratified by several majority voting procedures that incorporate it into a successful bill that the President then signs or vetoes. The level at which the unanimity criterion is applied in the two settings, however, is not the ratification of the exchange (or of the vote trade) but rather the exchange or vote trade itself.

127.   198 U.S. 45 (1905).

128.   300 U.S. 379 (1937).

129.   For one of the leading articles, see Peter H. Aranson, Ernest Gellhorn & Glen O. Robinson, *A Theory of Legislative Delegation*, 68 CORNELL L. REV. 1 (1982).

130.   Elhauge, *supra* note 47, at 101–08. For a more detailed analysis of Elhauge's argument, see MAXWELL L. STEARNS, PUBLIC CHOICE AND PUBLIC LAW: READINGS AND COMMENTARY 246–53 (1997).

131.   MUELLER, *supra* note 122, at 386; *see also* STEARNS, *supra* note 1, at 89 & n.119. For a discussion of the origins of this condition, see STEARNS, *supra* note 1, at 89–92, 349 n.130.

decision maker base her choice between each pair of presented alternatives solely upon the relative merits of those alternatives, without strategic considerations. Prohibited strategies can include trying to anticipate, and thus derail, a disfavored voting path by voting other than for one's first choice as needed to prevent an adverse outcome, or trying to improve one's utility through vote trading.

The independence criterion might well be the most counterintuitive and, indeed, controversial, of Arrow's fairness assumptions. The objection to independence can be expressed quite simply: If you or some other decision maker are influenced in selecting between options A and B by the presence (or absence) of option C, who is to say that C is irrelevant to your decision such that you should make your choice as between A and B as if you lacked this additional information? Despite this objection, both Condorcet and Arrow embraced independence, albeit for different reasons. Condorcet's intuition proves significant to evaluating Congress, while Arrow's intuition proves significant in evaluating the Supreme Court.

While range is generally relaxed in the Supreme Court in order to promote the Court's ability to ensure collective judgments in each case, it is generally honored in Congress, which has the power to remain inert when preferences cycle or to commodify preferences when cyclical preferences fail to capture the real stakes due to different preference intensities. The intuition underlying Arrovian independence is largely opposite. Subject to a caveat described below, Supreme Court Justices are generally presumed to adhere to independence, while members of Congress are understood to regularly violate independence.

Influenced by the republican philosopher, Jean–Jacques Rousseau, Condorcet proposed that in choosing among options, legislators should focus solely upon the merits of presented alternatives so that in each successive contest, better options are selected, until the best option emerges.[132] By Condorcet's understanding, individuals, upon entering the public sphere either as legislators or as voters, are expected to subordinate their personal objectives in favor of their assessment of the best interest of society.[133] In contrast, Arrow's intuition is not as obviously influenced by republican philosophy as by foundational assumptions of welfare economics. For Arrow, independence was necessary to avoid the difficulty that economists recognized in devising a system to allow government regulators to assess and weigh interpersonal utilities.[134] Of course in markets,

---

132. *See* Stearns, *supra* note 1, at 1250 n.108 (discussing Rousseau's influence on Condorcet and collecting authorities).

133. Keith Michael Baker, Condorcet: From Natural Philosophy to Social Mathematics 230 (1975) ("All men, Rousseau and Condorcet agreed, have the right to follow their own opinion. But reason dictates that on entering political society, they consent to submit to the general will—or, in Condorcet's phrase, 'the common reason'—those of their actions that must be governed for all according to the same principles.").

134. *See* Mueller, *supra* note 67, at 591 ("It was the desire to establish a welfare function that was not based upon interpersonal utility comparisons that first motivated Arrow."); Gary Lawson, *Efficiency and Individualism*, 42 Duke L.J. 53, 61 & n.26 (1992) (citing economists and legal scholars for the proposition that "it is impossible to make interpersonal comparisons of

individuals routinely signal their own relative utility through their willingness to pay, or what economists label "revealed preferences."[135] Indeed, to that extent, social choice theory provides a basis for understanding the comparative advantage of markets, at least under standard assumptions including no externalities and no coercion or duress, relative to other institutions in the creation of wealth. The problem that Arrow confronted was in seeking to develop a rule-making system that that lacked a pricing mechanism to allow expression of cardinal utility. The difficulty is that absent such a mechanism, systems that seek to quantify and compare interpersonal utilities are likely to invite posturing or other forms of strategic behavior. Does this help to explain the difficulties with the chocolate or vanilla cake hypothetical that opened this chapter? If so, how?

The unanimity and independence criteria operate in tension. Unanimity encourages methods that discover cardinal values and individual strategies that enhance individual utility. Independence demands nonstrategic or principled decision making without regard to effect on eventual outcomes. Within legislatures, individual legislators can vote sincerely or can enter into unanimous exchanges, or logrolls, thus voting strategically rather than sincerely on the merits of each proposal. The logrolling process demands careful attention to voting agendas and considerable foresight about the relationships between future options and immediate decisions. Effective legislating demands such vote trading and strategizing. Thus, while logrolling promotes unanimity, it thwarts independence.

---

utility" (internal citations omitted)). Consider also Robin West's discussion of interpersonal utility comparisons:

> As many modern moral philosophers have argued, and as (nonlegal) economists generally concede: we can make these comparisons, and we do make these comparisons, every day. We can sympathize with one person's subjective grief and another's subjective annoyance, compare the two subjective experiences, and decide the former is of greater weight, magnitude, intensity, and importance than the latter, even when neither subjective experience is reflected in a contract, a vote, or a price. We can even make comparisons of the intensity of that most arbitrary of subjective experiences, namely culinary taste: we might compare Johnny's revulsion to the taste of candy with Susan's indifference and decide that Johnny hates the candy more than Susan likes the bubble gum. We can do this even if neither party has committed to the trade.... We look at Johnny's scrunched-up face, and we share with him a pale version of his nauseous reaction to what is causing his physical response.

Robin L. West, *Taking Preferences Seriously*, 64 TUL. L. REV. 659, 683–84 (1990).

Of course Professor West is correct that individuals routinely make such comparisons. She is also correct that in assessing observed preferences, we actually do share a "pale version of" the other person's emotional reaction. For an accessible discussion, see Sandra Blakeslee, *Cells that Read Minds*, N.Y. TIMES, Jan. 10, 2006, at F1 (reviewing literature on mirror neurons). The concern Arrow and other economists have expressed however is that virtually any regulatory regime that includes preference intensities will invite strategic behavior among participants. Notice that West's familiar illustration (at least for those with children), involves the revelation of preferences after the fact that caused the sincere reaction. When asking children to select among several choices for dinner, each of which is one child's favorite, would we expect comparable expressions of candor to Johnny's unplanned "scrunched-up face." Why or why not? Notice also that the larger the regulatory stakes, the greater the incentives for such strategic behavior. Is this an adequate response to West? Why or why not? Is her argument an adequate response to Arrow's inclusion of Independence? Why or why not?

135. For discussions of revealed preferences, see John Beshears et al., *How Are Preferences Revealed?*, 92 J. PUB. ECON. 1787 (2008); Irina Georgescu, *On the Notion of Dominance of Fuzzy Choice Functions & Its Application in Multicriteria Decision Making*, in SYMBOLIC & QUANTITATIVE APPROACHES TO REASONING WITH UNCERTAINTY 257 (Lluís Godo ed., 2005); P.A. Samuelson, *A Note on the Pure Theory of Consumer's Behaviour*, ECONOMICA, Feb. 1938, at 61.

Conversely, norms against strategic judicial voting promote independence (an element of principled voting) at the price of sacrificing potentially unanimous vote trades that would improve the likelihood of ruling closer to the ideal point of the participating jurists.[136]

Legal academics commonly presuppose that judges engage in principled, rather than strategic, decision making.[137] And yet this raises a puzzle. Are appellate judges somehow less well equipped than legislators to engage in a process of vote trading? Appellate courts have substantially fewer members than most legislative bodies and the judges acquire substantial information regarding each others' preferences, and anticipate repeated rounds of play. Given that the circumstances are ripe for enforcing agreements, it is not difficult to imagine incorporating a judicial custom or norm that would facilitate some form of judicial logrolling. And yet, even in as high-stakes a context as the Supreme Court, documented instances of vote trading across cases, or even across issues within cases, are rare or nonexistent.[138]

To be sure, recent studies of the papers of retired Supreme Court Justices demonstrate that individual justices sometimes change their votes between their initial case assessments, as indicated in their preliminary post-argument conference votes, and the final case dispositions.[139] This tends to happen when justices need to compromise to secure a majority, without which the case would produce a holding but not establish a precedent. The result is often to produce a narrower holding, quite possibly a Condorcet winner, than the preferred broader holding for the justice making the compromise.[140]

How does this behavior relate to the Arrovian independence and unanimity? For example, do these judicial strategies contravene Arrovian independence in the same manner as logrolling in Congress? Can you identify relevant similarities and relevant differences? Are there specific judicial practices or norms that temper judicial opportunities for extreme vote-trading behavior, thus violating unanimity? Why is there so little, if any, evidence of Supreme Court Justices actually trading votes across cases or over issues within cases? Is it significant that appellate court judges, in contrast with legislators voting for bills, accompany their decisions with written statements (often published ones) explaining the basis for decision? Where does the presumption favoring written opinions in appellate courts come from?[141] Why do we not see members of Congress

---

136. *But cf.* COOTER, *supra* note 79, at 205–09 (presenting games in which jurists could improve the likelihood of achieving preferred policies within and across cases through vote trading).

137. *See, e.g.*, Lewis A. Kornhauser & Lawrence G. Sager, *The One and the Many: Adjudication in Collegial Courts*, 81 CAL. L. REV. 1 (1993).

138. For an informative discussion of Justice Powell's rejection of an overture for a vote trade by Justice Brennan, see JOHN C. JEFFRIES, JR., JUSTICE LEWIS F. POWELL, JR. 303–04 (1994).

139. *See generally* EPSTEIN & KNIGHT, *supra* note 79.

140. For a general discussion, see Maxwell L. Stearns, *The Case for Including* Marks v. United States *in the Canon of Constitutional Law*, 17 CONST. COMMENT. 321 (2000).

141. Of course there are notable exceptions to the norm of published opinions, and the resulting practices have been the subject of academic criticism. *See, e.g.*, William M. Richman &

justifying their votes in writing? Would requiring such statements be a good idea? Why or why not? Does the contrary practice suggest that legislators sometimes, or often, vote for or against proposed legislation for reasons *other than* a principled commitment to the cause? Should proposals to shift decision-making responsibility between these two institutions take account of these very different institutional norms?[142]

To the extent that there is a tension between unanimity and independence, which criterion is more important? Is it possible to answer that question outside a specific institutional context? Why or why not? If not, what does that suggest about the Arrow's Theorem conditions?

Nondictatorship: Nondictatorship is defined as follows: "No individual enjoys a position such that whenever he expresses a preference between two alternatives and all other individuals express an opposite preference, his preference is always preserved in the social ordering."[143] Nondictatorship appears the most obvious fairness condition in any collective decision-making institution. In fact, however, Arrow's Theorem proves that to preserve transitive orderings in a system that meets the other fairness conditions set out above, it is inevitable that someone be vested not merely with substantially disproportionate decisional authority, but also with authority that violates nondictatorship. While we do not suggest that all justices and all members of Congress have equal power in their respective institutions, as a formal matter both institutions satisfy the nondictatorship criterion.[144] By this we mean that while institutional practices vest disproportionate power in particular members, based for example on seniority status, these customs or rules do not give decisive significance to one participant at the expense of the contrary preferences of all members, at least not all of the time. And thus, no dictator's contrary preference is consistently preserved in the social ordering.

That said, it is worth discussing the occasional unequal power distributions within these institutions. In the Supreme Court, as in most appellate courts, the Chief Justice (or in the case of the federal circuits, the chief judge) truly is the first among equals in terms of the weight attached to his or her vote.[145] Even so, the Chief Justice does possess a significant source of disproportionate power, which occasionally vests to

---

William L. Reynolds, *Elitism, Expediency, and the New Certiorari: Requiem for the Learned Hand Tradition*, 81 CORNELL L. REV. 273 (1996) (criticizing the trend away from written opinions in all cases as unjust); Erica S. Weisgerber, Note, *Unpublished Opinions: A Convenient Means to an Unconstitutional End*, 97 GEO. L.J. 621, 626 (2009) (arguing that unpublished opinions written in the interests of efficiency are "of lesser quality"). Even unpublished slip opinions are accompanied by a judgment and thus a collective action on the part of the deciding court.

142. For a discussion of the role of published opinions as inhibiting vote trading, see STEARNS, *supra* note 1, at 92.

143. For a discussion of the origins of this condition, see *id.*, at 92–94, 339 n.130.

144. Of course Arrow's Corollary means that another condition is necessarily violated in each institution.

145. Compare, for example, this power to that of the Vice President in his capacity as President Pro Tem of the Senate, under which in the event of a tie, he casts the deciding vote.

other senior members of majority coalitions. When the Chief Justice votes with the majority, he assigns the opinion; when the Chief Justice votes in dissent, the senior Justice voting with the majority assigns the opinion.[146] While this practice does not violate nondictatorship, the power differential raises important questions.[147] More obviously, a minority of four is given power to control the Court's docket through the writ of *certiorari*. This also does not defy Arrovian nondictatorship because the Rule of Four, which governs the grant of *certiorari*, does not vest the same four justices with power over all certiorari petitions against the contrary will of the Court.[148] Those in a successful minority of four in one round might well find themselves in the unsuccessful majority of five in the next. Setting these practices aside, Supreme Court justices generally hold equal voting power.

Within Congress, the various structures that allow individual members to block legislation afford such members disproportionate power relative to their colleagues. While each member has an equal vote as a formal matter, Congress effectively allows some members to exert more power than their nominal votes might otherwise suggest. But here too, the power is not unlimited. As discussed above, in the event that a committee chair abuses his or her power, other members can engage in a variety of retaliatory measures intended to limit such abuses in the future.

IV. CONCLUDING COMMENTS AND SUMMARY

As stated above, the whole of Arrow's Theorem is greater than the sum of its parts. Even if one or more individual criteria are normatively suspect, the Theorem provides a framework for analyzing and comparing institutions in a manner that avoids the nirvana fallacy. It does so by demonstrating the ability of a given institution to relax criteria that are inessential to—or that might actually harm—its functioning. Table 3:2 summarizes the preceding discussion and analysis.[149] As you read the applications that follow in the remainder of this book, consider the implications of Arrow's Theorem and of Arrow's Corollary as a means of gaining insight into the relevant institutions and rules.

---

146. Saul Brenner & Harold J. Spaeth, *Majority Opinion Assignments and the Maintenance of the Original Coalition on the Warren Court*, 32 AM. J. POL. SCI. 72 (1988).

147. For example, the practice violates the Anonymity criterion of May's Theorem, *see supra* note 16, and cite therein.

148. For a general discussion, see Maxwell L. Stearns, *The Rule of Four*, *in* 4 ENCYCLOPEDIA OF THE SUPREME COURT OF THE UNITED STATES 298 (David S. Tanenhaus ed., 2008).

149. STEARNS, *supra* note 1, at 93 tbl.2.4.

Table 3:2. The Supreme Court and

Congress through an Arrovian Lens

Arrovian Criterion	Supreme Court	Congress
Range	Collective obligation to produce results prevents the Supreme Court from employing Condorcet-producing rules.	Collective ability to remain inert has allowed Congressional rules coupled with informal practices to evolve toward Condorcet criterion. In addition, cardinalization of preferences enables members of Congress to achieve collectively rational results while occasionally thwarting the Condorcet criterion.
Unanimity	Vote trading is inhibited in the Supreme Court by publication of written opinions and judgment-based decision making.	Vote trading is encouraged, thus producing *Pareto superior* legislative exchanges, which potentially undermine private market efficiency.
Independence of Irrelevant Alternatives	Judgment-based decision making and publication of written opinions raise the costs of strategic voting among justices; strategic interactions that remain are generally toward median position on the Court and operate along single-dimensional scale within individual cases.	Congressmen regularly vote strategically, thus cardinalizing their preferences over issues and bills.
Nondictatorship	Generally adhered to, opinion assignment power and power of certiorari provide occasional disproportionate power to minorities on the Court.	Compromised by practices that afford disproportionate power to committee chairs and to individual congressmen, limited by informal quasi-market checks when the stakes are high.
Condorcet Criterion	Evolution of important rules, including outcome voting and stare decisis are attributable to the Court's ability to employ Condorcet-producing rules. These rules should be evaluated in conjunction with companion rules, e.g., the narrowest grounds rule and standing, which help to improve the Court's overall rationality and fairness.	Important congressional voting rules have evolved toward Condorcet criterion, except when Congress lacks the power to remain inert, including, in selecting legislative leaders. Some limited rules appear to defy Condorcet criterion, but common voting practices provide quasi-market solution, thus restoring Condorcet criterion when stakes are high.

V. CASE AND STATUTORY ILLUSTRATIONS

The applications in this chapter examine the phenomenon of cycling as it relates to American bankruptcy law. Cycling over bankruptcy law potentially arises in two different contexts. First, Professor David Skeel has argued that the history of federal bankruptcy law in the United States illustrates the phenomenon of cycling. During the nineteenth century, Skeel argues, Congress cycled over whether the country should have a permanent national bankruptcy law. For much of the nineteenth century, Skeel maintains, there was no stable majority coalition in support of a permanent bankruptcy law. Instead, temporary coalitions formed during periods of national financial crisis, but once the crisis passed, the coalition in support of bankruptcy legislation would also lapse. Every state, however, had its own system of debtor-creditor laws, so that in the absence of a national bankruptcy law, debtor-creditor relations were governed by state laws. In 1898 Congress enacted a new bankruptcy law for the first time, that turned out to be permanent. The Bankruptcy Code that exists today is a direct descendent of the 1898 Bankruptcy Act. We will refer to the history that surrounds this legislation as a "macro" analysis of bankruptcy law.

Second, we look at the phenomenon of potential cycling *within* bankruptcy cases. The process of a successful Chapter 11 reorganization eventually culminates in the proposal of a plan of reorganization by the debtor, a process that is governed by a variety of complex substantive rules and which creditors and other claimants in the case must vote to approve. The Chapter 11 process itself is potentially susceptible to cycling among creditors. We examine several rules that govern the bankruptcy process to explore the question whether they reflect a concern about the potential for cycling in the contexts that give rise to bankruptcy cases and, if so, whether the bankruptcy rules satisfactorily address those concerns. We can conceive of this aspect of cycling as a "micro" analysis of bankruptcy law.

A. "MACRO" CYCLING: CYCLING OVER PROPOSED BANKRUPTCY LEGISLATION IN THE NINETEENTH CENTURY

The Bust-and-Boom Pattern of Nineteenth–
Century Bankruptcy Legislation[150]

The nineteenth-century bankruptcy debates have long been seen as fitting a loose, bust-and-boom pattern. In times of economic crisis, Congress rushed to pass bankruptcy legislation to alleviate widespread financial turmoil. Once the crisis passed, so too did the need for a federal bankruptcy law. Like Penelope and her weaving, Congress quickly undid its handiwork on each occasion only to start all over again when hard times returned. The traditional account is inaccurate in some respects and, as we will see, it does not explain why bankruptcy suddenly became permanent in 1898. But it provides

---

150. DAVID A. SKEEL, JR., DEBT'S DOMINION: A HISTORY OF BANKRUPTCY LAW IN AMERICA 24–47 (2001) (footnotes omitted).

a convenient framework for describing the first century of bankruptcy debate.

Agitation for bankruptcy legislation rose to a fever pitch at roughly twenty-year intervals throughout the nineteenth century. A depression starting in 1793 led to the first federal bankruptcy law in 1800—an act that Congress repealed three years later. Congress went back to the drawing board in the 1820s, when financial crisis and controversy over the Bank of the United States prompted calls for another bankruptcy law. The debates never came to fruition, however, and it was not until 1841, following the Panic of 1837, that Congress passed its second bankruptcy law. The 1841 act lasted only two years, when defections from the party that had won its passage, the Whigs, led to repeal. The cycle came around once more on the eve of the Civil War, with the Panic of 1857 putting bankruptcy back on the agenda, and setting the stage for the 1867 act. The 1867 act lasted longer than its predecessors, with a movement for repeal leading to an amendment instead in 1874. But by 1878, the nation was once again without a federal bankruptcy law.

All told, then, Congress passed three federal bankruptcy laws prior to 1898: the Bankruptcy Acts of 1800, 1841, and 1867. Together, the acts lasted a total of sixteen years. The absence of a federal bankruptcy law did not leave a complete vacuum in debtor-creditor relations, of course. Most states had insolvency laws on the books. Some of them, like Massachusetts's, predated the Revolution. In times of financial panic, states also responded by passing stay laws imposing moratoria on creditor collection. Proponents of federal bankruptcy legislation emphasized both the wide variation in these laws and their serious constitutional limitations, such as the inability of state law to bind out-of-state debtors.[151]

Skeel explains that today bankruptcy is seen primarily as a device for allowing debtors to discharge debt. Originally, however, one major purpose of federal bankruptcy law in America was to promote a more effective collection of debts, especially interstate collection. The inclusion of the Bankruptcy Clause as an enumerated power of the U.S. Constitution, for instance, was in large part designed to permit Congress to override debtor-friendly laws similar to those enacted by the states under the Articles of Confederation, most notably to protect farmers.[152] Not surprisingly, therefore, substantive views on the propriety of various proposed bankruptcy policies tended to divide based upon geographical region. Skeel writes:

> Because southerners feared that northern creditors would use bankruptcy law as a collection device to displace southern farmers from their homesteads, the strongest opposition to federal bankruptcy came from the South. Many western lawmakers opposed bankruptcy

---

151. *Id.* at 24–25 (footnotes omitted).

152. *See* Todd J. Zywicki, *Bankruptcy, in* THE CONCISE ENCYCLOPEDIA OF ECONOMICS 31 (David R. Henderson ed., 2d ed. 2008), *available at* http://www.econlib.org/library/Enc/Bankruptcy.html.

legislation for similar reasons. Lawmakers from the commercial
northeastern states, by contrast, were much more likely to view
federal bankruptcy legislation as essential to the promotion of commercial enterprise.

In addition to geography, lawmakers' views on bankruptcy also
tended to divide along party lines. The Federalists (later Whigs, and
then Republicans) promoted bankruptcy as essential to the nation's
commercial development. Jeffersonian Republicans (later Democratic
Republicans, and then Democrats), on the other hand, sought a more
agrarian destiny and insisted that bankruptcy legislation would encourage destructive speculation by traders. Northeastern Federalists
were the leading cheerleaders for federal bankruptcy legislation, and
southern and western Jeffersonians were the staunchest opponents.[153]

Skeel argues that the bankruptcy debates of nineteenth-century
America illustrate a phenomenon of legislative cycling:

> I have suggested thus far that the nineteenth-century debates
> pitted opponents of bankruptcy against bankruptcy advocates. In
> actuality, the debates were much more subtle. Rather than two
> positions, lawmakers divided into at least three camps, and sometimes
> more—and these camps crossed party lines. By considering the com-
> peting views in slightly more detail, and by analogizing these views to
> a voting irregularity that political scientists call *cycling*, we can begin
> to see how deeply unstable bankruptcy was for over a hundred years.
>
> ... Daniel Webster, like the famous Supreme Court justice Joseph
> Story, argued for an expansive and permanent federal bankruptcy
> framework. John Calhoun embodied the opposing view that federal
> bankruptcy legislation would be a serious mistake. Not coincidentally,
> Webster was a Whig from a commercial state, Massachusetts, whereas
> Calhoun was a states' rights advocate from the agrarian South.
>
> Senator Henry Clay of Kentucky, a Whig and member along with
> Webster and Calhoun of the "Great Triumvirate" of famous senators,
> represented a third, and similarly influential, view of bankruptcy.
> Clay was willing to support bankruptcy legislation, but only if the law
> was limited to voluntary bankruptcy. Clay shared the fear of many
> bankruptcy opponents that northern creditors would use bankruptcy
> to displace southern farmers from their homesteads, but he believed
> voluntary bankruptcy would minimize this risk while enabling finan-
> cially strapped debtors to obtain relief.
>
> Still other lawmakers adopted variations of these views. Demo-
> crat Thomas Hart Benton, another prominent senator ..., was a
> vocal opponent of bankruptcy. Here, as elsewhere, he frequently
> found himself allied with John Calhoun. But Benton also insisted
> that, if Congress did pass a bankruptcy law, it needed to include

---

153. SKEEL, *supra* note 150, at 26.

corporations as well as individuals. Bankruptcy, in his view, might be one way to [rein] in the excesses of the nation's growing corporate sector.[154]

Skeel describes the story as involving legislative cycling:

A vexing problem when lawmakers (or decision makers of any kind, for that matter) hold a multiplicity of views on a single subject is that their voting may lead to irrational or unstable outcomes. At its extreme, the competing views can lead to the phenomenon of cycling. In a pathbreaking book, the economist Kenneth Arrow demonstrated that no voting institution based on democratic principles can guarantee that voting irregularities of this sort will not arise. If everyone has an equal vote, and every option is available, the voting process may lead to chronically unstable results.

The views of nineteenth-century lawmakers on bankruptcy legislation provide a convenient illustration of the voting problems I have just described. Although the views will be described in stylized form, the overall pattern is not simply hypothetical. The senators I will use for purposes of illustration held views very close to the positions I will attribute to them, and Congress's ever-shifting stances on bankruptcy law in the nineteenth century may well have reflected the kinds of uncertainties we are about to explore.

Assume that three senators, Benton, Webster and Clay, must choose among three options: not passing any bankruptcy law (No Bankruptcy); passing a complete bankruptcy law [that permitted both voluntary and involuntary bankruptcy] (Complete Bankruptcy); or passing a law that permits only voluntary bankruptcy (Voluntary Only). As the careful reader will note, I have omitted a fourth option: providing for involuntary but not voluntary bankruptcy. As it turns out, the 1800 act adopted precisely this approach. Both for simplicity and because involuntary-only disappeared as a viable option by the middle of the nineteenth century, however, I will banish it from our discussion.

Of the three options we are considering, Benton would prefer not to pass any bankruptcy law (No Bankruptcy). If a bankruptcy law must pass, his next choice would be a complete bankruptcy law that included involuntary bankruptcy and brought corporations within its sweep (Complete Bankruptcy). His least favorite alternative is Voluntary Only.

As a fervent nationalist, Daniel Webster strongly favors an expansive bankruptcy law that provides or both voluntary and involuntary bankruptcy (Complete Bankruptcy). So strongly does he believe in the importance of bankruptcy to the health of the national economy that he would accept Voluntary Only bankruptcy as a second choice. His least favorite option is No Bankruptcy.

---

154. *Id.* at 28.

Henry Clay sees voluntary bankruptcy as an opportunity to alleviate the dire financial straits of many of his constituents. But he strongly opposes involuntary bankruptcy, fearing that many debtors who might otherwise recover from their financial distress would be hauled into bankruptcy court by their creditors. Clay's first choice is thus Voluntary Only, his second choice No Bankruptcy, and his last choice Complete Bankruptcy.

Table 3.A.1. Cycling Among Bankruptcy Options in the Nineteenth Century

Senator	First Choice	Second Choice	Third Choice
Benton	No Bankruptcy	Complete Bankruptcy	Voluntary only
Webster	Complete Bankruptcy	Voluntary Only	No Bankruptcy
Clay	Voluntary Only	No Bankruptcy	Complete Bankruptcy

The senators' views are illustrated in [Table 3.A.1]. The problem here is that the senators hold unstable preferences. To see this, consider what would happen if they held a series of [pairwise] votes on [any two of] the three options and each voted in accordance with his [sincerely held] preferences. In a vote between No Bankruptcy and Complete Bankruptcy, the winner would be No Bankruptcy, since both Benton and Clay prefer No Bankruptcy over Complete Bankruptcy. If the Senators then pitted the winner, No Bankruptcy, against Voluntary Only, Voluntary Only would emerge victorious on the strength of votes from Webster and Clay. At this point, Voluntary Only appears to be the winner. But if the senators held a vote between Voluntary Only and Complete Bankruptcy in order to complete the comparisons, both Benton and Webster would vote for Complete Bankruptcy. The senators prefer Complete Bankruptcy over Voluntary Only, but they like Complete Bankruptcy less than another option (No Bankruptcy) that Voluntary Only defeats.

If we were to study the alternatives a bit more closely, we would quickly see that Benton, Webster, and Clay could never choose a stable winner among the three alternatives.... For each option that two of the senators favor, there is always a choice that two of the senators like better. If the senators continued to vote and voted in accordance with their preferences, the votes would [disclose a] cycle.

This kind of voting irregularity can arise in either of two ways. If a group of existing voters hold inconsistent views, cycling can occur at the time of a particular vote, as in the illustration we have just considered. But cycling can also take place intertemporally. Even if a clear majority of legislators held Benton's views today, next year's majority might hold the views I have attributed to Webster; and two years down the road might be a Clay year.

I should emphasize—as several readers of this book emphasized to me—that true cycling only occurs under the restrictive conditions defined in Arrow's Theorem. If lawmakers agreed that one option belongs on the left, one in the center, and one on the right, for instance, their preferences would not be cyclical even if they sharply disagreed about the best choice. In view of this, let me emphasize that the principal point of this section is simply that the multiplicity of views contributed to Congress's inability to reach a stable outcome on federal bankruptcy legislation throughout the nineteenth century. Whether lawmakers' inconstancy reflected true cycling, or merely a garden-variety case of shifting legislative outcomes, the point remains the same.

Moreover, it is quite possible that the bankruptcy debates did indeed reflect true legislative cycling. If legislators hold consistent preferences, they will ordinarily gravitate toward a stable outcome even if there are sharply divergent views on what the outcome should be. Yet no such outcome emerged in the bankruptcy debates until late in the century. One is hard-pressed to think of another legislative issue on which Congress flip-flopped so continuously and for so long. (The closest analogue may be the debates whether to base the currency on gold alone, or to include silver as well; but these debates involved fewer shifts and moved more quickly to a relatively stable outcome.)

Rather than receding, the instability of the bankruptcy debates actually got worse as the century wore on. Ironically, as lawmakers came to see the Bankruptcy Clause as an expansive source of authority, and as this was vindicated by the Supreme Court, Congress's broad powers tended to complicate rather than to simplify it. Although the debates prior to the 1800 act were extremely controversial, most lawmakers viewed themselves as having only two options. They could pass a bill that provided for involuntary bankruptcy, or not pass any bill at all. Because it put more options at lawmakers' disposal— most importantly, the possibility of a Voluntary Only bill—the expanding view of Congress's powers exacerbated the existing instabilities.

From the 1830s on, lawmakers' views were repeatedly splintered among the options we have considered—Complete Bankruptcy, Voluntary Only, and No Bankruptcy—along with variations on these themes. In the twentieth century, Congress has developed institutional structures that can assure stability even in the face of inconsistent preferences. One of these, delegation of gatekeeping authority to a committee, dates back to the early nineteenth century. Because the relevant oversight committee determines whether existing legislation is reconsidered, committees have the power to prevent a new Congress from promptly reversing the enactments of its predecessor. In theory the Judiciary Committee, which has overseen bankruptcy issues since 1821, could have served this purpose. But committees played a less prominent role in the nineteenth century, in part because both Congress and congressional committees operated on a part-time basis. Neither the Judiciary Committee nor any stable block of lawmakers in Congress was in a position to act as agenda setter and provide the kind of stable outcome we see in other contexts where lawmakers hold inconsistent preferences.

Even a brief overview of the debates that led to the 1841 and 1867 acts gives a flavor of the instability that came from the multiplicity of views. The 1841 act was the brainchild of the Whig party, which had made bankruptcy law a crucial plank in the platform that brought them the presidency and control of the Senate the year before. In the face of strong opposition, the Whigs secured the necessary votes for enactment through a controversial log-rolling campaign that obtained votes for bankruptcy in return for votes on a land distribution bill. (Logrolling is another possible solution to cyclical preferences. Rather than voting their true preferences, lawmakers permit one bill to pass in return for a favorable vote on other legislation.)

Even before the bill took effect, a vote to repeal passed the House when a small group of southern Whigs reversed their earlier support for the legislation, and a similar proposal fell only one vote short in the Senate. The defection of several more Whigs, this time from the Midwest, brought the coalition tumbling down. Less than two years after it went into effect, President Tyler (who had assumed the presidency after President Harrison died) signed the repeal legislation and the 1841 act was gone. Just as the initial vote papered over a variety of strident dissenting views, the repeal illustrated just how quickly a majority coalition can collapse when lawmakers' underlying preferences are unstable.

The debates on the 1867 bankruptcy act, which dated back to the early 1860s, were complicated by the onset of the Civil War. When the war finally ended, the Republicans held large majorities in the House and Senate, which strengthened the support for a bankruptcy bill that included involuntary as well as voluntary bankruptcy. Northern lawmakers were particularly concerned that creditors would find it impossible to collect from southern debtors in the southern state courts. Yet a sizable group of lawmakers continued either to resist any bankruptcy legislation, or to insist that only voluntary bankruptcy be included.... Although it lasted longer than either of its predecessors, the 1867 act was deeply unstable from the moment it was enacted. In both 1868 and 1872, lawmakers amended the law to soften its effects on debtors, and a move to repeal it led to further concessions to debtors in 1874. By 1878, the act had few defenders, and it was repealed by large majorities of both parties in both houses.

The 1898 act would bring these instabilities to an end, but each of the competing views remained very much in evidence throughout the deliberations that preceded it.... [I]n debates that began in 1881 and spanned almost two decades, the Senate voted for ... Complete Bankruptcy in 1884, as did the House in 1890 and 1896, and Complete Bankruptcy finally prevailed in 1898 in the form of the 1898 act. Proponents of Voluntary Only bankruptcy ... also had their moments, as the House passed a Voluntary Only bill in 1894, and the Senate passed a somewhat similar bill before agreeing to Complete Bankruptcy in 1898. Throughout this time, opponents of bankruptcy managed (sometimes on the merits, sometimes because Congress ran out of time to act) to preserve the No Bankruptcy status quo.[155]

In 1898 Congress finally enacted a bankruptcy law that, with several major overhauls, has remained a permanent piece of legislation. Thus, the 1898 legislation brought an end to the century of legislative turmoil that had frustrated the enactment of a permanent bankruptcy law in the nineteenth century. As Skeel explains:

Most of us have childhood memories of a game called musical chairs. In musical chairs, children walk around a circle of chairs as long as the music continues to play. When the music stops, they scramble to sit in the chairs. There are enough chairs for all but one child. With each round of music, the child who fails to grab a seat is eliminated, until finally, when only two children and one seat remain, one child emerges at the winner.

By now, the similarity between musical chairs and the nineteenth-century bankruptcy debates should be obvious. The principal difference was that, rather than one game of musical chairs, the debates became an endless series of such games. The winning alternative one year might give rise to a new approach the next. When the music stopped in 1898, there was no obvious reason to believe the circling was over—that Complete Bankruptcy had won out for good. But it had.[156]

Skeel then asks, "Why, after a century of legislative turmoil, did Congress finally enact a permanent bankruptcy law in 1898?"[157]

Skeel identifies several factors that help to explain the stability of the 1898 legislation in contrast with its predecessors. First, the later half of the nineteenth century saw a dramatic growth in the number of commercial trade groups throughout the United States. These groups both benefited from and encouraged the continuing development of interstate commerce. This included an increasing recognition of the value of an integrated set of commercial laws, including bankruptcy laws. In particular, Skeel notes that "Merchants who engaged in interstate commerce complained bitterly and repeatedly that debtors played favorites when they

155. *Id.* at 28–33.
156. *Id.* at 35.
157. *Id.*

ran into financial trouble. The favorites [took the form of selective payments to] family members and local creditors, not [to] out-of-state merchants."[158] Merchants engaged in interstate commerce and the trade associations they comprised strongly urged Congress to enact a national bankruptcy law to ease these problems of interstate debt-collection and to thereby spur further commercial development. While these commercial interests played a major role in the ultimate success of the 1898 bankruptcy law, the final compromise that the act embodied reflects a balance of commercial interests with those of local agrarian communities and other groups that provided a countervailing set of pro-debtor interests. The stability of the eventual 1898 compromise legislation was enhanced by the long term Republican control of the Presidency, including the elections of President McKinley in 1898 and of Theodore Roosevelt in 1902 and 1906, and Republican control of Congress until 1910.

According to Skeel, the most important factor bringing about the permanence of the 1898 act was the growth of a specialized bankruptcy bar to administer the new system, a development that was triggered by the massive railroad reorganizations of the late-nineteenth and early-twentieth centuries. In short, bankruptcy lawyers had the incentive, organization, and political influence to retain a permanent bankruptcy law that earlier coalitions of interest groups had difficulty procuring in the first place. The bankruptcy bar exerted continuing influence by affecting a lawyer-centered litigation system that stands in stark contrast with the more typical administrative bankruptcy systems that characterize most western legal systems. This influence, Skeel notes, is reinforced by the historical accident that jurisdiction over bankruptcy law is in the Judiciary Committee of Congress, rather than such other committees as Banking or Financial Services. Lawyers are repeat players before the Judiciary Committee, thus possessing potentially greater influence there than would likely be the case on other subject-driven committees. On the Financial Services Committee, for example, banking interests are likely to exert comparatively greater influence than the organized bar. Finally, during the course of the twentieth century, bankruptcy law came to be seen as a highly technical, largely non-ideological area of law. This understanding of bankruptcy reinforced the influence of bankruptcy lawyers on the legislative process by allowing them to couch their recommendations in terms of nonpartisan technical advice. In reality, as Skeel notes, bankruptcy lawyers have an incentive to increase the scope of bankruptcy law along with the expense and complexity of bankruptcy procedures, as has been consistent with historical developments throughout the twentieth century.

To a certain extent, the observations about bankruptcy legislation are generalizable. Saul Levmore has argued more generally, for example, that the presence of legislative cycles might increase the influence of interest groups on the legislative process, and in fact, might help promote the formation of interest groups.[159] Levmore explains:

---

158. *Id.* at 36.

159. Saul Levmore, *Voting Paradoxes and Interest Groups*, 28 J. LEGAL STUD. 259 (1999).

Interest groups act where there are cycling majorities or other aggregation anomalies and, therefore, where there are excellent opportunities to influence agenda setters or to bargain for the formation of winning coalitions. Instability attracts political activity.[160]

The presence of underlying preferences that are susceptible of cycling, Levmore explains, suggests that legislative outcomes are often determined by "procedures and institutions," such as the presence of those with agenda-setting power or the structure of voting rules, "rather than coherent or stable majority preferences." Where this is the case, he argues, "Political activity is a relatively attractive investment."[161] Levmore provides two explanations:

> First, participation and subsequent investment may be most profitable when victory does not require overcoming a clear or stable majority winner.... As contributors and political entrepreneurs evaluate investments, it is likely to turn out that many of the best available projects are those in which costs are low because procedures, rather than underlying preferences, need to be influenced. This approach stresses a rational, or expected-value, calculation by contributors and groups.
>
> A second approach makes room for quasi-rational actors who choose strategies that might plausibly advance their ends efficiently, but in settings where there is insufficient pressure to root out imperfect strategies.... [I]mperfectly informed interest groups might invest where the probability of victory (rather than its expected value) is high—and ... where there is no stable winner the chance of bargaining for victory or influencing the agenda setter is greatest.
>
> If the focus is, instead, on the imperfect and expensive information citizens have about their political agents, then interest groups can be understood as sensibly investing in influencing politicians where these politicians can be influenced without upsetting their less-organized constituents. The idea is that interest groups might invest where their successes would not arouse suspicion by dispersed majorities or by other forces that might be motivated to diminish the power of interest groups in the longer run by changing various rules or political institutions. It seems likely that an interest group would have more trouble gaining for its members something that a majority of the citizenry (or legislature) unambiguously opposes than it would have extracting a law or subsidy that did not appeal to any absolute majority of the relevant voters but that was not opposed by a clear majority. The suggested link between cycling and rent seeking can therefore be seen in agency terms. It is more difficult to monitor an agent when the baseline for what to expect of the agent, or institution of which the agent is a part, is unclear. If an organized group seeks to capture an agent who controls the agenda of a legislative assembly,

---

160. *Id.* at 259.

161. *Id.* at 261.

for example, it might succeed most easily when there is no stable, majoritarian winner because the principals do not know what to expect of an uncorrupted assembly. Without this sort of baseline expectation it will be difficult to know when the assembly has been influenced in a manner contrary to its legal obligations or principals' preferences.[162]

Thus, Levmore concludes that in general:

[A]n interest group will invest more where procedure determines outcome, but it may invest either less or yet more depending on whether it also expects to be opposed by a competing organized group. Where there is no Condorcet winner and there is a competing organization, the probability of victory drops (compared to the case where there is no organized competition) but the likelihood of a loss increases if one does nothing. My secondary conjecture is that one should find increased investment where there is no Condorcet winner, regardless of expected opposition.[163]

In addition to Levmore's observations, Todd Zywicki argues that Skeel's historical discussion of the crucial role played by bankruptcy lawyers in ensuring the permanence of the American bankruptcy law in 1898 explains another link between legislative cycling and interest group activity.[164] Most of the primary actors in the legislative process, such as creditors, debtors (such as farmers), and corporate management, were willing to offer *conditional* support for a permanent bankruptcy system. Specifically, their support was conditioned on the superiority of the proposed regime to a continuation of the No Bankruptcy regime, meaning the continued reliance on state law over related matters of debt collection and debtor relief. As has been seen, during the nineteenth century, it was often the case that various groups preferred no bankruptcy system to the particular systems that were imposed during various economic crises.

Bankruptcy lawyers, in contrast, had an overriding preference for the maintenance of a bankruptcy system *as an end in itself*. Bankruptcy lawyers earn their living from bankruptcy filings; thus they have a direct stake in the continued existence of a bankruptcy system. The details of the particular system and the way it treated individual interest groups was (and is) of secondary importance to the mere existence of stable regulatory infrastructure for bankruptcy law that depends in large part for its administration on a developed bankruptcy bar. As a result, the bankruptcy bar served as a sort of residual claimant for the continued existence of the bankruptcy system itself, ensuring that even if legislative cycling or shifting preferences occurred, it did so *within* the accepted framework of the continued existence of some bankruptcy regime rather than taking the form of ongoing proposals to create, or displace, the bankruptcy system in

---

162.   *Id.* at 261–63 (footnote omitted).

163.   *Id.* at 272–73 (footnote omitted).

164.   *See* Todd J. Zywicki, Bankruptcy and Personal Responsibility: Bankruptcy Law and Policy in the Twenty-First Century (forthcoming 2010).

wholesale fashion. Bankruptcy lawyers also prefer a system that produces a greater number of bankruptcy filings and more expensive and complex bankruptcy procedures, goals that became more prominent during subsequent rounds of bankruptcy reforms during the twentieth century.

In 2005, Congress passed a comprehensive bankruptcy reform law that tempered some of the highly pro-debtor elements of the 1978 Code. Todd Zywicki has argued that the balance struck in this legislation can be explained by Skeel's basic model of an interaction between creditors, bankruptcy lawyers, and ideology.[165] In 2005, Zywicki argues, these same forces were present but the balance was struck differently. Most importantly, the Republican takeover of Congress in 1994 shifted the ideological center of gravity in Congress away from the debtor-friendly orientation of the past to a new focus on personal financial responsibility. Zywicki observes that the Republican Party is also generally tied less closely to lawyers than Democrats, and its electoral victory therefore weakened the interest group influence of lawyers over Congress. Finally, a dramatic growth in bankruptcy filings during the 1980s and 1990s, from about 250,000 annual consumer filings at the beginning of that period to about 1.5 million per year at the end, despite a period of steady prosperity and low unemployment, strengthened creditors' claims that the bankruptcy system was overly vulnerable to fraud and abuse. The interaction of these various factors produced a different winning coalition than in the past, pushing the bankruptcy laws in a more conservative direction.

DISCUSSION QUESTIONS

1. Skeel notes that during the nineteenth century the Supreme Court consistently adopted broader readings of the Bankruptcy Clause of Article I, Section 8 of the Constitution ("To establish ... uniform Laws on the subject of Bankruptcies throughout the United States"), thereby providing Congress broad latitude in crafting federal bankruptcy law. Skeel suggests that by increasing the *range* of options open to Congress, the expansive interpretation the Supreme Court gave to the Constitution's Bankruptcy Clause during the nineteenth century exacerbated the problem of instability and promoted cycling. Assuming that the Supreme Court could anticipate at the time of making a decision that one interpretation would be more likely to result in cycling than another, should it take this into account in its decision? Does social choice justify a normative conclusion that a judge should prefer a narrow interpretation that reduces the likelihood of cycling over a broader one that encourages cycling? In answering this question, note that a narrower interpretation of the Bankruptcy Clause promotes stability but does so by restricting the range of options available to Congress. Does social choice theory provide a normative basis for choosing between ensuring stability versus adhering to range?

2. Although Congress has exclusive power under Article I, Section 8, of the Constitution to enact laws on the subject of bankruptcies, this power is

---

165. Todd J. Zywicki, *The Past, Present, and Future of Bankruptcy Law in America*, 101 MICH. L. REV. 2016 (2003) (reviewing SKEEL, *supra* note 150).

layered over a preexisting foundation of state debtor-creditor law. This preexisting legal framework means that Congress's failure to enact a federal bankruptcy law creates a default rule of deferring to such state laws. Doing so may not result in an optimal bankruptcy regime, but it does create a functional status quo outcome meaning that the result need not be catastrophic. "No Bankruptcy" is therefore both a theoretical and practical option, although perhaps subject to certain substantive biases that render this system suboptimal (such as a tendency to prefer in-state interests over out-of-state interests). In this sense, the presence of a workable default rule made it less essential for Congress to act except in times of crisis. This combination of factors might have the unintended consequence of promoting cycling. Absent this workable *status quo*, would Congress have felt a greater urgency to reach agreement on bankruptcy law and to prevent cycling? Why or why not?

3. Skeel notes that given the presence of legislative cycling, one option available to legislators to break the cycle would be the adoption of some institutional rule or actor with the authority to limit *range* through agenda-setting power. If so, what practical alternatives can you identify for where to vest such power? Consider the following possibilities. First, some congressional committee (such as the Judiciary Committee) could use its agenda-setting power to prevent status quo-altering legislation from reaching the floor of Congress. Second, a well organized interest group (such as the bankruptcy bar) could use its external influence to restrict the range of practical outcomes available to Congress by effectively excluding the preferences of less organized groups from practical consideration. Third, the Supreme Court could through constitutional interpretation limit the range of options available for Congress to consider. Fourth, the Constitution could preempt any state authority with respect to debtor-creditor law, thereby eliminating "No Bankruptcy" as a theoretical or practical alternative. Finally, the legislature could permit log-rolling and thereby relax the requirement of sincere voting or "independence of irrelevant alternatives." Are these the only options? If not, what other options might have been available to nineteenth century lawmakers to create a stable bankruptcy law? What criteria might you use to select among these or other alternatives?

B. "MICRO" CYCLING: CYCLING INSIDE BANKRUPTCY

Consider whether the problem of cycling that characterized nineteenth century federal legislation is further endemic to the problem of bankruptcy itself. To illustrate, consider a stylized debtor-creditor arrangement in which the debtor owes $1.5 million but holds assets valued at $500,000, resulting from a combination of questionable business decisions and a failing economy. To simplify, assume three creditors, each owed $500,000. Each creditor wants to gain a maximum payoff even if this requires depleting the entire assets of the debtor's firm, while the debtor seeks to remain an ongoing concern. Assume that the three entities seek to resolve their financial relationships with a regime of majority decision-making over the debtor's assets. For any stable solution with majority support that is selected, a superior coalition can displace that proposed solution in favor of another majority preferred solution.

It is easy to translate this into a simple empty core bargaining game. If the two creditors, A and B, form a coalition to split all of the debtor's assets (250, 250), where each increment represents one-thousand dollars, then creditor C, can approach B and propose a superior coalition in which B receives 300, but leaves C with assets worth 200. Creditor A can now approach Creditor C and propose a new coalition in which C now receives a higher payoff of 300, while A receives a payoff of 200. Creditor B can now approach A and propose a superior payoff to A of 300, with B receiving 200. At this point the game has come full circle with coalitions AB, BC, CA, AB, but of course that result is no more stable than it was in the first round.

Within the Bankruptcy Code, there are numerous provisions that establish debt priorities and voting rules so that not all creditors sit in equal positions concerning a debtor. For instance, bankruptcy law generally requires that substantive entitlements that are created outside bankruptcy law are preserved in bankruptcy unless there is some compelling reason to alter the substantive rules in bankruptcy.[166] This rule is generally justified as a means of preventing the problem of "forum-shopping" between non-bankruptcy courts and bankruptcy courts with the goal of using bankruptcy proceedings to further non-bankruptcy objectives including redefining state law entitlements rather than to further bankruptcy policies. The so-called absolute-priority rule requires that all claimants with a higher level of priority against the debtor are supposed to be paid first before subsequent claimants are paid. For instance, under a strict application of the absolute priority rule, creditors are entitled to be paid in full before any assets of the estate are distributed to shareholders or the debtor. Courts have recognized some modest exceptions to the absolute priority rule.[167]

The rules for confirmation of a debtor's plan of reorganization are also complicated and contain numerous voting rules and substantive limitations. For instance, a debtor's plan can be confirmed by a bankruptcy judge only if at least one "impaired" class of creditors (i.e., a class of claimants that is paid less than full value for its claim) votes in favor of the plan.[168] An entire class of claims is deemed to accept a plan if the plan is accepted by creditors that hold at least two-thirds in amount and more than one-half in number of the allowed claims in the class.[169] To prevent "gerrymandering" of claims in order to engineer plan approval, one provision allows only "substantially similar" claims to be classed together.[170]

---

166. This rule is typically associated with the Supreme Court's decision in *Butner v. United States*, 440 U.S. 48 (1979).

167. For a discussion, see SKEEL, *supra* note 150, at 233–34.

168. 11 U.S.C. § 1129(a)(10) (2006). Under § 1126(f), holders of unimpaired claims are deemed to have accepted the plan.

169. 11 U.S.C. § 1126(c) (2006).

170. 11 U.S.C. § 1122(a) (2006).

Do you think that these provisions help to ameliorate the theoretical cycles described above? Why or why not? Why do the rules for approval of the plan by a class require a positive vote by both a majority of the claimants by number and a supermajority of the dollar amount of the claims? Bankruptcy practice also permits the selling of claims, thereby allowing original creditors of the bankrupt debtor to sell their claims in the case to others and thus permitting certain creditors to amass larger numbers of claims and claim amounts than would otherwise be the case. This also potentially gives the creditor greater authority over the plan's terms. Does social choice theory provide any insight on whether this "claims trading" activity is likely to be welfare-enhancing?

Is there any connection between the macro-and micro-analyses of bankruptcy law? Is it possible that bankruptcy regime ultimately adopted as a result of the history Professor Skeel describes forces pressure into the specific applications of bankruptcy within particular cases that have the potential to generate cyclical preferences? Stated differently, is it possible that the regime produces rules that embed cycles in the selected outcomes? Why or why not?

CHAPTER 4

ELEMENTARY GAME THEORY

■ ■ ■

Introduction

This chapter will introduce several basic tools from elementary game theory. As we have seen, the underlying intuitions from interest group theory and social choice theory rest upon insights drawn from other economic disciplines. Most notably, these disciplines include neoclassical economic theory, or price theory, and game theory. While each of these disciplines has its own specialized tools historically adapted to its own areas of inquiry, each shares an important set of common understandings growing out of economic reasoning.

Game theoretical literature has experienced a remarkable proliferation in recent decades that has influenced surprisingly diverse subject areas. These include behavioral economics, psychology, evolutionary biology, international relations, markets, and even the interpretation of biblical texts.[1] The legal literature applying game theory is sufficiently expansive that it could readily justify an independent course.[2] This chapter is not a substitute for such a course or for a course in game theory more generally. Instead, this chapter introduces a select subset of games and game theoretical concepts that complement the public and social choice concepts and applications developed in this book.

While game theory, like public choice, has important historical antecedents,[3] the formal discipline is generally traced to two mathematics

---

1. *See, e.g.*, COLIN F. CAMERER, BEHAVIORAL GAME THEORY: EXPERIMENTS IN STRATEGIC INTERACTION (2003) (applying game theory to behavioral economics); THOMAS C. SCHELLING, THE STRATEGY OF CONFLICT (1981) (applying game theory to psychology); Andrew M. Colman, *Thomas C. Schelling's Psychological Decision Theory: Introduction to a Special Issue*, 27 J. ECON. PSYCHOL. 603, 603–08 (2006) (same); JOHN MAYNARD SMITH, EVOLUTION AND THE THEORY OF GAMES (1982); RONALD FISHER, THE GENETICAL THEORY OF NATURAL SELECTION (complete variorum ed. 1999) (applying game theory to evolutionary biology); James D. Fearon, *Rationalist Explanations for War*, 49 INT'L ORG. 379, 379–414 (1995) (applying game theory to international relations); Alvin E. Roth, *Game Theory as a Tool for Market Design, in* GAME PRACTICE: CONTRIBUTIONS FROM APPLIED GAME THEORY 7–18 (Fioravante Patrone et al. eds., 2000) (applying game theory to markets); Alvin E. Roth, *The National Resident Matching Program as a Labor Market*, 275 J. AM. MED. ASS'N 1054, 1054–56 (1996) (applying game theory to labor markets); STEVEN J. BRAMS, BIBLICAL GAMES: GAME THEORY AND THE HEBREW BIBLE (rev. ed. 2002) (applying game theory to biblical texts).

2. For a book dedicated to that topic, see DOUGLAS BAIRD ET AL., GAME THEORY AND THE LAW (1994).

3. For an interesting overview, see Paul Walker, History of Game Theory (Oct. 2005), http://www.econ.canterbury.ac.nz/personal_pages/paul_walker/gt/hist.htm. For one fascinating illustra-

professors, the Hungarian-born John Von Neumann and the German-born Oskar Morgenstern.[4] After circulating a series of research papers that described specific games,[5] in 1944 Von Neumann and Morgenstern published a seminal book that pulled together various strands of the emerging discipline of game theory.[6] Social choice and game theory developed some closely related concepts during overlapping periods of time and yet they also developed independent terminologies and analytical techniques.[7] Given these connections, in this chapter, we will place some seemingly familiar concepts within a broader theoretical context and also introduce several new game theoretical concepts.

A great deal of game theoretical literature presents itself in the form of stylized and sometimes complex mathematical models. Such models allow scholars to eliminate unnecessary details and to focus instead on particular features of interest.[8] One important difference between game theory and neoclassical economic analysis involves assumptions concerning knowledge versus uncertainty. While law and economics scholars have tended to employ models premised upon complete knowledge (or costless information),[9] game theorists often design models specifically intended to explore the implications of incomplete knowledge, asymmetric information, or ignorance.[10] The game that is probably most familiar to readers, the prisoners' dilemma, models the predicted behavior of two prisoners each of whom lacks specific knowledge concerning the other prisoner's strategy.[11] In more complex games, game theorists study the implications of introducing degrees of certainty or uncertainty at different decision-

tion, Walker notes that Professors Robert J. Aumann and Michael Maschler have offered a compelling game theoretic account, grounded the outcome in the *nucleoli* of coalition games, of an otherwise anomalous Talmudic passage concerning the division of an estate among multiple creditors that appears to defy both equal and proportional division. *See* Robert J. Aumann & Michael Maschler, *Game Theoretic Analysis of a Bankruptcy Problem from the Talmud*, 36 J. Econ. Theory 195 (1985).

4. Robert J. Leonard, *From Parlor Games to Social Science: von Neumann, Morgenstern, and the Creation of Game Theory 1928–1944*, 33 J. Econ. Literature 730 (1995).

5. John von Neumann, *On the Theory of Parlor Games*, 100 Mathematical Annals 295 (1928).

6. Oskar Morgenstern & John von Neumann, Theory of Games and Economic Behavior (Princeton University Press 2004) (1944).

7. For example, the concept of cycling is analogous to the game theoretical concept of majority decisionmaking with an empty core. *See* Maxwell L. Stearns, *Standing Back from the Forest: Justiciability and Social Choice*, 83 Cal. L. Rev. 1309, 1313 n.4 (1995); *see also* Lynn A. Baker, *Direct Democracy and Discrimination: A Public Choice Perspective*, 67 Chi.-Kent L. Rev. 707, 726 n.63 (1991); Herbert Hovenkamp, *Rationality in Law & Economics*, 60 Geo. Wash. L. Rev. 293, 331–33 (1992).

8. Perhaps one irony of game theory is that the modeler's effort to streamline, and thus simplify complicating facts that tend to characterize real world phenomena, often results in mathematical models that those lacking specialized training view as inaccessibly complex.

9. Can you see why these are two ways of saying the same thing? Our distinction here is more a matter of emphasis than definition. Such economists as Frank Knight have studied the question of how to model behavior based upon incomplete information or ignorance. *See, e.g.*, Frank H. Knight, Risk, Uncertainty and Profit (1921). Rather, early law and economics scholarship has tended toward adopting complete information models.

10. Eric Rasmusen, Games and Information: An Introduction to Game Theory (4th ed. 2007).

11. For a more detailed analysis of the prisoners' dilemma, see *infra* pp. 171–96.

making junctures, referred to as "nodes."[12] This more nuanced analysis improves the realism of the models but at the cost of increased complexity. One reason is that in such games, which are sometimes formatted as a decision tree,[13] the ultimate resolution depends on the outcomes within each "subgame" that comprises the larger game. In addition, in more complex games, player strategies and combined outcomes—or equilibria— potentially turn on even slight alterations in assigned values.[14] In games played over extended periods of time, outcomes turn on the discount rate assigned for future benefits associated with cooperation or costs associated with punishment or defection.[15] As is generally true within economic analysis, adding precision to the model risks reducing the model's general applicability, but the converse is also true. More generalizable models sacrifice important institutional detail.

We will begin with some familiar games. In earlier chapters, we presented analyses that can now be formalized in terms of the prisoners' dilemma or the multiple Nash equilibrium bargaining game. A challenge for the legal theorist is selecting the most suitable game when analyzing a legal doctrine or decision-making rule. As Professors Douglas Baird, Robert Gertner, and Randal Picker have observed,[16] failing to appreciate the broader spectrum of available games when assessing questions of legal policy can result in wrongly assuming that coordination difficulties invariably reflect an underlying prisoners' dilemma.[17] Applying the incorrect game can lead to significant prescriptive errors concerning questions of legal policy.

This chapter proceeds in three sections, each of which develops one or more games in order of increasing complexity. The first section will focus on the prisoners' dilemma, in single period and in iterated form. This represents the simplest game because it conduces to a single dominant "Nash equilibrium" result. A Nash equilibrium is the outcome or set of outcomes that follow from each player's rational strategy in the absence of coordination with the other player or specific information concerning the other player's strategy, and in which no player has an incentive to deviate

---

12. For a general discussion, see RASMUSEN, *supra* note 10, at 43–46.

13. While we will present only simple form illustrations with single matrices. Decision tree presentations are referred to as "extended form" games. As Ian Ayres has explained, "Extensive form representation is especially appropriate for games with *asymmetric* or *incomplete* information." Ian Ayres, *Playing Games with the Law*, 42 STAN. L. REV. 1291, 1301 (1990) (reviewing RASMUSEN, *supra* note 10).

14. These values can, for example, represent degrees of knowledge or predictability. In the parlance of game theory, altering these values can affect which equilibria predominate both within sub-games and within the larger games that the sub-games comprise. *See* RASMUSEN, *supra* note 10.

15. For a discussion of discount rates, see *infra* p. 180.

16. BAIRD ET AL., *supra* note 2.

17. For a similar analysis, see Richard McAdams, *Beyond the Prisoners' Dilemma: Coordination, Game Theory, and the Law*, 82 S. CAL. L. REV. 209 (2009). A related insight from game theory shows that the payoffs attached to those options that the players in the game rationally avoid nonetheless can have profound effects on the ultimate outcome of a game. BAIRD ET AL., *supra* note 2, at 14–17 (providing illustration).

given the other player's strategy.[18] We will consider several variations on the prisoners' dilemma, including a game with endless iterations (or rounds of play) and a game with a known end period and show how those alternative sets of conditions affect the predictions of the model. The second section will present three games that are more complex in that each admits of more than a single Nash equilibrium. Instead, these games conduce to a combination of what game theorists refer to as "pure" Nash equilibria and non-equilibrium outcomes that can result when the players employ mixed strategies or incorrectly anticipate the other player's strategy, thus forcing the players outside the pure Nash solution.[19] These games include the driving game (or multiple Nash equilibrium bargaining game); the battle of the sexes; and the game of chicken (or Hawk–Dove). The third section will briefly revisit the empty core game, the game theoretical analogue to cycling introduced in chapter 3, to identify the conditions in which there is no dominant Nash strategy equilibrium.[20] For any given solution to this game, another has majority support. As a result, no outcome forms a stable solution, at least absent an external rule or norm preventing further rounds of play after an outcome has been selected.

In each section we introduce the terminology used to describe the games and their implications. Such concepts include normal form games, extended form games, single period games, iterated games, pure Nash equilibrium, mixed strategy equilibrium, backward induction, and unraveling. We also introduce several related concepts including Bayes' theorem, trigger strategy equilibria, and tit for tat strategies (and several variations on simple tit for tat). While our choice of selected games and concepts is not comprehensive, we refer to other works throughout our discussion that provide detailed presentations of other games. In sections I through III, we provide illustrations as appropriate to explaining the underlying concepts, and in section IV we offer additional materials that invite independent game theoretical assessment and analysis.

I. THE PRISONERS' DILEMMA

A. THE SINGLE PERIOD GAME

Certainly the single most well known game is the prisoners' dilemma. Imagine that Alex and Brad are arrested and held in separate cells. They

---

18. BAIRD ET AL., *supra* note 2, at 21 (describing Nash equilibrium as the solution concept to the principle that "The combination of strategies that players are likely to choose is one in which no player could do better by choosing a different strategy given the strategy the other chooses. The strategy of each player must be a best response to the strategies of the other"). KEN BINMORE, FUN AND GAMES: A TEXT ON GAME THEORY 12 n.8 (1992) (stating that Nash equilibrium "arises when each player's strategy choice is a best reply to the strategy choice of the other players."); MATTHEW RIDLEY, THE ORIGINS OF VIRTUE: HUMAN INSTINCTS AND THE EVOLUTION OF COOPERATION 58 (1996) ("The definition of a Nash equilibrium is when each player's strategy is an optimal response to the strategies adopted by other players, and nobody has an incentive to deviate from their chosen strategy.").

19. BAIRD ET AL., *supra* note 2, at 37 ("The alternative to a pure strategy equilibrium is a mixed strategy equilibrium, in which, in equilibrium, each player adopts a strategy that randomizes among a number of pure strategies.").

20. See *supra* chapter 3, section II.C.

cannot communicate and as a result they can neither make any agreements nor enforce any agreements that they might have made in the past. The police present each prisoner with the following identical offer. If both prisoners remain silent, each will be charged with a misdemeanor and face six months in prison. If Alex testifies against Brad and Brad remains silent, Alex will be released without charge (thus serving no time) and Brad will be charged with a class one felony and receive an expected sentence of five years. If Brad testifies against Alex and Alex remains silent, the payoffs are reversed with Brad receiving no time and Alex serving five years. If both prisoners testify then they will each be charged instead with a class two felony and face an equally certain sentence of three years. We present this simple form game in the following matrix.

Table 4:1. The Classic Prisoners' Dilemma

Payoffs for (Alex, Brad)	Brad cooperates	Brad defects
Alex cooperates	6 months, 6 months	5 years, no time
Alex defects	no time, 5 years	**3 years, 3 years**

Table 4:1 sets out the "payoffs," or expected results for each player based upon the combined strategies, in this game. Unless otherwise indicated, in this and all future matrices, the Nash outcome (or set of outcomes) is presented in bold. The payoffs, listed in the order of (column, row), are reciprocal, meaning that the incentives are the same for both Alex and Brad. In this game, the payoffs to cooperation and defection are viewed narrowly from the perspective of the opposing parties in the game, here the prisoners, rather than from that of other affected persons, for example the prosecutor or society. A prisoner cooperates by remaining silent, thus failing to incriminate the other prisoner and conversely a prisoner defects by testifying against the other prisoner so as to obtain a lighter sentence.

If both Alex and Brad cooperate, each receives a relatively lenient six month sentence. Alternatively, if Alex cooperates and Brad defects, Alex is given the harshest available sentence, five years, while Brad is released without charge. Conversely, if Alex defects and Brad cooperates, Alex is released while Brad is sentenced to five years. If both Alex and Brad defect, then each is sentenced to three years.

The prisoner's dilemma game is an example of a non-cooperative game with a single dominant Nash equilibrium. This unique solution arises because as a result of the payoffs, each player pursues a predictable strategy that is independent of the other player's actual strategy. Whether a given player cooperates or defects, it is rational for the other player to defect to obtain the benefit of a higher payoff. Because these payoffs are reciprocal, the incentives are identical for Alex and Brad. If Alex cooperates, Brad improves his payoff from 6 months to no time by defecting and if Alex defects, Brad improves his payoffs from 5 years to 3 years by defecting. The same incentives hold true for Alex in the event that Brad cooperates or defects. Thus, the optimal strategy for Alex is to defect regardless of what Brad does and the optimal strategy for Brad is to defect regardless of what Alex does.

It is important to consider the assumptions that underlie this game. First, the game assumes that each player seeks to maximize his *individual* payoffs without regard to the payoffs to the other player.[21] From the perspective of both players combined, the best outcome is mutual cooperation, with a total joint sentence of one year (six months each). If one cooperates and the other does not, the joint sentence is five years. And if both defect, the joint sentence is six years. Thus, mutual defection yields the lowest joint payoff of all combined strategies. And yet, mutual defection emerges as the dominant strategy.

Second, note that in this game what is optimal for the players may not be optimal from a larger social perspective. While the joint value to Alex and Brad is maximized when both cooperate, the joint value to society might well be maximized if both defect. This is certainly true if Alex and Brad are actually guilty of having committed a serious offense. Outside the criminal context, prisoners' dilemmas also have the potential to produce benign outcomes. Business cartels, for example, can be viewed as a multilateral prisoners' dilemma, subject to the same dynamics as the simpler prisoners' dilemma with two players. While the cartel as a whole benefits when members "cooperate," thus moving output and pricing from a competitive to a monopolistic level,[22] consumers benefit when the cartel members defect, thus restoring competitive production levels and pricing. Moreover, as with the basic prisoners' dilemma, the self-interest of cartel members will lead them to defect from the cartel by secretly increasing output and thus decreasing price. Defection will increase the cheater's share of the market but risks the eventual demise of the cartel. Because prisoners' dilemmas sometimes produce benign outcomes, an important public policy question involves identifying those circumstances in which placing individuals or institutions in a prisoners' dilemma (or conversely removing them from one they are already in) benefits society.

Third, the prisoner's dilemma game involves mutual ignorance in that neither player has specific knowledge concerning the other player's strategy. Even without such knowledge, however, this game produces a determinate outcome, referred to as a pure Nash strategy equilibrium. As previ-

---

21. One might couch this in terms of rationality, subject to the caveat that it is not necessarily irrational to hold preferences that include concern for the welfare of others. In this simple form game, however, the numbers are assumed to capture the full payoffs for each player.

22. For a general discussion, see *supra* chapter 1, section II.D.

ously stated, a Nash equilibrium is the outcome or set of outcomes that result from each player's rational strategy absent coordination or specific information about the other player's strategy and in which no player has an incentive to deviate given the other player's strategy.[23] Thus, a pure Nash outcome arises when no player, acting alone, could improve his or her payoff through a unilateral move to an alternative strategy.[24] Mutual defection, with each player being sentenced to three years, is a pure Nash strategy equilibrium in this game because neither player acting alone can improve upon it by altering her conduct. And yet, the outcome is inferior to the alternative strategy of mutual cooperation for both Alex and Brad. This undesirable outcome emerges from each player's rational strategy as a response to the payoffs and the other player's possible strategies.

This familiar game also provides a foundation for many basic features of game theoretical analysis. The prisoners' dilemma is a *normal form* game.[25] This form of game identifies the players, the available player strategies, and the payoffs that result from each combination of player strategies.[26]

While the prisoners' dilemma matrix specifies payoffs for each combined set of strategies, it is the relationship between and among payoffs, as opposed to the nominal payoffs, that motivate each prisoner's strategy. In this game, the combination of individual strategies drives the outcome toward mutual defection. We can change the nominal payoffs without changing the prisoners' dilemma provided that the numbers render defection the rational strategy for each prisoner without regard to the other prisoner's strategy.

As with any model or game, it is possible that the assumptions used to generate the payoffs fail to actually capture the stakes. Other factors not captured in these numbers might motivate one or both prisoners to respond differently, thus avoiding this seemingly problematic result. For example, it is possible that loyalty, morality, or guilt might motivate Alex or Brad to decline to testify against the other even despite the resulting personal consequences. In police dramas, for example, it is commonplace for a parent who feels guilty about the plight of his or her child to "take the fall" by declining to testify. And yet, if we focused only on the threatened sanctions that the police presented to each party and set aside emotional factors, the incentives would form the basis for a classic prisoners' dilemma.

By way of contrast, consider the doctrine of spousal privilege.[27] This rule prevents the state from forcing a husband and wife into a prisoners'

---

23. *See supra* at 18, and cites therein.

24. Some texts define the Nash concept to require that "each player adopts a particular strategy with certainty." BAIRD ET AL., *supra* note 2, at 313.

25. ROBERT GIBBONS, GAME THEORY FOR APPLIED ECONOMISTS 3 (1992); BAIRD ET AL., *supra* note 2, at 7–8, 312.

26. BAIRD ET AL., *supra* note 2, at 7–8.

27. FED. R. EVID. 501 incorporates common law privileges and has been construed to incorporate the longstanding spousal privilege. For a general discussion, see Bruce I. McDaniel,

dilemma, at least when prosecuting either spouse is impossible without the other spouse's incriminating testimony. Why might the legal system seek to avoid allowing prosecutors to construct a prisoners' dilemma as between husband and wife, but not as between a parent and child? Should there be a more general familial testimonial privilege? Why or why not?

While it is possible to incorporate psychological or other factors into the matrix payoffs, doing so has the potential to change the anticipated rational behavior. Depending upon the extent of such changes, altering the payoffs might transform the prisoners' dilemma into an altogether different game thus producing a different equilibrium solution. Nothing in game theoretical analysis should suggest that personal motivations are invariably simple or self interested. In constructing any game, however, it is important that the specified payoffs capture the incentives. Given the payoffs in prisoners' dilemma set out in Table 4:1, the dominant Nash equilibrium strategy operates to the detriment of each prisoner as compared with the alternative regime of mutual cooperation.

1. The Prisoners' Dilemma in a World of Organized Crime

For actual institutions that alter what otherwise might appear to be prisoners' dilemma games, consider the role of organized crime operations such as the Mafia or urban gangs. Assume two members of the mafia are arrested and that the police provide each with the necessary incentives to testify against the other or to remain silent so as to form a prisoners' dilemma. Further assume, however, that each mobster knows that if he defects, he will be subject to severe punishment from within the organized crime syndicate that far exceeds the maximum punishment that the prosecutor threatens to impose. The nature of organized crime thus changes the payouts in what otherwise might have looked like a prisoners' dilemma game thus limiting the prosecutor's ability to induce a defection strategy. In assessing the nature of this game, therefore, it is important to consider not only the payoffs that the prosecutor produces, but rather the *total* payoffs, including the private punishment imposed by the mob for defection.

The mob can also lower the cost of imprisonment, for example, by supporting an incarcerated mobster's dependents and promising work and income upon discharge.[28] In addition, because many organized crime organizations are family-based, psychological interdependency among the

---

Annotation, *Marital Privilege Under Rule 501 of Federal Rules of Evidence*, 46 A.L.R. FED. 735 (1980).

28. This is not to suggest, of course, that this form of employment insurance altogether diminishes the cost to the mobster of doing time. It might instead take the form of "an offer he can't refuse." *Cf.* THE GODFATHER (Paramount 1972) (depicting Don Corleone extending such an offer to a non-mobster). Inmates associated with organized crime, or with urban street gangs, might also experience other benefits within prison systems, including prestige and protections against violence given the risk of retaliation inside the prison, or upon release, by affiliated mob members.

members has the potential to alter payoffs that otherwise resemble a prisoners' dilemma by increasing the value of cooperative strategies.[29]

Finally, consider the famous "witness protection program," established by federal government.[30] To what extent does this program change the payoffs to cooperation as a countermeasure to mob-driven sanctions that otherwise inhibit the prosecutorial goal of encouraging mobsters to break ranks and defect? Does this program help to restore a benign prisoners' dilemma among coordinated criminals that organized crime has undermined? Why or why not?

B. THE ITERATED PRISONERS' DILEMMA: THE CASE OF PRECEDENT

We will now present a variation on the normal form prisoners' dilemma that involves endless iterations rather than a single round of play. To do so, we consider a highly stylized model of appellate court judging and the incentives of jurists to cooperate or defect from a regime of adherence to precedent. While the analysis that follows reveals a tension that can be characterized in terms of a prisoners' dilemma, we do not intend to suggest that an iterated game necessarily solves the difficulty that jurists confront regarding whether to adhere to a regime of precedent. As we will see later in this book, there is a large literature on the nature of precedent and the motivations of judges to follow precedent.[31] Instead, we use appellate court judging as a familiar context that allows us to present the differing dynamics that arise when the prisoners' dilemma is played in a single period, with endless iterations (and thus no known end period), and with a known end period.[32] When we revisit the discussion of precedent, we will consider a range of explanations, some relying on benefits to the judges themselves and some relying on benefits to society, for this common judicial practice.[33] We now begin by translating the single period prisoners' dilemma into a judicial context.

---

29. Consider for example the famous blood oaths that members of mob families take. The members of such organizations must swear absolute obedience to their superiors, putting the crime family ahead of their own family and being prepared to sacrifice their lives should the mafia boss order it, a result instilled in part through rituals involving blood oaths and religious iconography. Letizia Paoli, Mafia Brotherhoods: Organized Crime, Italian Style 5, 67–70 (2003).

30. This program was created as the product of a series of cases beginning in the 1960s through the work of, among others, Attorney General Robert Kennedy, as part of the war on organized crime. 18 U.S.C. § 3521 (2006). The Witness Security Program was authorized by the Organized Crime Control Act of 1970 and amended by the Comprehensive Crime Control Act of 1984. For a general discussion, see Douglas A. Kash, *Hiding in Plain Sight: A Peek into the Witness Security Program*, FBI Law Enforcement Bull. May 2004, at 25, 27–28.

31. *See infra* chapter 7, sections I.B. and I.C.

32. For a discussion of the historical origins of repeated games in the prisoners' dilemma context, see Ridley, *supra* note 18, at 58–60; *see also* William Poundstone, Prisoner's Dilemma 83–89; 101–31 (1992) (discussing history of prisoners' dilemma research including studies at RAND).

33. In chapter 7, we adapt the model set out below to study the scope of opinions, materiality, and vertical stare decisis on pyramidal common law courts. *See infra* chapter 7, section I.B.2. For general presentations of a similar game to that set out in the text, see Michael Abramowicz & Maxwell Stearns, *Defining Dicta*, 57 Stan. L. Rev. 953, 1004–11 (2005); Erin O'Hara, *Social Constraint or Implicit Collusion?: Toward a Game Theoretical Analysis of Stare Decisis*, 24 Seton

1. The Single–Period Judicial Prisoners' Dilemma

Imagine a judicial system in which each trial decision is subject to appeal before an appellate court consisting of a single judge. Each appellate court judge has the power to determine the legal principle used to decide the case before her, and also to determine the extent to which, if any, she should respect prior decisions on similar points of law issued by other appellate judges on the same court. To keep the exposition simple, we assume an appellate court with only two judges, Alice and Barb, each of whom adjudicates randomly assigned cases on appeal. The analysis to follow can be generalized to an appellate court with multiple judges. While some appeals present issues of first impression, meaning questions of law in the jurisdiction that have not previously been resolved, more often the appeals raise legal questions that either Alice or Barb have previously resolved in another case. Assume that Alice and Barb hold different views on the underlying questions of legal policy with respect to an important subset of such cases.

Now consider how the judges view their obligation with respect to adhering to each other's earlier decisions as precedent if they anticipate only a single round of play and how their incentives might change if they instead anticipate multiple rounds of play. We can easily translate the single period game into a classic prisoners' dilemma. Each judge prefers to decide cases consistently with her own view as to how the case should be resolved on the legal merits, without suffering whatever constraint her colleague's prior, and sometimes contrary, constructions of relevant legal materials would impose if those decisions were afforded precedential status.[34] At the same time, each judge prefers that the other judge respect her decisions as precedent in future cases that implicate the same governing principles of law because this form of judicial deference enhances her imprint on legal policy.

Even before formalizing this as a prisoners' dilemma, we can easily capture the game's intuition. Each judge prefers to constrain her colleague to her own prior construction of legal materials without being reciprocally constrained by her colleague in the same manner. Assuming that there is a benefit to a regime that respects precedent, these mutual incentives are likely to thwart that regime in favor of one in which each judge decides all cases as she prefers even when a given case presents a question of law that her colleague has previously resolved in a prior appeal.[35]

Hall L. Rev. 736 (1993); Eric Rasmusen, *Judicial Legitimacy as a Repeated Game*, 10 J.L. Econ. & Org. 63 (1994).

34. While there is a large literature that seeks to explore judicial motivations, for purposes of this game, it is unnecessary to engage this debate. *See infra* chapter 7 (reviewing literature). Imagine, for example, that Alice and Barb are legal realists who believe that the law is whatever they say it is in a particular case. Alternatively imagine that each judge views her role as substantially more constrained. Alice and Barb might eschew judicial policy making, but simply hold different views concerning how to construe the governing legal materials. Whether we view the judges as policy makers or as legal formalists who differ on substantive matters of construction, the stare decisis game we describe is the same.

35. To be clear, the judges might adhere to each other's decisions when they agree to them on the merits, but that is different than adhering to precedent because it is precedent. The obligation

To formalize the game, we will now translate the concepts of defection and cooperation into the context of judicial decision making. In this game, cooperation means adhering to the other's decisions as precedent and defection means disregarding such decisions, thus failing to afford them precedential status. In addition, we will specify the payoffs, meaning the anticipated benefits of cooperation and the anticipated costs of unilateral or mutual defection. For purposes of this game, there are two essential benefits associated with a precedent-based legal system.[36] First, a system of precedent affords each judge a more lasting imprint on the law, even though, at the same time, it prevents each judge from imposing her imprint in cases in which the other judge has already issued a binding precedent.[37] Second, a precedent-based regime generally enhances the stability of law. Those outside the legal system will benefit from knowledge that the particular rules of law that they are subject to are not a random consequence of which judge happens to decide a case affecting them, but rather are the product of a growing and stable body of precedent developed over the course of large numbers of cases.

Assume that each judge benefits from a regime of respect for precedent both in individual terms by having a more lasting impression on the law (the first benefit) and in institutional terms by being part of a judiciary that has the added prestige associated with more reliable case law upon which society can rely (the second benefit). Further assume that despite these benefits, at the level of the individual appeal, each judge continues to place a greater value on her own independent resolutions of questions of legal policy in deciding cases. As a result, each judge prefers that while the other judge respects her prior decisions as precedents, she maintains the flexibility to ignore those precedents with which she disagrees.

Assume that adhering to precedent provides payoffs to each judge of ten, but that a regime of unilateral defection produces payoffs of twelve for the defector and five for the cooperator. Even with unilateral defection, the cooperator receives the benefit of a more stable body of case law (the second benefit), but faces the prospect of losing her preferred imprint on substantial bodies of developing doctrine (the first benefit). In the event that neither judge adheres to precedent, each receives a payoff of seven,[38] which reflects some influence on the law, albeit in a random and temporary manner (unless and until the other judge decides a similar case to the contrary), without either the personal or general benefits of a precedent-based system.

---

of precedent assumes that judges will apply even those decisions with which they disagree simply because they resolved a materially indistinguishable point of law. O'Hara, *supra* note 33, at 736.

36. Of course there are other benefits to stare decisis, and not surprisingly there is a substantial literature on its costs and benefits. *See infra* chapter 7, section I.B and I.C. for a review of this literature.

37. Professor O'Hara aptly labels this benefit the elimination of "non-productive competition," meaning a constant state of flux in which each judge announces her preferred view of legal policy only to have it competed away by a colleague's contrary resolution in a subsequent round of play. O'Hara, *supra* note 33, at 738.

38. We assume that the benefit of this random influence on the law exceeds the cost of sacrificing the general benefit of precedent (the second benefit) in a regime that is dominated by the other judge.

Table 4:2 depicts the underlying judicial prisoners' dilemma.

Table 4:2. Prisoners' Dilemma Confronting Appellate Judges

Payoffs for (Alice, Barb)	Barb cooperates	Barb defects
Alice cooperates	10, 10	5, 12
Alice defects	12, 5	**7, 7**

While this game, unlike Table 4:1, depicts the payoffs with positive integers, both tables depict the same game. In this game, without regard to what the other judge does, it is rational for each of the two judges to defect and thus to avoid the obligation of precedent. If Alice adheres to precedent, then Barb can improve her payout from ten to twelve by defecting, and if Alice defects, Barb can improve her payout from five to seven by defecting. The payoffs are reciprocal, and thus the pure Nash equilibrium strategy is mutual defection, with payoffs of (7, 7). This result is a pure Nash equilibrium even though the judges would obtain higher individual and combined payoffs (10, 10) if they instead cooperated, thus respecting each other's opinions as precedent.

2.   The Iterated Judicial Prisoners' Dilemma

Let us now assume that Alice and Barb anticipate future interactions over multiple periods.[39] Each judge anticipates that her strategy in any given period, including the first period, potentially affects the other judge's incentives in a later period. Evaluating how future iterations affect judicial incentives and behavior therefore involves a two-step process. First we need to identify the changed incentives in future periods of play (or in the final period if we know when the game ends), and then, through a process of *backward induction*, assess the consequences of the outcome in each subsequent period on how the game is played in the immediately preceding round. We continue this process of backward induction until we return to the initial period of play.

We begin by assuming that the judges do not know when the game will end and that they therefore act in each round as if there will be a future round of play. Although obviously no game can go on forever, for expositional purposes, we will refer to this game as involving endless iterations. We then relax this assumption and consider how introducing an identified, or known, end period affects incentives in each round of play. To identify the payoffs in a late period (when the final period is unknown) or the final period (when it is known), we need to consider how the possibility of future iterations can alter the judges' incentives to cooperate by adhering to precedent, or to defect, thus producing a regime without

---

39.   For simplicity, we can imagine that each iteration represents a discrete number of cases or a specific judicial term. To maintain this as a single period, we might imagine that each judge issues all decisions on the same day at the end of the term.

the benefit of precedent. As we will see, the anticipated future interaction has the potential to alter the calculations in each period of play from those in a standard prisoners' dilemma to an alternative set of payoffs that yields mutual cooperation of the dominant pure Nash equilibrium strategy.

Assume first that there is no known end period and therefore that within any given round, the judges anticipate a subsequent round of play.[40] This version of the game produces a benefit from cooperation that the single period game, depicted in Table 4:2, does not capture. While we provide a matrix that expresses these payoffs numerically below, for now consider the intuition. The most notable factor influencing the change in payoffs is that mutual cooperation now produces an anticipated stream of future benefits over many periods, rather than just a one-shot benefit. Conversely, if defection produces an anticipated set of foregone benefits in the event that the game instead descends into an endless stream of mutual defections this provides a set of expected foregone benefits.[41] Robert Axelrod has aptly described this phenomenon as the "shadow of the future."[42] The difference in the anticipated benefits of repeated mutual cooperation versus repeated mutual defection in some cases will be sufficiently large to outweigh even the cost of enduring an isolated instance of the other player's defection in a given round of play. If so, then each player is rationally motivated to cooperate in each single round of play (or within each "subgame"). Notably, this result obtains whether or not the other player cooperates or defects in that subgame.

This result rests on an important assumption about the discount rate, meaning the present discounted value of the benefits of future cooperation or the present discounted cost of future defection.[43] To achieve the benefits of future cooperation, the discount rate must be low enough that players do not treat the repeated game as if only immediate payoffs are controlling. Depending upon how heavily one discounts the value of future rounds of play, game theorists can model the iterated prisoners' dilemma to produce mutual cooperation, mutual defection, or anywhere in between.[44] In the discussion that follows we assume a sufficiently low discount rate to generate the possibility of mutual cooperation as a

---

40. While these assumptions are obviously stylized, they have the benefit of allowing us to introduce an important benefit of cooperation that is not captured in the single period game, which as shown below has the potential to be eliminated through the process of backward induction or unraveling. *See infra* pp. 190–91 (describing unraveling).

41. As in the prior discussions, it is also important to emphasize here that in the payoff matrix, table 4:3, the numbers are relevant only for the relationships they create for the individual and combined strategies. They are not, for example, designed to reflect specific values with the discounted income stream from future cooperation or defection based upon the nominal original payoffs in table 4:2.

42. Robert Axelrod, The Evolution of Cooperation 12 (1984).

43. For a discussion of discount rates, see Rasmusen, *supra* note 10 at 486; Richard A. Ippolito, Economics for Lawyers 338–40 (2005).

44. This result is known as the folk theorem of the iterated prisoners' dilemma, because even before it was formalized, it formed part of the general understanding among those who employed game theoretical tools. Baird et al., *supra* note 2, at 307–08; *see also* Eric Rasmusen, *Folk Theorems for the Observable Implication of Repeated Games*, 32 Theory & Decision 147 (1992).

consequence of factoring in the "shadow of the future."[45] Based upon this assumption, the dominant pure Nash equilibrium strategy in this game shifts from mutual defection (the outcome of the single period game) to mutual cooperation (the outcome of a game with endless iterations).[46]

Let us now return to our two appellate judges, Alice and Barb. Alice rationally anticipates that Barb will obtain two benefits if Alice cooperates by adhering to Barb's opinions as precedent: first, the specific benefit of enhancing the value (or durability) of Barb's decisions, and second, the general benefit of improving reliance on the rule of law and thus the prestige of the court on which Alice and Barb sit. As a result, Alice anticipates that Barb will seek to reward her cooperative behavior in the next round by also adopting a similar cooperative strategy. Once again, these payoffs are reciprocal and so Barb anticipates that Alice has the same incentives to reward Barb's adherence to her cases as precedent. Based upon the preceding assumptions about the anticipated benefits of future cooperation, each judge is motivated to cooperate in each subgame whether or not the other judge cooperates (adheres to precedent) or defects (disregards precedent). Given these incentives, mutual cooperation emerges the dominant strategy as each judge seeks to avoid the danger of incurring the low payoffs of an endless future stream of defections.

Table 4:3. Iterated Prisoners' Dilemma Respecting Precedent

Payoffs for (Alice, Barb)	Barb cooperates	Barb defects
Alice cooperates	**15, 15**	10, 12
Alice defects	12, 10	8, 8

We can now translate this game into a matrix with altered payoffs and incentives. As shown in Table 4:3, if Alice cooperates, it is also in Barb's interest to cooperate because doing so raises her potential payoffs from ten to fifteen. This reflects the value of having her decisions honored as precedent and of anticipating a continued regime of adherence to precedent. Conversely, if Alice defects, thus reducing Barb's immediate influence on the law, it nonetheless remains in Barb's interest to cooperate. Despite the immediate short term loss, reflected in the reduced payoff from fifteen to ten, cooperation still produces the benefit of an anticipated

---

45. *See* AXELROD, *supra* note 42, at 126–32.

46. We will later demonstrate that even assuming a sufficiently high value from anticipated future cooperation to shift the pure Nash strategy from mutual defection to mutual cooperation, the result reverts back to mutual defection if the parties instead anticipate a known end period. *See infra* pp. 190–92.

stream of mutual cooperation in later rounds. By contrast, while punishment allows Barb an immediate imprint on the law in this round, that benefit is overwhelmed by the larger cost of inciting an endless stream of mutual defection, with the resulting lower payoff of eight.

Once again, these payoffs are reciprocal and so Alice and Barb have the same incentives. In this game, each judge is motivated to cooperate in each future round of play without regard to whether the other judge abides or avoids precedent in a given round of play. The mutual cooperation regime dominates as a result of the anticipated losses that punishment will invite in all future rounds.

While the preceding analysis suggests that under some circumstances each judge will suffer an isolated instance of defection from the other without imposing punishment, this does not mean that Alice or Barb will reward a constant stream of defection with cooperation. If Alice repeatedly defects, then beyond some point, Barb might punish that defection even at the risk of producing a perpetual stream of mutual defection, with correspondingly low payoffs. The number of defections required to generate punishment depends upon the value of cooperation and the optimal strategy employed by each player based upon the anticipated response by the other player. In the part that follows, we will consider several of the potential strategies that the players might employ.

a.   Tit for Tat Strategies: From Committed Pacifist to Grim Trigger

In Robert Axelrod's analysis of tit for tat strategies, he demonstrates a variety of circumstances in which the most effective strategy is to mimic the behavior of the other party to the game.[47] Cooperation yields cooperation and defection yields defection, and thus the strategy is referred to as tit for tat. In games yielding this strategy, imposing the "tit" as punishment for the "tat" is not an end in itself. Rather, the punishment forms a credible signal designed to motivate future cooperative behavior.

The Axelrod strategy can be understood as a form of contingent cooperation, meaning that each player signals a desire to behave cooperatively (or nicely) as a function of the other player's willingness to reciprocate. Axelrod has demonstrated that in a variety of contexts, tit for tat is

---

47. Robert Axelrod & William Hamilton, *The Evolution of Cooperation*, 211 SCIENCE 1390–96 (1981); AXELROD, *supra* note 42; Jonathan Bendor, *Uncertainty and the Evolution of Cooperation*, 37 J. CONFLICT RESOL. 709 (1993); Robert Axelrod & Douglas Dion, *The Further Evolution of Cooperation*, 242 SCIENCE 1385 (1988).

an optimal strategy, yielding the highest payoffs, *even though* it requires nothing more elaborate than simple period-by-period mimicking behavior.

It is important to note, however, that although tit for tat is an effective strategy over the long run, it is not necessarily optimal in all short-run instances or in all contexts. For instance, tit for tat is not likely to prove an effective strategy if the other player has bonded himself or herself to engaging in a defection strategy; if there is a high probability that the game will soon end; or if contrary to the game with Alice and Barb, the discount rate is sufficiently high. Thus, in some settings, it is better to follow a more aggressive punishment strategy, namely two tits for a tat or the more extreme grim trigger, while in others it is better to follow a more lenient strategy, for example a tit for two tats or the more extreme committed pacifism. Two tits for a tat punishes twice for one defection and a tit for two tats imposes punishment once after two defections. The most severe punishment strategy is grim trigger, which disallows the other player to induce cooperation after a single instance of defection. Conversely, the most lenient strategy is committed pacifism, meaning that regardless of what the other player does, no punishment will follow. We present a range at strategies, from strict to lenient, along a single dimensional spectrum in Figure 4:1.

Figure 4.1. Spectrum of Potential Punishment Strategies

Grim Trigger	Hair Trigger	Two tits for a tat	Tit for tat	Tit for two tats	Committed pacifism
Strict Punishment ←--→ Lenient Punishment					

The optimal strategy in any circumstance depends on a combination of factors, including the anticipated value of mutual cooperation, the plausibility that the other player will construe leniency as a signal to restore the benefits of mutual cooperation or as a sign of weakness to be exploited. Most importantly, except in the extreme cases of grim trigger and committed pacifism, the players have the potential to alter their strategies over time as they update their information about the other player's likely response to their selected strategy.

Axelrod has demonstrated that in general some form of "contingent nice" strategy, including tit for tat, tends to prevail over extreme strategies.[48] Can you identify circumstances favoring more extreme strategies? What about unilateral disarmament? Is this a beneficial strategy to avoiding war? Does the answer depend on whether the other side has armed solely as a defensive measure (a result dispelled by the disarmament) or instead has done so with aggression in mind? Conversely, a grim or even hair trigger—meaning a rapid punishment for even slight provocations that is just short of grim trigger—risks devastation when signals are potentially ambiguous and the other side's good faith disagreement is misread as an act of aggression. Does the generations-long family feud between the Hatfields and McCoys illustrate the dangers of hair-trigger strategies?[49] What about the three strikes rule, which results in permanent incarceration upon the third conviction, regardless of the severity of that offense? Is this game better characterized as a tit for three tats or as grim trigger on the third offense? If the latter, is there a sound justification for imposing a grim trigger strategy at that stage for a repeat offender? Why or why not? Is the contract law doctrine of anticipatory repudiation an illustration of "grim trigger"? Why or why not? How is the choice of strategy affected by the discount rate?

Let us now return to the judicial context. Depending on the payoffs from mutual cooperation, Alice and Barb might fear an end to precedent—the judicial equivalent to feuding—and thus engage in a softer strategy (between committed pacifism and grim trigger) hoping to restore the preferred regime of precedent. Notice also that if the iterated prisoners' dilemma game is played among a larger number of players, for example an appellate court with several judges rather than two, the risk of defection might be more severe. Without some degree of tolerance even a good faith dispute between or among a subset of judges might threaten to destroy a cooperative norm that is beneficial to the larger group. This is especially true if there is no practical means to mete out punishment to only a subset of the group, as might be the case for example if jurists meet in panels of three, rather than in isolation. And even with our two-judge illustration, some legitimate disagreements over the scope of governing precedent is inevitable. It might therefore be preferable to follow a "benefit of the doubt" strategy (a tit for several tats) rather than to assume that each contested application of precedent is necessarily a defection and thus to follow a simple tit for tat strategy.[50]

---

48. AXELROD, *supra* note 42, at 176.

49. While the Hatfield/McCoy feud is the most famous, such family feuds were not uncommon in the nineteenth century in the Appalachian region. For an analysis linking such feuding strategies to a Scottish highland culture in which fending off threats to goat herds demanded a reputation for the herder's immediate willingness to exact revenge, see MALCOLM GLADWELL, OUTLIERS: THE STORY OF SUCCESS 164–70 (2008).

50. The converse is also true; it is not even necessary that the defecting party actually intend to defect. Indeed, it is not necessary that she defect at all so long as any action is *perceived* as a defection by the other party, with the result of prompting retaliation.

Axelrod further suggests that cycles of retribution have the effect of leaving money on the table, meaning that the players forego valuable benefits of cooperative equilibria that can be obtained through more accommodating strategies. Depending upon the strategies that players follow, they might also invite other, competitor institutions to come in and employ more beneficial cooperative strategies at the expense of those who follow excessively myopic or grim forms of punishment. Alternatively, depending on the magnitude of the resulting losses from short-sighted punishment strategies, existing institutions might modify their structures to produce incentives facilitating more benign results.

Is it possible that common law judicial systems impose a strong cooperation (respect precedent) norm so that individual trigger-happy jurists (those who would punish perceived defection with actual defection) get reined-in, thus promoting a benefit of the doubt strategy that is conducive to mutual cooperation? If so, does that make the payoffs from Figure 4:3 more plausible in this context of precedent than those in Figure 4:2? Why or why not? If so, do such norms emerge as a consequence of the hierarchical judicial structure of common law systems and thus through vertical precedent, or through mutual cooperation in a repeat game among jurists on the same level court? Why? (We will reconsider these questions in Chapter 7). Can you identify circumstances in which groups trapped in a cycle of retaliation might simply be displaced by another group with more cooperative internal norms?[51]

b. *Trigger Strategy Equilibrium*

When players adopt an optimal set of strategies as needed to generate beneficial cooperation, the combined result is sometimes referred to as a "trigger strategy equilibrium." This means that the ultimate outcome of the iterated prisoners' dilemma game turns on the values associated with cooperation or defection and the optimal strategies needed to reward cooperation or to punish defection. As noted above, the maintenance of a cartel is an example of a prisoners' dilemma game. In the context of cartel enforcement, game theorists have relied upon the concept of trigger strategy equilibrium to identify optimal strategies for members of a cartel to monitor and punish defection from agreed-upon production quotas and thereby maintain a cooperative equilibrium.[52] Each individual member of

---

51. For a general discussion, see Todd J. Zywicki, *Was Hayek Right About Group Selection After All?*, 13 REV. AUSTRIAN ECON. 81 (2000).

52. For a general discussion, see, e.g., Robert Porter & Douglas Zona, *Detection of Bid Rigging in Procurement Auctions*, 101 J. POL. ECON. 518 (1993); Joseph E. Harrington, Jr., *Detecting Cartels* (Johns Hopkins Univ. Dep't of Economics, Working Paper Archive No. 526, 2005), *available at* http:// www.econ.jhu.edu/pdf/papers/WP526harrington.pdf.

the cartel has an incentive to cheat on the agreement by secretly boosting production and decreasing price. If the cartel members reciprocate defection with further defection, the cartel breaks down. If on the other hand cartel members never punish defection, then the result is a non-sustainable unilateral defection benefiting the defectors and harming the rest of the producers as the defectors benefit from the artificially raised price while also having a negative effect on that price through the higher production levels. In general, private cartels are very difficult to sustain, especially as the number of participants increases. And notice that as in the judging context, some good faith disputes inevitably emerge in which producers disagree whether particular production is or is not compliant with the terms established by the cartel. While some degree of tolerance might be necessary to sustain multilateral cartel relationships (thus avoiding grim trigger), endless tolerance makes the cartel impossible to sustain (thus avoiding committed pacifism). Trigger strategy equilibria solve the problem by devising an equilibrium solution for the problem of punishment in response to an instance (or several instances) of defection as required to bring the defector back into the fold of cooperation.

As applied to the context of judging, the analysis suggests that Alice will sometimes cooperate even in the face of some level of Barb's defection. It does not imply, however, that Alice's patience is unlimited. If Barb's defection extends beyond a certain level, Alice will punish Barb's defection by also defecting. As in the cartel, the goal is to calibrate the optimal level of tolerance for defection with the proper frequency (and level) of punishment. There is a spectrum of strategies that the players can employ.[53] As Axelrod demonstrates, however, neither extreme strategy is likely to produce the highest payoffs over time. Instead, the players are more likely to settle on some intermediate strategy that condones some defection but that beyond a certain point imposes punishment. Moreover, the optimal strategy might change over time as the other party alters his or her conduct, thus explaining why the extreme strategies of committed pacifism or grim trigger, which disallow such calibration over time, are rarely optimal strategies. To evaluate how strategies might change over time, it is helpful to consider the probabilistic framework known as Bayes' theorem.

c. *Bayes' Theorem: The Importance of Updating Information*

Bayes' theorem relies upon observation of the relationship between two random phenomena in the past to make predictions about the relationship between those phenomena in the future.[54] Whether we are discussing business cartels seeking to optimize output and price or appel-

---

53. For a general discussion, see James Friedman, *A Non-cooperative Equilibrium for Supergames*, 38 REV. ECON. STUD. 1 (1971).

54. Steven C. Salop, *Evaluating Uncertain Evidence with Sir Thomas Bayes: A Note for Teachers*, J. ECON. PERSP., Summer 1987, at 178.

late judges seeking to optimize the value of a precedent-driven system, each decision maker will rationally base his or her behavior on expectations concerning the behavior of other players in the game. Bayes' Theorem predicts the likely occurrence of observed phenomenon A based upon its degree of correspondence to observed phenomenon B. When A is observed along with B, the predictive force of the observed relationship concerning A is referred to as "conditional probability." When A is observed independently of B, the predictive force of the observed relationship concerning A is referred to as "marginal probability." Bayes' theorem posits that prior observed occurrences of A as a function of B and independent of B provide meaningful probabilistic data concerning the likelihood that A will occur in future periods. Most notably, the probabilities concerning A occurring in the future can change along with changed observations regarding the incidence of A as a function of, or independent of, B in the past.[55]

As applied to trigger strategy equilibria, Bayes' theorem implies that decision makers seeking to motivate others to cooperate will try to gauge the other party's cooperative behavior as a function of decisions to punish or not to punish defection. In other words, the purpose of punishment is not retribution, but to provide credible information that will make predictions of future behavior more reliable. For instance, the failure to respond to defection with punishment might provide a signal that one is a pushover who can be taken advantage of on a consistent basis, and responding with full force for even a slight provocation might signal recklessness and thus a person to be avoided. It is not necessary that one meet every defection with punishment, so long as the failure to do so does not cause the other party to believe that one will never respond with punishment.

In the context of appellate judging, if Alice observes Barb defecting and immediately punishes her, she might then witness Barb continuing to defect, leading to an endless stream of defection. Alternatively, if Alice does not punish Barb's defection, she might observe Barb cooperating in the next round. This might mean that she misread the earlier signal, and that the perceived defection was a good faith disagreement on the scope of a precedent. Alternatively, it might mean that Barb is only inclined to

---

55. Bayes' theorem does not imply a causal connection between A and B even when probabilistic data supporting conditional probabilities as between the two phenomena are highly significant. For example, the conditional probability that (A) people carry umbrellas when (B) drivers use windshield wipers is high. The fact that drivers use windshield wipers, however, does not cause people to carry umbrellas. And conversely the fact that people carry umbrellas does not cause drivers to use windshield wipers. Instead, rain, an independent factor, causes both observed phenomena, and for that reason, the correlation, or conditional probability, between the two events is significant. Despite the lack of a causal relationship, it is reasonable to predict that when we next observe drivers using windshield wipers (or people carrying umbrellas), we are likely also to observe people carrying umbrellas (or drivers using windshield wipers), based upon a high conditional probability. For a discussion of a similar example involving a claimed link between night time lighting for children and myopia, see Karla Zadnik et al., *Myopia and Ambient Night-time Lighting*, 404 NATURE 143 (2000) (providing alternative account linked to hereditary nature of myopia and an increased probability that myopic parents will use nighttime lighting for their children than nonmyopic parents).

defect on rare occasions, and that Alice is better off condoning such rare defections than risking an end to the general regime of mutual cooperation. If Alice continues to watch Barb and witnesses another defection, she might impose a punishment (a tit for two tats). If at this point, Barb declines to defect for an even longer period of time, Alice might infer that she has hit upon an effective strategy and thus continue to adhere to it. We do not, of course, intend to suggest that a single change in strategy will produce a stable and benign result. Instead, this is illustrative of the kind of adjustments that facilitate improved strategies over time.

This simple story suggests that in selecting among strategies, Alice benefits from observing Barb's behavior in each given round of play and updating her optimal response accordingly. It is possible that Alice's tit for two tats strategy yields a sufficiently low level of defection by Barb that Alice sticks with that strategy and views the occasional additional defection by Barb as the price of securing the larger benefits of mutual cooperation over time. Or it is possible that further refinements to Alice's strategy will be necessary in future periods of play.[56]

d. Quality–Adjusted Pricing as Affecting Success or Failure of Cartels

The ability of a party to defect from a cartel or other agreement is also affected by the likelihood that other members to the cartel can detect and punish cheating. As the cost of detecting cheating rises, it becomes easier to cheat and avoid punishment. This is most notable when cartel members have the capacity to cheat by adjusting the quality of the goods they sell, rather than simply by reducing price for goods of the same quality as sold by other cartel members. Thus, cartels are more likely to be sustainable in the context of commodities than in the context of more complex, or bundled, goods and services.[57] Where improving quality is a substitute for reducing price, these strategies are substitutes for gaining an advantage relative to other cartel members.

If, for example, airlines tried to fix the prices of fares, some airlines would be tempted to cheat on the agreement by providing tastier meals, better customer service, friendlier flight attendants, free movies, or more comfortable seating. Indeed, this is just what occurred in the 1970s, when prior to deregulation of the airline industry, the Civil Aeronautics Board (CAB) set the fares for all airline transportation at above-market rates.[58] Airlines competed for passengers by providing amenities such as in-flight

---

56. In this game, the conditional probability was how much defection follows from a given punishment, and the marginal probability is how much defection arises independently of punishment. This distinction is important because in a world with imperfect information, it is possible that judges appear to defect based upon good faith disagreement over whether a claimed precedent is controlling in the case they are deciding. If so, some defection arises with or without punishment simply due to disagreement, while other defection arises as a rational consequence of the selected punishment strategy.

57. For an example of a world-wide cartel in the production of the commodity lysine, see KURT EICHENWALK, THE INFORMANT (2000).

58. Paul L. Joskow & Roger G. Noll, *Economic Regulation*, *in* AMERICAN ECONOMIC POLICY IN THE 1980s, at 367, 380–82 (Martin Feldstein ed., 1995).

lounges and other luxuries, all of which disappeared following deregulation and the accompanying reduction in airline fares back toward a market-clearing price. Because it is more costly to monitor all aspects of quality with complex services like air transit, quality adjusted pricing makes cartel enforcement more difficult than for commodities.[59] Similarly, if it is difficult to punish a particular defector (say because that party is substantially larger than other members of the cartel or because it is a governmental entity), then the cartel will be unstable. Absent the ability to effectively monitor and punish cheating, cartels generally cannot be maintained over time.

In the context of judging, this analysis implies that Alice might not always be able to determine whether Barb has defected from a regime of mutual respect for precedent. The complexities of distinguishing holding and dicta and of determining whether case distinctions are legitimate or an effort to avoid precedent raise the cost of enforcing a regime of precedent and the risks associated with imposing punishment. Do these nuances make the task of developing a regime of precedent on the same level court implausible? Why or why not? If you conclude that they do, can you think of other mechanisms that create the benefits of precedent without imposing these costs?[60]

e.   *Extensive Form Games and Subgame Perfection*

As previously stated, one danger of an excessively strict punishment strategy is that premature punishment (following a good faith disagreement that was not intended as a defection) might wrongly signal a willingness to forego the benefits of mutual cooperation.[61] For simplicity, we continue to depict the game in normal form. The critical point is that for mutual cooperation to emerge the dominant strategy, each juncture, or subgame, in the iterated game must produce the result of mutual cooperation. Professor Eric Rasmusen has explained that to generate this seemingly happy outcome, the game must satisfy the condition of "subgame perfectness."[62] Rasmusen explains:

---

59. For a related discussion involving the difficulty of cartelizing to end payola, the practice of paying to get favored radio or other media play in the music industry, as a result of the difficulty in detecting cheating, see Ronald H. Coase, *Payola in Radio and Television Broadcasting*, 22 J.L. & ECON. 269 (1979).

60. We will revisit this question in chapter 7 (discussing pyramidal courts and vertical precedent).

61. Julio Rotemberg & Garth Saloner, *A Supergame–Theoretic Model of Price Wars During Booms*, 76 AM. ECON. REV. 390 (1986) (demonstrating that in cartel context, an observed production increase leads to an inference problem regarding cheating or to shock in demand and thus makes difficult assessing whether to pull the trigger strategy).

62. RASMUSEN, *supra* note 10, at 108. Note that while each subgame pure equilibrium is a Nash equilibrium, not all Nash equilibria are subgame pure equilibria. Instead, depending on such factors as discount rates and punishment strategies, some Nash solutions for the overall game might include rounds of play without subgame perfection. Robert Gibbons, *An Introduction to Applicable Game Theory*, J. ECON. PERSP., Winter 1997, at 127, 135 (noting that "to be subgame-perfect, the players' strategies must first be a Nash equilibrium and must then fulfill an additional requirement" and that "[t]he point of this additional requirement is, as with backward induction, to rule out Nash equilibria that rely on non-credible threats.")

A strategy profile is a **subgame perfect Nash equilibrium** if (a) it is a Nash equilibrium for the entire game; and (b) its relevant action rules are a Nash equilibrium for every subgame.[63]

This means that in each round of play, Alice and Barb need to give perceived defector the benefit of the doubt to avoid a cycle of defection. We do not mean to imply that it is impossible to recover from punishment following defection, but as previously stated, the likelihood of this result depends upon the value each side attaches to cooperation and defection and on how each side updates its strategies based upon information from the other player. Occasional defection followed by punishment might not render a cycle of defection inevitable, but it also does not render mutual cooperation inevitable. Depending on the valuations attached to the cooperation regime, there is a risk that the players might in fact wind up leaving the money on the table. In the next and final variation of the prisoners' dilemma, we consider another difficulty that can shift the potentially benign mutual cooperation outcome back to mutual defection.

f. Backward Induction and Unraveling

The final difficulty that can affect the outcome in an iterated prisoners' dilemma game is unraveling. Setting aside the various complexities discussed in the prior part, let us simply assume that in an endless iterated prisoners' dilemma, the result is mutual cooperation. This result follows from the assumption of endless rounds of play and the possibility of punishment in each future period. Of course there are never actual endless rounds of play in any game, although it is possible that neither player knows when the game will end, and thus whether she or the other player will make the final move. We will now assume instead that the players anticipate a specific period at which their interactions will end. In this variation on the game represented in Table 4:3, we can introduce the concepts of backward induction and unraveling to demonstrate how this changed assumption affects incentives at each decision node.

To simplify, assume that the judges anticipate six periods of play, after which the game stops. We begin by considering the players' incentives in the final known period, this time period 6.[64] In period 6, there is no longer any promise of reward or threat of punishment in the very next period, because there will be no period 7 in which such rewards or threats can be carried out. As a result, in period 6, the judges have the same incentives to cooperate or defect that they had in the single period prisoners' dilemma, depicted in Table 4:2. Now consider the incentives in the second to final period. In period 5, each judge knows that in the final period 6, the result will be mutual defection without regard to whether

---

63. RASMUSEN, *supra* note 10, at 109. *See also* Ayres, *supra* note 13, at 1305 ("A combination of strategies is a perfect Nash equilibrium if the strategies satisfy the Nash requirements for every subgame.").

64. Because the prior game did not have a known end period, we instead modeled incentives based upon a future period in which the players continued to anticipate future play.

she cooperates or defects in period 5. As a result, there is no effective possibility of reward for cooperation or punishment for defection. Regardless of what each player does, period 6 will produce a regime of mutual defection. Since the judges in period 6 will behave as if they had defected in period 5, regardless of what the other judge does, the dominant strategy is defection. Through backwards induction, we see that this game unravels, meaning that the benefits of an iterated prisoners' dilemma game, as reflected in Table 4:3, revert from the last period through the first to those of a standard prisoners' dilemma, as reflected in Table 4:2. The ultimate result is that in a game with a known end period, the incentives among the players are the same as if the game had only a single period. In effect, the anticipated benign outcome, mutual cooperation, from a game with endless iterations unravels in favor of mutual defection, beginning with the last known period of play all the way down to the initial period of play when there is a certain end period.

As the preceding discussion demonstrates, the game theoretical analysis does not suggest a simple binary choice between a game with endless iterations (yielding cooperation) or a game with a known end period (yielding mutual defection). Until now we have assumed that while the judges do not know each other's strategies, they do have information concerning whether there is an opportunity to reward cooperation or punish defection in a subsequent round of play. An alternative is to introduce uncertainty or a probablistic end period in the game itself. Game theorists have demonstrated that depending upon assumptions concerning degrees of certainty and the discount rate, it is possible to construct games in which absent complete information about when the game will end, parties nonetheless retain mutual incentives to engage in cooperative strategies.[65] As previously noted, within such games a great deal turns on the values assigned to the discounted future benefits of anticipated cooperation within each round of play. By changing those values, even slightly, modelers can affect outcomes within particular subgames and within the overall game, thus inviting once again concerns about subgame perfectness and perfectness for the overall game.

g. Questions and Comments

While Article III judges, who hold life tenure (and thus for whom there might be no known end period), embrace a regime of precedent, so too do state judges who are often appointed for previously identified terms of years.[66] Does this observation help to resolve the origins of precedent or does it make the problem more difficult? Does the preceding game theoretical analysis help to identify the conceptual origins of the common law regime of precedent?[67] Why or why not? Scholars also debate whether a

---

65. Drew Fudenberg & Eric Maskin, *The Folk Theorem in Repeated Games with Discounting or with Incomplete Information*, 54 ECONOMETRICA 533 (1986).

66. Gary M. Anderson, William F. Shughart II & Robert D. Tollison, *On the Incentives of Judges to Enforce Legislative Wealth Transfers*, 32 J.L. & ECON. 215, 220 (1989) (discussing variations in tenure of state court judges in contrast to the life tenure of federal judges).

67. To be clear, we are not drawing a historical distinction between precedent and stare decisis. In early jurisprudential history, precedent was linked to large bodies of case law relied

system of law founded on precedent generally provides better, more predictable, or more stable doctrine than civilian regimes, which nominally eschew precedent in favor of code law interpreted in decisions that, at least in theory, only govern the immediate case.[68] What are the tradeoffs between a precedent and non-precedent regime? Does the preceding analysis help to explain whether judges would rationally create a regime of precedent even if the obligation to respect precedent did not otherwise exist? Why or why not? We will revisit these questions in chapter 7. In a hierarchical judicial system, inferior judges obviously adhere to precedent when they fear reversal by a higher court. But do judges in fact adhere to horizontal precedent of a co-equal court? What about when precedent threatens to constrain the result in a particularly important case? What happens if a particular judge does not follow precedent? Do other judges on the same level court impose punishment, or does punishment, if imposed at all, arise from elsewhere? Is it possible to punish an isolated defector without harming the regime of precedent for the court as a whole? Why or why not? If not, does this mean that the regime of precedent operates independently of the actions of individual judges on the court? And if that is true, does that imply that precedent is more likely to take vertical or horizontal form? Why?

Which, if any, of the games described thus far is most relevant in answering these questions? Do judges only adhere to precedent when they anticipate endless future periods? Do judges ever anticipate that there will be no end point? What about state systems that appoint judges for periods of years? Why do they adhere to precedent? Does the unraveling problem prevent reliance upon game theory in developing a coherent account of precedent? If so, what alternative explanations can you devise? Is it possible that some structural features of the judiciary impose precedent without relying upon a trigger strategy equilibrium?[69]15 TXTH2⊡3.   Is the Prisoners' Dilemma Good or Bad?

We have now seen an illustration of a benign prisoners' dilemma (from a social perspective), namely the classic case involving persons who have committed serious offenses. And we have seen a potentially problem-

---

upon to establish a proposition of law. *See* Harold J. Berman & Charles J. Reid, Jr., *The Transformation of English Legal Science: From Hale to Blackstone*, 45 EMORY L.J. 437, 444–451 (1996). Stare decisis, meaning the obligation to abide by a particular decision on a point of law as precedent, is a more recent development. *See id.* at 513–16 (discussing use of case method in influencing conventional understanding of stare decisis); *see also* Hart v. Massanari, 266 F.3d 1155, 1175 (9th Cir. 2001) (Kozinski, J.) ("Case precedent at common law thus resembled much more what we call persuasive authority than the binding authority that is the backbone of much of the federal judicial system."). In modern jurisprudence, the terms are used interchangeably and we use them in that fashion in this discussion.

68. Abramowicz & Stearns, *supra* note 33, at 953; Todd J. Zywicki, *A Unanimity–Reinforcing Model of Efficiency in the Common Law: An Institutional Comparison of Common Law and Legislative Solutions to Large–Number Externality Problems*, 46 CASE W. RES. L. REV. 961, 996–1004 (1996); JOHN HENRY MERRYMAN & ROGELIO PÉREZ-PERDOMO, THE CIVIL LAW TRADITION: AN INTRODUCTION TO THE LEGAL SYSTEMS OF WESTERN EUROPE AND LATIN AMERICA (3rd ed. 2007).

69. *See infra* chapter 7, section I.B.5; *see also* Abramowicz & Stearns, *supra* note 33, at 953.

atical prisoners' dilemma involving the breakdown in the stability of precedent in the law. Can you identify other examples of prisoners' dilemmas that produce net positive and net negative results? Can you identify mechanisms that help to resolve the problems that prisoners' dilemmas create in the negative case, or mechanisms that help to facilitate a prisoners' dilemma in the positive case? Is it fair to say that one objective of a well functioning legal system is to facilitate beneficial prisoners' dilemmas and to devise solutions to problematical ones? If so, are judges well suited to the task of identifying good versus bad prisoners' dilemmas? Why or why not?

Consider the following additional examples of good and bad prisoners' dilemmas. Market competition rests on the fundamental mechanism that competition among sellers and among buyers is a prisoners' dilemma relationship. All firms would benefit if they could combine to restrict production and raise prices; all consumers would benefit if they could combine to coordinate demand and reduce prices. Antitrust law generally seeks to break up cartels, or to prevent firms from adopting schemes that result in monopolistic pricing strategies, in favor of a larger number of competitive firms or practices more likely to promote competitive pricing.[70] Competitive markets, by definition, involve a very large number of producers and consumers. While the standard prisoners' dilemma is generally presented with two players, competitive markets nonetheless have the characteristic features of a benign multilateral prisoners' dilemma. Given the large numbers of players involved in competitive markets, producers and consumers are unable to create effective agreements to coordinate behavior—either in terms of production levels (in the case of sellers) or consumption levels (in the case of buyers)—or to enforce any agreements that they wish they had made.[71] Assuming that these characterizations are fair, are restraints on monopoly or anticompetitive policies equivalent to a legal effort to create or perpetuate a benign prisoners' dilemma?

Promoting competition might also contradict other goals, thus complicating the claim that it is invariably a good prisoners' dilemma. Consider

---

70. As David Evans and Keith Hylton have observed, antitrust law does not prohibit every method of exploiting monopoly power, including most notably decisions to charge a monopoly price. While antitrust law regulates specific problematic conduct that results in monopolistic strategies, according to the authors it simultaneously balances the pricing concern against the dynamic incentives to undertake entrepreneurial efforts targeted toward innovation. Because the potential for monopoly profit is often an inducement to investing in an area characterized by high start up costs, large scale economies, and declining average cost, the authors maintain that antitrust law sometimes applies a lighter hand when pursuing individual firms with monopoly power than firms engaged in combined pricing strategies with other firms. *See* David S. Evans & Keith N. Hylton, *The Lawful Acquisition and Exercise of Monopoly Power and its Implications for the Objectives of Antitrust*, 4 COMPETITION POL'Y INT'L 203 (2008).

71. *See generally* Monroe Friedman, *Consumer Boycotts in the United States, 1970–1980: Contemporary Events in Historical Perspective*, 19 J. CONSUMER AFF. 96, 108 (1985) (acknowledging difficulty of measurement but positing that consumer boycotts are generally unsuccessful). For an interesting analysis of the various pressures that affect the success of boycotts, see Sankar Sen et al., *Withholding Consumption: A Social Dilemma Perspective on Consumer Boycotts*, 28 J. CONSUMER RES. 399 (2001).

an open-access resource, such as a fishery in a lake.[72] The fish in the lake should be harvested at a rate that maintains the long-term viability of the fish population in the lake, thereby maximizing the stream of revenues over time. A single owner of the lake would harvest the fish at this rate. Where the lake is open to anyone, however, fishermen are in a prisoners' dilemma problem with respect to one another. If one fisherman foregoes a catch or throws back a fish that is too small so that it can be caught at a more optimal time, he runs the risk that a subsequent fisherman will not be as restrained. Indeed, the incentive of each fisherman acting rationally would be to catch as many fish as possible before others do so, leading to a rapid depletion of the number of fish in the lake. If fishermen can overcome their collective-action problems and control access to the fishery, they can prevent the depletion of the resource. On the other hand, their efforts might run afoul of the antitrust laws, which forbid agreements to reduce competition. Some scholars have urged that the antitrust laws be modified or applied in such a manner as to permit private agreements among competitors when necessary to prevent the depletion of a common pool resource.[73]

Consider also the case of labor unions. To the extent that unions can be seen as cartelizing labor, can you identify policy reasons why the legal system might be willing to facilitate a solution to a supply side prisoners' dilemma affecting the sale of labor with its contrary inclination in the context of the production and sales of goods and services? To the extent that collective bargaining succeeds in raising wages above what would otherwise prevail in the free market, it has the potential to produce unemployment in the economy, especially among unskilled, young, and minority workers. Is permitting collective bargaining, and thereby restricting competition among employees for jobs and wages, a beneficial solution to a problematic prisoners' dilemma game or is it instead a means of allowing a cartel that thwarts what would otherwise be a socially beneficial prisoners' dilemma game akin to market competition more generally? How can you tell? To what extent, if any, are your answers to these questions informed by game theory? To what extent, if any, is it informed by interest group theory? Is this a context in which intuitions drawn from game theory and interest group theory run in different directions? If so, how should the resulting policy questions be resolved? And by whom?

Now consider various environmental enforcement regimes, for example, the Clean Air Act,[74] the Clean Water Act,[75] or the Endangered Species Act.[76] Are these statutes motivated by concerns that, left to their own devices, firms would engage in practices that thwart expressed societal

---

72. H. Scott Gordon, *The Economic Theory of a Common–Property Resource: The Fishery*, 62 J. POL. ECON. 124 (1954).

73. *See* Jonathan H. Adler, *Conservation Through Collusion: Antitrust as an Obstacle to Marine Resource Conservation*, 61 WASH. & LEE L. REV. 3 (2004). We will revisit this model of the common pool resource in the applications in this chapter.

74. 42 U.S.C. § 7401–7671 (2006).

75. 33 U.S.C. § 1251–1387 (2006).

76. 16 U.S.C. § 1531–1544 (2006).

interests in preserving the quality of water and air and endangered species and their habitats? Are they further motivated by the concern that again, left to their own devices, firms and states in which firms operate are in a prisoners' dilemma in which each would prefer that others comply with restrictive regulatory practices, while reserving the power to cheat in an effort to facilitate profitable economic activity in conflict with these policy concerns? Or are they devices to cartelize industries, raise prices, and create barriers to entry? Or both? Can you tell whether these regulations are solving a prisoners' dilemma game or creating a cartel in response to what otherwise would be a socially beneficial prisoners' dilemma game?

We do not intend to suggest that such large bodies of case law as antitrust, environmental law, and labor law can be understood entirely as a response to a very simple prisoners' dilemma analysis. Instead, we only wish to show that the prisoners' dilemma, along with the other games introduced in this chapter, can provide a helpful starting point or perspective in considering the normative foundations of these and other regulatory regimes. Consider as you go through the book whether you can identify other bodies of case law or regulatory law that can be explained in terms of the desire to create or thwart a prisoners' dilemma. Can you identify some contrary examples in which the legal system has facilitated a harmful prisoners' dilemma or undermined a beneficial prisoners' dilemma? If you do identify such cases, do the other tools introduced in this book help to explain the resulting anomaly?

4. The Prisoners' Dilemma and the Complexity of Games

As previously noted, this chapter is organized according to the increasing complexity of the games introduced. While the prisoners' dilemma game is likely the most familiar game to most readers, as the preceding discussion has demonstrated, even that game has the capacity for important and complex nuances. While the folk theorem demonstrates the possibility of virtually any outcome in an iterated game depending, for example, on the discount rate, under specified conditions, the prisoners' dilemma yields a single dominant Nash equilibrium outcome whether played in single period or iterated form. The prisoners' dilemma game presumes that the players are unable to coordinate their behavior and that, as a result of the payoffs, the combined effect of each player's independent but rational strategy produces an equilibrium result that each player would prefer to avoid as compared with another available set of combined strategies. Under specified conditions, the iterated game then shifts the dominant Nash outcome to a contrary regime of mutual cooperation. Finally, if we posit a known end period, then the game unravels. Once again, depending on the discount rate, the result is a single Nash equilibrium, this time restoring the lower right (mutual defection) regime.

In the games that follow in the next part, we look more systematically at games that lack a single dominant equilibrium outcome. While the following games produce pure Nash equilibrium outcomes, it is possible that the actual outcomes that obtain are instead mixed strategy equilibria.

These games raise important policy questions concerning the role of the state in facilitating regimes that increase the probability of a favored outcome or, instead, that allow a set of mixed outcomes.

II.   GAMES WITH MORE THAN ONE PURE NASH STRATEGY EQUILIBRIUM

The following games result in more than a single pure Nash equilibrium strategy and, in addition, raise the possibility of a result that thwarts any pure Nash strategy. The non-equilibrium strategy can arise when the players follow a "mixed strategy" such as randomizing over options (for example selecting either of two available strategies fifty percent of the time), in an effort to anticipate the likely strategy of the other player. While such strategies produce an expected (or ex ante) payoff, referred to as a "mixed strategy equilibrium," the actual (or ex post) value will depend on the actual strategy selected by the other player. Sometimes the mixed strategy will produce the desired payoff, but if so, it is only because of the fortuity of a correct guess. Alternatively, when the mixed strategy results in an incorrect guess, meaning a failure to match the strategy of the other player, the result is a lower set of payoffs for both players than would have been available had the players instead adopted strategies that resulted in the benefits of the higher payoffs produced from mutual cooperation. Once again, we will provide illustrations using normal form games, and then consider how the Nash concept conduces to a solution or set of preferred solutions in each game.

Again, we begin with the simplest version of games with multiple Nash equilibria and then add increasing complexity. We start with the driving game. This game involves an intuitive problem of pure coordination, one in which no one strategy is inherently superior to any other and the only basis for preference is assumed to be ensuring that the two players act consistently. As we will see, however, even a mutual desire for beneficial coordination does not ensure that the players succeed. One obvious function for government operating in its regulatory capacity is in facilitating incentives to ensure benign pure Nash equilibrium results in coordination games. We then introduce the battle of the sexes. The outdated label should not distract from the game's important central insight.[77] In contrast with the driving game, two players might agree on the benefit of accomplishing coordinated rather than mixed strategies, while disagreeing as to the relative benefits and burdens of the available coordinated strategies. And finally we introduce the game of chicken. This unfortunate normal form game depicts conditions under which two players seek to best each other in a context in which one or both players can adopt strategies that conduce to severe, even deadly, consequences. We then introduce an alternative equilibrium concept, non-myopic equilibri-

---

77. By way of example, while both authors of this book are men, one would generally prefer theater to most sporting events, while the other would prefer sporting events to most theater.

um,[78] to demonstrate why the apparent Nash outcome might not invariably obtain.

Together these games help to generalize the public policy inquiry with which we ended our discussion of the prisoners' dilemma. What role does the state have in seeking to transform problematical games into benign games that are more likely to produce beneficial results for the parties involved and for society? Within games that admit of more than a single pure Nash equilibrium strategy, what role does the state have in encouraging courses of play that lead players to preferred (pure) over disfavored (mixed) equilibrium outcomes?

A. THE DRIVING GAME

Assume that we are at early part of the twentieth century, with the advent of automobiles. While some relatively wealthy individuals drive, cars remain scarce and, as a result, rules governing their operation are rudimentary.[79] Assume that in a given jurisdiction there are no rules governing whether automobiles should be driven on the left or right side of the road. To simplify, assume that there are only two drivers, Anne (A) and Bob (B), and that neither much cares which side of the road he or she drives on. Both do care, however, that whichever convention one follows the other follows as well. Thus, while each driver least prefers that one drive on the left while the other drives on the right, each is indifferent as between a rule requiring both to drive on the left or both to drive on the right. Table 4:4 captures the payoffs in this game.

Table 4:4. The Driving Game

Payoffs for (A, B)	B drives left	B drives right
A drives left	**10, 10**	0, 0
A drives right	0, 0	**10, 10**

The payoffs reflect the intuition that the driving game involves a problem of pure coordination. If driver A drives left, and if driver B initially drives right, driver B can improve his payoffs from 0 to 10 by shifting and also driving left. Conversely, if driver A drives right, and driver B initially drives left, driver B can again improve his payoffs from 0 to 10, this time by shifting and also driving right. Neither left nor right is inherently superior but it is vital that both players follow the same strategy. The payoffs are reciprocal, and so if driver B is the initial mover,

---

78. STEVEN J. BRAMS, THEORY OF MOVES (1994).

79. In fact, in the earliest period there were no testing requirements for a driver's license and of course traffic rules were extremely limited. *See* M.G. LAY, WAYS OF THE WORLD 173–97 (1992) (describing the development of drivers' licenses as a "revenue raising measure" imposed on cabs but not private owners, and the gradual development of other rules of the road).

A's incentives to conform to *B's* behavior are the same. The effect is to motivate the second driver to follow the selected strategy of the first driver.

In contrast with the prisoners' dilemma, which when modeled with certain assumptions about the discount rate and the benefits of cooperation, potentially yields a single Nash equilibrium strategy in either single period or iterated form, the driving game produces two pure Nash equilibrium strategies (right/right or left/left) in a single round of play. And yet, it is not necessarily the case that the game will produce either of the available pure Nash equilibrium results. In the hypothetical, we assumed that either driver *A* or driver *B* was the initial mover. Imagine instead that the two drivers make their selection at the same time, and thus without the benefit of the first driver observing the other driver's selected strategy. In this case, each driver will rationally try to follow what he or she expects the other driver to do without knowing the other driver's selection and will have only a fifty percent chance of making the correct prediction. If, for example, driver *A* anticipates that driver *B* will drive right, driver *A* will drive right. Because driver *A* makes his choice without knowledge of driver *B's* actual strategy, however, it is possible that despite their best efforts to achieve a coordinated strategy, the two drivers inadvertently select opposite driving regimes to their mutual detriment. If the players follow a mixed strategy in which each randomizes over options (for example selecting right or left fifty percent of the time), then the result is known as a "mixed strategy equilibrium." Sometimes the mixed strategy will produce the desired effect (right/right or left/left), but when it does so, this results from the fortuity of a correct guess. Alternatively, when the mixed strategy results in an incorrect guess, meaning failing to match the strategy of the other player and thus yielding lower payoffs, the result is a lower set of payoffs for both players than would have been available had the players instead adopted a strategy that resulted in the benefits of the higher payoffs produced from mutual cooperation.

While each of the two disfavored results (left/right or right/left) represents a potential equilibrium solution, at least if the game is played in a single period, each rests outside the preferred pure Nash results that would obtain if the players had more information about the actions of the other player in advance of that round or if instead the game were played sequentially.

The most obvious illustration, for which the game was named, involves driving. State law regulates most aspects of highway safety, including selecting the side of the road on which to travel. While in the United States, we drive on the right side of the road (with left-side steering wheels), we know that this solution is not unique.[80] England and Australia, for example, employ the opposite, but still pure Nash equilibrium, regime of driving on the left side of the road (with steering wheels on the

---

80. The actual history of right side driving in the United States appears to be path dependent. Historians trace right driving to the technology of the Conestoga wagon, in the mid-eighteenth century. For a discussion, see LAY, *supra* note 79, at 199–200. Lay explains:

A major impetus for right-hand driving in the United States came from the design of the Conestoga wagon, which had led to the winning of the West. The wagon was operated either by

right). Neither of these two regimes is superior to the other, which is why each represents a pure Nash equilibrium strategy. But of course either is superior to the non-pure Nash outcomes of right/left or left/right driving.

A more complex illustration of the driving game arises in the context of the dormant Commerce Clause.[81] Numerous states have highway safety laws that specify particular means of transporting goods through the state. On occasion, the safety laws of one state run up against those of a neighboring state. When this occurs, the conflicting legal regimes threaten to impose considerable costs on those who engage in the valuable activity of transporting goods as part of interstate commerce. On several notable occasions, conflicting laws of this sort have given rise to constitutional challenges under the dormant Commerce Clause.[82] Two prominent illustrations are *Bibb v. Navajo Freight Lines*,[83] and *Kassel v. Consolidated Freightways*.[84]

In *Bibb*, Illinois had a law that required that trucks use only curved mudflaps. This law proved problematical because it conflicted with the contrary laws of forty-five other states that instead demanded straight mudflaps. It was not possible to comply with both legal regimes without considerable cost and effort, as one would have to change mudflaps at the border of Illinois and a neighboring state with a contrary law. In *Kassel*, Iowa prohibited, with notable exceptions,[85] the use of sixty-five foot twin

---

the postilion driver riding the left-hand near horse—called the wheel horse—or by the driver walking or sitting on a "lazy board" on the left-hand side of the vehicle. He kept to the left in both cases in order to use his right hand to manage the horses and operate the brake lever mounted on the left-hand side. Passing therefore required moving to the right to give the driver forward vision.

Id. at 199. *See also* Richard F. Weingroff, On the Right Side of the Road, http://www.fhwa.dot.gov/ infrastructure/right.cfm (Department of Transportation, Federal Highway Administration, Infrastructure) (last visited May 1, 2009).

As of this writing, for the first time in over forty years, a sovereign nation is planning a roadside driving switch. Prime Minister Tuilaepa Sailele Malielegaoi has ordered the tiny Pacific island nation of Samoa to switch from right to left driving (and a prospective switch from left to right steering wheels) effective September 9, 2009, as a means of encouraging the importation by Samoan workers in Australia and new Zealand of cheaper used cars from those nearby nations, which follow the British driving convention. *See* David Whitley, *Samoa Provokes Fury by Switching Sides of the Road*, July 3, 2009, http://www.telegraph.co.uk/motoring/news/5732906/ Samoa-provokes-fury-by-switching-sides-of-the-road.html. While this has met considerable internal resistance, in part due to the capital loss to left side steering wheel vehicle owners resulting from the altered secondary market, *see* Patrick Barta, *Shifting the Right of Way to the Left Leaves Some Samoans Feeling Wronged*, WALL ST. J., Aug. 24, 2009, at A1, the planned switch suggests that the path dependent account of coordinated driving regimes is not limited to contiguous states. *See infra* pp. 207–09.

81. The discussion that follows is based upon Maxwell L. Stearns, *A Beautiful Mend: A Game Theoretical Analysis of the Dormant Commerce Clause,* 45 WM. & MARY L. REV. 1 (2003).

82. The Commerce Clause states: "To regulate Commerce with foreign Nations, and among the several States, and with the Indian Tribes." U.S. CONST. art. I, § 6, cl. 3. While the clause thus takes the form of an express delegation of authority to Congress to regulate commerce, almost from its inception the Supreme Court has also construed the clause to limit the power of states to interfere with interstate commerce. For a detailed history and analysis, see Stearns, *supra* note 81.

83. Bibb v. Navajo Freight Lines, Inc., 359 U.S. 520 (1959).

84. Kassel v. Consol. Freightways Corp., 450 U.S. 662 (1981).

85. These exceptions included: the use of oversize vehicles for shipments from border cities to adjoining states, where the cities passed ordinances to permit their use; Iowa truck manufacturers shipping trucks up to seventy feet; and shipping oversized mobile homes from points in Iowa to Iowa residents. *Id.* at 666.

trailers, although the laws of the surrounding states permitted such rigs.[86] Once again, whatever the merits of the law as a safety measure, the law was problematical in that it ran up against those of the surrounding states that favored such means of transportation over other large rigs that they prohibited but that Iowa permitted.

How might you use game theory to characterize the challenged Illinois and Iowa laws? Are these seemingly noncompliant laws the product of a driving game or of some other game? If they are the product of a driving game, why then did Illinois and Iowa enact laws out of keeping with those of other, surrounding states, rather than trying to replicate the laws of such states in an effort to facilitate the flow of interstate commerce? Might there be situations in which particular states actually prefer to produce a mixed strategy equilibrium? If so, what would the benefits be to such a state? Consider the following analysis.[87]

Among the most elementary intuitions of economic analysis is the law of diminishing returns. As a general matter, as one acquires more units of a given good, the marginal value or utility that one derives from acquiring each successive unit declines.[88] There are, however, notable exceptions to this important principle. Marginal values have the potential to rise, rather than decline, in cases involving "positive network externalities" or "path dependence."[89] These related concepts are helpful in assessing the nature of the driving game as it is played among states, as opposed to the simpler example involving driving within a particular jurisdiction.

Assume a nation with two states in which State A enacts a policy of right driving (left steering wheels). This law provides a clear benefit to in-state drivers by inhibiting avoidable collisions caused simply by the absence of an announced coordinating strategy on the choice of the left or right side driving. But if neighboring State B possesses a contrary driving regime (left driving, right steering wheels), then the value of State A's law is limited to driving within a single jurisdiction. In this instance, the marginal value of the law rises if State B enacts a consistent law, thus facilitating the flow of vehicular traffic between and within the two bordering states. Now expand the scope to include a nation, like the United States, with a large number of contiguous states. The phenomenon of increasing marginal utility continues as other adjoining states, States C,

86. Note that in this case, other parts of the country, including all of New England and most of the Southeast, were consistent with the Iowa regime. *Kassel*, 450 U.S. at 687–88 (Rehnquist, J., dissenting).

87. This analysis is developed more fully *infra* pp. 207–09.

88. In fact, this insight resolves what Adam Smith considered a foundational anomaly of economics, namely why an essential good like water was relatively valueless as compared with such inessential luxuries as diamonds. KARL E. CASE & RAY C. FAIR, PRINCIPLES OF MACROECONOMICS 341 (7th ed. 2004); MAXWELL L. STEARNS, PUBLIC CHOICE AND PUBLIC LAW: READINGS AND COMMENTARY, at xxi (1997); ALFRED MARSHALL, PRINCIPLES OF ECONOMICS 13 (8th ed. 1920).

89. For general discussions of path dependence, see Maxwell L. Stearns, *Standing Back from the Forest: Justiciability and Social Choice*, 83 CAL. L. REV. 1309 (1995) (linking the modern standing doctrine to stare decisis-induced path dependence and the corresponding incentive of ideological interest groups to manipulate case orderings to effect favorable doctrine); Maxwell L. Stearns, *Standing and Social Choice: Historical Evidence*, 144 U. PA. L. REV. 309 (1995) (providing historical and case support for social choice theory of standing doctrine); Oona Hathaway, *Path Dependence in the Law: The Course and Pattern of Legal Change in a Common Law System*, 86 IOWA L. REV. 601 (2001) (reviewing various theories of path dependence as related to judicial behavior).

D, and E, for example, embrace the same driving regime. As each state enacts the consistent driving regime, initially selected by State A, the marginal utility for drivers, along with that of the affected states, increases.

In this instance, the driving regime's value is not a function of its merit in comparison with alternative driving regimes. Rather, the value is a function of the regime's coordination with those of adjoining states. Had the initial moving state instead elected a left driving regime (with right steering wheels), then the increasing marginal utility would have instead attached to the continued selection of that regime in the surrounding states. The value of the regime is thus independent of its normative merit and is instead dependent upon coordination resulting from the path of law that generated it.

The phenomenon of path dependence is also useful in assessing strategies for the implementation of newly developing technologies. Scholars have long noted, for example, that the modern typing keyboard, labeled "QWERTY" after the top left row of lettered keys, is a function of then nascent key punch technology designed to spread out the most commonly hit keys on a typewriter to avoid malfunctions due to jamming.[90] This concern became less of a problem when electronic typewriters replaced manual ones, and has been eliminated altogether in the modern age of digital word processing and computers, technologies that avoid mechanical hammering of letters.

August Dvorak devised a new typing system that reassigned the most commonly used letters to the strongest fingers. While this alternative never gained widespread popularity, numerous commentators maintain that in many respects, its operation is technically superior to the QWERTY keyboard.[91] One popular, albeit contested, account of this seeming anomaly is that whatever the respective merits of the two keyboard technologies, Dvorak was destined to fail as a result of path dependence.[92] This issue is not merely the somewhat significant personal learning curve for a given keyboard, but also the fact that virtually all text-based data entry systems throughout the world that rely upon the English alphabet, and even some that do not, have developed technologies around the QWERTY keyboard technology.[93] Path dependence implies that even a

---

90. Paul A. David, *Clio and the Economics of QWERTY*, 75 Am. Econ. Rev. 332 (1985); S.J. Liebowitz & Stephen E. Margolis, *The Fable of the Keys*, 33 J.L. & Econ. 1 (1990); *see generally* Michael L. Katz & Carl Shapiro, *Network Externalities, Competition, and Compatibility*, 75 Am. Econ. Rev. 424–40 (1985).

91. For detractors from this conventional account, see Stan J. Liebowitz & Stephen E. Margolis, Winners, Losers, and Microsoft: Competition and Antitrust in High Technology 140 (1999); Liebowitz & Margolis, *supra* note 90, at 21 ("[T]he evidence in the standard history of Qwerty versus Dvorak is flawed and incomplete.... [T]he claims for the superiority of the Dvorak keyboard are suspect.").

92. Richard Nelson & Sidney Winter, An Evolutionary Theory of Economic Change (1982); Paul A. David, *Path Dependence, Its Critics and the Quest for 'Historical Economics,'* in Evolution and Path Dependence in Economic Ideas: Past and Present (Pierre Garrouste & Stavros Ioannides eds., 2000).

93. Not only do other nations with romance languages use QWERTY, but systems with altogether different alphabets, e.g., Mandarin or Hebrew, code those alphabets on QWERTY keyboards. Even countries with languages other than English are locked into QWERTY. *See* Neville Holmes, *The Profession as a Culture Killer*, Computer, Sept. 2007, http://boole.computer.

superior technology developed at a later time might fail to be adopted if the industry path has already strongly favored an earlier (albeit inferior) technology. This is known as a "lock-in" effect, as the existing technology becomes locked-in.

The intuition underlying increasing marginal utilities resulting from path dependence can also be expressed in terms of *positive network externalities.* As more and more people began to use QWERTY, the cost of operating consistently with that technology was reduced while the marginal benefit of being part of a common system increased. Similar accounts relying upon path dependence and positive network externalities have been suggested to explain the dominance of VHS technology over Beta in recording video[94] and the use of Windows operating systems over alternatives offered, most notably, by IBM and Apple.[95]

1. Regulation versus Standards

The preceding analysis raises the question of when achieving the benefits of positive network externalities demands no more than a common standard or set of standards for conducting business or other legal affairs, on the one hand, versus when it is necessary for the government to issue binding regulations requiring the use of the common standard, on the other.[96] In the discussion that follows we provide illustrations of regimes in which a potential benefit follows the regulatory adoption of a national standard, rather than a mandated substantive rule governing how business should be conducted. To be clear, these examples are not intended as proof that the governmental provision was necessary to the creation of a standard, and it is possible, both theoretically and perhaps historically, that an alternative set of standards might have emerged through private market forces absent the government's imposed standard. The analysis does support the intuition that one potential benefit of a regulatory system is standard-setting, which can help to avoid various coordination difficulties.

---

org/portal/site/computer/index.jsp?pageID=computer_level1 & path=computer/homepage/Sept07 & file=profession.xml & xsl=article.xsl (discussing China's reliance on QWERTY).

94. Stanley M. Besen & Joseph Farrell, *Choosing How to Compete: Strategies and Tactics in Standardization,* J. ECON. PERSP., Spring 1994, at 117–118.

95. For related discussions, see John E. Popatka & William H. Page, *Microsoft, Monopolization, and Network Externalities: Some Uses and Abuses of Economic Theory in Antitrust Decision Making,* ANTITRUST BULL., Summer 1995, at 317, 321–23. Network externalities in the operating system market are tied not only to human investment, but also to the availability of other applications. *Id.* at 335–40. For an interesting first-person discussion of the economic effects that led to Windows dominance over OS/2, see Posting of Gordon Letwin to comp.os.ms-windows.misc (Aug. 17, 1995), http://groups.google.com/group/comp.os.ms-windows.misc/msg/d710490b 09745d5e5e. For a critical account of these path dependence claims, see Liebowitz & Margolis, *supra* 10 note 90, at 5.

96. For example, the United States and Europe have taken markedly different approaches to standard setting in cellular phone networks. For a discussion, see Neil Gandal et al., *Standards in Wireless Telephone Networks,* 27 TELECOMM. POL'Y 325 (2003). *See also* Dan Saugstrup & Anders Henten, *3G Standards: The Battle Between WCDMA and CDMA 2000,* INFO. 2006 Issue No. 4, at 10, 14–15.

Consider first the evolution of money as a means of facilitating trade and the role of government in standardizing money. Early historians claimed that money as a medium of exchange emerged through spontaneous ordering to allow individuals to coordinate their behavior into a larger coordinated network.[97] Because money serves both as a store of value and as a means of relative valuation, it creates the possibility of robust market exchange by avoiding the need for barter. Historically, units of currency have included such scarce goods as salt, clam shells, and beads. Over time, monetary systems have tended to standardize on the use of scarce metals, such as gold and silver.

The value of the standardization of money in promoting a system of exchange and in providing a means of storing value is demonstrated by the repeated "invention" of money throughout human history. In the United States throughout most of the nineteenth century, private banks issued paper currency backed by precious metals. Today, many banks issue credit cards and debit cards that are almost universally accepted and redeemed against the assets of the bank of issuance.

Over time, the central government has assumed the role of issuing various forms of currency. Inflationary government monetary policies during the eras of the Revolutionary War and Articles of Confederation led to a ban on issuance of paper currency in the Constitution.[98] Early governmental issuances of paper money during the first half of the nineteenth century were intended to fund government operations during emergencies (such as during the War of 1812), but were not declared legal tender. It was not until the issuance of "greenbacks" during the Civil War, which "postponed" the redemption of paper into gold, that the federal government first declared such currency to be legal tender. In 1870 the Supreme Court struck down the Legal Tender Act as violating the Constitution, only to reverse itself in 1871 following a change in the membership of the Court.[99] Within the United States today, the Federal Reserve issues currency that is declared "legal tender" for all debts public and private.[100]

What implications does this historical account hold for a regime in which the government standardizes currency by law? Would the United States be better served without a central unit of currency declared as legal tender by the federal government? If so, would you anticipate competition among states to serve this role? What about competition within private markets, perhaps among banks? If you conclude that there is a substantial

---

97. Carl Menger, *On the Origins of Money*, 2 ECON. J. 239 (1892).

98. *See* Todd J. Zywicki, *The Coinage Clause*, *in* THE HERITAGE GUIDE TO THE CONSTITUTION 114 (2005).

99. Hepburn v. Griswold, 75 U.S. (8 Wall.) 603 (1870) (invalidating the Legal Tender Act); Legal Tender Cases, 79 U.S. 457 (1871) (overruling *Hepburn*). A change in Court personnel involving the appointments of Justices William Strong and Joseph Bradley are credited as affecting this change in outcome. For an in-depth discussion of the process leading to this change, see Charles M. Fairman, *Reconstruction and Reunion: 1864–88*, 6 HISTORY OF THE SUPREME COURT OF THE UNITED STATES 713–63 (1971).

100. 31 U.S.C. § 5103 (2006).

benefit to private over government currency, can you explain why most nations have national currencies? Is this an (ironic) example of leaving money on the table? Or is this explained with a public choice story? And if so, who are the players? Are they the same from nation to nation? Or instead, is there an overriding benefit to some form of national currency standardization? Do central currencies reduce transactions costs by establishing a reliable standard against which all businesses can assess value? In the absence of a central currency, would a dominant substitute emerge, or instead would there be a large number of competing currencies and a corresponding need to translate currencies from different systems? Under which regime are creditors—or debtors—likely to be better off? Is the benefit of a central currency outweighed by the risk that the government will inflate the currency as needed to reduce its debt? Are there effective bonding mechanisms that governments can implement to gain the benefits of standardized currencies while controlling for the risk of inflation? Are governments or private entities better suited to issuing effective bonds against the devaluation resulting from inflation? Why?

For an interesting example of spontaneous use of a foreign national currency, consider the famous numismatic example involving the 1780 Maria Teresa Thaler coin. While the coin was first minted in 1741, the Austrian government continued to strike the coin with the same date, 1780, following Maria Teresa's death.[101] The Maria Teresa Thaler rapidly emerged as the leading coin throughout the Austrian empire and later through major parts of the Arab world. The coin set such a remarkable standard that the Austrian government continued issuing the 1780 imprint even after it was demonetized in the 1850s, for continued use as a trade coin.[102] In effect, the coin's prestige allowed it to emerge the dominant medium of exchange throughout a large part of the world. Indeed, it was so popular that other nations tacitly approved its use by declining to impose an alternative medium of exchange.

Can one tell an analogous story about the role of the United States dollar or the Euro today? Throughout many parts of the world, the dollar or Euro has become a *de facto* "coin of the realm" at least in major urban centers where such currencies are regarded as relatively stable gauges of value and can be converted at relatively low cost into local currency. In effect, at various times, systems around the world have customized their business financing around the standards set out by forms of currency issued by Austria, the United States, or the European Union, rather than based upon a superimposed regulatory system focused on a single mandated medium of exchange.

---

101. *See* Adrian Tschoegl, *Maria Theresa's Thaler: A Case of International Money*, 27 E. ECON. J. 443, 444–45, 452 (2001) (noting that while the Thaler was actually struck beginning in 1741, the date was fixed at 1780 upon Maria Theresa's death, and that even today the coin is still being struck in limited quantities for collectors).

102. Shepard Pond, *The Maria Theresa Thaler: A Famous Trade Coin*, BULL. BUS. HIST. SOC'Y, Apr. 1941, at 29. Numismatists are able to distinguish early coinage from later issuances bearing the same date. *Id.* at 26.

Also consider the flexibility among firms in choosing their state of incorporation and the ability of contracting parties in at least some circumstances to choose the governing legal regime through contractual choice of law. Delaware is a tiny state, but it has become the dominant standard for corporate chartering in the United States. Professor Roberta Romano has argued that Delaware emerged dominant because of the relatively high percentage of state revenue resulting from corporate chartering activity.[103] Because corporate chartering accounts for 16.9% of the state's revenue, Delaware has a credible bond against radical changes in its corporate law. While other states can copy Delaware Corporate Law (indeed Nevada has done so),[104] these states cannot issue a comparable bond given Delaware's relatively small size.

While incorporating in Delaware is notably more costly than in other states, for relatively large corporations, this nonetheless remains a minor expense.[105] Many companies with a more significant presence in other states nonetheless are legally based in Delaware, thus rendering their governance subject to Delaware law as a result of the internal affairs doctrine.[106] In the context of transacting, many parties include choice of law clauses that specifically rely upon the law of other jurisdictions to govern potential legal disputes that might arise. And in some instances, firms designate arbitration in lieu of a state-based legal system.[107]

Do these two illustrations—corporate chartering and contractual choice of law—support the intuition that at least in some circumstances, parties can benefit from a uniform standard, and thus from positive network externalities, without the burdens of mandatory regulation? Can you identify circumstances in which this is less likely to be true and when

---

103. Roberta Romano, *Law as a Product: Some Pieces of the Incorporation Puzzle*, 1 J.L. ECON. & ORG. 225, 240 (1985).

104. Jonathan R. Macey & Geoffrey P. Miller, *Toward an Interest–Group Theory of Delaware Corporate Law*, 65 TEX. L. REV. 469, 488 (1987).

105. Lucian Arye Bebchuk & Assaf Hamdani, *Vigorous Race or Leisurely Walk: Reconsidering the Competition over Corporate Charters,* 112 YALE L.J. 553, 573 (2002) (noting that "Incorporation in Delaware involves a franchise tax that is nonnegligible, though not substantial for most publicly traded firms."). The differential cost is not that of *establishing* a corporation, but results from "franchise fees" for Delaware firms. *See* ANTHONY MANCUSO, INCORPORATE YOUR BUSINESS app. A (2d ed. 2004). These fees can range from $75 to $165,000 based upon the number of shares in the incorporated Delaware firm. *See* Delaware Department of State, How to Calculate Franchise Taxes, http://corp.delaware.gov/frtaxcalc.shtml (last visited May 1, 2009). For a discussion of the incidence of such fees on various companies based upon size, see Marcel Kahan & Ehud Kamar, *The Myth of State Competition in Corporate Law,* 55 STAN. L. REV. 679, 690–99 (2002) (presenting tables showing marginal revenues from annual taxes and franchise fees by state).

106. For a general discussion of the Internal Affairs Doctrine, see Frederick Tung, *Before Competition: Origins of the Internal Affairs Doctrine*, 32 J. CORP. L. 33 (2006). *See also* LARRY E. RIBSTEIN & PETER V. LETSOU, BUSINESS ASSOCIATIONS (4th ed. 2003); Larry E. Ribstein & Erin A. O'Hara, *Corporations and the Market for Law*, 2008 ILL. L. REV. 661. George Stigler, *Public Regulation of the Securities Markets*, 37 J. BUS. 117 (1964) (same); George Benston, *Required Disclosure and the Stock Market: An Evaluation of the Securities Exchange Act of 1934*, 63 AM. ECON. REV. 132 (1972) (providing interest group account of Securities Act of 1934).

107. For informative discussions of contractual choice of law, see ERIN O'HARA & LARRY RIBSTEIN, THE LAW MARKET (2009); Andrew T. Guzman, *Choice of Law: New Foundations*, 90 GEO. L.J. 883 (2002); Erin A. O'Hara & Larry E. Ribstein, *From Politics to Efficiency in Choice of Law*, 67 U. CHI. L. REV. 1151 (2000).

it is better to have the legal system mandate the governing standard? Is game theory helpful in answering these questions?

Consider also the Securities and Exchange Commission (SEC). The SEC sets standards for publicly held corporations in a variety of contexts, including the sale and acquisition of stock. In addition, the SEC sets standards for domestic stock exchanges, including most notably the New York Stock Exchange (NYSE). As a result of these regulations, firms and individuals buying registered stocks do so knowing that the companies in question have satisfied detailed reporting requirements and are accountable for contravening various legal prohibitions, for example the prohibition against insider trading.

While this regime has the benefit of ensuring a common set of standards governing private market exchange for publicly held corporations, is uniform regulation *necessary* to achieving those goals? Legal historians have argued, for example, that the SEC was established in large part to impose barriers to entry protecting large securities dealers recognized by regulated exchanges.[108] Would competition among exchanges reduce such barriers to entry? To what extent are the potential benefits of competition weakened by the presence of a dominant exchange, such as the New York Stock Exchange, that might develop path-dependent or lock-in effects? Would competition increase the risk that those purchasing and selling shares do so absent a set of uniform regulations governing such matters as insider trading and corporate filings? If an unregulated (or privately regulated) system of securities exchange is welfare enhancing, why do all, or nearly all, large industrialized nations have regulated securities exchanges?[109] Is it possible that without the SEC, private organizations might emerge that would set quality standards for stocks in publicly held corporations? Is it possible that a central uniform standard is inferior to competing standards that might follow a federalist style approach to securities exchanges?

In other settings, private organizations create their own set of standards for the assessment of quality, for example, organizations that set standards for organic, vegetarian, and kosher foods; for fuel efficiencies in vehicles; and quality assessments for numerous goods and services. Why do many manufacturers tout their products as "approved by Underwriters Laboratory," rather than as "compliant with all applicable governmental regulations"? Which endorsement is the typical consumer likely to value more? Why? To what extent does game theory help in answering these questions? To what extent does interest group theory help? Do game

---

108. *See, e.g.,* Paul G. Mahoney, *The Political Economy of the Securities Act of 1933*, 30 J. LEGAL STUD. 1 (2001) (setting out interest group account of the founding of the SEC).

109. Franco Barbiero, *Federalizing Canada's Securities Regulatory Regime: Insights from the Australian Experience*, 24 NAT'L J. CONST. L. 89, 90 (2008) ("Since Australia centralized the regulation of its capital markets under a federal banner in 1991, Canada has remained the only developed country in the in the world with a provincially regulated regulatory regime."). Barbiero further notes that out of the 183 members of the International Organization of Securities Commissions, Canada and Bosnia–Herzegovina are the only two lacking a national securities regulator (Bosnia has 2). *See id.* at 90–91.

theoretical and interest group analyses coincide or diverge in this context? Why?

2. Overcoming Positive Network Externalities

Assuming that each of the prior illustrations of competing technologies or regulatory standards gave rise to a simple coordination game, then the early mover had a notable advantage over newer products placed in the market. Depending upon the strength of the positive network effect, this advantage might remain *even if* the later introduced product is regarded as technically superior. Consumers will weigh the benefits of sacrificing the positive network externalities against the marginal technological improvements associated with the later market entrants. Of course if the value of the new technology is substantial enough, this will eventually overwhelm the burden of departing from a path-induced technology regime.

For a simple and familiar illustration, consider some well known children's toys. Various toy systems have their own standards for interlocking with other toys by the same manufacturer and in some instances with similar products offered by competitors. While *Lego* building blocks will not interlock with *Playmobil*, *Lego* offers a large assortment of similar products that do interlock with their basic system. In contrast, while *Thomas the Train* and *BRIO* train systems are competitors, they interlock with each other, thus allowing the toys to be used interchangeably.

While systems involving interactive toys might appear trivial (although not to the authors' children!), they illustrate an important economic principle. Parents who purchase a basic *Lego* set will have some incentive to have the child acquire (or have relatives purchase) other *Lego* toys that operate consistently with that system. But if *Playmobil* offers a building set with features that *Lego* lacks (or the reverse) that the child very much wishes to have, relatively few parents would consider themselves permanently "locked in" to the exclusion of the other toy system. Of course for many parents (those to whom the manufacturers market their products), while children's toys can be costly, they are not prohibitively so, and thus many children have different toys operating on incompatible systems. For more expensive systems, however, purchasers might be less willing to acquire a new technology simply because it offers some marginal improvements over a costly system already in place. Few businesses, for example, are likely to offer their employees a menu of keyboard options that includes both QWERTY and Dvorak, in addition to any other that might come along. Indeed, many employers elect one among several competing word processing systems, for example Word or WordPerfect, to the exclusion of others, rather than allowing employees to make this election individually.

In each of these illustrations, market forces have primarily determined whether the continued benefit of positive network externalities outweighs the cost of declining to adapt to a newly developing technology. How, if at all, might this differ when lawmaking institutions must choose among two or more competing technologies? As we have already seen, state laws affecting various aspects of transportation have the potential for positive (or negative) network effects. In assessing claims under the dormant Commerce Clause doctrine that a contrary state law is designed to thwart beneficial coordination among states, the federal judiciary is called upon to assess whether the challenged law provides sufficient benefits to justify allowing it to thwart the common practices of other states. Does the inevitable conflict that results explain the Supreme Court's occasional application of a balancing test in such dormant Commerce Clause cases?[110] If so, what normative principles should the Court consider in striking an appropriate balance? Should the Court be skeptical of claims that state laws out of sync with those of most other states are genuinely motivated by highway safety concerns, rather than potential strategic considerations?

Does the creation of positive network externalities help further explain the cases of *Bibb* and *Kassel*? While highway safety laws that facilitate the flow of interstate commerce produce positive network effects for affected states, they also have the potential to impose burdens on pass-through states and corresponding opportunities for strategic behavior. Consider the perspective of a state that is primarily a throughway for interstate commerce benefiting surrounding states. For the pass-through state, the common regime might add to costs of highway maintenance and increase risks of vehicular accidents, all with relatively minor corresponding benefits to in-state residents or industry. While the surrounding states benefit from a common network of coordinated laws, deliberately departing from that framework, and thus forging a mixed strategy equilibrium, might provide a unique benefit to such a burdened state.[111]

Under existing dormant Commerce Clause doctrine, a state's desire to reduce the financial burdens of highway maintenance by shifting such burdens onto neighboring states, for example by discouraging in-state commercial traffic, is not a permissible justification for interfering with the coordinated regime of surrounding states. States that depart from otherwise common regulatory regimes must therefore defend their laws on alternative grounds, and will typically seek to do so based upon concerns for highway safety. When the Court confronts a dormant Commerce Clause challenge to such laws, however, it is forced to consider whether the claimed benefits of the nonconforming law outweigh the costs of burdening an otherwise common regulatory regime that facilitates the flow of commerce among states.

Does this analysis help to explain the Supreme Court's decisions to strike the challenged laws in *Bibb* and *Kassel*? Does it help to explain why

---

110. For an article claiming that the articulated doctrine notwithstanding, the Supreme Court does not in fact apply a balancing test in dormant Commerce Clause cases, see Donald H. Regan, *The Supreme Court and State Protectionism: Making Sense of the Dormant Commerce Clause*, 84 MICH. L. REV. 1091 (1986).

111. For a more elaborate account that develops this theory and evaluates it against the relevant case law, see Stearns, *supra* note 81.

the Court achieved these results using a balancing test even though the Court has routinely stated that highway safety laws are an area of deference to states? Whether or not this explains these rulings, does the analysis provide a sound normative justification? Why or why not? Do these cases suggest the need for central regulatory enforcement in the context of challenged state highway safety regulations, as opposed to a standard around which states can conform their conduct? Why or why not? Does your answer to the preceding questions help to explain why Congress has the power to overturn dormant Commerce Clause rulings?

B. THE BATTLE OF THE SEXES

We will now consider another simple form game that like the driving game has two pure Nash strategy equilibria and two non-Nash equilibria that can follow from the player's combination of mixed strategies. Unlike the driving game, however, the selection between these two pure Nash outcomes is not a simple matter of coordination. While the players care very much about having a coordinated strategy, they differ substantially on which available coordinated strategy to prefer.

Let us begin by considering a married couple. The wife is a football fan while the husband significantly prefers attending the theater. While each is willing, on occasion, to indulge the other's preference, the husband and the wife each derive significantly greater enjoyment from his or her preferred activity than from engaging in the spouse's preferred activity. At the same time, however, the level of satisfaction that each spouse derives from either activity depends in large measure on whether he or she is joined in that activity by the spouse. Thus, while the husband and the wife each prefer their own first choice activity, each would prefer to instead join the spouse in the second choice activity to engaging in the first choice activity alone. The payoffs in this game are reflected in Table 4:5 below.

Table 4:5. The Battle of the Sexes

Payoffs for (H, W)	W attends theater	W attends football
H attends theater	**10, 7**	5, 5
H attends football	3, 3	**7, 10**

In this game, the husband and wife (represented in Table 4:5 as H and W) each prefer different outcomes. If husband and wife each attend theater, husband's first choice activity, then husband receives the highest available payoff of ten, while wife receives the second highest available payoff of seven. Conversely, if both attend the football game, wife's first choice activity, these payoffs are reversed, with wife obtaining a payoff of ten and husband obtaining a payoff of seven. If the two attend separate events, and if each attends his or her first choice activity, then in this non-Nash outcome (arising from the players' combination of mixed strategies), each receives a payoff of five. Conversely, if each attends a separate event, but each goes to the event that he or she prefers less (husband going to the game; wife going to theater), then each receives a payoff of three. These latter outcomes are non-Nash because with knowledge of the other's strategy, either spouse could improve his or her payoff by conforming to that strategy. In addition, while the final combination of strategies—each going to their less preferred activity—might appear to be a null set, it is not. Imagine, for example, that each spouse is trying to anticipate the other's behavior but, unable to communicate and hoping to surprise the other, they each pursue the other spouse's first choice strategy. Alternatively, each spouse might mistakenly assume that the other has committed to his or her first choice strategy and thus try to mimic that strategy. Either approach generates the lower left hand solution.[112]

Given the payoffs in this game, each player hopes that both will engage in his or her first choice activity, but failing that hopes to engage together in the spouse's first choice (and his or her second choice) activity, rather than attending a first choice activity alone. And of course, the least preferred option is for each spouse to engage in the other's first choice activity alone.

One consequence of this game is the incentive to issue some kind of bond through which the husband or wife commit themselves to attending their first choice activity. Consider, for example, the husband's incentives when theater tickets become available. Assume that he purchases tickets and immediately notifies his wife, who believes he will not relinquish the tickets. The wife then confronts a choice of going to her preferred activity alone or joining her husband. Given the incentives, she gains more (with a payoff of seven) attending the theater than attending the football game alone (with a payoff of five). And because the payoffs are reciprocal, the same is true if instead the wife had purchased two football tickets on the same terms before the husband had an opportunity to buy the theater tickets. To what extent is repeat play a solution to the problem that this game presents? If it is not, would you be best off seeking guidance from a game theorist or a marriage counselor?

The battle of the sexes game nicely complements some of the insights of first generation law and economics.[113] Consider the Coase Theorem, which we introduced in chapter 1.[114] Recall that Coase explained that in a world with zero transactions costs and perfect information, resources will

---

112. For a more romantic literary illustration, consider *The Gift of the Magi,* in which the wife cuts off and sells her hair to purchase a watchband for her husband while the husband sells his watch to buy his wife a comb for her hair. O. HENRY, *The Gift of the Magi, in* THE COMPLETE WORKS OF O. HENRY 7 (Doubleday 1926) (1899). The authors thank Martin Kraus for bringing this illustration to their attention.

113. For a discussion of first generation law and economics scholarship, see GARY MINDA, POSTMODERN LEGAL MOVEMENTS: LAW AND JURISPRUDENCE AT CENTURY'S END 88–95 (1995).

114. *See supra* at chapter 1, section II.I.

flow to their most highly valued uses without regard to liability rules.[115] In theory, assuming that transactions costs are very low, including the cost of access to information, contract liability rules would have no bearing on how resources are finally allocated because in the event that the legal system places a property right in the party who places a lower value on it, the higher valuing user will have an incentive to purchase it and the other party would have an incentive to sell. This theoretically frictionless world gives legal rules only a trivial status, one belied by the enormous consequence that legal rules actually have in the real world, which is characterized by considerable transactions costs.

If we relax the assumption that all exchange is frictionless, the battle of the sexes suggests that parties will prefer clarity of legal rules to a state of contractual uncertainty. Consider a hypothetical contracting regime, for example, in which everything was literally and constantly up for grabs. One of the benefits of common law rules of contract, and also of Article II of the Uniform Commercial Code, is in specifying a set of off-the-rack rules that can fill in content in the event that the parties fail to anticipate potential contingencies that might arise at the stage of contract formation.

While contract law provides innumerable examples, we can select just a few to illustrate the essential point. Consider first a product advertisement. The legal system could treat this one of two ways, first as an offer for the sale of goods, that once a prospective buyer accepts, forms a contract, or second, as an invitation for the buyer to make an offer. If the advertisement were treated as an offer, the advertiser's failure to comply with the terms of the ad, for example, by failing to have sufficient goods available to satisfy all acceptances, would then provide the basis for a breach of contract action. As a matter of formal doctrine, the legal system does not treat advertisements in this manner, and instead treats them as invitations to prospective buyers to make an offer that the seller is then free to accept or reject.[116] Imagine that a seller advertises a loss leader, or even engages in a bait and switch, meaning advertising an item sufficiently attractively to pull people into the store in a ploy to divert their attention to other items that are less favorably priced, with the goal of never selling the advertised good at the listed price. From the perspective of a prospective buyer, the preferred rule is one that treats the advertisement as an offer and an unwillingness to sell following an acceptance as a

---

115. R.H. Coase, *The Problem of Social Cost*, 3 J.L. & Econ. 1 (1960).

116. It is hornbook law that an advertisement cannot be an offer, but the Minnesota Supreme Court in *Lefkowitz v. Great Minneapolis Surplus Store*, 86 N.W.2d 689 (Minn. 1957), found an exception where the advertisement was sufficiently specific so as to leave no room for further negotiation. Where an "offer is clear, definite, and explicit, and leaves nothing open for negotiation, it constitutes an offer, acceptance of which will complete the contract." *Id.* at 691. As Prof. Johnston has explained, "It is, of course, hornbook law that advertisements generally do not constitute offers," Jason Scott Johnston, *Communication and Courtship: Cheap Talk Economics and the Law of Contract Formation*, 85 Va. L. Rev. 385, 399 (1999), and thus *Lefkowitz* represents one of the "exceptions to the defaults." *Id.* at 396. For an interesting argument that although the rule is consistently stated that an advertisement is not an offer, they actually function as one, see Jay M. Feinman & Stephen R. Brill, *Is an Advertisement an Offer? Why It Is and Why It Matters*, 58 Hastings L.J. 61, 65 (2006) (positing that "*Lefkowitz* is particularly instructive because, to use the cliché, it is the exception that proves the rule.").

breach. From the perspective of the seller, however, the preferred rule is to treat the advertisement as an invitation to make an offer that the seller is free to reject. Without a clear rule, however, it is possible that both buyers and sellers will engage in constant challenges to the terms of doing business following advertisements.

While both sides have opposite preferences on the preferred rule, buyer and seller both benefit from clarity of the rule. In the event that the rule favors the buyer (an ad is an offer), the seller can include language in the advertisement specifying that "nothing in this ad should be construed as an offer" and that customers are free to make offers for any goods that the seller advertises here or elsewhere, subject to the seller's right to decline. Conversely, imagine that the legal rule provides that ads are only invitations to make an offer. This might discourage potential consumers from venturing into stores that advertise products on particularly attractive terms, for example, based upon an unusual buying opportunity or a liquidation sale. In this case, even a clear rule appearing to favor the seller would not prevent the seller from issuing a bond that ensures that buyers treat the ad as tantamount to an offer. For example, sellers could specify that the price will be available to the first one hundred customers; "while supplies last;" or even promise to issue rain checks in the event that the seller runs out of inventory on the day of the advertised sale.[117]

In this example, buyer and seller hold opposite views of the preferred rule on whether an ad should be treated as an offer but share a common interest in having a clear rule, especially one that the parties are free to negotiate around. Absent a clear rule, the seller would not be motivated to issue a disclaimer in the ad itself, anticipating that she will never honor the ad terms, and conversely will not seek to issue a bond to commit to ad terms as a device to pull consumers into the store. Conversely, absent a clear rule, buyer will not know how to construe the ad and will fear the risk of investing time and money on a fool's errand. So while the parties hold opposite views on the preferred legal rule, they hold a common interest in clarity, even if the rule initially appears to favor the other side. Returning to Table 4:5, the same payoffs in the battle of the sexes game characterize the incentives between buyer and seller in this basic issue of contract law. While each side most prefers his or her own rule, each side also prefers the rule favoring the other side to a state of uncertainty as to which rule governs. The states of uncertainty are captured in the mixed strategy equilibria where each side interprets the law either on terms favorable to him or her (the upper right solution), or alternatively on terms favorable to the other side (the lower left solution), and thus when the combined strategies do not match.

Let us now return to the dormant Commerce Clause cases described above. Are these cases better characterized in terms of the battle of the sexes or in terms of a pure coordination (driving) game? We might imagine

---

117. Another variation limits the number of items that a customer, or family, can purchase of the sale goods.

that while one state or group of states has a substantive preference for straight mudflaps or sixty-five-foot trailers, others prefer curved mudflaps or longer single trailers. If so, then these different substantive views of highway safety would yield payoffs that more closely resemble those in Table 4:5 (depicting the battle of the sexes) than those in Table 4:4 (depicting the driving game). The very worst result would arise if each state wrongly sought to anticipate the other state's laws (equivalent to the lower left solution), and an only slightly better result would arise if each stuck to its first choice without trying to coordinate with the other states. If the states did try to coordinate, then while some states might prefer a different legal regime, they would be willing to subordinate that concern in favor of the higher payoffs associated with a common regime that facilitates the flow of commerce among affected states.

While *Bibb* and *Kassel* might appear to fit this paradigm, consider the following rejoinder. In each case, the out of sync state enacted the challenged law against a background of laws of numerous states already in place that contradicted it. Passing laws is an extremely costly process, and it is difficult to do so in one state and especially difficult to enact coordinated laws across numerous independent state jurisdictions. The surrounding states had in place a well-established set of contrary laws at the time Illinois and Iowa enacted their challenged laws.[118] If these states were playing a battle of the sexes game, knowledge of the surrounding states' existing contrary laws would certainly have counseled in favor of acquiescing to receive the higher payoffs of coordination, even if Illinois and Iowa for some reason regarded those laws as inferior, rather than forging a mixed strategy equilibrium result that reduced payoffs for all of the states involved. Does it seem more plausible that the challenged law was motivated by the desire for a better policy, even if contrary to that of surrounding states, or by the desire to thwart a coordinated strategy? Does the fact that Illinois did not permit both types of mudflaps, as opposed to prohibiting the more commonly used mudflap, help to inform your answer to this question? Consider in this regard the following passage from Justice Douglas's opinion in *Bibb*:

> Such a new safety device—out of line with the requirements of the other States—may be so compelling that the innovating State need not be the one to give way. But the present showing—balanced against the clear burden in commerce—is far too inconclusive to make this mudguard meet this test.[119]

Does this passage lend support to the pure coordination or battle of the sexes account of *Bibb*? Why? Which account do you find more persuasive? Do you think *Bibb* and *Kassel* were correctly decided? Why or why not? To what extent is your answer informed by game theory? To what extent is it informed by interest group theory? What if subsequent evidence showed

---

118. *See* Kassel v. Consol. Freightways, 450 U.S. 662, 684 (1981) (noting that the Iowa law was out of keeping with those of surrounding states); Bibb v. Navajo Freight Lines, Inc., 359 U.S. 520, 529–30 (1959) (noting that Illinois law is out of keeping with that of almost all other states).

119. *Bibb*, 359 U.S. at 530.

the nonconforming standard to have greater benefits than originally believed? Might this help to explain the default nature of the dormant Commerce Clause doctrine, meaning the power of Congress to overrule such cases?

C. THE GAME OF CHICKEN (OR HAWK–DOVE)

1. The Basic Game

The chicken game, or its counterpart Hawk–Dove from evolutionary biology,[120] is different in an important respect from any of the games described thus far. Unlike the prisoners' dilemma, this game admits more than a single pure Nash equilibrium strategy. Unlike the driving game and the battle of the sexes, however, the game of chicken is an "anti-coordination" rather than a "coordination" game. By this we mean that the driving game and the battle of the sexes provide higher payoffs to each player if the players obtain the benefit of either of two coordinated strategies (same side driving or same choice of activity), which then forms the basis for the pure Nash equilibria. With complete information concerning the other player's strategy, these games are positive sum; both players improve their positions by adopting a coordinated, pure Nash equilibrium strategy.

In the game of chicken, the players receive relatively low (and potentially deadly) payoffs if they pursue a common, coordinated strategy. Instead, the two pure Nash equilibria arise when the players produce combined strategies that defy coordination. Whichever strategy player A anticipates player B to follow (or the reverse), it is rational to follow the opposite strategy. In its raw form, the game of chicken has the potential to result in the loss of life to one or both players.[121] Of course there are legal and other policy analogues to this game that do not result in loss of life, which we will consider. Once again, we begin with the normal form game.

Chicken is an unseemly game of nerve generally involving two drivers each seeking to outrank the other in an effort to attain status. In its traditional presentation, it is played in either of two ways. In the first illustration, both men, Albert and Bart, drive their cars toward a cliff. The last car to stop without going over is the winner. In the second illustration, the players drive at each other at considerable speed. The first to swerve is the loser. The dangers inherent in this game are obvious. Depending upon the guts (read stupidity) of the drivers, there is a substantial risk that one or both will take their cars over the cliff (in the first game) or that they will crash head-on (in the second). Winning the game of chicken requires that the other driver become unnerved suffi-

---

120. These two games are identical in structure, but were developed with different vocabularies and within different disciplines. *See* MARTIN J. OSBORNE & ARIEL RUBINSTEIN, A COURSE IN GAME THEORY 30 (1994).

121. The same is true for Hawk–Dove, except that birds, rather than people, risk the loss of life.

ciently early to prevent himself and the other player from continuing a course of play that leads to a devastating result, and potential loss of life.

Table 4:6 illustrates the payoffs in this game.

Table 4:6. The Game of Chicken

Payoffs for (Albert, Bart)	Bart Swerves	Bart does not Swerve
Albert Swerves	0, 0	**−25, 50**
Albert does not Swerve	**50, −25**	−100, −100

In this game, there are two pure Nash strategy equilibria and two non-Nash outcomes. As before, the non-Nash outcomes can also arise as mixed strategy equilibria if, for example, the players randomize over the available strategies and if the combined strategies produce a non-pure Nash outcome. As previously stated, this game differs from the preceding games in this section in that the pure strategies arise in the upper right and lower left boxes in which the players have failed to coordinate their conduct, such that one goes straight while the other swerves. In this game, if both Albert and Bart swerve, neither can claim victory, and each receives a payoff of 0, meaning that each winds up with the same status ranking as before playing the game. If one player swerves while the other does not, then the one who does not swerve greatly improves his status, thus receiving the highest payoff of 50, while the one who does swerve suffers a loss of status, with a payoff of -25. Finally, if neither player swerves, then they both are badly injured, or worse, with a payoff valued at -100.

Now consider the nature of the equilibrium results. Assume that Albert anticipates that Bart is going to drive straight no matter what. In that case, given the payoffs, Albert's rational strategy is to swerve, with the resulting payoffs of 50 to Bart, and -25 to Albert. This is not a great result, of course, but it is a stable equilibrium because given Bart's strategy, Albert would reduce his payoff to -100 (and risk death) by following the alternative strategy of also driving straight. Conversely, if Bart anticipates that Albert is going to become unnerved in the game and swerve no matter what, then the rational strategy is to drive straight, again securing a payoff (in the same box) of 50, with Albert suffering a loss of -25. For each player, this is a pure Nash equilibrium strategy given the anticipated strategy of the other player. The same is true of the lower left box, and here we need only reverse the names in the preceding discussion, this time with Albert predictably driving straight and Bart rationally responding by swerving, or with Bart predictably swerving, and Albert responding by driving straight.

For the same reason that the upper right and lower left boxes are pure Nash strategy equilibria, the upper left and lower right boxes are non-Nash. We begin with the upper left box in which both drivers swerve. Imagine that Albert anticipates that Bart will swerve no matter what. In this case, Albert receives a payoff of 0 by also swerving, but can improve that payoff to 50 by going straight, thus moving from the upper left box to the lower left box. Remember, the lower left box is a pure Nash strategy equilibrium, and so that remains a stable outcome. Conversely, if Bart anticipates that Albert will swerve no matter what, Bart would receive a payoff of 0 by also swerving, and could improve that payoff to 50 by driving straight, moving this time to the upper right box. That box is also a pure Nash strategy equilibrium.

The same analysis explains why the lower right box (-100, -100) is not pure Nash. Imagine that Albert anticipates that Bart will drive straight no matter what, for example, if Albert demonstrates his commitment by removing the steering wheel from the car. In that case, Bart faces a certain devastating consequence by also driving straight (with a payoff of -100), but can improve his payoff (to -25) by swerving, thus placing him in the upper right, pure Nash, box. The same result plays in reverse if instead Bart signals an absolute commitment to driving straight, this time with Albert improving his payoff from -100 to -25 by swerving, and moving from the lower right to the lower left, pure Nash, box.

As with the driving game and the battle of the sexes, while this game has two pure Nash and two non-Nash outcomes (or mixed strategy equilibria if the players randomize over options), depending upon how the game is played, there is no guarantee that the outcome will be pure Nash. If neither player has sufficient information to form a meaningful impression as to how the other will act, it is possible that one will misread the other, and that together they will find themselves in one of the two non-pure Nash boxes, either with both swerving (and accomplishing nothing), or with both driving straight and winding up dead.

2. Non–Myopic Equilibrium

The preceding analysis suggests that with knowledge as to the other player's bonded strategy, the drivers wind up in one of the two pure Nash strategy equilibria, and that without such knowledge they risk randomizing over any of the four options, depending upon how well they anticipate the other player's strategy. Let us now consider an alternative account that rests on an alternative equilibrium concept. In the conventional analysis, the (straight, swerve) or (swerve, straight) outcomes are pure Nash because if either player commits to a strategy, the other has no alternative that improves his payoffs. Now imagine that Albert and Bart play this game in a single period without any specific knowledge concerning the strategy of the other player. How might we expect them to respond?

Professor Steven Brams has analyzed the game of chicken using a dynamic equilibrium concept known as "non-myopic equilibrium."[122] To illustrate, we reproduce below the payoffs in Table 4:6, but this time with a series of arrows that suggest the possibility of thinking through the implications in each round of the combined strategies for each player.

Table 4:7. Non–Myopic Equilibrium in the Game of Chicken

Payoffs for (A, B)	Bart Swerves	Bart does not Swerve
Albert Swerves	$0\downarrow$, **0**→	-25, **50**$\downarrow$
Albert does not Swerve	50→, **−25**	$-100\searrow$, **−100**$\searrow$

To keep the exposition simple, we have italicized the payoffs for Albert and bolded the payoffs for Bart.[123] In each box, next to each relevant payoff, we have placed an arrow that signals the direction of an expected alternative strategy for a nonmyopic player. Unlike the standard Nash equilibrium analysis, which inquires whether for any given strategy by the other player, there is a move that will improve the decision maker's payoffs, in this game, we ask the following additional question. Given the payoffs from each combined set of strategies, how stable is the assumption concerning the strategy of the other player? Let us first illustrate by considering Albert's assessment of rational play given Bart's assessment of the combined strategies.

While we can begin the analysis at any strategic location, assume Albert positions himself in the lower left box hoping to drive straight while Bart swerves. Albert receives a payoff of 50 and Bart receives a payoff of -25. The problem is that while neither side knows the strategy that the other will adopt, both parties know the payoff schedule, which is reciprocal. Just as Albert pursues an initial strategy to get the favorable lower left payoffs (50, -25), Bart also pursues the inverse initial strategy to get the beneficial payoffs set out on the upper right (-25, 50). With this set of combined strategies, however, the result is to have both Albert and Bart drive straight, leading each to their worst possible result (-100, -100). If they anticipate this position, however, for each player it becomes rational to change strategies to swerving to avoid the potentially deadly result, thus moving to the upper left with payoffs of (0,0). Of course if Albert and Bart each anticipate that the other will pursue this strategy, each is then rationally motivated to drive straight once again to capture the higher payoffs associated with the lower left (for Albert) and upper

---

122. BRAMS, *supra* note 78, at 27–33, 127–38 (applying concept as applied in chicken game to the Cuban Missile Crisis).

123. Unlike in prior matrices, the bold in Table 4:7 is not intended to indicate a Nash equilibrium.

right (for Bart) solutions. And these combined strategies merely get the ball rolling again, as the combined set of strategies place Albert and Bart in the lower right $(-100, -100)$.[124]

In effect, Albert cycles from lower left to lower right to upper left, while Bart cycles from upper right to lower right to upper left. Thus to the extent that the players are non-myopic and anticipate not just the immediate payoff from a presumed strategy from the other player, but also the other player's equally dynamic assessment of the combined strategies, it is possible that neither settles on a stable outcome except by chance.

As you read each of the illustrations below, consider which equilibrium concept, Nash or non-myopic equilibrium, better captures the underlying features of the game. What, if anything, does the concept of non-myopic equilibrium suggest about the role of the state when confronted with situations that might be characterized in terms of a game of chicken? Can you think of ways to extricate parties from the seemingly intractable difficulties that such a game creates?

3. Cultural and Historical Illustrations

The game of chicken gained popular notoriety in the 1955 movie *Rebel Without a Cause*. In the movie, a new high school student, Jim Stark (played by James Dean), and a bully named Buzz Gunderson (played by Corey Allen) play the game by driving toward a cliff and the first to stop (or jump from the window) would lose. Buzz unsuccessfully tries to jump but his shirt sleeve gets caught taking him over the cliff to his demise. While the movie demonstrates the sometimes impetuous nature of young men, this should not mask the potential real stakes involved in such a game. Within evolutionary biology, status battles among alpha male chimpanzees can be modeled using the game of chicken (or Hawk–Dove), with the real stakes being sexual access to females.[125] From an evolutionary biology perspective, gaining the status of progenitor is hardly a trivial matter on par with challenging the local bully to fit in with a high school crowd. The Hawk–Dove version of the game places two birds in a potential battle over prey. If both play Hawk, they engage in a potentially deadly mutual attack and if both play Dove, they fail to get the prey as the price of avoiding a potentially deadly fight. If one plays Hawk while the other plays Dove, the Hawk gets the prey and the Dove flees. The payoff relationships are identical to those modeled in Table 4:6.[126] We might imagine that the alpha male chimpanzees are also playing this Hawk–

---

124. For an amusing theatrical account in which one player continues to non-myopically (but nonetheless futilely) move back and forth in evaluating his opponent's likely placement of the poisonous goblet, see The Princess Bride (Act III Communications 1987).

125. Martin A. Nowak, Evolutionary Dynamics: Exploring the Equations of Life 61 (2006) (depicting sexual competition among primates as Hawk–Dove game and observing that "Male chimpanzees fight for dominance of a group: the alpha male has to withstand challenges from other males, and in return gets a majority of the matings").

126. Recall that it is the payoff relationships rather than the nominal payoffs that create the game.

Dove game with the goal of sexual access in place of prey, and with considerably higher stakes than a single meal.

The chicken game also has an historical counterpart in the famous Alexander Hamilton–Aaron Burr duel, which took place on July 11, 1804. While neither contemporaneous accounts nor modern historical accounts of the duel are entirely consistent, in one version, duelists customarily missed firing or fired in a manner that imposed minimal injury, for example a shot in the leg. While the duel ended at that point, the duelists signified the requisite bravery to withstand the risk of fatal fire without having to kill or be killed.[127] Apparently, Hamilton, who shot first, instead shot into the air, but wide and well above Burr, who fired the second fatal shot into Hamilton's lower abdomen. While the conventional account of dueling expectations appears to translate roughly into a norm of mutual swerving, it is not entirely obvious that the result would have left both duelers in the same position in which they started. Consider that by willingly subjecting oneself to a potentially life threatening duel with a sworn enemy, even if both survive, each can claim honor among those who are most familiar with the factual circumstances that motivated the duel. In some sense, therefore, mutual swerving (throwing away both first shots) vindicates the honor of both duelists. While there was a move to end dueling prior to this most famous duel, the tragic consequence provided the a major impetus to end dueling within the United States, although by some accounts the practice, while increasingly rare, continued until the Civil War.[128]

4.   Legal Applications: Takings Redux

Let us now turn our attention to a legal context that potentially implicates the game of chicken, albeit without life-threatening consequences. In chapter 2 we explained how the Takings Clause might help the government to avoid the intractable difficulties that potentially arise in the context of a holdout game. The essential intuition is that an individual landowner in the middle of a lot that is intended for a major development, for example a highway or a park, might recognize that the project will be defeated, along with the conversion value of the remaining government-acquired parcels, if the landowner declines to acquiesce in the eventual sale. The same phenomenon arises in the context of private development. When the large developer, for example Disney or Universal Studios, offers a large number of adjoining lot owners a seemingly fair price (say fair market value plus some reasonable premium), one or more owners might rationally decline to accept. These owners might instead

---

127.   For an informative account, see generally JOANNE B. FREEMAN, AFFAIRS OF HONOR: NATIONAL POLITICS IN THE NEW REPUBLIC 179 (2002) ("Leg injuries were frequent enough to cast doubt on the power and meaning of the practice [of dueling]; hinting that affairs of honor entailed more pretense than peril, a newspaper editor jeered that one combatant 'was said to have received a wound in that fashionable part, *the leg.*' ").

128.   *See* C.A. Harwell Wells, Note, *The End of the Affair? Anti–Dueling Laws and Social Norms in Antebellum America*, 54 VAND. L. REV. 1805, 1838 (2001) ("Clearly, the Civil War killed the duel."); *see also* EDWARD L. AYERS, VENGEANCE AND JUSTICE: CRIME AND PUNISHMENT IN THE 19TH-CENTURY AMERICAN SOUTH 271 (1984).

elect to "hold out" for a substantially better offer. If the developer assembles all of the remaining parcels around the holdout, then in theory the holdout could prevent the developer from converting all of the acquired parcels to their higher value through the completion of the project.[129]

Certainly developers anticipate this problem and take steps to avoid or at least minimize the threat. For now, assume that a homeowner whose lot is in the middle of a proposed development believes (rightly or wrongly) that her lot is essential to whether the project succeeds or fails. As a result, she is unwilling to accept even a seemingly generous offer, say two to three times the property's pre-development fair market value. Is it possible that this scenario might threaten to convert what started as a holdout game into a game of chicken?

Consider the following argument. In this case, the developer and the property owner each have two available strategies that correlate to "drive straight" or "swerve." For the developer, swerving means acquiescing in the property owner's demands to acquire the remaining lot needed for the development. Driving straight means continuing with the development with or without acquiring the holdout's property. For the landowner, swerving means accepting a bid that, although attractive had this been an individual sale, fails to capture a larger portion of the seemingly enormous stakes involved in converting the entire set of acquired parcels into the proposed development. Conversely, driving straight means declining any offers that fail to convey a substantial portion of the overall project gains (or conversion value of all parcels) in exchange for the sale.

This game increasingly resembles a game of chicken when we consider what a mutual strategy of "drive straight" produces. In the event that the developer fails to up the ante and the holdout fails to accept the developer's increasingly generous offers, the consequence is extremely unfortunate for both parties. For the developer, the prospect is a theme park, golf course, or park constructed around a private residence. For the holdout, the prospect is a home in the middle of such a development, so that no other purchaser would seek to acquire the property *even at* the assessed fair market value prior to the development. Using the payoffs from Table 4:6, we can place this result in the lower right box (with payoffs of -100, -100). In contrast, mutual swerving means compromising and accommodating the other party's demands without the benefit to the holdout of an expected share of the full conversion value of the entire set of properties, and without the benefit to the developer of acquiring the holdout lot for a price that truly reflects its original fair market value. This correlates to the upper left box (payoffs at 0,0).

As in the game of chicken, neither mutual swerving nor mutual driving straight represents a pure Nash strategy. If the homeowner believes that no matter what, the developer will drive straight, she receives a substantially lower payoff by continuing to play the game

---

129. Recall that Disney actually employed straw purchasers to avoid this problem. *See supra* chapter 2, section II.E.1 and cite therein.

(diminishing the value of her property to zero), as compared with swerving and accepting the most recent reasonable offer. After all, few purchasers will acquire a home located in the middle of a theme park or other non-housing development.[130] This moves the game toward the lower left or upper right solutions in Table 4:6, which are Nash. Conversely, if the developer believes that no matter what, the homeowner will not swerve and will insist upon a portion of the larger conversion value, then it can also receive substantially higher value by cutting its losses and acquiescing to the owner's demands for a larger share of the prize, again producing a solution that is Nash.[131]

To what extent does the preceding analysis help to explain the Supreme Court's controversial takings decision, *Kelo v. City of New London*?[132] In *Kelo*, a private developer sought to purchase a number of contiguous parcels to create an urban restoration project.[133] The developer tried to deal with individual sellers through private contract, and perhaps not unexpectedly, encountered an apparent holdout. We use "apparent" to signal that in this case, and perhaps in others like it, the homeowner might elect to hold out for reasons unrelated to financial gain. Some holdouts might instead attach a high subjective value to their property that well exceeds what almost any other owner of the same property would consider an exceptional offer. Of course the legal system has no means of sorting those holdouts motivated by financial gain from those motivated by psychological or subjective considerations.[134] Whatever the property owner's personal motivations, from a game theoretical perspective the resulting dynamic is effectively the same.

The question in *Kelo* was whether the City of New London, Connecticut could exercise its eminent domain power to acquire a lot from a landowner to benefit a private developer, given that the Fifth Amendment, which applies to the states through the Fourteenth Amendment, states: "nor shall private property be taken for public use, without just compensation."[135] Specifically, Kelo challenged the taking on the ground that by converting her property from one private use to another private use, albeit one with higher financial value, the City of New London had exercised its power of eminent domain absent the requisite public use. In response, New London maintained that the higher tax revenues associated with the

---

130. Of course it is possible that through the doctrine of easement by necessity, the holdout will continue to have access to a main road, but even so, few if any buyers will be interested in acquiring a lot under these conditions. For a discussion of easements by necessity, see Hunter C. Carroll, *Easements by Necessity: What Level of Necessity Is Required?*, 19 AM. J. TRIAL ADVOC. 475 (1995). It is also possible, however, that if the surrounding development is attractive, for example a golf course or park, the holdout landowner retains marketable—or even more valuable—property.

131. This assumes that there is no prospect for regulatory intervention, a possibility discussed below. *See infra* chapter 3, section II.G.1, and accompanying text.

132. 545 U.S. 469 (2005).

133. *Id.* at 473–75.

134. How, if at all, does this observation relate to the discussion in chapter 3 of the difficulty in assessing interpersonal utility comparisons? *See supra* chapter 3, section III.B.

135. U.S. CONST. amend. V, cl. 4.

development, or the benefits associated with urban renewal, satisfied the public use doctrine.[136] As academic commentators have noted, however,[137] such arguments potentially eviscerate the public use doctrine, which is intended to ensure that the government actually deploy acquired parcels for a public use, rather than a more highly valued private use.

The *Kelo* decision has been widely condemned by legal academics, and in this discussion we do not intend to defend the decision on constitutional grounds. Our purpose is quite limited. We wish to suggest that game theory, and specifically a comparison of the holdout game and the game of chicken in the *Kelo* context, might provide a credible positive account of the decision. We begin with a challenge to the conventional holdout account.[138] In the conventional law and economics analysis,[139] eminent domain provides the government with the power to avoid intractable negotiations with potential holdouts who for fortuitous reasons hold the power to thwart the government's efforts to assemble contiguous parcels as needed to facilitate public development. But even if we accept one of the arguments for treating private-to-private land transfers as promoting the public use, does the holdout game necessarily justify this exercise of eminent domain power?

Consider Todd Zywicki's rejoinder. Before settling in New London, Connecticut, the developer had a wide range of options from which to select for development. Due diligence might have required the developer to assess not only which location was best suited to the planned development, but also which were more or less conducive to assembling the required parcels to allow that development to go forward. In this analysis, while Kelo might be a holdout, that is only because the City of New London, with the imprimatur of the *Kelo* Court, has assumed that the developer specifically requires her property to go through with the proposed development, rather than recognizing the developer's initial ability to pursue the development in any number of potential locations.

Now consider the following alternative account that views this from the perspective of the game of chicken. Once again, Person *A* owns property that is in the middle of a proposed theme park. She knows she would be foolish to sell right away, and so she holds out. She hopes that at some point the developer ups the ante, and not surprisingly the developer does. But the holdout is savvy, or so she thinks, and thus continues to hold out for a higher and higher offer. Eventually the developer thinks: "I can actually build around this property." So the developer alters his plans

136. 545 U.S. at 475–76.

137. *See, e.g.,* Charles E. Cohen, *Eminent Domain After* Kelo v. City of New London: *An Argument for Banning Economic Development Takings,* 29 HARV. J.L. & PUB. POL'Y 491, 496–97, 563–64 (2006); Timothy Sandefur, *The "Backlash" So Far: Will Americans Get Meaningful Eminent Domain Reform?,* 2006 MICH. ST. L. REV. 709, 730–32; Sonya D. Jones, *That Land Is Your Land, This Land Is My Land . . . Until the Local Government Can Turn it for a Profit: A Critical Analysis of* Kelo v. City of New London, 20 BYU J. PUB. L. 139, 151–55 (2005).

138. Posting of Todd Zywicki to The Volokh Conspiracy, http://volokh.com/archives/archive_2005_06_26-2005_07_02.shtml#1120162917 (June 30, 2005, 4:21 PM).

139. RICHARD A. POSNER, ECONOMIC ANALYSIS OF LAW 54–60 (6th ed. 2003).

with the intent of doing just that. At this point, both the parcel owner and the developer have committed to driving straight (without swerving), resulting in a figurative crash that produces a significant loss (the lower right solution) for both parties. Certainly the landowner has crashed, or driven over the cliff, at least financially. With the park around her house, the value has not only failed to increase, but actually it has moved from its one-time fair market value as a residence to zero. It is an asset that is only of value to the developer, but since no one else would be willing to purchase it, there is no longer any incentive to offer a premium, or even to reinstate the initial fair market value offer. At the same time, the developer has substantially compromised the terms of the development by constructing around a private residence, thus reducing substantially the value of the final development as compared with the original plan.

In this alternative account, the *Kelo* decision, which permits the use of eminent domain to facilitate a private-to-private transfer of property for the purpose of converting the property to a more valued use, effectively allows the City of New London to prevent Kelo from turning what began as a fairly conventional holdout game into a game of chicken. In doing so, it also prevents Kelo from moving the one-time fair market value of her property to zero and, at the same time, from substantially diminishing the value of the proposed development plan. The city anticipated this result following a series of actions that translated into a set of mutual bonds committing the developer to the project in exchange for tax breaks and other benefits. Against the backdrop of these commitments, one might view *Kelo* as a decision permitting the City of New London to take control of the wheel and to force Kelo to swerve into one of the pure Nash equilibrium results in the chicken game.

Recall that at the beginning of this chapter, we asked whether one important role of the regulatory state is to encourage benign games and to discourage illicit ones. Does *Kelo* illustrate this proposition? If so, is that sufficient for the Supreme Court to permit the City of New London to intercede in what is obviously a private-to-private land transfer through its power of eminent domain? What, if any, relationship does the game theoretical account of *Kelo* bear to the underlying constitutional question arising under the Fifth and Fourteenth Amendments? Does this analysis provide a normatively satisfying account of *Kelo*? Does it require that the government assume a paternalistic role in protecting property owners against themselves when confronted with an inevitable development? Does it matter if the development is in fact inevitable?

To help with this last question, compare the contrary outcome in Maryland in a case involving "quick-take condemnations."[140] These cases involved shortened processes for eminent domain to assemble properties with the eventual goal of facilitating private development. The Maryland Court of Appeals has suggested that the use of quick takes is subject to

---

140. *See* Mayor of Baltimore City v. Valsamaki, 916 A.2d 324 (Md. 2007).

close scrutiny and invalidated the particular application on the case facts.[141] Is this result distinguishable from *Kelo*? Consider this argument.

In the quick take case, no specific developer had (yet) made any of the bonding commitments that permitted regulators in the *Kelo* case to intervene and facilitate the transfer. As a result, these might look more like simple private-to-private transfers of property (and thus of wealth), without the threat to a seemingly misguided holdout whose risky behavior threatens a complete diminution of property value to the holdout, in addition to the associated loss to the developer. Thus, the quick-take decision might more closely resemble the case in which any potentially interested developer could choose among various sites (Zywicki's critique of the standard holdout analysis), and in which unless and until it settles on a given site, the developer can negotiate with whatever private land-owners happen to possess their desired property.

The essential step that might distinguish *Kelo* from the quick-take condemnation case in this analysis is the set of bonding commitments that the developer has already made—in purchasing surrounding lots, in securing municipal tax breaks, and in undertaking affirmative plans to begin the process of development—that together signal to the vast majority of affected property owners and to local government that the development is no longer speculative, but rather has become a *fait accompli*. The only party that appears not to recognize this is the final holdouts or set of holdouts against whom the local government—now sanctioned by the Supreme Court—has sought to exercise its power of eminent domain. Since there is no such developer, and no such bonding, in the quick-take case, the Maryland Court of Appeals declined to allow the private property transfer. Was *Kelo* rightly decided? Was the widespread public condemnation of this decision surprising? Why or why not? Was the Maryland case rightly decided? Why or why not? To what extent does game theory help in answering these questions?

III.   A GAME WITH NO PURE NASH EQUILIBRIUM STRATEGY: THE PROBLEM OF EMPTY CORE BARGAINING

As noted at the beginning of this chapter, many concepts in social choice and game theory developed along parallel tracks, albeit with different terminology and tools of analysis. This is especially notable when comparing the social choice concept of cycling with the game theoretical

---

141. The court determined that for the city to take possession under the statute, it must show sufficient reasons to support immediate possession, for example if the building or property is "immediately injurious to the health and safety of the public, or is otherwise immediately needed for public use." *Id.* at 356. The court ruled narrowly, finding that under the facts, the taking did not meet the requirements of the quick-take statute. *Id.* at 356. The court went on to state: "In essence, quick take procedures can be used inappropriately to destroy altogether the right of the property owner to challenge the public use prong of eminent domain." *Id.* at 347.

concept of empty core bargaining. As with the game of chicken and Hawk–Dove, discussed in the prior part, these concepts differ only in the contexts in which they are applied. Since we introduced the concept of cycling in chapter 3,[142] we do not offer an extended analysis. Instead, we offer some comments designed to draw out the connections between these concepts and explain their significance in comparative institutional analysis.

Among the core insights from social choice theory is that phenomena that cause one institution to cycle (*A* preferred to *B* preferred to *C* preferred to *A*) might inhibit cycling in another. The critical difference is one of timing. When a group of individuals seeks to allocate the benefits of an unanticipated capital gain, or the burdens of an unanticipated capital loss, in the absence of any rules that constrain strategic behavior, with sufficiently high stakes, groups disadvantaged by a seemingly fair solution might continue to push new allocations, with the effect of undermining any proposed outcome in favor of a cycle. Since for any proposed outcome another will have majority support, absent some stabilizing rule there is no pure Nash equilibrium outcome when preferences cycle. Instead, for any given outcome, some player can always improve his or her position by pushing for an alternative allocation. This can result in a series of seemingly endless iterations among changing coalitions concerning *ABC*, taking the form *AB, BC, CA, AB,* and so on.

Thus, the defining characteristic of empty core bargaining games, in contrast with the other games described in this chapter, is the lack of a pure Nash equilibrium strategy. For any given outcome, another superior coalition is poised to form and replace it with another outcome. But in doing so, such coalitions create their own alternative superior coalitions, and thus opportunities for yet another round of play. To the extent that these games are solvable, the solution invariably rests on external rules that place limits on the rounds of play, or through the interplay between complementary institutions that respond differently to factual prompts, which can lead one, but not the other, to cycle.[143]

Empty core bargaining games provide an important contrast with those games previously introduced that have pure and mixed Nash equilibrium strategies. Empty core games have no pure equilibrium strategies, and thus no dominant Nash equilibrium. That does not mean, however, that they invariably end without a solution. It means, instead, that the solution arises due to an equilibrating rule that is imposed from outside the institution subject to the cycling phenomenon. Not surprisingly, perhaps, the legal system is an important institution that facilitates outcomes that otherwise would have the potential to produce cycling results.

---

142. *See supra* chapter 3, section II.C.

143. For an alternative analysis suggesting that the risk of cycling itself will stabilize outcomes, see DANIEL A. FARBER & PHILIP P. FRICKEY, LAW AND PUBLIC CHOICE 52 (1991). This solution is most apt to work if, like the tit for tat game in an iterated prisoners' dilemma, the discounted future benefits of repeat play are lower than the gains from pushing the game another round. The difficulty, however, is that to achieve this, one must alter the payoffs in a manner that eliminates the very cycle that the risk of cycling is claimed to prevent. *See also supra* chapter 3, section II.E, n. 68.

Before closing this discussion, it is important to address a question of definition. One might imagine cycling to represent an endless stream of indecision in which we confront repeat iterations of proposals that are dismissed in favor of another, and another, and another, endlessly. But few institutions reveal such endless indecision. We have already confronted the famous inquiry by Gordon Tullock, *Why So Much Stability?*,[144] and the competing explanations that he, and others, have offered.[145] For now, the critical point is that cycling can be characterized not merely by a process that continues to demonstrate the superiority of new proposals over others on the table, but also by specific outcomes that embed information from which we can infer a suppressed alternative that some majority would have preferred to the eventual winner. As seen in the examples discussed in chapter 3,[146] an important question is whether we can identify rules that facilitate such outcomes and evaluate the normative soundness of those rules and of the outcomes the rules generate.

IV. APPLICATIONS

As you read the materials that follow, try to identify which, if any, of the games set out in this chapter could best be used to characterize the case facts. If you conclude that game theory applies, what benefit, if any, might there be to having had the court or legislature rely directly on game theory in undertaking its analysis?

Jacobson v. Massachusetts (1905)[147]

Mr. Justice **Harlan** delivered the opinion of the court:

This case involves the validity, under the Constitution of the United States, of certain provisions in the statutes of Massachusetts relating to vaccination.

The Revised Laws of that commonwealth, chap. 75, § 137, provide that 'the board of health of a city or town, if, in its opinion, it is necessary for the public health or safety, shall require and enforce the vaccination and revaccination of all the inhabitants thereof, and shall provide them with the means of free vaccination. Whoever, being over twenty-one years of age and not under guardianship, refuses or neglects to comply with such requirement shall forfeit $5.'

An exception is made in favor of 'children who present a certificate, signed by a registered physician, that they are unfit subjects for vaccination.' § 139.

---

144.   Gordon Tullock, *Why So Much Stability?*, 37 Pub. Choice 189 (1981).

145.   For a discussion of the logrolling and structure induced equilibrium accounts, see *supra* chapter 3, section II.E.

146.   *See supra* chapter 3, section II.C.

147.   Jacobson v. Massachusetts, 197 U.S. 11 (1905) (internal citations and quotation marks omitted).

[Pursuant to this state authority in 1902 the city of Cambridge passed a regulation requiring smallpox vaccinations. Jacobson, the plaintiff, refused to be vaccinated and challenged the law.]

. . . .

What, according to the judgment of the state court, are the scope and effect of the statute? What results were intended to be accomplished by it? These questions must be answered.

. . . .

[For] nearly a century most of the members of the medical profession have regarded vaccination, repeated after intervals, as a preventive of smallpox; that, while they have recognized the possibility of injury to an individual from carelessness in the performance of it, or even in a conceivable case without carelessness, they generally have considered the risk of such an injury too small to be seriously weighed as against the benefits coming from the discreet and proper use of the preventive; and that not only the medical profession and the people generally have for a long time entertained these opinions, but legislatures and courts have acted upon them with general unanimity. If the defendant had been permitted to introduce such expert testimony as he had in support of these several propositions, it could not have changed the result. It would not have justified the court in holding that the legislature had transcended its power in enacting this statute on their judgment of what the welfare of the people demands.

. . . .

[We] assume, for the purposes of the present inquiry, that its provisions require, at least as a general rule, that adults not under the guardianship and remaining within the limits of the city of Cambridge must submit to the regulation adopted by the board of health. Is the statute, so construed, therefore, inconsistent with the liberty which the Constitution of the United States secures to every person against deprivation by the state?

The authority of the state to enact this statute is to be referred to what is commonly called the police power,—a power which the state did not surrender when becoming a member of the Union under the Constitution. Although this court has refrained from any attempt to define the limits of that power, yet it has distinctly recognized the authority of a state to enact quarantine laws and 'health laws of every description;' indeed, all laws that relate to matters completely within its territory and which do not by their necessary operation affect the people of other states. According to settled principles, the police power of a state must be held to embrace, at least, such reasonable regulations established directly by legislative enactment as will protect the public health and the public safety. . . . It is equally true that the state may invest local bodies called into existence for purposes of local administration with authority in some appropriate way to safeguard the public health and the public safety. The mode or manner in which those results are to be accomplished is within the discretion of the state, subject, of course, so far as Federal power is concerned, only to the condition that no rule prescribed by a state, nor any regulation adopted by a local governmental agency acting under the sanction of state legislation, shall contravene the Constitution of the United States, nor infringe any right granted or secured by that instrument. A local enactment or regulation, even if based on the acknowledged police powers of a state, must always yield in case of conflict with the exercise by the general government of any power it possesses under the Constitution, or with any right which that instrument gives or secures. . . .

We come, then, to inquire whether any right given or secured by the Constitution is invaded by the statute as interpreted by the state court. The defendant insists that his liberty is invaded when the state subjects him to fine or imprisonment for neglecting or refusing to submit to vaccination; that a compulsory vaccination law is unreasonable, arbitrary, and oppressive, and, therefore, hostile to the inherent right of every freeman to care for his own body and health in such way as to him seems best; and that the execution of such a law against one who objects to vaccination, no matter for what reason, is nothing short of an assault upon his person. But the liberty secured by the Constitution of the United States to every person within its jurisdiction does not import an absolute right in each person to be, at all times and in all circumstances, wholly freed from restraint. There are manifold restraints to which every person is necessarily subject for the common good. On any other basis organized society could not exist with safety to its members. Society based on the rule that each one is a law unto himself would soon be confronted with disorder and anarchy. Real liberty for all could not exist under the operation of a principle which recognizes the right of each individual person to use his own, whether in respect of his person or his property, regardless of the injury that may be done to others. This court has more than once recognized it as a fundamental principle that 'persons and property are subjected to all kinds of restraints and burdens in order to secure the general comfort, health, and prosperity of the state; of the perfect right of the legislature to do which no question ever was, or upon acknowledged general principles ever can be, made, so far as natural persons are concerned . . . 'The possession and enjoyment of all rights are subject to such reasonable conditions as may be deemed by the governing authority of the country essential to the safety, health, peace, good order, and morals of the community. Even liberty itself, the greatest of all rights, is not unrestricted license to act according to one's own will. It is only freedom from restraint under conditions essential to the equal enjoyment of the same right by others. It is, then, liberty regulated by law.' In the Constitution of Massachusetts adopted in 1780 it was laid down as a fundamental principle of the social compact that the whole people covenants with each citizen, and each citizen with the whole people, that all shall be governed by certain laws for 'the common good,' and that government is instituted 'for the common good, for the protection, safety, prosperity, and happiness of the people, and not for the profit, honor, or private interests of any one man, family, or class of men.' The good and welfare of the commonwealth, of which the legislature is primarily the judge, is the basis on which the police power rests in Massachusetts.

Applying these principles to the present case, it is to be observed that the legislature of Massachusetts required the inhabitants of a city or town to be vaccinated only when, in the opinion of the board of health, that was necessary for the public health or the public safety. The authority to determine for all what ought to be done in such an emergency must have been lodged somewhere or in some body; and surely it was appropriate for the legislature to refer that question, in the first instance, to a board of health composed of persons residing in the locality affected, and appointed, presumably, because of their fitness to determine such questions. To invest such a body with authority over such matters was not an unusual, nor an unreasonable or arbitrary, requirement. Upon the principle of self-defense, of paramount necessity, a community has the right to protect itself against an epidemic of disease which threatens the safety of its members. It is to be observed that when the regulation in question was adopted smallpox, according to the recitals in the regulation adopted by the board of health, was prevalent to some extent in the city of Cambridge, and the disease was increasing. If such was the situation,—and nothing is asserted or appears in the record to the contrary,—if we are to attach, any value whatever to the knowledge which, it is safe to affirm, in common to all civilized peoples touching smallpox and the methods most usually employed to eradicate that disease, it cannot be adjudged that the present regulation of the board of health was not necessary in order to protect the public health and secure the public safety. Smallpox being prevalent and increasing at Cambridge, the court would usurp the functions of another branch of government if it adjudged, as matter of law, that the mode adopted under the sanction of the state, to protect the people at large was arbitrary, and not justified by the necessities of the case. We say necessities of the case, because it might be that an acknowledged power of a local community to protect itself against an epidemic threatening the safety of all might be exercised in particular circumstances and in reference to particular persons in such an arbitrary, unreasonable manner, or might go so far beyond what was reasonably required for the safety of the public, as to authorize or compel the courts to interfere for the protection of such persons.... There is, of course, a sphere within which the individual may assert the supremacy of his own will, and rightfully dispute the authority of any human government,-especially of any free government existing under a written constitution, to interfere with the exercise of that will. But it is equally true that in every well-ordered society charged with the duty of conserving the safety of its members the rights of the individual in respect of his liberty may at times, under the pressure of great dangers, be subjected to such restraint, to be enforced by reasonable regulations, as the safety of the general public may demand.... The liberty secured by the 14th Amendment, this court has said, consists, in part, in the right of a person 'to live and work where he will'; and yet he may be compelled, by force if need be, against his will and without regard to his personal wishes or his pecuniary interests, or even his religious or political convictions, to take his place in the ranks of the army of his country, and risk the chance of being shot down in its defense. It is not, therefore, true that the power of the public to guard itself against imminent danger depends in every case involving the control of one's body upon his willingness to submit to reasonable regulations established by the constituted authorities, under the sanction of the state, for the purpose of protecting the public collectively against such danger.

. . . .

Whatever may be thought of the expediency of this statute, it cannot be affirmed to be, beyond question, in palpable conflict with the Constitution. . . .

. . . .

A common belief, like common knowledge, does not require evidence to establish its existence, but may be acted upon without proof by the legislature and the courts. . . . The fact that the belief is not universal is not controlling, for there is scarcely any belief that is accepted by everyone.

. . . .

The defendant offered to prove that vaccination 'quite often' caused serious and permanent injury to the health of the person vaccinated; that the operation 'occasionally' resulted in death; that it was 'impossible' to tell 'in any particular case' what the results of vaccination would be, or whether it would injure the health or result in death; that 'quite often' one's blood is in a certain condition of impurity when it is not prudent or safe to vaccinate him; that there is no practical test by which to determine 'with any degree of certainty' whether one's blood is in such condition of impurity as to render vaccination necessarily unsafe or dangerous; that vaccine matter is 'quite often' impure and dangerous to be used, but whether impure or not cannot be ascertained by any known practical test; that the defendant refused to submit to vaccination for the reason that he had, 'when a child,' been caused great and extreme suffering for a long period by a disease produced by vaccination; and that he had witnessed a similar result of vaccination, not only in the case of his son, but in the cases of others.

These offers, in effect, invited the court and jury to go over the whole ground gone over by the legislature when it enacted the statute in question. The legislature assumed that some children, by reason of their condition at the time, might not be fit subjects of vaccination; and it is suggested-and we will not say without reason-that such is the case with some adults. But the defendant did not offer to prove that, by reason of his then condition, he was in fact not a fit subject of vaccination at the time he was informed of the requirement of the regulation adopted by the board of health. It is entirely consistent with his offer of proof that, after reaching full age, he had become, so far as medical skill could discover, and when informed of the regulation of the board of health was, a fit subject of vaccination, and that the vaccine matter to be used in his case was such as any medical practitioner of good standing would regard as proper to be used. The matured opinions of medical men everywhere, and the experience of mankind, as all must know, negative the suggestion that it is not possible in any case to determine whether vaccination is safe....

It seems to the court that an affirmative answer to these questions would practically strip the legislative department of its function to care for the public health and the public safety when endangered by epidemics of disease. Such an answer would mean that compulsory vaccination could not, in any conceivable case, be legally enforced in a community, even at the command of the legislature, however widespread the epidemic of smallpox, and however deep and universal was the belief of the community and of its medical advisers that a system of general vaccination was vital to the safety of all.

We are not prepared to hold that a minority, residing or remaining in any city or town where smallpox is prevalent, and enjoying the general protection afforded by an organized local government, may thus defy the will of its constituted authorities, acting in good faith for all, under the legislative sanction of the state.

. . . .

We now decide only that the statute covers the present case, and that nothing clearly appears that would justify this court in holding it to be unconstitutional and inoperative in its application to the plaintiff in error.

The judgment of the court below must be affirmed.

It is so ordered.

Mr. Justice **Brewer** and Mr. Justice **Peckham** dissent.

DISCUSSION QUESTIONS

1. Explain which game best describes the mandatory vaccine law and why. Does game theory provide a sufficient normative justification for the law? Why or why not?

2. Does the mandatory vaccine law qualify as an example in which the use of state police power solves a game theoretical problem?

3. The Court notes that the state's police power has long permitted it to effect quarantines. Is the analysis of a quarantine law the same as or different from a compulsory vaccination law? Why? Does game theory help to explain your analysis?

Under the National Childhood Vaccine Injury Act of 1986, Congress created a mechanism for persons injured through the mandatory vaccine process to obtain financial recovery without going through the tort system. On the webpage for the Vaccine Injury Compensation Fund, the program is described as follows:

About the National Vaccine Injury Compensation Program[148]

The VICP is a program designed to encourage childhood vaccination by providing a streamlined system for compensation in rare instances where an injury results from vaccination.

Over the past 12 years, the VICP has succeeded in providing a less adversarial, less expensive and less time-consuming system of recovery than the traditional tort system that governs medical malpractice, personal injury and product liability cases. More than 1,500 people have been paid in excess of $1.18 billion since the inception of the program in 1988.

Individuals who believe they have been injured by a covered vaccine can file a claim against the Department of Health and Human Services (HHS) in the U.S. Court of Federal Claims seeking compensation from the Vaccine Trust Fund. The Department of Justice (DOJ), which represents HHS, consistently works to ensure that fair compensation is awarded in every case that meets the eligibility criteria. If found eligible, claimants can recover compensation for related medical and rehabilitative expenses, and in certain cases, may be awarded funds for pain and suffering and future lost earnings. Often, an award is more than $1 million. By protecting the Trust Fund against claims by those who have not suffered a vaccine-related injury, DOJ helps to preserve the Fund for future deserving claimants. Regardless of a claimant's success under the Program, reasonable attorneys' fees and costs are paid.

---

148. National Vaccine Injury Compensation Program, About, http://www.usdoj.gov/civil/torts/const/vicp/about.htm (last visited July 17, 2009).

Vaccines covered under the program include those that protect against diphtheria, tetanus, pertussis (whooping cough), measles, mumps, rubella (German measles), and polio. The program continues to evolve consistent with medical science, and recently, HHS expanded coverage to four new vaccines: hepatitis B, varicella (chicken pox), Hemophilus influenzae type b, and rotavirus; pneumococcal vaccine will soon be covered, too.

Another positive result of the program is that costly litigation against drug manufacturers and health care professionals who administer vaccines has virtually ceased. Although an individual who is dissatisfied with the Court's final judgment can reject it and file a lawsuit in state or federal court, very few lawsuits have been filed since the program began. The supply of vaccines in the U.S. has been stabilized, and the development of new vaccines has markedly increased.

QUESTIONS

1. Does the availability of the fund inform the nature of the game involved in mandatory vaccines?

2. Does the fund demonstrate the soundness of a rule imposing limitations on who can opt out of the vaccine? If so, what alternatives are available to reduce the aggregate risk of disease?

3. The fund operates on a concept that economists refer to as "residual risk," meaning the inevitable risk that remains even after the relevant actors engage in the cost-effective safeguards against harm. In this case, overall risk is reduced by the vaccine, but at the price of forcing those subject to the law—and specifically those who would not do so but for the compulsion of law—to individually bear part of the residual risk. With the fund in place, those individuals continue to bear that risk, but in the event that the risk manifests itself in injury or death, the fund partially offsets the financial implications of the risk for the victim or his or her family by providing some financial compensation, albeit subject to a preset amount (akin to a regime of workers' compensation), rather than in tort. In the vaccine context, is it appropriate to allocate residual risk as between the government on the one hand and the individual on the other in this manner? Why or why not?

4. Is game theory helpful in answering these questions? Why or why not? What about interest-group analysis?

Offer and Acceptance: U.S. and Germany Compared

The United States has the mailbox rule, which generally means that an acceptance becomes legal at the time of mailing. The rule is set out in the *Restatement (Second) of Contracts* § 63, which provides as follows:

Unless the offer provides otherwise,

(a) an acceptance made in a manner and by a medium invited by an offer is operative and completes the manifestation of mutual assent as soon as put out of the offeree's possession, without regard to whether it ever reaches the offeror; but

(b) an acceptance under an option contract is not operative until received by the offeror.

In contrast, the German rule places acceptance at the time of receipt. Article 130 of the German Civil Code (BGB) states:

Section 130

Effectiveness of a declaration of intent to absent parties

(1) A declaration of intent that is to be made to another becomes effective, if made in his absence, at the point of time when this declaration reaches him. It does not become effective if a revocation reaches the other previously or at the same time.

(2) The effectiveness of a declaration of intent is not affected if the person declaring dies or loses capacity to contract after making a declaration.

(3) These provisions apply even if the declaration of intent is to be made to a public authority.[149]

Is either of these rules inherently superior to the alternative? If you were assessing these rules, as between a prisoners' dilemma, a pure Nash bargaining game, a battle of the sexes, or the game of chicken, which game would best characterize the relationship and why? Can you think of other rules that satisfy the same game?

Bankruptcy Revisited

In Chapter 3 we viewed bankruptcy through the lens of social choice and cycling and saw how bankruptcy procedures arguably operate to address cycling problems that might otherwise arise in the multi-party negotiations in bankruptcy. In the excerpt that follows, Professor Thomas Jackson approaches bankruptcy from a different perspective, as solving a collective action problem informed by the prisoners' dilemma or a common pool analysis. As you read the following excerpts, consider the relationship between these two accounts.

The Role of Bankruptcy Law and Collective Action in Debt Collection[150]

Bankruptcy law and policy have been subject to long-standing debate. This debate is not so much about whether bankruptcy law should exist at all but about how much it should do. All agree that it serves as a collective debt-collection device. Whether, when firms are involved, it should do more is the crux of the dispute. I plan to start

---

149. Juris, English Translation of German Civil Code (2008), *available at* http://www.gesetze-im-internet.de/englisch_bgb/englisch_bgb.html#Section% 20130.

150. The following discussion is taken from THOMAS H. JACKSON, THE LOGIC AND LIMITS OF BANKRUPTCY LAW 7-19 (1986).

by establishing what accepted wisdom already acknowledges—that bankruptcy's system of collectivized debt collection is, in principle, beneficial. . . .

Bankruptcy law is a response to credit. The essence of credit economies is people and firms—that can be called *debtors*—borrowing money. The reasons for this are varied. In the case of individuals credit may serve as a device to smooth out consumption patterns by means of borrowing against future income. In the case of corporations and other firms it may be a part of a specialization of financing and investment decisions. And just as the reasons for borrowing are varied, so, too, are the methods. The prototype creditor may be a bank or other financial institution that lends money, but that is only one of many ways in which credit is extended. An installment seller extends credit. So does a worker who receives a paycheck on the first of December for work performed in November. The government, in its role as tax collector, also extends credit to the extent that taxes accrue over a year and are due at the end. Similarly, a tort victim who is injured today and must await payment until the end of a lawsuit extends credit of sorts, although involuntarily and (probably) unhappily. Finally, credit is not extended just by "creditors." First-round purchasers of common and preferred stock of a corporation are also lending money to the debtor. Their repayment rights are distinct (they are the residual claimants), but it is proper to view them, too, as having defined rights to call on the assets of the debtor for payment.

Whatever the reasons for lending and whatever its form, the terms on which consensual credit is extended depend to a substantial extent on the likelihood of voluntary repayment and on the means for coercing repayment. We are not concerned here with the means for getting paid when the debtor is solvent—when it has enough assets to satisfy all its obligations in full—but is simply mean-spirited or is genuinely disputing whether it has a duty of payment (as the debtor might be with our putative tort victim or with a supplier who the debtor believes sold it defective goods). The legal remedies for coercing payment when the debtor is solvent concern the rights of a creditor to use the power of the state in pursuit of its claim. This is a question of debtor-creditor law and one to which bankruptcy law historically has had nothing to add, directly at least.

Bankruptcy law can be thought of as growing out of a distinct aspect of debtor-creditor relations: the effect of the debtor's obligation to repay Creditor A on its remaining creditors. This question takes on particular bite only when the debtor does not have enough to repay everyone in full. Even then, however, a developed system exists for paying creditors without bankruptcy. The relevant question is whether that existing system of creditor remedies has any shortcomings that might be ameliorated by an ancillary system known as bankruptcy law.

To explore that question, it is useful to start with the familiar. Creditor remedies outside of bankruptcy (as well as outside other formal, non-bankruptcy collective systems) can be accurately described as a species of "grab law," represented by the key characteristic of first-come, first-served. The creditor first staking a claim to particular assets of the debtor generally is entitled to be paid first out of those assets. It is like buying tickets for a popular rock event or opera: the people first in line get the best seats; those at the end of the line may get nothing at all.[151]

Professor Jackson proceeds to discuss the varieties of non-bankruptcy "grab" law, including security interests, judicial liens, garnishment, or statutory liens. In general, those rules provide that the first creditor to "perfect" its interest gets paid in full before any other "junior" claimants. Jackson explains:

> A solvent debtor is like a show for which sufficient tickets are available to accommodate all prospective patrons and all seats are considered equally good. In that event one's place in line is largely a matter of indifference. But when there is not enough to go around to satisfy all claimants in full, this method of ordering will define winners and losers based principally on the time when one gets in line.
>
> The question at the core of bankruptcy law is whether a *better* ordering system can be devised that would be worth the inevitable costs associated with implementing a new system. In the case of tickets to a popular rock event or opera, where there must be winners and losers, and putting aside price adjustments, there may be no better way to allocate available seats than on a first-come, first-served basis. In the world of credit, however, there are powerful reasons to think that there is a superior way to allocate the assets of an insolvent debtor than first-come, first-served.
>
> The basic problem that bankruptcy law is designed to handle, both as a normative matter and as a positive matter, is that the system of individual creditor remedies may be bad for the creditors *as a group* when there are not enough assets to go around. Because creditors have conflicting rights, there is a tendency in their debt-collection efforts to make a bad situation worse. Bankruptcy law responds to this problem. Debt-collection by means of individual creditor remedies produces a variant of a widespread problem. One way to characterize the problem is as a multiparty game—a type of "prisoner's dilemma." As such, it has elements of what game theorists would describe as an *end period* game, where basic problems of cooperation are generally expected to lead to undesirable outcomes for the group of players as a whole.[152] Another way of considering it is as

---

151. *Id.* at 7–9.

152. [After explaining the difference between a single period game, a game that is expected to be infinitely repeated, and a game with a known end period, Jackson explains:] "Although

a species of what is called a *common pool* problem, which is well known to lawyers in other fields, such as oil and gas.

This role of bankruptcy law is largely unquestioned. But because this role carries limits on what *else* bankruptcy law can do, it is worth considering the basics of the problem so that we understand its essential features before examining whether and why credit may present that problem. The vehicle will be a typical, albeit simple, common pool example. Imagine that you own a lake. There are fish in the lake. You are the only one who has the right to fish in that lake, and no one constrains your decision as to how much fishing to do. You have it in your power to catch all the fish this year and sell them for, say, $100,000. If you did that, however, there would be no fish in the lake next year. It might be better for you—you might maximize your total return from fishing—if you caught and sold some fish this year but left other fish in the lake so that they could multiply and you would have fish in subsequent years. Assume that, by taking this approach, you could earn (adjusting for inflation) $50,000 each year. Having this outcome is like having a perpetual annuity paying $50,000 a year. It has a present value of perhaps $500,000. Since (obviously, I hope) when all other things are equal, $500,000 is better than $100,000, you, as sole owner, would limit your fishing this year unless some other factor influenced you.

But what if you are not the only one who can fish in this lake? What if a hundred people can do so? The optimal solution has not changed: it would be preferable to leave some fish in the lake to multiply because doing so has a present value of $500,000. But in this case, unlike that where you have to control only yourself, an obstacle exists in achieving that result. If there are a hundred fishermen, you cannot be sure, by limiting your fishing, that there will be any more fish next year, unless you can also control the others. You may, then, have an incentive to catch as many fish as you can today because maximizing your take this year (catching, on average, $1,000 worth of fish) is better for you than holding off (catching, say, only $500 worth of fish this year) while others scramble and deplete the stock entirely. If you hold off, your aggregate return is only $500, since nothing will be left for next year or the year after. But that sort of reasoning by each of the hundred fishermen will mean that the stock of fish will be gone by the end of the first season. The fishermen will split $100,000 this year, but there will be no fish—and no money—in future years. Self-interest results in their splitting $100,000, not $500,000.

What is required is some rule that will make all hundred fishermen act as a sole owner would. That is where bankruptcy law enters the picture in a world not of fish but of credit. The grab rules of nonbankruptcy law and their allocation of assets on the basis of first-

insolvency may signal an end to relationships with one debtor, many creditors will still favor cooperation because of repeat dealings with each other. But not all will expect such repeat dealings, and destructive races to assets can be caused by a few 'bad apples.' "

come, first-served create an incentive on the part of the individual creditors, when they sense that a debtor may have more liabilities than assets, to get in line today (by, for example, getting a sheriff to execute on the debtor's equipment), because if they do not, they run the risk of getting nothing. This decision by numerous individual creditors, however, may be the wrong decision for the creditors as a group. Even though the debtor is insolvent, they might be better off if they held the assets together. Bankruptcy provides a way to make these diverse individuals act as one, by imposing a *collective* and *compulsory* proceeding on them. Unlike a typical common pool solution, however, the compulsory solution of bankruptcy law does not apply in all places at all times. Instead, it runs parallel with a system of individual debt-collection rules and is available to supplant them when and if needed.

This is the historically recognized purpose of bankruptcy law and perhaps is none too controversial in itself. Because more controversial limits on bankruptcy policy derive from it, however, less allegorical and more precise analysis is necessary. Exactly *how* does bankruptcy law make creditors as a group better off? To find the answer to that question, consider a simple hypothetical example involving credit, not fish. Debtor has a small printing business. Potential creditors estimate that there is a 20 percent chance that Debtor (who is virtuous and will not misbehave) will become insolvent through bad luck, general economic downturn, or whatever. (By insolvency, I mean a condition whereby Debtor will not have enough assets to satisfy his creditors.) At the point of insolvency ... the business is expected to be worth $50,000 if sold piecemeal. Creditors also know that each of them will have to spend $1,000 in pursuit of their individual collection efforts should Debtor become insolvent and fail to repay them. Under these circumstances Debtor borrows $25,000 from each of four creditors, Creditors 1 through 4. Because these creditors know that there is this 20 percent chance, they can account for it—and the associated collection costs—in the interest rate they charge Debtor. Assume that each party can watch out for its own interest, and let us see whether, as in the example of fishing, there are reasons to think that these people would favor a set of restrictions on their own behavior (apart from paternalism or other similar considerations).

Given that these creditors can watch out for their own interests, the question to be addressed is *how* these creditors should go about protecting themselves. If the creditors have to protect themselves by means of a costly and inefficient system, Debtor is going to have to pay more to obtain credit. Thus, when we consider them all together—Creditors 1 through 4 *and* Debtor—the relevant question is: would the availability of a bankruptcy system reduce the costs of credit?

. . . .

... The common pool example of fish in a lake suggests that one of the advantages to a collective system is a larger aggregate pie. Does that advantage exist in the case of credit? When dealing with businesses, the answer, at least some of the time, would seem to be "yes." The use of individual creditor remedies may lead to a piecemeal dismantling of a debtor's business by the untimely removal of necessary operating assets. To the extent that a non-piecemeal collective process (whether in the form of a liquidation or reorganization) is likely to increase the aggregate value of the pool of assets, its substitution for individual remedies would be advantageous to the creditors as a group. This is derived from a commonplace notion: that a collection of assets is sometimes more valuable together than the same assets would be if spread to the winds. It is often referred to as the surplus of a going-concern value over a liquidation value.

Thus, the most obvious reason for a collective system of creditor collection is to make sure that creditors, in pursuing their individual remedies, do not actually decrease the aggregate value of the assets that will be used to repay them. In our example this situation would occur when a printing press, for example, could be sold to a third party for $20,000, leaving $30,000 of other assets, but the business as a unit could generate sufficient cash so as to have a value of more than $50,000. As such it is directly analogous to the case of the fish in the lake. Even in cases in which the assets should be sold and the business dismembered, the aggregate value of the assets may be increased by keeping groups of those assets together (the printing press with its custom dies, for example) to be sold as discrete units.

This advantage, however, is not the only one to be derived from a collective system for creditors. Consider what the creditors would get if there were no bankruptcy system (putting aside the ultimate collection costs). Without a collective system all of the creditors in our example know that in the case of Debtor's insolvency the first two creditors to get to (and through) the courthouse (or to Debtor, to persuade Debtor to pay voluntarily), will get $25,000, leaving nothing for the third and fourth. And unless the creditors think that one of them is systematically faster (or friendlier with Debtor), this leaves them with a 50 percent chance of gaining $25,000, and a 50 percent chance of getting nothing. A collective system, however, would ensure that they would each get $12,500.

Would the creditors agree in advance to a system that, in the event of Debtor's insolvency, guaranteed them $12,500, in lieu of a system that gave them a 50 percent chance of $25,000—payment in full—and a 50 percent chance of nothing? Resolution of this question really turns on whether the creditors are better off with the one than the other. There are two reasons to think that they are, even without looking to the question of a going-concern surplus and without considering the costs of an individual collection system. First of all, if these creditors are risk averse, assurance of receiving $12,500 is better than a 50 percent chance of $25,000 and a 50 percent chance of nothing. Even if they can diversify the risk—by lending money to many people—it is probably preferable to eliminate it in the first place. This, then, represents a net advantage to having a collective proceeding.

One other possible advantage of a collective proceeding should also be noted: there may be costs to the individualized approach to collecting (in addition to the $1,000 collection costs). For example, since each creditor knows that it must "beat out" the others if it wants to be paid in full, it will spend time monitoring Debtor and the other creditors—perhaps frequently checking the courthouse records—to make sure that it will be no worse than second in the race (and therefore still be paid in full). Although some of these activities may be beneficial, many may not be; they will simply be costs of racing against other creditors, and they will cancel each other out. It is like running on a treadmill: you expend a lot of energy but get nowhere. If every creditor is doing this, each one *still* does not know if there is more than a fifty-fifty chance that it will get paid in full. But in one sense, unless the creditors can negotiate a deal with each other, the creditors have no choice. Each creditor has to spend this money just to stay in the race because if it does not, it is a virtual certainty that the others will beat it to the payment punch. Of course, a creditor could decide that it did not want to stay in the race, and just charge Debtor at the time of lending the money for coming in last should Debtor become insolvent. Debtor is not likely, however, to agree to pay a creditor that extra charge for having a lower priority provision, because, once paid that extra amount, the creditor may have an incentive to take steps to remain in the race and make money that way. For that reason it may be hard for a creditor to opt out of the race and get compensated for doing so.

These various costs to using an individual system of creditor remedies suggest that there are, indeed, occasions when a collective system of debt-collection law might be preferable. Bankruptcy provides that system. The single most fruitful way to think about bankruptcy is to see it as ameliorating a common pool problem created by a system of individual creditor remedies. Bankruptcy provides a way to override the creditors' pursuit of their own remedies and to make them work together.[153]

Viewing bankruptcy as solving a collective action problem, Jackson argues, helps to explains many of the important provisions of bankruptcy law:

---

153. JACKSON, *supra* note 150, at 9–17 (footnotes omitted) (citing Thomas H. Jackson, *Bankruptcy, Non–Bankruptcy Entitlements, and the Creditors' Bargain*, 91 YALE L.J. 857 (1982)). *See also* Garrett Hardin, *The Tragedy of the Commons*, 162 SCIENCE 1243 (1968); Gary D. Libecap & Steven N. Wiggins, *Contractual Responses to the Common Pool: Prorationing Crude Oil Production*, 74 AM. ECON. REV. 87 (1984); Alan E. Friedman, *The Economics of the Common Pool: Property Rights in Exhaustible Resources*, 18 UCLA L. REV. 855 (1971).

This approach immediately suggests several features of bankruptcy law. First, such a law must usurp individual creditor remedies in order to make the claimants act in an altruistic and cooperative way. Thus, the proceeding is inherently *collective*. Moreover, this system works only if all the creditors are bound to it. To allow a debtor to contract with a creditor to avoid participating in the bankruptcy proceeding would destroy the advantages of a collective system. So the proceeding must be compulsory as well. But unlike common pool solutions in oil and gas or fishing, it is not the exclusive system for dividing up assets. It, instead, supplants an existing system of individual creditor remedies, and . . . it is this feature that makes crucial an awareness of its limitations.

Note that the presence of a bankruptcy system does not mandate its use whenever there is a common pool problem. Bankruptcy law stipulates a minimum set of entitlements for claimants. That, in turn, permits them to "bargain in the shadow of the law" and to implement a consensual collective proceeding outside of the bankruptcy process. Because use of the bankruptcy process has costs of its own, if creditors can consensually gain the sorts of advantages of acting collectively that bankruptcy brings, they could avoid those costs. Accordingly, one would expect that consensual deals among creditors outside the bankruptcy process would often be attempted first. The formal bankruptcy process would presumably be used only when individual advantage-taking in the setting of multiparty negotiations made a consensual deal too costly to strike—which may, however, occur frequently as the number of creditors increases.

. . . .

Like all justifications, moreover, this one is subject to a number of qualifications. To say that a common pool problem exists is not to say that individual behavior is entirely self-interested or that legal rules can solve all collective action problems. We often observe people behaving in a cooperative fashion over time even if it appears contrary to their short-run interest. In the credit world, for example, creditors do not always rush to seize a debtor's assets whenever it seems to be in financial trouble. Yet despite this qualification the underlying point remains: sometimes people behave in a self-interested way and would be better off as a group if required to work together. The tragedy of the Texas oil fields in the first half of this century is a notable example of how self-interest led to the depletion of oil that otherwise could have been enjoyed by the group of oil field owners. Creditor relations almost certainly are another area where this essential truth has validity, especially given the fact that creditors may have fewer incentives to cooperate when a debtor is failing than they do when there are greater prospects of repeat dealings with a debtor.

. . . .

For now however, it is sufficient to ask whether there is in fact a common pool problem that cannot be solved by creditors contracting among themselves. If the number of creditors is sufficiently small and sufficiently determinate, it may be possible for them to negotiate a solution at the time of insolvency that would avoid many, if not most, of the costs of an individual remedies system, even if they were not bargaining in the shadow of the law. But in cases in which there are large numbers of creditors or the creditors are not immediately known at a particular time (perhaps because they hold contingent or nonmanifested claims), the ability of the creditors to solve the problem of an individual remedies system by an actual agreement may be lost. Bankruptcy provides the desired result by making available a collective system after insolvency has occurred.[154]

DISCUSSION QUESTIONS

1. Jackson argues that one justification for the normative force of a bankruptcy system is that creditors acting behind a "veil of ignorance" would implicitly consent to bankruptcy rules in the event of the debtor's insolvency because they all would be better off by being forced to participate in this collective system. Is that a satisfactory normative justification? Does that rationale apply for so-called involuntary creditors as well? If that is the case, why do creditors demand security interests and other provisions designed to improve their priority in bankruptcy?

2. Does the logic of Jackson's argument support making bankruptcy for insolvent firms a mandatory provision of all debtor-creditor contracts and relationships or should parties be allowed to contract out of that regime? For instance, what if a corporation's charter, one of its founding documents, provided, "In the event of insolvency, this corporation will not seek bankruptcy relief"? All subsequent consensual creditors, including workers, would thus have notice of such a provision when entering into contracts with that corporation. Would individual creditors be willing to contract with a firm with such a provision in its charter? If so, should such a provision be enforceable if a creditor subsequently sought to enforce it? Why or why not?

3. Jackson states: "The formal bankruptcy process would presumably be used only when individual advantage-taking in the setting of multiparty negotiations made a consensual deal too costly to strike—which may, however, occur frequently as the number of creditors increases." How does this analysis relate to the social choice account of bankruptcy rules as a function of cycling? More specifically, what is the relationship between Jackson's account of bankruptcy as seeking to avoid a prisoners' dilemma or common pool game, on the one hand, and the social choice account of bankruptcy as seeking to avoid a problem of legislative cycling or cycling over debtor/creditor financial interests, on the other? Is the risk of cycling preferences one of the factors that increases bargaining costs as the number of parties increases under Jackson's analysis? Why or why not?

---

154. *Id.* at 17–19.

CHAPTER 5

THE LEGISLATURE

■ ■ ■

Introduction

In this chapter, we consider how public choice analysis informs our understanding of the structure and processes of legislative decision making, with a particular emphasis on the United States Congress, and of the judicial interpretation of statutes. The chapter proceeds in three sections. In section I, we present two models that explain the legislative process.[1] We begin by returning to the public interest model of the legislative process, introduced in chapter 2.[2] Our earlier discussion was designed to contrast the descriptive claims of the public interest model with those drawn from interest group theory. In this chapter, we are primarily concerned with assessing competing normative, or prescriptive, proposals for the judicial construction of statutes that are informed by these competing understandings of legislative decision making.

To consider the normative implications of the public interest model, we turn to the influential Legal Process School developed in an unpublished, yet highly influential, manuscript by Professors Henry M. Hart, Jr. and Albert M. Sacks.[3] Hart and Sacks developed a comprehensive approach to statutory construction that rests on the supposition that both legislators and courts are primarily motivated to further public interest objectives in drafting and in interpreting statutes.

We also revisit the Wilson–Hayes matrix, introduced in chapter 2, which explores the implications of interest group dynamics for each of four analytical categories of legislation. The combined matrix provides a rough sketch of the legislative process that rests in tension with the supposition of public spiritedness that informs the Legal Process School. We begin with the original, static version of the Wilson–Hayes model. This model depicts the tendency among legislatures to oversupply or undersupply

---

1. In chapter 8, we also introduce the specific institutional feature of bicameralism. *See infra* chapter 8, section II.E.

2. *See supra* chapter 2, section I.

3. *See* HENRY M. HART & ALBERT M. SACKS, THE LEGAL PROCESS: BASIC PROBLEMS IN THE MAKING AND APPLICATION OF LAW 1374–80 (William N. Eskridge & Philip P. Frickey eds., 1994). While a tentative edition of these materials, which were developed beginning in the 1940s, circulated in two bound but unpublished volumes in 1958, thanks to the diligent efforts of Professors Eskridge and Frickey, they were finally, and posthumously, published as a course book in 1994.

certain categories of legislation. We then consider the implications of a dynamic version of this model, which highlights the important interrelationships among the identified legislative categories, and which explores the implications of those relationships for various proposals for the judicial construction of statutes.[4] The analysis exposes the difficulties in assuming that proposals designed to curb seemingly problematical features of the legislative process, including for example the tendency to produce private goods legislation or to avoid contentious policy making through delegation, can be implemented without producing other costs within the legislative process.

We can think of the Legal Process School and the Wilson–Hayes Matrix as endpoints on an analytical spectrum that depicts the extent to which observers view the legislature as furthering the public interest (the Legal Process School), or conversely, as willingly subordinating that interest in favor of narrow interest group objectives (the Wilson–Hayes Matrix). While most scholars hold views between these analytical endpoints, juxtaposing these contrasting views provides a means of assessing a range of scholarly proposals, each relying upon public choice, concerning the underlying motivation, or "purpose," of any given statute, as well as theories concerning how courts should engage in the task of statutory interpretation.

In section II, we present an array of normative theories concerning the judicial construction of statutes advanced by prominent judges, legal scholars, and political scientists, each of whom relies in varying degrees upon public choice tools and analyses to inform his or her discussion. A notable feature of this rich and varied literature is the range of perspectives that the scholars embrace as well as the often conflicting normative claims that they advance. We can divide these scholars in various ways, including a reference to particular public choice traditions, with the first group adhering more closely to the Chicago tradition, and a corresponding concern for legislative market failure, and the second group following more closely the Virginia tradition, with a stronger institutional focus and a somewhat more sanguine view of legislative bargaining processes. One might also view this from an ideological perspective, with the first group coming to public choice from the right and the latter coming to it from the left. If you find this characterization descriptive, consider the extent to which the authors rely upon public choice to reinforce preexisting ideological views.

The first group of scholars relies upon public choice to advance claims seeking to limit the reach of statutes, often with the effect of raising the costs of legislative bargaining. These scholars include Judges Frank Easterbrook and Richard Posner, of the United States Court of Appeals for the Seventh Circuit and members of the University of Chicago Law School faculty; Kenneth Shepsle, a political scientist at the Department of Gov-

---

4. Portions of this discussion are based upon Maxwell L. Stearns, *The Public Choice Case Against the Item Veto*, 49 WASH. & LEE L. REV. 385 (1992).

ernment at Harvard University; and Jonathan Macey, a professor at the Yale Law School.[5] While there are important differences, and indeed disagreements, among these jurists and scholars that we will emphasize in our presentation, there are also some helpful similarities. Each tends to hold the common law in high regard and thus to focus on the normative implications of public choice models for legislative processes that alter the background common law rules. These scholars question whether courts, in the interpretation of statutes, should be skeptical of claims that the legislature is generally motivated by the desire to further some aspect of the public interest, and thus whether statutory construction should be sparing, rather than an expansive effort to further some larger set of legislative objectives.

The second group of scholars generally offers a more optimistic view of both legislative processes and of the role of courts in furthering benign statutory objectives in the course of statutory interpretation.[6] These scholars include Professors Daniel Farber and Philip Frickey, of the University of California at Berkeley, Boalt Hall School of Law; Professor William Eskridge, of the Yale Law School; Professor Einer Elhauge, of the Harvard Law School; and McNollgast, an acronym for two political scientists at Stanford, Mathew D. *Mc*Cubbins and Roger *Noll,* and one at the California Institute of Technology, Barry Wein*gast.* While these scholars also hold varied and conflicting views concerning the proper role of courts in statutory interpretation, in a certain respect each can be viewed, at least in part, as heir to the Hart and Sacks Legal Process tradition.[7] These scholars tend to take a more sanguine view of the legislative process and of the capacity of judges to discern public interest objectives in assessing statutes that courts are called upon to interpret. Once again, each of these scholars claims support for this view in the public choice literature.

Given the varied perspectives that these scholars represent and the often directly conflicting normative claims that they advance in the name of public choice, this part raises important questions concerning the nature of public choice scholarship and of the legal applications of that scholarship. Is it possible to separate the ideological perspectives, or attitudes, of scholars relying on public choice from the specific normative claims that they advance? As applied to this chapter's more specific inquiry, is it possible to assess normative claims resting on public choice analysis of legislative processes, including matters of judicial statutory interpretation, independently of the (most often implicit) attitudinal base-

---

5. In some respects, Professor Macey could be placed in the latter camp, given his willingness to allow judges to read the overall legislative purpose broadly and to construe claimed payoffs consistently with that larger purpose. We have grouped him with the conservatives, however, because of the specific ends to which he seeks to have courts employ this arguably liberal set of interpretative techniques.

6. These scholars can also be described as heirs to the Virginia public choice tradition.

7. It should not be surprising, therefore, that two of these scholars, Professors Eskridge and Frickey, are the editors of the Hart and Sacks eventual published work. *See supra* note 3, and cite therein.

lines of the scholars advancing those claims?[8] If the answers to these
questions are "no," and thus if public choice does not provide its own set
of normative baselines against which to assess proposals for questions of
law or public policy, how can we best use public choice tools to meaningfully assess the competing claims among scholars who claim to rely upon
public choice?

Finally, in section III, we present two cases that test the positive
public choice models developed in section I and the normative theories
about statutory interpretation developed in section II. As you review these
cases, consider the following questions: Which of the various scholarly
approaches presented in section II are most helpful in assessing the cases
under review? To what extent are the intuitions respecting these cases
developed in the larger course of your legal training consistent or in
tension with insights respecting these cases that you have gained from
your study of public choice? In the event these intuitions conflict, which
should prevail? If you conclude that the legal framework should prevail,
what does that suggest about the value of public choice analysis? If you
instead conclude that the insights from public choice should prevail, how
could the underlying legal doctrines better reflect the relevant public
choice insights?

I. MODELS OF LEGISLATION AND LEGISLATIVE BARGAINING

A. THE LEGAL PROCESS SCHOOL

In the middle of the twentieth century, Professors Henry Hart and
Albert Sacks developed an influential framework designed in part to
describe actual judicial practices in construing statutes and in part to offer
a normatively promising theory of statutory construction.[9] While the
materials were written over a half century ago, the theory of statutory
interpretation that Hart and Sacks devised has continued to resonate with
an influential group of contemporary jurisprudential scholars. In a sense,
the Hart and Sacks approach gives normative content to the descriptive
claims embraced by those who support a public interest understanding of
legislative decision-making processes. The analysis is designed to inform
courts concerning how to construe statutes, what "attitudes" to bring to
this task, and how to identify the overall public-regarding design of
statutes that they are called upon to apply. The Legal Process School thus
provides an important normative gloss on the public interest theory of
legislation that instructs courts to construe statutes so as to further the
claimed underlying public interest objectives.[10]

Legal scholars routinely cite Hart and Sacks for the simple proposition that courts should "assume, unless the contrary unmistakably ap-

---

8. *Cf.* Einer R. Elhauge, *Does Interest Group Theory Justify More Intrusive Judicial Review?*,
101 YALE L.J. 31 (1991).

9. *See* HART & SACKS, *supra* note 3.

10. The discussion that follows is largely based upon the final section of the lengthy treatise,
entitled *Note on the Rudiments of Statutory Interpretation. See id.* at 1374–80.

pears, that the legislature was made up of reasonable persons pursuing reasonable purposes reasonably."[11] For Hart and Sacks, this premise is closely linked to the concept of legislative primacy, and thus to the role of the legislature as the "chief policy-determining agency of the society, subject only to the limitations of the constitution under which it exercises its powers."[12] The role of both the courts and agencies is to exercise "good faith and good sense" in construing statutes.

The authors summarize the proper task of legislative interpretation as follows:

1. Decide what purpose ought to be attributed to the statute and to any subordinate provision of it which may be involved; and then

2. Interpret the words of the statute immediately in question so as to carry out the purpose as best it can, making sure, however, that it does not give the words either—

   (a) a meaning they will not bear, or

   (b) a meaning which would violate any established policy of clear statement.[13]

Given the importance the authors ascribe to statutory language, it is perhaps not surprising that Hart and Sacks reject claims of linguistic indeterminacy in favor of the notion that language is a social construction.[14] The authors admonish courts to rely upon contemporaneous usages to inform intended statutory meaning. Hart and Sacks caution, however, that it is statutory text, and not "[u]nenacted intentions," that constitute governing law.[15] And yet, Hart and Sacks also instruct courts to avoid "linguistically permissible" constructions that produce "unusual meaning."[16] The authors identify two contexts in which courts should be cautious in ensuring that literal meaning does not produce unintended results. First, they observe that "words which mark the boundary between criminal and non-criminal conduct should speak with more than ordinary clearness." Second, they advise courts against interpreting legislation as "depart[ing] from a generally prevailing principle or policy of the law unless it does so clearly."[17]

---

11. *Id.* at 1378; *see also* Richard A. Posner, *Legal Formalism, Legal Realism, and the Interpretation of Statutes and the Constitution*, 37 Case W. Res. L. Rev. 179 (1986).

12. Hart & Sacks, *supra* note 3, at 1374.

13. *Id.*

14. For a general discussion about linguistic indeterminacy and its implications for law, see Timothy A.O. Endicott, *Linguistic Indeterminacy*, 16 Oxford J. Legal Stud. 667 (1996); Christian Zapf & Eben Moglen, *Linguistic Indeterminacy and the Rule of Law: On the Perils of Misunderstanding Wittgenstein*, 84 Geo. L.J. 485 (1996).

15. Hart & Sacks, *supra* note 3, at 1375.

16. *Id.* at 1376.

17. *Id.* at 1376–77. The authors trace these intuitions to Lord Blackburn's "golden rule," which they paraphrase as follows: "If Parliament means to produce an inconsistency, or absurdity, or very great inconvenience, it must be quite clear about it." *See id.* at 1209; *see also id.* at 1112 (quoting Blackburn). The authors describe their alternative formulation of the golden rule—"a statute ought always to be presumed to be the work of reasonable men pursuing reasonable purposes reasonably"—as an "even more radical suggestion." *Id.* at 1209.

Hart and Sacks link the second assertion, which they term a "golden rule," to an historically controversial canon of statutory interpretation: "statutes in derogation of the common law are to be strictly construed."[18] Without endorsing or rejecting this rule of construction, Hart and Sacks suggest that while legislatures can draw upon experience to change background suppositions regarding public policy, courts should not assume that a legislature has done so silently.

Against this background set of commands, the authors present the following passage, which contains the famous admonition that courts assume that legislatures comprise reasonable persons acting reasonably:

> In determining the more immediate purpose which ought to be attributed to a statute, and to any subordinate provision of it which may be involved, a court should try to put itself in imagination in the position of the legislature which enacted the measure.

> The court, however, should not do this in the mood of a cynical political observer, taking account of all the short-run currents of political expedience that swirl around any legislative session.

> *It should assume, unless the contrary unmistakably appears, that the legislature was made up of reasonable persons pursuing reasonable purposes reasonably.*

> It should presume conclusively that these persons, whether or not entertaining concepts of reasonableness shared by the court, were trying responsibly and in good faith to discharge their constitutional powers and duties.

> . . . The gist of this approach is to infer purpose by comparing the new law with the old. Why would reasonable men, confronted with the law as it was, have enacted this new law to replace it? Answering this question . . . calls for a close look at the "mischief" thought to inhere in the old law and at "the true reason of the remedy" provided by the statute for it.[19]

The authors also specifically address the questions concerning the proper role of legislative history in the judicial task of statutory interpretation:

> *First.* The history should be examined for the light it throws on *general purpose.* Evidence of specific intention with respect to particular applications is competent only to the extent that the particular applications illuminate the general purpose and are consistent with other evidence of it.

> *Second.* Effect should not be given to evidence from the internal legislative history if the result would be to contradict a purpose otherwise indicated and to yield an interpretation disadvantageous to

---

18. *Id.* at 1210.

19. *Id.* at 1378 (emphasis added).

private persons who had no reasonable means of access to the history.[20]

While Hart and Sacks did not suggest that subsequent legislative history informs specific statutory meaning, they do claim that "judicial, administrative, and popular construction of a statute, subsequent to its enactment, are all relevant in attributing a purpose to it."[21]

1. Discussion

Before turning to the public choice model of legislative processes, it is worth considering some of the underlying premises of the Hart and Sacks Legal Process model. While the authors are most often cited for the proposition that legislatures comprise reasonable people acting reasonably, read in its broader context, this assertion suggests something more fundamental concerning the authors' understanding of legislation. Hart and Sacks assert that courts should presume that legislation is intended to resolve some identified "mischief" in the law or public policy. In this analysis, not only judicial decisions, but also legislation, is presumed to be principled. And yet, Hart and Sacks are not so naïve as to imagine that statutory policy has not been influenced by the rough and tumble of political maneuvering. Instead, they claim that it is the job of courts to set aside knowledge of this maneuvering in favor of treating particular statutes under review as efforts to "solve" a specific problem of law or public policy.

While Hart and Sacks do not deny that political actors can sometimes behave in a self-interested fashion, they contend that this alone does not undermine larger and more public-spirited motives that courts can discern in construing statutes. Moreover, this might also require that in construing statutes, courts avoid literal objectives that threaten deeply problematical results. Part of this task, Hart and Sacks contend, includes the proper reliance upon legislative history.

Consider whether the following account provides a fair summary of the Legal Process school: The goal of statutory interpretation is to improve the prior state of the law informed by the statute that the courts are called upon to construe. If this is a fair account, how, if at all, does it differ from an understanding of statutory interpretation informed by public choice? How does one determine which constructions improve the state of the law? Can this be answered independently of the decision maker's normative premises concerning whatever values the law should reflect? If not, can Hart and Sacks avoid the argument that in the mind of a judge favoring a *laissez faire* philosophy, their "golden rule" admonishes construing statutes in derogation of the common law narrowly? Is that a problem? Why or why not?

---

20. *Id.* at 1379 (emphasis in original).

21. *Id.*

B. THE WILSON–HAYES MODEL REVISITED

We will now revisit the Wilson–Hayes model of legislative procurement introduced in chapter 2.[22] This model builds upon the insights of interest group theory to identify the conditions that are likely to give rise to various forms, or combinations, of legislation. The analysis divides legislation into four possible paradigms based upon whether the resulting benefits and costs are widely dispersed or narrowly concentrated. While the resulting matrix is stylized and admittedly simplistic, it nonetheless offers a helpful starting point in assessing public choice intuitions that sometimes operate in tension with the public interest, or Legal Process, understanding of legislation. In addition, the dynamic version of the Wilson–Hayes model provides the basis for a more nuanced understanding of the analytical categories themselves and the relationships among them in procuring desired legislation.

1. The Static Bargaining Model

The discussion that follows builds upon the following matrix below introduced in chapter 2.[23]

---

22. *See supra* chapter 2, section III.A. (discussing model based on JAMES Q. WILSON, POLITICAL ORGANIZATIONS (1973) and MICHAEL T. HAYES, LOBBYISTS AND LEGISLATORS: A THEORY OF POLITICAL MARKERS (1981)).

23. *See supra* chapter 2, section III.A. tbl. 2:1; *see also* Stearns, *supra* note 4, at 407.

Table 5:1. The Four Box Static Model

	Widely Distributed Benefits	Narrowly Conferred Benefits
Widely Distributed Costs	*Legislative Characteristics:* This desired category of legislation tends to be undersupplied as constituents express too little pressure in support; alternatively when pressure is brought on both sides, legislatures sometimes delegate to avoid the resulting conflict. *Illustrations:* Desired legislative responses to various environmental crises, e.g., waste management or global warming; and national fiscal management, e.g., social security reform.	*Legislative Characteristics:* Because small organized groups exert pressure disproportionately to numbers in political processes, legislatures tend to oversupply special interest legislation. *Illustrations:* Tariffs, industry subsidies.
Narrowly Conferred Costs	*Legislative Characteristics:* Given the fear that factional violence (Madison Federalist 10), or interest group politicking (the modern equivalent), will disadvantage unpopular minorities, congressional processes include numerous features that tend to enlarge successful coalitions above minimum winning size. *Illustrations:* Rent control, national health care reform.	*Legislative Characteristics:* Because intense interests directly conflict, legislators prefer to delegate to agencies, hoping to shift blame for resulting failures while claiming credit for resulting successes; legislators can also benefit from simply threatening regulatory delegation and can benefit from monitoring agencies. *Illustrations:* The National Labor Relations Board.

The Wilson–Hayes model returns us to a central premise of interest group theory, namely that we can gain insight into the political process by analogizing the legislature to a marketplace for the procurement of various forms of legislation. The model builds upon the incentives of those who demand legislation—constituents, interest groups, and lobbyists—and those who supply it—elected members of the legislature.

a. *The Demand Side*

The demand side of the model focuses on the tension that public choice highlights between the sorts of legislation we expect our representatives to provide and the incentives that the relevant constituencies have in pushing for desired legislation. It is a now familiar insight that the most public-spirited legislation, for example efforts to increase police protection and national defense, to ensure the solvency of Social Security, and to guard against environmental hazards, often confront substantial difficulty in garnering the necessary vigorous demand. The difficulty is that while such legislation benefits the public broadly, this very broad support, counterintuitively, undermines the demand function as each constituency, or each voter, anticipates that others will invest the necessary resources for procurement. As each potential beneficiary "free rides" on the efforts of others, the overall demand function for such broad-based general interest legislation suffers.[24]

Conversely, as Mancur Olson famously observed, the demand function for governmental action is positively correlated with the ability of groups to (1) organize, and (2) to monitor and punish those who do not do their fair share to contribute to the group's welfare.[25] While Olson is often presented as associating effective lobbying with a "size" principle, a more careful reading focuses on the susceptibility of the relevant interest groups to cohesion, organization and monitoring, and exclusion of noncontributors. While large groups are often dispersed and difficult to discipline, smaller groups are often more tightly organized and have greater capacity to identify and punish those who do not contribute to collective efforts at procuring quasi-private goods benefiting group members. To the extent that groups can punish non-contributors by excluding them from continued group affiliation or from sharing in the benefits of the group's lobbying successes, the more likely the group will avoid the free rider and collective action difficulties that plague larger constituencies that would benefit from the procurement of classic public goods.

The defining characteristics of public goods—value not diminished by consumption and an inability to exclude those who fail to contribute from receiving the benefits—are the same features that render general interest legislation difficult to procure.[26] Persons who do not contribute to national defense are equally protected as those who do contribute, and the protection of one house does not diminish the protection of its neighbor. The converse holds, however, for special interest legislation, as in the case of professional licensing or similar barriers to entry. Those who are not properly licensed or who do not anticipate the prospect of gaining such licensure are excluded from the resulting benefits. These benefits can include higher rates for member-provided services resulting from the effective elimination of competition that licensure provides.

Without suggesting that professional licensure provides benefits only to the affected professionals,[27] it is certainly the case that the American Medical Association ("AMA") and the American Bar Association ("ABA"), to name two prominent examples, are highly effective in pursuing the professional interests of group members. By contrast, while such organizations as the National Taxpayers Union, which seeks to promote tax fairness, and the Sierra Club, which seeks to improve the environment

---

24. These organizational difficulties may encourage political entrepreneurship in which politicians or political activists seek to motivate an identifiable constituency to support a particular cause. JOHN W. KINGDON, AGENDAS, ALTERNATIVES, AND PUBLIC POLICIES 122–24 (2d ed. 1995) (describing "policy entrepreneurs"); RUSSELL HARDIN, COLLECTIVE ACTION 35–37 (1982); Wendy J. Schiller, *Senators as Political Entrepreneurs: Using Bill Sponsorship to Shape Legislative Agendas*, 39 AM. J. POL. SCI. 186 (1995).

25. MANCUR OLSON, THE LOGIC OF COLLECTIVE ACTION: PUBLIC GOODS AND THE THEORY OF GROUPS (1971).

26. Paul A. Samuelson, *The Pure Theory of Public Expenditure*, 36 REV. ECON. & STAT. 387 (1954) (defining public goods).

27. *See supra* chapter 2, section II.A.

and to protect endangered species and their habitats, are undoubtedly prominent lobbying groups, to the extent that they are successful in their lobbying or other efforts, the benefits that they provide also accrue to nonmembers. As a result, these latter organizations likely confront different obstacles in disciplining those sympathetic to their cause to become members, and once members, to remain active contributors. For two intermediate cases, consider the National Association for the Advancement of Colored People ("NAACP") or the National Organization for Women ("NOW"). Both of these prominent national organizations seek to further the interests of identifiable, but rather large, groups: persons of color and women, respectively. While the potential beneficiaries of legislation that such groups seek to procure are more cohesive than the general public, consider the level of difficulty that such groups nonetheless confront concerning organization as a result of the size and diverse interests of potentially affected group members.

Can you identify strategies that this set of groups, or similar ones, have historically employed to foster more effective demand for their lobbying efforts? Are entrepreneurial efforts on behalf of prospective members of these groups consistent or in tension with insights drawn from public choice? Why? How might lawmaking efforts differ across such groupings as (1) the AMA and ABA, (2) the NAACP and NOW, and (3) Sierra Club and the National Taxpayers Union? What role, if any, might successful litigation on behalf of the interests these groups play in efforts to overcome free riding? What is the relationship between litigation and lobbying strategies for such groups? To what extent do such groups employ litigation as a means to encourage membership or to raise funds? Which sets of strategies are more likely to be successful in overcoming free rider problems?

Of course it is important not to construe the Wilson–Hayes model, or any other, in an excessively literal fashion. We do see substantial efforts, indeed often successful ones, to procure legislation that seeks to further public aims on statewide or national scale.[28] A more dynamic understanding of public choice will help to identify those processes that generate effective demand for public interest legislation. The analysis also demonstrates the importance of appreciating the analytical relationships between or among various categories of legislation that comprise the work of a given session of Congress.[29]

Consider, for example, how presidential versus non-presidential election cycles differ in the types of legislation they motivate. To what extent

---

28. While we do not dispute that others might quibble with any examples we could provide, we nonetheless offer as illustrations at the state level, laws funding programs for police and fire safety, criminal codes and highway safety regulations, and public education. At the federal level, consider the Gramm Rudman Hollings Act, national defense budgeting, and various environmental programs that states could not enact on their own without confronting coordination difficulties. Most recently (as of the publication of this book), consider the Troubled Assets Relief Program ("TARP") to bail out the financial sector and U.S. automobile industry. *See* Emergency Economic Stabilization Act of 2008, Pub. L. No. 110–343, §§ 101–136, 122 Stat. 3765.

29. This is the focus of the next subsection, introducing the dynamic version of the Wilson–Hayes matrix. *See infra* section I.B.

do presidential candidates assume the role of political entrepreneurs seeking to procure demand for categories of legislation that are harder to obtain in off-presidential elections, meaning elections on the alternative two-year cycle for the House of Representatives and for one third of the Senate in which there is no presidential election? How might one test the answer to this question empirically? What is the relationship between special interest legislation and legislation targeting a broad aspect of the public good? Are there mechanisms that limit the possibilities of special interest legislation while promoting other legislation that targets larger aims, however those aims are defined? To what extent are the problems exposed on the demand side reinforced by public choice dynamics on the supply side?

b. *The Supply Side*

While those seeking elective office certainly hold other, more laudable goals, some linked to desired legislation in furtherance of the public good, public choice theorists observe that politicians cannot achieve any goals unless they are successfully elected and reelected.[30] Candidates who subordinate the "electoral goal" in favor of other objectives when the choice proves decisive to electoral success risk falling off the political radar, as those political actors more willing to engage in conduct better targeted toward electoral success replace them.[31]

Of course legislators do in fact pursue many goals apart from electoral politics. Some legislators are more safely situated than others for reelection and as such have a greater degree of flexibility in focusing on larger issues related to their legislative agenda, or perhaps even the pursuit of higher elective office.[32] Those legislators who are new or otherwise vulnerable to electoral challenge, however, are most likely to pursue strategies that favor opportunities to claim credit with constituents for legislative successes.

Does the difference between the terms of office for the Senate (six years) versus the House of Representatives (two years) affect the ability of those in each office to pursue more public interested legislation? What sorts of studies could you devise to test your intuitions on this question?

1. *Credit Claiming*

Not all strategies for claiming legislative success are equally plausible. Most legislators are more likely to convince constituents of legislative

---

30. DAVID R. MAYHEW, CONGRESS: THE ELECTORAL CONNECTION 16 (2d ed. 2004); MORRIS P. FIORINA, REPRESENTATIVES, ROLL CALLS, AND CONSTITUENCIES 38–39 (1974).

31. Of course if one can pursue larger aims without compromising the prospect of electoral success, then the trade-off is not implicated.

32. The most recent election of President Barack Obama notwithstanding, the most current conventional wisdom suggests that the Senate has not proved an ideal stepping stone to the Presidency. *See* Barry C. Burden, *United States Senators as Presidential Candidates*, 117 POL. SCI. Q. 81, 81, 82 (2002) (noting that "it is almost unheard of for presidents to come directly from the Senate," although "the conventional wisdom holds that senators are prime presidential material.").

success with respect to localized items within bills than with respect to nationwide level accomplishments.[33] For this reason, both the demand and supply functions tend to favor special interest over general interest legislation. Legislators can more convincingly claim credit for matching funding for a highway or bridge repair, or a subsidy to local industry— benefits that are identifiable and excludable—than for laudable bills that help defense, promote fiscal soundness, or benefit the environment.

2. *Conflict Avoidance*

Successful legislators also seek to avoid unnecessary conflict among constituents. Such conflict can arise when broad legislation imposes costs on those in an identifiable, and narrow, constituency. Madison's *Federalist No. 10*,[34] which concerned the threat of factional violence, translates into a concern for legislation that provides wide benefits while imposing narrow costs. To avoid what Madison termed factional violence, he sought to impose impediments to the rapid formation of majoritarian politics operating to the detriment of discrete and identifiable classes.[35] While Madison's structural solution was to divide the legislature (bicameralism) and to afford the President a check (the veto) against surviving majoritarian legislation, other mechanisms have since developed in the Madisonian tradition that increase the needed size of governing coalitions and thus impose additional barriers to majoritarian politics or against Madison's feared factional violence.[36] In addition to bicameralism and presentment, such practices include calendaring rules, committee structures, seniority practices, the Senate filibuster, conference committees, and perhaps constitutional judicial review.[37] Together, these elaborate practices create the complex labyrinth—one that increases the size of governing coalitions— that bill sponsors must navigate to transform proposed bills into legislation, or in the case of the veto and constitutional judicial review, legislation that will endure post-enactment.

These institutional features also avoid Riker's theoretical prediction that in a zero-sum game, where side payments are permitted and where parties are rational and have complete information, the most stable

---

33. *See* Janet M. Box–Steffensmeier et al., *The Effects of Political Representation on the Electoral Advantages of House Incumbents*, 56 POL. RES. Q. 259, 265 tbl.2 (2003) (quantifying the effect of various activities of legislators on constituents' perceptions and finding that sponsorship of bills with local effects was the activity that caused the greatest increase in constituents' "reason for liking incumbent" and name recognition).

34. THE FEDERALIST NO. 10 (James Madison).

35. Madison was concerned, of course, with moneyed and landed classes and with proposals that would redistribute wealth from such classes to the public at large (majoritarian violence), but the principle can be generalized to discuss other "discrete and insular" minority groups. United States v. Carolene Prods. Co., 304 U.S. 144, 152–53 n.4 (1938).

36. Of course as Easterbrook and others have aptly noted, these mechanisms have created their own difficulties as they have become venues for special interest bargaining, thus facilitating payoffs in the concentrated benefit, dispersed cost category. Frank H. Easterbrook, *Foreword: The Court and the Economic System*, 98 HARV. L. REV. 4, 17 (1984).

37. While one can debate whether constitutional judicial review was anticipated at the framing, see, *e.g.*, THE FEDERALIST No. 78, as a formal matter the doctrine was established in a later period. *See* Marbury v. Madison, 5 U.S. 137 (1803).

legislative coalitions will approach minimum winning size.[38] Each of these legislative processes, also known as "veto gates," or "negative legislative checkpoints,"[39] raises the cost of procuring legislation by demanding support at various loci at which individual members of Congress are empowered to stop a bill in its tracks. By empowering sometimes even a single member of Congress in this manner,[40] these negative legislative checkpoints provide opportunities for those who might be disadvantaged by a proposed bill to bargain for favorable modifications as the price of allowing the bill to pass a particular veto gate and to move on to the next.

Because it is far easier to block than to pass proposed legislation—blocking requires only one successful veto gate, while successful passing requires surviving all veto gates—testing the theoretical insights of public choice can be a challenge.[41] The proof, after all, is often in what fails to make it into the pudding. The power to block, however, is real. Legislation rarely, if ever, passes in its initially proposed form and the ultimate shape that legislation takes is largely affected by the various loci at which potentially affected interests can exert or threaten the power to block. In some instances, blocking power can result in the defeat of proposed legislation, and in others, it can result in modifying that legislation relative to the "ideal point" of the original sponsors.[42] As we will see in the discussion of the dynamic model, "substantive bargaining" with adversely affected groups is one of the principal means of ensuring passage of proposed legislation, but has the effect of watering down bills relative to original proposals.[43] The softening of legislation from its original form moves bill sponsors off their ideal points, but at the same time avoids the harsh conflicts and the potential defeat that would occur if the sponsor insisted only on voting the bill in its original form.

---

38. WILLIAM H. RIKER, THE THEORY OF POLITICAL COALITIONS (1962). For the formal statement of conditions, see *supra* chapter 2, section B, at note 95.

39. For a discussion of these terms, see *supra* chapter 2, section B, at note 93, and cites therein.

40. This can occur for example with a committee chair who refuses to schedule a matter for debate, or with a Senator threatening a filibuster absent the requisite sixty-Senator supermajority required to invoke cloture. *See* United States Senate, Committee on Rules & Administration, Standing Rules of the Senate, http://rules.senate.gov/public/index.cfm?FuseAction=HowCongress Works.RulesOfSenate (last visited June 1, 2009) (Rules XII, Voting Procedure; and XXII, Precedence of Motions); *see also* Martin B. Gold & Dimple Gupta, *The Constitutional Option to Change Senate Rules and Procedures: A Majoritarian Means to Overcome the Filibuster*, 28 HARV. J.L. & PUB. POL'Y 205 (2004) (providing historical analysis of filibuster and cloture); John C. Roberts, *Majority Voting in Congress: Further Notes on the Constitutionality of the Senate Cloture Rule*, 20 J.L. & POL. 505 (2004) (providing history of the Senate's use of the filibuster and recommending modifications to filibuster and cloture rules).

41. Consider whether this helps to respond to some of the arguments that Green & Shapiro offer in their critique of public-choice based scholarship, *see supra* chapter 2, section V.B at note 95 (discussing critique of public choice by Professors Green and Shapiro).

42. An ideal point is the policy point that is the first choice preference of the bill sponsor. Ideal points are usually expressed along a unidimensional continuum, which can be general, for example, liberal to conservative, or specific, for example, high-to-low expenditure on a proposed project. The ideal point is the location on the relevant spectrum that represents the bill sponsor's first choice position concerning a given policy or basket of policies. *See supra* chapter 1, section III.A.3.

43. For a more detailed discussion, see Stearns, *supra* note 4, at 413–14 (describing substantive and length bargaining).

3. *Comparing State and Federal Legislative Processes*

As a general matter, state legislative processes are less cumbersome than those in Congress.[44] This might help to explain historical differences in legislation targeting identifiable constituencies that are relatively wealthy at the state versus federal level. While proposals to nationalize health care, and thus to limit the ability of physicians to continue to command market rates for their services, have met with repeated difficulties at the federal level,[45] several state and municipal governments have succeeded in targeting landlords as a class for rent control legislation.[46]

c. *Delegation*

Another conflictual difficulty arises when the political process directly pits opposing interests against one another. While legislators confront particular difficulty in attempting to resolve intense and narrow constituencies pressing opposing sides on the same issue, the same conceptual difficulty arises when the competing interests are relatively more dispersed. Within virtually every district, for example, the interests of labor conflict with those of management; the interests of landlords conflict with those of tenants; and the interests of those seeking environmental protection conflict with private interests seeking the benefits of economic development. And indeed, political entrepreneurs working on behalf of various interests seeking large-scale reform in such areas as the environment or tax law can effectively transform a political dynamic into one that closely resembles direct and narrow conflict. Legislators cannot "solve" the sometimes unavoidable conflict without incurring substantial political costs with the losing side.

When the affected constituents on both sides of an issue are roughly evenly balanced, whether the constituencies are broad or narrow, an attractive option for legislators will often be to avoid the conflict through delegation. Delegation affords legislators the opportunity to claim credit for facilitating a potentially responsive solution to the issues that the constituents raise, while at the same time also shifting blame to the agency when the results are other than what one side desires.[47] The conventional public choice account of delegation focuses on the power of legislators to claim credit and shift blame, a result that is unlikely to satisfy both sides, but that is likely to benefit the relevant political actors.

---

44. Paul Diller, *Intrastate Preemption*, 87 B.U. L. Rev. 1113, 1148 & n.174 (2007) (comparing state legislatures and Congress).

45. Jacob S. Hacker, *Learning from Defeat?: Political Analysis and the Failure of Health Care Reform in the United States*, 31 Brit. Med. J. 61, 72 (2001) ("In the late 1910s, the 1930s, the 1940s and the 1970s, comprehensive [healthcare] reform emerged on to the [United States] government agenda, only to slip from it without legislation action.").

46. A related public choice question is why rent control legislation can only be accomplished at the local level and why health care reform is widely understood to require a national solution. Can you think of an explanation for this intuition?

47. Peter H. Aranson, Ernest Gellhorn & Glen O. Robinson, *A Theory of Legislative Delegation*, 68 Cornell L. Rev. 1 (1982).

Agency decision making also implicates other branches of government, including especially the presidency. The President, after all, makes the major staffing decisions for agency appointments that affect policy making.[48] In this analysis, agency delegation shifts the policy focus from legislative lobbying to electoral politics, and particularly, presidential elections.[49]

An alternative analysis focuses on the implications of agency delegation for judicial decision making. In an important pair of administrative law decisions, the Supreme Court has admonished lower federal courts to exhibit deference to reasonable interpretations of ambiguous statutes,[50] but only to do so if Congress has delegated appropriate authority to the agency and the agency decision follows regularized agency procedures.[51] Thus while federal courts defer to substantive constructions of statutes that they might not have produced initially—provided agency law-making procedures are followed—they do not defer to the decisions of isolated agency decision makers, taking for example, the form of opinion letters.[52] While we will take up the *Chevron/Mead* doctrines in greater detail later in this chapter,[53] consider for now whether you can reconcile these doctrines based upon insights drawn from public choice? Can you reconcile them with the Legal Process School? Which model provides a more persuasive account of these doctrines? Why?

d. The Matrix Revisited

The preceding analysis provides the basis for the static Wilson–Hayes matrix. This model predicts tendencies of the legislative process with respect to particular categories of legislation. While the analysis forecasts an oversupply of special interest legislation and undersupply of general interest legislation, it is important to remember that any claims of these sorts rest upon some set of (usually unarticulated) background assumptions concerning the preferred levels of specific types of legislation that we expect an ideal legislature to provide.[54] Any baseline or set of baselines that one might suggest as a basis for comparison—for example majoritarianism, efficiency, welfare maximization, utilitarianism, or minimizing pork—is necessarily contestable. Different commentators will embrace different normative baselines, and assessing the merits of any arguments concerning such baselines requires an analysis that rests outside of the public choice model itself.

---

48. For an analysis of the role of the President in staffing executive and independent agencies, see *infra* chapter 6.

49. For a discussion of how a president embracing a deregulatory agenda might prefer staffing agencies with like-minded bureaucrats, rather than dismantling the agencies, see *infra* chapter 6, section III.C.

50. Chevron U.S.A., Inc. v. Natural Res. Def. Council, 467 U.S. 837 (1984).

51. United States v. Mead Corp., 533 U.S. 218 (2001).

52. *Id.* at 236 n.17.

53. *See infra* pp. 287–88.

54. This point was made effectively in Elhauge, *supra* note 8.

Because the model presumes that certain categories of legislation are over- or under-supplied, it is important to expose those assumptions that drive the Wilson–Hayes matrix. The model presumes that the legislature is supposed to provide public goods and services that private persons acting on their own will tend to undersupply because of the free rider and holdout phenomena. Consistent with this assumption, the Wilson–Hayes model reveals the anomaly that the very tendencies that plague private parties in their efforts to procure traditional public goods also manifest themselves within the legislative process such that free riders and hold-outs undermine effective lobbying efforts for the legislative procurement of such goods.

The analysis exposes a tendency to undersupply the very category of legislation that motivated the creation of the legislature in the first instance, namely general interest legislation, meaning legislation that imposes widely dispersed costs to provide broad benefits.[55] Instead, the legislature is prone to mimicking private market incentives in encouraging lobbying for narrow and discrete interests at the expense of the larger population. As a result of various structural impediments to the rapid passage of legislation, some discrete and narrow groups—those that are sufficiently organized and can capture the benefits of their legislative victories—are relatively well suited to protect themselves against majoritarian factions. While these features of the legislative process were specifically intended to avoid, or at least raise the cost of, factional politicking, they have, at the same time, created additional opportunities for special interests to gain access to legislative largesse at the expense of the public at large. As you evaluate Congressional bargaining processes, consider whether the system strikes the proper balance between protections against majoritarian violence on the one hand, and opportunities for special interest legislation on the other. Is it possible to maintain the protections that motivated Madison while also reducing pork barrel legislation? Why or why not? Finally, when interests directly conflict, the model predicts delegation as a solution to the political problem, even though the ultimate beneficiaries in this process might be the legislators rather than the affected constituent groups.

Let us now consider a dynamic model that builds upon the Wilson–Hayes matrix and that studies the interrelationships between and among the identified legislative categories.

2. The Dynamic Legislative Bargaining Model[56]

While public choice is both cited and faulted for exposing the sorts of tendencies within congressional processes that the Wilson–Hayes model captures,[57] the model itself might be prove more helpful in evaluating the

---

55. Glen O. Robinson, *Public Choice Speculations on the Item Veto*, 74 VA. L. REV. 403, 408–09 (1988).

56. Portions of this discussion are adapted from Stearns, *supra* note 4, at 401–22.

57. Daniel A. Farber & Philip P. Frickey, *Legislative Intent and Public Choice*, 74 VA. L. REV. 423, 424–25 (1988).

nature of legislative bargaining than in assessing any quantity of legislation within particular legislative categories. By transforming the static model into a dynamic bargaining model, we can see how legislative bargaining forges relationships among political actors, and additionally, among various legislative paradigms.

Assume that following *Massachusetts v. EPA*,[58] a case granting the Commonwealth of Massachusetts standing to challenge the EPA's failure to regulate mobile-sourced greenhouse gas emissions, the EPA proposes a set of regulations that leading members of the Democratically controlled Congress find entirely inadequate to deal with the threat of global warming. Senator Green, a liberal senator from a Democratic state, proposes the "Mobile–Sourced Greenhouse Gas Emissions Reductions Act." The Act would compel the EPA to implement regulations demanding a reduction of mobile-sourced greenhouse gas emissions for new vehicles by twenty percent within six months of the statute's enactment.

Assume that the proposed bill represents Senator Green's ideal point, meaning the precise policy that she prefers in light of her own assessment of the costs and benefits of the proposed regulation. The proposal itself falls well within the category of public interest legislation in that it addresses a problem that confronts all citizens, and indeed all persons. And because most adults drive vehicles that leave carbon footprints, the costs of the proposed reduction are similarly widely dispersed. Assume, however, that while the bill has broad support among members of the Democratically controlled Senate, where it was proposed, that support is insufficient for passage. Several powerful interest groups will suffer from the nearly immediate compliance requirement for the initial 20% emissions reduction. Further assume that those adversely affected interests— the automobile industry, the shipping industry, and the construction industry, to name a few—exert sufficient political pressure that without some effort to appease them, the bill is destined to fail.

a. *Substantive Bargaining*

The negative legislative checkpoints provide opportunities for these and other affected groups to engage in "substantive bargaining," meaning bargaining between Senator Green, the bill sponsor, and those interests who would be adversely affected if the proposed bill were passed in its initially proposed form. First, consider the suggested negotiations from Senator Green's perspective. While she would most prefer her original proposal, including the rapid 20% emissions reduction on new vehicles, Senator Green also knows that the negative legislative checkpoints afford various opposing interests the power to defeat her bill unless she engages in substantive compromise. The only way that she can achieve her larger legislative goal of imposing constraints on the EPA to motivate ambitious regulation is to water down the proposed bill, including the initial compli-

---

58.   549 U.S. 497 (2007).

ance requirements, in a manner that moves the bill away from her ideal point.

Table 5:2. Substantive Bargaining Over Emissions Reductions Bill

6 Month Compliance	1 Year Compliance (construction industry compromise)	3 Year Compliance (automobile industry compromise)	5 Year Compliance
Green's ideal point ←--→Interest groups' ideal point			

At the same time, however, there is a point beyond which she might no longer be willing to compromise on substance even if failing to do so means that the bill might not pass. If the adversely affected constituents insist upon the EPA's passive approach to emissions reductions (let us assume this requires a 20% reduction over a span of five years), Senator Green might prefer defeat to codifying a result so far from her preferred policy. At a minimum, this would produce a high profile campaign issue.

Assume that while the adversely affected interests prefer a five-year compliance schedule for the initial 20% reduction in mobile-sourced carbon emissions, they also realize that there is a risk that unless they agree to a compromise, some other coalitions will form that will cut them from the bargain. It is possible that the relevant interests split, such that the construction industry is willing to go along if the initial compliance is extended to one year, but that the automobile industry demands a full three years. If Senator Green requires only the support of one group to avoid a negative legislative checkpoint, then she will form a coalition with the construction industry, extending her initial compliance from six months to one year. Table 5:2 depicts both ideal points along with the potential compromises from those points. Of course this represents only a single bargain at a single locus, and there are many other potential loci at which similar substantive bargains, and compromises with similarly situated interest groups, might take place. Assume that following this successful negotiation with the construction industry, which allowed the bill to survive one negative legislative checkpoint, Senator Green's bill is still short of the votes needed to ensure passage. Further assume that Senator Green is unwilling to engage in any additional extensions for compliance and is therefore unwilling to entertain additional proposals for substantive compromise. Even at this point it remains possible for the bill to pass.

Senator Green and members of her now larger coalition can take a separate tack, which we will refer to as "length bargaining." Through length bargaining, when confronted with other negative legislative checkpoints that threaten the defeat of her bill, Senator Green can agree to tack on special interest items, or riders, as the precondition for support. This process will leave the substance of her bill unaffected while acquiring additional needed support for passage. These additional items might have some connection to environmental compliance legislation, for example tax credits for the cost of acquiring new technologies that reduce mobile-sourced emissions, or they might involve something else entirely, for example funding for a highway improvement project or bridge repair.[59]

Once again, now consider this bargain from Senator Green's perspective. Even though the bargaining does not alter the overall substance of the proposed legislation, which following the substantive bargain with the construction industry demands a 20% reduction in emissions from newly acquired mobile sources within one year of enactment, it does add a form of dead weight, namely costs attributed to the larger bill that add no value beyond enlarging the necessary coalition for passage. As with substantive bargaining, Senator Green might not be willing to add such additional weight to her bill beyond a certain point as a means of securing passage. But assuming that she is able to secure a successful coalition while still retaining the bill's larger objectives and without adding undue weight, then the combined processes of substantive and length bargaining enable her to move from her original bill, representing her ideal point, to a compromise bill that successfully withstands the various bargaining loci within the Senate. The bill is now ready to be forwarded to the House for similar consideration and perhaps further bargaining.

Table 5:3. Length Bargaining Over Emissions Reductions Bill

No special interest riders	Low intermediate riders	High intermediate riders	Many riders
Green's ideal point ←---→ Interest groups' ideal point			

Table 5:3 depicts the resulting length bargaining process. As with the substantive bargaining model, we depict the preferences, or ideal points, this time concerning length bargaining, for Senator Green and for interest groups seeking to use the bill as a means of securing passage of favored riders, along with two intermediate positions, one favoring each side. Before leaving this model and exploring its normative implications, consider also that while Senator Green was trying to "sell" her bill and "buy" votes in this example, with respect to other statutes, she is a seller whose votes other bill sponsors seek to buy. Through the process of "logrolling," bill sponsors will exchange support for other bills to gain support for their own. This implies that not all compromise is reflected in the text of the bill that ultimately becomes law, since some compromise will involve offering support for an altogether different bill, or (complicating things further) perhaps even declining to vote against another bill. And negotiations do not necessarily stop here since it is also possible to negotiate

---

59. It is not uncommon to have riders that bear little or no relationship to the substance of the bill to which they are attached.

support for important committee posts, for various scheduling matters, and for decisions not to exercise the filibuster on this or some other bill. And the list goes on.

3. Assessing the Static and Dynamic Wilson–Hayes Model

As we will see in the next section, scholars have relied upon intuitions drawn from the Wilson–Hayes model to offer normative assessments concerning the proper judicial task in the course of statutory interpretation. Before considering some of the more noteworthy proposals, it will be helpful to consider your own independent assessment of the Hart and Sacks model and the two variations on the Wilson–Hayes model. To what extent are these models in conflict and to what extent are they mutually reinforcing? What are the normative implications of the Wilson–Hayes model, whether presented in its static or dynamic form? How does the Wilson–Hayes model inform the interpretive tools that Hart and Sacks develop in the Legal Process model? If you find the models inconsistent, what is the basis for your conclusion? Is it possible to reconcile them, and if so, what assumptions must you make about the role of the judge to do so? If you believe that the models are not consistent, what is the basis for that conclusion? To the extent that the models diverge, which should be preferred in the course of statutory construction and why?

II. NORMATIVE PROPOSALS FOR STATUTORY INTERPRETATION

In this part we present several scholarly works relying upon the implications of public choice for the judicial construction of statutes. As previously noted, it is possible to divide these scholars in various ways. Some are more skeptical that legislation embeds overarching public purposes and view the political process as a venue for interest group bargaining. Others view legislation as more closely resembling a pursuit of the public good, albeit one that must confront the difficulties of interest group influence along the way. While we have presented the Legal Process School and the Wilson–Hayes models as analytical endpoints, most scholars are somewhere in the middle of this spectrum. Even so, we can think of these scholars as forming clusters. The first group expresses a greater distrust of the legislative process, and a corresponding willingness to raise barriers to the cost of interest group bargaining. Conversely, the second group, generally more sanguine about legislative bargaining, is willing to lower the cost of legislative procurement through the exercise of judicial construction of statutes. As you read these materials, consider whether such labels as ''conservative'' or ''liberal'' are helpful in categorizing the various scholars. Assuming that these labels are helpful, to what extent do these scholars rely upon public choice to advance their preexisting ideological predilections? What, if anything, does your answer to the preceding question suggest about the nature of public choice?

A. SCHOLARS EXPRESSING SKEPTICISM ABOUT THE LEGISLATIVE PROCESS

We begin with a group of scholars who contend that insights from public choice demonstrate the inability of courts to infer meaning beyond what is expressed in the written terms of the statute. As a result, these scholars tend to advocate that courts construe statutes narrowly. They are also generally distrustful of extraneous sources of information—those that go beyond the text or historical context of the statute—although they are generally open to extrinsic sources of contemporaneous meaning.

We can roughly place these scholars into three subgroups: (1) Those who interpret public choice as suggesting the impossibility of ascribing collective meaning beyond the literal text of statutes and who thus impose a very strict form of judicial minimalism to the task of judicial interpretation. In this camp, we place Kenneth Shepsle and Judge Frank Easterbrook. (2) Those who are skeptical of the notion of legislative intent, but who continue to believe that collective meaning can extend beyond the literal text and who are therefore willing to entertain some contemporaneous sources to support such broader constructions. In this camp, we place Judge Richard Posner and McNollgast. And (3) those who are willing to engage in a kind of admitted legal fiction in which courts can focus on expressly stated intent to further articulated benign statutory objectives, even when doing so might subordinate payoffs to groups who negotiated them during the complex processes of legislative bargaining. In this camp, we place Jonathan Macey.

Overall, these scholars share a general distrust of legislative processes and therefore seek to raise the cost of obtaining narrow interest group payoffs through the judicial system. And yet, as we will see, these scholars offer very different perspectives on how judges should go about this task.

1. Textual Minimalists

a. Kenneth Shepsle

In his aptly titled essay, *Congress Is a "They" not an "It": Legislative Intent as an Oxymoron*,[60] Professor Kenneth Shepsle offers a broadside attack against those who would seek to ascribe legislative intent to federal statutes. Shepsle's essential insight, which he develops from his application of Arrow's Theorem to the question of legislative intent, is that it is mistaken to anthropomorphize an institution, and that this is especially true for a highly complex institution like the United States Congress. Because Congress comprises 535 separate actors, each holding his or her own separate set of intents, and because Congress affords opportunities for agenda setting, strategic manipulation of procedures, and voting for reasons that transcend the merits of proposed bills or other legislative

---

60. Kenneth A. Shepsle, *Congress Is a "They," Not an "It": Legislative Intent as an Oxymoron*, 12 INT'L REV. L. & ECON. 239 (1992).

matters, legislative outcomes cannot be interpreted to hold meaning beyond the specific language of enacted statutes. Consider the following excerpt:

> It is evident that Congress is composed of *many* majorities.... And each majority is composed of many individuals.... When some point ... defeats the status quo, we only know two things for certain. First, one majority prevailed, but there were clearly others that could have, except for "other factors" (unknown, and possibly unknowable). Second, the winning majority consists of many legislators; their respective reasons for voting against the status quo may well be as varied as their number.
>
> The first claim should raise some doubts about the normative status of any particular victor. For unspecified reasons a particular majority was assembled around a particular replacement for the status quo. Why that particular majority? Hard to say. It could be for Chicago School interest group reasons. But then again it could be because some particular majority had procedural advantages....
>
> The second claim adds an independent indictment to reading much, either substantively or normatively, into winning policy. With $(n + 1)/2$ or more individuals in the winning coalition, there is not a single legislative intent, but rather many *legislators'* intents. *Congress is a 'they,' not an 'it.'*[61]

Shepsle compares the task of statutory interpretation to that of filling in incomplete contracts. Shepsle considers the implications for several specific tools of statutory interpretation, none of which he endorses entirely:

> Perhaps the most extreme is the "plain meaning" doctrine, according to which ... neither intention nor prediction play a role. In the circumstances of cases apparently falling in the interstices of a statute, the Court must resist bringing the case under the statute's rubric. It may neither generalize the language of a statute, read intent into its words other than what is explicitly stated, nor forecast what the enacting majority (or some other majority for that matter) might have ruled. If the plain meaning of the statute's language does not cover a circumstance, then the statute is inapplicable. In a sense, this position, a minimalist one for courts, asserts that the *legislature* must complete otherwise incomplete statutes, not the courts. In either the interstitial case or the circumstance in which different statutes, with different dispositional implications for the case at hand, apply, it is the Court's obligation to seek further legislative guidance.[62]

While Shepsle concedes that some might regard his view as extreme and possibly impractical, he claims that if adopted, it will motivate

---

61. *Id.* at 244 (third emphasis added).
62. *Id.* at 252–53 (footnote omitted).

rational legislators to "make their statutes plainer and more meaning-ful."[63]

b. *Frank Easterbrook*

Judge Frank Easterbrook expresses similar sentiments in his famous essay, *Statutes' Domains*.[64] Easterbrook begins with the question "When does a court construe a statute, treaty, or constitutional provision and when hold it inapplicable instead?"[65] Easterbrook contends that this is an overlooked question and that the general presumption that when parties rely upon a statute for relief a court is duty-bound to "construe" it is incorrect. He explains:

> Yet to construe a statute at all is to resolve an important question in favor of the party invoking it. The interesting questions in litiga-tion involve statutes that are ambiguous when applied to a particular set of facts. The construction of an ambiguous document is a work of judicial creation or re-creation. Using the available hints and tools—the words and structure of the statute, the subject matter and general policy of the enactment, the legislative history, the lobbying positions of interest groups, and the temper of the times—judges try to deter-mine how the Congress that enacted the statute either actually resolved or would have resolved a particular issue if it had faced and settled it explicitly at the time. Judges have substantial leeway in construction. Inferences almost always conflict, and the enacting Congress is unlikely to come back to life and "prove" the court's construction wrong. The older the statute the more the inferences will be in conflict, and the greater the judges' freedom.

> If, however, the court finds the statute inapplicable to the subject of the litigation, it never begins this task of creative construction. Even if the judge *knows* how Congress would have handled the question presented, the court will do nothing. It will say to the litigant: "Too bad, but legislative intentions are not legal rules." Whoever relies on the statute loses. . . .

> The choice between construction and a declaration of inapplicabil-ity thus may make all the difference to the case.[66]

Easterbrook concedes that some readers might be troubled by his claimed distinction and conclude that "to declare a statute inapplicable to a dispute *is* an act of construction, and that [he is] therefore talking nonsense."[67] To support his claimed distinction, Easterbrook offers the following illustration:

> Consider, for example, whether a statute providing for the leash-ing of "dogs" also requires the leashing of cats (because the statute

---

63. *Id.* at 253.

64. Frank H. Easterbrook, *Statutes' Domains*, 50 U. CHI. L. REV. 533 (1983).

65. *Id.* at 533.

66. *Id.* at 553–34 (footnote omitted).

67. *Id.* at 534–35.

really covers the *category* "animals") or wolves (because the statute really covers the *category* "canines") or lions ("dangerous animals"). Most people would say that the statute does not go beyond dogs, because after all the verbal torturing of the words has been completed it is still too plain for argument what the statute means. Perhaps it is a quibble, but in my terminology this becomes a decision that the statute "applies" only to dogs. For rules about the rest of the animal kingdom we must look elsewhere.[68]

Easterbrook's larger argument is that judges should presume against construing statutes in those cases in which the statutes, properly read, do not appear to apply to the case before them. Like Shepsle, based upon such problems as cycling, agenda control, and procedural obstacles affecting statutory outcomes, Easterbrook claims that legislative outcomes cannot be presumed rational attempts to further some larger objective that extends beyond the actual statutory language.

Easterbrook therefore proposes that Congress can ensure that courts provide the proper "domain" to statutes in either of two ways. First, they can identify specific policy goals and instruct courts precisely how to pursue those goals in the text of the statute such as the precise rules governing tender offers under the national securities laws.[69] Alternatively, they can set out the statutory goals and instruct courts to develop the necessary rules in furtherance of those goals. This is more akin to delegating a form of rule-making power to courts. The Sherman Act has largely been interpreted as falling into this latter category.[70]

Easterbrook contends that if the statute in a case falls into the first category, then courts should enforce the statute as written but do no more than that. Easterbrook holds to this position whether the underlying statute is more properly classified as special or public interest legislation. If it is special interest legislation, the court serves societal interests in limiting interest group payoffs to those expressly set out in the statute itself. If instead it is public benefiting legislation, the court errs if it fails to recognize that from the perspective of the enacting legislature, more of a good thing can at some point become a bad thing. Easterbrook explains:

> Legislators seeking only to further the public interest may conclude
> that the provision of public rules should reach so far and no farther,

---

68. *Id.* at 535 (footnote omitted).

69. *See* Williams Act, 15 U.S.C. §§ 78m(d)-(e), 78n(d)-(f) (2006); and accompanying regulations at 17 C.F.R. §§ 240.14d–1 to–10 (2008); 17 C.F.R. §§ 240.14e–1 to–8 (2008).

70. *See* Sherman Act, 15 U.S.C. §§ 1–38 (2006). *See* National Soc'y of Prof'l Eng'rs. v. United States, 435 U.S. 679, 688 (1978) ("Congress, however, did not intend the text of the Sherman Act to delineate the full meaning of the statute or its application in concrete situations. The legislative history makes it perfectly clear that it expected the courts to give shape to the statute's broad mandate by drawing on common-law tradition."); United States v. Associated Press, 52 F. Supp. 362, 370 (S.D.N.Y. 1943) (Hand, J.) ("Congress has incorporated into the Anti–Trust Acts the changing standards of the common law, and by so doing has delegated to the courts the duty of fixing the standard for each case."). *But see* Robert H. Bork, The Antitrust Paradox: A Policy at War with Itself 53 (1978) ("Congress, by its use of common law terminology in the Sherman Act, most certainly did not delegate any such free value-choosing role to the courts. And if it had attempted to do so, the courts should have refused the commission.").

whether because of deliberate compromise, because of respect for private orderings, or because of uncertainty coupled with concern that to regulate in the face of the unknown is to risk loss for little gain. No matter how good the end in view, achievement of the end will have some cost, and at some point the cost will begin to exceed the benefits.[71]

Easterbrook instructs courts to apply a very different mode of reasoning when statutes fall into the second category involving delegating to courts the authority to construct the means of effectuating Congress's specified objectives. In those instances, courts should instead fill in the statute with its own rules that are based upon the contemporary (the time of decision), rather than contemporaneous (the time of statutory enactment) wisdom. That is because the fact of delegation to courts legitimates the value added from the new judicial construction of the legislation by a body "long prorogued."[72]

Easterbrook rejects arguments that in the event of a seeming "blank" or interstitial gap, it is the job of courts to fill in based upon construction. Easterbrook claims that the courts have no authority to fill in the blank by trying to figure out how the legislature *would have* filled the blank if it had done so. Easterbrook instead proposes that courts should leave the blank and not try to construe it because the only legitimate basis for doing so would be to further legislative intent. As a result of agenda control, logrolling, or *ad hoc* special interest influence, Easterbrook claims that it is not possible to identify a coherent majority will and that the notion of a public purpose that a statute seeks to serve is incoherent.

Easterbrook maintains that logrolling makes legislative majorities seem more coherent (since the practice provides broader support for enacted bills), but at the same he cautions that the process makes the notion of legislative intent less coherent (since the apparent support is very likely motivated by non-merits considerations). In a regime typified by logrolling, attempts to fill in statutory gaps become little more than "wild guesses" as to how the legislature *would* have wanted to decide questions that it did not actually decide.[73]

Finally, consider the following related passage:[74]

Because legislatures comprise many members, they do not have "intents" or "designs," hidden yet discoverable. Each member may or may not have a design. The body as a whole, however, has only outcomes. It is not only impossible to reason from one statute to another, but also impossible to reason from one or more sections of a statute to a problem not resolved.

71. Easterbrook, *supra* note 64, at 541.
72. *Id.* at 545.
73. *Id.* at 548.
74. *Id.* at 547–48.

This follows from the discoveries of public choice theory. Although legislators have individual lists of desires, priorities, and preferences, it turns out to be difficult, sometimes impossible, to aggregate these lists into a coherent collective choice. Every system of voting has flaws. The one used by legislatures is particularly dependent on the order in which decisions are made. Legislatures customarily consider proposals one at a time and then vote them up or down. This method disregards third or fourth options and the intensity with which legislators prefer one option over another. Additional options can be considered only in sequence, and this makes the order of decision vital. It is fairly easy to show that someone with control of the agenda can manipulate the choice so that the legislature adopts proposals that only a minority support. The existence of agenda control makes it impossible for a court—even one that knows each legislator's complete table of preferences—to say what the whole body would have done with a proposal it did not consider in fact.

One countervailing force is logrolling, in which legislators express the intensity of their preferences by voting against their views on some proposals in order to obtain votes for other proposals about which their views are stronger. Yet when logrolling is at work the legislative process is submerged and courts lose the information they need to divine the body's design. A successful logrolling process yields unanimity on every recorded vote and indeterminacy on all issues for which there is no recorded vote.

In practice, the order of decisions and logrolling are not total bars to judicial understanding. But they are so integral to the legislative process that judicial predictions about how the legislature would have decided issues it did not in fact decide are bound to be little more than wild guesses. . . . [75]

Easterbrook further contends that these seemingly arbitrary practices render reliance upon legislative history illegitimate. Consider the following passage from *Statutes' Domains* discussing whether the Federal Communications Act, which authorizes the Federal Communications Commission to regulate television and radio broadcasts, also authorizes it to regulate cable television:

Suppose that within a month after Congress passed the Communications Act a court declares the statute inapplicable to cable television. The FCC consequently lacks regulatory jurisdiction. Immediately thereafter, during the same session of Congress that passed the Communications Act, the pertinent committee in each house of Congress reports out a short amendment giving the FCC jurisdiction. The texts of the amendment are identical, and the unanimous committee reports state that the amendment is necessary to correct a terrible oversight. Each report states that the committee originally intended to confer on the FCC jurisdiction over cable systems, but that during

75. *Id.*

the session members of the staff charged with drafting the language to implement the design resigned, and their successors, unaware of the original plan, had not carried it out. As a result the legislation did not implement the agreed-upon plan, and this technical amendment would perfect the statute.

Suppose further that the leaders of both parties endorse the amendment, and the President expresses willingness to sign it when it reaches his desk. Yet although the amendment encounters no opposition, it also does not pass. Perhaps it never is scheduled for time on the floor because other, more pressing legislation consumes the remainder of the session. Perhaps members who support the amendment hold it hostage in an effort to secure enactment of some other bill over which there is vigorous debate. Perhaps the bill is *so* popular that it becomes the vehicle for a school prayer amendment or some other factious legislation, in the hope that it will carry the disputed legislation with it, but the strategy succeeds only in killing both proposals. There are a hundred ways in which a bill can die even though there is no opposition to it.[76]

Easterbrook maintains that judicial gap-filling fails to appreciate that specific legislative sessions expire. Because no legislature has time to decide every issue, Easterbrook claims that judicial gap-filling improperly reduces the cost of passing legislation.[77] If each legislature possessed unlimited time and foresight, then it is just as possible that subsequent legislatures would repeal earlier legislation as it is that the original legislature would have enacted more legislation or filled in more blanks. In effect, Easterbrook argues, judicial blank-filling based on vague "legislative intent" improperly empowers a legislature to legislate beyond its actual term and to avoid submitting this "new" legislation to consideration by the executive veto.

c. *Questions and Comments*[78]

Do you agree with Shepsle that minimalist judicial construction of statutes will force Congress to legislate with greater precision? Why? Whether it will or will not, should present litigants be subject to narrow interpretations due to the inability of the enacting Congress to specifically include textual language resolving their dispute? Why or why not?

Consider Easterbrook's distinction between construction and nonconstruction, including his opening illustration concerning the dog leash law. Assume that you are clerking for a judge who is called upon to resolve a case involving a claim that the statute demanded the leashing of an

---

76. *Id.* at 537–38 (footnotes omitted).

77. For a very different normative understanding of this observation about legislative sessions, consider EINER ELHAUGE, STATUTORY DEFAULT RULES: HOW TO INTERPRET UNDER LEGISLATION 9–10 (2008) (proposing that courts should generally construe ambiguous statutory provisions based upon contemporary enactable legislative preferences).

78. This discussion is adapted from MAXWELL STEARNS, PUBLIC CHOICE AND PUBLIC LAW: READINGS AND COMMENTARY 631–35 (1997).

animal other than a dog, perhaps a Vietnamese Pig, and that leashing the animal would have avoided a bite, thus constituting negligence per se. If you were clerking for Judge Easterbrook, how would you draft the opinion in a manner that successfully avoided statutory construction? If you were clerking for a judge who instructed you to interpret the statute against the claimant, how would you draft the opinion in a manner that properly construed the statute? Would both opinions articulate as the basis for denying relief, at least with respect to the claim that failing to abide the dog leash law in the case of the pig was negligence per se, that the statute demands the leashing of dogs, not pigs? If so, how if at all do these two approaches differ? Perhaps Easterbrook's argument suggests that absent the statute, the court is called upon to apply the common law in assessing the underlying legal claim. If so, however, does this avoid the implicit construction in setting aside the statutory basis for relief as a prelude to reaching the underlying common law issue? If not, are the approaches two ways of saying the same thing? Why or why not? If so, is Easterbrook "talking nonsense"?

Consider Easterbrook's argument against reliance upon legislative history. To focus the analysis, let us generalize Easterbrook's Communications Act hypothetical as follows. In Time Period 1 (T1), Congress enacts Statute A. In T2, the Supreme Court determines that on a given set of facts, Facts X, Statute A produces a particular result, Result Y. In T3, the same Congress seeks to amend Statute A to correct the Supreme Court's error to instead say the following: On Facts X, Statute A produces the opposite result from that announced by the Supreme Court, or Result *not-Y*. Despite otherwise sufficient consensus, and the willingness of the President to sign the relevant legislation into law, due to any number of procedural problems, the proposed amendment in T3 fails to pass. In T4, the Supreme Court once again gets a case presenting Facts X, and must decide whether to rely upon the subsequent legislative history from T3 as a means of avoiding the problematical precedent in T2.

Judge Easterbrook explains that there is a nearly universal judicial consensus *against* reliance on subsequent legislative history and uses this to bolster his claim against legislative history. Consider his argument:

> If such powerful evidence of the intent of Congress about the domain of its statutes is not dispositive in matters of construction versus inapplicability, the usual kind of evidence is even less helpful. To delve into the structure, purpose, and legislative history of the original statute is to engage in a sort of creation. It is to fill in blanks. And without some warrant—other than the existence of the blank—for a court to fill it in, the court has no authority to decide in favor of the party invoking the blank-containing statute.[79]

Consider the following response. The subsequent legislative history that Easterbrook describes is extremely "helpful" in discerning legislative intent respecting Statute A. The problem is that it is inadmissible for

---

79. Easterbrook, *supra* note 64, at 539.

independent reasons. The fact that the evidence of legislative intent, as revealed in P3, is not "dispositive" in case 2, therefore, says very little about whether other evidence of legislative intent—evidence that does not suffer from the same evidentiary defect associated with legislative history—is or is not helpful. The real difficulty with subsequent legislative history is that bills frequently die for procedural reasons that have little or nothing to do with support (or lack thereof) on the merits. Moreover, some sections within bills are attached in the amending process to gain support for the overall bill even though those sections, if freestanding, would not garner independent majority support.[80] Ultimately, Easterbrook's analysis might counsel against admitting evidence of the shadow history concerning bills not passed, or of provisions that passed as part of a larger legislative bargain, as evidence of legislative intent. Can you identify reasons for the general understanding that evidence of this sort is generally impermissible? How, if at all, does this vary from the sorts of evidence of legislative intent that, for example, Hart and Sacks are likely to find admissible and useful to statutory interpretation? If you conclude that they are different, can you articulate a rule that would draw out the distinction?

Returning to Judge Easterbrook's hypothetical, imagine instead that well documented evidence of legislative intent for Statute *A* demonstrated a substantial likelihood that on Facts *X*, Congress intended Result *not-Y*, but that the statute itself was not precise on the question. Assume for example, that this position was articulated without opposition on the floor of the Congress and was recorded, also without opposition, in the committee report. Assume once again that Case 1 arises before the Supreme Court. Does Judge Easterbrook's argument against the subsequent legislative history shed light on the potential value of relying upon the actual legislative history in this case? Assuming that Judge Easterbrook is correct that it is extremely difficult for Congress to overturn a judicial decision even with broad Congressional consent to do so, does this counsel in favor of or against using available evidence of legislative history as a means of approximating legislative preferences?[81]

Also consider Judge Easterbrook's argument that as a result of the procedural and other complexities in Congress that public choice exposes in the legislative process, it is not possible to assess intensities of preference. Might efforts to include misleading assertions in the legislative record prompt other counter-statements that would signal credibility problems to courts? Easterbrook also claims that legislative decision making is particularly agenda prone. Does this mean that prior to the formal implementation of a voting path by a committee chair, those who might be adversely affected are not able to negotiate a more favorable path? If they are able to negotiate the voting path, what does that suggest

---

80.   Stearns, *supra* note 4, at 397.

81.   Consider these questions also when we discuss Einer Elhauge's analysis of enactable preferences, *infra* pp. 286–89.

about Easterbrook's argument concerning the inability of legislators to register intensities of preferences concerning legislative proposals? What about logrolling? Does this process limit or further the power of litigants to register intensities of preference? Why?

2. Legislative Skeptics Influenced by the Legal Process School

We now consider the approaches to statutory interpretation offered by Judge Richard Posner, Professor Jonathan Macey, and McNollgast. These scholars also express a distrust of legislative processes, especially when compared to the process of common law decision making. And yet, based in part on intuitions from the Legal Process School, these scholars propose methods of teasing out public-regarding purposes in the judicial construction of statutes. As you read their proposals, consider how their views of the judicial task differ from those advanced by Professor Shepsle or Judge Easterbrook.

a. Judge Richard Posner and McNollgast

Before evaluating Judge Posner's normative analysis of statutory interpretation, it is important to set out his premise about the fundamental differences between the common law as a logical system and statutory law as a strictly textual system. Posner claims that because the common law is a conceptual system, in contrast with authoritative written legal texts, it exists independently of any particular verbal formulations:

> The concepts of negligence, of consideration, of reliance, are not tied to a particular verbal formulation, but can be restated in whatever words seem clearest in light of current linguistic conventions. Common law is thus unwritten law in a profound sense. There are more or less influential statements of every doctrine but none is authoritative in the sense that the decision of a new case must be tied to the statement, rather than to the concept of which the statement is one of an indefinite number of possible formulations.[82]

By contrast, Posner maintains that statutory and constitutional law cannot be understood separately from the governing text:

> Statutory and constitutional law differs fundamentally from common law in that every statutory and constitutional text—the starting point for decision, and in that respect (but that respect only) corresponding to judicial opinions in common law decision-making—is in some important sense not to be revised by the judges. They cannot treat the statute as a stab at formulating a concept which they are free to rewrite in their own words.... [T]here is no such thing as deduction from a text. No matter how clear the text seems, it must be interpreted (or decoded) like any other communication, and interpretation is neither logical deduction nor policy analysis.[83]

---

82. Posner, *supra* note 11, at 186.

83. *Id.* at 187 (footnote omitted).

While Posner describes the common law as a logical system separate from any particular verbal formulation contained in a judicial opinion, as you read the following passage, consider the extent to which this ultimately rests on a particular normative conception of the common law.

> The modern exemplar of formalism in common law is the positivist economic analysis of that law which Professor Landes and I and others have expounded. Taking as our premise the claim that the common law seeks to promote efficiency in the sense of wealth maximization (that is, abstracting from distributive considerations), and adding some data and assumptions about technology and human behavior, we deduce a set of optimal common law doctrines and institutions and then compare them with the actual common law. I use "deduction" in a literal sense. Microeconomic theory is a logical system like calculus or geometry (hence economic theory can be and often is expressed mathematically); more precisely a family of such systems.[84]

Do you agree with Posner's distinction between the common law as a logical system and statutes as purely text based? To the extent that the common law departs from normative claims identifying optimal, or efficient, common law rules, what does that suggest about whether the common law is "unwritten in a profound sense?" Is the common law unwritten, or is the notion of an efficient common law unwritten? Are there other potential benchmarks for evaluating common law rules that are similarly "unwritten," and that can be used as a basis for evaluating actual common law rules as distinguished from efficient common law rules? What about statutes as pure text based systems? To the extent that legislation effectively delegates specific policy goals to courts, what does that suggest about Posner's claim that judges cannot "rewrite [statutory objectives] in their own words"? Is it possible that even statutes that do not take the form of broad judicial delegations contain premises that can be applied beyond their literal wording?

Judge Posner's understanding of legislation as a textual system suggests that efforts to find "purposes" in legislation inappropriately apply common law logical reasoning to statutes. Nonetheless, Posner balks at dismissing the notion of legislative purpose. Posner claims that the "purpose" of the law, broadly defined, provides some of the context for interpreting ambiguous legislative communications. Consider Judge Posner's response to those who reject reliance upon legislative history based upon arguments drawn from public choice:

---

84. *Id.* at 185 (footnote omitted).

Then there is the growing skepticism about the traditional props of statutory interpretation, such as reference to purpose, to legislative history, and to rules of interpretation. Public-choice theory makes the attribution of unified purpose to a collective body increasingly difficult to accept—though I think it is possible to overdo one's skepticism in this regard. Institutions act purposively, therefore they have purposes. A document can manifest a single purpose even though those who drafted and approved it have a variety of private motives and expectations.[85]

Now consider McNollgast's complementary analysis:[86]

[A]s social choice theorists have known since Condorcet, majority-rule decisionmaking in the absence of agenda control can be unstable. But these observations do not imply that the concept of statutory intent lacks content. In the first place, that legislators all have different intentions does not imply that they do not or cannot strike bargains in order to construct a common understanding of the intention of a particular statute.... The number of legislators does not change the basic dynamic of policymaking: in the U.S., it is Congress as a whole that makes laws, not individual members of Congress. The fact that a particular agreement about intention might be defeated by another intention in a majority rule process with no agenda control does not mean that an enacted bill lacks meaning, just as a collective bargaining agreement does not lack meaning because a majority of union members might vote for an alternative that was not presented to them. To deny that a single, common intention for a statute is possible is to deny as well that Congress can legislate or that private parties can contract, a claim that is patently false.[87]

Judge Posner supports his argument concerning legislative intent using an analogy involving a platoon commander seeking to decode an ambiguous command:

[The] military analogy ... may help make clear that in arguing that judges have a duty to interpret, even when the legislative text is unclear, I am not arguing for judicial activism. The relationship between a military officer and his superiors and their doctrines, preferences, and values is, after all, the very model of obedience and deference. But the relationship does not entail inaction when orders are unclear. On the contrary, it requires "interpretation" of the most creative kind. And nothing less will discharge the judicial duty, even for those who believe, as I do, that self-restraint is, at least in our day, the proper judicial attitude. Creative and willful are not synonyms. You can be creative in imagining how someone else would have acted

---

85. *Id.* at 195–96.

86. McNollgast, *Legislative Intent: The Use of Positive Political Theory in Statutory Interpretation*, LAW & CONTEMP. PROBS., Spring 1994, at 3.

87. *Id.* at 19.

knowing what you know as well as what he knows. That is the creativity of the great statutory judge.[88]

Judge Posner also criticizes Easterbrook's suggested division between statutes that delegate policy making to courts and those that create their own underlying policies:

> If adopted, this proposal might well reduce the effective power of the legislative branch. In the class of statutes that judges classified as authorizing common law, the legislature would have little or no effect on policy; policy would be made by the courts. In the residual class the legislature would have little power also, for its statutes would be given no effect beyond the applications "expressly addressed" by the legislators.[89]

While Judge Posner rejects the Hart and Sacks premise that "courts deem the enacting legislators reasonable persons intending reasonable results in the public interest,"[90] he nonetheless considers himself at least partially heir to the Legal Process tradition:

> Far from thinking interpretation irrelevant, [Hart and Sacks] devote most of their discussion of statutory interpretation to techniques for "decoding" the statutory communication. It is only when all else fails that a court is to assume that the legislators were trying to do the same thing that courts do; it is only the most difficult, the indeterminate, issues of statutory interpretation that are to be subjected to common law formalist-realist reasoning. The fact that the court is to decode first, and reason in common law fashion only if the effort to decode fails, suggests that Hart and Sacks were well aware that not all legislation is reasonable in a common law sense.[91]

McNollgast go one step further and suggest that with a nuanced understanding of Congressional processes, judges can use the intricacies of bargaining to gain insights into legislative intent:

> In general, an observer (a jurist) who is informed (for example, about legislative intent) can learn from a signal of an informed party (a legislator) in either of two circumstances. First, the observer can learn whether the informed party bore some cost to communicate the signal. Although the content of the signal may be meaningless to the observer, the fact that the informed party bore a cost to communicate it nonetheless tells the observer that the informed party believed that the benefit of communicating would likely outweigh the cost incurred to do so. Second, if the informed party can be punished for sending

---

88. Posner, *supra* note 11, at 200.

89. *Id.* at 198.

90. *Id.* at 192.

91. *Id.* at 193. Posner goes on to explain that the authors' "discussion implies a more comfortable and confident view of 'interpretation' (broadly conceived) than is likely to gain many adherents today." *Id.* at 193–94. Posner ascribes this to a variety of challenges to traditional interpretive claims, including the assumption that statutes are generally welfare enhancing, the problem of understanding intent, and the problem of reliance on evidence of legislative intent described more fully in the text.

false signals, the observer can conclude that some lies are unprofitable for the informed party (those for which the expected benefit for lying is less than the expected penalty). This reasoning allows the observer to conclude that certain signals are more likely to reflect the truth than others.[92]

For McNollgast, this intuition follows from the fact that there are reliable, or pivotal, members of Congress who play a key role in transforming proposals into law. Ironically, perhaps, this is due to the very veto gates, or negative legislative checkpoints, that public choice reveals to be essential in Congressional bargaining processes. In effect, their analysis of the proper reliance upon legislative history is tied to the intuitions underlying the dynamic legislative bargaining model.[93] McNollgast explain:

> We use the term "pivotal" in a broader sense than simply the "swing" voters in Congress who must be induced to vote for a bill if it is to be enacted. As we use the term, anyone who occupies a "veto gate" in the institutional structure of legislative decisionmaking is also pivotal. Think of the legislative process as a decision tree, in which different members of the legislature are assigned different responsibilities at various nodes. A pivotal member is one whose action at a particular node can determine which branch of the tree the process will subsequently follow.[94]

The authors add that "The single most important feature of the legislative process in the House and Senate is that, to succeed, a bill must survive the gauntlet of veto gates in each chamber, each of which is supervised by members chosen by their peers to exercise gatekeeping authority."[95] According to McNollgast, identifying pivotal nodes and the actors who control them can provide valuable information concerning which sources of legislative history are more or less creditable.

To what extent do you read the Posner and McNollgast analyses as critiques of the Easterbrook and Shepsle approaches to statutory interpretation? How might Easterbrook and Shepsle respond? Which set of positions do you find more persuasive and why? Which do you find more consistent with the lessons of public choice theory? Which do you find more consistent with the lessons of the Legal Process School? Why?

b. Professor Jonathan Macey[96]

Professor Jonathan Macey relies upon public choice to take up the Hart and Sacks challenge directly.[97] Macey's project is to encourage courts to construe statutes so as to further whatever public interest objects they

---

92. McNollgast, *supra* note 86, at 8.

93. *See supra* pp. 254–57.

94. McNollgast, *supra* note 86, at 7.

95. *Id.* at 18.

96. Portions of this discussion are adapted from STEARNS, *supra* note 78, at 637–39.

97. Jonathan R. Macey, *Promoting Public-Regarding Legislation Through Statutory Interpretation: An Interest Group Model*, 86 COLUM. L. REV. 223 (1986).

appear to contain while at the same time limiting some of the more egregious payoffs necessary to secure the legislative deal. Macey argues that the enterprise of statutory interpretation by the judiciary requires judges to reconcile what he presents as two competing goals under the Constitution: (1) honoring the primary authority of the legislature to create policy, and (2) checking against legislative excesses, including reducing interest group influence, thus making legislation more public regarding. Macey claims that those advocating what he terms the "legislation-as-contract" approach, including Easterbrook,[98] seek to vindicate the terms of the statutory bargain struck between the legislature and interest groups and, if necessary, are willing to delve into the statutory history to uncover the full terms of the bargain. Macey argues that this approach honors the first principle (legislative supremacy) but violates the second (checking interest-group activity). Conversely, Macey claims that those who urge greater judicial activism in striking down special-interest legislation on constitutional grounds, as occurred during the *Lochner* era, vindicate the second principle but fail to properly weigh the first.

Macey claims that between these two extremes lies the "traditional" approach to statutory interpretation which "refers to the classic, time-honored methods of statutory interpretation that judges actually employ to decide cases."[99] Under this approach, which is informed by the Legal Process school, Macey claims that judges should apply the statute as written but should not try to vindicate interest-group purposes that lie beyond the statutory language. Macey argues that this approach promotes the public interest by seeking out the public-regarding features of statutes that were motivated in part to benefit narrow interest groups and therefore that it properly balances the two goals described above.

Macey divides statutes into three categories: (1) public interest statutes; (2) "open-explicit" statutes that make clear and direct payoffs to interest groups; and (3) "hidden-implicit" statutes that embed more obscure payoffs to interest groups that courts might or might not choose to enforce. Where the terms and intent of the statute advance the public interest, Macey claims that judges should simply enforce the statute as written since the two competing goals are not in conflict. The two remaining subcategories present a more difficult judicial task.

Macey argues that where the statute is unambiguous and the terms, including the payoffs, of a special-interest bargain are clear, meaning that the bargain is "open-explicit," judges are duty bound to honor the terms of the bargain as needed to advance the goal of legislative primacy in policymaking. Where instead the terms of the special interest bargain are more obscure or are "hidden-implicit," Macey argues that judges should instead construe the statute consistently with its stated public-regarding purpose even if doing so frustrates the terms of the embedded special interest bargain.

---

98. Macey uses this term to characterize the argument in Easterbrook, *supra* note 36, *see* Macey, *supra* note 97, at 226.

99. Macey, *supra* note 97, at 227.

Macey maintains that this approach furthers the public interest because open-explicit bargains are much more costly for interest groups to acquire than hidden-implicit bargains since the former are more likely to bring about public opposition. Macey observes:

> When the legislature has passed a statute that claims to be in the public interest but in fact benefits an interest group, that interest group may meet with frustration in the courts when it tries to enforce the statute. The statute is unlikely to serve the ends it claims to serve and at the same time enrich a particular group. When the court interprets the statute so as to serve the public, the court may ... inadvertently invalidate a legislative bargain. But when this happens it is all to the common good.[100]

Professor Macey claims support for his analysis and for this assertion about the proper judicial role in policing—or at least raising costs respecting—special interest legislation in the following passage from the *Federalist* No. 78 (Hamilton)[101]:

> But it is not with a view to infractions of the Constitution alone that the independence of judges may be an essential safeguard against the effects of occasional ill humors in the society.... [T]he firmness of the judicial magistracy is of vast importance in mitigating the severity and confining the operation of such laws. It not only serves to moderate the immediate mischiefs of those which may have been passed but it operates as a check upon the legislative body in passing them; who, perceiving that obstacles to the success of an iniquitous intention are to be expected from the scruples of the courts, are in a manner compelled, by the very motives of the injustice they mediate, to qualify their attempts.

In evaluating Macey's claim respecting this passage, it will be helpful to compare the following alternative analysis offered Judge Posner:

> Another general problem of interpretation is that no one knows for sure whether the framers of the Constitution intended federal courts merely to translate (so far as they were able) the specific commands of Congress into particular case outcomes, or instead, as suggested by Alexander Hamilton [in the passage quoted above], to exert a civilizing influence—to act as a buffer between the legislators and the citizenry even when no constitutional issue was raised. The role of the judge in "civilizing" statutes was not problematic for Hart and Sacks because they were willing to assume in all doubtful cases that the statute was intended to achieve the civilized result. On such an assumption there is no difference between being a translator and being a buffer, so Hamilton could be left in peace.[102]

---

100. *Id.* at 254.

101. THE FEDERALIST No. 78 (Alexander Hamilton).

102. Posner, *supra* note 11, at 195 (footnote omitted).

c. *Discussion Questions*

What are the fundamental differences between Posner and Macey concerning the proper judicial task in statutory interpretation? Which is closer to the position advanced by Easterbrook and Shepsle? Which is closer to the position advanced by the Legal Process school? Which of the approaches among these groups of scholars is best informed by public choice analysis? Which is more persuasive as a matter of legal policy? Are the last two questions the same? Why or why not? Has Macey adequately supported his conclusion that it is the role of courts to provide an additional check against interest group payoffs secured in the political process? Is Macey correct that this is a constitutional goal? Can you identify any potential adverse consequences that might flow from Macey's regime? How, if at all, is his proposed regime different from the constitutional regime associated with *Lochner v. New York*? Is Macey's willingness to allow interest group payoffs when the terms of the interest group bargain are open/explicit sufficient, but not when they are hidden/implicit, sufficient to distinguish *Lochner*? How, if at all, is Macey's proposal different from the common law canon demanding that statutes in derogation of the common law be narrowly construed? Does the answer to this question inform whether Macey is operating in the Legal Process tradition? Why or why not?

B. SCHOLARS EMBRACING A MORE OPTIMISTIC VIEW OF THE LEGISLATIVE PROCESS

We now turn to a group of scholars who generally embrace a more optimistic view of the legislature and a greater willingness to allow courts to further legislative objectives through the interpretation of statutes. We begin with Professors Daniel Farber and Philip Frickey, who we can describe as falling within the Legal Process tradition or alternatively within the tradition of small "r" republicanism.[103] These scholars criticize the Chicago public choice school and claim that a broader reading of public choice supports a more substantial judicial role using statutory construction to further active political participation. In addition, we consider the work of William Eskridge, who more transparently than other scholars relies upon the Wilson–Hayes model to advance a comprehensive theory designed to carve out particular rules of judicial construction of statutes depending upon the analytical category into which the underlying legislation falls. Finally, we consider an analysis of statutory interpretation by Professor Einer Elhauge that challenges the foundational assumption among most scholars that the proper referent for statutory construction is the set of preferences of the enacting, or contemporaneous legislature, rather than those of the current legislature at the time of the judicial decision, or some other proxy for what he terms "enactable preferences."

---

103. Not to be confused with large "R" Republican politics.

1. Farber and Frickey

Professors Daniel Farber and Philip Frickey advance several claims that are intended to dispel the conclusion that public choice compels ascribing no more to statutes than literal meaning based strictly upon the written text. Instead, on both theoretical and pragmatic grounds, the authors claim that public choice is consistent with a more active judicial role in construing statutes that is consistent with common judicial practices, including reliance upon legislative history. The authors summarize their position as follows:

> We believe ... that public choice theory is compatible with a more respectful attitude toward legislative intent. In our view, public choice theory is consistent with a flexible, pragmatic approach to statutory construction, in which legislative intent plays an important role.[104]

Consider the authors' challenge to Chicago public choice arguments respecting legislative coherence and the possibility of discerning legislative intent beyond a statute's literal meaning. The authors reject the claim that the possibility of cycling preferences, or other difficulties revealed by social choice, undermine the concept of legislative intent. Farber and Frickey base their analysis upon a body of literature that describes three related concepts: the uncovered set, the yolk, and the strong point. The authors explain:

> [T]he uncovered set consists of outcomes that could survive sophisticated voting procedures by "dominating" other outcomes. The yolk is the smallest sphere that intersects all of the median planes, where a median plane is one that divides the voters' ideal points (each voter's most preferred outcome) into groups of equal size. In a rough sense, the center of the yolk is the median of the various voters' ideal outcomes. The strong point is the one that beats the most alternatives in pairwise voting.
>
> Remarkably these very different definitions turn out to describe very similar outcomes.[105]

The authors add: "We do not suggest that courts perform the elaborate calculations involved in these mathematical models. We believe that many judges will, however, have a good intuitive sense of the legislative center of gravity."[106]

How, if at all, does this framing relate to the McNollgast decision-node analysis? Does the concept of a decision node suggest that bargains might reflect outcomes not captured in such concepts as the uncovered set, strong point, or yolk? In a regime of active legislative bargaining, is it possible to determine whether specific interest group payoffs reflect out-

---

104. Farber & Frickey, *supra* note 57, at 424.

105. *Id.* at 433. *See also* William Panning, *Formal Models of Legislative Processes, in* HANDBOOK OF LEGISLATIVE RESEARCH (Gerhard Loewenberg et al. eds., 1985).

106. Farber & Frickey, *supra* note 57, at 437.

comes that rest on some notion of a legislative center of gravity? Why or why not? Which of these approaches is more likely to be intuitive to judges in the construction of statutes? Why?

In addition, as discussed in chapter 3, Farber and Frickey maintain that a fairness norm conduces toward stability even when one can construct a set of preferences that reveal the formal conditions for a cycle. By fairness, the authors imagine that when confronted with various empty core bargaining games, participants are quite likely to split any resulting super-additive gains evenly,[107] rather than introducing continual options that hold temporary majority support, but will then be superseded by a series of plays taking the form of a cycle. The authors explain:

> The incentive to move away from these "natural" equilibria [meaning equal division as a fairness solution] is small because the ensuing cycling is likely to send the outcome back into the equilibrium area anyway. Rational behavior calls for quickly finding and sticking with the equilibrium area.[108]

Farber and Frickey maintain that this intuition is closely tied to appreciating institutional rationality and to the processes through which institutions select decision-making rules. The authors maintain that " 'natural selection' would eliminate any legislature that failed to develop defenses to cycling and instability,"[109] and ask "What purpose is served by a legislature the outcomes of which are entirely unpredictable and fortuitous?"[110]

Does social choice support the authors' claim that legislative decision-making is likely to evolve in a manner that thwarts cycling? Are fairness norms likely to limit cycling? How, if at all, does this social choice analysis inform the proper judicial construction of ambiguous statutory provisions? Consider also Professor Shepsle's response to the Farber and Frickey cycling analysis, presented more fully in chapter 3.[111] Recall that Shepsle contends that Arrow's result "does not entail constant flux and indeterminacy,"[112] but that it might call into question the normative merit of particular outcomes that embed cycling preferences.

Which positive account of the relative infrequency of cycling, that offered by Farber and Frickey or the response by Shepsle, do you find more persuasive? Which is more consistent with public choice theory? While Shepsle argues that the method through which institutions avoid cycles is influenced by factors that render outcomes "arbitrary or other-

---

107. Super-additivities mean the gains that arise from various superior coalition strategies that are available to replace existing coalition strategies in an empty core game. *See* Maxwell L. Stearns, *The Misguided Renaissance of Social Choice*, 103 YALE L.J. 1219, 1236–40 (1994).

108. Farber & Frickey, *supra* note 57, at 434–35. *See also* WILLIAM N. ESKRIDGE, JR., DYNAMIC STATUTORY INTERPRETATION (1994).

109. Farber & Frickey, *supra* note 57, at 435. Professor William Eskridge advances a similar argument in his book, *Dynamic Statutory Interpretation*. *See* Maxwell L. Stearns, *Book Review*, 86 PUB. CHOICE 379 (1996) (reviewing ESKRIDGE, *supra* note 108).

110. Farber & Frickey, *supra* note 57, at 435.

111. *See supra* chapter 3, section II.E.

112. Shepsle, *supra* note 60, at 242 n.6.

wise morally indefensible,"[113] is it possible that the processes through which those outcomes are achieved nonetheless legitimate those outcomes? Might the "manner in which majority cycling is resolved" give outcomes a "compelling" or at least adequate "normative justification"? Is it possible to justify such outcomes without redefining a non-Condorcet winner to nonetheless describe a legislative center of gravity, for example, as reflected in such concepts as uncovered sets, strong points, or yolks? In other words, might we distinguish the merits of particular outcomes that are the product of cycling and voting paths from the merits of processes that create outcomes in general even when we find particular outcomes problematic? How might Farber and Frickey respond to this analysis? How might Shepsle respond? Can the legislative bargaining processes themselves—either length bargaining or substantive bargaining—lend normative legitimacy to outcomes that would not arise independently of those decision-making processes? Why or why not? Do group outcomes ever exist independently of the processes that generate them? Why or why not?

2. William Eskridge

We will now turn to Professor William Eskridge's arguments advocating a more active judicial role in furthering objectives contained in statutes. Eskridge initially developed his thesis in an article, *Politics Without Romance: Implications of Public Choice Theory for Statutory Interpretation*,[114] and later extended his thesis in a book length treatment, *Dynamic Statutory Interpretation*.[115] For our purposes, this article is particularly important because it sets out the most ambitious comprehensive normative assessment of the Wilson–Hayes model for statutory interpretation.[116]

Eskridge maintains that presumptive judicial deference to Congress is inappropriate given that unlike courts, Congress has the capacity, and frequently the tendency, to remain inert. He explains:

> Perhaps the most important lesson of public choice theory for statutory interpretation is that it deepens our understanding of the court-legislature dialogue. A court is often tempted to finesse a hard interpretational choice by "leaving it to the legislature." This is frequently the worst place to leave the choice. Before doing that, the court ought to consider the legislature's incentives to act (and to act constructively) or not to act.[117]

Eskridge continues:

---

113. *Id.*

114. William N. Eskridge, Jr., *Politics Without Romance: Implications of Public Choice Theory for Statutory Interpretation*, 74 VA. L. REV. 275 (1988).

115. ESKRIDGE, *supra* note 108.

116. For a discussion of Eskridge's analysis of how majority voting in a legislature can produce a social welfare loss, see *supra* chapter 3, section II.F.

117. Eskridge, *supra* note 114, at 279.

[T]he mandatory jurisdiction of federal cases makes it difficult for judges—unlike legislators—to avoid the task of updating statutory policy. Litigants before a court are entitled to a decision, and devices to avoid the merits (such as questions of standing) are invoked only in exceptional cases.

> ... [C]ourts behaving in a common law manner have a comparative advantage over Congress in updating symmetrical, public goods laws.... [118]

Eskridge maintains that the political insularity of federal judges provides a further benefit in encouraging courts to update statutory policy. He explains:

> The very nonaccountability of judges gives them—unlike legislators— the freedom to make hard policy choices without falling athwart the dilemma of the ungrateful electorate. Their relative nonaccountability also leaves them with few incentives to cozy up to interest groups, who can in most instances do them no good. In short, precisely because they are not subject to reelection pressures, judges avoid a major force skewing legislators' views.[119]

Eskridge also claims that the different nature of interest group involvement within each institution favors judicial, as opposed to legislative, updating of statutes:

> Although interest groups play a role in the judicial process, it appears that the incidence and influence of group behavior are different in the judicial (in comparison to the legislative) arena. To begin with, there is less likely to be the same high degree of asymmetry of viewpoints in litigation that there routinely is in legislation. Courts generally have at least two parties representing opposing interests in a litigated case, and a court will refuse to hear a case that does not reflect a truly adversarial controversy.[120]

Finally, Eskridge offers a comprehensive synthesis of various scholarly works resting upon public choice, which takes the form of an updated Wilson–Hayes matrix.[121] As you review this matrix, consider its relationship to the approaches to statutory interpretation offered by Hart and Sacks. Consider its relationship to prior presentation of the static and dynamic Wilson–Hayes models. Finally, compare the approach depicted in the matrix with those of the various other scholars relying upon public choice. Notice that Eskridge claims to integrate the approaches of various scholars within his larger framework. Does he succeed? Why or why not?

---

118. *Id.* at 303.

119. *Id.* at 305 (footnote omitted).

120. *Id.* at 303–04.

121. The following is adapted from *id.* at 299 and 325. Eskridge presents this in two forms, and for ease of comparison, we have marked the original as such, and the other entries are from the version that appears later in the same article. We have reoriented the matrix, reversing the upper right and lower left corner to match our earlier presentation, but we have not altered its content.

Which of these approaches is more consistent with your own assessment of the teachings of public choice? Why? Which approach is most sound as a matter of policy? Why?

Table 5:4. Dynamic Statutory Interpretation

Distributed benefit/distributed cost	Concentrated benefit/distributed cost
Original: Interpret in a common law fashion, limited by the statutory language, updating to reflect changed circumstances (similar to Posner's theory). **Danger:** The legislature's failure to update the law as society and the underlying problem change. **Response:** Courts can help maintain a statute's usefulness by expanding it to new situations and by developing the statute in common law fashion. **Caveat:** Courts should be reluctant to create special exceptions for organized groups.	**Original:** Interpret narrowly and refuse to provide special benefits unless clearly required by statute (similar to Easterbrook's view). **Danger:** Rent seeking by special interest groups at the expense of the general public. **Response:** Courts can narrowly construe the statute to minimize the benefits. Court should err in favor of stinginess with public largesse.
Distributed benefit/concentrated cost	**Concentrated benefit/concentrated cost**
Original: Interpret to effectuate stated public purposes and to reflect changing legal or constitutional values, within the frame of ongoing agency implementation (similar to Macey's theory). **Danger:** Regulated groups' evasion of duties; as agencies are "captured" by groups, regulation becomes a means to exclude competition. **Response:** Courts can monitor agency enforcement and private compliance, and can open up procedures to allow excluded groups to be heard. Courts should seek to make the original public goal work.	**Original:** Interpret to effectuating original deal among interest groups effectuating the stated purposes of the statute within the frame of ongoing agency interpretation (similar to Macey's theory). **Danger:** The statutory "deal" often grows unexpectedly lopsided over time. **Response:** Err against very much judicial updating, unless affected groups are systematically unable to get legislative attention.

3. Einer Elhauge

In a recently published book, Harvard Law Professor Einer Elhauge has offered a novel theory of statutory interpretation that in some respects builds upon intuitions drawn from Professor Eskridge. Whereas Professor Eskridge seeks to update statutory policy to overcome perceived legislative bargaining problems that public choice helps to identify, Professor Elhauge offers a two-part prescription for legislative interpretation.[122] In the first part he maintains that overall legislative satisfaction is enhanced when the judiciary does not seek to further the interests of the enacting, or contemporaneous, legislature in the construction of ambigu-

---

122. *See* ELHAUGE, *supra* note 77, at 9–10.

ous statutory provisions, but rather when courts construe such provisions with reference to what he terms the "enactable preferences" of the sitting legislature at the time of the judicial decision. In the second, he argues that when it is not possible to identify enactable legislative preferences, courts sometimes optimize satisfaction by announcing rules that are "preference eliciting," meaning that the judicial decision motivates a legislative response with the effect of formally enacting present legislative preferences into law.

We begin with Elhauge's thesis concerning enactable preferences:

> My first major point will be that the default rules that overall best maximize the political preferences of the *enacting* legislative polity turn out to track the preferences of the *current* legislative polity when the latter can be reliably ascertained from official action. By "official action," I mean either agency decisions interpreting the statute or subsequent legislative statutes that help reveal current enactable preferences even though they do not amend the relevant provision.
>
> This argument for current preferences default rules may be the most counterintuitive of my claims. Why wouldn't the enacting legislative polity want its *own* political preferences followed? The key to the answer is that the question here is not what result the enacting legislative polity would most likely want for the *particular* statute; if that were the question then it would be true that the legislature would want its own preferences followed. However, the question here is instead what *general* rules for resolving uncertainties about statutory meaning—including uncertainties in older statutes that are being interpreted and applied during the time that the enacting legislative polity holds office—would most maximize the political satisfaction of the enacting legislative polity? In choosing such general statutory default rules, the enacting legislative polity would prefer *present* influence (while it exists) over *all* the statutes being interpreted, rather than *future* influence (when it no longer exists) over the *subset* of statutes it enacted.[123]

Elhauge further contends that when neither current nor enactable preferences are clearly discernible, political satisfaction is sometimes maximized when the judiciary rules contrary to anticipated and strongly held legislative preferences with the result of eliciting a contrary legislative response. Elhauge recognizes the potential risk associated with this proposed default rule, and counsels a narrow set of applications:

> Preference-eliciting default rules will … enhance political satisfaction only when the chosen interpretation is more likely to elicit a legislative response, by a margin sufficient to outweigh a weak estimate that another interpretation is more likely to match enactable preferences. In other words, a necessary condition for applying a preference-eliciting default rule is the existence of a significant differ-

---

123. *Id.* at 9–10 (italics in original).

ential likelihood of legislative correction. Where that and other conditions are met, a preference-eliciting default rule can create statutory results that reflect enactable preferences more accurately than any judicial estimate of current or enactor preferences possibly could.[124]

Consider one prominent illustration of each of Elhauge's default rules, first the enactable preference rule and then the preference eliciting rule. Elhauge contends that absent statutory guidance on the sitting legislature's preferred interpretation of an existing statute, agency interpretation offers a useful proxy for enactable preferences because agency policy is generally made by political appointees who are therefore at least indirectly subject to some degree of political accountability.

The Supreme Court has issued two major decisions that relate to the question of when federal courts should defer to agency interpretations of statutes. In *Chevron U.S.A. Inc. v. Natural Resources Defense Council, Inc.*,[125] the Court announced a general policy of deferring to agency construction of ambiguous statutory provisions even if the agency construction differs from that which the federal court would have produced as an initial matter.

Elhauge explains the intuition underlying *Chevron* as follows:

> . . . *Chevron* deference depends on agencies being fairly accurate barometers of current enactable preferences, or at least more accurate than judicial estimates would be. Although the phrase "legislative preferences" is often used as a shorthand for enactable preferences, in systems like the United States' the set of preferences that are actually enactable is strongly influenced not just by legislators but also by the executive, who has the powers to veto legislation and put issues on the public agenda. Each is in turn influenced by outside political forces, which lobby, organize, contribute, and otherwise constrain the actions of both legislators and executives. In such a system, agencies must be responsive to executive, legislative, and general political influences for their actions to be likely to minimize the dissatisfaction of enactable political preferences in a way that merits *Chevron* deference.[126]

In *United States v. Mead Corp.*,[127] the Supreme Court announced a major exception to the *Chevron* agency deference rule, holding that when the agency policy is not adopted through formal processes, the announced policy is not subject to *Chevron* deference.[128] The *Mead* Court ruled that *Chevron* deference does not apply to "agency letter rulings, opinion letters, policy statements, manuals, and enforcement guidelines."[129]

---

124. *Id.* at 12.

125. 467 U.S. 837 (1984).

126. ELHAUGE, *supra* note 77, at 99.

127. 533 U.S. 218 (2001).

128. We will set out a more thorough examination of *Chevron* and *Mead*, *infra* chapter 6 (the executive branch and agencies).

129. ELHAUGE, *supra* note 77, at 91. The *Mead* Court stated: "Interpretations such as those in opinion letters—like interpretations contained in policy statements, agency manuals, and enforce-

Elhauge reconciles the two cases as follows:

> This distinction—between individualized determinations and rulemaking for a general class of persons—may not make much sense if we focus on the coercive effect of the decision, but is entirely understandable if we instead understand this doctrine as a current preferences default rule. Individualized determinations cannot be said to reflect the current enactable preferences of any general set of interested parties. One-shot individualized interpretations are also unlikely to provoke any legislative oversight. They thus do not suffice to justify judicial application of a current preferences default rule, especially since adopting that default rule would create an interpretation that would be binding on the general class of affected persons.[130]

In addition to analyzing the enactable preferences default rule, Elhauge evaluates those limited circumstances in which he encourages courts to rule in a manner that elicits an intended legislative response, even though the elicited legislative response contradicts the initial judicial ruling.[131] Professor Elhauge explains his intuition as follows:

> Suppose a statute has two plausible meanings: option A is 60% likely to reflect enactable preferences, and option B is 40% likely to do so. Suppose also that, if option A turned out not to conform to enactable preferences, the odds are 0% that the legislature might correct it. In contrast, if option B did not match enactable preferences, the odds are 100% that the legislature would correct it. If the court chooses option A, then the expected political satisfaction will be 60%, because in the 40% of cases where this interpretation did not match enactable preferences, the legislature would not correct it. However, if the court chooses option B, then the expected political satisfaction will be 100%, because in the 40% of cases where the default rule does turn out to match enactable preferences, the legislature will leave it in place, where as in the 60% of cases where the default rule does not match enactable preferences, the legislature will replace it with option A. Choosing preference-eliciting option B will thus ultimately increase the expected satisfaction of enactable preferences, even though option B itself is less likely to reflect enactable preferences than A.[132]

Elhauge goes on to explain:

> The existence of preference-eliciting default rules means that an ex post statutory override does not prove that the judicial interpretation was mistaken, as is often supposed. To the contrary, such

---

ment guidelines, all of which lack the force of law—do not warrant *Chevron*-style deference." United States v. Mead Corp., 533 U.S. at 236 n.17 (quoting Christensen v. Harris County, 529 U.S. 576, 587 (2000)).

130. ELHAUGE, *supra* note 77, at 94.

131. As an illustration, Elhauge discusses the decision to grant relief to the Guantanamo detainees in the *Hamdan* case, a result that elicited a rather immediate Congressional response. *Id.* at 163–64.

132. *Id.* at 153.

statutory overrides mean that the preference-eliciting default rule achieved its purpose: forcing explicit decisionmaking by the political process.[133]

Professor Elhauge distinguishes this analysis from Professor Macey's interpretive rule encouraging courts to further the claimed public regarding purpose of statutes containing hidden implicit bargains. The critical difference, Elhauge explains, is that while Macey places the burden of clarification on the parties seeking the benefit of the interest group bargain, Elhauge would place the burden on those challenging the unpopular payoff as a means of encouraging legislative overruling.[134]

Elhauge claims that his analysis helps to explain the rule of lenity. The purpose of the rule is not the relief afforded to an unpopular criminal defendant. Instead, it is the motivation that the ruling creates in the sitting legislature to enact a contrary rule by statute. Elhauge explains:

> [P]reference-eliciting analysis provides a ready justification for this counterintuitive canon. By providing the most lenient reading in unclear cases, the rule of lenity forces legislatures to define just how anti-criminal they wish to be, and how far to go with the interest in punishing crime when it runs up against other societal interests. If instead courts broadly (or even neutrally) interpreted criminal statutes in cases of unclarity, this would often produce an overly broad interpretation that would likely stick, because there is no effective lobby for narrowing criminal statutes. In contrast, an overly narrow interpretation is far more likely to be corrected by statutory interpretation, because prosecutors and other members of anti-criminal lobbying groups are heavily involved in legislative drafting and can more readily get on the legislative agenda to procure any needed overrides.[135]

4. Questions and Comments[136]

Let us now compare the approaches to statutory interpretation offered by Farber and Frickey, Eskridge, and Elhauge. Recall that Professors Eskridge and Frickey ultimately published the Hart and Sacks Legal Process course materials. It is not surprising, therefore, that these authors view themselves as heirs, at least in part, to the Hart and Sacks scholarly tradition. We will begin with Farber and Frickey. To what extent are their assumptions about the legislative process informed by public choice and to what extent by other sources of political theory? Consider, for example, their claim that political actors will be motivated to produce fairness solutions rather than forcing empty core games back into the throes of cycling. Are the Farber and Frickey intuitions about the institutional implications of fairness grounded in social choice theory? Is their under-

---

133. *Id.* at 154 (footnote omitted).

134. *See id.* at 163.

135. *See id.* at 169.

136. Portions of the discussion that follows are based upon STEARNS, *supra* note 78, at 712–24.

standing of fairness consistent with Arrow's specified fairness criteria, and their linkage to democratic norms, or is it instead linked to some other set of normative considerations? If the latter, what are those normative considerations?

Consider also their argument concerning the evolution of institutions away from procedural devices that conduce to cycling. As previewed in chapter 3, some institutional decision-making rules can be explained as mechanisms to avoid cycling. In elections, for example, rules that would produce cycling would risk failing to select a candidate when voter preferences cycled. As we will see in chapter 7, within appellate courts, such rules as outcome voting and stare decisis formalize outcomes in a manner that limits the appearance of cycling and thus that promotes stable doctrine. Still other institutions employ rules that exhibit a strong status quo preference. As we have seen in the study of parliamentary rules, even motion-and-amendment procedures that formally limit votes relative to options can permit the requisite number of binary comparisons to disclose cycles when we consider the possibility of informal practices that allow actors to identify their preferences in advance of formal agenda setting or voting.

How, if at all, does the Farber and Frickey analysis distinguish the evolutionary paths of courts and legislatures? Do you agree with Farber and Frickey that institutional evolution would prefer legislatures that avoid cycling even when the underlying preference structures do not demonstrate support for any single outcome representing a change from the status quo? Are there, instead, reasons why we might prefer legislatures to have an institutional status quo bias under these conditions? Is Shepsle's response to Farber and Frickey helpful in answering these questions?[137] Why or why not?

Whether or not Farber and Frickey have captured the underlying intuitions concerning the evolutionary paths of legislatures, might one still find appealing their normative intuitions concerning the role of courts in construing statutes? To what extent does their assertion favoring a more respectful role for the use of legislative history turn on their public choice analysis of the legislature? Do you agree that courts are well suited to intuitively locate the center of legislative gravity, whether characterized in terms of the uncovered set, yolk, or strong point? How do these concepts relate to the locating a Condorcet winner? Notice that Farber and Frickey do not claim that these outcomes are preferred to all available alternatives, and thus they can be applied even when preferences cycle. As a result, such outcomes are necessarily disfavored to some alternative option, but within the relevant models are treated as stable. Does this suggest that such regimes must relax range to effectuate outcomes?[138] If so, what are the mechanisms for imposing such a range restriction? Are those mechanisms likely present in Congress? Why or why not?

---

137. Shepsle, *supra* note 60, at 242 n.6.

138. *See supra* chapter 3, section II.B. (discussing range).

Now consider Professor Eskridge's arguments for dynamic statutory interpretation. Eskridge offers an ambitious analysis that requires identifying the analytical category into which each statute, or relevant statutory provision, falls using the Wilson–Hayes analysis. Let us begin with Eskridge's analysis of institutions. Eskridge maintains that public choice reveals a considerable basis for caution in ascribing benign motives to at least some categories of legislation.[139] Recall from chapter 3 Eskridge's hypothetical in which A and B succeed in securing Decision 1, with a shared payoff of 100, to the detriment of C and a corresponding societal welfare loss of 20, as compared with Decision 3.[140] In a robust legislature with a tradition of vote trading, is this welfare-reducing outcome likely to occur? Why or why not? Applying the McNollgast analysis, if we assume a vote on Decision 1 at a given decision node, what could C do to reduce the risk of an adverse outcome? Is it possible (if somewhat ironic) that Eskridge's dynamic statutory analysis rests upon an unduly static conception of Congressional bargaining? In effect, Eskridge's analysis is premised upon a political market failure. But consider whether his analysis successfully captures political market dynamics. As previously explained, this danger only arises if the successful coalition is willing to leave money on the table, foregoing potential gains from trade that are available if A and B include this isolated bill among a broader set of bills over which all three members, including C, could enhance their utility, thus improving social welfare for all participants. And notice that it is the self-interest of A and B in this analysis that ultimately promises a better potential outcome for C.

More generally this suggests the danger in evaluating truncated legislative enactments in isolation from other legislative components. How does this question relate to Eskridge's larger project captured in his (now combined) analytical matrices? We can approach this analysis at both a micro- and macro-level. We will begin, for example, by inquiring about the same premises that underlie the related political market failure analyses suggested by Judge Easterbrook and Professor Macey. Specifically, within each of the four boxes of Eskridge's modified Wilson–Hayes matrix, we could inquire about the market failure premises and about how the proposed rule of statutory construction works toward improving upon those claimed defects. This is of course a worthwhile exercise, and yet, we would like to also encourage assessing Eskridge's project by viewing it with a wider lens.

Specifically, consider the nature of using the Wilson–Hayes matrix to demarcate specific analytical categories for evaluating the proper judicial response in construing legislation. The Wilson–Hayes matrix is a helpful heuristic in considering possible endpoints along two combined analytical spectrums: narrowly or broadly spread costs and narrowly or widely spread benefits. The broader question is whether this combined set of

---

139.   It is for this reason that Eskridge borrows from Buchanan and Tullock the title "Politics without Romance." Eskridge, *supra* note 114.

140.   *See supra* chapter 3, section II.F.

analytical devices translates into literal commands that courts can employ when evaluating isolated categories of legislation based upon the claimed political defects that each category is presumed to depict. To answer this question, it is helpful to revisit both the discussion in section I on substantive and length bargaining and the McNollgast decision node analysis in section II. Assume that such bargaining at a particular decision node results in negotiations to support or decline to support more than a single bill. Is it possible in such a dynamic bargaining regime to know whether any given piece of legislation pits narrow or broad beneficiaries against narrow or broad cost bearers? Why or why not? How does the answer to this question inform Eskridge's larger project of tailoring judicial responses to the nature of the legislation under review? How does it inform the analysis within each of the four micro-categories for Eskridge and for those upon whom Eskridge relies?

Consider also Eskridge's evolutionary analysis of courts and legislatures. While Farber and Frickey suggest that legislative adaptation favors cycle-avoiding decisional rules, Eskridge appears to suggest the opposite. Legislatures, unlike courts, have a built-in status quo bias as a result of which, Eskridge maintains, courts have a comparative advantage in updating statutes. This is because unlike legislatures, courts usually have mandatory jurisdiction in the cases that they are called upon to decide. In addition, Eskridge maintains that the judiciary guarantees a broader range of perspectives—at a minimum two parties are generally represented in any given case—than do legislatures. Do you find these arguments persuasive? Does social choice analysis give any guidance as to why courts, unlike legislatures, are generally required to resolve cases and issues within properly docketed cases? Does it give any guidance as to why legislatures, unlike courts, are empowered to avoid collective decisions on bills absent a majority or Condorcet winner, or absent a set of vote trades that achieve majority support over a larger number of formally separate bills? How, if at all, does this analysis inform proposals, like Eskridge's, to rely upon the judicial obligation to resolve cases as an argument for encouraging courts to affirmatively update statutes? How does this analysis link to the earlier discussion comparing Farber and Frickey with Shepsle about the difference between the merits of substantive outcomes and the legitimacy of the processes that produce those outcomes?

Finally, consider whether Eskridge's analysis is consistent with the Legal Process school. Does his analysis rest upon the Hart and Sacks presumption that legislators are reasonable persons acting reasonably? Do you think that Hart and Sacks would have endorsed Eskridge's dynamic statutory interpretive regime? Why or why not?

Now let us turn our attention to Professor Elhauge's enactable preferences and preference-eliciting default rules. Recall that in his earlier article, *Does Interest Group Theory Justify More Intrusive Judicial Review?*,[141] Elhauge inquired whether those who rely upon interest group

---

141.   Elhauge, *supra* note 8.

theory to advocate more stringent judicial review of statutes were relying upon a (most often unstated) normative baseline about the appropriate extent of interest group influence in the political process. What baseline is Elhauge employing in advancing his two suggested statutory default rules? Whether or not the two rules he advocates—the enactable preference rule or the preference eliciting rule—maximize present political satisfaction, is it obvious that present political satisfaction is the proper normative baseline against which to gauge default rules for statutory interpretation? Can you identify any normative difficulties with that baseline? To what extent does Elhauge's implicit baseline rest upon, or operate in tension with, the lessons of public choice theory? Why?

Professor Elhauge suggests that most legislators would prefer temporary influence over all ambiguous statutory provisions subject to judicial resolution during the period of time that they are in office to an indefinite, or at least prolonged, influence on ambiguous statutory provisions that they enacted, long after their terms expire. Is it possible to know whether this is correct? Is it possible that legislators would prefer a longer influence respecting those policy issues that they chose to address in the statutes that they had a role in passing, rather than a shorter lived influence over statutes that were the object of their predecessor legislatures' attention but that was subject to litigation during their terms in office?

If we treat the assumption that legislators would prefer a present influence over a larger number of statutes than a future influence over a smaller number of statutes as Elhauge's hypothesis, is it falsifiable? If so, can you think of an appropriate test? Can you identify institutional mechanisms that improve the likelihood that courts construe ambiguous statutory provisions consistently with enactable preferences? Can you identify institutional mechanisms that have the opposite effect, namely encouraging courts to weigh the preferences of the enacting legislature to the extent that they can discern those preferences? Is the presence or absence of these possible institutional mechanisms relevant to testing whether Elhauge's suggested default rule rests upon sound premises?

In considering these questions, consider a famous article on the federal judiciary by Professor William Landes and Judge Richard Posner. Landes and Posner posit that one of the principal benefits of an independent federal judiciary is that it prolongs the payoffs of bargains made—including interest group bargains—in the political process.[142] The analysis is fairly straightforward. While no one imagines that judges are entirely immune from political influences, Article III tenure provides as effective a means as practicable of political insulation since Congress has no truly effective means of punishing federal judges for decisions that Congress

---

142. We will evaluate this thesis more closely in chapter 8, and specifically consider arguments by Macey and others that this claimed benefit operates to the detriment of more benign rules of judicial construction by prolonging narrow interest group payoffs. *See supra* pp. 277–80 (discussing Macey thesis). For now it is sufficient to observe that the longer payoff might not be intended to benefit interest groups for their own sake. Instead, that payoff might motivate political involvement that helps facilitate the procurement of desired general interest legislation.

objects to politically.[143] As a result, Article III tenure increases the probability that in enforcing statutes, federal judges will be more likely to weigh the intentions of those who drafted them, as opposed to those of present legislators, as compared with a regime that does not afford such political insulation. If Elhauge has identified an appropriate normative baseline with which to evaluate the meaning of ambiguous statutory provisions, would the framers have created a judiciary that was relatively more removed from, or relatively closer to, present (or contemporary) legislative processes? Is the answer to this question helpful in assessing whether Professor Elhauge's normative baseline is testable?

Elhauge responds to the Landes and Posner model as follows: "[i]n the cases at issue in [Elhauge's] book, the statutory meaning is uncertain, and thus a particular resolution of that uncertainty was never bid for, nor resolved, by the original bargaining."[144] Is that an adequate response? Is it likely that the framers only intended to prolong the original meaning with respect to the narrow class of expressly articulated interest group bargains or more generally with respect to the application of policies embedded in federal statutes? Is the intuition that underlies the Landes and Posner thesis limited to interest group payoffs, or does it suggest something more general about the judicial incentives to vindicate the preferences of the enacting, rather than the contemporary, Congress?

As a purely descriptive matter, Elhauge's asserted baseline has an intuitive appeal. Past Congresses lack present political power. While Article III courts are substantially removed from present political processes, it would be naïve to suggest that they are therefore immune from present political influence. And yet, present political will rarely points in a single direction. As Professor Matthew Stevenson has observed, *Chevron* deference advantages the executive branch's interpretation of ambiguous statutory provisions, rather than present political preferences more generally.[145] In the event that the executive and legislative branches are controlled by the same party, this might not be problematical to Elhauge's thesis. What does Stevenson's analysis suggest, however, when the two political branches are controlled by different parties? Would an unelected judiciary with *Chevron* deference or an elected judiciary without *Chevron* deference be more likely to infuse ambiguous statutory provision with present *enactable* legislative preferences? Why?

Now consider Elhauge's preference-eliciting statutory default rule. Are the courts well equipped to gauge the conditions under which their decisions are likely to prompt subsequent corrective legislative action? If there is strong support for a pro-criminalizing measure, is the rule of lenity a good means of triggering that political force into legislation? Is

---

143. Impeachment has proved almost entirely ineffective as a means of disciplining judges based upon the substance of their decisions, and to punish judges with reduced benefits, Congress would have to punish the entire judiciary, not simply the judges with whom a majority disagrees.

144. ELHAUGE, *supra* note 77, at 53.

145. Matthew Stephenson, *Legislative Allocation of Delegated Power: Uncertainty, Risk, and the Choice Between Agencies and the Courts*, 119 HARV. L. REV. 1035, 1065–68 (2006).

there a risk that such a rule might lead to legislative over-compensation given that resulting legislative action will be motivated by a politically unpopular judicial ruling, for example releasing a convicted criminal for an egregious crime based upon the failure of the statute in question to cover the precise details of the underlying acts? Is there a risk that such rulings might instead motivate another form of political market failure, for example, a cascade effect favoring over-criminalization, or excessive relaxation of protections against civil liberties, than would be the case if such policies were announced in more dispassionate circumstances?

Consider also whether the rule of lenity is compelled by considerations disconnected from the desire to maximize present political satisfaction.[146] To what extent is the rule compelled by *ex post facto* clause,[147] which prevents retroactively criminalizing conduct? To what extent is it motivated by the Due Process Clause?[148] Might courts employ the rule of lenity in spite of their own preferences as a means of furthering these independent constitutional considerations, rather than to trigger a corrective legislative response? Professor Elhauge provides probabilistic estimates designed to show that such rulings potentially produce legislative overrides in a high percentage of cases.[149] Is this argument sufficient to support Elhauge's broader thesis? Are the data equally consistent with the claim that the rule of lenity is motivated by independent constitutional considerations?

Finally, consider the relationship between this statutory default rule and default constitutional doctrines, such as the dormant Commerce Clause doctrine. In this area, the federal courts announce rules that Congress has the constitutional authority to override with ordinary legislation. Congress rarely does so. Does this suggest that the Court has correctly identified enactable legislative preferences, or alternatively, does it suggest that these cases are not politically salient and that most of the time inertia will favor whatever results obtain in federal courts? Is there a way to test which of these accounts provides a better explanation for the results? Overall, do you find Elhauge's suggested default rules of statutory construction compelling? Why or why not?

---

146. *See, e.g.,* Keeler v. Superior Court, 470 P.2d 617 (Cal. 1970) (finding due process violation in prosecution of man charged with murder of fetus, since the statutory definition of murder did not include victims that were fetuses); 1970 Cal. Stat. ch. 1311 § 1 (codified at CAL. PENAL CODE § 187) (expanding the definition of murder to include the killing of a fetus).

147. U.S. CONST. art. I, § 10, cl. 1 ("No State shall ... pass any ... ex post facto law....").

148. In *Bouie v. City of Columbia,* 378 U.S. 347 (1964), the Supreme Court infused the ex post facto principle into the Fourteenth Amendment Due Process Clause to prevent the retroactive judicial relaxation of a prosecutorial standard. In *Marks v. United States,* 430 U.S. 188 (1977), the Supreme Court applied *Bouie* to reverse a conviction where the prosecutor retroactively lowered the standard for an obscenity prosecution based upon a rejection of a narrowest grounds plurality ruling established in *Memoirs v. Massachusetts,* 383 U.S. 413 (1966).

149. Einer Elhauge, *Preference–Eliciting Statutory Default Rules,* 102 COLUM. L. REV. 2162, 2176 (2002) (specifying conditions such that "a preference-eliciting default rule that only provoked ex post legislative correction 20% of the time would actually be 92% successful at provoking legislative reconsideration of all kinds").

C. OTHER CONNECTIONS

1. Hart and Sacks Revisited

Consider also the analytical connection between the theses advanced by Farber and Frickey, Eskridge, and Elhauge, on the one hand, and the Legal Process School, on the other. Which set of proposals is more consistent with the suggestions advanced by Hart and Sacks? Why? Do these scholars works provide a theoretical basis grounded in public choice for the normative prescriptions of the Legal Process School? Why or why not?

2. Coase Revisited[150]

Finally, let us return to the Coase theorem, introduced in chapter 1. Coase observed that in a world without transactions costs and perfect information, resources will flow to their most highly valued uses regardless of which party bears the property right. In effect, absent barriers to bargaining, those who would gain by reallocating the property right will be motivated to do so in an effort to secure their share of the resulting welfare-enhancing gains from trade. Conversely, however, when transactions costs are high, a legal regime that rests the property right in the wrong party (meaning the one who places a lower value on it) might entrench that rule by preventing such parties from transferring the resulting right to its more highly valued location. In some contexts, where there are effective means of bargaining, the clarity of rules might prove more important than whether they accurately reflect the affected parties' preferences, as parties can avoid disfavored rules through contract. In other contexts, however, those in which transactions costs are high, a clear but wrong rule can produce an ongoing social welfare loss.

In this context, consider whether the relevant institutions, Congress and the federal judiciary, are like actors in a low or high transactions cost world respecting the rules of statutory construction. Easterbrook and Shepsle suggest that the optimal interpretive rules are quite narrow, and that Congress must specifically delegate to the courts policy-making powers if it wishes to have the courts engage in "construction" beyond literal wording. Macey would afford courts flexibility provided that Congress makes plain (or open-explicit) its payoffs to interest groups. Otherwise, however, he would suppress such payoffs to the extent that they are in tension with the statute's larger stated objectives.

Whatever one might think of the wisdom or lack thereof of these various policy proposals, it is worth considering their Coasian implications. Even if we assume that a proposed alternative respecting statutory interpretation is normatively superior, if only a small number of courts adopt it, does the change make it more difficult for Congress to legislate against a known set of judicial practices? Consider for example the extent

---

150. Portions of the discussion that follows is adapted from STEARNS, *supra* note 78, at 719–23.

to which members of Congress who are dissatisfied with the present regime, which looks to a host of sources to inform statutory meaning (including what Judge Posner identifies as the "traditional props of statutory interpretation"[151]), can minimize the impact of such sources within the framework of existing rules. While Congress and the federal judiciary do not "bargain" over indicia of legislative intent, individual congressmen can include statements in the legislative record, either on the floor of the relevant house or in the relevant committee reports. If particular assertions included in the record are dubious, other members of Congress can include opposing statements. Does this suggest that a default rule permitting or excluding reliance on legislative history is more effective in lowering the relevant transactions costs? Why?

Consider also the more ambitious legislative proposals that would allow courts to update statutes without regard to the preferences of the enacting legislators. Are there comparable mechanisms that would allow members of Congress to insist that they do not want the statutes they enact updated? For instance, consider the unusual admonition in the legislative history to the Civil Rights Act of 1991:

> No statements other than the interpretive memorandum appearing at Vol. 137 Congressional Record § 15276 (daily ed. Oct. 25, 1991) shall be considered legislative history of, or relied upon in any way as legislative history in construing or applying, any provision of this Act that relates to Wards Cove—Business necessity/cumulation/alternative business practice.[152]

Does this example help in identifying the preferred default rule? From a Coasian perspective, which of the various sets of approaches to statutory interpretation offered in this chapter seems optimal? Why? Is your answer to this question consistent with the teachings of public choice? Is it consistent with the legal process school? Why? Can the two be reconciled? Why or why not?

III. STATUTORY INTERPRETATION CASES

A. STATUTORY INTERPRETATION AND INTEREST–GROUP DYNAMICS

Consider the following cases in light of the discussion in this chapter. We present two opinions from the first case, the panel opinion in *Mississippi Poultry Ass'n, Inc. v. Madigan*,[153] and the *en banc* opinion from the same case.[154] *Mississippi Poultry* raised the issue of how a judge should deal with a question of statutory interpretation in a situation where there was substantial reason to believe that interest-group politics were at work. Applying the *Chevron* doctrine, the Court in the case was required to

---

151. Posner, *supra* note 11, at 195.

152. Civil Rights Act of 1991, Pub. L. No. 102–166, Sec. 105(b), 105 Stat. 1071, 1075.

153. 992 F.2d 1359 (5th Cir. 1993).

154. 31 F.3d 293 (5th Cir. 1994).

determine whether the United States Department of Agriculture's regulation providing that foreign poultry inspection rules must be "at least
equal to" the American regime was a reasonable interpretation of federal
law requiring foreign poultry inspection regimes to be "the same as" those
under domestic law. The Mississippi Poultry Association challenged the
USDA's regulation, claiming that it was inconsistent with the plain
language of the statute, and that the phrase "the same as" required the
inspection regime to be identical to the domestic regime. In response to
this claim, the USDA argued that such an interpretation would be an
"absurd" interpretation of the law because it would bar poultry inspected
under rules superior to the American system. As we will see, answering
this challenge required the Court to determine what exactly the purpose
of the law is. We also present an excerpt from the Fifth Circuit's *en banc*
opinion in the case, which achieved the same result as the panel court but
did so based upon an alternative analysis. As you read these opinions,
consider how the various theorists we have described, such as Easterbrook, Posner, Macey, and Hart and Sachs, would go about interpreting
the statute in question.

The second case is *Powers v. Harris*.[155] In the opinions presented
below, the judges offer three different approaches to the appropriate
judicial role when reviewing the constitutionality of a statute that appears
to be the product of special-interest group influence. The majority opinion
of Chief Judge Tacha acknowledged that the law under review was plainly
the product of interest group influence, yet concluded that under the
Supreme Court's established jurisprudence, judges are constrained from
striking down such laws and that a legislative desire to create a regime of
intrastate protectionism and to enrich in-state special interest groups at
the expense of in-state consumers is a legitimate governmental purpose
that does not run afoul of the Constitution. In a separate concurrence,
Judge Tymkovich offered an alternative approach. While Judge Tymkovich generally appeared to share the majority's view about the motivations
and effects of the law, he would not go so far as to describe it as having *no*
purpose other than to enrich an influential interest group at the expense
of the public at large. Instead, he suggested that it is inappropriate for
judges to "call out" the interest-group influences that might have animated and preserved a given law over time, especially if the Court then goes
on to uphold the law as consistent with the Constitution. Judge Tymkovich's opinion might imply that when necessary, judges should engage in
the "noble lie" in which despite a potential interest group motivation
behind a statute, the court seeks to identify a legitimate governmental
purpose. And only if the court is unable to do so should it strike the law
down. As you read his opinion, consider why Judge Tymkovich might urge
this approach rather than adopting the one taken by the majority, which
provides the court a more active role in policing interest group bargains.
Finally, the case summarized the holding of the Sixth Circuit in *Craig-*

---

155.   379 F.3d 1208 (10th Cir. 2004).

miles v. Giles,[156] in which the statute in question and facts of the case are virtually identical to *Powers*. Contrary to the Tenth Circuit's holding in *Powers*, however, Judge Danny Boggs held that the statute advances no cognizable public purpose and thus struck down the prohibition as violating the rational basis test.

Mississippi Poultry Ass'n, Inc. v. Madigan[157]

Weiner, Circuit Judge.

This is an appeal from the district court's grant of summary judgment rejecting the Secretary of Agriculture's interpretation of a critical inspection standard contained in the Poultry Products Inspection Act (PPIA). Like Pertelote, we heed Chanticleer's clarion call to resolve the central issue of this most recent in a long and illustrious line of gallinaceous litigation: whether the interpretation of poultry importation standards by the Defendant–Appellant Secretary of Agriculture (the Secretary) is entitled to deference under *Chevron USA v. Natural Resources Defense Council*. Finding the language employed by Congress both clear and unambiguous, we conclude not only that we owe no such deference to the Secretary's interpretation, but also that his interpretation is unsupportable under the plain language of the statute.

At issue in this appeal is the interpretation of § 17(d) of the PPIA and the implementing regulation promulgated jointly by the Secretary and the Food Safety and Inspection Services (FSIS) (collectively, "the Agency"). Section 466(d) provides that all imported poultry products

> shall ... be subject to *the same* inspection, sanitary, quality, species verification, and the residue standards applied to products produced in the United States; and ... have been processed in facilities and under conditions that are *the same as* those under which similar products are processed in the United States.

The Agency promulgated a regulation interpreting the foregoing statutory language as requiring that "[t]he foreign inspection system must maintain a program to assure that the requirements referred to in this section, *at least equal to* those applicable to the Federal System in the United States, are being met."

During the required notice and comment period, the FSIS received thirty-one comments on the proposed rule, more than 75% of which opposed the "at least equal to" language. Nonetheless, in the preamble to the final rule, the FSIS stated that it did not believe that a literal application of the term "the same as" was the intent of Congress, although the FSIS acknowledged that "there are certain

---

156. 312 F.3d 220 (6th Cir. 2002).

157. 992 F.2d 1359 (5th Cir. 1993).

features that any system must have to be considered 'the same as' the American system."

Congress reacted to the effrontery of the "at least equal to" language in the regulation by enacting § 2507 of the Food, Agriculture, Conservation, and Trade Act of 1990 (1990 Farm Bill). In that section, Congress addressed the Agency's interpretation, stating that "the regulation promulgated by the Secretary of Agriculture, through the [FSIS], with respect to poultry products offered for importation into the United States does not reflect the intention of the Congress." It then "urge[s]" the Secretary, through the FSIS, to amend the regulation to reflect the true legislative intent. Further, in the House Conference Report accompanying the 1990 Farm Bill, Congress declares that although certain technical deviations from United States standards, such as dye color and materials used for knives, may be acceptable, the "fundamental inspection system, intensity, procedures, and food safety standards, ... should be *the same as* those prevalent in the United States for any such country to be certified for export to the United States." The Agency resisted Congress' expressed wishes, however, and the regulation remained unchanged.[158]

In addition, § 2507(b)(2) of the Farm Bill "urge[d] the secretary ... to repeal the October 30, 1989 regulation and promulgate a new regulation reflecting the intention of the Congress."

Two nonprofit trade associations representing domestic poultry producers, the Mississippi Poultry Association, Inc., and the National Broiler Council (the "Associations"), challenged USDA regulation as arbitrary and capricious under the Administrative Procedure Act. The Associations argued that the statutory language requiring that foreign poultry inspection regimes be "the same as" those in the United States meant that foreign poultry regimes must be *identical* to that in the United States, thus barring the USDA standard which only demanded that the foreign scheme be "at least equal to" the domestic scheme. The district court had agreed with the Associations' argument and held that USDA's regulation violated the plain language of the statute and that therefore no *Chevron* deference was owed.

Writing for the Fifth Circuit, Judge Weiner agreed that the statutory language was unambiguous and barred the USDA's regulation. After discussing various dictionary definitions of "the same," Weiner concluded that it was unambiguously meant "identical." Judge Weiner also pointed to Congress's rebuke in the 1990 Farm Bill as corroborating his interpretation:

In that Act, Congress stated emphatically and unequivocally that the Agency has misinterpreted the "same as" standard. The Agency's efforts to make much of Congress' failure actually to amend the statute is a red herring. There simply was no need for Congress to amend the statute; it already stated precisely what Congress wanted

---

158. *Id.* at 1360–62 (footnotes omitted).

it to state. Congress desired the "same as" language, and that is the language it placed in the statute. It is not required to respond to the Agency's disregard of unequivocally expressed congressional intent by amending a statute that is both clear and unambiguous on its face.

In response, the government argued that this literalist interpretation would produce absurd results, such as barring the importation of poultry products processed under superior inspection systems. Judge Weiner responded that this would be the case only if the purpose of the law was believed to be the advancement of health and safety goals. Weiner stated:

> Even if the Agency is correct, however, we cannot agree that the result is absurd. Had the Agency labeled the actions of Congress *protectionism*, we would not necessarily disagree. But, while that may be deemed in some quarters to be unwise or undesirable, it cannot be labeled "absurd" in the context of divining the *result intended by Congress*. The Agency's complaint, therefore, is one implicating the clear policy choice of Congress—a choice made, undoubtedly, in response to effective lobbying by domestic poultry producers. It is not within the purview of the Agency, however—or of the courts for that matter—to alter, frustrate, or subvert congressional policy. Our "third branch" role under the constitutional scheme of separation of powers is limited—as is the role of the Agency—to determining whether that policy is clearly expressed. We conclude that it is in this instance.
>
> . . . .
>
> This final argument exposes the true nature of this case as a dispute between the Executive and Legislative branches over the propriety of Congress' policy choices. Although the Agency makes a compelling argument that the "at least equal to" language is the better standard, it simply is not the court's role to judge which branch has proposed the preferable rule. Congress has made clear that "the same as" requires *identical* inspection and processing procedures, and the fact remains that it is Congress that has the right to make the choice, even if it proves to be the wrong choice.[159]

Weiner concluded:

> . . . After application of the traditional tools of statutory construction, we conclude that the plain language of § 466(d) of the PPIA clearly demonstrates that Congress intended "the same as" to be a synonym for "identical." Any lingering doubt as to Congress' intent is dispelled by its subsequent passage of the 1990 Farm Bill in which it expressly rejected the Agency's unilateral mutation of "the same as" standard to the "at least equal to" language in its regulation.

The Agency's attempts to conjure up ambiguity are unavailing. As we find under the first step of the *Chevron* methodology that the language of the statute is unambiguous, there is neither need nor

---

159. *Id.* at 1365, 1367–68 (footnotes omitted).

authority for us to proceed further. We therefore owe no deference to the Agency's interpretation and grant none.

For the foregoing reasons, the district court's summary judgment is AFFIRMED.[160]

Judge Reavley issued a dissenting opinion in which he argued that as a matter of plain language, the phrase "the same as" was ambiguous and that Congress had not actually chosen "identicality over equivalence."[161] Reavley explained:

> In describing the statutory structure in which Congress placed "same" in section 466(d), the majority ignores an argument that contravenes its decision. In 21 U.S.C. § 451, Congress bases the entire PPIA on its finding that "[u]nwholesome, adulterated, or misbranded poultry products" hurt people and destroy markets for poultry. . . . [T]he Secretary's interpretation of "same" to mean "equivalent" results in wholesomeness, absence-of-adulteration, and proper-marking qualities which *meet* or *better* the results of an identicality standard. In fact, the *only* result of substituting an identicality standard for the Secretary's equivalence standard is to erect a trade barrier, as the majority recognizes.
>
> While the majority claims to strictly adhere to the principle that words "take their purport from the setting in which they are used," it ignores the fact that section 466(d) appears in a poultry-inspection act which is expressly based upon Congress' exclusive finding that *unwholesome, adulterated, and misbranded* poultry must be eliminated to protect people and poultry markets. Where is the majority's explanation of how an identicality standard is consistent with section 451?
>
> My analysis of the extant structural arguments shows that the ones relied upon by the majority are inconclusive, and the section 451 argument indicates that Congress did not choose identicality. Thus, even under the majority's understanding of "make[s] some sense," the Secretary's interpretation of "same" is entitled to deference. . . .[162]

Judge Reavley also examined the legislative history and policy of the statute and concluded that it supported his argument that Congress had not foreclosed the USDA's regulation through the plain language of the statute. In particular, Reavley argues that the legislative history reveals no evidence that Congress intended this measure to serve as a form of backdoor trade protectionism for the benefit of the domestic poultry industry.

> Legislative history and policy together affirmatively establish that Congress has *not* "directly spoken to the precise question" of whether "same" means "identical" or "equivalent" in section 466(d). The *only*

---

160. *Id.* at 1368 (footnote omitted).

161. *Id.* (Reavley, J., dissenting).

162. *Id.* at 1374–75 (citations and footnotes omitted).

rational policy effect of choosing identicality over equivalence is that fewer foreign birds will enter the United States under an identicality standard than would enter under an equivalence standard. By definition, the Secretary's equivalence standard results in poultry that is *at least* as safe and correctly-packaged as that produced under federal standards. If Congress chose between identicality and equivalence in enacting section 466(d) as the majority holds, it must have done so because of the trade implications of an identicality standard. No one suggests another reason. But there is no record anywhere of any congressional consideration of the trade implications of an identicality standard before Congress passed section 466(d). This wholesale lack of attention to the *only* rational policy difference between identicality and equivalence establishes that Congress never chose between identicality and equivalence.

The majority evades this critical point with the truism that neither courts nor agencies can alter policy choices made by Congress. This truism does not alter the fact that we sit to determine *whether* Congress has in fact made a policy choice, regardless of the merit of that choice. I would decide this case according to the simple logic that if Congress wanted to erect a trade barrier, someone, somewhere, would have said something about why a barrier was justified, what it was supposed to accomplish, or how its effectiveness would be monitored.

Judge Reavley noted that from 1972 to 1984, the Secretary applied an equivalence standard to foreign poultry. Reavley explains:

While the 1985 Farm Bill was under consideration on the Senate floor, Senator Helms offered an amendment which substituted "the same as" for "at least equal to" in the portion of the 1985 Farm Bill that became section 466(d). Senator Helms explained that his amendment was "purely technical" and intended to "clarif[y] the provision to reflect the original intent of the provision as adopted by the committee in markup." Without any debate, further explanation, or recorded vote, the Senate adopted Senator Helms's amendment. A conference committee adopted the Senate's version of what became section 466(d) without any recorded consideration of the effect of Senator Helms's amendment.

Either Senator Helms meant to incorporate an identicality standard in section 466(d) by amending the statute to use "same," or he did not intend to incorporate an identicality standard. He did not affirmatively indicate that he desired an identicality standard or that he wanted to change the substance of the Agriculture Committee's equivalence standard. Nor did he mention the trade consequences of a substantive change. Instead, he said that he wanted the provision to reflect the Agriculture Committee's "original intent," which it expressed in an equivalence standard. These points indicate that Senator Helms did not subjectively desire an identicality standard.

But even if Senator Helms harbored this subjective intent, are we to attribute it to Congress *as an institution* when Senator Helms indicated that his amendment was of minimal importance, failed to call Congress' attention to the major trade consequences of such an interpretation of the amendment, and most importantly, *used equivocal language* to institute an identicality standard? The facts of this case provide no basis on which to hold that Congress "directly spoke[] to the precise question" of whether section 466(d) mandates identicality.

Finally, Judge Reavley addresses the 1990 "sense of Congress" resolution:

> Predictably, the majority turns to section 2507 of the 1990 Farm Bill, where Congress declares that its "sense" is to "urge" the Secretary to substitute "same" for the equivalence standard challenged in this case. But a careful study of section 2507 and its background teaches that section 2507 better explains why the Secretary clings to an equivalence standard rather than adopting the position that the majority would have him take.

> Section 2507 undeniably has the force of federal law. But by its own terms, this "law" only states a fact that the 101st Congress believes to be true and makes a suggestion to the Secretary. The plaintiffs do not contend that Congress established an identicality standard in section 2507; in their complaint, they only seek a declaratory judgment that 9 C.F.R. § 381.196 is inconsistent with the *PPIA*, which includes section 466(d) and does not include section 2507.

> The plaintiffs contend that the intent of the 101st Congress as expressed in the 1990 Farm Bill is relevant to determine what the intent of the 99th Congress was in drafting the 1985 Farm Bill. I am aware of no case where any court has held that subsequent legislative history is at all relevant to cases like this one, where, rather than determine what a statute means, we must determine "whether Congress has directly spoken to the precise question at issue." Even the most unambiguous intent in 1990 cannot establish the intent of a different group of people five years earlier. Section 2507 has no bearing on our present inquiry. ...

Nowhere in section 2507 or its history does Congress suggest that the Secretary adopt an identicality standard, even though the Secretary publicly explained in 1989 that he understood his choices to be between identicality and equivalence. Instead of helping the Secretary interpret "same," Section 2507 and its history simply "urge" the Secretary to adopt a "same" standard, and to ignore technical deviations from this standard. But the Secretary understood his equivalence standard to operate just like a "same" standard that permits various technical deviations. If Congress demands something different, it has yet to say so.[163]

Judge Reavley concluded his dissent by stating:

> The decision of what "same" means should remain with the Secretary until Congress says otherwise, and no one contends that the Secretary's choice has an unreasonable effect. I would reverse the district court's decision and render judgment for the Secretary.[164]

The Fifth Circuit reheard *Mississippi Poultry en banc*. While the *en banc* decision vacated the panel decision, in this case it achieved the same result. More notably, while Judge Weiner, who authored both the majority panel decision and the majority decision for the *en banc* court, applied different reasoning. The Court reiterated the panel decision's argument concerning Congress's power to enact a protectionist measure, but added a second rationale: Congress demanded identicality to reduce the administrative costs associated with reviewing different inspection regimes.

Mississippi Poultry Ass'n v. Madigan (En Banc)[165]

Weiner, Circuit Judge:

> Under the PPIA, Congress devised a two-track system for regulating domestic poultry production: Domestic producers who wish to sell products *inter* state must comply with the *federal* standards embodied in the federal regulatory program; domestic producers who wish to sell products only *intra* state may do so by complying with any *state* regulatory program with standards "at least equal to" the federal program. Reduced to the simplest terms, Congress thus subjected all domestic poultry production sold in *inter*state commerce to a single, federal program with uniform standards.
>
> Congress also addressed the issue of foreign standards. Under § 17(d) of the PPIA, Congress directed the Secretary to require imported poultry products to be "subject to *the same* ... standards applied to products produced in the United States." Were that congressional mandate to be enforced strictly, all poultry sold in *inter* state commerce—whether produced in this country or anywhere else in the world—would be inspected pursuant to the uniform federal standards. Despite this congressional command, however, the Secretary promulgated the challenged regulation allowing foreign—but not domestic—poultry products to be imported and sold in interstate commerce, even though such poultry is inspected under *different* standards, as long as the foreign standards are determined by the Secretary to be "at least equal to" the federal standards. Given the plain language and structure of the PPIA, we conclude that this regulation cannot withstand the instant challenge. Because the phrase "at least equal to," as used in the PPIA, inescapably infers the

---

163. *Id.* at 1377–80 (citations and footnotes omitted).

164. *Id.* at 1380.

165. 31 F.3d 293 (5th Cir. 1994).

existence of a *difference*—and the phrase "the same as," as used in the PPIA, eschews any possibility of more than a technical or de minimis difference, neither phrase can ever be synonymous with the other in the PPIA.

. . . In 1957 Congress enacted the PPIA, thereby establishing a comprehensive federal program for the regulation of poultry products. The PPIA was enacted to serve a two-fold purpose: To protect consumers from misbranded, unwholesome, or adulterated products, and to protect the domestic poultry market from unfair competition.

Typically, the safety and unfair competition goals are closely related. Of significance here, however, was Congress' concern with more than differences in *product* when it addressed unfair competition. Specifically, Congress also recognized that differences in *regulation* could also cause unfair competition. Indeed, in its original form, § 2 of the PPIA justified regulation of poultry sold in "large centers of population" on the belief that uninspected poultry products—regardless of whether such products were unsafe—adversely affected the national market for inspected poultry products.[166]

Weiner explained that in 1968 Congress established a two-tier system of poultry inspection. This regime applied the federal inspection standards to poultry sold in interstate commerce and "large centers of population" affecting interstate commerce. For poultry traveling only in intrastate commerce, however, Congress permitted the relevant state inspection regime to govern provided that regime was "at least equal to" the federal regulatory regime. Judge Weiner observed that against this background of jockeying between state and federal inspection regimes loomed a separate question concerning the applicable regulatory standards for imported foreign poultry. Weiner explained:

The 1968 amendments did not alter the standards for imported poultry products. The House Report accompanying these amendments candidly states the then-extant trade considerations underlying this omission:

The committee concluded that more stringent regulation of imports, when not required might result in the enactment of measures abroad which could hamper the exportation of U.S. slaughtered poultry and poultry products, the volume of which far exceeds the imports.[167]

This hybrid system required the USDA to oversee two distinct poultry inspection programs: the federal program for interstate sales and state programs for intrastate sales that were required to be "at least equal to" the federal program. In 1985 Congress passed the law requiring imported poultry to be subject to "the same" inspection standards as poultry produced and processed in the United States. Judge Weiner continued:

---

166. *Id.* at 295–96 (footnotes omitted).

167. *Id.* at 296.

Despite Congress' command to hold foreign producers of poultry destined for interstate commerce in this country accountable to "the same" standards as domestic producers of poultry destined for that market, in 1989 the Secretary and the Food Safety and Inspection Service ("FSIS") (collectively, the "Secretary") promulgated the challenged regulation, thereby retaining the subjective "at least equal to" standard. Congress reacted to that effrontery the following year by enacting § 2507 of the Food, Agriculture, Conservation, and Trade Act of 1990 ("1990 Farm Bill"). In that section, Congress addressed the Secretary's interpretation, stating that "the regulation promulgated by the Secretary of Agriculture, through the [FSIS], with respect to poultry products offered for importation into the United States *does not reflect* the intention of the Congress." It then "urge[d]" the Secretary, through the FSIS, to amend the regulation to reflect the true legislative intent. The Secretary ignored Congress' entreaty, however, and allowed the regulation to remain unchanged.[168]

Judge Weiner reiterated, as in his vacated panel opinion, that the plain language of "the same as" prohibited the USDA's proffered reading as "at least equal to."

The structure of the PPIA is plain: Domestic poultry producers who comply with state inspection programs that are "at least equal to" the standards in the federal program may sell their products, but only *intra* state. If a domestic poultry producer wishes to sell his product *inter* state, he must comply with "the same" standards that are embodied in the federal program.

The history of the PPIA regarding imports is likewise plain. When the Secretary in 1972 adopted (and in 1989 readopted) standards for imported poultry he had two choices: Either to require imported poultry to comply with the standards applied to all poultry sold in interstate commerce—i.e., the federal standards—or to adopt an "at least equal to" standard as used for poultry sold in *intra* state commerce under state programs. To the surprise and dismay of Congress and the domestic poultry industry, the Secretary followed the *intra* state, state-standards approach by promulgating the "at least equal to" standard.

Not to be outdone, Congress in 1985 rejected the "at least equal to" approach and explicitly provided that imported poultry must meet "the same ... standards applied to products produced in the United States." The language of the statute is critical here because the *only* standards applicable to domestic poultry products sold in interstate commerce are the federal standards that make up the federal program: There are no parallel or alternative state programs or state

168. *Id.* at 297–98 (footnotes omitted).

standards applicable to poultry sold interstate. As all imported poultry is free to be sold in interstate commerce, only one, inescapable conclusion can be reached: When Congress stated "the same" standards it meant for imported poultry to be held to those federal program standards.

The referent for the phrase "the same" is thus unmistakably clear. It is also clear that there would be no way for imported poultry sold interstate and domestic poultry sold interstate to be treated "the same" under the PPIA's structure if imported poultry were allowed to be imported under the "at least equal to" standard. Under such an approach, imported poultry, which the Secretary would attempt to regulate under myriad programs that are "at least equal to" the federal program, could move in interstate commerce, whereas domestic poultry that is likewise regulated under "at least equal to" programs could move only in *intra* state commerce. In short, by adopting the "at least equal to" standard, the Secretary is or could be treating imported and domestic interstate poultry in a substantially different manner. Such diverse treatment can never properly be viewed as applying to imported poultry "the same ... standards [as are] applied to products produced in the United States." Accordingly, when § 17(d) is read in light of the structure of the PPIA as a whole, the unavoidable conclusion is that the words "the same" as used in § 17(d) cannot be stretched to include "at least equal to."[169]

Judge Weiner maintained that the 1990 Farm Bill confirmed his reading that with respect to foreign poultry imports, the 1989 "same as" requirement demanded identicality rather than equivalency:

[The [1990 Farm Bill was enacted,] not surprisingly, within one year following the Secretary's promulgation of the "at least equal to" regulation. In § 2507 of the 1990 Farm Bill Congress first reiterated the facts of this inter-branch dispute: In 1985 Congress had enacted a statute requiring imported poultry to meet "the same" standards as domestic interstate poultry, and in 1989 the Secretary had promulgated a regulation imposing merely "at least equal to" standards. Congress then stated in plain, direct, and unequivocal language that the Secretary's regulation "does not reflect the intention of the Congress."

Congress' store of "institutional knowledge" is important. Accordingly, courts have long held that subsequent legislation is relevant to ascertaining the intent of Congress. Although subsequent legislation has been characterized as being anything from of "great weight" or having "persuasive value," to being of "little assistance" to the interpretative process, resolution of the proper weight to be accorded such legislation depends on the facts of each case. Here, given: 1) the substantial overlap in membership between the Congress that passed the 1985 Farm Bill and the Congress that passed

---

169. *Id.* at 301–02 (footnotes omitted).

§ 2507;[170] 2) the close temporal proximity between the passage of the 1985 Farm Bill and of § 2507; 3) the unmistakable specificity and directness with which § 2507 addressed the Secretary's interpretation; and 4) the alacrity with which Congress through § 2507 responded to the Secretary's interpretation, we find § 2507 to be highly persuasive, albeit not per se binding. Further, given the structure and history of the PPIA discussed earlier, we also conclude that § 2507 merely states the obvious: That the Secretary's adoption of the "at least equal to" standard "does not reflect" the intent of Congress as plainly expressed in § 17(d) of the PPIA.[171]

Finally, Judge Weiner rejected what he regarded as the USDA's attempt to rewrite the statute to bring about a more desirable policy:

> The Secretary strenuously argues that an "at least equal to" standard protects American consumers from "unhealthful, unwholesome, or adulterated" products while allowing foreign poultry products to be imported at reasonable costs. In contrast, the Secretary asserts that imposition of "the same" standards with accompanying "jot for jot" identicality would raise these costs to a prohibitive, protectionist level without any concomitant increase in the safety and quality of the imported product. According to the Secretary, holding foreign poultry producers to "the same" standards even contains the seed of an absurdity: That such a practice would prohibit the importation of poultry products produced under *superior* foreign standards!

> Even though there is superficial appeal to some of the Secretary's policy arguments, they are overdrawn. As a preliminary matter, we observe that although the Secretary places much weight on his prohibiting-superior-standards-is-absurd argument, he has failed to cite even one instance in which a foreign country actually uses a superior standard. All we have been offered is hypotheticals. As the Secretary must certify the production and inspection practices in foreign countries—and hence is presumably familiar with such practices—we find this omission strange.

> . . . .

> As a parting comment, we also observe that the Secretary's arguments fail to account for the various legitimate reasons why Congress might want to hold imported poultry to the federal standards. For example, requiring such congruity between foreign and federal standards means that *all* poultry—domestic and foreign—sold *inter* state must be produced and inspected according to *one* set of rules. Accordingly, such an approach maintains uniformity in the national market, thereby presumably engendering the lowered infor-

---

170. Four hundred and thirty-five members of the Congress that passed § 2507 [in 1990] were members of the Congress that added 'the same' language to § 17(d) as part of the 1985 Farm Bill.

171. *Id.* at 302–03 (footnotes omitted).

mation costs and enhanced consumer confidence commonly associated with such uniformity.

In addition, adopting such an approach offers the traditional advantage associated with "bright line" rules—agency personnel would no longer be required to make subjective, fact-specific judgments as to whether one country's standards are somehow in globo "at least equal to" federal standards. If we operate from the uncontested assumption that the Secretary has devised a federal program that ensures safety, then lessening of subjectivity here also reduces the risk that unsafe products might be imported—i.e., that agency personnel might err, even once, in concluding that a foreign program which differs substantially from our own nevertheless offers safety standards "at least equal to" the federal program.

Finally, we note that—as a matter of policy—there would be little reason for the Secretary to single out domestic "state program" poultry producers, who must likewise meet an "at least equal to" standard to sell intrastate, and prevent them from entering the interstate market. Of course, there is a simple rebuttal to this argument: The statute prevents such producers from selling their products interstate. And that rebuttal applies equally to the Secretary's impassioned plea for the "at least equal to" standard for foreign poultry producers: The statute flatly forbids it! These points place the foregoing policy discussion in proper perspective. Although such a discussion is helpful to our understanding of the PPIA and § 17(d)—and is necessary as a check for any "absurdities"—these policy concerns cannot control the disposition of this case. Policy choices are for Congress—not the courts. And here Congress has chosen—twice.[172]

Judge Weiner concluded:

For the foregoing reasons, the district court's summary judgment holding that the Secretary's 1989 regulation implementing § 17(d) was arbitrary and capricious and thus invalid is

AFFIRMED.[173]

Judge Higginbotham issued a dissenting opinion in which he determined that the statute was ambiguous and that the USDA's interpretation, and promulgated regulation, was reasonable. Even though the *en banc* opinion downplayed the protectionism rationale for insisting upon an identicality standard, Judge Higginbotham argued that protectionism was a forseeable consequence of such a reading and that absent explicit congressional guidance, the court should not lightly infer an intent to produce this result. Higginbotham explained:

This case is simple. Congress has insisted that foreign poultry meet the "same" standards as domestic poultry. It did so in a statute

---

172. *Id.* at 308–10 (footnotes omitted).

173. *Id.* at 310.

addressed to "unwholesome, adulterated or misbranded poultry prod-ucts." Our court today holds that under this statute, the Department of Agriculture must forbid the importation of all foreign poultry produced by quality standards higher and lower than those in the United States. It reads "same" standards to mean identical processes and identical plants. Make no mistake about it: as the majority interprets the statute, virtually all importation of poultry is illegal. The majority insists on this literalism despite the common sense reading of "same" in the context of standards of quality to mean the same minimum level of wholesomeness, that is, "at least equal to." This absurdity is a lion in the street for the majority, and it never deals with it. It does not because it cannot. The Department of Agriculture has implemented the statute by regulations that allow importation of poultry produced by standards "at least equal to" our own. Dictionaries of the English language permit not "different in relevant essentials," or "equivalent" as meanings of the word "same." This reference to dictionary meanings is quite different from a game-like use of "modify." Rather, these are meanings as old as the republic. The choice of meanings is found in context.

Higginbotham considered the political implications of the majority ruling:

> Deny, deny, explain, explain—the inescapable reality is that un-der the majority's view, we must tell France and Israel, for example, that they may not import poultry into the United States because their standards for cleanliness and wholesomeness are higher or lower than those in the United States. The standards are not, and it is doubtful if they could be, implemented in identical "facilities" and under identi-cal "conditions," as the majority insists they must be. Further, by the majority opinion, we allow Canada and Mexico [under the North American Free Trade Agreement (NAFTA)] to meet some undefined, but lesser standard. First the panel opinion, and now the en banc opinion, hints at a latent congressional purpose of trade protection-ism. It is indeed a curious blend of protectionism that would protect American poultry interests from the threat of foreign poultry that is superior because it is healthier for the consumer. This insistence that a foreign producer lower its standards of health to meet the statutory command of sameness may be a form of trade protectionism, but it remains an absurdity.[174]

Judge Higginbotham then argued that the statutory language does not recognize the majority's distinction between state and federal stan-dards. The only policy purpose expressly recognized in the legislative history was the protection of consumers from unsafe poultry products. In contrast, there was no mention in the legislative history of a protectionist purpose.

---

174. *Id.* at 310–11 (Higginbotham, J., dissenting) (footnotes omitted).

If Senator Helms in submitting his amendment or Congress in adopting it intended to embed a protectionist measure in a bill dedicated to health issues, neither gave any sign or signal.

. . . .

The majority's second argument, as I understand it, is that by using alternative processes to ensure the quality of poultry, a foreign nation might gain some strategic advantage. That the statute does not say same processes, but same standards, does not slow the majority. Congress might indeed be unhappy if it unwittingly deprived domestic poultry producers of processes for ensuring the quality of chickens that were less expensive than, and as effective as, those required by federal law. If foreign poultry producers adopted these processes of poultry production, and thereby increased their sales in the United States, Congress might well respond. It could do so by banning the less expensive foreign poultry, the approach the majority opinion takes, or by allowing American poultry producers to adopt the foreign process, the approach I myself would think preferable. It is crucial to point out, however, that Congress has not as of yet done either. The majority has simply grafted onto the PPIA its own policy concern, reading it into the word "same," and never, I repeat, confronting the question—same as what?[175]

Judge Higginbotham concluded his dissent by questioning the majority's use of subsequent legislative enactments:

The majority relies on legislation passed subsequent to the PPIA to support an identicality standard. Congress responded to the Secretary's regulation in section 2507 of the Food, Agriculture, Conservation, and Trade Act of 1990 by stating that the regulation "does not reflect the intention of Congress" and "urg[ing] the Secretary . . . to repeal the October 30, 1989 regulation and promulgate a new regulation reflecting the intention of Congress." Congress did not purport to amend the PPIA nor did it make a finding as to its intentions at the time it passed the PPIA. The Secretary did not change the regulation in response to Congress' admonition.

The Supreme Court has made clear how to approach this legislation. "If th[e] language [of the 1990 Act] is to be controlling upon us, it must be either (1) an authoritative interpretation of what the [1985] statute meant, or (2) an authoritative expression of what the [1990] Congress intended. It cannot, of course, be the former, since it is the function of the courts and not the Legislature . . . to say what an enacted statute means." Nor can it be the latter because the 1990 Act made no claim to enact a new or to alter an old law. The language of the Act is clear: Congress urged the Secretary of Agriculture to repeal the October 30, 1989 regulation and to promulgate a new one.

---

175. *Id.* at 313–14 (footnotes omitted).

If, as I believe, the language of the PPIA permitted the Secretary's interpretation, Congress's later urging did not alter that fact.[176]

DISCUSSION QUESTIONS

1. How would the various commentators we have interpreted the statute at issue here? Consider the following possibilities. Judge Easterbrook would follow the majority panel opinion and read the statute as having a protectionist purpose. On this reading, "same" means "identical." Judge Posner would instead agree with the reasoning of the *en banc* majority, acknowledging the dual purposes of the law (consumer protection and economic protectionism) while also recognizing that Congress could elect a bright-line rule for administrative convenience. It is less clear whether Posner would find the law to be ambiguous and thus subject to administrative interpretation. Professor Macey would agree with the holding of the dissent from the *en banc* opinion. He would stress that if Congress had a protectionist intent, that intent was "hidden-implicit." The court therefore should enforce law's stated purpose of consumer protection, or perhaps the USDA interpretation, which advances the public interest. Finally, Hart and Sachs, and perhaps those scholars who consider themselves heir to the Legal Process tradition, would side with the dissenting opinion, reading the law to advance the public interest goals of consumer welfare and to prevent "unfair" competition (rather than competition *per se*). Can any of these approaches be said to be "correct"?

2. In the panel opinion, Judge Weiner observes that the definition of "same" as "identical" is not absurd if the judge recognizes that one purpose of the law was protectionism. Writing in dissent, Judge Reavley, however, claims that this protectionist purpose is nowhere expressly stated. To what extent should a Court try to infer implicit interest-group purposes of legislation when the legislation is not explicit on the point?

3. Following the initial promulgation of the USDA's regulation, Congress announced a "Sense of Congress" resolution that criticized the USDA's interpretation. Congress did not, however, amend the statute or take other corrective action. The *en banc* opinion notes that the Congress that enacted the "Sense of Congress" resolution was virtually identical to the composition of Congress that enacted the initial legislation (with 435 members of the 1985 Congress who supported the original legislation also supporting the "Sense of Congress" resolution as active members of both houses in 1990). What relevance, if any, should a subsequent statement of Congress have in interpreting legislation? Should the degree of continuity in the composition of the Congress make a difference?

4. What weight might Easterbrook attach to the "sense of Congress" resolution? How does the question relate to his analysis of the hypothetical failure to amend the Communications Act after a court, apparently contrary to congressional intent, held it inapplicable to cable[177]? From a public choice perspective, if it is the case that the poultry industry sought protectionism through this legislation, would it be easier to overturn the USDA's definition

---

176. *Id.* at 314 (footnotes omitted).

177. *See supra* pp. 269–70.

of "same" as meaning "at least equal" or "identical"? Should that make a difference in how the court interprets the statute?

5. In the majority panel opinion, Judge Weiner justifies his reading of the law by emphasizing its implicit protectionist purposes. In his *en banc* opinion reaching the same result, however, he instead emphasizes a claimed public interest justification for the law, namely that it will serve to minimize administrative costs in monitoring different poultry inspection regimes. Why might Weiner, on further consideration, have based his opinion on a public interest justification for the law? Might this have been necessary to forge a majority coalition on the *en banc* court, but not for a majority panel decision? If so, why might that difference in bargaining dynamics have arisen?

B. CONSTITUTIONAL JUDICIAL REVIEW OF INTEREST–GROUP LEGISLATION

The next case, *Powers v. Harris*,[178] from the United States Court of Appeals for the Tenth Circuit, considers the constitutional implications of interest-group theory for constitutional judicial review of interest-group driven legislation. The various opinions in *Harris* also consider a related case from the United States Court of Appeals for the Sixth Circuit, *Craigmiles v. Giles*.[179]

The *Harris* opinions present three different approaches to the question of the appropriate judicial role when reviewing a statute that appears to be the product of special-interest group influence. Writing for a majority, Chief Judge Tacha acknowledges that the enacted statute is a protectionist measure. He concludes, however, that under established Supreme Court case law, a legislative scheme that benefits an in-state interest group at a cost imposed upon in-state consumers does not violate the Constitution.

While Judge Tymkovich, writing in concurrence, generally shares the majority's reading of the statute as motivated by interest group pressures, he would not go so far as to describe it as having *no* other purpose than to pay off an influential interest group at the expense of consumers. Instead, he suggests that it is inappropriate for judges to "call out" the interest group influence underlying the law especially when the court proceeds to sustain the statute against a constitutional challenge. On one reading, Judge Tymkovich encourages judges to engage in the noble lie that interest group driven laws nonetheless further a legitimate governmental purpose. Alternatively, Tymkovich's opinion might be construed to imply that if the court can locate no such legitimate purpose, it should then proceed to strike down the challenged law. As you read his opinion, consider why Tymkovich might urge this choice rather than allowing a frank acknowledgement of an interest group payoff while still sustaining the challenged law.

---

178. 379 F.3d 1208 (10th Cir. 2004).

179. 312 F.3d 220 (6th Cir. 2002).

Finally, the *Powers* majority distinguished its holding from that of the Sixth Circuit in *Craigmiles v. Giles*,[180] a case presenting nearly identical facts. In contrast with *Harris*, however, Judge Danny Boggs, writing for the *Craigmiles* Court, struck down the challenged law as violating rational basis scrutiny.

Powers v. Harris dealt with an Oklahoma law, similar to those in other states, demanding that funeral caskets only be sold by licensed funeral directors operating a funeral home. This regulation did not apply to other related merchandise, including urns, grave markers, and monuments. The prohibition also did not apply to "pre-need" sales, meaning caskets sold in connection with funeral arrangements prior to a person's death, but only to "time-of-need" sales.

The Oklahoma State Board of Embalmers and Funeral Directors, which was empowered to enforce the legislation, limited its application to intrastate casket sales. As a result, an unlicensed Oklahoman could sell a time-of-need casket to a customer *outside* Oklahoma; an unlicensed *non-Oklahoma* salesman could sell a time-of-need casket in Oklahoma; and an unlicensed person could sell a *pre-need* casket within Oklahoma. As a result, the requirement that a salesperson possess both a funeral director's license and operate out of a licensed funeral home only applied to the intrastate sale of time-of-need caskets between an Oklahoma seller and an Oklahoma consumer.

Obtaining a funeral director's license was both time consuming and expensive, and most of the relevant training did not relate to casket sales. Applicants were required to complete sixty credit hours of specified undergraduate training, a one-year apprenticeship that included embalming no fewer than twenty-five bodies, and to pass both a subject-matter and an Oklahoma law exam. Finally, businesses seeking to be licensed funeral homes were required to have a fixed physical location, a preparation room that met embalming requirements, a merchandise room with an inventory of no fewer than five caskets, and suitable areas for public viewing of human remains.

The plaintiff in the case was an Oklahoma corporation that sought to sell funeral merchandise, including caskets, over the Internet. Judge Tacha, writing for the *Harris* majority, held that the law was not unconstitutional.[181] Tacha explained:

> Hornbook constitutional law provides that if Oklahoma wants to limit the sale of caskets to licensed funeral directors, the Equal Protection Clause does not forbid it. . . .
>
>   . . . .
>
> In *United States v. Carolene Products Co.*, the Court held, pursuant to rational basis review, that when legislative judgment is called into question on equal protection grounds and the issue is debatable,

---

180.   312 F.3d 220 (6th Cir. 2002).

181.   379 F.3d 1208 (10th Cir. 2004).

the decision of the legislature must be upheld if "any state of facts either known or which could reasonably be assumed affords support for it." Second-guessing by a court is not allowed.

Further, rational-basis review does not give courts the option to speculate as to whether some other scheme could have better regulated the evils in question. In fact, we will not strike down a law as irrational simply because it may not succeed in bringing about the result it seeks to accomplish, or because the statute's classifications lack razor-sharp precision. Nor can we overturn a statute on the basis that no empirical evidence supports the assumptions underlying the legislative choice.

Finally, "because we never require a legislature to articulate its reasons for enacting a statute, it is entirely irrelevant for constitutional purposes whether the conceived reason for the challenged distinction actually motivated the legislature." "[T]hose attacking the rationality of the legislative classification have the burden 'to negative every conceivable basis which might support it[.]' " As such, we are not bound by the parties' arguments as to what legitimate state interests the statute seeks to further. In fact, "this Court is *obligated* to seek out other conceivable reasons for validating [a state statute.]" Indeed, that the purpose the court relies on to uphold a state statute "was not the reason provided by [the state] is irrelevant to an equal protection inquiry."

These admonitions are more than legal catchphrases dutifully recited each time we confront an equal protection challenge to state regulation—they make sense. First, in practical terms, we would paralyze state governments if we undertook a probing review of each of their actions, constantly asking them to "try again." Second, even if we assumed such an exalted role, it would be nothing more than substituting our view of the public good or the general welfare for that chosen by the states. As a creature of politics, the definition of the public good changes with the political winds. There simply is no constitutional or Platonic form against which we can (or could) judge the wisdom of economic regulation. Third, these admonitions ring especially true when we are reviewing the regulatory actions of states, who, in our federal system, merit great respect as separate sovereigns.

Thus, we are obliged to consider every plausible legitimate state interest that might support the [Funeral Service Licensing Act] FSLA—not just the consumer-protection interest forwarded by the parties. Hence, we consider whether protecting the intrastate funeral home industry, absent a violation of a specific constitutional provision or a valid federal statute, constitutes a legitimate state interest. If it does, there can be little doubt that the FSLA's regulatory scheme is rationally related to that goal.[182]

---

182. *Id.* at 1211, 1216–18 (citations and footnotes omitted).

After reviewing various justifications offered for the law, the court turned to the key proffered justification, which was whether the desire to transfer wealth from in-state consumers to an in-state interest group (in this case, licensed funeral home directors) was a legitimate state interest. Judge Tacha held that it was:

> Implicit in Plaintiffs' argument is the contention that intrastate economic protectionism, even without violating a specific constitutional provision or a valid federal statute, is an illegitimate state interest. Indeed, Plaintiffs describe Oklahoma's licensure scheme as "a classic piece of special interest legislation designed to extract monopoly rents from consumers' pockets and funnel them into the coffers of a small but politically influential group of businesspeople—namely, Oklahoma funeral directors." Amici are not so coy. In their view, Oklahoma's licensure scheme "is simply ... protectionist legislation[,]" and "[u]nder the Constitution, ... economic protectionism is not a legitimate state interest."[183]

The court then considered whether the Supreme Court's dormant Commerce Clause opinion, *H.P. Hood & Sons*, relied upon by the *Craigmiles* court, provided the basis for relief on the case facts:

> ... The *Craigmiles* court cites to the following passage from *H.P. Hood & Sons*, which is clearly limited to the regulation of *interstate* commerce, to support its conclusion that *intrastate* economic protectionism is an illegitimate state interest:
>
>> This principle that our economic unit is the Nation, which alone has the gamut of powers necessary to control of the economy, including the vital power of erecting customs barriers against foreign competition, has as its corollary that the states are not separable economic units....
>
> When read in context, *H.P. Hood & Sons*'s admonition is plainly directed at state regulation that shelters its economy from the larger national economy, i.e., violations of the "dormant" Commerce Clause.
>
> ... As such, these passages do not support the contention espoused in *Craigmiles* ... that intrastate economic protectionism, absent a violation of a specific federal statutory or constitutional provision, represents an illegitimate state interest. Our country's constitutionally enshrined policy favoring a national marketplace is simply irrelevant as to whether a state may legitimately protect one intrastate industry as against another when the challenge to the statute is purely one of equal protection....
>
> In contrast, the Supreme Court has consistently held that protecting or favoring one particular intrastate industry, absent a specific federal constitutional or statutory violation, is a legitimate state interest....
>
> ....

---

183. *Id.* at 1218 (citations omitted).

We also note, in passing, that while baseball may be the national pastime of the citizenry, dishing out special economic benefits to certain in-state industries remains the favored pastime of state and local governments. While this case does not directly challenge the ability of states to provide business-specific economic incentives, adopting a rule against the legitimacy of intrastate economic protectionism and applying it in a principled manner would have wide-ranging consequences. Thus, besides the threat to all licensed professions such as doctors, teachers, accountants, plumbers, electricians, and lawyers, *see, e.g.*, Oklahoma Statutes, title 59 (listing over fifty licensed professions), every piece of legislation in six states aiming to protect or favor one industry or business over another in the hopes of luring jobs to that state would be in danger. While the creation of such a libertarian paradise may be a worthy goal, Plaintiffs must turn to the Oklahoma electorate for its institution, not us.[184]

Judge Tacha added:

... [We] part company with the Sixth Circuit's *Craigmiles* decision, which struck a nearly identical Tennessee statute as violating the Equal Protection Clause and substantive due process. Our disagreement can be reduced to three points. First, as noted by the District Court, *Craigmiles*'s analysis focused heavily on the court's perception of the actual motives of the Tennessee legislature. "The state could argue that the Act as a whole ... actually provides some legitimate protection for consumers from casket retailers. The history of the legislation, however, reveals a different story...." The Supreme Court has foreclosed such an inquiry. Second, the *Craigmiles* court held that "protecting a discrete interest group from economic competition is not a legitimate governmental purpose." As discussed above, we find this conclusion unsupportable. Third, in focusing on the actual motivation of the state legislature and the state's proffered justifications for the law, the *Craigmiles* court relied heavily on *Cleburne v. Cleburne Living Center, Inc.* We find this emphasis misplaced....

Despite the hue and cry from all sides, no majority of the Court has stated that the rational-basis review found in *Cleburne* and *Romer v. Evans* differs from the traditional variety applied above. Perhaps, as Justice O'Connor suggests, *Cleburne* and *Romer* represent the embryonic stages of a new category of equal protection review. But "[e]ven if we were to read *Cleburne* to require that laws discriminating against historically unpopular groups meet an exacting rational-basis standard," which we do not, "we do not believe the class in which [plaintiffs] assert they are a member merits such scrutiny."

On the other hand, *Romer* and *Cleburne* may not signal the birth of a new category of equal protection review. Perhaps, after considering all other conceivable purposes, the *Romer* and *Cleburne* Courts

184. *Id.* at 1219–22 (citations and footnotes omitted).

found that "a bare ... desire to harm a politically unpopular group," constituted the only conceivable state interest in those cases. Under this reading, *Cleburne* would also not apply here because we have conceived of a legitimate state interest other than a "bare desire to harm" non-licensed, time-of-need, retail, casket salespersons.

Finally, perhaps *Cleburne* and *Romer* are merely exceptions to traditional rational basis review fashioned by the Court to correct perceived inequities unique to those cases. If so, the Court has "fail[ed] to articulate [when this exception applies, thus] provid[ing] no principled foundation for determining when more searching inquiry is to be invoked." Regardless, the Court itself has never applied *Cleburne*-style rational-basis review to economic issues. Following the Court's lead, neither will we. Thus, we need not decide how *Cleburne* alters, if at all, traditional rational-basis review because, even under a modified rational basis test, the outcome here would be unchanged.[185]

Judge Tacha concluded:

We do not doubt that the FSLA "may exact a needless, wasteful requirement in many cases. But it is for the legislature, not the courts, to balance the advantages and disadvantages of the [FSLA's] requirement[s]." Under our system of government, Plaintiffs " 'must resort to the polls, not to the courts' " for protection against the FSLA's perceived abuses.

As Winston Churchill eloquently stated: "[D]emocracy is the worst form of government except for all those other forms that have been tried." Perhaps the facts here prove this maxim. A bill to amend the FSLA to favor persons in the Plaintiffs' situation has been introduced in the Oklahoma House three times, only to languish in committee. While these failures may lead Plaintiffs to believe that the legislature is ignoring their voices of reason, the Constitution simply does not guarantee political success.

Because we hold that intrastate economic protectionism, absent a violation of a specific federal statutory or constitutional provision, is a legitimate state interest and that the FSLA is rationally related to this legitimate end, we AFFIRM.[186]

Judge Tymkovich offered a concurring opinion.[187] While he agreed with the holding, he was troubled by the majority's candid acknowledgement of a protectionist purpose. Tymkovich explained:

... I write separately because I believe the majority overstates the application of "intrastate economic protectionism" as a legitimate state interest furthered by Oklahoma's funeral licensing scheme.

The majority opinion usefully sets forth an overview of the rational basis test. Under the traditional test, judicial review is

---

185. *Id.* at 1223–25 (citations and footnotes omitted).

186. *Id.* at 1225 (citations omitted).

187. *Id.* at 1225 (Tymkovich, J., concurring).

limited to determining whether the challenged state classification is rationally related to a legitimate state interest. As the majority explains, and I agree, courts should not (1) second-guess the "wisdom, fairness, or logic" of legislative choices; (2) insist on "razor-sharp" legislative classifications; or (3) inquire into legislative motivations. I also agree that the burden rests with the challenger to a legislative classification "to negative every conceivable basis" supporting the law. Courts should credit "every plausible legitimate state interest" as a part of their judicial review under this deferential standard.

Where I part company with the majority is its unconstrained view of economic protectionism as a "legitimate state interest." The majority is correct that courts have upheld regulatory schemes that favor some economic interests over others. Many state classifications subsidize or promote particular industries or discrete economic actors. And it is significant here that Oklahoma's licensing scheme only covered intrastate sales of caskets. But all of the cases rest on a fundamental foundation: the discriminatory legislation arguably advances either the general welfare or a public interest.

The Supreme Court has consistently grounded the "legitimacy" of state interests in terms of a public interest. The Court has searched, and rooted out, even in the rational basis context, "invidious" state interests in evaluating legislative classifications. Thus, for example, in the paradigmatic case of *Williamson v. Lee Optical, Inc.*, the Supreme Court invoked consumer safety and health interests over a claim of pure economic parochialism. Rather than hold that a government may always favor one economic actor over another, the Court, if anything, insisted that the legislation advance some public good.

While relying on these time-tested authorities, the majority goes well beyond them to confer legitimacy to a broad concept not argued by the Board—unvarnished economic protectionism. Contrary to the majority, however, whenever courts have upheld legislation that might otherwise appear protectionist, as shown above, courts have always found that they could also rationally advance a *non-protectionist* public good. The majority, in contrast to these precedents, effectively imports a standard that could even credit legislative classifications that advance no general state interest.

The end result of the majority's reasoning is an almost per se rule upholding intrastate protectionist legislation. I, for one, can imagine a different set of facts where the legislative classification is so lopsided in favor of personal interests at the expense of the public good, or so far removed from plausibly advancing a public interest that a rationale of "protectionism" would fail. No case holds that the bare preference of one economic actor while furthering no greater public interest advances a "legitimate state interest."

We need not go so far in this case for two reasons. First of all, the record below and the district court's findings of fact support a conclusion that the funeral licensing scheme here furthers, however imperfectly, an element of consumer protection. The district court found that the Board had in fact brought enforcement actions under the Act to combat consumer abuse by funeral directors. The licensing scheme thus provides a legal club to attack sharp practices by a major segment of casket retailers. Secondly, the history of the licensing scheme here shows that it predates the FCC's deregulation of third-party casket sales or internet competition, and, at least in the first instance, was not enacted solely to protect funeral directors facing increased intrastate competition. I would therefore conclude that the district court did not err in crediting the consumer protection rationale advanced by the Board.

The licensing scheme at issue here leaves much to be desired. The record makes it clear that limitations on the free market of casket sales have outlived whatever usefulness they may have had. Consumer interests appear to be harmed rather than protected by the limitation of choice and price encouraged by the licensing restrictions on intrastate casket sales. Oklahoma's general consumer protection laws appear to be a more than adequate vehicle to allow consumer redress of abusive marketing practices. But the majority is surely right that the battle over this issue must be fought in the Oklahoma legislature, the ultimate arbiter of state regulatory policy.

I therefore conclude that the legislative scheme here meets the rational basis test and join in the judgment of the majority.[188]

Finally, consider the following brief excerpt from Judge Danny Boggs opinion in *Craigmiles v. Giles*[189]:

Finding no rational relationship to any of the articulated purposes of the state, we are left with the more obvious illegitimate purpose to which licensure provision is very well tailored. The licensure requirement imposes a significant barrier to competition in the casket market. By protecting licensed funeral directors from competition on caskets, the FDEA harms consumers in their pocketbooks. If consumer protection were the aim of the 1972 amendment, the General Assembly had several direct means of achieving that end. None of the justifications offered by the state satisfies the slight review required by rational basis review under the Due Process and Equal Protection clauses of the Fourteenth Amendment. As this court has said, "rational basis review, while deferential, is not toothless."

Judicial invalidation of economic regulation under the Fourteenth Amendment has been rare in the modern era. Our decision today is not a return to *Lochner,* by which this court would elevate its economic theory over that of legislative bodies. No sophisticated

---

188. *Id.* at 1225–27 (citations and footnote omitted).

189. 312 F.3d 220 (6th Cir. 2002).

economic analysis is required to see the pretextual nature of the state's proffered explanations for the 1972 amendment. We are not imposing our view of a well-functioning market on the people of Tennessee. Instead, we invalidate only the General Assembly's naked attempt to raise a fortress protecting the monopoly rents that funeral directors extract from consumers. This measure to privilege certain businessmen over others at the expense of consumers is not animated by a legitimate governmental purpose and cannot survive even rational basis review.[190]

DISCUSSION QUESTIONS

1. Together, *Powers* and *Craigmiles* suggest three possible approaches to judicial review of rent-seeking legislation: (1) Determining that the judiciary has no role in policing rent-seeking legislation; (2) Deferring generally to legislative rent seeking unless the court cannot identify any other legitimate purpose (however implausible) that is independent of payoffs to a special interest group; or (3) Engaging in a less deferential and more searching inquiry to determine the actual purposes of the statute, including rent seeking, and invalidating the statute if that appears to be the sole motivation. Which approach is most consistent with the insights of public choice theory? Is it possible to select among these options without first having adopted a normative baseline premise concerning the appropriate (or at least tolerable) extent of interest group involvement in legislative processes? It is possible to select among these options without first embracing an independent theory concerning the role that interest groups play in the process of legislative procurement? For example, will you reach a different result if you view interest groups as necessary facilitators of overall legislative processes that help to produce general interest legislation, on the one hand, or if you instead view interest groups solely as securing rents, without providing any corresponding benefits to the legislative process, on the other?

2. In *Powers* the court observed that legislation to repeal the restriction on casket sales had been introduced into the state legislature three times, only to "languish in committee" each time. Does this result reflect a lack of public support for repeal of the regulation? Is the court correct in thinking that the legislature will repeal the restriction if it fails to advance the public interest or becomes obsolete (as suggested by the concurring opinion)? Does the failure to repeal suggest that this might be a suitable case for a more dynamic judicial role, per Eskridge; for weighing enactable preferences, per Elhauge; or for a more cautious judicial approach, per Farber and Frickey? Why?

3. *Powers* rests on the assumption that the effects of the legislation in question are purely intrastate, merely transferring wealth from in-state consumers to in-state funeral home directors. Is that assumption correct? If so, does it support the ruling?

4. Consider Judge Tacha's analysis of whether *Cleburne* and *Romer* demand a more exacting rational basis scrutiny test. Tacha concludes that the Supreme Court has never applied the test announced in these cases, triggered

---

190. *Id.* at 228–29 (citations omitted).

by a conclusion that the law was motivated by a "bare ... desire to harm a politically unpopular group," in a case involving economic regulation. How does this relate to the suggestion in chapter 2 by Bruce Ackerman and Geoffrey Miller that insularity is a strength rather than a weakness in the context of legislative participation?[191] Does Tacha's analysis of when the *Cleburne* and *Romer* test does and does not apply support the claim that these scholars might be committing a category error within the framework of the Wilson–Hayes model? Why or why not?

---

191. *See supra* chapter 2, section IV.C (discussing Ackerman and Miller).

CHAPTER 6

THE EXECUTIVE BRANCH AND AGENCIES

■ ■ ■

INTRODUCTION

Under the United States Constitution, the President is afforded broad powers through which to influence the creation, interpretation, and execution of federal laws. Article I, § 7, which articulates the processes through which Congress enacts statutes, provides the President veto power over bills approved in both Houses of Congress, thus making the President a *de facto* third legislative house. Article II, § 2 empowers the President, with the advice and consent of the Senate, to appoint Officers of the United States. While the Senate holds the power of advice and consent respecting cabinet level appointments (although not with respect to "inferior officers") the President alone is charged with the power to remove cabinet officers who report to him unless the cabinet official is impeached. Finally, the Constitution provides the President the power, once more with the advice and consent of the Senate, to appoint Article III judges, who serve for a period of "Good Behaviour."[1] Among the most important practical consequence of this constitutional structure for modern analysis of government is the twentieth century growth of the vast administrative state. This includes the creation of a myriad of so-called independent agencies whose members are protected from removal by the President and whose internal decision making is to a considerable extent insulated from outside review. This chapter focuses on the internal operations of the executive branch, especially department and agency decision making and regulatory policy making within bureaucracies.

In terms of their influence on law and policy, administrative agencies have become the functional equivalent of a fourth branch of the federal government. For instance, as the 110th Congress was reaching its conclusion, it had passed 294 public laws.[2] And the Supreme Court now decides fewer than 100 cases per year. By contrast, a recent count finds 319 administrative agencies.[3] In 2006, the number of pages included in the

---

1. U.S. CONST. art. III, § 1. Relationships and interactions among the branches, including the executive veto, are discussed in chapter 8.

2. Elizabeth Williamson, *As U.S. Economic Problems Loom, House, Senate Sweat the Small Stuff*, WALL ST. J., Aug. 19, 2008, at A1.

3. ROBERT A. LEVY & WILLIAM MELLOR, THE DIRTY DOZEN: HOW TWELVE SUPREME COURT CASES RADICALLY EXPANDED GOVERNMENT AND ERODED FREEDOM 68 (2008).

Code of Federal Regulations was about six times that of the United States Code. The 2006 *Federal Register*, which lists agency-proposed regulations, rulings, and other activities, was 69,248 pages long!

The modern administrative state is premised on the intuition that addressing problems in the complex modern world requires reliance on disinterested experts insulated from the rough and tumble of electoral politics and market incentives. The civil service system, which insulates bureaucrats from political pressures and from the use of government resources for partisan political purposes, grows out of this tradition. This principle reached its apex in the United States during the first half of the twentieth century with the establishment of "independent agencies" such as the Federal Trade Commission and the Securities and Exchange Commission, with Commissioners who are appointed for terms of years, sometimes with rules that require partisan political balance. Unlike executive branch appointments, officers of independent agencies are substantially insulated from pressures associated with the prospect of presidential removal power. As you read the materials that follow, consider the extent to which the intuition that agencies facilitate expert government removed from political influence is borne out by current Supreme Court doctrines respecting matters such as the scope of removal powers and respect for agency rulemaking. Also consider whether the intuition is consistent or in tension with the models presented in this chapter. Does public choice help to test the underlying assumptions that motivated the rise and perpetuation of the administrative state? Why or why not? If you conclude that public choice analysis is not consistent with the original justification for the administrative state, does it nevertheless provide the basis for an alternative justification?

Given the central role that presidential politics plays in the direction of regulatory policy, our analysis necessarily begins by considering the nature of presidential politics itself. We begin with a spatial model that grows out of the median voter analysis presented in chapter 3,[4] but then examine how the temporal staging of presidential elections into primaries and general elections changes the predictions of the basic median voter analysis and the implications of this analysis for the formation of federal policy, both at the agency level and through judicial construction of statutes. Unlike the basic median voter model, which predicts policy convergence by the two candidates, a two-staged election with parties predicts policy divergence between the two candidates. This analysis proves important in assessing the normative foundations, and implications, of agency deference rules that largely insulate both executive and independent agencies in their interpretation and implementation of federal statutes.

We then examine the preferences and motivations of bureaucrats in light of their institutional incentives. We begin with the general question, "What do *bureaucrats* maximize?" As before, we look at features of

---

4. *See supra* chapter 3, section I.B.

institutional design that affect the motivations of rational policymakers operating within an agency setting. We also examine how the executive branch uses agency decision making to interact with other branches of government including, most notably, Congress. Finally, we examine the decision by Congress to delegate and the nature of such delegations. We close with several case studies that will allow you to test the various theories of bureaucratic behavior developed in this chapter.

Beginning with a series of cases concerning Congress's power to limit the President's ability to terminate officers, the Supreme Court has drawn a distinction between executive and independent agencies. Executive agencies are those in which the agency head (often a cabinet official) serves at the pleasure of the President. Given the direct political accountability of executive agencies, those who head them are obviously expected to pursue the President's policy initiatives. Although executive agency heads are subject to congressional oversight, their more pressing concern generally is political accountability to the President. While there is undoubtedly agency cost slippage (meaning that the cabinet members have some power to depart from strict presidential preferences), the boundaries for pursuing objectives contrary to presidential preferences are more constrained than in the context of independent agencies.

Independent agencies are those in which the senior officials are protected by statute from unilateral executive removal power and thus from many of the direct political pressures experienced by those heading executive agencies. The Chairs and Commissioners on independent agencies—such as the Federal Trade Commission ("FTC"), Securities and Exchange Commission ("SEC"), and Federal Communications Commission ("FCC")[5]—are typically appointed for a term of years and otherwise removable "for cause" or some similar standard. Many independent agencies are required to have partisan balance or representation, thereby giving the party out of power minority representation and some corresponding influence over agency policy. The incentives of those who head independent agencies are more difficult to assess than for executive officials. It is not obvious to whom they are accountable, and regulatory oversight often appears to be weak. Historically, the consequences of agency scrutiny have varied considerably. The Civil Aeronautics Board ("CAB") and the Interstate Commerce Commission ("ICC"), both of which were subject to intense media and political criticism, were eventually terminated. Other agencies that have been subject to similar scrutiny, such as the FTC, were dramatically reformed in the face of heavy political and public pressure. Still others, such as the SEC and the FCC, whose performance has been long criticized, have been subject to only modest reforms and remain a frequent target of criticism. What do these varied results suggest about the likely differences in agency slack as between

---

5. For a listing of executive and independent agencies housed in the executive branch, see Appendix A (available online).

executive and idependent agencies? To whom are independent agencies accountable? What motivates or constrains those who head them?

I. THE MEDIAN VOTER THEOREM MEETS NON–MEDIAN PRESIDENTIAL CANDIDATES

In chapter 3, we introduced the median voter theorem. That simple spatial model demonstrates that in a system in which the head of state is selected through a direct election, the result is likely to be a stable two-party system. The model also predicts considerable, if not complete, policy convergence among the leading candidates, each of whom is motivated to capture a majority of the electorate, represented along a single dimensional ideological spectrum. A major difficulty that theorists confront is that within the United States, where the President is elected by the citizenry, rather than, for example, a minimum winning parliamentary coalition,[6] there is often substantial policy divergence between the leading candidates. This difference between the predictions of the median voter model and observed political behavior is important not only for revisiting assumptions about how the President is elected, but also for considering the President's role in influencing the formation of regulatory policy.

The simple model of the median voter theorem predicts that the policy platforms of presidential nominees of two major parties will tend to converge toward the preferences of the median voter, leaving only narrow policy differences. In practice, however, the Democratic and Republican presidential nominees often hold sharp policy disagreements. This divergence between the predictions of the simple median voter model and observed electoral politics can be explained in substantial part by the two-staged electoral system by which presidential candidates are selected. This system combines primaries (or caucuses)[7] with a general election among each party's primary winners.[8] The two-stage election process creates countervailing pressures that pull the major party candidates toward and

---

6. For a discussion of the differing implications of parliamentary designation of the head of state, see *infra* chapter 8, section II.H. This description leaves aside of course, the formality of the Electoral College.

7. *See* WILLIAM G. MAYER & ANDREW E. BUSCH, THE FRONT-LOADING PROBLEM IN PRESIDENTIAL NOMINATIONS 19–20 (2004). The authors note, "[U]nlike presidential primaries, which occur on a single, definite date, caucuses are multistage affairs, in which meaningful delegate selection decisions are made over a period of several months. . . . (footnote omitted). As a consequence of the larger investment required to participate in a caucus versus a primary, what implications does the chance hold for the extent to which the results will be more consistent with the preferences of the median as base voters in the relevant party? *Id.*

8. For related works that consider the impact of two-stage elections on candidate locations using the general framework of the median voter theorem, see Donald Wittman, *Candidate Motivation: A Synthesis of Alternative Theories*, 77 AM. POL. SCI. REV. 142 (1983); James Adams, Thomas L. Brunell, Bernard Grofman & Samuel Merrill, III, Move to the Center or Mobilize the Base? (August 31, 2006) (unpublished manuscript), *available at* http://www.all academic. com/meta/p_ mla_ apa_ research_ 1citation/1/5/2/3/0/ p152307_ 1index.html; Gilles Serra, Primary Divergence: The Effects of Primary Elections on Candidate Strategies in the Downsian Model (Apr. 2, 2007) (unpublished manuscript), *available at* http://convention3. allacademic.com/meta /p_mla_ apa_research_ 1citation1/1/9/8/3/7/ p198378_ index.html.

away from the competing ideal points of their respective party base and of the general election's median voter.

The analysis explains why the prediction of the simple median voter model of candidate convergence does not hold in practice and why elections do not witness complete ideological fluidity of candidates moving as far in the direction of the party base as needed to secure the nomination and then all the way back to the general election's median voter to secure victory in the general election. After reviewing the basic two-staged model, which identifies factors that encourage just these sorts of identifiable ideological shifts, we set out a more detailed analysis that identifies factors that temper complete fluidity at each election stage. While the precise equilibrium—in both primaries and in the general election—will of course vary for each election cycle, as demonstrated below, the net effect of the combined processes is substantially greater candidate policy divergence than the single period median voter hypothesis predicts.

The sometimes sharp divergence between the policy positions of the leading presidential candidates has the potential to produce wide policy swings when the party of presidential administration changes hands. One might assume that the life-tenured federal judiciary would temper broad agency-driven policy swings. And yet, important administrative law doctrines related to agency deference have just the opposite effect of reinforcing the control of agencies over regulatory policy, thereby tending to amplify rather than dampen policy swings when the Presidency changes parties.

An important pair of administrative law cases holds that when an agency uses proper agency procedures to provide a reasonable construction of an ambiguous federal statute, a federal court is obligated to defer to the agency's interpretation even if the result that the agency obtains contradicts what a federal court would have ruled as a matter of first impression.[9] In a more recent case, the Supreme Court has gone further and held that even if the Supreme Court had previously construed an ambiguous federal statute in a manner that a federal agency later interprets differently, the agency interpretation, rather than the Court's, controls.[10] The combination of three factors—(1) potentially substantial policy divergence between leading presidential candidates, (2) significant presidential influence over the direction of agency policy, and (3) presumptive judicial deference to agency policy affecting the construction of federal statutes—demonstrates the importance of properly modeling the presidential selection process in an effort to better understand agency incentives.

A. THE MEDIAN VOTER THEOREM REVISITED

1. Predicting Complete Convergence in a Single–Staged Election

We begin with a single-stage presidential election and then introduce a two-stage election, including a primary and general election. The analy-

---

9. *See* United States v. Mead Corp., 533 U.S. 218 (2001); Chevron U.S.A. Inc. v. Natural Res. Def. Council, Inc., 467 U.S. 837 (1984).

10. *See* National Cable & Telecomms. Ass'n v. Brand X Internet Servs., 545 U.S. 967, 980–86 (2005).

sis begins with figure 6:1, reproduced from chapter 3, which depicts the median voter theorem in a single period election. The model rests on the following premises: (1) a single dimensional liberal-to-conservative continuum; (2) two candidates whose ideal points (meaning their preferred set of packaged policy positions) occupy opposing ends of the ideological spectrum; and (3) presidential candidates who behave rationally in pursuit of winning the election.[11] The Democratic candidate (D) occupies the liberal (L) end of the spectrum (to the left), while the Republican candidate (R) occupies the conservative (C) end of the spectrum (to the right).

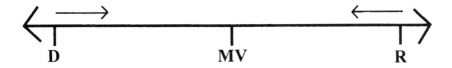

D   **MV**   **R**

Key: **MV = Median Voter**
            D = Liberal (Democratic) Candidate
            R = Conservative (Republican) Candidate

Figure 6:1

Based upon these assumptions, the model predicts that as each candidate seeks to capture larger segments of the electorate, he or she will move toward the position embraced by the general election's median voter (MV). The model further assumes that as each candidate takes on more moderate views relative to his or her ideal point (with R moving left and D moving right), those voters who prefer a more extreme candidate (or one whose ideal point occupies the relevant endpoint of the ideological spectrum) will continue to support a candidate who remains ideologically less distant, rather than vote for the opposite candidate (or not vote at all) as a result of the preferred candidate's decision to moderate his or her views.

The median voter model helps to explain the persistence of the two-party system within the United States, as the major party candidates effectively squeeze out the necessary policy space that would allow a stable third party candidacy to flourish.[12] And yet, as Donald Wittman has

---

11. *See supra* chapter 3, section I.B.

12. Duverger's law predicts direct elections generally yield two party systems, a phenomenon that is closely linked to the insights of the median voter theorem. *See* MAURICE DUVERGER, POLITICAL

observed, the model fails to explain the frequently observed divergence in party platforms in actual presidential elections.[13]

2. Predicting Policy Divergence in a Two–Staged Election

Let us now adapt figure 6:1 to account for two-staged elections. Gilles Serra has extended Donald Wittman's intuition that the median voter theorem fails adequately to capture the ideological distance observed between major party platforms by developing a two-staged election model operating in a single dimensional plane.[14] We begin with a simple adaptation of the Serra model that accounts for ideological candidate location. In the discussion that follows, we begin with a simple two-staged model and then consider the implications of relaxing some of the underlying assumptions for the eventual ideological placement of the major party candidates in any given presidential election.

Figure 6:2 depicts a truncated ideological spectrum for each of the two major parties that emerge in the United States system of direct presidential election, and relates the primary spectrum for each party to the larger spectrum for the general presidential election, depicted in Figure 6:1.

PARTIES: THEIR ORGANIZATION AND ACTIVITY IN THE MODERN STATE 216–28 (Barbara & Robert North trans., Methuen & Co. 2d ed. 1959) (1951) (setting out thesis later referred to as Duverger's law); *see also* William H. Riker, *Political Science and Rational Choice, in* PERSPECTIVES ON POSITIVE POLITICAL ECONOMY 163, 177–81 (James E. Alt & Kenneth A. Shepsle eds., 1990) (describing Duverger's law). This does not imply that a third party candidate can never prevail in a system of direct election, as occurred, for example, in the election of Jesse Ventura in the Minnesota gubernatorial race as a member of the Reform Party in 1998. In that election, however, Ventura won a plurality of the votes, and might well not have been a Condorcet winner had the election produced a runoff between the two leading contenders. *See, e.g.,* Jodi Wilgoren, *Gov. Ventura Says He Won't Seek Re-election,* N.Y. TIMES, June 19, 2002, at A14. A start-up party also might replace one of the two existing parties if that party fails to converge sufficiently toward the party median. Examples are the supplanting of the Whig party by the Republican party in the United States and the Liberal Party in Great Britain. In the end, however, both systems returned to a stable but reformulated two-party system.

13. *See* Wittman, *supra* note 8 at 143 (positing that rational major party candidates who are motivated to win the general election will take positions during primaries to secure the party nomination that "maximize[] the expected utility of the party's median voter").

14. *See* Serra, *supra* note 8, at 6–8. Serra predicts that in a highly competitive primary race, the result is a commitment to the position of the party median voter, which can change in cases of incumbency. *See id.* at 13–18. Serra further explains that because incumbency limits primary competition, this poses a threat to the preferred ideological positioning of the party base. The essential difference between Serra's model and the model developed here is that Serra assumes full voter participation and presents the spatial dimension of each party as starting at the extreme right or left and ending at the precise location of the general election median voter. Our analysis instead treats voter turnout as dependent on candidate location along the ideological dimension and further assumes that there are some crossover voters, which allows for some left of center Republican voters and some right of center Democratic voters. The authors thank Gilles Serra for his generous assistance in helping to develop portions of this discussion.

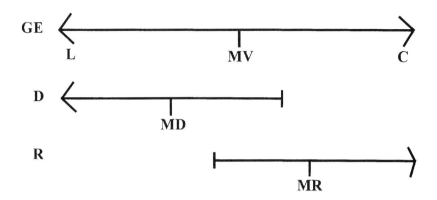

Key: GE = General Electorate
        D = Registered Democratic Voters (as compared with General Electorate)
        R = Registered Republican Voters (as compared with General Electorate)
        MV = Median General Electorate Voter
        MD = Median Democratic Voter
        MR = Median Republican Voter

Figure 6:2

In this model, the Republican spectrum begins at the far right of the larger spectrum depicted in figure 6:1 and continues slightly to the left of *MV*, and the Democratic spectrum begins at the far left of the large spectrum and continues slightly to the right of *MV*. Notice that in this model, each primary spectrum includes at least some voters who are on the side opposite the party's base constituency. As a result, the generally liberal Democratic Party includes some moderate to conservative Democratic voters, and the generally conservative Republican Party includes some moderate to liberal Republican voters. One benefit of this assumption, as shown in the next part, is that it allows for an observed phenomenon in actual elections, namely the ability of major party candidates to appeal to "crossover voters," meaning those who in a given election might vote either for a Republican or Democratic candidate.[15]

In this simple model, the predictable result appears to be some degree of candidate divergence as each candidate positions himself or herself at or near his or her party's median voter along the relevant truncated ideologi-

---

15. At various points in history, the degree of distance on the side opposite the party base has varied considerably. Southern Democrats, for example, potentially occupied positions quite far to the right of the general electoral median voter, while "Rockefeller" Republicans occupied positions substantially to the left of the general electoral median voter, at least over some issues. For an informative book that touches on these themes, see JAMES L. SUNDQUIST, DYNAMICS OF THE PARTY SYSTEM: ALIGNMENT AND REALIGNMENT OF POLITICAL PARTIES IN THE UNITED STATES (rev. ed. 1983). The empirical incidence of such voters is less important than is realizing that neither party cuts off at the precise point that represents the general election's theoretical median voter. As a consequence, in any general election, crossover voters have the potential to support either major party candidate, based on any number of variables, including but not limited to ideological distance from his or her ideal point.

cal spectrum to secure the relevant nomination. The distance between the median Democratic and median Republican voter is considerably greater than the complete policy convergence that the single-stage application of the median voter theorem depicted in figure 6:1 predicts. If we continue to assume full electoral participation, this time within each party, then ultimately successful primary candidates will rationally move toward the median party voter as they compete with other primary candidates for the nomination. As in the single-staged median voter analysis, those voters within each party who prefer a more ideologically extreme candidate— generally thought of as the party base—will nonetheless vote for those candidates who have moderated their positions by moving toward the party's median voter, rather than declining to vote or voting for a primary candidate whose views are on the opposite side of the party's median voter.

Assuming that this analysis captures the dynamics of presidential primaries, it highlights a substantial difficulty for the nominated candidate. Once each major party candidate secures the nomination, the same analysis would suggest that he or she is rationally motivated to converge back toward MV in an effort to win the general election. If the candidate is assumed to act rationally at each stage, then the model implies complete candidate fluidity as candidates will move along the single-dimensional ideological spectrum toward the party's median voter (or perhaps even further if, as suggested below, the party's base turns out to vote in disproportionate numbers), as needed to secure the nomination, and then back toward MV as needed to win the general election. In this analysis, the two-staged model does no better at explaining major candidate divergence than the one-staged model.

3. Complexities in the Two–Stage Model

We now modify the two assumptions that undergird both the single-staged and two-staged electoral models to restore the intuition that introducing a primary (or caucus) stage produces a more stable policy distance between major party candidates than a single-stage election. The analysis demonstrates that while the precise issue locations of each candidate will vary from election to election, there are predictable forces that simultaneously pull toward the general electoral median voter and toward the extreme positions of each party's base. The predictable net effect of the two-staged system limits the probability of complete policy convergence by the major party candidates, thus reinforcing the basic intuition underlying the two-staged model.

a. *The Voter Probability Distribution Function*

The preceding analysis assumes an even distribution of voters across the ideological spectrum for the general election and also for the truncated spectra for the primary elections. Consider the possibility, however, that a larger number of voters occupy a relatively moderate ideological position than occupy the ends of the ideological spectrum in the general election. If so, we can depict the general electorate in the form of a probability distribution function (PDF), which assumes a bell shape form. The PDF is shown in figure 6:3.

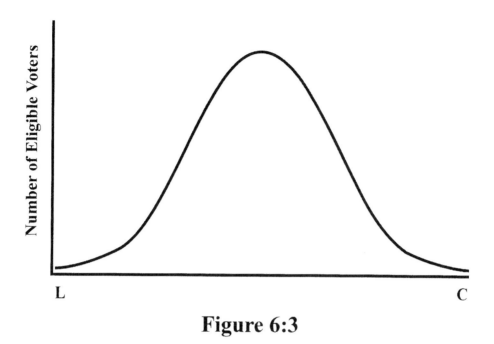

Figure 6:3

If we continue the assumption of full voter participation, this standard bell-shaped PDF would enhance the tendency of the candidates, after having secured the relevant party nomination, to move toward *MV*. Such moves would improve their efforts to capture a larger and larger number of general electoral voters. Moreover, as William Niskanen has demonstrated, it would give a potentially enhanced payoff because a "flipped" crossover voter is the equivalent of two votes—one vote gained plus one taken from the other side—whereas a voter lost due to diminished enthusiasm is simply one vote lost.[16]

Niskanen's intuition is strengthened to the extent that there are voters in each party whose positions are distant from the party base in a moderate direction, which enhances the possibility of appealing to voters registered to the other party as one moves in the direction of *MV* in the general election. If we continue to assume full voter participation, an assumption we relax below, these factors encourage moves toward *MV* as each candidate rationally seeks to capture potential moderate voters. Obviously, the result would thwart the interests of those who sought to secure a candidate committed to their party's core values. The question

---

16. *See* William A. Niskanen, *U.S. Elections Are Increasingly Biased Against Moderates*, 23 CATO J. 463 (2004), *reprinted in* WILLIAM A. NISKANEN, REFLECTIONS OF A POLITICAL ECONOMIST: SELECTED ARTICLES ON GOVERNMENT POLICIES AND POLITICAL PROCESSES 237 (2008).

thus arises how voter turnout however, may temper the candidate's motivation to move toward the position of *MV*.

b. Non–Uniform Electoral Turnout (or Challenging the Assumptions of a Single Dimensional Scale)

A competing consideration for candidates seeking a major party nomination is that while ideologically extreme voters might be fewer in number, as demonstrated in the bell-shaped PDF, studies demonstrate that the party base participates in politics in a manner disproportionate to their numbers.[17] Assuming that this higher incidence of general political participation translates into disproportionate turnout in general elections, then each candidate's rational ideological placement might be endogenous to anticipated voter turnout. In this context, endogeneity means that rather than assuming universal turnout, candidates recognize that electoral turnout is a function of (or is endogenous to) where they position themselves along the ideological spectrum, and conversely, candidate positioning is a function of the expected impact on voter turnout.

This analysis provides an alternative perspective on Niskanen's observation about the two-to-one payoff for "flipping" a moderate voter relative to turning out a voter from the candidate's core constituency.[18] In this analysis, the cost of flipping a moderate voter might be higher than that of securing two base voters because both major candidates are competing for general electorate's moderate voters, while each candidate is alone in courting his or her base voters. It is also likely to be easier to appeal to the relatively more homogenous base voter constituency with targeted campaigning. Courting moderates also risks diminishing enthusiasm among the party base.

Assuming that voters holding more extreme ideological views tend to be more politically engaged, candidates also confront the risk that moving toward the center of the ideological spectrum during the general electoral cycle will have a disproportionate dampening effect on those eligible voters most likely to become actual voters in the general election. Political candidates ultimately are concerned with capturing a majority of *actual* voters as needed to win the general election, rather than with appealing to a majority of *eligible* or *potential* voters, only some of whom turn out at the polls. The tradeoff is reflected in figure 6:4 below.

---

17. For an article summarizing this literature, see Elisabeth R. Gerber & Rebecca B. Morton, *Primary Election Systems and Representation*, 14 J.L. ECON. & ORG. 304, 309 (1998) (presenting studies that show "voters with strong partisan ties are much more likely to participate in political activities than are other voters"; that in 1988, voter turnout was about 50% but over 80% for strong partisans; and that "one group of party elites—convention delegates and caucus participants—have more extreme issue positions than the general electorate"). The authors claim that these studies imply that "the ideal point of the closed primary election median voter is likely to diverge substantially from the ideal point of the general election median voter." *Id.* at 310.

18. *See supra* note 16 and accompanying text.

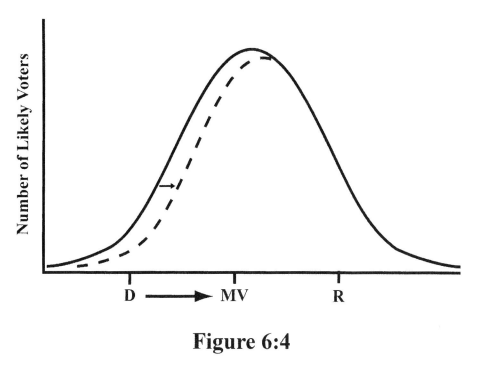

Figure 6:4

Figure 6:4, which focuses on the Democratic candidate, reveals the disproportionate tempering effect on more ideologically liberal voters as the candidate moves toward the ideal point of the general election's median voter. Together, figures 6:3 and 6:4 reveal that while general election candidates seek to capture the larger percentage of eligible voters bunched toward the middle of the bell-shaped PDF (and the two-for-one arithmetic of flipped voters), they have to rationally weigh this incentive against the corresponding risk of sacrificing support among the "party base" or "party faithful," meaning those voters who, although a smaller percentage of the general electorate, might be more likely to become actual voters than other registered voters.[19] The question remains, however, whether the party faithful retain control over the party nominee past the point of nomination.

19. For an interesting, related study on the 2002 congressional elections, see Niskanen, *supra* note 16. Niskanen observes that in that election, candidates most "at risk" were those reputed to be moderates, a result that he claims is in tension with the median voter hypothesis. Niskanen attributes the failure of the median voter theory to explain the 2002 election results, which displaced some moderate incumbents, to the assumption underlying the median voter theorem that voter turnout is exogenous to a candidate's ideological placement. Niskanen explains that if instead "the decision of *whether* to vote is [dependent] of the issue positions of the candidates," then "candidates have an incentive to choose an issue position closer to the median of their party base than to the median of the total electorate (in the relevant constituency)." *See id.* at 239–40. Are there reasons why moderate congressional candidates might be more vulnerable in general elections than moderate presidential candidates, assuming such a candidate secures his or her party nomination? One interesting consequence of the Niskanen study is that it suggests that Congress as an institution is more politically polarized than the general electorate. Does this help to answer the preceding question? Why or why not? Might it matter that 2002 was an "off-year" congressional election with no presidential election, when overall turnout tends to be lower?

c. Two–Staged Presidential Elections as a Multi–Period Game

Assume that each two-staged election is a single-period game. This means that after each election cycle, voters experience a sort of collective amnesia and confront the next election cycle uninformed by what happened in the past. With this sort of electoral myopia, we might well imagine that the two-party system provides the party faithful no meaningful power to rein in their party's nominee. Once the candidate is chosen, the voters confront anew the incentives set out in the single period model and are forced, in effect, to support their party's candidate regardless of policy convergence, so long as the two major candidates do not cross paths with each other. The question then is why we do not witness complete convergence (or even flipping) along the relevant ideological spectrum? Are there mechanisms that reward candidates who adhere to commitments made in the primary campaign and that punish defections during the general election?

Consider the extent to which primaries allow a set of commitment strategies played out over multiple elections. If we view each individual election as a round of play in a multi-period game, this has the potential to raise the cost—although it certainly does not eliminate all risk—of a candidate moving from the primary ideal point (associated with each party's median voter) to a substantially more moderated position, closer to that of the general election median voter, during the general election. To what extent is the primary system, with the party base committing to active participation not only in the general election but also in later primaries, a vehicle for encouraging enforceable commitments? Does the two-staged election regime limit complete candidate fluidity not only in the primary (as moving too far toward the base is costly given the risk of having to renege in the general election), but also in the general election (as moving toward MV threatens diminished turnout among the base)?

Does treating the election as a multi-period game help to restore the intuition that the two-staged election system promotes meaningful policy distance between the leading presidential candidates? Can you identify particular devices at the primary stage that operate to bind presidential candidates from straying too far from positions taken to secure the party nomination?

d. Turnout and Dimensionality

The preceding discussion raises several empirical issues: (1) what is the ideological incidence of voters along the ideological spectrum; (2) how fluid is candidate placement from the primary to the general election cycle; and (3) to what extent are base voters willing to abstain in response to what they view as excessive moderation in the general election cycle. It is nonetheless fair to assume that the net effect of the factors set out above produces a result that is more consistent with the observed divergence between major party candidates in recent presidential electoral cycles than the simple median voter hypothesis operating alone would predict.

Is it realistic to assume that base party voters will ever decline to support—some might say "punish"—a candidate by abstaining when doing so is tantamount to supporting the candidate for the other side? Consider the possibility that such a strategy is rational if the liberal to conservative ideological spectrum does not capture the entire stakes for the party faithful. In this analysis, the question of turnout is equivalent to the question of dimensionality.[20]

Consider the possibility that base voters care about retaining long-term control over the party and its ideological positioning even if that results in a loss in a particular general election.[21] How plausible is it that base voters care more about control than electoral victory in a particular election cycle? Are those committed to such core issues as "right to life," "freedom of choice," and "anti-" or "pro-death penalty" behaving irrationally if they view themselves as "single issue" voters? Are single issue voters the sort of voters who elevate issues of party control over the concern for party victory in the general election?

Are there other factors that affect issues of party control? Available data demonstrate that during the 2008 Obama–McCain election, voter turnout was the most diverse in history, with African American voters setting a "historic first" by having the "highest turnout rate" among "young eligible voters."[22] The African American community had long been considered a core constituency of the Democratic Party. Does the differential turnout in the 2008 general election as compared with prior elections demonstrate that African American voters can be turned out in higher numbers than they have been historically—and to that extent are not captured—based upon the enthusiasm for the selected candidate and his or her policies? Why or why not? How might this relate to the broader question of dimensionality and party control?

Consider also state laws governing the nature of party candidate selection. States have adopted a variety of approaches to selecting candidates for general elections, including primaries, caucuses, conventions, or a combination. Some of these processes are "closed," meaning that only registered party members can participate, while others are "open," meaning that voters registered to other parties or as independent can also participate.[23] What are the tradeoffs involved in selecting between open

---

20. For a discussion of dimensionality, see *supra* chapter 3.

21. For a related discussion, see David Brooks, Op–Ed., *Road to Nowhere*, N.Y. TIMES, Jan. 1, 2008, at A17 (positing that while Republican Party leaders supporting Mitt Romney knew that he would not win the general election if nominated, "some would rather remain in control of a party that loses than lose control of a party that wins").

22. MARK HUGO LOPEZ & PAUL TAYLOR, PEW RESEARCH CTR., DISSECTING THE 2008 ELECTORATE: MOST DIVERSE IN U.S. HISTORY 6 (2009). According to this study, which is based on Census Bureau data, "[v]oter turnout rates among black, Latino and Asian eligible voters were higher in 2008 than in 2004.... The voter turnout rate among black eligible voters was 5 percentage points higher in 2008 than in 2004...." *Id.* at 4.

23. *See, e.g.*, Karen M. Kaufmann et al., *A Promise Fulfilled? Open Primaries and Representation*, 65 J. POL. 457, 459 (2003).

and closed primaries? Caucuses versus primaries? Do closed primaries help the base retain control of the party even at the risk of defeat in general elections, or does it ensure higher levels of turnout by the party base? More generally, does the existence of a variety of mechanisms suggest that none of these options is necessarily "superior" to others? Should states be allowed to compel political parties to hold open primaries in which those registered to another party or as independents can participate? Why or why not? To what extent was the nomination of John McCain, viewed by many as a moderate Republican, helped by open primary voting? Does the foregoing analysis provide any guidance to a judge considering a constitutional challenge to a law requiring open, or blanket, primaries?[24]

B. PRESIDENTIAL POLITICS AND REGULATORY POLICY REVISITED

The various policy commitment strategies made during the primary stage—and specifically the predicted divergence between the policy positions of the major party candidates—has a potentially significant effect on the likely regulatory policies that the President and those he or she appoints to various agencies will pursue in the course of his or her administration. Securing the support of industry against environmentalists, or the reverse; the support of labor over management, or the reverse; the drug industry, or consumers seeking stringent drug regulations, have the effect of making departures from these positions costly as a political matter. While there is some observed policy convergence in the general election cycle, the two-staged electoral system makes complete policy convergence less likely. Judicial doctrine has developed so as to make candidate policy distancing highly relevant to changes in regulatory policy.

Under the *Chevron* doctrine,[25] the federal judiciary is obligated to give deference to a reasonable agency interpretation of an ambiguous federal statutory provision. This holds even if that interpretation differs from the construction that the federal court would provide in the first instance. Under *Mead*,[26] *Chevron* deference is not appropriate if an agency uses an insufficiently formal instrument to announce its interpretation, but an attenuated degree of deference (known as *Skidmore* deference) nonethe-

---

24. Some state political parties have challenged state laws regulating the conduct of primary elections, including "open" primaries, which allow voters registered to one party to vote in the primary of the other party, or "blanket" primaries, which allow states to treat primaries of different parties uniformly for purposes of deciding who runs in the general election. For a recent case upholding Washington State's law requiring a blanket primary system, which demands that the two top vote-getters in the primaries run off in the general election without regard to their party affiliation, see Wash. State Grange v. Wash. State Republican Party, 128 S. Ct. 1184 (2008). In that case, the Court, with Justice Thomas writing, rejected the argument that the rule prevented parties from selecting their own candidates, allegedly in violation of the rule established in Cal. Democratic Party v. Jones, 530 U.S. 567 (2000), and instead ruled that the parties remain free to select their candidates outside the primary system but remain subject to the top vote-getting rule in the general election. *Grange*, 128 S. Ct. at 1192–95.

25. Chevron U.S.A. Inc. v. Natural Res. Def. Council, Inc., 467 U.S. 837 (1984).

26. United States v. Mead Corp., 533 U.S. 218 (2001).

less may be applicable. And under *National Cable & Telecommunications Ass'n v. Brand X Internet Services*,[27] the Supreme Court will even disregard its own prior interpretation of an ambiguous federal statute if an agency acting within the scope of its proper jurisdiction subsequently provides a different, yet reasonable, interpretation.

As you read the materials that follow, consider the impact of presidential elections in affecting the "meaning" of federal statutes as a result of the President's central role in staffing agencies. On one account of the preceding model, the primary system has the effect of preserving substantial policy distance between the two major parties with the predictable result of fairly considerable policy swings when the party controlling the White House changes hands. Judicial deference rules add one level of magnitude to the significance of these policy swings by effectively removing final interpretive authority over ambiguous statutory provisions from Article III courts and conferring it instead upon executive and independent agencies. Because the President has a more immediate effect in staffing agencies than in staffing the judiciary (given the life tenure of judges and thus the reduced incidence of replacements), the President has a greater likelihood of affecting administrative interpretations than judicial constructions of statutes.[28]

Of course, the President does appoint federal judges (with Senate approval), but the effect of such appointments on the construction of statutes is likely to be felt over a longer period of time and often with the result of a considerable lag between presidential administrations.[29] Within the federal judiciary, the Supreme Court's interpretation of statutes is otherwise final (barring congressional override), and presidential appointments to that Court arise stochastically.

---

27. 545 U.S. 967 (2005).

28. For a recent article that considers the implications of presidential policy swings from the ideal point of the general election's median voter, see Matthew C. Stephenson, *Optimal Political Control of the Bureaucracy* 107 MICH. L. REV. 53 (2008). Stephenson is not concerned with the causes of predictable presidential policy divergence from the preferences of the median voter. *Id.* at 83 n.81 and cites therein. Instead, he is concerned with the consequence of that divergence for the claim that tighter presidential control over agency policies promotes majoritarian bureaucratic accountability. Stephenson maintains that under specified assumptions some degree of insulation from presidential control is more likely, counterintuitively, to increase bureaucratic tracking of majoritarian policy preferences. Stephenson claims that those advocating a unitary executive, or what he terms strong presidentialism, commit the analytical error of equating "the *expected value of the distance* between two variables" with "the *distance between the expected value* of these two variables." *Id.* at 73 (emphasis in original). Because Presidents tend to represent ideal points, perhaps for reasons set out in the text that are closer to the median party voter and thus some distance to one side or the other of the general election's median voter, an insulated bureaucracy is more likely over time to track the true median voter's ideal point than is an agency increasingly subject to the control of changing presidential administrations. Stephenson's largely positive account rests on the premise that bureaucratic action is intended to reflect the preferences of the median voter, rather than, for example, that of the successful political coalition as one of the several means of encouraging democratic engagement.

29. The interaction between the judiciary and agencies does seem to matter, however, as there is some empirical evidence that judges act more deferentially toward regulations issues by a President of their own party, which might further exacerbate policy swings. *See* discussion *infra* at notes 178–186 and accompanying text.

Why might the Supreme Court have articulated a set of doctrines that effectively vests construction of statutes in the very agencies whose interpretations are subject to judicial review? Recall that under the Landes and Posner model, the independent judiciary prolongs the meaning of statutes as envisioned by the drafters, at least when compared with the alternative of a *dependent* judiciary.[30] Recall also that in the Elhauge model, *Chevron* deference promotes political satisfaction as gauged against what he terms "enactable preferences."[31] Which of these models does the preceding analysis of the role of two-staged presidential elections in affecting policy change tend to support? Bear this question in mind as you read the rest of this chapter and consider the incentives of the bureaucrats themselves in the course of agency construction of statutes.

More generally, does the preceding analysis help to explain the nature of bureaucratic behavior? Does the answer to this question depend on whether we are discussing executive or independent agencies? Why or why not? We now turn to the second inquiry, namely, what motivates the agencies themselves.

II. CHARACTERISTICS OF BUREAUCRATIC ACTION

In chapter 5, we began with the premise that the overarching incentive of legislators is to be elected and re-elected. While legislators undoubtedly hold other, more lofty, objectives, in a competitive political system, those politicians unwilling to behave *as if* they are primarily motivated to be elected and re-elected will eventually fall off the radar of electoral politics. In this sense, the assumption that legislators act as if they are motivated by the goal of re-election is analogous to the assumption in the study of private markets that although firms might hold a range of objectives, to survive in a competitive market, they must behave as if they are primarily motivated to maximize profits, and thus their behavior can be modeled as if they consciously seek this end.[32] Those that fail to act as if they are maximizing profits otherwise will be out-competed by those that do.

Unlike legislators, bureaucrats do not face direct electoral constraints, and unlike firms, they do not face external market pressures. The vast majority of governmental employees are non-political and are protected by civil service regulations from direct partisan political pressure.[33] Senior governmental officials and agency heads typically serve at the discretion of

---

30. *See also infra* chapter 8, section IV.B (providing more detailed discussion of Landes and Posner model).

31. For discussion, *see supra* chapter 5, section II.B.3.

32. *See* Armen A. Alchian, *Uncertainty, Evolution, and Economic Theory*, 58 J. POL. ECON. 211 (1950).

33. It is estimated that about ninety percent of civilian federal government employees are protected by the Civil Service Act. Herbert Kaufman, *Major Players: Bureaucracies in American Government*, 61 PUB. ADMIN. REV. 18, 20–21 (2001).

those who appoint them (usually the President) or for a set term of years. But civil service protections limit the power of senior officials to hire and fire subordinates beyond their immediate staff members. In addition, within the United States, as in most countries, professional bureaucrats are relatively constrained in their ability to earn income beyond their fixed salary. Compensation is often seniority-based, and bureaucrats have limited opportunities for financial reward resulting from exemplary performance or for financial punishment for substandard performance. In general, therefore, bureaucrats are largely immune from the direct electoral or financial incentives that motivate either elected officials or private market actors.

The American administrative state dates back to the Progressive Era of the early twentieth century as embodied in the intellectual and political influence of Woodrow Wilson. Before entering politics, Wilson was a leading academic who urged the study of the "science of administration" and the implementation of policy by a trained corps of unbiased and disinterested experts, a model inspired by the German administrative state.[34] The model of bureaucracy advanced during the Progressive Era implicitly assumed that unbiased experts, insulated from political and market pressures and guided by proper procedures and rules, would best discern and pursue the public interest. The civil service reforms and the creation of independent agencies, such as the Interstate Commerce Commission (1887), the Federal Trade Commission (1914), and later the multiple "alphabet soup" agencies created during the New Deal, were designed to produce the benefits of insulation from political pressure and to base government employment on merit-based criteria, such as competitive examinations, rather than through political party affiliation (the "spoils" system).[35] Once insulated from improper influences, bureaucrats were expected to be able to identify and pursue the public interest in a relatively selfless and disinterested manner. These assumptions about bureaucratic motivations came to dominate analyses of agency decision-making during the first half of the twentieth century and reached their zenith in the proliferation of new expert agencies during the New Deal and continued (and even accelerated) through the Johnson and Nixon Administrations.[36] Some recent commentators have applied the insights of public choice theory and the related field of "positive political theory" to suggest that even though the naïve model of delegation may no longer be

---

34. Woodrow Wilson, *The Study of Administration*, 2 POL. SCI. Q. 197 (1887); *see also* JAMES M. LANDIS, THE ADMINISTRATIVE PROCESS 46 (1938) ("The administrative process is, in essence, our generation's answer to the inadequacy of the judicial and the legislative processes.").

35. For a recent summary of this period and the philosophy that supported it, see John F. Duffy, The Death of the Independent Regulatory Commission (And the Birth of a New Independence?) (June 9, 2006) (unpublished manuscript), *available at* http://www.law.georgetown. edu/ faculty/documents/duffy_ paper.pdf.

36. For an informative discussion that claims the scope of regulatory expansions during the late Johnson and Nixon administrations eclipsed that of the New Deal, see Theodore J. Lowi, *Two Roads to Serfdom: Liberalism, Conservatism and Administrative Power*, 36 AM. U. L. REV. 295, 298–99 (1987) ("Depending on who is doing the counting, an argument can be made that Congress enacted more regulatory programs in the five years between 1969 and 1974 than during any other comparable period in our history, including the first five years of the New Deal.").

valid, continued delegation to agency specialists is consistent with public preferences.[37]

As noted in chapter 1, public choice theory rejects the assumption that governmental actors are selfless, disinterested actors motivated purely by the pursuit of the public interest, even assuming we could agree as to how to define such terms. And yet, it is true that bureaucrats are not primarily motivated by the desire to maximize income and that they are not subject to electoral pressures. What then do bureaucrats maximize? There are three main hypotheses about what motivates bureaucratic action: (1) agency expansion, (2) autonomy maximization, and (3) congressional control. We review each in turn.

A. THE AGENCY–EXPANSION HYPOTHESIS

Writing in the late nineteenth century, the German political economist Max Weber posited that in general bureaucrats seek to maximize power.[38] Modern public choice theorists have essentially adopted, and elaborated on, Weber's intuition, offering a number of specific corroborating studies.[39]

In his 1971 book *Bureaucracy and Representative Government*,[40] William Niskanen provided the first systematic effort to study bureaucracies within a public choice framework. Niskanen began by specifying the likely variables that influence a bureaucrat's utility function: "salary, perquisites of the office, public reputation, power, patronage, output of the bureau, ease of making changes, and ease of managing the bureau."[41] Niskanen linked many of these factors to agency size. James Q. Wilson summarized Niskanen's view, stating, "The utility of a business person is assumed to be profits; that of a bureaucrat is assumed to be something akin to profits: salary, rank, or power."[42] Wilson added: "Since both bureaucrats and business executives are people, it makes sense to assume that they prefer more of whatever they like to less."[43] Niskanen relied upon this utility function to model how a rational individual would behave

37. *See* David B. Spence & Frank Cross, *A Public Choice Case for the Administrative State*, 89 GEO. L.J. 97 (2000); *see also* Jonathan Bendor & Adam Meirowitz, *Spatial Models of Delegation*, 98 AM. POL. SCI. REV. 293 (2004).

38. Max Weber, *Bureaucracy*, in FROM MAX WEBER: ESSAYS IN SOCIOLOGY 196, 233–34 (H.H. Gerth & C. Wright Mills eds., trans., 1946); *see also* DENNIS C. MUELLER, PUBLIC CHOICE III, at 360 (2003).

39. Portions of the discussion that follows and the use of the *term* "empire building" summarize Niskanen's views are adapted from Todd J. Zywicki, *Institutional Review Boards as Academic Bureaucracies: An Economic and Experiential Analysis*, 101 Nw. U. L. REV. 861 (2007).

40. WILLIAM A. NISKANEN, JR., BUREAUCRACY AND REPRESENTATIVE GOVERNMENT (1971).

41. *Id.* at 38.

42. JAMES Q. WILSON, BUREAUCRACY: WHAT GOVERNMENT AGENCIES DO AND WHY THEY DO IT, at xviii (1989).

43. *Id.*

within a bureaucratic environment. Niskanen's model predicts that bureaucrats are primarily engaged in "empire building," meaning that they seek to maximize the size of their budgets and the scope of their agency's jurisdictional domain.

Within Niskanen's model, rational bureaucrats seek to maximize the bureau's budget during a given bureaucrat's tenure in office. With the exception of two variables in the bureaucrat's utility function—the ease of making policy changes and the ease of bureau management, which also depends on the actions of others—the remaining variables are positively correlated to the "total budget of the bureau during the bureaucrat's tenure in office."[44] As with public choice models of other governmental actors, it is not necessary that every bureaucrat share the same motivation. Some bureaucrats, for example, might seek higher salaries, others more power. Regardless of their ultimate motives, however, Niskanen argues that budget-maximization advances these other goals. After all, larger budgets permit a bureau to undertake more activities than they could with a smaller budget. Thus even public-interested bureaucrats will tend to favor budgetary expansion.

Niskanen suggests that in an important respect bureaucratic management is subject to the same sorts of "survivor" biases witnessed in electoral politics or market competition. Even if bureaucrats do not consciously seek to maximize agency budgets, only those bureaucrats willing to "play the game" of competing for larger budgets and power will survive in the sharp-elbowed world of political conflict. There is some empirical support for Niskanen's model. For instance, there is "ample evidence that bureaucrats systematically request larger budgets" and that they often succeed in having budgets set at the maximum politically feasible level.[45] Bureaucrats also have a "substantial impact on budgetary outcomes,"[46] generally producing larger budgets.

Because of their independence, bureaucrats are largely insulated from direct public pressure. As a result, the two primary constituencies with whom bureaucrats interact are agency employees and members of Congress, who confirm nominations and provide administrative oversight. Niskanen contends that those constituencies also tend to support enhanced agency budgets. Agency employees will prefer agency expansions, especially into novel areas, to enhance their prospects for internal promotion as part of a growing enterprise and their post-government career prospects in the private sector. For example, attorneys who participate in regulatory drafting will be in high demand by law firms involved in advising clients on matters of regulatory compliance.[47]

---

44. NISKANEN, *supra* note 40, at 38 (emphasis omitted). Niskanen further observes that while the exceptional elements of the utility function are not primarily furthered by budgetary concerns, larger budgets ameliorate these concerns as well.

45. André Blais & Stéphane Dion, *Conclusion: Are Bureaucrats Budget Maximizers?, in* THE BUDGET-MAXIMIZING BUREAUCRAT: APPRAISALS AND EVIDENCE 355, 355 (André Blais & Stéphane Dion eds., 1991) [hereinafter BUDGET-MAXIMIZING BUREAUCRAT] (emphasis omitted).

46. *Id.* at 358 (emphasis omitted).

47. The precise manner in which "revolving door" incentives might influence policy will vary among agencies. *See* PAUL J. QUIRK, INDUSTRY INFLUENCE IN FEDERAL REGULATORY AGENCIES 143–74

Congressional overseers also will tend to support larger budgets. Most regulatory oversight is performed at the committee level.[48] Committee membership typically is self-selected and, not surprisingly, legislators generally serve on committees that are considered most important to their constituencies. For instance, representatives of agricultural districts typically serve on agriculture committees; representatives from western districts serve on committees related to public lands; representatives of districts with military bases or large military contractors generally serve on military committees; and representatives of urban districts generally serve on committees dedicated to banking, housing, and welfare policy. Niskanen argues that this self-selection means that oversight committee members tend to support the missions of the agencies under their jurisdiction and thus to support larger budgets relative to the median legislator. Niskanen further observes that even the process of consolidating previously dispersed agency functions into a single department tends to result in increased expenditures rather than improved administrative efficiency.

Professor Tim Muris has offered an alternative explanation of increased regulatory expenditures that is linked to changes in the federal budget process.[49] Muris observes that "For most of our nation's first century, a single committee in each house controlled almost all spending authority." After reviewing the history of shifts between decentralization and centralized congressional spending power, Muris turned to the relevant modern history:

> Unfortunately, the process of spreading spending jurisdiction among committees began anew in 1932 when the Reconstruction Finance Corporation was created and financed outside normal appropriations channels. Decentralization accelerated during the next four decades, particularly between 1965 and 1975. By the mid 1970s, most substantive congressional committees had authority to report legislation to the floor committing funds from the U.S. Treasury. In 1932, the Appropriations Committees controlled 89 percent of outlays through the annual federal budget process. By 1992, fewer than 40 percent of federal outlays resulted from decisions under the Appropriators' control.
>
> This balkanization of spending authority creates a "common pool" problem. When no one owns a common resource, such as the fish in a lake, there is an incentive for too much fishing, depleting the population. With the budget, the common resource is general-fund revenue. As the Appropriations Committee controls less and less

---

(1981); *see also* Robert A. Katzmann, *Federal Trade Commission, in* THE POLITICS OF REGULATION 152 (James Q. Wilson ed., 1980); Suzanne Weaver, *Antitrust Division of the Department of Justice, in* THE POLITICS OF REGULATION, *supra*, at 123.

48. William A. Niskanen, Jr., *Bureaucrats and Politicians*, 18 J.L. & ECON. 617 (1975), *reprinted in* WILLIAM A. NISKANEN, JR., BUREAUCRACY AND PUBLIC ECONOMICS 243 (1994).

49. *Budget Process Reform: Hearing before the H. Comm. on Rules*, 106th Cong., 1st Sess. 120 (1999) (prepared statement of Timothy J. Muris, Foundation Professor, George Mason University School of Law); *see also* W. Mark Crain & Timothy J. Muris, *Legislative Organization of Fiscal Policy*, 38 J.L. & ECON. 311 (1995).

spending, and, correspondingly, other congressional committees control more and more, no one committee has the incentive to restrain spending because the total level of spending is no longer the responsibility of any one committee. To the contrary, the resulting competition among committees to spend results in more spending than would otherwise occur, increasing deficit spending.[50]

Does this history counsel in favor of a renewed call for tightened central control of congressional budgeting processes, including centralizing all or most spending decisions to a single committee? Would such a change have the potential to improve not only fiscal discipline, but also regulatory discipline given the potential mismatch that might then arise between regulatory policy and the means with which to effectuate that policy? Why or why not?

Whatever the root cause, the process of agency expansion also provides congressional overseers with opportunities for rent extraction.[51] Agencies can threaten regulatory activity, thus encouraging members of Congress to offer their constituents benign intervention by holding the agency at bay. Morris Fiorina notes that Congress can even initiate this rent-extraction process by enacting vague legislation, knowing in advance that the regulators will inevitably make mistakes, at which point Congress can intervene to "piously [denounce] the evils of bureaucracy" and set matters right: Fiorina claims that this process allows Congressmen to "take credit coming and going."[52] Once again, this process also provides oversight officials with regulatory expertise that proves of value in the private market.

Over time, Niskanen modified his model, claiming that bureaucrats seek to maximize their *discretionary* budget, rather than their overall budget. Thus, for instance, agencies would not necessarily seek to acquire large budgetary responsibilities connected to ministerial activities such as processing food stamps or Social Security checks, as these mechanical functions do not have a substantial discretionary component that will augment the agency's power or prestige. Niskanen defines discretionary budget as "the difference between . . . total budget and the minimum cost of producing the expected output. . . ."[53] In effect, this is equivalent to the agency-cost slack between the legislature and the regulatory agency. The discretionary budget thus permits the bureaucrat to enlarge his perquisites and other benefits to the status of the agency. In general, enhanced agency budgets correlate with enhanced discretion since effective monitoring becomes more difficult as a function of agency growth. Niskanen argues:

---

50. *Budget Process Reform: Hearing before the H. Comm. on Rules, supra* note 49, at 121; *see also* Crain & Muris, *supra* note 49, at 311.

51. For a related discussion, see *supra* chapter 2, section II.6 (discussing rent extraction).

52. MORRIS P. FIORINA, CONGRESS: KEYSTONE OF THE WASHINGTON ESTABLISHMENT 46–47 (2d ed. 1989).

53. Niskanen, *supra* note 48, at 245.

Some part of this discretionary budget will be spent in ways that serve the bureau, such as additional staff, capital, and perquisites. The remainder will be spent in ways that serve the interests of the political review authorities. The distribution of this surplus between spending that serves the interests of the bureaus and that which serves the interests of the review authorities, as in any bilateral bargaining, will depend on the relevant information, alternatives, and bargaining strategies available to the two parties.[54]

Niskanen's model has been criticized on several grounds. Bureaucrats themselves do not obtain obvious direct benefits from increased agency budgets, thus raising questions about their incentives to seek larger budgets. Although growing budgets might offer greater opportunities for promotion for rank-and-file employees, salaries of governmental employees vary little based on agency size.[55] Those who work in larger agencies are unlikely to earn higher salaries (or have opportunities for more non-pecuniary income, such as leisure) as compared with those who work in smaller agencies. Moreover, federal bureaucrats do not have particularly generous perquisites, such as ornate offices or cushy travel arrangements. As compared with the private sector, working conditions in governmental agencies are relatively spare. And yet, large and growing agencies might be intrinsically more prestigious thus provide greater opportunities for lucrative post-governmental employment. But even here there are exceptions. Comparatively small agencies such as the SEC are quite powerful and prestigious and provide substantial opportunities for lucrative post-governmental employment.

B. THE AGENCY–AUTONOMY HYPOTHESIS

James Q. Wilson has challenged Niskanen's assumption that bureaucrats are primarily motivated to maximize budgets. He writes, "[B]ureaucrats have a variety of preferences; only part of their behavior can be explained by assuming they are struggling to get bigger salaries or fancier offices or larger budgets."[56] Bureaucrats might instead be motivated by ideological views or professional norms.[57] Indeed, contrary to Niskanen's predictions, agencies sometimes resist expansions to their authority and scope.[58]

Wilson argues that rather than being imperialistic, bureaucrats tend to be averse to risk and conflict with other agencies. Bureaucrats thus tend to avoid pursuing larger budgets and responsibilities if the result

---

54. William A. Niskanen, *A Reflection on* Bureaucracy and Representative Government, *in* BUDGET–MAXIMIZING BUREAUCRAT, *supra* note 45, at 19.

55. *See* Ronald N. Johnson & Gary D. Libecap, *Agency Growth, Salaries and the Protected Bureaucrat*, 27 ECON. INQUIRY 431 (1989); Robert A. Young, *Budget Size and Bureaucratic Careers*, *in* BUDGET–MAXIMIZING BUREAUCRAT, *supra* note 45, at 33.

56. WILSON, *supra* note 42, at xviii.

57. Spence & Cross, *supra* note 37, at 117.

58. *See infra* notes 67–69 and accompanying text.

generates conflict. Wilson claims that a more accurate model of agency behavior rests on "autonomy" or "independence," rather than jurisdictional or budgetary expansion.[59] Wilson defines autonomy as:

> [A] "condition of independence sufficient to permit a group to work out and maintain a distinctive identity." There are two parts to [this] definition, an external and an internal one. The external aspect of autonomy, independence, is equivalent to "jurisdiction" or "domain." Agencies ranking high in autonomy have a monopoly jurisdiction (that is, they have few or no bureaucratic rivals and a minimum of political constraints imposed on them by superiors). The internal aspect of autonomy is identity or mission—a widely shared and approved understanding of the central tasks of the agency.[60]

Autonomy takes many forms, such as independence from oversight, external constituencies, or rivalry from other agencies. According to Wilson, successful bureaucracies resist incursions onto their turf and avoid taking on tasks that are not at the heart of their institutional mission or that "will produce divided or hostile constituencies."[61] Rational bureaucrats will resist proposals to expand agency budgets or jurisdiction that risk creating conflict with rival agencies, undertaking new and difficult tasks, or producing problematic constituency relations.[62]

Agency expansions thus have costs as well as benefits. A relatively small agency, for example, might have effective "monopoly" power in a given regulatory field, a satisfied clientele, and considerable policy expertise. Specialization allows the regulators to navigate congressional oversight procedures and to better manage potential jurisdictional conflict with other agencies. Agency expansion might provoke interagency conflict by forcing the agency into regulatory areas in which it lacks both expertise and clientele support. Wilson observes, for example, that when the United States Department of Agriculture ("USDA") began to administer the Food Stamp program, it encountered new conflicts with various congressional oversight committees, interest groups, and clientele concerned with welfare programs for lower-income groups, as opposed to its previous clientele who were focused on farming and agricultural products. Agency expansions also threaten a less satisfactory and less cost-effective administration of assigned regulatory functions, thus inviting heightened public and congressional scrutiny. The combined effects might also harm the agency's public reputation and bring its leaders under scrutiny, a foreseeable result that bureaucrats would prefer to avoid.

Wilson observes that these complications might lead agencies to resist expansion of their budget and authority if expansion compromises their autonomy or other beneficial aspects of agency culture. In contrast with

---

59. WILSON, *supra* note 42, at 182.

60. *Id.* (quoting PHILIP SELZNICK, LEADERSHIP IN ADMINISTRATION 121 (1957)).

61. *Id.* at 191.

62. For a largely complementary analysis, see *id.* at 179 (citing MORTON H. HALPERIN, BUREAUCRATIC POLITICS AND FOREIGN POLICY 51 (1974) (positing that bureaucracies "are often prepared to accept less money with greater control than more money with less control")).

Niskanen, Wilson contends that "[g]overnment agencies are more risk averse than imperialistic. They prefer security to rapid growth, autonomy to competition, stability to change."[63] Agencies pursuing expansion, he argues, are characterized by especially "benign environments—strong public support and popular leadership."[64] The typical bureaucracy is "defensive, threat-avoiding, scandal-minimizing," not " 'imperialistic' or expansionist."[65] "In short," Wilson writes, "agencies quickly learn what forces in their environment are capable of using catastrophe or absurdity as effective political weapons, and they work hard to minimize the chances that they will be vulnerable to such attacks."[66]

Contrary to Niskanen's hypothesis, Wilson argues that the typical bureaucracy will be reluctant to take on activities that embrace seemingly intractable problems and that are fraught with the danger of unintended consequences including regulatory failure and criticism. Wilson notes, for example, that the Federal Bureau of Investigation ("FBI") originally resisted investigating narcotics and organized crime because the potential costs (broadly understood) exceeded the benefits to the agency. According to Wilson, the FBI feared that narcotics trafficking could not be "solved" in the same way as kidnappings and bank robberies, thus risking public criticism. The Bureau also feared the potential for corruption associated with drug and Mafia investigations and the complex new demands that undertaking such responsibilities would pose, including undercover operations, which "make the internal management of the organization more difficult or even threaten the existence of its shared sense of mission."[67] The result of the FBI's resistance to agency expansion was the creation of the Drug Enforcement Agency ("DEA"). Thus, while Wilson agrees that "[a]ll else being equal, big budgets are better than small," his model is premised on the intuition that "all else is not equal"[68] and that "[a]utonomy is valued at least as much as resources, because autonomy determines the degree to which it is costly to acquire and use resources."[69] As a result, the agency is unlikely to sacrifice its autonomy to secure more resources or an enlarged jurisdiction.

The bureaucratic preference for autonomy over empire-building is also consistent with the greater opportunities of governmental employees to consume leisure or to shirk in performing one's duties compared to comparable workers in the private sector. Civil service protections not only insulate governmental employees from improper political and market pressures but they also weaken incentives for productivity and reduce accountability for rank-and-file bureaucrats. At a minimum, civil service

63. James Q. Wilson, *The Politics of Regulation, in* THE POLITICS OF REGULATION, *supra* note 47, at 357, 376 (footnote omitted).

64. *Id.*

65. *Id.* at 378.

66. *Id.* at 377.

67. WILSON, *supra* note 42, at 182–83.

68. *Id.* at 182.

69. *Id.* at 195.

protections reduce incentives to expend greater than average effort. In fact, government employees may self-select for positions that provide security and reduced accountability in place of the higher potential remuneration, greater accountability, and reduced job security that characterize comparable employment in the private sector.

Studies of government-owned corporations indicate that as compared with otherwise similar private market actors, government employees tend to work less and at lower efficiency, while drawing higher salaries for any given level of professional responsibility.[70] Dennis Mueller reviewed seventy-one academic studies comparing work incentives in private firms and government bureaucracies. Mueller found that only five studies found that public firms operated with a greater level of cost effectiveness than comparable private firms and only ten found no difference in cost effectiveness.[71] In each of the remaining fifty-six studies, "state-owned companies were found to be significantly less efficient than privately owned firms supplying the same good or service."[72] Mueller concludes, "The provision of a good or service by a state bureaucracy or by a state-owned company generally leads to lower residual profits, and/or higher costs and lower productivity."[73] Scholars have claimed that workers in firms in regulated industries protected from competition exhibit similar inefficiencies.[74]

Do you find these claims persuasive? Are there contexts in which a governmental employee's output should be gauged against criteria other than efficiency? If so, what are those criteria? To what extent are the claimed findings of comparative bureaucratic or government-owned inefficiencies generalizable? Would you expect to find similar results in other areas of employment in which the incentives for productivity are attenuated, at least as compared with traditional firm settings, including, for example, university professors (especially those with tenure)? What about unionized work forces that provide relatively higher degrees of job seniority? What does the model suggest about the behavior of life-tenured judges?

C. CONGRESSIONAL CONTROL MODEL

Models of budget-maximizing, autonomy-maximizing, or leisure-maximizing bureaucrats assume that congressional oversight of agency activity is lax and passive, enabling bureaucrats to pursue their own agendas

---

70. For a general discussion of government-owned corporations, see FROM BUREAUCRACY TO BUSINESS ENTERPRISE: LEGAL AND POLICY ISSUES IN THE TRANSFORMATION OF GOVERNMENT SERVICES (Michael J. Whincop ed., 2003).

71. MUELLER, *supra* note 38, at 373.

72. *Id.*

73. *Id.* Mueller observes, for example, that the public school system in the United States has been criticized as "fai[ling] its citizens not by educating too many students, but educating them poorly" as compared with what he claims are more efficiently organized private schools". *Id.* at 384 (citing JOHN E. CHUBB & TERRY M. MOE, POLITICS, MARKETS, AND AMERICA'S SCHOOLS (1990)).

74. For summaries of this literature, see Sandra E. Black & Philip E. Strahan, *The Division of Spoils: Rent–Sharing and Discrimination in a Regulated Industry*, 91 AM. ECON. REV. 814 (2001); James Peoples, *Deregulation and the Labor Market*, J. ECON. PERSP., Spring 1998, at 111.

rather than those of Congress or the public at large.[75] Congress holds relatively few and generally perfunctory oversight hearings that focus primarily on such matters as budgets and confirmations of agency heads. This ineffective and *ad hoc* oversight is said to result from three factors:

> First, agencies control information from their policy area. Second, access to clientele fosters agency-clientele alliances to protect agencies from their nominal overseers in Congress. And third, the high cost of passing new legislation to redirect agency policy limits congressional action in all but the most important cases. The resulting bureaucratic insulation affords bureaucrats a degree of discretion which, in turn, is used to pursue their own private goals rather than the public purposes for which they were originally created.[76]

Thus, it is argued that lax and ineffective congressional oversight enables inefficient agency expansion or deviation from preferred congressional policies.

Other scholars have questioned this model of congressional passivity, arguing that Congress, behaving rationally, will seek to limit agency departures from its preferred policies. Because bureaucrats and members of Congress are repeat players, it is unlikely that Congress would tolerate ongoing deception and inefficiency, as would be required to maintain continuous regulatory expansion or shirking.[77] Moreover, when Congress decides to delegate authority to an agency, it should take into account any agency biases toward inefficient regulatory expansion.[78]

In a case study of the FTC, Weingast and Moran argued that focusing on the absence of active formal oversight overlooks important informal dynamics in the relationship between agencies and Congress. Instead, the authors propose a ''[c]ongressional dominance'' model that focuses on the informal relationships between congressional committees and agencies.[79] The authors describe the model as follows:

> [C]ongressmen—or, more specifically, particular congressmen on the relevant committees—possess sufficient rewards and sanctions to create an incentive system for agencies. Agency mandate notwithstanding, rewards go to those agencies that pursue policies of interest to the current committee members; those agencies that fail to do so are confronted with sanctions. It follows that if the incentive system worked effectively, then agencies would pursue congressional goals even though they received little direct public guidance from their overseers. Congressmen on the relevant committees may appear ignorant of agency proceedings because they gauge the success of pro-

---

75. *See* THEODORE J. LOWI, THE END OF LIBERALISM: THE SECOND REPUBLIC OF THE UNITED STATES (2d ed. 1979).

76. Barry R. Weingast & Mark J. Moran, *Bureaucratic Discretion or Congressional Control? Regulatory Policymaking by the Federal Trade Commission*, 91 J. POL. ECON. 765, 767 (1983).

77. *See* Gary J. Miller & Terry M. Moe, *Bureaucrats, Legislators, and the Size of Government*, 77 AM. POL. SCI. REV. 297 (1983).

78. *See* Spence & Cross, *supra* note 37, at 117–18.

79. *See* Weingast & Moran, *supra* note 76, at 768.

grams through their constituents' reactions rather than through detailed study. Public hearings and investigations are resource-intensive activities, so they will hardly be used by congressmen for those policy areas that are operating smoothly (i.e., benefiting congressional clientele). Their real purpose is to police those areas functioning poorly. The threat of ex post sanctions creates ex ante incentives for the bureau to serve a congressional clientele.[80]

The authors claim that their view carries the following "striking implication: the more effective the incentive system, the less often we should observe sanctions in the form of congressional attention through hearings and investigations."[81] Stated differently, "direct and continuous monitoring of inputs rather than of results is an inefficient mechanism by which a principal constrains the action of his agent."[82] In Weingast and Moran's analysis, the absence of visible congressional monitoring counterintuitively suggests that the agency is abiding congressional priorities. Only when informal constraints break down must Congress rely upon formal oversight mechanisms. Thus, Weingast and Moran challenge the inference that the absence of aggressive, public, congressional oversight reflects agency independence from congressional control.

Weingast and Moran argue that congressional control over independent agencies actually is pervasive albeit not always visible. They identify several mechanisms through which Congress influences agency behavior. First, agencies are subject to a competitive budgetary process. Few agencies stand in the position of a bilateral monopoly with Congress; instead, the various agencies compete with each other for budgetary allocations, and Congress should favor those that perform their duties in a relatively more cost-effective manner. The resulting competition constrains individual agencies seeking to increase their size and budgets and also reduces the information asymmetries between Congress and the agency by forcing the agency to explain its operations in order to justify its budget request.[83] Second, Congress can and does exert formal oversight control when necessary through hearings and investigations. Third, Congress can "make life miserable for an agency by endless hearings and questionnaires."[84] The best way to avoid this harassment is "to further congressional interests."[85] Finally, Congress can use its power to confirm appointments to negotiate with the President over nominations. Thus, even though confirmation hearings often appear perfunctory, the formal hearings do not necessarily reflect the extensive private negotiations that precede the hearings.

---

80. *Id.* at 768–69.

81. *Id.* at 769.

82. *Id.*

83. *See* DONALD A. WITTMAN, THE MYTH OF DEMOCRATIC FAILURE: WHY POLITICAL INSTITUTIONS ARE EFFICIENT 95 (1995).

84. McNollgast, *The Political Economy of Law*, *in* 2 HANDBOOK OF LAW AND ECONOMICS 1651, 1705 (A. Mitchell Polinsky & Steven Shavell eds., 2007).

85. *Id.*

Although bureaus compete for congressional resources, members of Congress are motivated to reduce agency conflict and can use the committee process to do so. The congressional committee system allows individual members of Congress to create what amounts to a system of congressional mini-monopolies that oversee particular agencies and departments with minimal inter-jurisdiction conflict. As previously noted, self-selecting on committees gives members of Congress disproportionate influence over issues that matter most for electoral support. The committee system also reduces the information asymmetries between Congress and agencies by allowing committee overseers to develop the requisite expertise with which to effectively monitor agency performance.[86]

Because oversight committees exert disproportionate influence over agency policy as compared with Congress more generally, Weingast and Moran predict that changes in committee preferences should translate into changes in agency policy. Conversely, stable committee membership promotes stable agency policy, even if agency leadership changes. The agency independence model would predict that agency leadership should matter more.

Weingast and Moran test their model with evidence of the FTC's behavior in the late 1970s and early 1980s. During the late 1970s, the FTC aggressively asserted authority over broad segments of the American economy. The Commission launched investigations of "advertising aimed at children ..., the used car market, the insurance industry," and professional licensing organizations, as well as launching major antitrust suits against the nation's largest oil companies and breakfast cereal manufacturers.[87] After encouraging these efforts for many years, congressional overseers reversed course, publicly lambasting the FTC for overreaching and passing targeted legislation to halt several FTC investigations. At one point, Congress even refused to authorize the FTC's budget, temporarily suspending the agency's activities (the funding was later reauthorized). The FTC responded to this pressure by closing nearly all of its controversial rulemaking investigations and suspending what many considered its most ambitious and controversial antitrust prosecutions.

Weingast and Moran argue that the FTC's behavior during this period contradicts the predictions of the agency independence model.[88] Under the agency independence view, Congress intervened only after the FTC had operated independently for a decade, by which time it had severely strayed from preferred congressional policy. In this analysis, the FTC was the exception that proved the rule: Had it been more restrained in its

---

86. *See* DAVID EPSTEIN & SHARYN O'HALLORAN, DELEGATING POWERS: A TRANSACTION COST POLITICS APPROACH TO POLICY MAKING UNDER SEPARATE POWERS 166–67 (1999); Albert Breton & Ronald Wintrobe, *The Equilibrium Size of a Budget Maximizing Bureau: A Note on Niskanen's Theory of Bureaucracy*, 83 J. POL. ECON. 195 (1975); Rui J.P. de Figueiredo, Jr., Pablo T. Spiller & Santiago Urbiztondo, *An Informational Perspective on Administrative Procedures*, 15 J.L. ECON. & ORG. 283 (1999).

87. Weingast & Moran, *supra* note 76, at 776.

88. Weingast and Moran's critique is specifically targeted against KENNETH W. CLARKSON & TIMOTHY J. MURIS, THE FEDERAL TRADE COMMISSION SINCE 1970: ECONOMIC REGULATION AND BUREAUCRATIC BEHAVIOR (1981) and ROBERT A. KATZMANN, REGULATORY BUREAUCRACY: THE FEDERAL TRADE COMMISSION AND ANTITRUST POLICY (1980). Weingast & Moran, *supra* note 76, at 776.

activities, it could have continued to act indefinitely unimpeded by congressional interference. Most agencies, in contrast, operate unchecked by avoiding extreme positions that alienate important constituencies and congressional overseers.

Weingast and Moran instead claim that the FTC's behavior is better captured by the congressional dominance model. In their analysis, the agency's behavior in both the earlier activist and later retrenchment periods reflect congressional preferences or, more specifically, those of the relevant oversight committee members. Weingast and Moran demonstrate that the preferences of the oversight committee changed from supporting to opposing FTC activism, thus changing agency policies. Whereas in 1977, Congress "consistently criticized the FTC for lack of progress on their many investigations," the authors observe that these were the "very investigations that drew so much criticism [two] years later."[89] The change in the FTC's behavior reflected the rapid change in Congress during this period:

> Between 1976 and 1979, the dominant coalition on the relevant congressional committees changed from favoring to opposing an activist FTC. This resulted from the nearly complete turnover of those on and in control of the relevant Senate oversight subcommittee. None of the senior members of the subcommittee responsible for major FTC legislation and direction for the previous decade returned after 1976. Those previously in the minority took control of the subcommittee and began reversing the policies initiated by their predecessors. The 1979 and 1980 hearings were simply the most visible culmination of this process.
>
> The congressional choice explanation suggests that the FTC initiated controversial policies because it got strong signals to do so from Congress. Far from roaming beyond its congressional mandate as an exercise in bureaucratic discretion, the FTC aggressively implemented its new authority in concert with its congressional sponsors. With the turnover in 1977, however, the FTC lost its congressional support and thus was vulnerable to the subsequent reversals.[90]

In fact, Weingast and Moran observe that many of those on the FTC oversight committee during the 1970s were champions of consumer protection legislation who sponsored major pieces of pro-consumer legislation that characterized the era of regulatory expansion. Indeed, those members urged the FTC to be more active, as was reflected in the agency's consumer protection agenda.

From 1977 to 1979, however, there was a dramatic turnover of membership on the Senate Commerce Committee and Subcommittee on Consumer Affairs that included a rapid replacement of liberals with conservatives. From 1966 to 1976, members of the subcommittee were substantially more liberal than the Senate as a whole. By 1979, however,

---

89. Weingast & Moran, *supra* note 76, at 777.

90. *Id.* at 777–78.

the pendulum swung in the opposite direction with the result that subcommittee members were substantially more conservative than the Senate as a whole. Weingast and Moran conclude that the FTC's crisis resulted from changes in congressional preferences rather than the agency's activities, a finding that is consistent with the congressional control model but not the agency independence model.

Other studies have corroborated substantial congressional influence over the FTC. Roger Faith, Donald Leavens, and Robert Tollison found that congressional influence helps to explain the pattern of FTC merger enforcement.[91] Unlike Weingast and Moran, however, Faith, Leavens, and Tollison concluded that constituent politics played a larger role than ideology. The authors found that an FTC merger challenge was significantly more likely to be dismissed if the headquarters of a merging firm was located within the district of one of the congressional oversight subcommittee members than if it was not.[92] They conclude that this finding is potentially consistent with either the budget-maximizing or congressional oversight models, but is inconsistent with the autonomy model. They further conclude that their analysis supports Richard Posner's observation that Congress often spurred FTC antitrust investigations at the behest of firms located in their district in order to gain a competitive advantage.[93]

Timothy Muris, who served as Chairman of the FTC from 2001 to 2004, has challenged the congressional control model, claiming that it overstates congressional influence on FTC policymaking.[94] Muris argues that agency outputs reflect the interaction of several internal and external constituencies: Congress, courts, the President, and the internal staff itself. Muris further notes that Congress itself does not speak with a unified voice. Indeed, its members represent different, and conflicting, constituent interests. In addition, the FTC responds to two other principals: the President (who appoints the Chairman), and the judiciary, which in proper cases ensures that FTC actions fall within the agency's statutory mandate. Moreover, agencies have their own independent bureaucratic culture:

> What Weingast and Moran miss in explaining the FTC, however, is the importance of the agency's staff, both in its ideological character and in its career goals. During the early 1970s, for example, numerous liberal employees were drawn to the "revitalized" commission. . . . [T]his new blood [made the agency more liberal], paralleling the increased [liberalism] of both the Senate and House subcommittees

---

91. Roger L. Faith, Donald R. Leavens & Robert D. Tollison, *Antitrust Pork Barrel*, 25 J.L. & ECON. 329 (1982).

92. *Id.* at 335–42.

93. Richard A. Posner, *The Federal Trade Commission*, 37 U. CHI. L. REV. 47 (1969). Subsequent research has further illuminated the political constraints on the FTC as well as the agency's internal conflicts. *See* Malcolm B. Coate et al., *Bureaucracy and Politics in FTC Merger Challenges*, 33 J.L. & ECON. 463 (1990).

94. Timothy J. Muris, *Regulatory Policymaking at the Federal Trade Commission: The Extent of Congressional Control*, 94 J. POL. ECON. 884 (1986).

overseeing the FTC. While the composition of these subcommittees became more conservative in the late 1970s, the composition of the FTC staff remained liberal. Thus, contrary to the approach of Weingast and Moran, we would expect to find a more dramatic shift in FTC caseload in the early 1970s, when *both* Congress and the FTC staff changed politically, than we would find in the late 1970s, when only Congress changed. The evidence available supports this prediction.[95]

Muris thus argues that the agency bureaucracy has an internal dynamic of its own that is at least partially independent of congressional incentives. Sometimes congressional and agency preferences push in the same direction, thereby amplifying policy swings. Other times, however, they push against each other so that even if agency policy moves in the same general direction as Congress, the bureaucracy may moderate the extent of the swing.

Niskanen also has challenged the assumptions that underlie the congressional control model. From the perspective of individual members of Congress, monitoring is a public good because any resulting savings inure to the benefit of Congress or the nation as a whole.[96] Like other public goods, monitoring is subject to collective action and free riding problems. Thus, although Congress as a whole might have incentives to monitor agency waste and inefficiency, individual members of Congress do not, or at least do not to the same extent.[97] Agency monitoring is costly and requires allocation of time and staffing resources that could be rationally dedicated to other tasks that promote legislators' interests more directly, such as constituent service or legislative activity. Niskanen contends that members of Congress will rationally monitor agency behavior only up to the point where a member's private marginal costs exceed the member's private marginal benefits. As compared with activities that produce discrete and excludable benefits for which members of Congress can claim credit with constituents, monitoring activities tend to be undersupplied. Rational legislators are likely to prefer responding to constituent complaints as a low cost source of information from which to sort potential targets of abusive or inefficient exercises of agency powers, often referred to as a "fire alarm" theory of oversight.

Which model seems to best explain the behavior of agencies and bureaucrats—the budget-maximization hypothesis, the autonomy hypothesis, or the congressional control hypothesis? To what extent are these models mutually exclusive and to what extent are they complementary? Are there conditions, or periods of time, when one of the models is likely to be more robust in explaining agency behavior than another? How, if at all, is your answer related to presidential and non-presidential election cycles? Why? How might these various models apply in other contexts,

---

95. *Id.* at 888–89.

96. *See also* Gordon Tullock, *Public Decisions as Public Goods*, 79 J. POL. ECON. 913 (1971).

97. *See* Niskanen, *supra* note 48, at 249–54.

such as managerial incentives in large, nonprofit organizations such as charities or universities?

Should these models, individually or in combination, influence the judicial response to agency activities? Should it affect, for example, agency deference rules under the *Chevron* and *Mead* doctrines? Should it affect the attitude of courts toward the so-called non-delegation doctrine? Why or why not? How does the selection among these models help to frame the inquiry as to which types of policy domains Congress is more prone to delegate to agencies and under which circumstances? Why? How might it affect whether particular regulatory policies are, or should be, vested in executive or independent agencies? Why?

D. MONITORING BY THE PUBLIC

Bureaucrats are probably even more insulated from effective monitoring by the public than are elected officials, and as a result, agencies are also potentially subject to a corresponding increase in interest group influence. Citizens do not vote directly for bureaucrats and as a result, the policymakers lack direct electoral accountability for their decisions. In general, federal agencies receive less popular attention than Congress and the complex regulatory labyrinth often makes the processes and outcomes of regulatory activity difficult for most people to comprehend. Moreover, the processes of agency rulemaking are more opaque than elections, and agency responsiveness to the general public is therefore all the more attenuated. Former Administrators of the Office of Information and Regulatory Affairs ("OIRA") Christopher DeMuth and Douglas Ginsburg have observed that as a practical matter, "public" participation in administrative rulemaking process "is limited to those organized groups with the largest and most immediate stakes in the results."[98] They observe:

> Although presidents and legislatures are themselves vulnerable to pressure from politically influential groups, the rulemaking process— operating in relative obscurity from public view but lavishly attended by interest groups—is even more vulnerable. A substantial number of agency rules could not survive public scrutiny and gain two legislative majorities and the signature of the president.[99]

Judge Ralph Winter also has commented on the divergence of agency rulemaking from public preferences:

> Much has been made of the consumer's inability to affect his market destinies and his lack of product information. Yet surely these criticisms are even more cogent where government is involved. A product which does not satisfy consumers is far more likely to disappear than a government ruling. When the [Interstate Commerce Commission "I.C.C."] prohibits new truckers from entering the market, consum-

---

98. Christopher C. DeMuth & Douglas H. Ginsburg, *White House Review of Agency Rulemaking*, 99 HARV. L. REV. 1075, 1081 (1986).

99. *Id.*

ers rarely know of the ruling—much less why it was made—and, of course, can do nothing to change it.[100]

Moreover, even if citizens were able to acquire meaningful information regarding regulatory policy, the agencies themselves would still have minimal incentive to seek input from average citizens on regulatory matters. As Steven Croley has observed:

> Direct citizen participation in regulatory decisionmaking is thus both rare—taking place only as often as elections for political representatives—and very crude—citizens vote for political candidates with very little information about those candidates' positions on regulatory issues, and must moreover vote for a mixed bundle of such policies at once.[101]

Croley concludes:

> Because most citizens are largely uninformed about most regulatory decisions, and because they moreover lack incentives to become sufficiently informed to reward legislators who do not shirk, legislators do not—cannot—protect the broad regulatory interests of their constituencies. This is true because organized interest groups—industry groups, occupational groups, and trade associations—who *are* informed because they have an especially high demand for regulatory goods do monitor legislators, punishing those who consistently fail to provide such goods and rewarding those who provide favorable regulation. Thus interest groups capitalize on the opportunities created by principal-agent slack, made worse by most voters' collective action problems, in order to buy regulatory goods that advantage them.[102]

David Spence and Frank Cross have challenged this description of agency indifference to public preferences.[103] They acknowledge that the public itself is rationally ignorant about agency activities; nonetheless, they contend that the public might support delegation on the belief that expert decision makers have more expertise on a given issue than Congress and that, as a result, the agency is more likely to get the "correct" answer. The median voter in the electorate often will have no particular substantive preference on a given issue, but instead will prefer that government experts select the policy that they determine to be best. Spence and Cross further argue that voters will prefer to rely upon skilled experts rather than generalist elected representatives to make these policy decisions. If so, voters will support broad discretion for agency decisionmaking even if congressional oversight is limited and bureaucratic control attenuated.

Consider Winter's claim that citizens cannot move agency behavior. To what extent, if any, is this in tension with the history of the Gay

---

100. Ralph K. Winter, Jr., *Economic Regulation vs. Competition: Ralph Nader and Creeping Capitalism*, 82 YALE L.J. 890, 894 (1973).

101. Steven P. Croley, *Theories of Regulation: Incorporating the Administrative Process*, 98 COLUM. L. REV. 1, 38 (1998).

102. *Id.* (footnote omitted).

103. Spence & Cross, *supra* note 37; *see also* Bendor & Meirowitz, *supra* note 37.

Rights lobby on the issue of speeding up access to the AIDS cocktail through fast-track FDA approval?[104] The result was to speed up approval of the AIDS cocktail relative to the ordinary regulatory processes, which are both extremely expensive and often take decades to accomplish. Does this example run counter to Winter's thesis or does it confirm Winter's thesis? Is the AIDS-activist lobby the type of group that Winter was describing? If not, what characteristics might distinguish this group politically and account for their success?

To what extent do the insights from these models help to explain opportunities for citizen watchdog groups? Do these groups emerge as political entrepreneurs who are able to capitalize on the inability of private citizens to effectively monitor agency conduct? Are such groups effective at harnessing citizen demand for regulatory reform? Why or why not? To what extent do activist monitoring groups have their own institutional interests in maximizing their group's influence or budgets that might lead them to deviate from the interests of the public generally?[105] Would you anticipate that such groups are effective in securing promises during presidential primaries that subsequently affect the direction of regulatory policy? If so, does this counsel in favor or against agency deference rules? Why?

III. CHARACTERISTICS OF AGENCY BEHAVIOR

Public choice theorists generally claim that observed features of bureaucratic behavior are at odds with the public interest model of politics. Specifically, the motivation and opportunity to shirk produces incentives that depart from majoritarian or efficiency objectives. In this part, we address these claims.

A. SYSTEMATIC BIAS IN DECISION–MAKING

Economists have predicted that the incentive structure faced by bureaucrats will lead to unduly risk-averse decision-making, producing an inefficiently high level of regulation.[106] The concepts of Type I and Type II error help to explain the precise nature of the competing risks that regulators seek to avoid.

Type I errors, also referred to as "false positives," arise when a regulatory burden is sub-optimally high and, as a result, certain safe goods

---

104. Wendy K. Mariner, *Activists and the AIDS Business*, 257 SCIENCE 1975 (1992) (reviewing PETER S. ARNO & KARYN L. FEIDEN, AGAINST THE ODDS: THE STORY OF AIDS DRUG DEVELOPMENT, POLITICS AND PROFITS (1992)) (observing that AIDS activists, such as ACT UP, successfully pushed FDA to change trial and approval processes in the late 1980s to allow fast track approval of AIDS cocktail).

105. Todd J. Zywicki, *Baptists? The Political Economy of Environmental Interest Groups*, 53 CASE W. RES. L. REV. 315 (2002).

106. *See* Sam Peltzman, *An Evaluation of Consumer Protection Legislation: The 1962 Drug Amendments*, 81 J. POL. ECON. 1049 (1973); *see also* MUELLER, *supra* note 38, at 370–71 (summarizing literature).

or services are classified by the regulator as unreasonably dangerous. Type II error produces "false negatives," meaning an erroneous conclusion that dangerous goods are safe. Type II error arises when the regulatory burden is sub-optimally low and, as a result, dangerous goods are classified by the regulator as safe. Both types of errors—Type I and Type II—impose costs on consumers either by prohibiting the sale of safe goods or permitting the sale of dangerous goods. The total economic cost of a regulatory regime will include the sum of these two errors multiplied by the harm to consumers that the errors produce plus the administrative costs of making the decisions.

These error costs need not be symmetrical. For instance, for criminal law enforcement, the American legal system accepts as a foundational premise that the cost of false positives (the erroneous conviction of innocent defendants) exceeds the cost of false negatives (the erroneous acquittal of guilty defendants). This assumption is reflected in the aphorism that it is better to allow ten (or one hundred) guilty men to go free than to wrongly convict one innocent man.[107] As a result of the asymmetrical assessment of these competing costs, the American legal system imposes a substantially higher standard of proof for convictions in criminal cases (beyond a reasonable doubt) than in civil cases (preponderance of the evidence).

Strict cost-benefit analysis suggests that social welfare is maximized when regulators act in a risk-neutral manner. This means that regulators are expected to weigh the opportunity costs of delayed approval in preventing suffering or saving lives equally with the costs to those who might be injured by premature approval of a drug. From the perspective of individual bureaucrats, however, private cost may not be aligned with public costs, and instead a bureaucrat might be systematically risk-averse. From the perspective of the individual bureaucrat, erroneously approving a harmful drug by setting the regulatory bar too low threatens public condemnation, regulatory oversight, and potentially major negative career consequences. In contrast, the delay of a useful drug for further testing, while also producing potentially significant social costs, might be harder to identify and thus be less likely to invite criticism. For instance, the Food and Drug Administration might be overly cautious in approving valuable new medications, requiring extensive testing and limiting the claims for which the new drugs may be approved even though the delay and even disapproval of a life-saving medicine results in harm to consumers (taking the form of Type I error), possibly of comparable magnitude to that resulting from setting the regulatory bar too low (taking the form of Type II error).

Empirical studies tend to support the theoretical claim that regulators are unlikely to be risk neutral as between these two kinds of error, and instead that regulation is systematically biased in favor of avoiding the more tangible harm associated with Type II error than the abstract and

---

107. *See* WILLIAM BLACKSTONE, 4 COMMENTARIES *358; *see also* Alexander Volokh, *n Guilty Men*, 146 U.PA. L.REV. 173 (1997) (reviewing different articulations of the phrase over time).

generally unobservable harm from Type I error.[108] For instance, one group of scholars has argued that this intuition explains resource allocation at the Immigration and Naturalization Service ("INS").[109] Measuring the number of people caught illegally entering the United States is easier than measuring the number of illegal immigrants already present. As a result, it is argued, the INS tends to devote greater resources to preventing illegal entry than to capturing and deporting those who are here. Similarly, the Department of Housing and Urban Development ("HUD") tends to allocate funds to cities with less risky investment projects to avoid the criticism that funded projects have failed, notwithstanding the claimed goal of using program funding to help "distressed" cities. Not surprisingly, housing projects in cities that are distressed are far more likely to be characterized as high risk.[110]

John Allison, Chairman of the BB & T Bank Corporation provides another example of how the risk aversion of bureaucrats can create agency costs that can contradict preferred Executive Branch policy.[111] In September 2008, in response to the American financial crisis at the time, the government enacted the Trouble Asset Relief Program ("TARP"), which was intended to stabilize the financial sector and avert bank failures.[112] The administrations of both President George W. Bush[113] and Barack Obama[114] stated that an additional justification for infusing capital into the financial sector was to encourage banks to make new loans. Allison, however, notes that the private incentives of ground level bank examiners directly contradicted this goal. Whereas the President was encouraging greater lending in order to jump-start the economy, individual bank examiners were primarily motivated to make sure that the banks that they oversaw would not take any risks that might lead to failure and jeopardize their individual standing. As a result, the actions of local examiners were forcing banks to tighten lending standards and to curtail lending. Allison argues that one effect of the inspectors' overly cautious attitude was to cause his bank to not make loans that it would have made otherwise, which probably caused some businesses to fail that otherwise would not have.

108. *See* MUELLER, *supra* note 38, at 370–71.

109. Alberto Dávila et al., *Immigration Reform, the INS, and the Distribution of Interior and Border Enforcement Resources*, 99 PUB. CHOICE 327 (1999).

110. John R. Gist & R. Carter Hill, *The Economics of Choice in the Allocation of Federal Grants: An Empirical Test*, 36 PUB. CHOICE 63 (1981).

111. John Allison, Chairman, BB&T Corporation, Keynote Address, The Competitive Enterprise Institute's 25th Anniversary Gala (June 11, 2009) (transcript on file with authors); *see also* Judith Burns, *BB&T Chair Blasts TARP as a "Huge Rip–Off"*, WALL ST. J., June 12, 2009, http://online.wsj. com/article/ SB1244 82152 282410185.html (summarizing Allison's remarks).

112. Emergency Economic Stabilization Act of 2008, Pub. L. No. 110–343, §§ 101–136, 122 Stat. 3765–800.

113. *See* Press Release, Remarks by Secretary Henry M. Paulson, Jr. on Financial Rescue Package and Economic Update (Nov. 12, 2008), http://www.ustreas.gov/press/releases/hp1265.htm.

114. *See* Press Release, Secretary Geithner Introduces Financial Stability Plan (Feb. 10, 2009), http://www.treasury.gov/press/releases/tg18.htm.

Does the assumption that risk neutrality is welfare enhancing always hold? Are there circumstances in which societal welfare is enhanced by discounting one form of error in favor of another? Is the different standard of proof in the criminal and civil context an illustration of this proposition? Why or why not? If it is, is that context unique, or are there other regulatory contexts in which the danger of false positives is greater than those of false negatives? Does the reverse also hold? Are there conditions under which the dangers of false negatives exceed those of false positives? Why or why not?

Political actors hold other biases that affect policy making. Senior political officials and legislators, for example, are predicted to exhibit a short term bias, selecting policies with benefits that materialize during the official's expected tenure in office (or before the next election), with substantial discounting for costs that are incurred beyond her term of office. "Politicians and regulators . . . have an incentive to maximize their political and financial support in the next electoral cycle, whether two, four, or six years" later.[115] Persistent budget deficits that result from providing benefits today at the expense of voters in the future is perhaps the most obvious example. Other policy decisions also reflect this tendency toward short-run vote-maximization. Thus, for instance, the federal government historically has a poor record of managing federal lands for long-term benefit. Grazing, logging, and mining rights on federal lands traditionally have been sold for below-market prices to win political support from extractive business interests, leading to overuse of those resources. As a result of these subsidies, the direct costs of running those federal programs exceed the revenues generated. Although these subsidies are difficult to justify from an environmental or financial perspective, they appear to generate political benefits to regulators and their political overseers. As is the case with the tendency for the government to accrue budget deficits, federal resource policy thus tends toward the promotion of short-term political goals at the expense of long-term environmental and economic goals.

B. MARGINALITY AND COST EXTERNALIZATION

Commentators have also observed that bureaucrats tend to exhibit an imperfect understanding of marginal costs and benefits of regulation.[116] Justice Stephen Breyer has argued, for example, that policy makers select issues for their regulatory agenda based upon such random factors as media attention, rather than based upon a systematic cost-benefit analy-

---

115. Todd J. Zywicki, *Environmental Externalities and Political Externalities: The Political Economy of Environmental Regulation and Reform*, 73 TUL. L. REV. 845, 900 (1999); *see also* John A. Baden & Richard L. Stroup, *The Environmental Costs of Government Action*, POL'Y REV., Spring 1978, at 23.

116. *See* W. Kip Viscusi, *The Dangers of Unbounded Commitments to Regulate Risk*, *in* RISKS, COSTS, AND LIVES SAVED: GETTING BETTER RESULTS FROM REGULATION (Robert W. Hahn ed., 1996); Christopher C. Demuth, *The Regulatory Budget*, REGULATION, Mar.–Apr. 1980, at 29, 34–36.

sis.[117] One barrier to effective cost-benefit analysis of regulation is the absence of a price signal to convey to regulators the relative benefits and costs. In addition, many regulatory costs are borne by private market actors, rather than by the agency, further inhibiting feedback signals concerning the optimal scope and form of regulation.

Numerous efforts have been made to identify substitutes for market valuation in the regulatory context. These include devices intended to provide proxies for marginal costs and benefits of regulations, such as the Paperwork Reduction Act, which aims to measure the administrative costs of regulations on private actors. While these methods improve estimates of the costs of regulation on private actors, they offer at best crude measures. Cost benefit analysis is often inconsistently applied, thus producing unpredictable results. While some life-saving regulations are implemented at low cost, commentators observe that other regulations fail cost-benefit analysis.[118]

Regulatory compliance also has distributional effects. For instance, certain types of regulation (such as command-and-control environmental regulation) impose compliance costs largely without regard to the scale of the firm installing it.[119] Regulatory compliance requirements that demand fixed capital investments, therefore, tend to place disproportionate burdens on small businesses that must amortize those costs over a smaller production schedule as compared with larger competitors.[120] Paperwork and other regulatory compliance measures also impose many fixed costs and studies have found that larger companies spend proportionately less on legal services (as a percentage of sales) than do small companies.[121] In contrast, other forms of regulation deliberately take account of firm size, such as taxes on the volume of pollution emitted as a by-product of a factory's production. Taxes based on production tend to have less severe distributional consequences than those that impose burdens independent of output.

The focus on governmental regulation also might ignore alternative market-based means for accomplishing regulatory goals, such as investments in name brands and third-party rating agencies, such as Consumer Reports.[122] Providing unsafe products or services, or simply products of low quality, can result in effective financial penalties from diminished

117. *See* STEPHEN BREYER, BREAKING THE VICIOUS CIRCLE: TOWARD EFFECTIVE RISK REGULATION 19–29 (1993).

118. *See* W. Kip Viscusi et al., *Measures of Mortality Risk*, 14 J. RISK & UNCERTAINTY 213, 228 tbl.9 (1997).

119. Zywicki, *supra* note 115, at 864–66.

120. One estimate, for instance, found that complying with environmental laws was $717 annually per employee for firms over 500 employees and $3,228 per employee for firms under twenty employees. LEVY & MELLOR, *supra* note 3, at 69–70.

121. B. Peter Pashigian, *A Theory of Prevention and Legal Defense with an Application to the Legal Costs of Companies*, 25 J.L. & ECON. 247 (1982).

122. *See generally* REPUTATION: STUDIES IN THE VOLUNTARY ELICITATION OF GOOD CONDUCT (Daniel B. Klein ed., 1997); Benjamin Klein & Keith B. Leffler, *The Role of Market Forces in Assuring Contractual Performance*, 89 J. POL. ECON. 615 (1981).

demand for those goods or services and a corresponding decline in the value of the firm's stock. The resulting financial losses often will greatly exceed civil liability and government penalties and fines.[123] Although regulatory oversight undoubtedly provides important benefits in terms of consumer safety in a broad range of areas, regulators might tend to overlook or discount non-governmental alternatives that serve similar functions, thereby leading to inefficient levels or types of regulation.

C. SELECTION BIAS AND COMMITMENT TO REGULATORY MISSION

An additional potential problem for bureaucratic actors is a tendency toward "tunnel vision," meaning too narrow a focus on their particular regulatory agenda at the expense of alternative policy goals.[124] Over forty years ago, Anthony Downs claimed that bureaucrats' "views are based upon a 'biased' or exaggerated view of the importance of their own positions 'in the cosmic scheme of things.' "[125] This sense of regulatory mission might be reinforced by a selection bias in the types of matters and parties that regularly appear before regulators as a result of particular agency objectives.

In some settings, bureaucratic tunnel vision might create or exacerbate risks in one sector while seeking to eliminate or to reduce it in another. For instance, excessively rigorous, intrusive, and time-consuming airport security regulations might dissuade some potential air travelers in favor of longer automobile trips, with corresponding risks of highway fatalities and the possible net result of raising the overall societal death rate.[126] Improving auto safety might cause drivers to feel more confident and thus to drive faster and less cautiously, thereby increasing risks to pedestrians.[127] Increasing gas mileage requirements for cars also reduces the marginal cost of driving, creating a "rebound effect" of encouraging commuters to drive more, carpool less, or drive larger cars, thereby offsetting some of the conservation benefits of improved gas mileage. Increased environmental protection also might conflict with other goals, such as economic growth or national security.[128]

---

123.   *See* Mark L. Mitchell, *The Impact of External Parties on Brand–Name Capital: The 1982 Tylenol Poisonings and Subsequent Cases*, 27 ECON. INQUIRY 601 (1989); Mark L. Mitchell & Michael T. Maloney, *Crisis in the Cockpit? The Role of Market Forces in Promoting Air Travel Safety*, 32 J.L. & ECON. 329 (1989).

124.   *See* BREYER, *supra* note 117, at 10–19; *see also* Zywicki, *supra* note 39.

125.   ANTHONY DOWNS, INSIDE BUREAUCRACY 107 (1967).

126.   *See* Robert W. Hahn, *The Cost of Antiterrorist Rhetoric*, REGULATION, Fall 1996, at 51; *cf.* Garrick Blalock et al., The Impact of 9/11 on Driving Fatalities: The Other Lives Lost to Terrorism (Feb. 25, 2005) (unpublished manuscript), *available at* www.news.cornell.edu/stories/March05/Sept11driving.pdf. Breyer provides the example of a proposed sewage disposal regulation designed to save one life every five years but that would create incentives to incinerate the waste, thereby causing two additional cancer deaths annually. BREYER, *supra* note 117, at 22.

127.   Sam Peltzman, *The Effects of Automobile Safety Regulation*, 83 J. POL. ECON. 677 (1975).

128.   *See* Zywicki, *supra* note 105.

Consider how government makes agriculture policy.[129] The FTC has focused its efforts on improving consumer economic welfare and, as a result, has tended to favor increased competition and lower prices for agricultural products. In contrast with the FTC, the United States Department of Agriculture ("USDA") is highly concerned with the welfare of farmers, who are its primary constituency, even if policies that help farmers result in higher average consumer prices. Rather than pursuing policies designed to lower prices for all consumers, as the FTC does, the USDA might prefer reduced competition and higher agricultural prices with a food stamp program that maintains demand among low income consumers. Each agency tends to emphasize its particular regulatory mission and constituencies, even if those objectives conflict with other agencies.

Economic theory predicts that organizations will tend to attract individuals with a comparative advantage at—and a considerable interest in and commitment to—the tasks that they are called upon to perform. Employment generally provides two types of remuneration: monetary income and non-monetary or psychic income, such as intrinsic satisfaction or a sense of "doing good." As Spence and Cross observe, "That agencies are systematically more loyal to their basic mission seems persuasive, even obvious. People who are sympathetic to that mission are more likely to be attracted to work at the agency."[130] A principled commitment to the value of an agency's mission also might reconcile the apparent anomaly that bureaucrats seek increased budgets even if they do not personally benefit.[131] Larger budgets and a broader scope of authority will give the agency greater ability to pursue their desired regulatory objectives and to that extent reinforce a bureaucrat's sense of beneficial accomplishment.

Bureaucrats also pursue ideological and political objectives.[132] One study of public employees in eleven countries found them to be more politically left of center than the general population and to generally support a larger government role in the economy.[133] A study by Donald Blake also found a general tendency of government employees to lean ideologically left of center.[134] This orientation might result from either self interest (within various governmental systems, political parties to the left of center generally tend to support larger public sectors) or ideology. The direction of causation is largely irrelevant, however, as the ideological orientation of employees might both reflect and cause a preference for larger and more activist government. For instance, Tim Muris has argued

---

129. This paragraph is based on Zywicki's personal experience at the FTC.

130. Spence & Cross, *supra* note 37, at 120 (emphasis omitted); *see also id.* at 115 n.76 (providing examples).

131. Blaise & Dion, *supra* note 45, at 356–57.

132. *See, e.g.,* William W. Buzbee, *Remember Repose: Voluntary Contamination Cleanup Approvals, Incentives, and the Costs of Interminable Liability*, 80 MINN. L. REV. 35, 82–96 (1995).

133. André Blais, Donald E. Blake & Stéphane Dion, *The Voting Behavior of Bureaucrats, in* BUDGET-MAXIMIZING BUREAUCRAT, *supra* note 45, at 205.

134. Donald E. Blake, *Policy Attitudes and Political Ideology in the Public Sector, in* BUDGET-MAXIMIZING BUREAUCRAT, *supra* note 45, at 231.

that one possible explanation for what he characterizes as the FTC's extreme activist tilt during the late–1970s was the influx of many new "Naderite," ideologically-motivated consumer activist lawyers into the agency.[135]

Regulators can also structure regulation so as to create ongoing demand for their services. As Richard Harris and Sidney Milkis have observed, "Because the lifeblood of bureaucratic entities is administrative programs, bureaucrats enhance their position by helping to develop new programs and protect their current position by opposing the destruction of existing programs."[136] Todd Zywicki has observed that by writing highly complex, detailed, and specific regulations, bureaucrats can build "obsolescence" into regulations, thereby requiring their ongoing services to update them.[137] This might explain the historical preference among environmental regulators for economically inefficient, technology-based, command-and-control regulation rather than more cost effective decentralized market-based schemes. Technology-based standards place an ongoing demand for regulatory services as technology changes. Thus, Zywicki notes that each technological development will initiate a new round of conflict among competing interest groups, with some urging the adoption of the new technology and others supporting the status quo.

If these characterizations are sound, what do they suggest about the nature of those prone to pursuing careers as agency bureaucrats? Are agencies generally biased in favor of regulatory expansion? What about those who joined the ranks of federal bureaucracy during such conservative administrations as Ronald Reagan or George W. Bush?[138] Did those administrations attract bureaucrats who enjoyed psychic income from pursuing deregulatory agendas? Consider also why the Reagan and Bush II administrations did not dismantle agencies whose earlier, more liberal, policies they sought to reverse, instead staffing those agencies with bureaucrats favoring a deregulatory agenda. Is this consistent with the theories advanced by Harris and Milkis, and Zywicki, that bureaucrats pursue policies that promote continued demands for their services? Dismantling an agency as a means of deregulation makes it more difficult for another administration to sharply reverse the direction of regulatory policy.[139] By retaining the agencies but staffing with deregulators, however, these administrations were able to demand ongoing support to main-

---

135. *See* Muris, *supra* note 94; *see also* RICHARD A. HARRIS & SIDNEY M. MILKIS, THE POLITICS OF REGULATORY CHANGE: A TALE OF TWO AGENCIES 154–80 (2d ed. 1996).

136. HARRIS & MILKIS, *supra* note 135, at 47.

137. Zywicki, *supra* note 115, at 894.

138. *See* HARRIS & MILKIS, *supra* note 135, at 181–224.

139. Does this help to explain the phenomenon of "midnight regulations"? *See* Elizabeth Kolbert, Comment, *Midnight Hour*, NEW YORKER, Nov. 24, 2008, at 39, *available at* http://www.newyorker.com/talk/comment/2008/11/24/081124taco_talk_kolbert (discussing the history of midnight regulations since Jimmy Carter).

tain deregulatory policies over time. Do you find this analysis persuasive? Why or why not?

Do the same arguments concerning the absence of pricing mechanisms in affecting the level of governmental regulation and services apply to those bureaucrats who are inclined to pursue either regulatory or deregulatory agendas? Is it possible that the zeal for deregulation will be applied without adequate consideration of the costs of removing regulatory protections already in place? Why or why not? Which of the preceding models, if any, is most helpful in answering these questions? Why?

D.   EXECUTIVE BRANCH RESPONSE TO AGENCY COSTS

The growth of the administrative state since the New Deal has created special challenges for the President in seeking to coordinate the various regulatory initiatives throughout the executive branch.[140] Although it is difficult for the President to closely supervise the thousands of ongoing regulatory, adjudicatory, and other processes within the executive branch, in the end it is the President who bears political responsibility for those activities. Several departments and agencies may share overlapping jurisdiction over an issue, reviewing the same issue from a variety of perspectives and with different objectives and preferences.

This problem of creating coherent regulatory policy has been chronic, and Presidents have given this responsibility to different offices over time, including the Vice–President.[141] In recent decades, the primary office performing this duty has been the OIRA. Growing out of an informal regulatory review process in Richard Nixon's Office of Management and Budget, OIRA was established as part of the 1980 Paperwork Reduction Act. OIRA reviews all economically significant regulations proposed by executive branch agencies, and its central tasks have been supported by Presidents of both parties for the past thirty years.[142] Sally Katzen, OIRA Administrator during the Clinton Administration, described the importance of its oversight process as follows:

> The agencies focus like a laser, as they should, on their statutory missions—in the case of EPA, protecting the environment. The White House and OIRA take a broader view and consider how, for example, an environmental proposal will affect energy resources, tax revenues, health policy, etc. Stated another way, EPA is pursuing a parochial

---

140. *See* DeMuth & Ginsburg, *supra* note 98, at 1079–80.

141. *See* Keith Werhan, *Delegalizing Administrative Law*, 1996 U. ILL. L. REV. 423, 425–31.

142. *See* Exec. Order No. 12,866, 3 C.F.R. 638 (1993), *reprinted as amended in* 5 U.S.C. § 601 (2006); *see also* Lisa Schultz Bressman & Michael P. Vandenbergh, *Inside the Administrative State: A Critical Look at the Practice of Presidential Control*, 105 MICH. L. REV. 47 (2006); Steven Croley, *White House Review of Agency Rulemaking: An Empirical Investigation*, 70 U. CHI. L. REV. 821 (2003); Sally Katzen, *A Reality Check on an Empirical Study: Comments on "Inside the Administrative State,"* 105 MICH. L. REV. 1497 (2007).

interest; OIRA is tempering that with the national interest, as it should.[143]

Assuming this is correct, the analysis raises an important question: What does the head of OIRA rationally seek to maximize? To what extent does the preceding analysis imply that a given Administration's regulatory priorities are likely to affect any seemingly independent analysis of the relative costs and benefits of various agency activities that have the potential to produce regulatory conflict? In the event that two or more agency programs conflict, how is that conflict likely to be resolved? To what extent is public choice analysis helpful in answering this question? To what extent is the spatial model of presidential selection that opened this chapter helpful in answering this question? Given the potential conflicts among agencies respecting overlapping areas, is it possible that the agency deference rules announced in *Chevron* and *Mead* promote a race to regulate first? Does this raise analytical difficulties for judicial deference? Why or why not? Keep these questions in mind as you review the next set of materials, discussing competing theories of delegation.

IV. DELEGATION

We now leave aside the question of bureaucratic incentives and constraints and turn to the congressional decision whether to delegate rulemaking authority to agencies in the first instance. Congress might pursue a course of delegation for benign reasons: to take advantage of an agency's policy expertise, to minimize costly legislative processes, or to reduce its workload in an effort to focus its limited resources on higher priorities.[144] Congress might also delegate for more problematic reasons: to avoid making hard choices, to avoid responsibility for unpopular decisions, or to facilitate a rent-extraction scheme. Even if delegation is done for beneficial purposes, from the legislature's perspective, delegation raises the problem of agency costs, as bureaucratic decision-making might depart from Congress's expected or preferred outcomes.

A. CONGRESSIONAL CONTROL OF DELEGATED AUTHORITY

Congress can reduce the problem of agency costs by making narrow and tightly circumscribed delegations, thus spelling out the scope of the delegation in precise detail. Narrowly-defined delegations circumscribe the discretion not only of the current bureaucracy, but also of future bureaucrats. Greater restrictions on agency discretion, however, might reduce the benefit to Congress of delegating in the first place. Restrictive delegations substitute congressional mandates for agency expertise and force Congress to expend more time and resources on articulating and enforcing limits on

---

143. Katzen, *supra* note 142, at 1505.

144. *See* David Epstein & Sharyn O'Halloran, *Administrative Procedures, Information, and Agency Discretion*, 38 AM. J. POL. SCI. 697, 698 (1994) (summarizing rationales for delegation).

agency discretion, thereby reducing the anticipated workload savings resulting from delegation and reducing the agency's flexibility to respond to changing circumstances. Congress thus confronts a tradeoff in the decision to delegate: It must delegate enough authority to be able to capture the benefits of delegation, but at the same time it must constrain excess bureaucratic agency costs. Terry Moe summarizes the resulting tradeoff as follows:

> The most direct way [to control agencies] is for today's authorities to specify, in excruciating detail, precisely what the agency is to do and how it is to do it, leaving as little as possible to the discretionary judgment of bureaucrats—and thus as little as possible for future authorities to exercise control over, short of passing new legislation. . . .
>
> Obviously, this is not a formula for creating effective organizations. In the interests of political protection, agencies are knowingly burdened with cumbersome, complicated, technically inappropriate structures that undermine their capacity to perform their jobs well.[145]

Once Congress has delegated authority to an agency, it can control agency discretion to deviate from Congress's preferred policy either through *ex ante* controls or *ex post* ongoing oversight. *Ex ante* controls involve "issues of agency design," such as reporting and consultation procedures that an agency must follow in making policy.[146] Congress may also exert control over the establishment of new departments, the location of new agencies within the executive branch, and how far down the organizational hierarchy political appointments will reach. As with using narrow delegations to control agency discretion, *ex ante* controls are not costless. For example, greater constraints limit agencies from adapting to new situations.

Ex post controls include those institutional features that check agency actions on a regular basis, such as congressional oversight and annual budget appropriations. The federal judiciary also exerts ongoing control through the enforcement of administrative law requirements, and the President exerts control through his power of appointment (subject, where applicable, to the confirmation process).

Because exercising control (whether *ex ante* or *ex post*) has costs, Congress must anticipate a certain amount of agency slack. Thus, Congress will be more willing to delegate when it can exercise control at low cost and be less willing to delegate when ensuring compliance is costly. Congress also will be less willing to delegate discretion where there is a large information asymmetry between Congress and the agency, which further raises monitoring costs. Thus, the value to Congress of *ex post* oversight controls will increase as the anticipated disparity in policy preferences between Congress and the agency increases and as informa-

---

145. Terry M. Moe, *Political Institutions: The Neglected Side of the Story*, 6 J.L. ECON. & ORG. 213, 228 (1990).

146. Epstein & O'Halloran, *supra* note 144, at 698–99.

tion asymmetries between Congress and the agency decrease.[147] Where it is difficult to monitor and control the use of agency discretion, Congress will delegate less and stipulate more clearly what is to be done. When delegation occurs despite information asymmetries, such as where reliance on technical expertise is necessary, Congress tends to hold more oversight hearings to monitor agency behavior.[148]

Tighter *ex ante* controls, such as statutory precision or increased control over appointments, reduce agency costs by giving Congress greater control over agency policies. Conversely, narrow delegations raise the risk of "legislative" or "coalitional drift." Legislative drift is a change over time in regulatory policy from changes in the ideological composition of Congress or of the relevant oversight committees. Thus, if the median member of Congress or the applicable oversight committee changes, the desired scope of agency delegations and the preferred approach to agency oversight will change as well. In addition, as discussed in Chapter 2, one element of the willingness of interest groups to lobby for favorable legislation is the legislation's expected durability, i.e., how long the stream of benefits will be produced.[149] Thus, interest groups will provide greater support for legislation with a long expected life than a shorter one. The fear that a future Congress will reverse the decision of the current Congress reduces the expected value of the legislation and hence the support that interest groups will provide. Rational members of Congress therefore are likely to prefer policies that reduce the threat of legislative drift in the future, thereby increasing the value of their services today.

The risk of legislative drift can be distinguished from "bureaucratic drift." Bureaucratic drift occurs when Congress delegates authority but the agency subsequently pursues policies inconsistent with the enacting Congress's expectations. Broader delegations reduce the risk of legislative drift by insulating the agency from subsequent changes in congressional preferences, but at the same time, increase the risk of bureaucratic drift. Congress can mitigate the risk of bureaucratic drift through monitoring and oversight. Doing so, however, is costly and difficult, especially with respect to those complex and rapidly changing areas of regulation where delegation is considered most appropriate. Thus, where delegations are not carefully constrained and specified at the outset, the risk of bureaucratic drift is most acute.

Legislative and bureaucratic drift are thus mirror images.[150] David Epstein and Sharyn O'Halloran explain:

> In order to check runaway bureaucracies, *legislatures must structure agency decision-making to be responsive to congressional demands.* However, this ensures that future Congresses will be able to influence

---

147. *Id.* at 708.

148. *See* Epstein & O'Halloran, *supra* note 86, at 207–11.

149. *See supra* chapter 2.

150. Kenneth A. Shepsle, *Bureaucratic Drift, Coalitional Drift, and Time Consistency: A Comment on Macey,* 8 J.L. Econ. & Org. 111 (1992).

policy outcomes, thereby exacerbating the consequences of coalitional drift. [Thus], ex ante decisions about bureaucratic structure are intimately linked with issues of ongoing oversight.[151]

There is a sharp difference between the two sets of monitoring tools. Tight *ex ante* controls can be reversed only by subsequent legislation, an expensive and time-consuming process. As a result, such controls risk becoming entrenched. Conversely, broader delegation with intensive *ex post* oversight requires discretion on the part of contemporary members of Congress, which might produce policy that departs from that preferred by the enacting legislature.[152]

B. POSITIVE THEORIES OF DELEGATION

Epstein and O'Halloran conclude that these tradeoffs describe many observed patterns of delegation. They find that "Congress delegates less and constrains more under divided government" (when Congress and the Presidency are controlled by different parties) and thus when the risk of bureaucratic drift is high.[153] Congress also tends to delegate less discretion when legislation is passed over a presidential veto or in the face of a presidential veto threat because the veto threat signals presidential hostility to the act and a high risk that the executive branch will use its discretion in a manner inimical to the enacting Congress's wishes. Finally, divided government also affects the structure of delegation. Under divided government Congress is less likely to delegate to executive branch departments and is more likely to delegate to independent agencies or even state governments. Thus, Epstein and O'Halloran conclude that Congress's decision to delegate is not explained primarily by a desire to rely on agency technical expertise or constraints on Congress's time. Instead, it is strategic: Congress is aware that agencies make political decisions and, therefore, Congress's willingness to delegate depends on the degree of policy agreement between Congress and the President.

Congress might sometimes be forced to delegate more discretionary authority than it would prefer as the price for implementing a policy that it seeks to pursue but that the President at least initially disfavors. Epstein and O'Halloran claim that agriculture subsidies illustrate the idea.[154] Farm subsidies as they exist today are widely viewed as a distributional "pork barrel" program that confers significant financial benefits upon farmers with little if any apparent public benefits. Congress often supports distributive programs that allow members to claim credit with their constituencies for conferring the legislative benefits while imposing dispersed costs that incur relatively minor political opposition. Farm subsidies require minimal expertise or discretion by the President and thus would seem to require little discretionary delegation. According to

---

151. Epstein & O'Halloran, *supra* note 144, at 712 (emphasis added).

152. *Id.* at 713.

153. *See* EPSTEIN & O'HALLORAN, *supra* note 86, at 11, 121–62.

154. *Id.* at 220–21.

Epstein and O'Hallaron, however, the President has an unexpectedly high amount of discretion over the program's implementation, which the authors explain as the President's price for acquiescing in the congressional bargain. They contend that the President, who is elected by the nation as a whole, will be reluctant to endorse pork barrel projects that favor narrow regional interests, and thus will be reluctant to go along with the deal. The authors conclude, "The untold story of agricultural policy, then, is that it relies heavily on executive discretion for implementation, this authority being supplied as a bribe for presidential support of agricultural programs."[155]

Aranson, Gellhorn, and Robinson ("AGR") challenge the conclusion that the President will be hostile to pork barrel legislation because the private goods nature of electoral processes applies with equal force to the President as to members of Congress.[156] If it is true that the President has a high degree of discretion in implementing the farm subsidy program, how might AGR explain this fact? Can you explain why Presidents tend to be more supportive of free trade policies than Congress? McCubbins, Noll, and Weingast ("McNollGast") argue that "because of the importance, visibility, historical significance and clear accountability of the office, the President's personal reputation hinges much more on the broad performance of the government than is the case for legislators."[157] Does that help to explain this phenomenon? Does it seem correct in general? Why or why not?

Would a legislature specifically concerned about agency capture be more likely to prefer *ex ante* or *ex post* controls on agency decision-making? Terry Moe has argued, for instance, that in setting up the EPA, Congress spelled out voluminous and detailed *ex ante* procedural regulations that create a complicated and lengthy procedure for regulatory approval. The EPA gave environmental interest groups a substantial voice in the regulatory process through a variety of mechanisms for public participation.[158] Complex regulatory procedures enable Congress to achieve substantive goals indirectly while also affording favored interest groups a de facto veto over adverse agency action.[159] Can you explain why Congress might facilitate this result? Is it relevant that EPA was created in the early–1970s, at the time that policy makers were highly concerned with the risk of industry capture of the regulatory process? To what extent is this system dependent on the assumption that there are minimal agency costs between environmental interest groups and the public?

---

155. *Id.* at 221.

156. *See* Peter H. Aranson, Ernest Gellhorn & Glen O. Robinson, *A Theory of Legislative Delegation*, 68 CORNELL L. REV. 1, 41–43 (1982).

157. McNollgast, *supra* note 84, at 1689–90.

158. *See* Terry M. Moe, *The Politics of Bureaucratic Structure*, *in* CAN THE GOVERNMENT GOVERN? 267, 310–20 (John E. Chubb & Paul E. Peterson eds., 1989).

159. *See* McNollgast, *supra* note 84, at 1710–13.

C. CONGRESSIONAL RESPONSES TO AGENCY DRIFT

In theory, Congress can rectify any agency deviation from its preferences with *ex post* oversight. McNollgast have argued, however, that reliance on *ex post* monitoring might not allow Congress to fully rectify bureaucratic drift because Congress frequently will be unable to "reproduce the policy outcome that was sought by the [original] winning coalition...."[160] As a result of congressional turnover, some members of the initially successful legislative coalition might no longer be in Congress, and the new members who replaced them might hold different preferences, leading to a shift in the preferences of the median member of Congress. The agency's regulatory policy might have mobilized a previously unorganized or dormant constituency that prefers the agency's selected policy. Some members of the original coalition might have changed their views to favor the new regulatory policy and thus oppose efforts to rein in the agency. As a result of congressional bargaining processes, including veto gates or negative legislative checkpoints (as described in Chapter 2), a successful exercise of blocking power by a member of Congress or a presidential veto is sufficient to protect agency policy against congressional override. Does this explain the popularity of the so-called "one-House veto"? Does it call into question the soundness of the Supreme Court decision invalidating this practice in *INS v. Chadha*?[161] Why or why not?

Consider McNollgast's analysis in the context of *Mississippi Poultry Ass'n, Inc. v. Madigan*, presented in Chapter 5.[162] Recall that the United States Department of Agriculture ("USDA") promulgated regulations governing poultry inspections that defined the legislative term "the same as" to mean "at least equal to." The initial statute was adopted with strong support, and some members of Congress criticized the USDA's regulatory interpretation when it was adopted on the ground that it deviated from the original intent of the statute. Despite this, no legislation was passed to overrule the agency interpretation. The USDA adopted Congress's apparent preferred meaning only when ordered to do so by the United States Court of Appeals for the Fifth Circuit. Does this case support McNollgast's intuition that it is more difficult for Congress to police departures from intended policy positions *ex post* than to constrain agency discretion *ex ante*? Why or why not?

Given the difficulty of attempting to reverse an agency action, McNollgast argue that one purpose of administrative procedures may be to "erect a barrier against an agency carrying out such a *fait accompli* by forcing the agency to move slowly and publicly, giving politicians (in-

---

160. Matthew D. McCubbins, Roger G. Noll & Barry R. Weingast, *Structure and Process, Politics and Policy: Administrative Arrangements and the Political Control of Agencies*, 75 VA. L. REV. 431, 433 (1989).

161. 462 U.S. 919 (1983). For a more detailed presentation of *Chadha* and the one-house veto, *see infra* chapter 8. For a related analysis of how the one-house veto allows Congress to move the scope of delegation closer to its ideal point rather than that of the President, as compared with the post-*Chadha* regime, see William N. Eskridge, Jr., & John Ferejohn, *The Article I, Section 7 Game*, 80 GEO.L.J. 523 (1992).

162. *See supra* chapter 5.

formed by their constituents) time to act before the status quo is changed."[163] Administrative rulemaking requires cumbersome, but public and deliberative, processes. Before an agency can enact a new policy, it must first announce that it is considering a new rule and solicit the views of interested parties. This often takes the form of notice and comment rule-making, which requires the agency to publicize the proposed rule and solicit comments. In some cases, the agency must also hold public hearings. Finally, the agency must produce a record setting forth the reasons for its decision and explaining why it rejected alternative proposals. Often, legislation expressly mandates consultation with designated stakeholders elsewhere in the government, or with affected private interests, thereby entrenching interests that were part of the initial legislative coalition. The authors explain:

> These procedures allow politicians to prevent deviations before they occur. The members of the coalition enacting the policy can adopt a blanket agreement to inhibit all possible deviations while the nature of the deviation is still in doubt and the coalition has not yet formed that might support the deviation. Delay gives the old coalition time to mobilize its constituents before the agency undermines it by enunciating a noncomplying policy that changes the status quo.[164]

Much bureaucratic delay is ascribed to the pursuit of other objectives, for example due process concerns, or to bureaucratic incentives or agency costs. McNollgast argue, however, that this delay and inefficiency might be *intentional* in order to slow the pace of agency action and thereby provide Congress and interest groups with the time and means to prevent departures from preferred policy outcomes before they occur.

Finally, Jonathan Macey has argued that through the use of agency structure, an enacting Congress can simultaneously address the problems of both agency and legislative drift.[165] Macey argues that Congress can achieve this result by intentionally structuring agency jurisdiction and operations in a manner that *increases* the likelihood that it will be captured by identifiable special-interest groups. If a group that is favorably inclined toward the agency's mission is essentially hard-wired into the agency's architecture, then this will help to keep the agency focused on its mission.

Macey argues that the most effective vehicle for synchronizing agency mission with interest group monitoring is defining that mission narrowly, for example giving it jurisdiction over one identifiable industry, as is the case with the Securities Exchange Commission ("SEC"), Commodities Futures Trading Commission ("CFTC"), and Office of the Comptroller of the Currency ("The Comptroller"), rather than defining the agency's scope by function, as is the case with the FTC. Macey explains:

---

163. McCubbins, Noll & Weingast, *supra* note 160, at 442 (emphasis added).

164. *Id.* (footnote omitted).

165. Jonathan R. Macey, *Organizational Design and Political Control of Administrative Agencies*, 8 J.L. ECON. & ORG. 93, 100–04 (1992).

The ability to structure an administrative agency as a single-interest or a multi-interest organization enables Congress to exert greater ex ante control over the outcomes generated by the agency. Congress accomplishes this by controlling the ability of outside interest groups to exert political pressure on the agency, and by reducing the incentive of new interest groups to form to protest the agency's actions.

In general, then, where a single interest group dominates the original decision-making process in Congress that leads to a particular legislative enactment, the resulting administrative agency will be a single-interest-group agency. Where the original decision-making process in Congress involves a compromise among a large number of interest groups, the resulting administrative agency will provide access to all of these groups. This is an as-yet-unrecognized manifestation of the well-known congressional tendency to create regulatory structures that "mirror" the political environment existing at the time of the initial statutory enactment.[166]

Macey further explains:

The initial jurisdictional design of an agency will determine which interest groups will have ready access to the agency, and on what terms. In this way, the enacting legislators can, to a large degree, determine in advance the extent to which, and the terms on which, the agency will be "captured" by the groups it regulates. The enacting coalition therefore can minimize the amount of bureaucratic drift and legislative drift likely to occur.[167]

Macey identifies several tools that the legislature has at its disposal when setting up an agency. First is the initial hardwiring of the agency to determine its degree of responsiveness to different interest groups. Macey offers as an example the establishment of a central bank. In general, there is an inverse correlation between the independence of a central bank from political pressure and the inflation rate: More independent central banks tend to have lower inflation rates. Macey notes that this has significant implications for the expected degree of influence debtors are likely to exert over monetary policy. Macey argues that if creditor interest groups have higher influence relative to debtor interest groups at the bank's inception, then the bank will likely be more independent in its structure, and conversely, if debtor interest groups are more influential, then the bank will likely be less independent. The influence of interest groups through this initial agency hardwiring can then be reinforced, as desired, through agency procedural rules that may either enfranchise or disenfranchise interest groups to influence agency decision-making.

Macey argues that more specialized agencies are prone to interest group capture. An agency whose scope is defined by the industry it regulates, rather than the functions it performs, will be relatively more likely to be staffed by experts drawn from that industry. Thus, the

Comptroller is likely to be staffed by employees either drawn from, or by those who anticipate seeking post-governmental employment in, the banking industry. Such persons are likely to hold particular biases about the importance of the national banking industry and to draw on industry professionals and trade publications for information about the industry. Conversely, defining the agency's jurisdiction to regulate a number of competing industries will predictably reduce the likelihood that the agency will be dominated by the representatives of a single industry.

A final factor affecting Congress's choice of agency scope is the effect on inter-agency competition. Macey argues that affected industry under single industry agencies tend to become partisans for that agency, such that the interest group will support that agency in intra-governmental battles. Macey illustrates the point with the conflict among the SEC, the CFTC, and the Comptroller over the question of whether futures contracts for the delivery of securities should be treated as futures (subject to CFTC oversight) or securities contracts (subject to SEC oversight) for regulatory purposes. As might be expected, securities dealers argued that they were securities contracts and advocated for SEC regulation, while those interests regulated by the CFTC (such as the Chicago Board of Trade) argued for that agency's jurisdiction. Congress could have avoided these conflicts by combining regulatory authority over options, futures, and securities into a single agency, but elected otherwise.[168] Macey thus suggests that by structuring an agency with a single-industry jurisdiction, Congress can simultaneously reduce agency and legislative drift. This in turn increases the expected durability of the legislation and thus the present value of the rents that the legislation is expected to produce. On the other hand, hardwiring the agency in this manner reduces agency discretion, with the attendant costs of reducing agency flexibility and subsequent opportunities for rent-extraction from regulated industries.

A related question is the initial decision by Congress whether to establish an agency's responsibilities according to "function-specific" regulation or "industry-specific" regulation. Function-specific regulation is defined with reference to the regulatory body's scope and function rather than a particular industry. Thus, the authority of agencies such as the EPA, the Occupational Safety and Health Administration ("OSHA"), Equal Employment Opportunity Commission ("EEOC"), and the FTC is defined by function and thus cuts across industry boundaries. Agencies that engage in industry-specific regulation define their jurisdiction by the industries they regulate, as illustrated by the SEC, CFTC, FCC, or the Comptroller.

Function-based versus industry-based regulation presents important tradeoffs. An industry-specific agency might have more expertise regarding the particular structure and idiosyncrasies of the industry but might also have a greater propensity to be captured by that industry, whereas the general jurisdiction agency might have a greater expertise in the

---

168. The Seventh Circuit finally held that the CFTC had exclusive jurisdiction over trading in investment vehicles that could be characterized both as securities and investment contracts. Chicago Mercantile Exch. v. SEC, 883 F.2d 537 (7th Cir. 1989).

application of the principles and policies it implements generally but less detailed knowledge of specific industries.[169] Consider the formation of competition policy. Under federal law, there are a variety of agencies that regulate mergers for compliance with antitrust laws. The FTC and the Antitrust Division of the Department of Justice hold concurrent jurisdiction over mergers. And this jurisdiction is also shared with many other agencies on an industry-specific basis. For instance, the FCC reviews mergers in the telecommunications industry, the Department of Transportation ("DOT") reviews mergers in the airline industry, and the Federal Reserve Board reviews mergers in the banking industry. The FTC and Antitrust Division might have more expertise in the application of antitrust law and policy, and the industry-based regulator might know more about the particular industry but also might be more prone to industry capture. From a public interest perspective, what factors would be relevant in determining whether to regulate a given industry through a specific sector-based agency or through a multi-industry, function-based agency? Consider whether the same questions of capture apply to the decision of whether to establish specialized courts to hear certain types of cases, such as the Federal Circuit (to hear patent appeals) or Bankruptcy Courts, versus having those cases heard by courts of general jurisdiction.[170]

V. JUDICIAL REVIEW OF AGENCY ACTION

The analysis of regulation has gone through three basic phases over the past century: (1) the "public interest era" of the post-New Deal period, (2) the "capture era" of the 1960s and 1970s, and (3) the modern "public choice era" since the 1980s. What implication have these intellectual changes had for law?

A. INFLUENCE OF REGULATORY THEORIES ON COURTS

Thomas Merrill has argued that the intellectual development of these three theories of governmental regulation helps to explain the evolution of legal doctrine concerning judicial oversight of agencies during the twentieth century.[171] Even if judges did not consciously apply these theories in

---

169. *See* Todd J. Zywicki, Dir., Office of Policy Planning, FTC, Address at the Japan Fair Trade Commission Inaugural Symposium on Competition Policy: Competition Policy and Regulatory Reforms: Means and Ends (Nov. 20, 2003), *available at* http://www.ftc.gov/speeches/other/031120zywickijapanspeech.pdf.

170. For arguments that the Federal Circuit is prone to capture by the interests of the patent bar, see Stuart Minor Benjamin & Arti K. Rai, *Fixing Innovation Policy: A Structural Perspective*, 77 GEO. WASH. L. REV. 1, 17–18 (2008); Arti K. Rai, *Engaging Facts and Policy: A Multi-Institutional Approach to Patent System Reform*, 103 COLUM. L. REV. 1035, 1110 (2003); John R. Thomas, *Formalism at the Federal Circuit*, 52 AM. U. L. REV. 771, 792–94 (2003); *see also* G. Marcus Cole & Todd J. Zywicki, *The New Forum–Shopping Problem in Bankruptcy* (working paper, June 10, 2009), *available at* http://papers.ssrn.com/sol3/papers.cfm?abstract_id=1417621) (discussing bankruptcy courts).

171. Thomas W. Merrill, *Capture Theory and the Courts: 1967–1983*, 72 CHI.-KENT L. REV. 1039 (1997).

their decision-making, Merrill suggests, judicial doctrines implicitly reflect the prominence of these underlying theories in different historical periods.

Merrill argues that at the dawn of the administrative state during the New Deal, courts were imbued with the ethic of the public interest model of government. As a result, they tended to exhibit substantial deference to agency decision-making and congressional delegation, based upon the Progressive Era presumption that regulatory policy should be made by disinterested experts. This mindset is reflected in the Legal Process School, described in Chapter 5.[172] As a matter of judicial doctrine, this school stressed the need for transparency and procedural regularity in agency decision-making and exhibited great deference to resulting regulatory policies. Although Hart and Sacks did not imagine that regulatory experts were immune to special interest pressures, they encouraged judicial constructions that brought out the public interest elements of enacted regulatory policies. Otherwise, they favored a minimal role for judicial oversight of agency decision-making that emphasized the centrality of policy making by regulators and deference by judges.

Beginning in the 1960s, however, judges and scholars increasingly realized that regulatory results in practice often diverged from public interest objectives. This development led to a questioning of public interest theory and a shift toward capture theory. The capture critique of the administrative state corresponded with the consumer protection movement led by Ralph Nader, who bemoaned the capture of regulatory agencies by the business interests that they were established to regulate. Merrill argues that many of the judges of the D.C. Circuit during the 1960s and 1970s, who were themselves veterans of the New Deal and sympathetic to Nader's goals, were distressed by the apparent evolution of regulation away from New Deal and Progressive goals. Some of these judges, including perhaps most notably J. Skelly Wright, came to implicitly embrace capture theory. A natural consequence of this reconceived understanding of agency dynamics, Merrill claims, was heightened judicial oversight of agency processes to try to prevent interest group capture of regulation. Judges influenced by capture theory, however, tended not to abandon their earlier intuitions informed by public interest theory as to the proper *ends* of government; instead, they were increasingly vigilant in ensuring that bureaucrats were not distracted from their regulatory missions by what they regarded as excessive interest group influence.

Merrill describes the intellectual transition from public interest to capture theory as follows:

> Notice that capture theory . . . also contains a theory of comparative institutional advantage. Implicit in capture theory is the understanding that the central problem of the administrative state is a relatively limited one. Only administrative agencies are subject to the unique pathologies of bureaucracy such as interest group capture. Rival institutions, like the legislature and the courts, were implicitly

---

172. *See supra* chapter 5.

regarded as being immune from these pathologies or at least as suffering from them to a significantly diminished degree. Moreover, in terms of interest group influence, the problematic actor was seen to be the business lobby. Other groups, such as labor unions or advocates for civil rights or the environment, were tacitly assumed to be champions of the public interest.

[This intuition] created an ideal atmosphere for vigorous reform efforts. For example, one solution might be for Congress to enact more detailed legislation, thereby helping to ensure that policy is made by a healthy democratic institution (the legislature), and leaving comparatively little room for the corrupted institution (the agency) to undermine that policy. And in fact, there was a decisive move in the early 1970s toward enacting longer and more detailed regulatory statutes, in order to constrain the discretion of agencies. These statutes typically provided for policy to be made by informal rulemaking open to all, and included strict deadlines for the adoption of rules that could be enforced by citizen suits in court.

More importantly for present purposes, capture theory also suggests that aggressive judicial oversight and control of agencies is needed in order to counteract the distortions of the administrative process introduced by interest group capture and other pathologies. Specifically, by forcing agencies to adopt an administrative process that is more open and to give greater consideration to underrepresented viewpoints in that process, courts may be able to counteract the distortions emphasized by the theory.[173]

Merrill argues that the mid–1980s began the "public choice" era. During this time (which presumably continues today), there was a retreat from the capture theory-inspired position that had prompted robust judicial review of agency action. Merrill posits that the economic theory of regulation differs from capture theory in two significant ways. First, capture theory is narrowly focused on the dysfunctions of administrative agencies alone, whereas the economic theory of regulation applies its tools to governmental action generally, including the actions of legislatures and courts. Thus, capture theory accepts the public interest premises on which Congress establishes regulatory agencies in the first instance, but seeks to avoid what it regards as excessive interest group influence affecting the ends of agency regulation. Public choice theory, in contrast, questions the motivating goals of regulation, focusing on forms of regulation that ultimately benefit the very industries that agencies are called upon to regulate. Second, capture theory is concerned with the undue influence of one particular group—producers—whereas public choice considers the influence of all organized groups, "including not just business and producer groups, but also environmental groups, labor unions, civil rights groups, and rent control activists...."[174]

---

173. Merrill, *supra* note 171, at 1051–52 (footnotes omitted).

174. *Id.* at 1069.

Merrill asserts that the interest group theory of regulation has motivated a judicial retrenchment from the activist agency oversight that typified the capture era. This followed from judicial and academic commentary expressing skepticism of all organs of government, including the judiciary. This retrenchment was not marked, however, by a return to the earlier era of deference to legislatures and bureaucrats that characterized those influenced by the public interest model. Merrill explains:

> The decline of judicial assertiveness in the recent period, and the partial return of authority and autonomy to agencies ... cannot be considered in any sense a revival of the public interest conception of the administrative state, or a rehabilitation of administrative agencies as institutions in the eyes of the judiciary. Rather, it is a product of a deeper and more generalized pessimism about the administrative state, and in particular, of a spreading disenchantment with all forms of activist government. I ... refer to this shift in attitudes as a movement toward a "public choice" conception of the administrative state, although I hasten to add that I do not mean to imply that (most) judges have either studied or become practitioners of formal public choice theory.... I simply mean a conception that is skeptical about the capacity of *any* governmental institution to serve the public interest, primarily because all governmental institutions—agencies, legislatures, the White House, and even the courts—are subject to manipulation by organized groups, and hence cannot be regarded as dispassionate guardians of the public interest.[175]

"In effect," Merrill concludes, "capture theory's pessimism about the performance of administrative agencies has been generalized to include all political institutions."[176] Merrill further concludes that just as the pessimism of the "capture era" brought about recommendations to relocate some decision-making authority from agencies to courts, the "public choice era" brought about support for a more general reallocation of authority from government to private market actors and institutions.

If public choice identifies difficulties in the decision-making processes of agencies, Congress, and courts, might the theory counsel in favor of clear rules concerning which institution holds primary lawmaking responsibility? Does the *Chevron* doctrine, for example, improve political accountability by designating the agency as the central focus of administrative law making within its scope or does it reduce accountability by permitting Congress to shift responsibility for controversial decisions? Merrill maintains that if there is no basis for preferring one institution over another, then there is also no justification for reviving the nondelegation doctrine, which would shift decision-making authority from one flawed decision-maker (agencies) to another (legislatures). Do you agree with this conclusion? Why or why not?

---

175. *Id.* at 1044.

176. *Id.* at 1053.

Are Merrill's intuitions about the extent to which public choice calls into question the institutional competence of each governmental institution persuasive? Does social choice provide a means of comparing institutions that avoids the claim that all institutions are inherently or equivalently defective?[177] Are actors within institutions as likely to be aware of the limitations of their own institutional capabilities as they are of others? As a descriptive claim about judicial perceptions of institutional competence, whose analysis is more persuasive? Given that courts are not steeped in public choice, as Merrill concedes, is there reason to believe that courts might regard themselves as above the sort of interest group influences that some public choice theorists claim characterize agencies and Congress? Why or why not? If you conclude that they would, what alternative explanations might account for the reticence of courts in the public choice period to continue to ensure stringent rulemaking processes? Might judges be concerned that intervening to police rent-seeking activity might motivate interest groups to direct their efforts toward courts after having failed in the legislative process?

B. COURTS AND ADMINISTRATIVE RULEMAKING

Courts are also important players in the production of regulation as they interact with Congress and the executive branch. Thus, judicial attitudes toward regulation have a major impact on the formation of regulatory policy. Professor Richard Revesz has examined the role of judicial ideology in the judicial review of administrative decision-making. Analyzing rulings of the United States Court of Appeals for the District of Columbia Circuit on the validity of regulations issued by the EPA, Revesz concludes that judges' ideology significantly influence that court's decision-making on administrative law issues.[178] Revesz finds that during periods in which Republican-appointed judges controlled that court, it was more likely to reverse an EPA rule when the challenger represented industrial interests and that when Democratic-appointed judges controlled the court, it was more likely to reverse when the challenger represented environmental interests. Revesz finds no evidence of a consistent pattern of deference to the EPA by judges of either party, as he claims would be the case if judicial behavior were motivated by a general theory concerning the relationships among the branches of government. If, for example, Republican judges were generally more deferential to the executive branch, then it should not matter who the challenging party is. Instead, for judges of either party, Revesz concludes that deference turns on the identity of the challenging party.

Revesz also finds ideological voting to be more prevalent in cases raising procedural rather than substantive challenges. Judges can impose

---

177. *See generally* chapter 3. For an article that addresses this question, see Maxwell L. Stearns, *The Misguided Renaissance of Social Choice*, 103 YALE L.J. 1219 (1994).

178. Richard L. Revesz, *Environmental Regulation, Ideology, and the D.C. Circuit*, 83 VA. L. REV. 1717 (1997).

their ideological views through either substantive interpretation of enabling acts or by the degree of deference courts afford agencies on procedural grounds. By basing deference on procedural rules, courts can affect administrative outcomes without having to take responsibility for substantive rulings. Revesz further hypothesizes that judges will prefer such procedural rulings to substantive rulings as the former are less apt to be reviewed by the United States Supreme Court. Revesz argues that the use of procedural gambits to resolve controversial cases supports the intuition that judges not only are voting based upon ideological considerations but also voting in a strategic manner, disguising their decisions in a manner that reduces the effectiveness of further review.

Revesz finds that individual judges are more likely to vote ideologically when there are other like-minded judges on the panel. For instance, in the cases that Revesz reviewed, a Republican judge was much more likely to reverse in a case involving an industry challenge to an EPA regulation when there was at least one other Republican on the panel, and a Democratic judge was significantly less likely to reverse in such a case when there was at least one other Democrat on the panel. A Democrat sitting with two Republican judges tends to vote more conservatively than a Republican sitting with two Democrats. From this evidence, Revesz concludes that while both individual ideology and panel composition have important effects on judicial behavior, the ideology of colleagues proves more significant than personal ideology in predicting actual voting patterns.

Revesz concludes that because judges appear to take the likelihood of Supreme Court reversal into account before deciding whether to allow ideology to affect voting behavior, his findings support the hypothesis that "D.C. Circuit judges employ a strategically ideological approach to judging, versus either a nonideological or a naively ideological approach."[179] Revesz concludes that the different behavior exhibited in procedural versus nonprocedural cases indicates that D.C. Circuit judges "regard the Supreme Court as the primary reviewer of their decisions, rather than Congress."[180]

In a subsequent article, Professors Frank Cross and Emerson Tiller found further support for the claim that D.C. Circuit judges vote ideologically in cases reviewing administrative agency decisions.[181] They conclude that the willingness of judges on the D.C. Circuit to grant deference to administrative agencies depends to a significant extent on whether the agency action is consistent with the ideological preferences of the reviewing judge. But the authors also find that judges on panels with judges all appointed by Presidents of the same party are twice as likely to vote ideologically as are judges on divided panels, meaning panels in which

---

179. *Id.* at 1766–67.

180. *Id.* at 1768. Supreme Court review of circuit court decisions is rare, however, suggesting that the constraining effect of even this review is attenuated.

181. Frank B. Cross & Emerson H. Tiller, *Judicial Partisanship and Obedience to Legal Doctrine: Whistleblowing on the Federal Courts of Appeals*, 107 YALE L.J. 2155 (1998).

judges are appointed by Presidents of different parties. The authors label this the "whistleblower" phenomenon, meaning that the presence of a potential dissenting judge on a panel who will signal that other panelists are following their ideological preferences rather than the law inhibits ideological behavior.

Recent research has confirmed the basic empirical findings of these studies. In *Are Judges Political? An Empirical Analysis of the Federal Judiciary*,[182] Cass R. Sunstein, David Schkade, Lisa M. Ellman and Andres Sawicki ("SSES") examine judicial decisions across a number of subject areas and confirm the basic findings that for most areas of law (including administrative law) judicial ideological preferences influence outcomes. SSES find that judges also are influenced by the ideological preferences of *other* judges on their panel, in some cases even more so than by their personal preferences. When three judges of the same party sit together, for example, they tend to vote more ideologically, a phenomenon that SSES refer to as "ideological amplification."[183] Where a judge of one party sits with two judges of another party, the minority judge tends to vote more like the majority judges. The authors label this effect "ideological dampening."[184] In addition, SSES find that judges are more likely to uphold the agency interpretations of administrations headed by members of the same political party as the President who appointed the judge to the bench (i.e., judges appointed by Republican Presidents are more likely to uphold agency interpretations by Republican administrations, and Democratic-appointed judges are more likely to uphold agency interpretations by Democratic administrations).

In a spirited response to the articles by Revesz and Cross and Tiller (and anticipating the later findings by SSES), then-Chief Judge Harry T. Edwards of the D.C. Circuit challenged the conclusions that the findings demonstrated strategic and ideologically-based judging.[185] Edwards argued that the claimed "panel composition effects" might reflect deliberative judicial processes rather than ideologically motivated decision-making. Edwards writes:

> My own view is that if panel composition turns out to have a "moderating" effect on judges' voting behavior, this is a sign that panel members are behaving collegially: that is, they are discussing the case with each other and reaching a mutually acceptable judgment based on their shared sense of the proper outcome. In such a collegial deliberative process, we would expect to find that the presumed political views of different judges push the outcome towards the center of the spectrum (where there is a spectrum). The Revesz and

---

182. CASS R. SUNSTEIN, DAVID SCHKADE, LISA M. ELLMAN & ANDRES SAWICKI, ARE JUDGES POLITICAL? AN EMPIRICAL ANALYSIS OF THE FEDERAL JUDICIARY (2006).

183. *Id.* at 9.

184. *Id.* at 8–9.

185. Harry T. Edwards, *Collegiality and Decision-Making on the D.C. Circuit*, 84 VA. L. REV. 1335 (1998).

the Cross and Tiller studies are both consistent with the phenomenon of collegiality.

In explaining my view of collegiality I start with three observations drawn from many years of working and talking with my colleagues on the D.C. Circuit. First, judges on my court who are convinced that the law requires a certain result in a case do not decline to take a position simply to avoid registering a dissent. Second, judges who are in the majority and convinced that the law requires a certain result do not moderate their views because they fear that a dissent will somehow draw attention to flaws in the majority opinion. Finally, the judges on a panel usually agree on the correct result in a case. And when there is initially no clear view as to what the judgment should be in a particular case, we normally work hard in our deliberations to find the correct result.[186]

Are you more persuaded by the explanation that judges vote strategically and ideologically or by Judge Edwards's response that the statistical findings demonstrate collegiality and compromise? Is there any empirical test that might distinguish Judge Edwards's theory of collegiality on one hand and the ideological and strategic-voting theories offered by Revesz and Cross and Tiller on the other?

VI. APPLICATIONS

A. DEFERENCE TO AGENCY DECISION-MAKING

Perhaps the most crucial and contested issue that arises with respect to agency decision-making is the degree of deference owed by courts to agency interpretations of enabling statutes. Two approaches have been offered: the "*Chevron* standard" and the "*Skidmore* standard." As you read the following two cases, consider the extent to which public choice theory provides support for one standard over the other and the extent to which public choice insights inform, or should inform, the Supreme Court's decision.

Chevron U.S.A. Inc. v. Natural Resources Defense Council[187]

Chevron U.S.A. Inc. v. Natural Resources Defense Council, Inc. is one of the most important Supreme Court cases of recent decades. *Chevron* arose in response to new regulations established by the EPA interpreting the Clean Air Act. The specific issue in *Chevron* was review of the decision by the EPA to amend its earlier regulatory definition of a "stationary source" of air pollution, which had defined each individual source of pollution in a plant (e.g., each smokestack) as a "stationary source," to instead allow a state to treat the entire plant as a "stationary source." The new regulation produced a figurative "bubble" over the entire plant.

---

186. *Id.* at 1358–59 (footnote omitted).

187. 467 U.S. 837 (1984).

As a result, an existing plant that contained several pollution-emitting devices could install or modify one piece of equipment without meeting the permit conditions if the alteration would not increase the total emissions from the plant. The Court held that the change in the definition was permissible. Justice Stevens, writing for a unanimous Supreme Court, wrote:

> When a court reviews an agency's construction of the statute which it administers, it is confronted with two questions. First, always, is the question whether Congress has directly spoken to the precise question at issue. If the intent of Congress is clear, that is the end of the matter; for the court, as well as the agency, must give effect to the unambiguously expressed intent of Congress. If, however, the court determines Congress has not directly addressed the precise question at issue, the court does not simply impose its own construction on the statute, as would be necessary in the absence of an administrative interpretation. Rather, if the statute is silent or ambiguous with respect to the specific issue, the question for the court is whether the agency's answer is based on a permissible construction of the statute.
>
> "The power of an administrative agency to administer a congressionally created ... program necessarily requires the formulation of policy and the making of rules to fill any gap left, implicitly or explicitly, by Congress." If Congress has explicitly left a gap for the agency to fill, there is an express delegation of authority to the agency to elucidate a specific provision of the statute by regulation. Such legislative regulations are given controlling weight unless they are arbitrary, capricious, or manifestly contrary to the statute. Sometimes the legislative delegation to an agency on a particular question is implicit rather than explicit. In such a case, a court may not substitute its own construction of a statutory provision for a reasonable interpretation made by the administrator of an agency.[188]

After concluding that the regulation was not inconsistent with the statutory language or legislative history of the Clean Air Act, the Court also specifically noted that it would not second guess the policy conclusions of the EPA:

> The arguments over policy that are advanced in the parties' briefs create the impression that respondents are now waging in a judicial forum a specific policy battle which they ultimately lost in the agency and in the 32 jurisdictions opting for the "bubble concept," but one which was never waged in the Congress. Such policy arguments are more properly addressed to legislators or administrators, not to judges.
>
> In these cases, the Administrator's interpretation represents a reasonable accommodation of manifestly competing interests and is entitled to deference: the regulatory scheme is technical and complex,

---

188. *Id.* at 842–44 (citation and footnotes omitted).

the agency considered the matter in a detailed and reasoned fashion, and the decision involves reconciling conflicting policies. Congress intended to accommodate both interests, but did not do so itself on the level of specificity presented by these cases. Perhaps that body consciously desired the Administrator to strike the balance at this level, thinking that those with great expertise and charged with responsibility for administering the provision would be in a better position to do so; perhaps it simply did not consider the question at this level; and perhaps Congress was unable to forge a coalition on either side of the question, and those on each side decided to take their chances with the scheme devised by the agency. For judicial purposes, it matters not which of these things occurred.

Judges are not experts in the field, and are not part of either political branch of the Government. Courts must, in some cases, reconcile competing political interests, but not on the basis of the judges' personal policy preferences. In contrast, an agency to which Congress has delegated policymaking responsibilities may, within the limits of that delegation, properly rely upon the incumbent administration's views of wise policy to inform its judgments. While agencies are not directly accountable to the people, the Chief Executive is, and it is entirely appropriate for this political branch of the Government to make such policy choices—resolving the competing interests which Congress itself either inadvertently did not resolve, or intentionally left to be resolved by the agency charged with the administration of the statute in light of everyday realities.

When a challenge to an agency construction of a statutory provision, fairly conceptualized, really centers on the wisdom of the agency's policy, rather than whether it is a reasonable choice within a gap left open by Congress, the challenge must fail. In such a case, federal judges—who have no constituency—have a duty to respect legitimate policy choices made by those who do. The responsibilities for assessing the wisdom of such policy choices and resolving the struggle between competing views of the public interest are not judicial ones: "Our Constitution vests such responsibilities in the political branches."

We hold that the EPA's definition of the term "source" is a permissible construction of the statute which seeks to accommodate progress in reducing air pollution with economic growth.[189]

United States v. Mead Corp.[190]

In *United States v. Mead Corp.*, the Supreme Court was confronted with the question of the scope of *Chevron*. The issue in *Mead* was whether a tariff classification ruling by the United States Customs Service should be afforded *Chevron* deference. Justice Souter, writing for the *Mead* majority, concluded that under the facts as presented in *Mead*, *Chevron*

---

189. *Id.* at 864–66 (citation and footnotes omitted).

190. 533 U.S. 218 (2001).

deference would not apply. Instead, the Court applied the doctrine of *Skidmore v. Swift & Co.*,[191] that "the ruling is eligible to claim respect according to its persuasiveness."[192] The Court drew the distinction as follows:

> We granted certiorari in order to consider the limits of *Chevron* deference owed to administrative practice in applying a statute. We hold that administrative implementation of a particular statutory provision qualifies for *Chevron* deference when it appears that Congress delegated authority to the agency generally to make rules carrying the force of law, and that the agency interpretation claiming deference was promulgated in the exercise of that authority. Delegation of such authority may be shown in a variety of ways, as by an agency's power to engage in adjudication or notice-and-comment rulemaking, or by some other indication of a comparable congressional intent. The Customs ruling at issue here fails to qualify, although the possibility that it deserves some deference under *Skidmore* leads us to vacate and remand.
>
> When Congress has "explicitly left a gap for an agency to fill, there is an express delegation of authority to the agency to elucidate a specific provision of the statute by regulation," and any ensuing regulation is binding in the courts unless procedurally defective, arbitrary or capricious in substance, or manifestly contrary to the statute. But whether or not they enjoy any express delegation of authority on a particular question, agencies charged with applying a statute necessarily make all sorts of interpretive choices, and while not all of those choices bind judges to follow them, they certainly may influence courts facing questions the agencies have already answered. "[T]he well-reasoned views of the agencies implementing a statute 'constitute a body of experience and informed judgment to which courts and litigants may properly resort for guidance,'" and "[w]e have long recognized that considerable weight should be accorded to an executive department's construction of a statutory scheme it is entrusted to administer...." The fair measure of deference to an agency administering its own statute has been understood to vary with circumstances, and courts have looked to the degree of the agency's care, its consistency, formality, and relative expertness, and to the persuasiveness of the agency's position. The approach has produced a spectrum of judicial responses, from great respect at one end, to near indifference at the other. Justice Jackson summed things up in *Skidmore* v. *Swift & Co.*:
>
>> "The weight [accorded to an administrative] judgment in a particular case will depend upon the thoroughness evident in its consideration, the validity of its reasoning, its consistency with

191. 323 U.S. 134 (1944).

192. *Mead*, 533 U.S. at 221.

earlier and later pronouncements, and all those factors which give it power to persuade, if lacking power to control."[193]

The Court concluded:

Underlying the position we take here, like the position expressed by Justice Scalia in dissent, is a choice about the best way to deal with an inescapable feature of the body of congressional legislation authorizing administrative action. That feature is the great variety of ways in which the laws invest the Government's administrative arms with discretion, and with procedures for exercising it, in giving meaning to Acts of Congress. Implementation of a statute may occur in formal adjudication or the choice to defend against judicial challenge; it may occur in a central board or office or in dozens of enforcement agencies dotted across the country; its institutional lawmaking may be confined to the resolution of minute detail or extend to legislative rulemaking on matters intentionally left by Congress to be worked out at the agency level.

Although we all accept the position that the Judiciary should defer to at least some of this multifarious administrative action, we have to decide how to take account of the great range of its variety. If the primary objective is to simplify the judicial process of giving or withholding deference, then the diversity of statutes authorizing discretionary administrative action must be declared irrelevant or minimized. If, on the other hand, it is simply implausible that Congress intended such a broad range of statutory authority to produce only two varieties of administrative action, demanding either *Chevron* deference or none at all, then the breadth of the spectrum of possible agency action must be taken into account. Justice Scalia's first priority over the years has been to limit and simplify. The Court's choice has been to tailor deference to variety. This acceptance of the range of statutory variation has led the Court to recognize more than one variety of judicial deference, just as the Court has recognized a variety of indicators that Congress would expect *Chevron* deference.[194]

Writing in dissent, Justice Scalia argued that *Skidmore* deference to agency action was, among other things, inconsistent with the purposes of permitting delegation in the first place, namely to allow Congress to rely on agency expertise in crafting regulations. Moreover, by treating different types of agency actions differently, the Court's rule provides administrative agencies with incentives to try to strategically manipulate their rulemaking procedures so as to fit their rules into the preferred category. He wrote:

Another practical effect of today's opinion will be an artificially induced increase in informal rulemaking. Buy stock in the GPO. Since informal rulemaking and formal adjudication are the only more-or-

193. *Id.* at 226–28 (citations and footnotes omitted).
194. *Id.* at 235–37 (footnotes omitted).

less safe harbors from the storm that the Court has unleashed; and since formal adjudication is not an option but must be mandated by statute or constitutional command; informal rulemaking—which the Court was once careful to make voluntary unless required by statute—will now become a virtual necessity. As I have described, the Court's safe harbor requires not merely that the agency have been given rulemaking authority, but also that the agency have *employed* rulemaking as the means of resolving the statutory ambiguity. (It is hard to understand why that should be so. Surely the mere *conferral* of rulemaking authority demonstrates—if one accepts the Court's logic—a congressional intent to allow the agency to resolve ambiguities. And given that intent, what difference does it make that the agency chooses instead to use another perfectly permissible means for that purpose?) Moreover, the majority's approach will have a perverse effect on the rules that do emerge, given the principle (which the Court leaves untouched today) that judges must defer to reasonable agency interpretations of their own regulations. Agencies will now have high incentive to rush out barebones, ambiguous rules construing statutory ambiguities, which they can then in turn further clarify through informal rulings entitled to judicial respect.

Worst of all, the majority's approach will lead to the ossification of large portions of our statutory law. Where *Chevron* applies, statutory ambiguities remain ambiguities subject to the agency's ongoing clarification. They create a space, so to speak, for the exercise of continuing agency discretion. As *Chevron* itself held, the Environmental Protection Agency can interpret "stationary source" to mean a single smokestack, can later replace that interpretation with the "bubble concept" embracing an entire plant, and if that proves undesirable can return again to the original interpretation. For the indeterminately large number of statutes taken out of *Chevron* by today's decision, however, ambiguity (and hence flexibility) will cease with the first judicial resolution. *Skidmore* deference gives the agency's current position some vague and uncertain amount of respect, but it does not, like *Chevron*, *leave* the matter within the control of the Executive Branch for the future. Once the court has spoken, it becomes *unlawful* for the agency to take a contradictory position; the statute now *says* what the court has prescribed. It will be bad enough when this ossification occurs as a result of judicial determination (under today's new principles) that there is no affirmative indication of congressional intent to "delegate"; but it will be positively bizarre when it occurs simply because of an agency's failure to act by rulemaking (rather than informal adjudication) before the issue is presented to the courts.

One might respond that such ossification would not result if the agency were simply to readopt its interpretation, after a court reviewing it under *Skidmore* had rejected it, by repromulgating it through one of the *Chevron*-eligible procedural formats approved by the Court today. Approving this procedure would be a landmark abdication of judicial power. It is worlds apart from *Chevron* proper, where the court does not *purport* to give the statute a judicial interpretation—except in identifying the scope of the statutory ambiguity, as to which the court's judgment is final and irreversible. (Under *Chevron* proper, when the agency's authoritative interpretation comes within the scope of that ambiguity—and the court therefore approves it—the agency will not be "overruling" the court's decision when it later decides that a different interpretation (still within the scope of the ambiguity) is preferable.) By contrast, under this view, the reviewing court will not be holding the agency's authoritative interpretation within the scope of the ambiguity; but will be holding that the agency has not used the "delegation-conferring" procedures, and that the court must therefore *interpret the statute on its own*—but subject to reversal if and when the agency uses the proper procedures.

... I know of no case, in the entire history of the federal courts, in which we have allowed a judicial interpretation of a statute to be set aside by an agency—or have allowed a lower court to render an interpretation of a statute subject to correction by an agency.... There is, in short, no way to avoid the ossification of federal law that today's opinion sets in motion. What a court says is the law after according *Skidmore* deference will be the law forever, beyond the power of the agency to change even through rulemaking.

And finally, the majority's approach compounds the confusion it creates by breathing new life into the anachronism of *Skidmore*, which sets forth a sliding scale of deference owed an agency's interpretation of a statute that is dependent "upon the thoroughness evident in [the agency's] consideration, the validity of its reasoning, its consistency with earlier and later pronouncements, and all those factors which give it power to persuade, if lacking power to control"; in this way, the appropriate measure of deference will be accorded the "body of experience and informed judgment" that such interpretations often embody. Justice Jackson's eloquence notwithstanding, the rule of *Skidmore* deference is an empty truism and a trifling statement of the obvious: A judge should take into account the well-considered views of expert observers.

It was possible to live with the indeterminacy of *Skidmore* deference in earlier times. But in an era when federal statutory law administered by federal agencies is pervasive, and when the ambiguities (intended or unintended) that those statutes contain are innumerable, totality-of-the-circumstances *Skidmore* deference is a recipe for uncertainty, unpredictability, and endless litigation. To condemn a vast body of agency action to that regime (all except rulemaking, formal (and informal?) adjudication, and whatever else might now and then be included within today's intentionally vague formulation of affirmative congressional intent to "delegate") is irresponsible.[195]

DISCUSSION QUESTIONS

1.   From a public choice perspective, as a general rule, which form of deference, *Chevron* or *Skidmore*, makes the most sense? Does the Court in *Chevron* assume that when Congress delegates it does so based on the traditional model of delegation, rather than the strategic models of delegation suggested by some public choice theorists? In determining the deference owed to an agency interpretation, should it matter why Congress delegates?

2.   The Court writes in *Chevron* that the reasons for Congress's decision to delegate rulemaking authority is unknown: Congress might have done so to make use of EPA's expertise, Congress might have done so without considering the policy question resolved by EPA and called into question in *Chevron*, or Congress might have done so after failing to resolve offsetting interest-group pressures and so the interests "on each side decided to take their chances with the scheme devised by the agency," a sort of regulatory "lottery."[196] More importantly, the Court argues that the reason why Congress chose to delegate is irrelevant: "For judicial purposes, it matters not which of these things occurred." Do you agree with that conclusion? If you think that the reasons for the delegation should matter, do you also think that judges are capable of determining such motivations? Assuming that Courts can distinguish delegations for "good" reasons (such as reliance on agency expertise) from "bad" reasons (as a result of interest-group capture or to play the "delegation lottery") should the degree of judicial deference to agency decision-making turn on the quality of the reasons for the delegation? Why or why not? If Congress delegates in order to avoid blame for enacting controversial policies, as some public choice theorists argue, should this have any implications for the appropriate degree of deference owed to an agency? Should judges try to prevent Congress from delegating in order to avoid political accountability? If not, should judges try to articulate rules that heighten agency accountability?

3.   Prior to becoming a Judge (and later Justice), Justice Scalia edited the journal *Regulation*, a public choice-influenced academic journal that studies regulation and the regulatory process, suggesting at least some formal familiarity with public choice scholarship. As this chapter discusses, before joining the judiciary, Justice Breyer also had considerable scholarly familiarity with regulation and public choice scholarship. Yet as illustrated in *Mead*— where Breyer joined the majority opinion while Scalia, writing alone, dissented—these Justices disagree on fundamental questions of judicial deference to agency decision-making. To what extent, if at all, does their disagreement arise from differences in their understanding of the regulatory process and the ability of the judiciary to improve it? Can either of their views be said to be more compatible with the insights of public choice theory? Do either of their views tend to confirm Merrill's hypothesis about the influence of public choice theory on judicial doctrine?

---

195. *Id.* at 246–50 (Scalia, J., dissenting) (citations omitted).

196. For an analysis of delegation as a form of "regulatory lottery" favored by interest groups and Congress when Congress is unable to strike a political coalition, see Aranson, Gellhorn & Robinson, *supra* note 156.

4. Justice Scalia argues that the *Skidmore* doctrine provides agencies with an incentive to "rush out barebones, ambiguous rules construing statutory ambiguities, which they can then in turn further clarify through informal rulings entitled to judicial respect." Scalia's concern implicitly assumes that agencies act strategically in the manner and timing of issuance of regulations. Is this statement consistent with public interest theories of delegation? Public choice theories? If agencies do act strategically in the issuance of regulations, should that affect whether, or the degree to which, judicial deference should be granted?

5. Which of the various agency delegation theories is most consistent with *Mead*? Do you agree with Elhauge that the combined *Chevron/Mead* regime promotes enactable preferences by allowing rules to develop consistently with the best available proxy for contemporary (but not necessarily contemporaneous) congressional intent[197]? Why or why not? Do you agree that it is an appropriate normative benchmark? Why or why not?

B. DEFERENCE TO AGENCY SELF INTEREST

One area in which public choice insights have influenced governmental regulation involves judicial deference to agency decision-making in contexts that implicate agency self interest, a situation that arises in various settings.[198] For instance, some cases directly involve an agency's financial self interest, such as the interpretation of a contract entered into between an agency and a private party or the interpretation of a statute that may affect the agency's contractual obligations. Sometimes an agency competes with private parties in the marketplace, and again the interpretation of relevant statutes potentially affects the agency's competitive position.

A more interesting and far-reaching situation, however, is whether *Chevron* deference is owed to an agency's interpretation of its jurisdiction, even before reaching the substance of its regulation. As a matter of public choice theory, the analysis turns on whether agencies are thought to seek expansion or autonomy and independence. As you read the cases presented, consider which of the theories of agency incentives by Niskanen, Wilson, or others, best explains the agencies' decisions whether to assert jurisdiction. Consider also the normative question as to whether public choice theory suggests a need for a different degree of deference depending on whether an agency is seeking to expand or to contract its regulatory jurisdiction.

We present two cases: *FDA v. Brown & Williamson Tobacco Corp.*[199] and *Massachusetts v. EPA.*[200]

---

197. *See supra* chapter 5, section II.B.3.

198. *See* Timothy K. Armstrong, Chevron *Deference and Agency Self–Interest*, 13 CORNELL J.L. & PUB. POL'Y 203 (2004); *see also* Nathan Alexander Sales & Jonathan H. Adler, *The Rest Is Silence:* Chevron *Deference, Agency Jurisdiction, and Statutory Silences* (George Mason Univ. Law & Econ., Research Paper No. 08–46, 2008), *available at* http://papers.ssrn.com/sol3/papers.
cfm?abstract_id=1213149.

199. 529 U.S. 120 (2000).

200. 549 U.S. 497 (2007).

FDA v. Browne Williamson Tobacco Corp.[201]

Brown & Williamson addressed the question of whether the FDA had the authority to regulate tobacco and, specifically, to regulate cigarettes and smokeless tobacco as "devices" that deliver nicotine to the body. The FDA asserted the authority to do so, a position that the United States Supreme Court ultimately rejected.

Under the Food and Drug Act, the FDA must ensure that any product regulated by it must be "safe" and "effective" for its intended use. Thus, the Act generally requires the FDA to prevent the marketing of any drug or device where the potential for inflicting death or physical injury is not offset by the potential therapeutic benefit. In its rulemaking proceeding, the FDA determined that " 'tobacco products are unsafe,' 'dangerous,' and 'cause great pain and suffering from illness.' "[202] It further found that the consumption of tobacco products presents " 'extraordinary health risks,' and that 'tobacco use is the single leading cause of preventable death in the United States.' "[203]

Writing for the Court in *FDA v. Brown & Williamson Tobacco Corp.*, Justice O'Connor determined that given FDA's statutory mandate and its factual findings respecting cigarettes and smokeless tobacco products, if those products were classified as "devices" under the statute, the "FDA would be required to remove them from the market."[204] However, she noted, Congress has made clear its intent that tobacco products not be removed from the market and, in fact, had enacted several pieces of legislation since 1965 related to the problem of tobacco and health, legislation that was predicated on the assumption that tobacco products would remain legal. Justice O'Connor wrote:

> In determining whether Congress has spoken directly to the FDA's authority to regulate tobacco, we must also consider in greater detail the tobacco-specific legislation that Congress has enacted over the past 35 years. At the time a statute is enacted, it may have a range of plausible meanings. Over time, however, subsequent acts can shape or focus those meanings. The "classic judicial task of reconciling many laws enacted over time, and getting them to 'make sense' in combination, necessarily assumes that the implications of a statute may be altered by the implications of a later statute." This is particularly so where the scope of the earlier statute is broad but the subsequent statutes more specifically address the topic at hand. "[A] specific policy embodied in a later federal statute should control our construction of the [earlier] statute, even though it [has] not been expressly amended."
>
> Congress has enacted six separate pieces of legislation since 1965 addressing the problem of tobacco use and human health. . . .

---

201.   529 U.S. 120 (2000).

202.   *Id.* at 134.

203.   *Id.*

204.   *Id.* at 135.

In adopting each statute, Congress has acted against the backdrop of the FDA's consistent and repeated statements that it lacked authority under the FDCA ["Food Drug and Cosmetics Act"] to regulate tobacco absent claims of therapeutic benefit by the manufacturer. In fact, on several occasions over this period, and after the health consequences of tobacco use and nicotine's pharmacological effects had become well known, Congress considered and rejected bills that would have granted the FDA such jurisdiction. Under these circumstances, it is evident that Congress' tobacco-specific statutes have effectively ratified the FDA's long-held position that it lacks jurisdiction under the FDCA to regulate tobacco products. Congress has created a distinct regulatory scheme to address the problem of tobacco and health, and that scheme, as presently constructed, precludes any role for the FDA.[205]

Justice O'Connor further observed that until this case, the FDA consistently and expressly disavowed jurisdiction to regulate tobacco. In fact, Congress's actions over time made clear "Congress' intent to preclude *any* administrative agency from exercising significant policymaking authority on the subject of smoking and health."[206] For instance, when the Federal Trade Commission at one point moved to regulate cigarette labeling and advertising, "Congress enacted a statute reserving exclusive control over both subjects to itself."[207] The Court notes:

Taken together, these actions by Congress over the past 35 years preclude an interpretation of the FDCA that grants the FDA jurisdiction to regulate tobacco products. We do not rely on Congress' failure to act—its consideration and rejection of bills that would have given the FDA this authority—in reaching this conclusion. Indeed, this is not a case of simple inaction by Congress that purportedly represents its acquiescence in an agency's position. To the contrary, Congress has enacted several statutes addressing the particular subject of tobacco and health, creating a distinct regulatory scheme for cigarettes and smokeless tobacco. In doing so, Congress has been aware of tobacco's health hazards and its pharmacological effects. It has also enacted this legislation against the background of the FDA repeatedly and consistently asserting that it lacks jurisdiction under the FDCA to regulate tobacco products as customarily marketed. Further, Congress has persistently acted to preclude a meaningful role for *any* administrative agency in making policy on the subject of tobacco and health. Moreover, the substance of Congress' regulatory scheme is, in an important respect, incompatible with FDA jurisdiction. Although the supervision of product labeling to protect consumer health is a substantial component of the FDA's regulation of drugs and devices, the FCLAA ["Federal Cigarette Labeling and Advertising Act"] and the CSTHEA ["Comprehensive Smokeless Tobacco Health Education Act

---

205. *Id.* at 143–44 (citations omitted).

206. *Id.* at 149.

207. *Id.*

of 1986"] explicitly prohibit any federal agency from imposing any health-related labeling requirements on cigarettes or smokeless tobacco products.

> Under these circumstances, it is clear that Congress' tobacco-specific legislation has effectively ratified the FDA's previous position that it lacks jurisdiction to regulate tobacco.[208]

In addition to criticizing the FDA for this sudden reversal of position, the Court questioned whether Congress would have delegated to the FDA the authority to regulate or even to ban tobacco. The Court concluded that it was highly implausible that Congress would have impliedly delegated such a far-reaching authority to the FDA, especially in such a cryptic manner:

> Finally, our inquiry into whether Congress has directly spoken to the precise question at issue is shaped, at least in some measure, by the nature of the question presented. Deference under *Chevron* to an agency's construction of a statute that it administers is premised on the theory that a statute's ambiguity constitutes an implicit delegation from Congress to the agency to fill in the statutory gaps. In extraordinary cases, however, there may be reason to hesitate before concluding that Congress has intended such an implicit delegation.

> This is hardly an ordinary case. Contrary to its representations to Congress since 1914, the FDA has now asserted jurisdiction to regulate an industry constituting a significant portion of the American economy. In fact, the FDA contends that, were it to determine that tobacco products provide no "reasonable assurance of safety," it would have the authority to ban cigarettes and smokeless tobacco entirely. Owing to its unique place in American history and society, tobacco has its own unique political history. Congress, for better or for worse, has created a distinct regulatory scheme for tobacco products, squarely rejected proposals to give the FDA jurisdiction over tobacco, and repeatedly acted to preclude any agency from exercising significant policymaking authority in the area. Given this history and the breadth of the authority that the FDA has asserted, we are obliged to defer not to the agency's expansive construction of the statute, but to Congress' consistent judgment to deny the FDA this power.

> . . . .

> [W]e are confident that Congress could not have intended to delegate a decision of such economic and political significance to an agency in so cryptic a fashion. To find that the FDA has the authority to regulate tobacco products, one must not only adopt an extremely strained understanding of "safety" as it is used throughout the Act—a concept central to the FDCA's regulatory scheme—but also ignore the plain implication of Congress' subsequent tobacco-specific legisla-

---

208. *Id.* at 155–56 (citations omitted).

tion. It is therefore clear, based on the FDCA's overall regulatory scheme and the subsequent tobacco legislation, that Congress has directly spoken to the question at issue and precluded the FDA from regulating tobacco products.

By no means do we question the seriousness of the problem that the FDA has sought to address. The agency has amply demonstrated that tobacco use, particularly among children and adolescents, poses perhaps the single most significant threat to public health in the United States. Nonetheless, no matter how "important, conspicuous, and controversial" the issue, and regardless of how likely the public is to hold the Executive Branch politically accountable, an administrative agency's power to regulate in the public interest must always be grounded in a valid grant of authority from Congress. And " '[i]n our anxiety to effectuate the congressional purpose of protecting the public, we must take care not to extend the scope of the statute beyond the point where Congress indicated it would stop.' "[209]

Massachusetts v. EPA[210]

A few years later in *Massachusetts v. EPA* the Supreme Court revisited the question of an agency's authority to determine its jurisdiction, but in the context of an agency's *refusal* to assert jurisdiction. The case arose when Massachusetts and several other states sued the EPA, requesting that it be ordered to regulate certain "greenhouse gases," including carbon dioxide, that were alleged to cause global climate change that harmed the party states. Section 202(a)(1) of the Clean Air Act requires that the EPA "shall by regulation prescribe . . . standards applicable to the emission of any air pollutant from any class . . . of new motor vehicles . . . which in [the EPA Administrator's] judgment causes[s], or contribute[s] to, air pollution . . . reasonably . . . anticipated to endanger public health or welfare."[211] The EPA refused to regulate on the basis that is was not authorized to do so under the Clean Air Act and that even if it had such power, it was a reasonable exercise of its discretion to refuse action in light of what it viewed as the uncertainty of climate change science as well as the practical difficulties associated with various proposed regulatory solutions.

Writing for the majority of the *Massachusetts* Court, Justice Stevens held that EPA did have authority to regulate under the statute and that its refusal to do so was not based on specific findings about the lack of scientific evidence. The Court opened by noting the high importance of the issue:

> A well-documented rise in global temperatures has coincided with a significant increase in the concentration of carbon dioxide in the atmosphere. Respected scientists believe the two trends are related.

---

209. *Id.* at 159–61 (citations omitted).

210. 549 U.S. 497 (2007).

211. 42 U.S.C. § 7521(a)(1) (2006).

For when carbon dioxide is released into the atmosphere, it acts like the ceiling of a greenhouse, trapping solar energy and retarding the escape of reflected heat. It is therefore a species—the most important species—of a "greenhouse gas."

Calling global warming "the most pressing environmental challenge of our time," a group of States, local governments, and private organizations, alleged in a petition for certiorari that the Environmental Protection Agency (EPA) has abdicated its responsibility under the Clean Air Act to regulate the emissions of four greenhouse gases, including carbon dioxide. Specifically, petitioners asked us to answer two questions concerning the meaning of § 202(a)(1) of the Act: whether EPA has the statutory authority to regulate greenhouse gas emissions from new motor vehicles; and if so, whether its stated reasons for refusing to do so are consistent with the statute.[212]

Justice Stevens first determined that the Commonwealth of Massachusetts had standing to present the challenge in its sovereign capacity and as owner of coastal property allegedly subject to erosion as a consequence of global warming. The Court also noted that it was taking the case despite reservations more generally about whether specific plaintiffs had standing because of the "unusual importance of the underlying issue...."[213] The Court noted the immense international debate on the issue and ongoing efforts to address the issue through legislative and international action. The majority opinion continued:

Congress ... addressed the issue in 1987, when it enacted the Global Climate Protection Act. Finding that "manmade pollution—the release of carbon dioxide, chlorofluorocarbons, methane, and other trace gases into the atmosphere—may be producing a long-term and substantial increase in the average temperature on Earth," Congress directed EPA to propose to Congress a "coordinated national policy on global climate change," and ordered the Secretary of State to work "through the channels of multilateral diplomacy" and coordinate diplomatic efforts to combat global warming. Congress emphasized that "ongoing pollution and deforestation may be contributing now to an irreversible process" and that "[n]ecessary actions must be identified and implemented in time to protect the climate."

Meanwhile, the scientific understanding of climate change progressed. In 1990, the Intergovernmental Panel on Climate Change (IPCC), a multinational scientific body organized under the auspices of the United Nations, published its first comprehensive report on the topic. Drawing on expert opinions from across the globe, the IPCC concluded that "emissions resulting from human activities are substantially increasing the atmospheric concentrations of ... greenhouse gases [which] will enhance the greenhouse effect, resulting on average in an additional warming of the Earth's surface."

212. Massachusetts v. EPA, 549 U.S. 497, 504–05 (2007) (footnotes omitted).
213. *Id.* at 506.

Responding to the IPCC report, the United Nations convened the "Earth Summit" in 1992 in Rio de Janeiro. The first President Bush attended and signed the United Nations Framework Convention on Climate Change (UNFCCC), a nonbinding agreement among 154 nations to reduce atmospheric concentrations of carbon dioxide and other greenhouse gases for the purpose of "prevent[ing] dangerous anthropogenic [*i.e.*, human-induced] interference with the [Earth's] climate system." The Senate unanimously ratified the treaty.

Some five years later—after the IPCC issued a second comprehensive report in 1995 concluding that "[t]he balance of evidence suggests there is a discernible human influence on global climate"—the UNFCCC signatories met in Kyoto, Japan, and adopted a protocol that assigned mandatory targets for industrialized nations to reduce greenhouse gas emissions. Because those targets did not apply to developing and heavily polluting nations such as China and India, the Senate unanimously passed a resolution expressing its sense that the United States should not enter into the Kyoto Protocol. President Clinton did not submit the protocol to the Senate for ratification.[214]

After disposing of several questions involving standing, the Court turned to the merits of the case:

On the merits, the first question is whether § 202(a)(1) of the Clean Air Act authorizes EPA to regulate greenhouse gas emissions from new motor vehicles in the event that it forms a "judgment" that such emissions contribute to climate change. We have little trouble concluding that it does. In relevant part, § 202(a)(1) provides that EPA "shall by regulation prescribe ... standards applicable to the emission of any air pollutant from any class or classes of new motor vehicles or new motor vehicle engines, which in [the Administrator's] judgment cause, or contribute to, air pollution which may reasonably be anticipated to endanger public health or welfare." Because EPA believes that Congress did not intend it to regulate substances that contribute to climate change, the agency maintains that carbon dioxide is not an "air pollutant" within the meaning of the provision.

The statutory text forecloses EPA's reading. The Clean Air Act's sweeping definition of "air pollutant" includes "*any* air pollution agent or combination of such agents, including *any* physical, chemical ... substance or matter which is emitted into or otherwise enters the ambient air...." On its face, the definition embraces all airborne compounds of whatever stripe, and underscores that intent through the repeated use of the word "any." Carbon dioxide, methane, nitrous oxide, and hydrofluorocarbons are without a doubt "physical [and] chemical ... substance[s] which [are] emitted into ... the ambient air." The statute is unambiguous.

Rather than relying on statutory text, EPA invokes post-enactment congressional actions and deliberations it views as tantamount

---

214. *Id.* at 508–09 (citations and footnotes omitted).

to a congressional command to refrain from regulating greenhouse gas emissions. Even if such post-enactment legislative history could shed light on the meaning of an otherwise-unambiguous statute, EPA never identifies any action remotely suggesting that Congress meant to curtail its power to treat greenhouse gases as air pollutants. That subsequent Congresses have eschewed enacting binding emissions limitations to combat global warming tells us nothing about what Congress meant when it amended § 202(a)(1) in 1970 and 1977. And unlike EPA, we have no difficulty reconciling Congress' various efforts to promote interagency collaboration and research to better understand climate change with the agency's pre-existing mandate to regulate "any air pollutant" that may endanger the public welfare. Collaboration and research do not conflict with any thoughtful regulatory effort; they complement it.[215]

The Court then addressed the apparent inconsistency with *FDA v. Brown & Williamson Tobacco Corp.*:

> EPA's reliance on *Brown & Williamson Tobacco Corp.*, is ... misplaced. In holding that tobacco products are not "drugs" or "devices" subject to Food and Drug Administration (FDA) regulation pursuant to the Food, Drug and Cosmetic Act (FDCA), we found critical at least two considerations that have no counterpart in this case.

> First, we thought it unlikely that Congress meant to ban tobacco products, which the FDCA would have required had such products been classified as "drugs" or "devices." Here, in contrast, EPA jurisdiction would lead to no such extreme measures. EPA would only *regulate* emissions, and even then, it would have to delay any action "to permit the development and application of the requisite technology, giving appropriate consideration to the cost of compliance." However much a ban on tobacco products clashed with the "common sense" intuition that Congress never meant to remove those products from circulation, there is nothing counterintuitive to the notion that EPA can curtail the emission of substances that are putting the global climate out of kilter.

> Second, in *Brown & Williamson* we pointed to an unbroken series of congressional enactments that made sense only if adopted "against the backdrop of the FDA's consistent and repeated statements that it lacked authority under the FDCA to regulate tobacco." We can point to no such enactments here: EPA has not identified any congressional action that conflicts in any way with the regulation of greenhouse gases from new motor vehicles. Even if it had, Congress could not have acted against a regulatory "backdrop" of disclaimers of regulatory authority. Prior to the order that provoked this litigation, EPA had never disavowed the authority to regulate greenhouse gases, and in 1998 it in fact affirmed that it *had* such authority. There is no reason,

---

215. *Id.* at 528–30 (citations and footnotes omitted).

much less a compelling reason, to accept EPA's invitation to read ambiguity into a clear statute.

EPA finally argues that it cannot regulate carbon dioxide emissions from motor vehicles because doing so would require it to tighten mileage standards, a job (according to EPA) that Congress has assigned to DOT. But that DOT sets mileage standards in no way licenses EPA to shirk its environmental responsibilities. EPA has been charged with protecting the public's "health" and "welfare," a statutory obligation wholly independent of DOT's mandate to promote energy efficiency. The two obligations may overlap, but there is no reason to think the two agencies cannot both administer their obligations and yet avoid inconsistency.

While the Congresses that drafted § 202(a)(1) might not have appreciated the possibility that burning fossil fuels could lead to global warming, they did understand that without regulatory flexibility, changing circumstances and scientific developments would soon render the Clean Air Act obsolete. The broad language of § 202(a)(1) reflects an intentional effort to confer the flexibility necessary to forestall such obsolescence. Because greenhouse gases fit well within the Clean Air Act's capacious definition of "air pollutant," we hold that EPA has the statutory authority to regulate the emission of such gases from new motor vehicles.[216]

The EPA further argued that even if it had legal authority to regulate greenhouse gases, it was a reasonable exercise of its discretion to decline to act. The Court rejected this claim, writing:

> Nor can EPA avoid its statutory obligation by noting the uncertainty surrounding various features of climate change and concluding that it would therefore be better not to regulate at this time. If the scientific uncertainty is so profound that it precludes EPA from making a reasoned judgment as to whether greenhouse gases contribute to global warming, EPA must say so. That EPA would prefer not to regulate greenhouse gases because of some residual uncertainty—which, contrary to Justice Scalia's apparent belief, is in fact all that it said—is irrelevant. The statutory question is whether sufficient information exists to make an endangerment finding.

> In short, EPA has offered no reasoned explanation for its refusal to decide whether greenhouse gases cause or contribute to climate change. Its action was therefore "arbitrary, capricious, ... or otherwise not in accordance with law." We need not and do not reach the question whether on remand EPA must make an endangerment finding, or whether policy concerns can inform EPA's actions in the event that it makes such a finding. We hold only that EPA must ground its reasons for action or inaction in the statute.[217]

---

216. *Id.* at 530–32 (citations omitted).

217. *Id.* at 534–35 (citations omitted).

In one of two dissenting opinions in the case, Justice Scalia argued that nothing in the statute compels the EPA Administrator to determine whether a given substance creates a public health risk, only that the EPA must act if such a judgment is made. Thus, Scalia maintained, the EPA Administrator has discretion whether to make any such judgment in the first place, especially given the contentious nature of the underlying scientific claims about global climate change and the difficulties of identifying a workable regulatory solution to the problem. Scalia explained:

> The provision of law at the heart of this case is § 202(a)(1) of the Clean Air Act (CAA), which provides that the Administrator of the Environmental Protection Agency (EPA) "shall by regulation prescribe ... standards applicable to the emission of any air pollutant from any class or classes of new motor vehicles or new motor vehicle engines, which *in his judgment* cause, or contribute to, air pollution which may reasonably be anticipated to endanger public health or welfare." As the Court recognizes, the statute "condition[s] the exercise of EPA's authority on its formation of a 'judgment.' " There is no dispute that the Administrator has made no such judgment in this case.

> The question thus arises: Does anything *require* the Administrator to make a "judgment" whenever a petition for rulemaking is filed? Without citation of the statute or any other authority, the Court says yes. Why is that so? When Congress wishes to make private action force an agency's hand, it knows how to do so. Where does the CAA say that the EPA Administrator is required to come to a decision on this question whenever a rulemaking petition is filed? The Court points to no such provision because none exists.[218]

Scalia continues, "I am willing to assume, for the sake of argument, that the Administrator's discretion in this regard is not entirely unbounded—that if he has no reasonable basis for deferring judgment he must grasp the nettle at once."[219] But, he continued:

> The Court dismisses this analysis as "rest[ing] on reasoning divorced from the statutory text." "While the statute does condition the exercise of EPA's authority on its formation of a 'judgment,' ... that judgment must relate to whether an air pollutant 'cause[s], or contribute[s] to, air pollution which may reasonably be anticipated to endanger public health or welfare.' " True but irrelevant. When the Administrator *makes* a judgment whether to regulate greenhouse gases, that judgment must relate to whether they are air pollutants that "cause, or contribute to, air pollution which may reasonably be anticipated to endanger public health or welfare." But the statute says *nothing at all* about the reasons for which the Administrator may *defer* making a judgment—the permissible reasons for deciding not to grapple with the issue at the present time. Thus, the various

---

218. *Id.* at 549–50 (Scalia, J., dissenting) (citations omitted).

219. *Id.* at 550.

"policy" rationales that the Court criticizes are not "divorced from the statutory text," except in the sense that the statutory text is silent, as texts are often silent about permissible reasons for the exercise of agency discretion. The reasons EPA gave are surely considerations executive agencies *regularly* take into account (and *ought* to take into account) when deciding whether to consider entering a new field: the impact such entry would have on other Executive Branch programs and on foreign policy. There is no basis in law for the Court's imposed limitation.

EPA's interpretation of the discretion conferred by the statutory reference to "its judgment" is not only reasonable, it is the most natural reading of the text. The Court nowhere explains why this interpretation is incorrect, let alone why it is not entitled to deference under *Chevron U. S. A. Inc.* v. *Natural Resources Defense Council, Inc.* As the Administrator acted within the law in declining to make a "judgment" for the policy reasons above set forth, I would uphold the decision to deny the rulemaking petition on that ground alone.[220]

On remand to the EPA, the EPA issued a Notice of Proposed Rulemaking that solicited comments on the possible health effects of greenhouse gases but refused to make any conclusions or findings on the issue.[221] The Notice was prefaced with the following statement by the EPA Administrator:

> EPA's analyses leading up to this ANPR ["Advance Notice of Proposed Rulemaking"] have increasingly raised questions of such importance that the scope of the agency's task has continued to expand. For instance, it has become clear that if EPA were to regulate greenhouse gas emissions from motor vehicles under the Clean Air Act, then regulation of smaller stationary sources that also emit GHGs [greenhouse gases]—such as apartment buildings, large homes, schools, and hospitals—could also be triggered. One point is clear: the potential regulation of greenhouse gases under any portion of the Clean Air Act could result in an unprecedented expansion of EPA authority that would have a profound effect on virtually every sector of the economy and touch every household in the land.

> This ANPR reflects the complexity and magnitude of the question of whether and how greenhouse gases could be effectively controlled under the Clean Air Act. This document summarizes much of EPA's work and lays out concerns raised by other federal agencies during their review of this work. EPA is publishing this notice today because it is impossible to simultaneously address all the agencies' issues and respond to our legal obligations in a timely manner.

> I believe the ANPR demonstrates the Clean Air Act, an outdated law originally enacted to control regional pollutants that cause direct

---

220. *Id.* at 552–53 (citations omitted).

221. Regulating Greenhouse Gas Emissions Under the Clean Air Act, 73 Fed. Reg. 44,354 (July 30, 2008).

health effects, is ill-suited for the task of regulating global greenhouse gases. Based on the analysis to date, pursuing this course of action would inevitably result in a very complicated, time-consuming and, likely, convoluted set of regulations. These rules would largely pre-empt or overlay existing programs that help control greenhouse gas emissions and would be relatively ineffective at reducing greenhouse gas concentrations given the potentially damaging effect on jobs and the U.S. economy.[222]

The Notice was followed by a Proposed Rule, issued after the inter-vening change in presidential administrations. The new Proposed Rule differed significantly from the previous Notice. It stated:

> Today the Administrator is proposing to find that greenhouse gases in the atmosphere endanger the public health and welfare of current and future generations. Concentrations of greenhouse gases are at unprecedented levels compared to the recent and distant past. These high atmospheric levels are the unambiguous result of human emissions, and are very likely the cause of the observed increase in average temperatures and other climatic changes. The effects of the climate change observed to date and projected to occur in the future— including but not limited to the increased likelihood of more frequent and intense heat waves, more wildfires, degraded air quality, more heavy downpours and flooding, increased drought, greater sea level rise, more intense storms, harm to water resources, harm to agricul-ture, and harm to wildlife and ecosystems—are effects on public health and welfare within the meaning of the Clean Air Act. In light of the likelihood that greenhouse gases cause these effects, and the magnitude of the effects that are occurring and are very likely to occur in the future, the Administrator proposes to find that atmo-spheric concentrations of greenhouse gases endanger public health and welfare within the meaning of Section 202(a) of the Clean Air Act.[223]

The Administrator also proposed to find that the emissions of some greenhouse gases from motor vehicles contribute to the overall mix of greenhouse gases in the atmosphere: "Thus, she proposes to find that the emissions of these substances from new motor vehicles and new motor vehicle engines are contributing to air pollution which is endangering the public health and welfare...."[224]

DISCUSSION QUESTIONS

1. In *FDA v. Brown & Williamson Tobacco Corp.*, the FDA asserted jurisdiction to regulate that the Court subsequently said that it lacked. In *Massachusetts v. EPA*, the EPA refused to assert jurisdiction that there was

---

222. *Id.* at 44,354–55.

223. Proposed Endangerment and Cause or Contribute Findings for Greenhouse Gases Under Section 202(a) of the Clean Air Act, 74 Fed. Reg. 18,886, 18,886 (proposed Apr. 24, 2009).

224. *Id.*

strong reason to believe it possessed. Moreover, on remand to the EPA, the Administrator still refused to assert jurisdiction. Do any of the models discussed in this chapter provide a consistent explanation for the decisions of the agencies in these cases?

2.   In *Brown & Williamson* the extreme public importance of the issue and the dramatic consequences that would flow from a ruling led the Court to infer that Congress did not intend for the FDA to regulate tobacco. In *Massachusetts v. EPA*, the Court noted the extreme importance of the issue and suggested that this might indicate Congress's intent to have the EPA regulate greenhouse gas emissions. Can the two cases—and the premises upon which the opinions rest—be reconciled? What does public choice and other theories of delegation say about whether Congress generally does or does not intend to delegate on extremely important and controversial issues?

3.   In *Massachusetts v. EPA*, Justice Scalia argues that if Congress wanted EPA to regulate greenhouse gases, it could simply mandate that the Administrator make a judgment as required by the statute or alternatively simply order EPA to regulate. Scalia suggests that given the high-profile nature of the issue, Congress's failure to take such steps suggests that Congress did not intend for the EPA to regulate greenhouse gases. Do any of the models discussed in this chapter explain why the EPA Administrator refused to make this judgment? Or why Congress did not order EPA to make that judgment?

4.   On remand, the EPA Administrator originally expressed the opinion that regulation of greenhouse gases is an issue that should be left to Congress and not undertaken by the EPA. Why do you believe that he expressed that view? Why might Congress be willing to allow the EPA to issue regulations on this issue rather than undertake to enact legislation as requested by the EPA Administrator?

5.   Is it relevant to the determination of whether Congress intended EPA to act that the Senate specifically refused to ratify the Kyoto Treaty? Why or why not?

6.   In *Brown & Williamson*, Justice O'Connor noted that on an issue as important and high-profile as the possible banning of tobacco, it would be illogical to assume that Congress would permit an agency to act without a clear expression of congressional intent. In *Massachusetts v. EPA*, in contrast, Justice Stevens stressed the public and economic importance of the issue and that when the Clean Air Act was enacted, given the scientific knowledge of the time, Congress could not have anticipated that greenhouse gases (such as carbon dioxide) might later be considered a pollutant. Justice Stevens further reasoned that when Congress delegates, it does so broadly in order to allow agencies to react to changing conditions. Based on the models discussed in this chapter, which of the underlying assumptions—those expressed by Justice O'Connor or by Justice Stevens—concerning congressional behavior is more plausible?

7.   To what extent can the decisions in these cases be explained by the models of ideological judging discussed in this chapter? Keep this question in mind as you read the "attitudinal model" of judicial behavior in chapter 7.

8.   In *Whitman v. American Trucking Associations, Inc.*,[225] the Supreme Court addressed a nondelegation challenge to certain rules issued by the EPA

---

225.   531 U.S. 457 (2001).

under the Clean Air Act. Under the Act, the Administrator of the EPA is required to set national ambient air quality standards (NAAQS) for each air pollutant for which "air quality criteria" have been issued. Once NAAQS have been promulgated, the Administrator must review the standard and the criteria on which it is based every five years. In 1997, EPA revised the NAAQS for particulate matter and ozone. The American Trucking Associations challenged the EPA action on the ground that the delegation of this authority to the EPA was made without an "intelligible principle" and therefore was an improper delegation under the Supreme Court's precedent in *J.W. Hampton, Jr., & Co. v. United States*, 276 U.S. 394, 409 (1928).

Several states joined the American Trucking Association (the "ATA") in challenging the rules. In *Massachusetts v. EPA*, the named plaintiff and several other states joined in bringing the action to try to force the EPA to regulate greenhouse gases (several other states filed an *amicus* brief supporting the EPA). In *American Trucking*, Michigan, Ohio, and West Virginia opposed the EPA's regulation. In *Massachusetts*, the states bringing the action included California, Connecticut, Illinois, Maine, Massachusetts, New Jersey, New Mexico, New York, Oregon, Rhode Island, Vermont, and Washington. Those who filed *amicus* briefs opposing the action in *Massachusetts* included Alaska, Idaho, Kansas, Michigan, Nebraska, North Dakota, Ohio, South Dakota, Texas, and Utah. Does public choice help to provide an explanation of the various states' positions in these two cases?

Professor Todd Zywicki has offered the following hypothesis: Environmental regulation can be very costly. States that adopt stricter environmental regulations such as regulation of greenhouse gases, whether for practical or ideological reasons, thereby create a competitive disadvantage for in state businesses.[226] Other states, notably rural states with low population densities, will be less concerned about issues of ambient air quality and greenhouse gases and will thus oppose strict environmental regulations for economic or ideological reasons. Producers of raw materials (such as coal) or other products (such as automobiles or auto parts) that are likely to be adversely affected by such regulations were they to be promulgated also will oppose stricter regulation.

On this account, states that unilaterally enact strict environmental regulations will support federal action that enables them to export the cost of their regulations onto states with different policy preferences, which Zywicki calls "political externalities." Does this breakdown of state economic interests provide the basis for a persuasive account of the lineup of states in *Massachusetts* and *American Trucking*? If so, does Zywicki's thesis provide any normative insight with respect to the nondelegation doctrine and the allocation of decision-making authority among Congress, agencies, and the courts? Which body is in the best position to respond to the inevitable distributional consequences of any proposed regulation? Why?

---

226. *See* Zywicki, *supra* note 115; Jason Scott Johnston, *Climate Change Hysteria and the Supreme Court: The Economic Impact of Global Warming on the U.S. and the Misguided Regulation of Greenhouse Gas Emissions Under the Clean Air Act* (Univ. of Pa. Law Sch. Inst. for Law & Econ., Research Paper No. 08–04, 2008), *available at* http://ssrn.com/abstract=1098476; Henry N. Butler & Todd J. Zywicki, *Expansion of Liability Under Public Nuisance*, 20 S. CT. ECON. REV. (forthcoming 2011).

In *American Trucking*, Justice Breyer wrote a concurring opinion uphold-ing the delegation. Breyer reasoned that the statute affords the EPA Adminis-trator wide latitude to update the requirements of the Clean Air Act and to weigh those standards that " 'protect the public health' with 'an adequate margin of safety' " against other values such as economic effects and feasibili-ty.[227] Can those tradeoffs be resolved as a matter of "technical expertise"? Does the EPA's technical expertise include assessing the economic effects of its regulatory policies? Breyer also argues that given the substantial effect of ambient air quality standards on "States, cities, industries, and their suppli-ers and customers, Congress will hear from those whom compliance deadlines affect adversely, and Congress can consider whether legislative change is warranted." Should this "fire alarm" theory of delegation, meaning that in the event of a significant and unintended result, affected parties will notify Congress, be relevant to the question of whether a court should uphold a delegation? Why or why not?

---

227.   531 U.S. at 494.

CHAPTER 7

THE JUDICIARY

■ ■ ■

Introduction

In this chapter we apply the various tools of public choice to study the behavior of judges and to explain several prominent features of hierarchical common law judicial systems. While there is substantial variation among judicial systems, in this chapter we focus on several important features that common law systems tend to share. We also discuss several institution-specific features and identify noteworthy differences among judicial systems where appropriate. Our approach in this chapter is to offer a series of discrete models and applications in succession. This allows us to proceed from more general to increasingly specific features of the models and systems under review.

The main section of this chapter is divided into four principal subsections. The first section considers how to apply the economist's understanding of rationality to judges. If we consider the United States judiciary as an example, Article III tenure substantially removes judges from the pressures associated with electoral political processes and from any forces that influence most private market actors. Not all judicial systems afford judges the equivalent of lifelong tenure and protection against salary reduction that Article III tenure provides.[1] Even those systems with more limited judicial terms or with elected judiciaries, however, employ codes of professional conduct that are largely designed to remove judges from the sorts of ideological or interest group pressures that commonly characterize ordinary partisan politics.[2] Within judicial systems that provide judges with life tenure, the degree of political insulation is simply more pronounced. To the extent that judges are removed from pressures that characterize electoral politics, the question arises how to construct public choice models that build upon the rationality postulate in a manner that

---

1. U.S. CONST. art. III, § 1 ("The judges, both of the Supreme and inferior courts, shall hold their offices during good behavior. . . .").

2. See MODEL CODE OF JUDICIAL CONDUCT (2007). See also Matthew J. Streb & Brian Frederick, *Judicial Reform and the Future of Judicial Elections, in* RUNNING FOR JUDGE 204 (Matthew J. Streb ed., 2007) (detailing the efforts of states to maintain an impartial elected judiciary); Mary L. Volcansek, *Appointing Judges the European Way,* 34 FORDHAM URB. L.J. 363 (2007) (describing the approaches used in several European countries to protect judicial selection from partisan influence).

effectively captures judicial motivations and that translates those motivations into identifiable maximands.

In the second subpart, we offer a series of models that are designed to explain stare decisis or precedent. Once again, not all judicial systems have precedent, at least as a formal constraint. Even in civil law regimes, however, which formally eschew precedent, commentators have observed that judges treat the decisions of prior courts on similar questions of law as important and influential sources of authority, with the effect of affording such decisions a hybrid status not unlike precedent.[3] Of course even common law systems, which are largely defined by adherence to precedent,[4] vary considerably in the presumptive strength that they attach to the doctrine. Given the pervasive nature of some form of precedent within most judicial systems, legal scholars and economists have developed a variety of explanations or models intended to explain the development and persistence of this important judicial norm. These include: (1) that judges have developed the doctrine on their own to enhance their individual ideological imprimatur on developing doctrine; (2) that society has imposed the obligation on courts to gain the benefit of stable legal doctrine; and (3) that the doctrine has emerged historically within English practice as a result of intra-jurisdictional competition favoring those courts that, by offering more stable doctrine, were able to expand in jurisdictional scope by drawing away cases from other courts.[5] The stare decisis analysis will also provide important insights into the pyramidal nature of judicial hierarchies and into the legal concept of materiality.

In the third subsection we focus largely on the works of Professor Maxwell Stearns and his two complementary social choice models designed to explain persistent yet anomalous features of decision making in the United States Supreme Court. The anomalies include outcomes that sometimes appear to thwart the preferences of identifiable majorities within and across cases; processes that sometimes empower discrete minorities to define and resolve dispositive case issues; and substantive outcomes that appear to be influenced by the order in which cases are presented for review. The first set of models explains the Supreme Court's individual case decision-making rules, including outcome voting and the narrowest grounds doctrine. The second set explains rules affecting larger bodies of case law over extended periods of time, including horizontal stare decisis and standing. While this subsection centers on United States Supreme Court decision-making rules, many of the case anomalies and judicial decision-making rules it describes have substantially broader application, in some instances to other multimember courts of final resort,

---

3. For a general discussion, see FRANCESCO PARISI, LIABILITY FOR NEGLIGENCE AND JUDICIAL DISCRETION 381–95 (2d ed. 1992); JOHN HENRY MERRYMAN & ROGELIO PÉREZ-PERDOMO, THE CIVIL LAW TRADITION: AN INTRODUCTION TO THE LEGAL SYSTEMS OF EUROPE AND LATIN AMERICA 39–47 (3d ed. 2007).

4. Jonathan R. Macey, *The Internal and External Costs and Benefits of Stare Decisis*, 65 CHI.-KENT L. REV. 93 (1989).

5. Later in this chapter, we introduce a social choice model that explains horizontal stare decisis as a partial solution to the problem of cycling judicial preferences over multiple cases. *See infra* pp. 458–64.

and in others to intermediate courts of appeal. We also consider a competing social choice account by Judge Frank Easterbrook of these judicial decision-making phenomena. Finally we evaluate recent normative proposals by several scholars to modify individual case decision-making rules based upon the occasional anomalies that outcome voting produces, and consider competing accounts of several phenomena under review.

The fourth subpart considers an ongoing debate among law and economics scholars seeking to explain why the common law is widely understood to produce efficient doctrine. Once again, we consider models on both the supply side—*What motivates judges to provide efficient common law?*—and the demand side—*Do litigants actually demand efficient common law?* We also evaluate recent scholarly arguments drawing on public choice theory that call into question whether the common law as it presently exists is efficient.

We conclude this chapter with three case presentations. We begin with *Bush v. Gore*,[6] the controversial Supreme Court decision that effectively resolved the presidential election in the year 2000 by suspending a mandated Florida recount of undervotes and thus solidifying the victory of George W. Bush. We then consider *Adarand Constructors, Inc. v. Pena*,[7] a case that definitively resolved the standard of review in cases involving the benign use of race in federal racial set-aside programs in favor of strict scrutiny. Finally, we consider an issue that arises as a result of Justice Clarence Thomas's concurring opinion in *Gonzales v. Carhart*,[8] a case that sustained a federal statute banning partial birth abortion. Together, these cases will allow us to test several of the models and doctrines evaluated throughout this chapter.

I. MODELS OF JUDICIAL DECISION MAKING
A. JUDICIAL RATIONALITY

We begin once more with the following inquiry: What does rationality mean, this time in the context of judicial decision making? Jurists, legal scholars, political scientists, and economists have expressed sharp disagreement on this question. In large part this is due to the inevitable difficulty of identifying an acceptable proxy for rationality that we can translate into a plausible maximand for judicial behavior. It is by now a familiar observation that while economic models are reductionist, the simplifying assumptions allow us to explain or emphasize notable features of the processes under review, whether in markets or governmental institutions. The most important, and the most controversial, aspect of developing such models involves identifying and relying upon proxies for rational behavior. Thus far we have seen public choice models that rest on one or more of the following simplifying assumptions:

6.   531 U.S. 98 (2000).

7.   515 U.S. 200 (1995).

8.   550 U.S. 124 (2007).

(1) Firms seek to maximize profits,

(2) Individuals seek to produce and enjoy wealth,

(3) Legislators seek to be elected and re-elected, and

(4) Bureaucrats seek to expand the scope of their agency's budgets or their autonomy.

Most would likely agree that these admittedly general claims have some foundation as used to characterize the incentives of large numbers of actors. And yet, with respect to specific firms or individuals, each generalization is contestable. These underlying assumptions are therefore best understood as stylized or heuristic devices that allow public choice theorists to model and test how particular policy proposals might further or compromise the claimed purposes of those advancing them. While individual persons and firms are motivated by a variety of objectives, identifying a plausible set of simplifying maximands allows us to construct models that render the resulting analyses more manageable.

1. What Do Judges Maximize?[9]

How then does rationality-based modeling help to inform our understanding of judges, especially those who have Article III tenure or comparable tenure in another system?[10] Is it possible to identify credible proxies or maximands for judges, especially those for whom the usual carrots and sticks that motivate other private or governmental actors have been effectively removed? With rare exceptions, Article III judges have practically no meaningful prospect of career advancement as a result of providing excellent service, have a vanishingly small prospect of losing their jobs or job benefits as a result of substandard performance, and are unlikely to enhance their salaries other than by longevity of service.[11] Given the important role that judges play in our system of lawmaking,[12] is it possible to identify a sufficiently plausible proxy or set of proxies for rationality that provides the basis for constructing meaningful public choice models designed to study judicial behavior?

---

9. Richard A. Posner, *What Do Judges and Justices Maximize? (The Same Thing Everybody Else Does)*, 3 SUP. CT. ECON. REV. 1 (1993).

10. *See supra* note 1, and cite therein. *See also* Denise Dancy, *Judicial Selection, in* NATIONAL CENTER FOR STATE COURTS, FUTURE TRENDS IN STATE COURTS: 20TH ANNIVERSARY PERSPECTIVE 12–13 (2008), *available at* http://www.ncsconline.org/D_KIS/Trends/index.html (listing the various methods other countries use to choose their judges); Roy A. Schotland, *New Challenges to States' Judicial Selection*, 95 GEO. L.J. 1077, 1084–85 (2007) (noting that judges are appointed in eleven states, face retention elections in nineteen states, and face contestable elections—some partisan, some nonpartisan—in nineteen states).

11. The salaries of Article III judges are fixed by Congress based upon duration on the level court on which the judge serves. *See* 28 U.S.C. § 5 (2006) (Supreme Court Justices); § 44 (circuit court judges); § 135 (district court judges). Note the recent push by Chief Justice Roberts for a 50% salary increase for Article III judges. *See* CHIEF JUSTICE JOHN G. ROBERTS, 2007 YEAR-END REPORT ON THE FEDERAL JUDICIARY 6–8 (2008), *available at* http://www.supremecourtus.gov/publicinfo/year-end/2007year-endreport.pdf.

12. One interesting question is whether judges in other systems, in particular civilian regimes, and regimes with separate constitutional courts, are subject to different maximands than those that we might apply in modeling common law judges.

In an intriguing article, *What do Judges and Justices Maximize? (The Same Thing as Everybody Else)*, Judge Richard Posner describes the underlying puzzle as follows:

> At the heart of economic analysis of law is a mystery that is also an embarrassment: how to explain judicial behavior in economic terms, when almost the whole thrust of the rules governing compensation and other terms and conditions of judicial employment is to divorce judicial action ...—to take away the carrots and sticks.... The economic analyst has a model of how criminals and contract parties, injurers and accident victims, parents and spouses—even legislators, and executive officials such as prosecutors—act, but falters when asked to produce a model of how judges act.[13]

Posner compares judges to actors who are generally understood to work within contexts removed from ordinary private market incentives or from incentives associated with most political actors. These actors include directors of nonprofits, electoral voters, and spectators at sporting events.

Posner begins by considering the theory of nonprofits offered by Professor Henry Hansmann of the Yale Law School. Hansmann claims that for benefactors who are unable to monitor the distribution of their contributions to the ultimate beneficiaries, the nonprofit form improves the likelihood of the intended distribution because it prevents directors from the possibility of profiting from residual income.[14] At one level, the nonprofit form provides a compelling analogy to judging, given that the public, like the charitable benefactor, has little practical means of effectively monitoring the dispensation of justice. At the same time however, removing incentives that motivate other governmental actors, for example the political accountability of elected officials, invites the risk of judicial slack. Posner suggests that to some extent, this concern can be ameliorated through careful judicial screening.

Posner emphasizes that in constructing a judicial utility function, he seeks to explain the motives of what he describes as "ordinary," rather than "extraordinary" judges. For this more common group, Posner claims, the relevant factors include popularity, prestige, pursuit of the public interest, the desire to avoid overruling (more pronounced for district court than appeals court judges at the federal level),[15] reputation, and leisure.[16]

---

13. Posner, *supra* note 9, at 2.

14. *See* Henry B. Hansmann, *The Role of Nonprofit Enterprise*, 89 YALE L.J. 835 (1980).

15. Posner explains:

Judges don't like to be reversed (I speak from experience), but aversion to reversal does not figure largely in the judicial utility function. It is nonexistent in the case of Supreme Court Justices, and fairly unimportant in the case of court of appeals judges because reversals of appellate decisions by the Supreme Court have become rare and most reflect differences in judicial philosophy or legal policy rather than mistake or incompetence by the appellate judges. Hence they are not perceived as criticism. [One study] found that reversal rates do not affect district judges' chances of promotion.

Posner, *supra* note 9, at 14–15 (citing Richard S. Higgins & Paul H. Rubin, *Judicial Discretion*, 9 J. LEGAL STUD. 129 (1980) (additional citations omitted)). While Posner maintains that Supreme Court reversal of appellate court judges is regarded largely as political, what about en banc reversal? Would appellate judges view that in the same manner? Why or why not?

16. *Id.* at 13–15, 20–23. While modern judges today draw the same salary regardless of how hard or conscientiously they work, this was not always the case. For much of the history of the

Posner also compares judges to those who vote in political elections. Posner observes that this is "a valued consumption activity of many people," and explains that judges "are constantly voting."[17] Posner suggests that for most judges, even those on the Supreme Court, the joy of voting comes not from the often supposed power play associated with resolving disputes, but rather from the sense of "satisfaction from casting votes that are not merely symbolic expressions, but count."[18] Posner adds that for judges who craft their own opinions, judging provides the additional satisfaction of being a published author. Posner further explains why appeals court judges sometimes defer to one member who holds particularly strong views on a case. "Going-along" or "live and let live" voting is different from legislative logrolling, Posner claims, because the former is "leisure-serving" while the latter is "power-maximizing."[19]

Posner contends that an important characteristic of judging, much like serious sports fandom or attendance at the theater, rests on ensuring compliance with the rules of the game or on suspending disbelief as needed to appreciate the tensions and nuances in a presented work of fiction.[20] Posner goes on to explain that "The pleasure of judging is bound up with compliance with certain self-limiting rules that define the 'game' of judging," and claims:

> It is a source of satisfaction to a judge to vote for the litigant who irritates him, the lawyer who fails to exhibit proper deference to him, the side that represents a different social class from his own; for it is by doing such things that you know that you are playing the judge role, . . . and judges for the most part are people who want to be—judges.[21]

Do you find the various analogies that Posner identifies—directors of nonprofits, electoral voters, and fans of sports or the arts—persuasive in considering likely judicial motivations? Why or why not? Can you identify significant considerations that enter a judicial utility function that are absent in these contexts? If so, can you think of reasons why Posner might have omitted them from his model?

---

common law, judges drew some of their salaries from the filing fees paid by litigants. *See* discussion *infra* pp. 468–471, and accompanying text.

17. Posner, *supra* note 9, at 16.

18. *Id.* at 18.

19. *Id.* at 22.

20. *Id.* at 25–26. Posner also notes that this analogy is overlooked because legal academics who are the main analysts of judicial behavior give excessive focus to written opinions, which for judges form a relatively smaller slice of the overall drama to which the judge is a part, and for whom, "as for Hamlet, 'the play's the thing.' " *Id.* at 26 (quoting WILLIAM SHAKESPEARE, HAMLET act 2, sc. 2).

21. *Id.* at 28. For the formal exposition of Posner's judicial utility function, see *id.* at 31, which includes income, reputation, popularity, prestige, and avoiding reversal. *See id.*

2. The Attitudinal Model: Sincere versus Strategic Voting on the Supreme Court

One aspect of judging that plays a subordinate role in Posner's judicial utility function is seeking to influence legal policy through case decision making.[22] Indeed, the desire to influence legal policy is often seen as an overriding judicial maximand. An increasingly influential body of political science scholarship studies "judicial politics."[23] As the label implies, these scholars tend to view judging as a quasi-political activity in which judges are primarily motivated to affect the legal policy relevant to the cases that they are called upon to decide. And yet, while many political scientists accept the premise that Supreme Court Justices seek to affect legal policy, they are nonetheless split on whether the Justices further this objective by voting in a straightforward fashion reflecting their sincerely held ideological preferences or, if instead, they interact strategically in an effort to move doctrine in their preferred direction.

Adherents to the influential "Attitudinal Model,"[24] posit that in the United States Supreme Court, the most robust predictor of case votes and outcomes rests on the ideological predilections—or "attitudes"—of the deciding justices, whose primary motivation is assumed to be infusing their preferences into legal doctrine.[25] The model generally assumes that Supreme Court decisions, and the justices that decide them, are almost uniformly susceptible of measurement along a single normative liberal-to-conservative ideological spectrum. Based upon this premise, attitudinal scholars contend that if each justice votes honestly with respect to his or her preferred ideological view in each case, the outcome will reflect the preferences of a majority based upon the coalition members' attitudinal predilections.

The Attitudinal model raises a difficult methodological question of measurement.[26] Judges are defined as "liberal" (or "conservative") because they author or join decisions that are coded as liberal (or conserva-

---

22. While Posner does not ignore this point, *see, e.g., id.* at 27 (observing that ideologues are more likely than others to be appointed at a young age because of the stronger indication of likely views that will be carried onto the bench), it does not form a separate element in his utility function.

23. LAWRENCE BAUM, AMERICAN COURTS: PROCESS AND POLICY (6th ed. 2008); LEE EPSTEIN & JACK KNIGHT, THE CHOICES JUSTICES MAKE (1998).

24. JEFFREY A. SEGAL & HAROLD J. SPAETH, THE SUPREME COURT AND THE ATTITUDINAL MODEL REVISITED (2002).

25. Attitudinalists and other judicial politics scholars often pit their supposition against what they describe as the "Legal Model." They claim that the legal model holds that judges neutrally apply governing law based upon the dispassionate application of governing legal authority, including statutes, regulations, or governing precedents. *See* Tracey E. George, *Developing a Positive Theory of Decisionmaking on U.S. Courts of Appeals*, 58 OHIO ST. L.J. 1635 (1998); Tracey E. George & Lee Epstein, *On the Nature of Supreme Court Decision Making*, 83 AM. POL. SCI. REV. 323 (1992). To be clear, Attitudinal scholars do not claim that the left-right ideological axis captures all votes or outcomes, but rather they contend that particular case facts as compared with political attitudes are more robust than alternative predictors of votes among Supreme Court Justices. *See* Lee Epstein et al., *The Political (Science) Context of Judging*, 47 ST. LOUIS U. L.J. 783, 794–95 n.46 (2003).

26. *See* SEGAL & SPAETH, *supra* note 24, at 320–21 (discussing circularity criticism and responses).

tive) in the relevant database.[27] And outcomes are coded as liberal or conservative based upon whether liberal or conservative Justices form the majority coalition. As a way out of this seeming loop, Attitudinal scholars have sought external corroborating data to use in coding judicial ideology. These include past voting behavior (prior to joining the Supreme Court) and newspaper editorials.[28] The Segal–Cover scoring system seeks external confirmation of ideological coding in pre-confirmation newspaper editorials respecting Supreme Court nominees.[29] In addition, the recently developed Martin–Quinn scoring index[30] relies upon Bayesian statistical analysis[31] to track each Justice's "ideal point," or preferred policy position, over time relative to the other members of the Court for each year he or she serves on the Court.[32] One interesting feature of the Martin–Quinn system is in exposing the degree to which the ideal points of the various members of the Court "drift" over time, as compared with other members of the Court, raising the question whether predictions based upon corroborating data that remain fixed after members have joined the Supreme Court retain substantial predictive power.[33]

Political scientists have also called into question the attitudinal assumption that the Justices further their preferred policy views by voting consistently with their attitudes and thus without engaging in strategic voting behavior. Building upon insights from Walter F. Murphy's landmark work, *Elements of Judicial Strategy*,[34] which likened Supreme Court Justices to other policy-minded officials who engage in strategic voting behaviors to further desired policy objectives, an emerging group of political scientists has sought to demonstrate similar strategic interactions among members of the Supreme Court. The recently available papers of various former Justices, including Brennan, Marshall, and Powell,[35] have provided rich data to use in the pursuit of this important research project.

---

27. *See* HAROLD J. SPAETH, THE UNITED STATES SUPREME COURT JUDICIAL DATABASE 1953–2007 TERMS: DOCUMENTATION (2008), *available at* http://www.cas.sc.edu/poli/juri/allcourt_codebook.pdf (describing the structure and use of the database); U.S. Supreme Court Judicial Database (Harold J. Spaeth comp.), http://www.cas.sc.edu/poli/juri/sctdata.htm (last visited Mar. 9, 2009).

28. SEGAL & SPAETH, *supra* note 24, at 320–24; Jeffrey A. Segal & Albert D. Cover, *Ideological Values and the Votes of U.S. Supreme Court Justices*, 83 AM. POL. SCI. REV. 557 (1989); Saul Brenner & Theodore S. Arrington, *Ideological Voting on the Supreme Court: Comparing the Conference Vote and the Final Vote with the Segal–Cover Scores*, 41 JURIMETRICS J. 505 (2001).

29. Segal & Cover, *supra* note 28, at 559.

30. Andrew D. Martin et al., *The Median Justice on the United States Supreme Court*, 83 N.C. L. REV. 1275 (2005).

31. For a discussion of Bayesian analysis, see *supra* chapter 4, section I.B.2.C.

32. Martin et al., *supra* note 30, at 1296–98.

33. *Id.* at 1301–02. The critical point is that those corroborating data that rest on information that is complete prior to the time that a Justice joins the Supreme Court are unable to account for ideological drift. And yet, such Justices as Felix Frankfurter, Byron White, Harry Blackmun, John Paul Stevens, and David Souter have experienced substantial ideological drift during their tenure on the Court that strict reliance on such factors as party of appointing president and even contemporaneous news accounts would not predict. For a general discussion of ideological drift, see Maxwell L. Stearns, *Standing at the Crossroads: The Roberts Court in Historical Perspective*, 83 NOTRE DAME L. REV. 875, 922–37, 950–54 (2008); Lee Epstein et al., *Ideological Drift Among Supreme Court Justices: Who, When, and How Important?*, 101 NW. U. L. REV. 1483 (2007).

34. WALTER F. MURPHY, ELEMENTS OF JUDICIAL STRATEGY (1964).

35. CONNIE L. CARTLEDGE, THURGOOD MARSHALL: A REGISTER OF HIS PAPERS IN THE LIBRARY OF CONGRESS (2001), *available at* http://lcweb2.loc.gov/service/mss/eadxmlmss/eadpdfmss/2001/ms

Drawing upon positive political theory, and studying these new data, Professors Lee Epstein and Jack Knight claim that Justices sometimes press insincere views in their effort to pursue an acceptable outcome that is likely to gain majority support even when that position diverges from their ideal point.[36] Professors Forrest Maltzman, Paul Wahlbeck, and James Spriggs have relied upon some of the same data to support their "collective decision-making postulate."[37] The postulate holds that individual justices will seek to further their own policy preferences based upon a careful consideration of the policy preferences and strategies of other members on the Court. The authors demonstrate the importance of careful timing given the limited opportunities to influence opinion drafts, opportunities that effectively evaporate once the opinion author secures a majority coalition.

An important feature of both works is the nature of the judicial interactions these political scientists rely upon to illustrate judicial strategy. Epstein and Knight rely upon *Craig v. Boren*,[38] a case presenting an equal protection challenge to a state law that imposed different age restrictions based upon sex for access to so-called nonintoxicating or 3.2% beer.[39] The authors show that Brennan's papers reveal that he originally advanced an intermediate scrutiny test in the hope of forging a successful majority coalition, rather than insisting upon his sincerely held view, which preferred strict scrutiny.[40] Maltzman, Spriggs, and Wahlberg offer a similar account of Brennan's voting behavior that draws upon *Pennsylvania v. Muniz*.[41] In that case, Justice Brennan successfully formed a majority coalition that recognized but limited a routine booking exception to the requirement of *Miranda* warnings,[42] even though the position he claimed to prefer was the one expressed in Marshall's dissent, which disallowed the exception altogether.[43]

Legal scholars have questioned the foundations of such political science accounts of Supreme Court voting behavior by challenging the

---

001047.pdf; Powell Papers, Washington & Lee Univ. School of Law, http://law.wlu.edu/powellarchives/page.asp?pageid=236 (last visited Mar. 10, 2009); AUDREY WALKER & MICHAEL SPANGLER, WILLIAM J. BRENNAN JR.: A REGISTER OF HIS PAPERS IN THE LIBRARY OF CONGRESS (2001), *available at* http://lcweb2.loc.gov/service/mss/eadxmlmss/eadpdfmss/2002/ms002010.pdf.

36. *See* EPSTEIN & KNIGHT, *supra* note 23.

37. *See* FORREST MALTZMAN, JAMES F. SPRIGGS II, & PAUL J. WAHLBECK, CRAFTING LAW ON THE SUPREME COURT: THE COLLEGIAL GAME 17 (2000).

38. 429 U.S. 190 (1976).

39. *Id.* at 192.

40. MALTZMAN, SPRIGGS, & WAHLBECK, *supra* note 37, at 6–9.

41. 496 U.S. 582 (1990).

42. Miranda v. Arizona, 384 U.S. 436 (1966).

43. *See* MALTZMAN, SPRIGG & WAHLBECK, *supra* note 37, at 3–4. One interesting question is why the authors assume that the sincere position was expressed in correspondence to Marshall, which is, after all, cheap talk, rather than in the final opinion, which actually has the potential to constrain future decision making.

assumption that jurists are primarily motivated to influence legal policy.[44] Is it possible to reconcile the common supposition among lawyers that judges are expected to behave "judicially" with the premise that they are first and foremost policy makers for whom preexisting attitudinal views are the most robust predictor of case outcomes? If the primary motivation of judges is to influence legal policy, what does this suggest about such traditional understandings as constrained decision making, judicial modesty, abiding precedent, and respect for separation of powers? Is it possible to reconcile the political scientists' understanding of judicial motivation with widely shared intuitions within the legal community concerning a properly limited judicial role? Are the political scientists unduly "cynical" or are the lawyers excessively "naïve"? Does the last question present a false choice? Why or why not?

As noted above, attitudinalists, and other judicial politics scholars, generally pit their accounts of judicial behavior against what they label the "Legal Model."[45] This model presents law as a kind of scientific or deductive process such that in any given case, the neutral application of shared legal principles is expected to produce a correct, or at least preferred, result. In our post-Realist legal culture,[46] very few legal scholars would subscribe to such a view, which appears at best a caricature of the legal process, a process that is more aptly characterized by contentious claims about the meaning of legal doctrine. Is it possible to reject the Attitudinal Model without reverting to an unrealistic, or hopelessly naïve, vision of the judicial process, as for example, that suggested in the so-called Legal Model? Is it possible to identify a plausible judicial maximand that does not require assuming that judges are primarily motivated to affect legal policy?

One possible escape valve is to assume that for some judges, ideological predilections, or attitudes, are equivalent to assuming a modest, non-policy making, role in resolving cases. If so, one can accept the notion that judges seek to advance their own attitudes in resolving cases with the notion that for some, and perhaps many, judges, judicial attitudes incorporate important notions of judicial restraint. Might judges who hold such a view be the "ordinary" judges Posner seeks to describe? Might this explain his omission of the desire to influence legal policy as an independent factor in his judicial utility function? Whether this analytical move

---

44. It is of course important to distinguish arguments that the attitudinal assumption is normatively problematic—judges should not seek to infuse their preferences into the law—from arguments that it is not accurately descriptive—judges do not in fact seek to infuse their preferences into the law. *See* Frank B. Cross, *Political Science and the New Legal Realism: A Case of Unfortunate Interdisciplinary Ignorance*, 92 Nw. U. L. Rev. 251 (1997) (arguing that the attitudinal approach is incomplete without considering the effects of legal rules); Charles Gardner Geyh, *The Endless Judicial Selection Debate and Why It Matters for Judicial Independence*, 21 Geo. J. Legal Ethics 1259, 1272 (noting that a judge who decides cases solely on attitudinal or political considerations would be violating the *Model Code of Judicial Conduct*).

45. *Id.* at 86; George & Epstein, *supra* note 25, at 326–28.

46. For an informative history of the legal realism movement, see Laura Kalman, Legal Realism at Yale 1927–1960 (1986). Some maintain that we are all realists, or post realists, now. *Id.* at 229 (" 'We are all realists now.' The statement has been made so frequently that it has become a truism to refer to it as a truism."). *See also* Patrick McKinley Brennan, *Locating Authority in Law, and Avoiding the Authoritarianism of "Textualism"*, 83 Notre Dame L. Rev. 761, 762 (2008); Mark A. Hall & Ronald F. Wright, *Systematic Content Analysis of Judicial Opinions*, 96 Cal. L. Rev. 63, 77 (2008).

explains the attitudes of a small number of judges, the vast majority of judges, or somewhere in between, is of course an empirical question.[47] In addition, it is important to consider whether the notion of constraint-as-attitude is more likely to explain judges on particular kinds of courts.

Attitudinal scholars limit to the Supreme Court their formal claim that the most robust predictor of case outcomes is judicial attitudes.[48] To the extent that this limitation is appropriate, is it because only judges sitting on the highest level court are interested in imbuing the law with their preferred ideological cast, or is it because only such judges have a meaningful opportunity to do so? Might Supreme Court Justices, for example, be more inclined to infuse attitudes with their own normative conceptions of legal policy than district court judges, whose decisions are more closely constrained by precedent and often must be sustained on appeal? In contrast, Supreme Court cases stand absent the relatively rare event of a subsequent overruling by the Court itself, or the even rarer occurrence of *political* overruling by legislation or constitutional amendment.[49]

What about federal circuit court judges? Given the relative rarity of Supreme Court review,[50] is there any reason to think that these judges are less prone to infusing decisions with their preferred understandings of legal policy? Is en banc review within a circuit an effective means of disciplining appeals court judges who seek to embed preferred policy preferences into case law?

The attitudinal model's assumption—that the primary motivation affecting judicial decision making is to affect legal policy—has a significant counterpart within more than one legal scholarly tradition. Consider, for example, how this assumption relates to the claim within Critical Legal Studies that "law is politics."[51] Is it possible to embrace the assumption

---

47. Can you think of a way to test this empirical question?

48. Thus, the attitudinal model is applied to the Supreme Court, rather than to judges more generally. Specifically, attitudinal scholars limit the model to judges who satisfy the following conditions: (1) complete docket control; (2) judges with life tenure; (3) judges without further career ambition; and (4) judges who sit atop the judicial hierarchy and thus who cannot be overturned by a higher court. Within the United States, and possibly the world, this might limit the model to the Supreme Court. The authors thank Lee Epstein for this clarification. *See* SEGAL & SPAETH, *supra* note 24, at 92–93.

49. Statutory cases can be overruled through ordinary legislation, while constitutional rulings require a constitutional amendment to overturn, something that has occurred only four times in the entire history of the Supreme Court. These include the Eleventh Amendment (limiting federal court jurisdiction in suits against states); the Fourteenth Amendment (rendering all persons born or naturalized in the United States citizens of the United States and of the state in which they reside); the Sixteenth Amendment (enhancing Congressional taxation power); and the Twenty–Sixth Amendment (lowering voting age to eighteen years).

50. *See* JAMES C. DUFF, ADMINISTRATIVE OFFICE OF THE U.S. COURTS, 2006 JUDICIAL BUSINESS OF THE UNITED STATES COURTS 101 tbl.A–1, 102 tbl.B (2006), *available at* http://www.uscourts.gov/judbus 2006/completejudicialbusiness.pdf (noting that the Supreme Court heard ninety cases in the 2005 October term, compared to more than 66,000 cases filed in the Courts of Appeal in the year ending Sept. 2006).

51. For simplicity, we are grouping together schools that employ a critical perspective, including critical race theory and certain strands of feminist theory. While these schools are by no means equivalent, they do share certain important characteristics related to the normative

that jurists seek to influence legal policy based upon their ideological predilections without equating the normative legitimacy of judicial and legislative policymaking? If so, what are the bases for distinguishing these two lawmaking functions?

As we will see in the materials that follow, some scholars writing within the law and economics community also claim that judges are largely motivated to influence legal policy. And yet, such scholars often hold sharp normative disagreements concerning legal policy with those whose work is informed by a critical perspective. What accounts for these differences? Is it simply a function of the different ideological perspectives—or attitudes—of the legal scholars themselves?

B. ECONOMIC MODELS OF STARE DECISIS

We begin by briefly revisiting the game theoretical models of stare decisis, introduced in chapter 4 to describe the single-period and iterated prisoners' dilemmas. These models are designed to explain an apparent anomaly operating within common law based judicial systems.[52] Assuming that judges are motivated to embed their preferred legal policy preferences into case outcomes, why then do judges adhere to a regime of stare decisis, which prevents them from doing so in those cases in which a contrary precedent prevents a preferred outcome?

1. Internal Foundations Revisited: The Game Theoretical Origins of Stare Decisis

While we have previously presented the formalized models developed by Professors Erin O'Hara and Eric Rasmusen, for our immediate purposes we can summarize the essential intuition. The authors suggest that each judge prefers to constrain her colleague to her own prior construction of legal materials as precedent without being reciprocally bound by her colleague's construction in cases subject to her colleague's adverse precedent. The resulting set of mutual incentives is likely to thwart a regime of precedent in favor of one in which each judge decides cases on his or her own, unconstrained by any obligation of precedent.[53] The effect, however, is to provide each jurist a temporary imprimatur on a larger number of cases, rather than a more lasting imprint—one adhered to by other judges in the form of precedent—over the relatively smaller number of cases in which the issue presented has not yet been resolved as a matter of stare decisis.

---

foundations of legislative and judicial lawmaking. For a helpful overview of the critical legal studies movement, see MARK KELMAN, GUIDE TO CRITICAL LEGAL STUDIES (1990).

52. *See supra* chapter 4, section I.B.

53. To be clear, the judges might adhere to each other's decisions when they agree to them on the merits, but that is different than adhering to precedent because it is precedent. The obligation of precedent assumes that judges will apply even those decisions with which they disagree simply because they resolved a materially indistinguishable point of law. Erin O'Hara, *Social Constraint or Implicit Collusion?: Toward a Game Theoretic Analysis of Stare Decisis*, 24 SETON HALL L. REV. 736, 737–38 (1993).

One difficulty with this analysis is that while it exposes an important tension among judges operating on the same level court, the resulting regime of mutual defection within a prisoners' dilemma framework provides the seeds of its own destruction as a means of providing precedent with a game theoretical foundation. Even if we extend the game to include multiple iterations, unless we assume endless iterations, the game threatens to unravel to the initial single period prisoners' dilemma game in which mutual defection again emerges the dominant outcome.[54]

As we have also seen, however, game theoretical analysis does not force a simple binary choice between a single period prisoners' dilemma or a game in which players anticipate endless iterations. More sophisticated modelers have assessed the implications of probabilistic end periods and trigger strategy equilibria.[55] If we assume that the players receive some benefit from appearing cooperative, then these models suggest the possibility that discounting the payoffs of defection in future rounds of play allows the players to avoid the low payoffs associated with triggering mutual defection equilibrium outcomes. If so, then these models also imply that such players, possibly those whose utility functions include some payoff from abiding by precedent, will yield a positive set of cooperative behaviors in at least some circumstances.

Several commentators have suggested for example that jurists observe precedent in part because doing so is consistent with collegiality and is thus properly judicial.[56] While such accounts possess an admittedly circular quality (judges observe stare decisis because they prefer collegiality and collegiality includes observing stare decisis), in our view it would be mistaken to entirely dismiss such claims. Certainly it is the case that judges are generally the sorts of professionals who enjoy engaging in those behaviors that are most likely to be considered judicial, and all that implies. Consistent with Posner's model of judging, adhering to precedent might be one of the rules of the game the adherence to which enhances judicial satisfaction. But even accepting this premise begs the question why such norms emerge as "judicial" behaviors in the first instance.

2.   A Comment on the Scope of Opinions and the Importance of Legal Materiality

Before discussing alternative accounts of stare decisis, it is important to consider a related anomaly that Professors Erin O'Hara and Eric Rasmusen address. O'Hara and Rasmusen inquire why rational judges, when deciding cases subject to precedent, generally decline to overreach— or at least to do so dramatically—when articulating holdings in opinions.[57] To take an extreme example, imagine a case involving whether an offer to

---

54. *See supra* chapter 4, section I.B.2.F.

55. *See supra* chapter 4, section I.B.2.C and I.B.2.F.

56. RICHARD A. POSNER, THE FEDERAL COURTS: CHALLENGE AND REFORM 381–82 (1996); Harry T. Edwards, *The Effects of Collegiality on Judicial Decision Making*, 151 U. PA. L. REV. 1639 (2003).

57. O'Hara, *supra* note 53, at 741–42; Eric Rasmusen, *Judicial Legitimacy as a Repeated Game*, 10 J.L. ECON. & ORG. 63, 67 (1994).

repay a previously forgiven debt provides the basis for consideration in a later contract. Imagine that Judge A, to whom this case is assigned, uses it to also resolve the policy question whether the appropriate standard in a tort suit involving an inherently dangerous activity should be negligence or strict liability.

Professor O'Hara suggests that rational jurists might decline to overreach in such cases if they anticipate some difficulty in predicting how the present case might influence future doctrine. In our hypothetical, we might imagine that Judge A imposes strict liability in a context that erroneously raises the cost of some dangerous activities for which potential tort victims could take low cost precautions to reduce risk and thus inhibits worthwhile investment in economically valuable activity. In this account, a judge's own lack of prescience might provide an internal source of limitation on overreaching.[58] In Professor Rasmusen's alternative account, individual judges limit the scope of their opinions to leave sufficient legal policy space open for all jurists so that each judge has the potential to meaningfully influence developing doctrine. In effect, Rasmusen argues that judicial self restraint promotes a benign mutual accommodation that allows all jurists to make law within the confines of those cases that they are called upon to decide.[59]

Does game theory help to assess these accounts? Might some jurists willingly fill obvious legal policy voids within case law when other jurists are reticent as a result of their perceived inability to appropriately forecast the development of future caselaw? Are some jurists more confident than others that they possess appropriate normative frameworks for assessing broad bodies of law affecting open legal policy? If so, would this justification provide judges with an equal opportunity to influence the law as O'Hara and Rasmusen suggest? Does Rasmusen's analysis provide a stable equilibrium result? What would prevent those judges who do not share the concern about leaving sufficient legal policy space open for future judging from producing opinions that dramatically overreach? Can you articulate this in terms of either the single period or iterated prisoners' dilemma game? Which game better captures the stakes for rational jurists? Does the result differ depending on whether we are discussing Posner's ordinary judge or a more intellectually ambitious jurist, including for example Posner?

---

58. Todd Zywicki and Anthony Sanders suggest a similar justification for precedent based upon information costs that confront judges attempting to determine whether a proposed legal innovation will actually improve the law overall as a result of the co-evolution of legal rules in disparate settings. Given the complex interactions between legal rules and the manner in which they feed back into individual expectations and planning, the authors claim that judges apply stare decisis to avoid the uncertainty associated with potentially welfare reducing consequences elsewhere in the legal system of changes in legal rules subject to precedent. *See* Todd J. Zywicki & Anthony B. Sanders, *Posner, Hayek, and the Economic Analysis of Law*, 93 IOWA L. REV. 559 (2008).

59. Keep Rasmusen's account in mind as you consider Professor Jonathan Macey's suggestion, discussed below, that stare decisis improves judicial specialization. *See infra* pp. 428–429.

Now consider the following alternative account of why judges do not systematically overreach in crafting opinions.[60] Judges tend not to overreach because if they were to do so, they would risk encouraging other judges not only to avoid their opinions that do overreach, but also, and more importantly, to decline to give even their legitimate holdings proper stare decisis effect. In the prior hypothetical involving announcing a tort rule in a contract case, we might well imagine Judge B in a later case squarely presenting the need to resolve the choice between negligence or strict liability in the context of inherently dangerous activities, issuing an opinion that contains the following passage: "Nothing in Case 1 compelled Judge A to pronounce on tort law because that case turned on a question of contract law. As a result, we do not treat any assertions about the choice of negligence or strict liability as expressing the holding in that earlier case."

Judge A might rightly fear that if she routinely or egregiously overreaches, Judge B will not only fail to provide stare decisis effect to those holdings that are obviously excessively broad, but also that Judge B will distrust her opinions in general. As a result, Judge A is rationally motivated to defend the scope of her legitimate holdings. To do so, she will explain why announcing each holding is necessary in light of the material facts of the case that she was called upon to decide. In this analysis, each judge fears that absent a clear exposition of material facts demonstrating the need to announce the specific holding in each case, her colleagues will not afford her holdings stare decisis effect. As a result, each judge is rationally motivated not only to decline to overreach, but also to articulate the justification of her holding, grounded in material case facts in her written opinions.

Do you find the materiality account of the scope of opinions persuasive? Why or why not? Does it help to explain the nature of written judicial opinions? How does it differ from the account that O'Hara and Rasmusen offer? Which is more consistent with observed judicial practice? Which provides the basis for a more persuasive normative justification for stare decisis? Can you articulate the relationship between the proper scope of opinions and the stare decisis norm?

3. The Game Theoretical Origins of Pyramidal Courts

Let us now turn to an alternative analysis of stare decisis that returns us to the apparent prisoners' dilemma among judges on the same level court regarding precedent. In this analysis, the prisoners' dilemma motivates the development of pyramidal judicial hierarchies. The analysis begins with the insight that while district court judges do not routinely abide each other's precedents, appeals courts in common law systems (and perhaps to some extent even in civilian systems) do abide precedent, both horizontally (meaning they adhere to their own earlier decisions) and vertically (meaning they adhere to binding precedents of higher level

---

60. Portions of this discussion are based upon Michael Abramowicz & Maxwell Stearns, *Defining Dicta*, 57 STAN. L. REV. 953 (2005); MAXWELL L. STEARNS, PUBLIC CHOICE AND PUBLIC LAW: READINGS AND COMMENTARY 540–47 (1997).

courts). Is it possible to use game theoretical analysis to explain this phenomenon?

In an important article, William Landes and Richard Posner identified the prisoners' dilemma that confronts judges in the construction of precedent.[61] The authors suggested a very different mechanism that helps judges avoid what O'Hara described as non-productive competition.[62] Instead, Landes and Posner suggest that the resulting competition encourages the formation of pyramidal judicial hierarchies.

To illustrate, imagine a group of jurists, perhaps mediators, who implicitly recognize the prisoners' dilemma associated with horizontal precedent. In effect, they realize that each jurist will continue in the role of mediator, meaning that he or she will resolve specific disputes but will not transform her adjudications into rules that bind other mediators in future disputes that implicate similar issues.

We might imagine that a group of such mediators discuss their frustration over the temporary impact they have in resolving specific disputes in a manner that lacks the more lasting form of opinions that "make law." In effect, they seek to elevate their function from resolving disputes to actual judging, and include in that some role in using cases to make law. They discuss differing strategies, perhaps including a group admonition to take more seriously the legal bases of prior rulings when deciding similar disputes, but ultimately recognize that this will not likely produce the desired result of transforming their individual decisions into precedents. And so they try an alternative approach. The mediators will take turns meeting as an appellate tribunal, in randomly drawn groups of three to avoid the appearance of arbitrariness and the risk of ties, and in that capacity will resolve disagreements among the mediators over legal policy arising in resolved disputes. The appellate resolutions will form binding precedents for the individual mediators, but will do so as a matter of vertical (top-down) precedent, rather than through a system of horizontal precedent among the individual mediators themselves.[63]

We might also imagine that as the regime becomes more sophisticated, different appellate panels will themselves express occasional disagreements over legal policy, and seek to impose constraints on future panels that depart from earlier panel decisions as precedent. As we will later see in the discussion of the social choice analysis of judicial decision making,[64] horizontal stare decisis—meaning stare decisis by appellate courts respect-

---

61. William M. Landes & Richard A. Posner, *Legal Precedent: A Theoretical and Empirical Analysis*, 19 J.L. & ECON. 249 (1976).

62. *Id.* at 273 (arguing that "the free-rider problem" of judges who do not wish to follow precedent "is held in check by the structure of appellate review [and that] decision according to precedent will often constitute rational self-interested behavior of judges who personally disagree with the precedent in question").

63. In a regime of courts engaged in competition, based for example on filing fees, jurisdiction, or other incentives, *see infra* pp. 468–471, we might also imagine mimicking behavior to the extent that those courts developing a pyramidal form do better, and thus increase the scope of their dockets or jurisdiction, as a result of providing more stable doctrine.

64. *See infra* pp. 468–471.

ing the same court's earlier decisions—can be understood as a mechanism that avoids some of the potential difficulties that intransitive judicial preferences might pose for the stability of legal doctrine. This problem can arise within en banc supreme courts; en banc appeals courts; and among differently constituted appellate tribunals, for example, randomly drawn panels of three within larger courts of appeals. For now, however, let us simply assume that the benefits of the vertical stare decisis regime—from appeals court to trial court—do not ensure doctrinal consistency among differently constituted appellate tribunals. A partial solution to this problem is adding one more step to the judicial hierarchy. By adding a single larger panel supreme court, presumably of at least five members,[65] the judicial system can then enforce stare decisis from the supreme court to the appellate courts and from the appellate courts to the trial courts. And notably the regime emerges as stable with only these three steps in the judicial hierarchy. This is a pervasive judicial structure, not merely within the United States, but throughout western democracies.[66]

Once this regime is established, the intermediate appellate court and the supreme court are likely to assume a more professional and thus more specialized form. Judges, or justices, will be appointed to their specific positions within the judicial hierarchy, rather than occupying them on a temporary or randomly drawn basis from a lower rung on the ladder. The skills associated with adjudicating trials and appeals are notably different and it is not surprising therefore that judges will experience significant career specialization—and even some degree of jealous professional rivalry—regarding their respective spheres of influence in the resolution of disputes on the one hand and in the creation of binding precedents on the other.

The resulting set of institutional arrangements also has the important effect of enhancing the stability and thus the value of individual adjudications. Rather than simply affording judicial resolution of disputes between the parties, the regime creates a vehicle for the anticipated application of an emerging body of precedent. This allows the parties, or their representatives, to better ascertain the probable outcomes of potential legal disputes, and thus to make more reasoned assessments concerning how to conduct their personal and business affairs and also whether to take a cases to trial or to settle.[67] A major benefit of the resulting judicial hierarchy, therefore, is in enhancing the overall value of the judicial outputs relative to the mediation regime and, in effect, moving the regime from mediation to judging.

65. If drawn from the ranks of the courts of appeals, at least as an interim measure, a minimum of five reduces the risk that the Supreme Court will be controlled by a single appellate tribunal as it can overrule, for example, a two-to-one majority decision with a larger majority.

66. Michele Taruffo, *Institutional Factors Influencing Precedents*, in INTERPRETING PRECEDENTS: A COMPARATIVE STUDY 437 (D. Neil MacCormick & Robert S. Summers eds., 1997).

67. *See* Bruce H. Kobayashi, *Case Selection, External Effects, and the Trial/Settlement Decision*, in DISPUTE RESOLUTION: BRIDGING THE SETTLEMENT GAP 17 (David A. Anderson ed., 1996); Leandra Lederman, *Precedent Lost: Why Encourage Settlement, and Why Permit Non–Party Involvement in Settlements?*, 75 NOTRE DAME L. REV. 221 (1999); George L. Priest & Benjamin Klein, *The Selection of Disputes for Litigation*, 13 J. LEGAL STUD. 1 (1984).

4. Questions and Comments

Do you believe that game theory helps to explain stare decisis within our judicial system? Why or why not? If you believe it is helpful, which of the models do you find more persuasive and why? Can you identify benefits to the absence of precedent at the trial level within judicial hierarchies? Is consistency more valuable at the appellate than the trial level? If so, why? Why do separate circuits operating in the United States Courts of Appeals fail to adhere to each other's precedents? Is stare decisis more valuable at the Supreme Court level than across differing courts of appeals? Do different circuit courts decline to follow each others' precedents for the same reasons that district court judges on the same court fail to abide each other's precedents?

5. External Foundations of Stare Decisis

The preceding discussion centered on the internal origins of a regime of stare decisis,[68] and specifically, on how the regime of precedent, whether operating in horizontal or vertical form, benefits the judges themselves. The question was why judges are motivated to *supply* a precedent-driven legal regime. In the discussion that follows, we consider the external benefits, or policy justifications, for stare decisis. Here we focus instead on why society might *demand*, or at least prefer, a judicial system that includes as a substantial component, the doctrine of stare decisis.

In an exchange of articles, Professors Lewis Kornhauser and Jonathan Macey relied upon game theoretical and traditional law and economics analyses to assess the normative merit of stare decisis within common judicial systems. While Professor Kornhauser maintains that stare decisis has the potential to provide stability when the legal regime confronts more than one pure Nash strategy equilibrium as a solution to a game that we can characterize in terms of a battle of the sexes, he also identifies conditions under which stare decisis threatens the paradoxical result of locking in regimes favoring inferior technologies. We begin with Kornhauser's positive account of the doctrine, which tracks two of the games introduced in Chapter 4: (1) the pure coordination Nash equilibrium game, and (2) the battle of the sexes.

a. *Stare Decisis and the Pure Nash Strategy Equilibrium Game*

Recall that in a multiple Nash bargaining game, there arises the potential for more than a single pure Nash equilibrium strategy as well as for more than a single mixed strategy equilibrium. The classic model, reproduced from chapter 4, involves two drivers each deciding whether to drive on the right or left hand side of the road.

---

68. This includes the discussion of stare decisis in chapter 4, section I.B.

Table 7:1. The Driving Game

Payoffs for (A, B)	B drives left	B drives right
A drives left	**10, 10**	0, 0
A drives right	0, 0	**10, 10**

In this game, the two pure Nash equilibrium strategies are depicted in the upper left and lower right boxes, with payoffs of (10,10). The game is assumed to be one of simple coordination, meaning that each player is indifferent to the choice of right or left driving, but does hold a strong preference (indicated by the dramatic differences in the payoffs between the pure and mixed strategy equilibrium outcomes) for coordinated versus non-coordinated driving.[69] In contexts like the driving game, a stare decisis regime can induce stability once the pure Nash strategy equilibrium result is announced, at least assuming that decisions are sequential rather than simultaneous.[70] As Kornhauser recognizes, however, the narrow range of legal contexts involving simple coordination problems highlights the limited nature of this normative account of stare decisis.[71]

b. Stare Decisis as a Means of Stabilizing Battle of the Sexes Games

Kornhauser also suggests a game justifying stare decisis that can readily be expressed in terms of a battle of the sexes. The game involves the judicial selection of two presumptive, or off-the-rack, contract liability rules governing the purchase of goods: caveat emptor (buyer beware) or caveat venditor (seller beware).[72] In its simplest form, caveat emptor means that the buyer assumes all risk of defects following point of sale. This can be expressed in terms of an "as is" contract that places all duties to inspect on the buyer prior to execution of the contract. In contrast, caveat venditor can be viewed as a form of strict products liability, coupled with a full set of warranties for nonconformities.[73] These two rules represent endpoints on a spectrum of potential off-the-rack contracting rules that could include an intermediate set of solutions, including for example, a buyer's right of inspection and a seller's liability for concealed defects or a set of limited warranties depending upon the use to which the goods are put, with the burden on the buyer for risks associated with nonconforming uses.

---

69. For a general discussion, see Lewis A. Kornhauser, *An Economic Perspective on Stare Decisis*, 65 CHI.-KENT. L. REV. 63, 79–80 (1989).

70. If decisions are simultaneous, then it is possible that each party will attempt to anticipate the other party's strategy, but will do so incorrectly, thus risking a mixed strategy equilibrium. *See supra* chapter 4, section II.

71. *See* Kornhauser, *supra* note 69, at 80.

72. While Kornhauser does not present the game as a battle of the sexes, the discussion in the text provides a basis for this classification.

73. *See* DAVID G. OWEN, PRODUCTS LIABILITY LAW § 1.2, at 17–18 (2005).

For expositional purposes, Kornhauser assumes that the more ex-treme regimes, caveat emptor and caveat venditor, are the only available off-the-rack contract rules for the sale of goods that provide clearly identifiable and predictable outcomes for buyers and sellers. This assump-tion is important because without it, it is not obvious that any potential intermediate set of outcomes necessarily disadvantages both buyer and seller, relative to each of their preferred endpoints. Kornhauser presents the following table to illustrate the resulting game[74]:

Table 7:2. Caveat Emptor versus Caveat Venditor

Payoffs are (Row, Column)	a	b	c
A	**5,3**	7,1	1,2
B	3,2	4,6	0,4
C	4,3	3,2	**2,5**

Kornhauser explains that the upper left and lower right corner solutions, presented in bold, are the only pure Nash strategy equilibria:

> In [Table 7:2], (A,a) is an equilibrium because Row cannot improve upon her payoff of 5, conditional on Column's choice of strategy a. If Row chooses B rather than A she would receive 3; if she chooses C rather than A she would receive 4. Similarly, Column cannot improve his payoff of 3, conditional on Row's choice of strategy A. If Column chooses b rather than a, he receives 1 rather than 3; if he chooses c rather than a, he receives 2 rather than 3. A parallel argument reveals that (C,c) is also an equilibrium.

> No other pair of choices meets this criterion of each actor's choice being her best response to her opponent's chosen strategy. Consider for example the strategy pair (B,b) which makes Column best off. This pair is not an equilibrium because, conditional on Column's choice of b, Row does best to choose A, which gives her a payoff of 7 rather than 4.[75]

This game, and its corresponding justification for stare decisis, differs from the pure coordination Nash equilibrium game in an important respect. While driving is a simple coordination game, in this game, the players care very much about and indeed hold opposite views concerning the choice of legal regime. And yet, once the legal regime is selected, stare decisis locks that regime in place as a pure Nash strategy equilibrium, at least absent either legislative or judicial overruling, because any unilateral move would make the moving party worse off.

---

74. Table 7:2 is reproduced from Kornhauser, *supra* note 69, at 81.

75. *See id.* at 81 n.29.

The battle of the sexes game suggests the potential for a far broader set of applications than does the driving game because when parties litigate, they do so hoping to obtain a sufficient advantage to justify the investment of litigation resources. It is difficult to imagine a case in which parties will invest such resources to obtain judicial resolution concerning legal regimes the content of which is a matter of indifference to them.[76] It is a common observation that contract rules favoring one side nonetheless are potentially welfare enhancing to the extent that the resulting certainty reduces the cost of contracting from those rules to others that the parties instead prefer. The battle of the sexes game can be generalized to a broader set of contexts involving such games in which each party prefers his or her own off-the-rack rule but would prefer the other side's off-the-rack rule to a state of uncertainty respecting future contract negotiations.

c. *Stare Decisis and the Risk of Entrenching Inferior Technologies*

Let us now consider the case that Kornhauser claims is more difficult for stare decisis. Kornhauser begins with the premise that the legal regime seeks to optimize social welfare and must select among two competing legal regimes that affect liabilities, and thus the relative values, of driving and walking during an era of technological change. Kornhauser first considers a regime in which driving is uncommon, for example in the advent of the driving era at the beginning of the twentieth century, or in a remote location with unpaved roads and few cars. When walking is the more highly valued activity, the optimal rule is presumed to be strict liability with dual contributory negligence, and when driving is more highly valued, the optimal rule is presumed to be negligence with contributory negligence. We can depict the two regimes in a single matrix that embraces all four negligence/non-negligence combinations and that identifies potential driver liability in each category under each set of rules[77]:

Table 7:3. Alternative Tort Regimes: Negligence with Contributory Negligence (Rule 1) and Strict Liability with Dual Contributory Negligence (Rule 2)

(Rule 1; **Rule 2**)	Driver Negligent	Driver non-negligent
Pedestrian negligent	no liability; **liability**	no liability; **no liability**
Pedestrian non-negligent	liability; **liability**	no liability; **liability**

Because either driver or pedestrian can be negligent or nonnegligent, there are four resulting combinations for either legal regime. The liability

---

76. To be fair, this does not fully characterize the driving game. The drivers might be indifferent ex ante, but each driver, having selected a side of the road, cares deeply that the legal system ratify his or her choice following an accident.

77. This table is taken from STEARNS, *supra* note 60, at 548 tbl.3.

as between the two parties only changes in two of the four categories as a result of a change in these two liability rules. The table lists only driver's liability (the inverse liability is that of pedestrian) in the event of an accident with pedestrian, with the payoff for the first rule set out in Roman typeface and for the second rule set out in bold. In the upper right and lower left boxes, where only one of the two parties is negligent, the choice of rule does not affect the outcome. In either case, the negligent party bears the full risk of the accident. In contrast, when neither or both parties to the accident are negligent, the selection of liability rule determines which party bears the risk.

When walking is the more highly valued activity, the operative regime is strict liability with dual contributory negligence. In this regime, when both the driver and pedestrian are negligent, or when neither is negligent, the driver bears the burden of the accident, with the liability rule set out in bold. Conversely, when driving becomes the more highly valued activity, the operative regime is negligence with contributory negligence. In this regime, when neither or both are negligent, the pedestrian bears the risk of accidents, with the results set out in Roman typeface.

Kornhauser explains the resulting anomaly as follows:

> Suppose the court announces a rule of negligence. Then, if the value of driving is high, the statically (second-)best rule will prevail. If, on the other hand, the value of driving is low, negligence will be far from the statically (second-)best rule. The higher the probability that driving will have a high value, the more preferable will negligence (with stare decisis) be to strict liability (with stare decisis).

> Whether stare decisis should be adopted however will depend on the nature of the first-best optimum. Suppose the valuations of activities are such that both injurer and victim should adopt moderate (or low) levels of the activity. Under stare decisis, the actor who escapes liability will always adopt a high level of activity. Under a practice of no stare decisis, however, each actor will be uncertain whether she will bear the cost of an accident.... For certain relative values of activities, then, the uncertainty over the legal rule induces the actors to adopt activity levels closer to the social optimum.[78]

In effect, Kornhauser argues that while the stability that stare decisis provides is welfare enhancing in the two Nash games—the pure coordination and battle of the sexes—stare decisis-induced stability can be welfare reducing in an era of technological change. This seemingly paradoxical result arises from the problem of adverse reliance upon an inferior—or outdated—legal regime that continues to elevate the legal status of the lesser valued activity.[79] Counterintuitively, perhaps, a regime without

---

78. *See* Kornhauser, *supra* note 69, at 85–86 (footnote omitted).

79. For an early case demonstrating the relative undervaluation of vehicular traffic, and of the need to impose safety measures, such as gates at railroad crossings, to protect drivers and passengers, see Baltimore & Ohio R.R. v. Goodman, 275 U.S. 66 (1927). Writing for the majority,

legal certainty would encourage the parties to consider on their own the relative values of the activities in which they are engaged, without regard to which activity the legal system, strengthened by stare decisis, had selected as more highly valued some time in the past.

d. Macey's Critique and the Use of Stare Decisis in Promoting Judicial Specialization

In a responsive essay, Professor Jonathan Macey rejected Kornhauser's claim that stare decisis risks entrenching an inferior legal regime following an era of technological change. The difficulty that Kornhauser identifies, Macey posits, arises only if stare decisis operates as an absolute rule, favoring specific activities like driving or walking. Instead, legal rules are frequently expressed at a higher level of generality.[80] Imagine, for example, that the underlying substantive rule to which stare decisis applied was construed as protecting the more highly valued activity. If so, stare decisis itself will allow a change in the specific liability rule as between two competing activities depending upon their relative value in a period of technological progress. With this level of flexibility in the stare decisis regime, the pedestrian will alter her conduct at the very least in the period in which driving is clearly more highly valued, and quite likely also in periods of uncertainty in which judges could reasonably determine that either activity is more highly valued.

Translating this into common law doctrine, we might imagine that the duty to use reasonable care in tort includes an assessment of the relative value of the two competing activities that pose reciprocal risk.[81] A regime that in one period placed presumptive liability on vehicles (strict liability with dual contributory negligence) would not necessarily induce excessive pedestrian reliance in a period of technological progress that later places a higher value on driving and a correspondingly greater duty on pedestrians to avoid unnecessary risks (negligence with contributory negligence). Undue reliance is avoided if pedestrians realize that the increased prevalence of vehicular traffic imposes greater duties on the pedestrians themselves to avoid careless strolls (for example, in the street at night with dark clothing) that might result in avoidable accidents.

Professor Macey goes further and identifies four important functions that stare decisis serves: (1) minimizing error costs; (2) increasing the public goods aspects of decisions; (3) minimizing the costs of judicial review; and (4) increasing the power of courts relative to that of the

---

Justice Holmes rejected the negligence claim of a surviving spouse of a man killed by an oncoming train at a railroad crossing, stating:

> In such circumstances it seems to us that if a driver cannot be sure otherwise whether a train is dangerously near he must stop and get out of his vehicle, although obviously he will not often be required to do more than to stop and look. It seems to us that if he relies upon not hearing the train or any signal and takes no further precaution he does so at his own risk.

Id. at 70.

80. Macey, *supra* note 4, at 104. The following discussion is based in part on STEARNS, *supra* note 60, at 549–50.

81. *See* Macey, *supra* note 4, at 103–04.

legislature. While each of these arguments provides an important means of assessing stare decisis, given our focus on judicial behavior, Macey's error cost justification is particularly important to our analysis:

Macey explains:

[J]udges apply two sorts of legal skills when deciding a case. One sort of legal skill is the skill involved in formulating, articulating, and applying substantive legal doctrine to a particular legal dispute. The second set of legal skills allows the judge to determine what sorts of cases are alike, in order to "check" his result in the first case.

. . . It is easy to see that stare decisis can be extremely valuable to a legal system. In developed legal systems judges will be checking their opinions against several, perhaps hundreds of similar cases that have evolved in the common-law process over hundreds of years. If we retain our assumption that other judges usually are correct when they reach legal decisions, then the prevailing substantive legal rule on a particular issue is very likely to be correct.

. . . Clearly, not even the best judges go about formulating what they believe to be the substantively correct legal result in every case, and then checking that result with the relevant precedents. Instead, judges generally employ stare decisis precisely because it enables them to *avoid* having to rethink the merits of particular legal doctrine. Instead of rethinking, the judges can "free-ride" on the opinions of previous judges.

At the same time, however, judges are likely to feel more confident about their abilities and instincts when deciding certain sorts of cases than when deciding others. For those classes of cases about which judges feel they have a particular expertise, the idealized checking process described above is a valid portrayal of the judging process. Thus a practice of stare decisis not only permits judges to conserve judicial resources, it allows them to specialize in particular areas of the law.

Judges can free-ride on the expertise of other judges in those areas in which they do not specialize, and create new law in those areas in which they feel they have expertise. This phenomenon is particularly obvious in multi-judge panels such as those that exist on federal circuit courts of appeals. . . . Stare decisis may be viewed as a legal innovation that allows judges to expand the process of trading experience and expertise over time and across jurisdictions.[82]

e. A Comment on the Condorcet Jury Theorem and the Nature of Judicial Reliance

Professor Macey's analysis rests upon an important understanding about the nature of judicial decision making in generating reliable information to judges operating within the judicial system. While he does not

---

82. Macey, *supra* note 4, at 102–03 (footnote omitted).

couch his analysis in terms of the Condorcet Jury Theorem, it is helpful for our purposes to consider the role of that theorem in supporting or challenging Macey's intuition. Condorcet posited that in the context of a decision admitting of two answers one of which is correct, when members of a jury are at least 50% likely to select the correct answer, the probability that the jury selects the right answer increases as the size of the jury increases.[83]

The intuition is fairly easy to explain. Imagine that there are two options, A and B, and that each juror is at least 50% likely to know that the correct answer is A. The jurors who actually know A to be correct will select it. The jurors who do not know will split approximately evenly over A and B. As the size of the jury is enlarged, the risk that random error will result in the jury preferring the wrong answer is reduced because the "bump" that distinguishes the right answer from the wrong answer as a consequence of correct voting among those who actually know that answer to be correct correspondingly increases.[84] Two critical assumptions underlie the jury theorem, first that the question admits of a correct answer, and second, that each juror, who is expected to be at least 50% likely to know the right answer, independently derives that answer, meaning that he or she is not influenced by the (potentially erroneous) decisions of other members of the jury. Otherwise, information cascades risk producing a wave in favor of an initial erroneous answer.[85]

Macey suggests that stare decisis allows judges to employ analogical reasoning, rather than analysis from first principles, as they progress from

---

83. Saul Levmore, *Ruling Majorities and Reasoning Pluralities*, 3 Theoretical Inquiries L. 87 (2002); Maxwell L. Stearns, *The Condorcet Jury Theorem and Judicial Decisionmaking: A Reply to Saul Levmore*, 3 Theoretical Inquiries L. 125 (2002).

84. This can be generalized to more than two answers. The once popular American game show, *Who Wants to Be a Millionaire?*, the Indian version of which inspired the Academy Award winning *Slumdog Millionaire*, involved trivia questions in which the players were offered three "lifelines": phone a friend, eliminate two responses, and ask the audience. Ask the audience was often the best choice. The format presented questions with four multiple choice answers, one of which was correct. Assume that the audience members were 25% likely to get the correct answer. As you increase the size of the audience, you increase the number of audience members who give that answer a distinguishing bump. The rest of the audience will roughly split evenly over the other all four answers, exposing the correct answer to be just that. Two limitations apply, first a credible decoy that could serve as a Schelling point and mislead a sufficiently large segment to select it, and second, a very obscure question that very few audience members know the answer to and for which an expert is required. For the first error, elimination would work, but only if the decoy response is removed, and for the second error, phone a friend would work if the friend shared the relevant obscure expertise. For academic literature on the Condorcet Jury Theorem as applied to law, see John O. McGinnis & Michael Rappaport, *The Condorcet Case for Supermajority Rules*, 16 Sup. Ct. Econ. Rev. 67 (2008); Eric A. Posner & Cass R. Sunstein, *The Law of Other States*, 59 Stan. L. Rev. 131 (2006); Adrian Vermeule, *Common Law Constitutionalism and the Limits of Reason*, 107 Colum. L. Rev. 1482 (2007). For a modern popular study that explores conditions under which groups produce more accurate data than individuals, see James Surowiecki, The Wisdom of Crowds 10 (2004) (identifying the following as necessary conditions to the wisdom of crowds: diversity of opinion, independence, decentralization, and aggregation); *see also id.* at 3–4 (discussing *Who Wants to Be a Millionaire*).

85. Lisa R. Anderson & Charles A. Holt, *Information Cascades in the Laboratory*, 87 Am. Econ. Rev. 847 (1997); Sushil Bikhchandani et al., *Learning from the Behavior of Others: Conformity, Fads, and Informational Cascades*, J. Econ. Persp., Summer 1998, at 151; Timur Kuran & Cass R. Sunstein, *Availability Cascades and Risk Regulation*, 51 Stan. L. Rev. 683 (1999); Beth Z. Shaw, *Judging Juries: Evaluating Renewed Proposals for Specialized Juries from a Public Choice Perspective*, 2006 UCLA J.L. & Tech. 3.

case facts to outcomes. If we assume that common law judges confront groups of similar fact patterns over time and that they make independent assessments concerning how to resolve these cases (or assessments concerning which facts are material or immaterial for purposes of selecting governing precedent), then the large corpus of case decisions on related questions of common law rules will provide highly valuable information to jurists concerning how to resolve particular disputes. This will hold even if the jurists themselves lack the technical competence to reason to the outcome based upon foundational analytical reasoning.

6. Questions and Comments

Can you identify the differing assumptions concerning judicial rationality that inform the stare decisis analyses that O'Hara, Rasmusen, Kornhauser, and Macey offer? Are their analyses consistent or in tension with your own assessment of the concept of judicial rationality? Why? After reviewing the arguments, do you believe it more accurate to describe the judicial obligation of stare decisis as internally constructed or externally imposed? Why? Is it necessary to select between these two approaches to stare decisis? Why or why not? If not, how can the two sets of models be reconciled? Which of the specific justifications for stare decisis do you find most persuasive?

Do you find the various games that Kornhauser relies upon compelling in justifying or in criticizing stare decisis? In the context of pure coordination games, like driving, which institution, courts or the legislatures, generally provides the stable outcome? In games in which legislatures do not specify outcomes, does this suggest that something other than pure coordination is at stake? If legislatures do provide outcomes in such games, how is this relevant to Kornhauser's claim concerning the merits of stare decisis?

Now consider the battle of the sexes game. Is the choice of liability rule in a contract setting a good illustration of the benefits of stare decisis? How, if at all, does this argument for stare decisis differ from the argument that there is a general benefit to clarity in the construction of contract rules?

Do you find Macey's error cost justification for stare decisis persuasive? Does the Condorcet Jury Theorem support or undermine the assumptions required to generate the sort of judicial specialization that Macey suggests? Why? Can the Condorcet Jury Theorem explain the relative size of appellate court and supreme court panels? Why or why not?

7. An Interest–Group Perspective on Precedent

Todd Zywicki has relied upon interest-group theory to suggest that the conventional law and economics account of stare decisis described above might fail adequately to consider the incentives that the doctrine creates for parties seeking to manipulate the creation of favorable legal doctrine through investments in strategic litigation.[86] Zywicki models the common law process of rule generation through litigation in a similar manner to modeling rulemaking in the legislature. In both contexts, the value of the stream of rents an interest group obtains is a function of two variables: (1) the value of the rent in each period, multiplied by (2) the number of periods over which the rents are expected to be paid. So viewed, the present value of a wealth transfer to an interest group can be enlarged by increasing either the per-period payout or the payout duration. Zywicki further notes that the same collective action problems that affect legislative rent-seeking are likely to apply in the litigation context as discrete, well-organized interest groups are better suited to organize, and thus manipulate, the favorable development of preferred doctrine than more dispersed heterogeneous groups.[87]

One implication of Zywicki's model is that strict adherence to stare decisis has the potential to increase the stability of both efficient and inefficient precedents, including those that result from rent-seeking litigation. Moreover, although a stronger stare decisis doctrine increases the societal costs of rent-producing precedents by making overruling more difficult, it simultaneously increases the value of the "prize" by increasing the precedent's lifespan. Zywicki contends that to the extent that rent-seeking litigation dynamics approximate those in legislatures in favoring well-organized discrete groups, the result is to increase the production and maintenance of inefficient precedents relative to efficient precedents. Zywicki posits, therefore, that interest groups might prefer a more costly common law ex ante that produces more stable rules (and hence longer payouts) ex post and that this is most likely to hold for those groups that are better suited than their competitors to engage in judicial rent-seeking.

As a result, Zywicki claims, it is not clear that strict stare decisis is an optimal rule. Instead, Zywicki argues, the preferred rule might be a relatively weak form of precedent. He envisions, for example, a regime in which legal rules do not gain precedential status until they are reaffirmed by several independent judges considering the issue, and in which individual precedents can be revisited. As an historical matter, Zywicki observes, during the formative centuries of common law development, precedent was relatively weak, while the stricter stare decisis model observed today emerged in the late-nineteenth century. It was during the earlier period, Zywicki claims, that most of the economically efficient doctrines of the common law were developed. In contrast, Zywicki claims, rent-seeking litigation and inefficient legal rules have become increasingly prevalent in the United States over the past century.

Do you find Zywicki's account of stare decisis persuasive?[88] While Zywicki claims that the past century has produced increasingly inefficient

86. Todd J. Zywicki, *The Rise and Fall of Efficiency in the Common Law: A Supply–Side Analysis*, 97 Nw. U. L. Rev. 1551 (2003).

87. *See also* Mancur Olson, The Logic of Collective Action (1965).

88. As you read the materials on the efficiency of the common law, *infra* pp. 464–71, consider the following additional question: Can you reconcile Zywicki's analysis with Priest's claim that

precedent, this raises the question, as compared with what? For example, is it possible to determine whether the common law is more or less efficient than statutory law? Is it possible to assess whether the relative efficiencies of these two general categories of law has changed over the relevant historical periods that Zywicki has studied? Is answering these questions relevant to Zywicki's thesis? Why or why not?

8. Attitudinal Accounts of Stare Decisis

Before leaving the stare decisis analysis, it is worth considering the Attitudinal account of precedent on the Supreme Court. While Attitudinal scholars have leveled numerous challenges, both theoretical and empirical, to the constraining influence of precedent,[89] we consider two principal arguments. Professors Jeffrey Segal and Harold Spaeth have argued that precedent is not a meaningful constraint on judicial behavior because robust data suggest that both sides of any dispute are able to locate and cite to available precedents to support their preferred case positions. The authors explain:

> Though precedent, like plain meaning and intent, looks backward, it does not appreciably restrict judicial discretion for a number of reasons. First, and most basic, precedents lie on both sides of most every controversy, at least at the appellate level. If losing litigants at trial did not have authority to support their contentions, no basis for appeal would exist. . . .
>
> As further evidence that precedents exist to support the contentions of both parties, merely consult any appellate court case containing a dissenting opinion. This, as well as the majority opinion, will likely contain a substantial number of references to previously decided cases. Reference to these cases will undoubtedly show that those cited by the majority support its decision, whereas those specifically cited by the dissent bolster its contrary position.[90]

In a later edition of the same work, the same authors modify this argument, observing: "Since there are always some cases supporting both sides in virtually every conflict decided by the Court, [a definition of precedent that rests on a jurist's citation to consistent case authority] turns stare decisis into a trivial concept, at least for explanatory purposes."[91] The authors then suggest the following analysis:

> Rather, the best evidence for the influence of precedent [established in a case] must come from those who dissented from the majority

---

while judges can generate inefficient precedents in relatively small numbers, increasing the number of inefficient precedents creates welfare enhancing opportunities for displacing inefficient rules with efficient precedents?

89. *See, e.g.,* SAUL BRENNER & HAROLD J. SPAETH, STARE INDECISIS: THE ALTERATION OF PRECEDENT ON THE SUPREME COURT, 1946–1992 (1995).

90. *See* JEFFREY A. SEGAL & HAROLD J. SPAETH, THE SUPREME COURT AND THE ATTITUDINAL MODEL 45–46 (1993).

91. *See* JEFFREY A. SEGAL & HAROLD J. SPAETH, THE SUPREME COURT AND THE ATTITUDINAL MODEL REVISITED 294 (2002).

opinion in the case under question, for we *know* that these justices disagree with the precedent. If the precedent established in the case influences them, that influence should be felt in that case's progeny, through their votes and opinion writing. Thus, determining the influence of precedent requires examining the extent to which justices who disagree with a precedent move toward that position in subsequent cases.[92]

Based upon these arguments, and statistical inference from the Supreme Court Database, the authors maintain that ideological predilection rather than precedent, proves the overriding determinant of Supreme Court decision making.

Consider the following response respecting the first argument. Jurists tend to give extensive citation respecting divisive issues or respecting issues most subject to ambiguity within cases they are deciding. In the context of a constitutional challenge to a state statute restricting access to abortion procedures, for example, there are a large number of issues over which legal propositions are well settled. These include, as illustrations, the Supreme Court's power of constitutional judicial review, the incorporation of many provisions of the Bill of Rights against the states, the existence of a right of privacy, the inclusion of the abortion right as part of the right of privacy, and many others. In most cases, precedent operates as a set of agreed-upon background principles that help frame those issues that ultimately prove decisive. In many cases, most or all issues are well settled, but not surprisingly, in the Supreme Court, the number of cases presenting important unsettled issues is larger. Will citation counting give a reasonable proxy for whether arguments for or against the abortion statute are supported by precedent? Why or why not? Even in divisive Supreme Court cases, precedent plays a significant role that the citation count methodology cannot take into account.

With respect to the second argument, is the fact that the Justices, acting individually, seek to preserve the opportunity to limit a precedent by continuing to distinguish cases that they disagreed with initially, or even by advocating overruling, sufficient to claim the precedent is not a constraint? Is inquiring whether dissenting Justices move to embrace contrary majority decisions the correct test of the doctrine of stare decisis? Why or why not? Is the Supreme Court itself the best institution for assessing the constraining effect of stare decisis within the judiciary? Why or why not?

After *Gregg v. Georgia*,[93] which overruled *Furman v. Georgia*[94] and upheld the constitutionality of the death penalty, Justices Brennan and Marshall took turns producing dissenting opinions that insisted, consistent with their votes in each of these cases, that the death penalty violated the Eighth Amendment prohibition against cruel and unusual punishment

---

92. *Id.* at 292.

93. 428 U.S. 153 (1976).

94. 408 U.S. 238 (1972).

as applied to the states via the Fourteenth Amendment.[95] What does this practice suggest about stare decisis? Should justices adhere to their own personal "precedents" or to the majority precedents of the Supreme Court? As a normative matter, should Justices operate consistently in this regard, either always following their initially articulated views or always changing their votes to reflect contrary majority views? Why? Please keep these questions in mind as you evaluate the social choice analysis of Supreme Court decision-making rules that follows.

C. A SOCIAL CHOICE ANALYSIS OF SUPREME COURT DECISION–MAKING RULES[96]

In this part we will consider the implications of social choice for assessing a variety of decision-making rules. While our emphasis will be on the United States Supreme Court, several of the insights set out in this part will apply to other levels of the judicial hierarchy and will also apply more generally to other judicial systems. In this subpart, we consider the social choice model developed by Maxwell Stearns of several anomalous features of Supreme Court decision-making involving individual cases and groups of cases over time; works by Judge (then-Professor) John Rogers, Professors David Post and Steven Salop, Lewis Kornhauser and Lawrence Sager, and Jonathan Remy Nash, offering and critiquing a set or proposed alternative voting protocols for individual Supreme Court cases; and a social choice analysis of the Supreme Court decision-making proposed by Judge (then-Professor) Frank Easterbrook.

For ease of presentation, we will divide this presentation into two main parts: (1) a static or micro-theory that explains the Court's decision-making processes in individual cases; and (2) a dynamic or macro-theory that explains the Court's decision-making processes over larger numbers of cases over time. In terms of doctrine, the first set of models focuses on the Court's reliance (and that of appeals courts more broadly) on outcome rather than issue-voting rules and the development of the narrowest grounds doctrine, articulated in *Marks v. United States*.[97] The second set of models focuses on the Court's reliance upon horizontal stare decisis— meaning the Supreme Court's presumptive adherence to its own previously announced precedents—as a means of stabilizing developing doctrine, and its reliance upon standing (and other justiciability) rules to limit the ability of ideological litigants to favorably time cases to benefit from the inevitable path dependence that stare decisis produces.

---

95. *See, e.g.*, McCleskey v. Bowers, 501 U.S. 1281, 1281–82 (1991) (Marshall, J., dissenting from denial of certiorari); Clemons v. Mississippi, 494 U.S. 738, 755–56 (1990) (Brennan, J., dissenting); Saffle v. Parks, 494 U.S. 484, 515 (1990) (Brennan, J., dissenting); Hildwin v. Florida, 490 U.S. 638, 641 (Brennan, J., dissenting) (Marshall, J., dissenting).

96. Portions of the analysis to follow are based upon Maxwell L. Stearns, Constitutional Process: A Social Choice Analysis of Supreme Court Decision-Making (2000); *see id.* at 97–156 (describing static constitutional process involving resolution of individual cases); *see also id.* 157–211 (describing dynamic constitutional process involving how groups of cases are decided over time).

97. 430 U.S. 188, 193 (1977).

1. Micro–Analysis: How the Supreme Court Decides Individual Cases

In chapter 3, we saw that under certain conditions, groups of individuals who hold internally consistent, or transitive preferences, will discover that their combined preferences are intransitive, or "cycle," when aggregated through voting procedures commonly associated with majority rule. The Condorcet paradox shows that with persons holding the following ordinal preferences over options ABC (P1: ABC; P2: BCA; and P3: CAB), the group as a whole cycles such that ApBpCpA, where p means preferred to by simple majority rule. In contrast, with the following more well-behaved preferences over the same options, shifting only P3's second and third ordinal ranking (P1: ABC; P2: BCA; and P3: CBA), B emerges a Condorcet winner, defeating A and B in direct binary comparisons.

Arrow's Theorem generalizes the paradox of voting in the following sense: Any external rule that is intended to ensure that the members' preferences do not cycle will inevitably run up against some other important norm associated with fair or democratic decision-making. A group of three or more persons selecting among three or more options cannot ensure transitive (or noncyclical) outputs without violating at least one, and possibly more than one, of the following conditions:[98] (1) *Range*: The collective decision-making rule must select its outcome in a manner that is consistent with the members' selection from among all conceivable ordinal rankings over three available alternatives; (2) *Independence of irrelevant alternatives*: In choosing among paired alternatives, participants are assumed to decide solely based upon the merits of those options and without regard to how they would rank options that might be introduced later; (3) *Unanimity*: If a change from the status quo to an alternate state will improve the position of at least a single participant without harming anyone else, the decision-making body must so move; and (4) *Nondictatorship*: The group cannot consistently vindicate the preferences of a member against the contrary will of the group as a whole.[99]

Maxwell Stearns has argued that while legislatures routinely avoid *Independence* in their decision-making processes—consider the discussion of vote trading or logrolling in chapter 5[100]—appellate courts, including the United States Supreme Court, have important institutional norms that encourage compliance with *Independence* but that relax *Range*. Stearns maintains that this operates at both the level of micro- and macro-voting rules. To see why, we will consider three paradigm cases that Stearns uses to demonstrate the significance of the cycling problem for Supreme Court decision making in individual cases.

Before doing so, however, it will help to consider Stearns's larger presentation of the categories of cases that the nine-member Supreme

---

98. This presentation is reproduced from chapter 3, section I.E and III.A.

99. *See id.*; STEARNS, *supra* note 96, at 41–94 (providing more detailed presentation, and comparison with Arrow's original presentation).

100. *See supra* chapter 5, section I.B.2.A.

Court has the potential to issue. The Court can issue unanimous, majority, and fractured panel opinions.[101] It can also issue three-judgment cases in which there is no majority for a single judgment. A social choice problem only arises when there is no first choice majority candidate, and, as a result, Stearns argues, the difficulties associated with aggregating collective preferences do not arise in either unanimous or majority opinion cases.[102] In addition, as explained below, Stearns demonstrates that the Court has developed an informal norm that has effectively solved the difficulty in three-judgment cases.

As a general matter, Stearns explains, within the fractured panel category, the Court will issue a combination of opinions that will usually include the following: a plurality opinion, one or more concurrences in the judgment,[103] and one or more dissents. In many instances, individual opinions will combine elements from more than a single category, for example an opinion that concurs in part, concurs in the judgment in part, and dissents in part, but to clarify the presentation, it is helpful to focus on the basic categories.[104]

The social choice problem (meaning the problem of aggregating collective preferences into a meaningful social outcome) instead arises in the context of cases that lack a majority winner, and that offer at least two alternative justifications for reaching the judgment, in addition to the possibility of an opposite judgment. The simplest case involves a plurality, a concurrence in the judgment, and a dissent. Not all such cases will produce cycling preferences and indeed most such cases are likely to possess an implicit Condorcet winning opinion. As Stearns demonstrates, however, in an identifiable subset of fractured panel cases, it is plausible to identify reasonable conditions that expose the absence of a Condorcet winner. The social choice analysis helps to identify those conditions and their significance in assessing Supreme Court decision-making rules.

We will illustrate the analysis with a stylized presentation of three actual Supreme Court decisions. The presentation is intended to focus on

---

101. By fractured panel opinions, we mean opinions that have a majority for one judgment, but lack a majority opinion consistent with that judgment.

102. Cycles can also arise across two more separate majority decisions. For a discussion, see *infra* pp. 460–64 (discussing Washington v. Seattle Sch. Dist. No. 1, 458 U.S. 457 (1982), and Crawford v. Bd. of Educ., 458 U.S. 527 (1982)).

103. A concurrence in the judgment is distinct from a simple concurrence. The Justice concurring in the judgment agrees with the judgment issued by the plurality opinion or other opinion issuing the judgment, but provides an independent rationale, while a concurring Justice also joins the opinion issuing the judgment, but offers additional analysis in his or her separate opinion.

104. Other combinations are possible. For example, there can be an opinion that issues the judgment even if it is not a plurality opinion, and there can be concurrences, partial concurrences and partial dissents, and even partial concurrences, partial concurrences in the judgment, and partial dissents. It is also possible that all jurists agree to the same outcome such that there is either a majority opinion or a plurality opinion, along with several concurrences or concurrences in the judgment, but no dissents. *See, e.g.*, Washington v. Glucksberg, 521 U.S. 702 (1997). In addition, it is possible to have multiple opinions of equal size coalitions such that there is no plurality opinion. *See, e.g.*, Miller v. Albright, 523 U.S. 420 (1998) (presenting three opinions for two Justices each consistent with the judgment and two dissenting opinions written or joined by the remaining three Justices in dissent).

the inherent aggregation problems that arise as a consequence of the collective nature of the Supreme Court's decision-making processes. The first case, based upon *Kassel v. Consolidated Freightways Corp.*,[105] will demonstrate the probability of cyclical preferences contained across the separate opinions in a single case.[106] The second case, based upon *Planned Parenthood of Southeastern Pennsylvania v. Casey*,[107] will demonstrate the conditions under which even a nonmajority opinion can yield a stable outcome consistent with the Condorcet criterion. In many respects, we might think of *Casey* as the "normal" case and *Kassel* as something of an aberration, although it is by no means unique. As we will see, the Supreme Court's narrowest grounds rule will succeed in the normal cases in selecting the opinion that expresses the Court's dominant, or Condorcet winning, holding. The final case, based upon *Arizona v. Fulminante*,[108] is a subset of the larger corpus of aberrational cases and illustrates an alternative approach that individual justices have sometimes taken to try to avoid the seeming anomaly that such cases produce. Such efforts produce their own anomalies and controversy concerning how judges should resolve cases. After presenting these cases, we will tie them into Stearns's larger model of outcome voting and the narrowest grounds rule, and consider several alternative normative assessments that other scholars have advanced concerning the implications of social choice for Supreme Court decision making.

a. *Kassel v. Consolidated Freightways*

Kassel involved a dormant Commerce Clause challenge to an Iowa law that prevented sixty-five-foot twin trailers from traveling through the state, with exceptions that benefited various in-state interests.[109] The law imposed substantial burdens on interstate truckers because the rigs prohibited in Iowa were permitted in the surrounding states. As a result, truckers traveling with nonconforming rigs from one side of Iowa to the other had to make the choice to either go around the state or to alter their rigs and make separate runs with the cab pulling the trailers separately. Either alternative substantially raised the cost of shipping goods in commerce.

---

105. 450 U.S. 662 (1981).

106. Each of the case discussions is simplified to present the critical preference aggregation features that highlight the social choice difficulty raised in the various opinions. For more detailed treatments of the cases, see STEARNS, *supra* note 96, at 99–106 (discussing *Kassel*); *id.* at 16–23, 129–30 (discussing *Planned Parenthood of Southeastern Pa. v. Casey*); *id.* at 146–47, 149–52 (discussing *Arizona v. Fulminante*).

107. 505 U.S. 833 (1992).

108. 499 U.S. 279 (1991).

109. The exceptions allowed such vehicles to benefit border cities, for Iowa shippers seeking an exemption for a vehicle up to seventy feet long, and for intrastate transit of mobile homes to Iowa residents. *Kassel*, 450 U.S. at 665–67. The statutory history is somewhat unusual in that the challenge rested in part on legislative history concerning the governor's decision not to sign into law a bill that would have repealed the challenged statute. For Stearns's more detailed presentation of this case, see Maxwell Stearns, *The Misguided Renaissance of Social Choice*, 103 YALE L.J. 1219, 1256–57, 1267–70 (1994).

Consolidated Freightways, an international shipping company, challenged the Iowa law as violating the dormant Commerce Clause doctrine. The difficulty was that under traditional dormant Commerce Clause analysis, state highway safety laws were subject to low level rational basis scrutiny. After the Iowa Supreme Court sustained the state law against the dormant Commerce Clause challenge, Consolidated Freightways petitioned for writ of certiorari in the United States Supreme Court. The Supreme Court reviewed the case and ultimately issued three separate opinions, none commanding majority support.

Writing for a plurality of four, Justice Powell voted to strike down the challenged law as violating the dormant Commerce Clause. Powell rejected low level rational basis scrutiny in favor of the somewhat stricter balancing test that permitted the Court to weigh the claimed safety benefits of the law against the burdens that the law posed for commerce. Powell further determined that in applying that test, the Court was permitted to weigh arguments that were not raised in the legislature at the time that the law was passed, but rather that were raised for the first time by trial counsel. Based upon his own independent assessment under the balancing test, Powell rejected the state's proffered justification for the challenged law, thus voting to strike the law down.

In an opinion concurring in the judgment, Justice Brennan, writing for two, expressly disagreed with Powell's resolution of both dispositive issues. Brennan concluded that it was not the Court's job to independently weigh safety benefits against burdens on commerce, instead reasoning that the issue was whether the enacting legislature had a rational basis in support of the law. Brennan also rejected Powell's willingness to entertain newly constructed arguments of trial counsel that were not offered as a contemporaneous justification at the time that the truck ban was enacted. Because Brennan found that the actual arguments in support of the law evinced a protectionist motivation, he concluded that even under low level rational basis scrutiny, the law was virtually *per se* unconstitutional.

Finally, writing for three Justices, then-Associate Justice Rehnquist dissented. Rehnquist agreed with Justice Brennan that the Court should not independently weigh safety benefits against burdens on commerce, and thus concluded that the appropriate test was rational basis scrutiny. Rehnquist agreed with Powell, however, that in seeking to determine whether the state satisfied the selected test, the Court was free to consider not only contemporaneous legislative justifications, but also newly constructed arguments submitted by trial counsel. Based upon newly introduced safety justifications, Rehnquist determined that the legislature could have had a rational justification in support of the challenged law, thus voting to sustain it against the dormant Commerce Clause challenge.

Stearns argues that the *Kassel* case presents an anomaly that with some reasonable assumptions can readily be transformed into a voting paradox. The analysis begins with a proposition that is consistent with all three of the opinions that the Justices either wrote or joined: If the Court applied low level rational basis scrutiny (the more lenient of the two available substantive tests) and if it willingly entertained novel safety justifications not presented to the legislature (the more lenient of the two available evidentiary rules), then the Court should sustain the challenged law. Conversely, applying at least one of the less lenient rules is sufficient to strike the law down.

Applying this premise against the separate opinions, Stearns demonstrates that while Powell and Brennan each struck the law down on the ground that one of the two conditions was not met (Powell applied the more stringent substantive test and Brennan applied the more stringent evidentiary rule), separate majorities supported the necessary preconditions for sustaining the law. Brennan plus Rehnquist, for a total of five Justices, supported rational basis scrutiny, and Powell plus Rehnquist, for a total of seven Justices, supported considering newly constructed evidence. Although Justice Rehnquist implicitly recognized the resulting anomaly,[110] the Court issued a judgment in tension with the separate majority resolutions of the two issues that the three opinions identified as decisive to the outcome in the case.

Stearns explains the voting anomaly by treating the three opinions as packages of resolved issues, each leading to a preferred case judgment, as set out in Table 7:4[111]:

Table 7:4. *Kassel* in Two Dimensions

	Rational Basis	Balancing Test
Allow Novel Evidence	C. Rehnquist (for 3)	A. Powell (for 4)
Exclude Novel Evidence	B. Brennan (for 2)	

Powell sets out package A (lenient evidentiary rule, strict substantive rule), leading to striking the challenged law down; Brennan expresses option B (strict evidentiary rule, lenient substantive rule), also leading to striking the challenged law down; and Rehnquist set out package C (lenient evidentiary rule, lenient substantive rule), leading to sustaining the challenged law. Based upon the previously articulated assertion about the proposition that is consistent with all three opinions,[112] Stearns shows

---

110. Thus, Justice Rehnquist stated:

It should not escape notice that a majority of the Court goes on record today as agreeing that courts in Commerce Clause cases do not sit to weigh safety benefits against burdens on commerce when the safety benefits are not illusory.... I do not agree with my Brother Brennan, however, that only those safety benefits somehow articulated by the legislature as *the* motivation for the challenged statute can be considered in supporting the state law.

450 U.S. at 692 n.4.

111. STEARNS, *supra* note 96, at 101 tbl.3.1 (presenting table).

112. See *id.* at 100.

that while each opinion is internally consistent, the combined logic of the opinions reveals separate majority preferences for a lenient evidentiary rule (Powell plus Rehnquist) and for a lenient substantive rule (Brennan plus Rehnquist). If an individual Justice made these independent issue determinations (as does Rehnquist), he would have dissented.

Stearns further explains the possibility of voting cycle in *Kassel* as follows. Imagine that each opinion-writing Justice must ordinally rank his second and third choices over the remaining alternatives. Assume that Powell determines that he cares more about the outcome than about the reasoning to achieve that outcome. If so, his ordinal preferences are (ABC). Assume that Brennan is more concerned with selecting the preferred substantive standard (rational basis scrutiny) than with the outcome. If so, his ordinal preferences are (BCA). Finally, assume that Rehnquist, who is inevitably forced to choose opinions leading to a contrary result, is more concerned about the evidentiary issue than the choice of substantive standard. If so, his ordinal preferences are (CAB). These combined preferences are the paradigm case for collective intransitivity, such that $ApBpCpA$. Nothing in the opinion proves that these jurists embrace the particular ordinal rankings described here. It is possible, for example, to construct the following hypothetical preferences, which combine to produce a reverse cycle: Powell (ACB), Brennan (BAC), Rehnquist (CBA), thus generating the (reverse) cycle $ApCpBpA$. And it is also possible to imagine combinations that avoid a cycle.

The larger point of the analysis is that any set of combinations rests upon equally plausible (or implausible) assumptions about how the Justices would rank order their preferences over the three packaged alternatives. The apparent voting anomaly in *Kassel* illustrates the problem of multidimensionality and asymmetry, introduced in chapter 3.[113] There are two issue dimensions captured in the two substantive issues, and in this instance, Powell and Brennan express opposite views on these two issues, but their opposite resolutions lead, counterintuitively, to the same result. The anomaly arises because *a priori*, as a second choice, there is no way to know if a given judge with these ordinal preferences would prefer an opinion in agreement on a single issue but producing an opposite judgment or an opinion in disagreement on both issues but leading to the same judgment. Stearns explains that this unusual, but not unique, combination of preferences gives rise to the possibility of multidimensional and asymmetrical preferences for the Court as a whole, thus producing a possible embedded cycle.

After reviewing two other case paradigms, we will discuss the larger thesis explaining why the Court employs voting rules capable of generating this anomaly. As we will see below, in the ordinary nonmajority opinion case, these peculiar ordinal ranking combinations are less plausi-

---

113. *See supra* chapter 3, section II.G.1. For a more detailed exposition, see STEARNS, *supra* note 96, at 67–77; *see also* Maxwell L. Stearns, *Should Justices Ever Switch Votes?: Miller v. Albright in Social Choice Perspective*, 7 SUP. CT. ECON. REV. 87 (1999).

ble, with the result of generating a stable median, or Condorcet-winning, outcome.

b. *Planned Parenthood v. Casey*

We will now consider an alternative nonmajority opinion case that Stearns relies upon to demonstrate when the conditions required to produce a cycle appear unlikely.[114] This discussion is based upon the famous Supreme Court decision, *Planned Parenthood of Southeastern Pennsylvania v. Casey*.[115] In that case, the Supreme Court, with seven out of nine members appointed by Republican Presidents, was presented with what many contemporaneous commentators regarded as the clearest opportunity to overrule *Roe v. Wade*,[116] the controversial 1973 decision announcing the right to abortion.[117]

The *Casey* decision produced five separate opinions, none containing majority support. To simplify the analysis, Stearns suggests combining those joining these opinions into three main camps: liberal (Blackmun and Stevens); moderate (O'Connor, Kennedy, and Souter); and conservative (Rehnquist, Scalia, Thomas, and White).[118] While this does not alter the substantive analysis, it allows for a simpler comparison of *Casey* to *Kassel*.

Casey involved a challenge to five provisions of the Pennsylvania abortion statute: (1) informed consent; (2) parental notification for minors; (3) spousal notification for married women; (4) an exemption from the first three provisions in the event of a medical emergency; and (5) reporting requirements. Ultimately, a majority comprising the moderate and liberal camps voted to strike down the spousal notification provision, and a majority comprising the moderate and conservative camps voted to sustain the remaining provisions. More important than the specific holdings on the challenged Pennsylvania statute, Stearns claims, was the effect of collective decision making on the Court's revision of the framework for assessing the challenged abortion statute under *Roe v. Wade*.

The *Roe* Court held abortion to be a fundamental right, protected within the constitutional zone of privacy first articulated in *Griswold v. Connecticut*.[119] Applying strict scrutiny, the *Roe* Court determined that the state's identified interests in regulating abortion did not become compelling—and were therefore inadequate to countervail the woman's

---

114. *See* STEARNS, *supra* note 96, at 129–30 (presenting *Casey* as a unidimensional case).

115. 505 U.S. 833 (1992).

116. 410 U.S. 113 (1973).

117. Ruth Marcus, *Preelection Ruling Likely on Abortion: Pennsylvania Asks High Court Review*, WASH. POST, Dec. 10, 1991, at A1 ("At least four justices are believed to be ready to overrule *Roe*, an outcome that [the ACLU's] Kolbert predicted yesterday is 'highly likely' in the Pennsylvania case"); David G. Savage, *The Rescue of Roe vs. Wade: How a Dramatic Change of Heart by a Supreme Court Justice Saved Abortion—Just When the Issue Seemed Headed for Certain Defeat*, L.A. TIMES, Dec. 13, 1992, at A1 (expressing surprise at *Casey* holding).

118. To be clear, this is not to suggest that each of these justices is necessarily part of a broader coalition associated with the ideological label. Instead, as seen below, this simple categorization helps to explain the relationships among the various camps in the *Casey* opinions.

119. 381 U.S. 479 (1965).

right to abort—until specific points in the pregnancy. Because the risks associated with abortion was lower early in a pregnancy than carrying the fetus to term, the state could not regulate abortion to further its interest in maternal health until the end of the first trimester. The Court further determined that the state's interest in the potential life represented by the fetus did not become compelling until the fetus is capable of meaningful existence outside the mother's womb, namely the point of viability, which coincides with the end of the second trimester.

In *Casey*, Justices O'Connor, Kennedy, and Souter issued a joint opinion that considered first whether to adhere to *Roe v. Wade* as a matter of precedent. The joint opinion rejected various arguments for declining to adhere to *Roe*, but did not accept the opinion in its entirety. Instead, the Court adhered to what it characterized as *Roe*'s "essential holding."[120] Most notably, this did not include the trimester framework or the characterization of abortion as a fundamental right. Instead, the joint authors found that because technology rendered late abortions safer and also rendered viability earlier, the trimester framework proved increasingly unworkable.[121] In addition, the joint authors reasoned that the *Roe* Court had given inadequate weight to the state's interest in the potentiality of human life. Because the joint authors determined that abortion was a liberty interest rather than a fundamental right, they applied the newly formulated undue burden test, rather than strict scrutiny, to assess the challenged law. Under this test, the Court found that only the spousal notification provision posed an undue burden, thus striking that provision but sustaining the remainder of the Pennsylvania statute.

Justices Stevens and Blackmun, in contrast, wrote a partial concurrence and partial dissent, in which they rejected the join authors' revision of *Roe* in favor of the original doctrinal formulation. That formulation included the trimester framework and the viability test for evaluating whether the state's interest in potential life becomes compelling. Finally, Rehnquist, Scalia, Thomas, and White rejected the joint authors' stare decisis analysis, preferring to overturn *Roe* outright. Because they viewed abortion as a mere liberty interest, subject to low level scrutiny, the conservatives would have sustained the challenged Pennsylvania law in its entirety. Stearns presents the *Casey* opinions along the following single dimensional table.[122]

---

120. Planned Parenthood of Se. Pa. v. Casey, 505 U.S. 833, 846 (1992).

121. *Id.* at 860.

122. *See* Stearns, *supra* note 96, at 129.

Table 7:5. The *Casey* Decision in One Dimension

A Blackmun, Stevens (Liberal)	B. O'Connor, Kennedy, Souter (Moderate)	C. Rehnquist, Scalia, White, Thomas (Conservative)
Strike down all restrictive provisions based upon either stare decisis or analysis of merits of original *Roe* decision	Strike down only spousal notification provision, based upon stare decisis revision of *Roe*	Uphold all provisions based upon critical analysis of original *Roe* decision
Broad abortion right◄─────────────────────────►Narrow abortion right		

Table 7:5, which depicts *Casey*, is notably different from Table 7:4, which depicts *Kassel*. Like *Kassel*, *Roe* presented more than a single issue. At a minimum, it presented the following issues: (1) Does stare decisis require adhering to *Roe*?; (2) What is the relevant test for evaluating the abortion right?; and (3) Under the selected test, how do each of the challenged provisions fare? And yet, it is intuitive to present the resolutions of these issues by each camp along a single normative dimension that is easily captured according to the breadth or narrowness of the protected abortion right.[123] While both the Liberal and Conservative camps were critical of the Moderate camp's stare decisis analysis and decision to revise *Roe*, consistent with the prior analysis, the fundamental issue is how each of those camps would choose, if forced to rank ordinally the remaining opinions. In this case, the answer is quite intuitive. The liberals, A, would almost certainly prefer the partial relief afforded in the revised *Roe* formulation that the moderates provide, B, to overturning *Roe* as embraced by C. Conversely, the conservatives would almost certainly prefer the moderates' revision of *Roe*, and its demotion of abortion to a liberty interest protected by the lesser undue burden standard, B, to the original *Roe* formulation advocated by the liberals, A. The second and third ordinal rankings of the moderates are irrelevant; either way, B is the Condorcet winner.

Stearns argues that the same underlying intuition used to analyze *Casey* further explains the narrowest ground rule articulated in *Marks v. United States*.[124] While the details of *Marks* are unnecessary for our purposes, suffice it to say that the Court evaluated an opinion that possessed the characteristic features of *Casey* in that the separate opinions could be cast along a single normative spectrum. The issue in the case was whether a criminal defendant could rely upon the narrowest grounds holding in a Supreme Court plurality opinion, which had afforded a relatively higher level of protection than a later majority decision, which

---

123. Recall that in chapter 3 we presented a stylized version of *Casey* that illustrated the median voter theorem. *See supra* chapter 3, section I.B. and I.G.1.

124. 430 U.S. 188 (1977). For a more detailed analysis of this case, see Maxwell L. Stearns, *The Case for Including* Marks v. United States *in the Canon of Constitutional Law*, 17 CONST. COMM. 321 (2000).

retroactively lowered the relevant prosecutorial standard.[125] The prosecutor maintained that only majority decisions produced binding precedents, but the Court, with Justice Powell writing, instead stated:

> When a fragmented Court decides a case and no single rationale explaining the result enjoys the assent of five Justices, "the holding of the Court may be viewed as that position taken by those Members who concurred in the judgments on the narrowest grounds...."[126]

Stearns contends that the *Marks* narrowest grounds rule can be translated as follows. In a case that sustains a law against a constitutional challenge, locate the controlling opinion that would sustain the fewest laws and in a case that strikes down a law on constitutional grounds, locate the controlling opinion that would strike down the fewest laws. In effect, the opinion consistent with the outcome that would have the least effect on extant law is the narrowest grounds opinion.

In *Casey*, it is easy to see the application of the doctrine. Of the opinions sustaining the challenged provisions of Pennsylvania law, the plurality would apply a stricter test and thus sustain fewer such laws than the conservatives. Of the opinions striking down the spousal notification provision, the plurality would apply a more deferential standard than the liberal's preferred strict scrutiny test and thus would strike down the fewest laws. Notice that the joint opinion, which represents the Condorcet winner (or dominant second choice), states both holdings for the Court under the narrowest grounds rule.

Now consider whether *Marks* can be applied in *Kassel*. The Court resolved two issues in *Kassel*: (1) which of two substantive standards to apply, the more lenient rational basis or the stricter balancing test; and (2) which of two evidentiary rules to apply, the more lenient rule allowing novel evidence or the stricter rule excluding such evidence. Under the *Marks* rule, the opinion consistent with the outcome that resolves the case on the narrowest grounds states the holding. The two opinions consistent with the outcome of striking down the challenged Iowa statute are those of Powell and Brennan. But notice that the Powell opinion is narrower on the question of the evidentiary rule—the more relaxed test would sustain more challenged laws—while the Brennan opinion is narrower on the question of the substantive rule—the more relaxed evidentiary rule would sustain more challenged laws. Stearns explains that the *Marks* doctrine does not apply in cases like *Kassel* because of the problem of dimensionality and asymmetry. The two opinions consistent with the outcome resolve the two issues in opposite fashion, but achieve the same result. Neither of the opinions resolves the case on narrower grounds; rather each resolves it on opposite grounds. While one might say that Rehnquist would resolve the case on narrower grounds, applying the more relaxed substantive and

---

125. In 1957, the Supreme Court held that the government could prosecute materials as obscene that violated "contemporary community standards." *See* Roth v. United States, 354 U.S. 476, 489, 492 (1957). In 1966, a controlling plurality of the Supreme Court elevated the prosecutorial standard to demand that the materials alleged to be obscene be "utterly without redeeming social value." Memoirs v. Massachusetts, 383 U.S. 413, 418 (1966). And in 1973, the Supreme Court, in a majority opinion, reverted to a modified version of the *Roth* contemporary community standards test, a laxer prosecutorial standard. Miller v. California, 413 U.S. 15, 24 (1973).

126. *Marks*, 430 U.S. at 193 (quoting Gregg v. Georgia, 428 U.S. 153, 169 n.15 (1976)).

evidentiary rules, his opinion is ineligible to state the holding under *Marks* because it is in dissent.

Stearns thus shows that while the *Marks* rule works properly in those cases that rest along a single dimensional continuum, it fails in the relatively narrow class of cases that present multidimensionality and asymmetry. As a result of the sometimes displeasing results in such cases, individual jurists have sometimes engaged in a kind of vote-switch mechanism. This invites its own anomalies, as the next case aptly illustrates.

c. *Arizona v. Fulminante*

In *Arizona v. Fulminante*,[127] a man was convicted of capital murder and sentenced to death following a trial in which the prosecution admitted two confessions, the first of which Fulminante maintained had been coerced and the second of which he claimed was fruit of the poisonous tree.[128] The question before the Supreme Court was whether admitting an allegedly coerced confession provides the basis for reversing a capital murder conviction. The three Justices who produced opinions, Chief Justice Rehnquist, Justice Kennedy, and Justice White, distilled the case to three issues: (1) was the first confession coerced?; (2) if so, does harmless error analysis apply?; and (3) if so, on these facts is the admission harmless error? Following the same analysis, Stearns explains that all three opinions are consistent with the following proposition: If the confession was coerced, and if harmless error analysis did not apply (such that the admission itself was reversible error) or if harmless error analysis applied but the admission of the confession into evidence was not harmless error, the conviction should be reversed. Conversely, if the confession was not coerced, if harmless error analysis did apply, and if the admission was harmless error, then the result should be to affirm.

Writing in part for a majority of five that did not include Justice Kennedy, Justice White determined that the confession was coerced. Justice Kennedy, writing separately, concluded that the confession was not coerced. Consistent with that conclusion, Justice Kennedy should have voted to affirm because harmless error analysis is irrelevant to the admission of a voluntary confession. In part of his opinion for a majority of five, the Chief Justice determined that if the confession is coerced, harmless error analysis applies. In part of his opinion for a differently constituted majority of five that did include Justice Kennedy, Justice White further determined that admitting the coerced confession was not harmless error. In his separate opinion, Justice Kennedy stated the following:

> My own view that the confession was not coerced does not command a majority.

---

127. 499 U.S. 279 (1991). For a more detailed discussion, see STEARNS, *supra* note 96, at 146–47, 149–52; Stearns, *supra* note 113, at 136–39.

128. 499 U.S. at 284.

In the interests of providing a clear mandate to the Arizona Supreme Court in this capital case, I deem it proper to accept in the case now before us the holding of five Justices that the confession was coerced and inadmissible. I agree with a majority of the Court that admission of the confession could not be harmless error when viewed in light of all the other evidence; and so I concur in the judgment. . . . [129]

Table 7:6 is helpful to the discussion that follows:[130]

Table 7:6. *Arizona v. Fulminante*

	Confession coerced	Confession not coerced
Admission not Harmless	B. Marshall, Brennan, Stevens, White, *[Kennedy]*	A. *Kennedy* (moves left)
Admission Harmless	C. Scalia	D. Rehnquist, O'Connor, Souter

Had Kennedy stuck to his original position and not reached the admissibility question, or expressed it strictly as dictum, the *Fulminante* decision would have presented the same voting paradox that Stearns demonstrated arises in *Kassel*. While separate majorities determined that the confession was coerced (camps B and C) and the admission of the confession was not harmless (camps B and A), only four Justices would have embraced both positions as required to reverse the conviction. As in *Kassel*, camps A and C would have reached the same outcome, affirm, based upon opposite resolutions of the each of the two dispositive case issues. Scalia determined that despite the coerced confession, the admission is harmless. Kennedy would have determined that the confession is not coerced, thus avoiding the harmlessness question altogether. Instead, Kennedy switched his vote to join the Brennan camp, based upon the contrary majority determination on coercion (camps B and C), with the result that he joined a majority finding that admitting the now-coerced confession could not be harmless error. Thus, rather than affirming, the Court reversed the conviction based upon Justice Kennedy's vote switch.

2. Normative Implications of Supreme Court Voting Anomalies

Legal scholars have drawn differing implications from these and similar voting anomaly cases. Judge (then-Professor) John Rogers has criticized Justice White for a similar vote switch in *Pennsylvania v. Union*

---

129.   499 U.S. 279, 313 (1991) (Kennedy, J., concurring in the judgment).

130.   Table 7:8 is reproduced from Stearns, *supra* note 113, at 139.

Gas Co.,[131] claiming that the decision to acquiesce in a contrary majority's resolution of an underlying issue was an abdication of the judicial obligation to resolve cases in a principled fashion.[132] Professors David Post and Steven Salop, in contrast, defended Justice White's vote switch and suggested that in cases producing such voting anomalies, an alternative voting protocol, which they term "issue voting," is normatively preferable to outcome voting.[133] Professors Lewis Kornhauser and Lawrence Sager have suggested a meta-vote on the voting rule in cases that appear poised to present the voting anomaly to determine whether to apply the ordinary outcome-voting rule or instead an issue-voting rule. And most recently, Professor Jonathan Nash has suggested a "context specific voting protocol" that would automatically facilitate a switch to an issue-voting regime under specified conditions. We now consider the description by these scholars of their preferred alternative voting protocols:

Professors David Post and Steven Salop advance the following approach:

> An alternative approach [to resolving voting anomaly cases] would have the court as a whole ... assess each of the legal issues raised in the case and reach collective decisions on each of those issues, again by majority vote. The court's judgment then would be determined by the result it reached on each of the underlying issues. We call this "issue voting" in our analysis.[134]

Defending this protocol, the authors further assert:

> [O]utcome-voting by appellate courts is deeply flawed. It is arguably no fairer than issue-voting to the individual litigants before the court. More importantly, it is fundamentally inconsistent with an appellate court's role of providing guidance to lower courts and the community as a whole as to the legal consequences of specific actions.[135]

By contrast,[136] Professors Lewis Kornhauser and Lawrence Sager decided against resolving the choice of voting protocol with a fixed rule.

---

131. 491 U.S. 1 (1989).

132. John M. Rogers, *"I Vote this Way Because I'm Wrong": The Supreme Court Justice as Epimenides,* 79 Ky. L.J. 439, 442 (1990–1991) ("[A] Supreme Court justice should not vote contrary to his own stated analysis, because such action is harmful and destabilizing to the determinacy of the law.").

133. David Post & Steven C. Salop, *Rowing Against the Tidewater: A Theory of Voting by Multijudge Panels,* 80 Geo. L.J. 743, 752 (1992) ("[B]y voting to affirm the court of appeals, Justice White allowed the Court to preserve the outward appearance of outcome-voting. Given the Court's apparent predisposition toward outcome-voting, Justice White was forced to vote against his own analysis of the case in order to reach the result the Court would have reached under an issue-voting rule.").

134. *Id.* at 744. The authors refer to such cases as presenting "paradoxical holdings." *Id.* at 766.

135. *Id.* at 745. The authors add that in such cases incoherence arises from "path dependence, precedent inconsistency, and paradoxical holdings," with the result that "it is obvious that outcome-voting should be disfavored." *Id.* at 770.

136. Lewis A. Kornhauser & Lawrence G. Sager, *The One and the Many: Adjudication in Collegial Courts,* 81 Cal. L. Rev. 1 (1993).

Instead, in those cases that the authors characterized as presenting the doctrinal paradox, the authors have proposed the following meta-vote regime:

> In a paradoxical case . . . the question of collegial agency is open and problematic. In such a case, a multi-judge court ought to make that question and its resolution an explicit, reflective, articulated, and formal part of its decision of the case. The judges should deliberate about the appropriate collegial action to take in the case before them, given their convictions about all those matters that they would be called on to determine were they deciding the case as individuals rather than as a group. They should vote on the question of collegial action as they would any other question, and they should proffer an opinion or several opinions justifying their metavote.[137]

In a critique of these articles,[138] John Rogers argued as follows:

> [F]or Professors Post and Salop to advocate issue voting in all cases, they must accept some results that will deeply embarrass the judicial system. If, for instance, there are three constitutional challenges to a criminal defendant's capital conviction and different groups of only three justices agree with each challenge, the criminal could be executed although all justices independently find the conviction unconstitutional. Post and Salop basically say, why not? One answer is that the polity that ultimately must accept judicial decisions will have a hard time accepting such a result. The only way to defend headlines like "JONES EXECUTED; ALL JUSTICES AGREE CONVICTION UNCONSTITUTIONAL" would be to explain that the justices voted issue-by-issue on what the law is, and the application of this law requires execution. But who made the decision? Who did the applying? Each justice can say that if the court had agreed with him or her, the defendant would not have been executed. But this is not how the public thinks judges should act. Judges should not be voting on the law like legislators but should be applying the law and bearing responsibility for the proper application of the law. It would fundamentally undermine the responsibility of the judiciary to permit, or require, judges to vote for results that they oppose.[139]

Rogers also criticized the Kornhauser and Sager proposed meta-voting regime:

> How should the metavote be taken if there are different majorities on determinative issues in the metavote? Should there be issue voting or outcome voting on the metavote? Neither answer is fully satisfactory. Outcome voting on the metavote could lead to the very sort of path

---

137. *Id.* at 30.

138. John M. Rogers, *"Issue Voting" by Multimember Appellate Courts: A Response to Some Radical Proposals*, 49 VAND. L. REV. 997 (1996). For a separate and comprehensive article in which Professor Rogers critiqued individual vote switches by justices seeking to avoid anomalous results in cases presenting the voting paradox, and claiming the absence of support in case history for those vote switches, see Rogers, *supra* note 132, at 439.

139. Rogers, *supra* note 138, at 1022 (footnotes omitted).

dependence that Kornhauser and Sager are trying to address. But deciding whether to have issue voting might require a meta-metavote. Nightmares of infinite regression are conceivable.[140]

Responding to a separate argument that issue voting is itself indeterminate because one can divide issues at multiple levels, in a later article Post and Salop advanced what they describe as an "issue decomposition rule":

> A *primary* issue on which multimember courts should vote is a question of law presented by a case that (a) is logically independent of any other questions presented by the case, in the sense that the question can be resolved as a logical matter without reference to any other accompanying questions, (b) is potentially dispositive of the outcome of the case, in the sense that resolution of the question can uniquely determine the outcome of the case, and (c) cannot be further decomposed into separate subquestions that fulfill criteria (a) and (b).[141]

The authors concede that this rule is only a partial solution to the indeterminacy objection, stating:

> This issue decomposition rule will produce a unique set of primary issues defined vertically. That is, it provides a manageable "stopping rule" for the vertical issue decomposition process. However, cases may present alternative primary issues at any level of decomposition defined horizontally.[142]

More recently, Professor Jonathan Remy Nash has proposed a "context-sensitive voting protocol," that he maintains avoids some of the difficulties with prior issue-voting proposals while presenting what he maintains is a preferred alternative to outcome voting.[143] Nash explains:

> Pure questions of law (once isolated in respect of separate causes of action or charges) should be treated without decomposition—that is, under outcome-based voting with respect to each question of law. [Such questions] present a setting where the risk of an intractable guidance problem flowing from the use of outcome-based voting is relatively low (though not . . . nonexistent).

> After outcome-based voting has been used to establish the proper (pure) legal standard governing a particular cause of action or charge, every application of law to fact under that standard should be determined separately, using issue-based voting. These situations are the counterpoint to pure questions of law: Application of issue-based voting is more likely to be fair, while outcome-based voting is more

---

140. *Id.* at 1025.

141. David G. Post & Steven C. Salop, *Issues and Outcomes, Guidance, and Indeterminacy: A Reply to Professor John Rogers and Others*, 49 VAND. L. REV. 1069, 1078 (1996).

142. *Id.* at 1083.

143. Jonathan Remy Nash, *A Context–Sensitive Voting Protocol Paradigm for Multimember Courts*, 56 STAN. L. REV. 75 (2003).

likely to generate guidance problems, especially for courts on remand and future courts.[144]

Professor Stearns has suggested a different approach to analyzing the seemingly anomalous results represented in both the voting paradox and vote-switch cases. The analysis, which relies upon social choice theory, is intended as a positive, or explanatory, account of existing Supreme Court voting protocols. This analysis explains appellate court reliance upon the combined regime of outcome and the narrowest grounds doctrine, rather than issue voting,[145] along with other anomalies that arise over larger groups of cases over time.

In Stearns's analysis, the Court's rules are best understood as staged responses to specific collective decision-making anomalies that social choice proves uniquely well suited to explain. Each incremental improvement presents another social choice difficulty that becomes the target of the next staged judicial response. The net result of the staged decision-making rules is to substantially narrow—without ever entirely eliminating—the inherent difficulty in transforming the aggregate judicial preferences in specific cases into outcomes that generally (but again, imperfectly) satisfy the Arrovian conditions of rationality and fairness.

3.   A Social Choice Account of Supreme Court Voting Rules

Stearns's analysis returns us to the paradox of voting. Recall that when individuals hold the following preferences (P1: ABC, P2: BCA; P3: CAB), there is an intransitivity such that ApBpCpA. In contrast, when we change the preferences of P3 to CBA, option B emerges the Condorcet winner, defeating both A and C in direct binary comparisons. Neither of these two preference sets—that which contains and that which lacks a Condorcet winner—includes a first choice majority candidate. And yet, the principle of majority rule produces a meaningful social choice in the second case where option B is a dominant second choice of P1 and P3.

When the Supreme Court issues unanimous or majority decisions, there is no social choice problem. In either instance, a majority of the Court agrees with a single rationale justifying the case judgment. The social choice difficulty thus arises in a smaller subset of cases in which there is not a single majority opinion. Within that category, there are two paradigmatic cases. In the first, the Court typically issues a plurality opinion and one or more concurrences in the judgment that together form the majority for the case judgment. In the second, the Court fractures not merely on rationale, but also on the judgment itself.

In practice, the three-judgment case has not proved a serious problem.[146] In each case that has split the Court over three judgments—affirm, remand, reverse—none with majority support, one or more Justices em-

---

144. *Id.* at 147–48 (footnotes omitted). For a critique of the Nash proposal and others, see Michael I. Meyerson, *The Irrational Supreme Court*, 84 NEB. L. REV. 895, 949–51 (2006).

145. 430 U.S. 188 (1977).

146. *See* STEARNS, *supra* note 96, at 153–54; Stearns, *supra* note 113, at 109.

bracing one of the more extreme positions (affirm or reverse) has opted to vote for the intermediate remand outcome. This problem has tended to arise in criminal cases, and the jurist who has exhibited a willingness to depart from his ideal point on the judgment has stated that it would not be acceptable in such a case for the Court to decline to give clear guidance on how to formally dispose of the case.[147]

This informal solution in three-judgment cases might be less counter-intuitive than it first appears. On the narrow question of judgment, especially in a criminal case, most jurists would likely view the choice among the three judgments as resting along a single normative dimension, captured by pro-defendant to pro-government on the particular set of case facts. Those who would embrace one extreme position are quite likely to prefer a middle ground (pro-defendant unless ... or pro-government unless ...) to a position that embraces the opposite judgment (absolutely pro-defendant or absolutely pro-government). If we imagine three camps, one favoring each judgment, and if P1 seeks to affirm (A), P2 seeks to remand (B), and P3 seeks to reverse (C), the likely preferences are P1: ABC and P3: CBA. The ordinal rankings for P2 do not matter because in either event (BCA or BAC), B emerges the Condorcet winner.

This is not to suggest that there are no conditions under which it is plausible to imagine a jurist preferring one extreme (affirm or reverse) to the opposite extreme (reverse or affirm) to the seeming middle ground (remand). A Justice might, for example, prefer to have a broad constitutional protection in a given area of constitutional law, but if not successful, prefer to cut off litigation rather than invite a complex body of constitutional common law. Or conversely, a Justice might hold the opposite view, preferring to close off a body of constitutional doctrine, but preferring a clear set of protections to a complex body of constitutional law. However plausible such preferences might be, Stearns demonstrates that they have not manifested themselves in any actual Supreme Court decision. Instead, through this sort of informal accommodation, the justices have effectively "solved" the theoretical difficulty that three-judgment cases appear to present. The social choice problem is more significant, however, with respect to a subset of cases within the remaining category, involving fractured panel decisions.

As we have previously seen, this subgroup of cases divide into two general categories. The more common category involves cases resting along a unidimensional issue spectrum. In such cases, it is most plausible to intuit a set of preferences over the various opinions that generate stable outcomes similar to that in the three-judgment case. To take a simple paradigm, one that finds reflection in *Casey*, imagine that one group of Justices seeks to affirm a murder conviction finding that the claimed

---

147. This presents an interesting doctrinal question. Although the formal rule articulated in *Marks* only applies when a majority agrees to a single judgment, would a lower court be justified in applying the logic of the narrowest grounds rule in a three-judgment case in which no justice solved the problem by moving toward the median to nonetheless select the remand as the controlling outcome? Why or why not?

Fourth Amendment violation does not apply to state courts; a second group of Justices seeks to reverse the conviction on the ground that it rested on the admission of evidence obtained without a warrant, and thus in violation of the Fourteenth Amendment, which through the incorporation doctrine applies the Bill of Rights to the states; and a third group accepts the incorporation doctrine, but would allow the state to avoid the obligation of a warrant in exigent circumstances, which it finds lacking on the case facts. For simplicity, we can label the first group as Liberal, the second as Conservative, and the third as Moderate. Stearns explains that in such cases it is most intuitive to imagine that the first group would rank its preferences Liberal, Moderate, Conservative, and the second group would rank its preferences Conservative, Moderate, Liberal. The ordinal rankings of the middle group do not matter; either way, that position emerges the Condorcet winner.

In such cases, under the *Marks* rule, the Moderate opinion expresses the Court's holding. Of the two opinions consistent with the outcome, the Liberal and the Moderate opinions, the latter would reverse fewer convictions on constitutional grounds because it finds some cases in which the state can secure evidence without a warrant. Notice that in this hypothetical, while the opinions can be cast along single normative issue dimension, the case presents more than a single dispositive legal issue.[148] The Justices have to determine if the Fourth Amendment applies, and if so, if it provides the basis for relief on the case facts.[149] While we do not have complete information for each camp, with reasonable assumptions, we can intuit these preferences. The Liberals find the Fourth Amendment applies via incorporation and that it provides relief on the case facts. The Conservatives find it not to apply, but we could infer that if they had to assess the merits of the claim, they would find that the absence of the warrant was justified on the case facts. If so, then the Liberal and Conservative camps would have resolved both issues in opposite fashion, and those contrary issue resolutions would have led them to opposite judgments with the Liberals seeking to reverse and the Conservative seeking to affirm.[150]

Based upon the preceding analysis, Stearns explains that Supreme Court decision-making rules, which have developed in response to specific problems that social choice helps to identify, produce ongoing difficulties in aggregating judicial preferences only in an exceedingly narrow category class of cases. Ongoing difficulties do not arise in unanimous, majority, or three-judgment cases (this last one for practical, rather than theoretical,

---

148. For a discussion of the difference between dimensionality as used to express issues and as used to express the preconditions to cycling, see *supra* chapter 3, section II.G.1.

149. In a separate work, Stearns further divides the categories into unidimensionality, multidimensionality and symmetry, and multidimensionality and asymmetry. The second category, like the first, conduces to a Condorcet winner, captured in the narrowest grounds rule. STEARNS, *supra* note 96, at 77; Stearns, *supra* note 113, at 109.

150. In his article on vote switching, Professor Stearns formalized this as presenting a case of multidimensionality and symmetry, meaning that opposite issue resolutions produce opposite judgments. Stearns, *supra* note 113, at 117–21.

reasons). Instead, they arise only in fractured panel cases. And even within that narrow category, the problems arise in a small subset. The Court does not confront any difficulty aggregating preferences in those cases in which the issues (even if multiple) can be cast along a single normative dimension, for example, the scope of abortion protection, per *Casey*, or the scope of Fourth Amendment protection, per the preceding hypothetical. Instead, the Court only confronts difficulty in a very narrow category in which the opinions of the Justices rest along more than a single issue dimension, and in which the opinions possess the defining characteristics of multidimensionality and asymmetry.[151] As previously explained, asymmetry implies that those Justices who hold opposite preferences concerning the resolution of dispositive case issues nonetheless agree to the case judgment, while the Justices in dissent resolve one issue in favor of each camp favoring an opposite judgment. We have seen this in the presentation of *Kassel*.

Recall that in that case, Justice Brennan determined that the relevant substantive test in evaluating the challenged Iowa statute was the less strict rational basis test, and that the relevant evidentiary rule was the stricter rule, preventing the introduction of newly developed trial evidence that was not considered by the enacting legislature. In contrast, Justice Powell determined that the relevant test was the stricter balancing test and that the relevant evidentiary rule was the less strict rule allowing newly presented trial evidence. Justice Rehnquist, writing in dissent, applied the less strict version of both tests. While Justices Brennan and Powell resolved both issues in opposite fashion, their opposite resolutions nonetheless led them to the same judgment. In contrast, Justice Rehnquist resolved one issue in favor of Brennan (the more relaxed substantive test) and one issue in favor of Powell (the more relaxed evidentiary rule), and yet voted for the opposite judgment.

Stearns further explains that the voting anomaly manifests itself in *Kassel* for an important reason. In order to determine the logical ordinal rankings over these opinions, we would need to know whether Justices Powell and Brennan are more concerned with having one of the two substantive issues resolved in their preferred manner (in which case they rank the Rehnquist opinion second and each other's opinion third), or instead are more concerned with how the case as a whole is resolved (in which case they rank each other's opinion second, and Rehnquist's opinion third). Of course it is possible that one cares more about one of the substantive issues, while the other cares more about the case judgment. As we have previously shown, based upon reasonable assumptions along these lines, it is possible to construct a forward or a backward cycle.

Once again, this analysis does not rest upon the validity of specific assumptions made to demonstrate intransitive judicial preferences. Because of the actual Supreme Court decision-making rules, which limit the information that the Justices produce, it is not possible to know how each

---

151. For a discussion of dimensionality and symmetry, see *supra* chapter 3, section II.G.1.

camp would rank the packaged set of alternative issue resolutions presented in the various opinions. Instead, the analysis demonstrates a narrower point concerning the precise conditions under which one can reasonably infer intransitive judicial preferences.[152] It is the combination of multidimensionality and asymmetry that produces the anomaly. No single Justice writing in *Kassel* would apply the more lax substantive test (rational basis) and the more lax evidentiary rule (allowing in new evidence) to strike down the challenged Iowa statute. And yet, that is precisely what the combined logic of the opinions suggests. This is indeed a problem of social choice, but an exceedingly narrow one that arises as a consequence of the Court's sequential decision-making rules.

Consider once more the literature concerning the choice of issue versus outcome voting. Stearns suggests that we imagine locking the Justices into agreeing that the two identified issues in *Kassel*—the choice of substantive test and the choice of evidentiary rule—are controlling. We could then embrace either of two voting regimes. First, we could hold a controlling vote on the outcome—affirm or reverse—and then assess the various independent rationales at the opinion stage. This is the actual regime that the Court employs. Alternatively, we could have the Justices vote on the identified controlling issues and allow the logic of the separate issue resolutions to control the case outcome with no separate outcome vote. Or we could define categories in which each voting protocol applies. These are the rules advocated by those preferring issue voting, either as a general rule (Post and Salop), through a meta-vote (Kornhauser and Sager), or through a context specific protocol (Nash). In cases like *Kassel*, the choice of protocol controls the ultimate case disposition. Under outcome voting, the result is to strike down the challenged Iowa statute. Under any of the identified issue-voting regimes, the result (at least assuming that the justices use their meta-vote as intended) is to instead sustain the challenged law.

While the outcome- and issue-voting rules lead to opposite outcomes, Stearns claims that it is important to recognize an important feature that these rules hold in common. Remember that social choice reveals that to determine if an outcome is a socially significant choice or the arbitrary product of a voting regime, we must allow as many binary comparisons as options. Rules that satisfy the Condorcet criterion or, using Arrow's terminology, that satisfy range, meet this condition. Recall that range requires that the decision-making rule select an outcome that is consistent with each person's ordinal rankings over three or more options.[153] *Kassel* presents no fewer than three questions that control the case outcome. While this can be presented in various ways, the following phrasing is helpful in highlighting the voting anomaly:

(1) Should the Court apply the more lenient substantive test (rational basis)? Yes.

---

152. As previously shown, the assumptions necessary to posit a cycle are no more or less reasonable than those necessary to posit a stable second choice.

153. *See supra* chapter 3, section III.B.

(2) Should the Court apply the more relaxed evidentiary rule (admitting novel evidence)? Yes.

(3) Should the Court sustain the challenged Iowa statute? No.

With all three questions permitted, Stearns demonstrates, we see that separate majorities answer yes to questions (1) (Brennan and Rehnquist) and (2) (Powell and Rehnquist). As a logical matter, this would lead to sustaining the challenged statute, the result obtained under the issue-voting regime defined above. But taking the third vote produces the opposite "no" outcome (Brennan and Powell), the actual result under outcome voting in *Kassel.*

Stearns explains that both voting regimes provide stable outcomes. Each does so by preventing the requisite number of binary comparisons to reveal a cycle. For this reason, both voting rules also defy the Arrovian range criterion. Once again, each does so by effectively preventing an outcome consistent with the preferences of all jurists over all conceivable rank orderings, since that would threaten an intransitive, and thus unstable, outcome. Given that both of these voting rules equally defy range (and the Condorcet criterion) and equally ensure a stable outcome (at least on the assumption that we know the dispositive issues), why has the Supreme Court, along with virtually all appellate courts, opted for outcome voting *especially given* that this rule is susceptible of such anomalous outcomes as seen in *Kassel* and *Fulminante?*

Stearns argues that the answer rests with an analytical flaw in the issue-voting arguments, which economists refer to as "endogeneity."[154] Endogeneity, in this context, means that some outcomes arise as a function of the internal processes that produce them. Conversely, an outcome is exogenous when it exists in a consistent form without regard to the decision-making rule. Stearns demonstrates that the selection of an issue-voting rule has the potential to motivate the Justices to identify issues differently than they presently do under the outcome-voting rule.[155] Justices who are more concerned with a case judgment than with how the case issues should be resolved will attempt to forge a voting path that leads to their preferred case judgment. The resulting selection of issues might well be different than those that obtain in the present regime, which effectively gives Justices the following command: Identify your preferred *outcome* and then construct the most persuasive opinion that will encourage a majority of your colleagues to join you (or that will retain your initial majority coalition)[156] in achieving that outcome. Stearns contends that advocates of the various issue-voting regimes have failed to appreciate that the issues over which judicial preferences occasionally cycle in voting paradox cases arise as an endogenous function of the Supreme Court's outcome-voting rule. Consider in this regard, for exam-

154. *See* Maxwell L. Stearns, *How Outcome Voting Promotes Principled Issue Identification: A Reply to Professor John Rogers and Others,* 49 VAND. L. REV. 1045 (1996).

155. *See id.*

156. For a study of coalition formation in the Supreme Court, see MALTZMAN, SPRIGGS, & WAHLBECK, *supra* note 37.

ple, the concession by Professors Post and Salop that while their issue decomposition rule works *vertically*, it will not ensure a stable resolution of issues defined *horizontally*.[157] As the authors use these terms, which level of division is more likely to match cases in which cycling is apt to occur?

Most importantly, Stearns argues, the selection of issue versus outcome voting *will not* merely affect the choice of voting regime in the narrow class of cases in which the voting paradox arises. Instead, because it creates an opportunity for the strategic identification of governing issues, it will also present the opportunity to affect the far larger corpus of cases—those presently captured by a fractured panel on a single issue dimension, majority, and even unanimity cases—by inviting Justices to identify issues strategically, rather than in a principled effort to devise the most persuasive means of forging or retaining a successful coalition in favor of a preferred case resolution. By effectively divorcing the selection of case outcome from the identification of a voting path, Stearns argues, outcome voting encourages principle rather than strategy as the primary determinant governing the identification of dispositive issues. While judicial preferences occasionally cycle over the identified governing issues, that is an inevitable outcome of a collective decision-making process. Fixing it, however, might create incentives to behave strategically over the larger body of Supreme Court case law.

Now let us return to the social choice account of the narrowest grounds rule. The Supreme Court occasionally issues fractured panel decisions under the outcome-voting regime and a small subset of such cases—those characterized by multidimensionality and asymmetry—produce a voting anomaly. Stearns demonstrates that when the Supreme Court issues a fractured panel (or non-majority) decision, the *Marks* rule ensures that those cases that possess a stable center of gravity (a Condorcet winner), will express that opinion in the form of a holding. The combined effect of outcome voting and the narrowest grounds rule, therefore, is to encourage case resolutions (relaxing range and the Condorcet criterion), while promoting principled decision making (adhering to what Arrow defined as independence of irrelevant alternatives).[158] And at the same time, in the majority of cases in which there actually is a Condorcet winning opinion, the narrowest grounds rule comes in at the end to locate it and give it controlling status. In this analysis, only in the narrow class of fractured panel cases in which the opinions cannot be cast along a common normative dimension and in which preferences are assymetrical, does the voting anomaly—and thus an analytical impasse under *Marks*—have the potential to arise.

---

157. *See supra* p. 436. For a discussion demonstrating the ability to use creative issue definitions in *National Mutual Insurance Co. v. Tidewater Transfer Co.*, 337 U.S. 582 (1949), a case presenting a voting paradox, so as to forge an unintended outcome under the proposed issue-voting regime, see Stearns, *supra* note 154, at 1059–61.

158. *See supra* chapter 3, section III.B.

4. Questions and Comments

Do you think that the social choice analysis is sufficient to counter arguments for issue voting as a general alternative to outcome voting? Is it sufficient to counter arguments for a meta-voting rule, per Kornhauser and Sager or a context-specific use of issue voting, per Nash? If so, what are the difficulties with the various issue-voting proposals? If not, what is the difficulty with the social choice analysis?

Do you agree with Judge Rogers that Justices should not defer to contrary majorities in the resolution of dispositive case issues? Why or why not? Do you agree with Rogers that such a vote switch is unprincipled? What does Rogers mean by unprincipled? What is the proper normative baseline for making the assertion as to principled or unprincipled voting? Are there any circumstances in which a vote switch is appropriate? Is there a principled way to narrow the class of such cases for which vote switching is or is not proper and if so, how would you articulate the distinction?

Are Supreme Court Justices generally likely to be more concerned with case outcomes or with the resolution of controlling issues within cases? How does your answer to this question affect your choice of issue versus outcome voting? How does it affect the answer to whether you would condone frequent or occasional vote switching?

Is the narrowest grounds rule normatively defensible? Do cases like *Kassel* and *Fulminante*, in which the doctrine's underlying logic fails, undermine the rule's validity? If you conclude that it is not defensible, what rule would you replace it with? Is plurality rule better than the narrowest grounds rule for fractured panel Supreme Court cases? Why or why not?

D. MACRO–ANALYSIS OF SUPREME COURT VOTING RULES: A SOCIAL CHOICE ACCOUNT OF HORIZONTAL STARE DECISIS AND STANDING

1. Ways of Criticizing The Court: The Social Choice Case Against Strict Stare Decisis

Judge (then-Professor) Frank Easterbrook has relied upon social choice to challenge, among other things, the logical foundations of stare decisis in the Supreme Court.[159] His analysis rests on a dynamic account of developing doctrine and provides the basis for an important comparison with the Stearns's social choice analysis of Supreme Court decision-making rules. Easterbrook maintains that all of Arrow's fairness conditions—range, independence of irrelevant alternatives, unanimity, and nondictatorship—apply. As a resulting positive matter, Easterbrook claims that it is not possible for the Court to ensure transitive or rational doctrine. Easterbrook suggests therefore that over time the Court might develop a stock of precedent that will "allow[] the Justices to 'prove'

---

159. *See* Frank H. Easterbrook, *Ways of Criticizing the Court*, 95 HARV. L. REV. 802 (1982).

anything they like, without fear of contradiction."[160] As a normative matter, Easterbrook criticizes the value of adhering to stare decisis in those cases in which, as a result, doctrine is affected by the order of precedent. Easterbrook states:

> The upshot of stare decisis is that the meaning of . . . [some] constitutional [doctrines] . . . [is] uncertain; everything depends on the fortuitous order of decision. Yet this is plainly unsatisfactory; no sensible theory of constitutional adjudication, interpretive or noninterpretive, allows such happenstance to determine the course of the law. The order of decisions has nothing to do with the intent of the framers or any of the other things that might inform constitutional interpretation.[161]

Easterbrook argues that the "best way out of the trap of path dependence (but not out of the problem of cycling) is to relax or abandon stare decisis when there are three or more competing positions."[162] Easterbrook further notes that in some contexts, the Justices express views in separate opinions—sometimes leading to fractured decisions for the Court as a whole—that do not accord with existing precedent. Easterbrook states:

> This is essentially what the Court has done, and the result is exactly what the critics decry: plurality decisions with each of three (or more) positions expressed; Justices who adhere to their views despite intervening cases' apparently inconsistent decisions; the revisiting of rules adopted and abandoned in the past. . . . For all the objections to this outcome, it seems preferable to an aggravated form of path dependence, under which the Court adopts and adheres to positions that a majority of the Justices find constitutionally untenable.[163]

Are you persuaded by Easterbrook's positive account of Supreme Court decision making? Why or why not? Are you persuaded by his suggestion that the Court should relax precedent to avoid path dependence? Bear these questions in mind as you read Professor Stearns's alternative social choice account presented below.

In contrast with Easterbrook, who claims that the Supreme Court adheres to all of Arrow's fairness conditions, but relaxes transitivity, Stearns claims that the Supreme Court relaxes range, thus allowing the court to produce generally (but not perfectly) stable doctrine (thus pro-

---

160. *Id.* at 831.

161. *Id.* at 819–20.

162. *Id.* at 820.

163. *Id.* at 820–21. Easterbrook's analysis raises an additional question about collegial courts such as the Supreme Court, namely *whose* precedents should count? Easterbrook notes that some Justices adhere to their previously expressed opinions consistently despite contrary precedent for the Court as a whole. *See supra* pp. 434–35 (illustrating with opinions by Justices Thurgood Marshall and William Brennan, who regularly claimed that the death penalty violated the Eighth Amendment prohibition against cruel and unusual punishment despite clear contrary Supreme Court rulings). Such Justices evidently believe that they are furthering the goals of stare decisis by adhering to consistency with their "personal" precedents, rather than the Court's precedents. Is this position defensible? Why or why not?

moting transitivity) over considerable bodies of case law. Stearns thus offers both a differing set of premises and a differing set of normative conclusions about Supreme Court decision-making rules than Easterbrook, notably including the implications of social choice analysis for the doctrine of stare decisis.

2. Constitutional Process: A Positive Social Choice Account of Stare Decisis and Standing

In his dynamic model of Supreme Court decision making, Stearns demonstrates that the problem of intransitive judicial preferences can arise not only within individual cases, as shown above, but also across groups of cases over time. Stearns offers a social choice assessment of Supreme Court voting rules affecting the larger development of constitutional doctrine, with a particular emphasis on horizontal stare decisis and standing. The analysis is analytically parallel to the prior social choice account of outcome voting and the narrowest grounds rule.

Even in cases in which the Court issues majority decisions, there are circumstances in which the Court's members manifest intransitive preferences over larger groups of cases. To illustrate, consider two actual cases that the Court decided on the same day in 1982, *Washington v. Seattle School District No. 1*[164] and *Crawford v. Board of Education*.[165] Both cases involved the question whether a state that was not previously subject to de jure segregation, but which had taken affirmative steps to integrate its public schools, could be prevented by a state constitutional amendment or a statewide initiative from taking further integrative steps beyond that which is constitutionally required without running afoul of the requirements of equal protection set out in the Fourteenth Amendment or, in the case of Washington State, that plus the parallel state equal protection requirement.

In *Crawford*, California had passed a state constitutional amendment that prevented state courts from ordering integrative busing unless the court first determined that a federal court would find that the order was necessary to remedy a violation of the Fourteenth Amendment Equal Protection Clause. Writing for a majority of six, Justice Powell sustained the amendment against a federal equal protection challenge. Brennan wrote a concurrence for two, and Marshall dissented alone. In *Seattle*, the state passed a statewide referendum that prevented local school boards from ordering integrative busing unless necessary to avoid a violation of either the state or federal equal protection requirements. Writing for a majority of five, Justice Blackmun struck down this referendum. Powell wrote a dissent for four. To explain the voting anomaly that these cases present, Stearns presents the following voting line-up in the two cases: [166]

---

164. Washington v. Seattle Sch. Dist. No. 1, 458 U.S. 457 (1982).

165. Crawford v. Bd. of Educ., 458 U.S. 527 (1982).

166. STEARNS, *supra* note 96, at 28 tbl.1.2.

Table 7:7. Supreme Court Voting Line-up in *Seattle* and *Crawford*

Seattle		
Majority		*Dissent*
Blackmun Marshall* Brennan White Stevens		Powell* Burger* Rehnquist* O'Connor*

Crawford		
Majority	*Concurrence*	*Dissent*
Powell* Burger* Rehnquist* O'Connor* Stevens White	Brennan Blackmun	Marshall*

In Table 7:7, asterisks appear next to the names of five Justices, Chief Justice Burger and Justices Powell, Rehnquist, and O'Connor, who joined the majority opinion in *Crawford* and the *Seattle* dissent, and Justice Marshall, who joined the majority in *Seattle*, and who alone dissented in *Crawford*. In his dissenting opinion in *Crawford*, Marshall maintained that although the Court had decided *Crawford* and *Seattle* in opposite fashion, the two cases were constitutionally indistinguishable. In his dissenting opinion in *Seattle*, Justice Powell rejected each argument offered to distinguish the two cases. As a matter of substantive equal protection law, one can certainly debate whether the two cases are indistinguishable, but for purposes of the social choice analysis, resolving this debate is unnecessary. Whatever the merits of arguments drawn to distinguish the cases, a majority of the Court—Powell, Burger, Rehnquist, O'Connor, and Marshall—conclude that the cases should be decided in the same manner. And yet, the Court as a whole, in two separate majority opinions issued on the same day, resolved them in opposite fashion.

At this point, the social choice implications should be intuitive. Stearns identifies three separate and overlapping majorities. One majority seeks to sustain the *Crawford* amendment against the equal protection challenge. A second majority seeks to strike down the *Seattle* initiative based upon equal protection. And a third majority seeks to resolve these cases in a consistent fashion such that either both are upheld or both are struck down. Obviously it is not possible to simultaneously satisfy all three majorities.

To highlight the anomaly, imagine that the two cases were issued sequentially, one year apart, rather than on the same day. If we assume that the Justices vote consistently with their preferences as expressed in the opinions that they drafted or joined in the actual *Crawford* and *Seattle* case, the order in which the cases were presented for decision would have fully controlled the outcomes in both cases. Thus, if *Crawford* arose first, the Court would have sustained the challenged law. If *Seattle* came up one year later, the five Justices with asterisks next to their names would not have asked how to resolve the case as a matter of first impression, but rather, they would have asked whether *Crawford* controlled *Seattle*. Stearns observes that if we assume that the Justices resolved this sincerely (according to the expressed views in the actual cases and thus consistently with the independence criterion), they would answer yes, and based upon stare decisis, would vote to sustain the *Seattle* initiative, with the result that both laws are sustained. Conversely, if *Seattle* were decided first, a majority would have voted to strike down the challenged initiative. One year later when *Crawford* is presented, the same five Justices would ask if *Seattle* governs *Crawford*, and applying the same logic, would vote to strike down the *Crawford* amendment as well, with the result that both laws are struck down. The actual cases were presented at the same time, such that neither case was a controlling precedent on the other. As a result, Stearns explains, the *Crawford* amendment was sustained and the *Seattle* initiative was struck down, thus thwarting the crossover majority of Justices who determined that the cases should have been decided in like manner.

Now consider the implications of this analysis for the doctrine of stare decisis. As we have already seen, social choice demonstrates the need for the same number of binary comparisons as options if we seek to determine the social significance of the eventual outcome or set of outcomes. Within legislatures, for example, it is commonplace to limit the number of votes relative to options through any number of formal rules, for example, a limit on amendments, or a prohibition on reconsideration of defeated alternatives.[167] If there are more options than permitted amendments, or if defeated options cannot be resurrected and pitted against the option poised to be chosen, it is not possible to know whether the outcome is a Condorcet winner or the product of a voting path. The common practice of preventing reconsideration of defeated alternatives thus ensures an outcome, but does so at the cost of uncertainty as to that outcome's social significance. Relying on this analysis, Stearns presents stare decisis as the judicial equivalent of this time-honored cycle-breaking rule that works to ensure that an option defeated in a prior case cannot be brought back to undermine a later judicial outcome.

Crawford and *Seattle* illustrate the analysis. These two cases presented three binary choices: (1) uphold or strike the California amendment (*Crawford*); (2) uphold or strike the Washington referendum (*Seattle*); and

---

167. William H. Riker, *The Paradox of Voting and Congressional Rules for Voting on Amendments*, 52 AM. POL. SCI. REV. 349 (1958) (discussing Congressional rule limiting votes relative to options); *see also supra* chapter 3, section II.G.

(3) decide the cases consistently or inconsistently (stare decisis). The rule of stare decisis effectively takes one of the options off the table, namely the choice to decide the second case—the one subject to prior precedent—on its independent merits without regard to the obligation of precedent. In doing so, stare decisis has the potential to ground substantive case outcomes in the order in which the cases are presented and decided. *Crawford* followed by *Seattle* produces opposite holdings in both cases as compared with *Seattle* followed by *Crawford*.

Stearns maintains that the social choice analysis demonstrates that while stare decisis renders the substantive evolution of doctrine path dependent—meaning that the outcomes will be affected by the order of cases—the real problem is not the fortuitous effect of timing on doctrine. Recall that the fortuity of decision was the normative basis for Easterbrook's claim that social choice provides a basis for relaxing stare decisis.[168] In contrast, Stearns argues that as a normative matter, some degree of doctrinal arbitrariness dictated by the fortuitous order of case decisions in a regime of stare decisis is acceptable, provided that the process through which case orders are set is accepted as legitimate. In Stearns's analysis, the primary difficulty that stare decisis creates is not path dependence, but rather is the resulting incentive among ideological interest groups to time cases for maximal doctrinal effect. In short, litigants intuitively grasp the significance of case orderings as a consequence of stare decisis in formulating test cases and in seeking to present the most favorable cases first. Stearns also notes that stare decisis is a presumptive doctrine that stabilizes doctrine over the short to moderate term, which the Court sometimes relaxes (formally overruling in only a small number of cases) when over time cycles eventually manifest themselves doctrinally.

Stearns argues that at a time when the Court is particularly prone to possessing cyclical preferences, the Court had an incentive to erect defenses to potential litigant path manipulation. Stearns's social choice analysis demonstrates that the Supreme Court's standing rules operate to improve the likelihood that fortuitous historical events—an act producing an injury that is caused by someone else and that is susceptible of meaningful judicial redress—rather than the desire to present better cases early on in an effort to develop preferred doctrine, presumptively control the order of cases that have the potential to affect substantive doctrine. In Stearns's analysis, the standing rules do not prevent doctrinal path dependence, which is an inevitable consequence of stare decisis, but rather they raise the cost of deliberate path manipulation.[169]

---

168. *See* Easterbrook, *supra* note 159, at 818.

169. Stearns also explains stare decisis within (but not across) circuit courts as consistent with this social choice account. *See* STEARNS, *supra* note 96, at 197–98. Stearns explains:

Because the evolution of legal doctrine within the circuit will sometimes be the arbitrary product of path dependence, the Supreme Court has [an incentive] ... to ensure that the doctrine of stare decisis is adhered to *within* but not *among* the circuits. *Intra-* but not *inter-* circuit stare decisis avoids the indeterminacy that would result from cyclical preferences within each circuit. At the same time, the regime ensures that path-dependent iterations, which

Once again, in Stearns's analysis, social choice suggests that through staged rules, one rule breaking down cyclical preferences—outcome voting in individual cases and stare decisis in groups of cases over time—the Supreme Court improves the rationality of its outcomes. And then a second rule—the narrowest grounds rule in individual cases and standing in groups of cases over time—improves the fairness of the process through which substantive outcomes are selected.[170]

3. Questions and Comments

Standing is among the most contentious Supreme Court doctrines. Legal scholars fault the doctrine for inconsistent applications and claim that the results are often the product of political rather than principled concerns. Does Stearns's social choice analysis avoid these criticisms of standing doctrine? Does social choice provide a means of reconciling the seeming inconsistencies of standing with a principled set of normative justifications?

Does the social choice analysis of stare decisis help to explain the doctrine's evolution within pyramidal courts? Does it help to explain why the doctrine applies within appellate panels—either of three or en banc—when it does not apply among individual jurists acting as trial courts? Can you explain why federal circuit courts do not give stare decisis effect to each other's opinions, while they do so internally? Does social choice help to answer this question? Why or why not?

Easterbrook claims that the Supreme Court adheres to all Arrovian fairness conditions, but relaxes transitivity, while Stearns claims that the the Supreme Court generally relaxes range, but adheres to the other Arrovian conditions, including independence of irrelevant alternatives. Which account provides a stronger positive account of Supreme Court doctrines affecting individual cases? Which provides a stronger positive account of Supreme Court doctrines over groups of cases over time? Which offers the basis for a stronger normative argument concerning the role of stare decisis and standing? Why?

E. IS THE COMMON LAW EFFICIENT?

We now turn from the Supreme Court to common law courts. The question addressed in this subsection is whether common law courts are rationally motivated to produce (or not produce) efficient doctrine. While Judge Posner's focus was Article III rather than common law judges, his question—*What do judges maximize?*—is also relevant in evaluating judi-

---

produce arbitrary bodies of law within a given circuit, are not automatically replicated across the circuits.

Id. at 197.

170. Stearns further explains the complementary nature of certiorari and standing doctrine in minimizing the most egregious effects of litigant path manipulation. *See* STEARNS, *supra* note 96, at 197 (demonstrating that with only certiorari but no standing, ideologically motivated litigants could effectively time circuit splits in a manner that would render Supreme Court docket control illusory).

cial motivations to move the common law toward, or away from, efficiency. The first "wave" of law and economics scholarship was motivated to explain common law rules in terms that transcended the doctrinal accounts expressed in published judicial opinions. Early law and economics scholars used neoclassical microeconomic theory to identify linkages between bodies of case law and incentives to move resources to their most highly valued uses, whether the relevant body of doctrine involved contract, tort, or property.

Our focus here is not on the specific efficiency analyses of common law doctrines. We are instead interested in the nature of the institutions, or the decision-making processes, that effect the development of efficient—and sometimes inefficient—common law rules. Using the principles of economic reasoning, is it possible to identify conditions that are likely to render common law courts more or less prone to producing case results— even if not captured in formally articulated doctrines—that prove consistent with an efficient understanding of governing rules? What are those conditions likely to be? How have they changed over time?

1. A Supply Side Analysis of Common Law Efficiency

In earlier scholarship, then-Professor Richard Posner posited that judges are likely to prefer supplying efficient rules because such rules are welfare enhancing.[171] Thus, Posner states: "[T]he economic norm I call 'wealth maximization' provides a firmer basis for a normative theory of [judge-made] law than does utilitarianism."[172]

Todd Zywicki has suggested several problems with this argument:[173]

First, it is difficult to verify because we cannot read judges' minds to determine their preferences or the extent to which their preferences explain case outcomes. Second, Posner's assumption seems inconsistent with the observation that many judges are at least as concerned with redistributive goals as efficiency goals. In fact, common experience indicates that many judges have strong tastes for distributional goals, and that they pursue these goals in their judicial role. Third, it fails to explain why the common law might evolve in an efficient manner at some times during history, but inefficiently at other times.... Fourth, it is questionable whether even the most well-intentioned judge possesses the expertise and knowledge to devise efficient legal rules where he or she desires to do so.[174]

Whatever the merits of Posner's account, notice that it is ultimately operates on the supply side, asking what motivates judges to provide efficient common law rules.

---

171. Richard A. Posner, *Utilitarianism, Economics, and Legal Theory*, 8 J. LEGAL STUD. 103 (1979).

172. *Id.* at 103.

173. *See* Zywicki, *supra* note 86, at 1563.

174. *Id.* (footnote omitted).

2.   A Demand Side Analysis of Common Law Efficiency[175]

Professor Paul Rubin, an economist, sought to untangle the common law efficiency question in a manner that avoids the assertion that the common law is efficient because judges seek efficiency.[176] Rubin instead proposed a demand side explanation of common law efficiency where the tendency toward the efficiency in the common law arises from an "invisible hand" process of private litigation, and thus without regard to the preferences of individual jurists.

Rubin claimed that common law efficiency is affected by the balance of interests on the two sides of litigation. As noted above, a precedent can be expressed as a capital good that generates a stream of rents taking the form of judicial rulings. Favorable precedents are of the greatest value to those who anticipate being repeat players. For instance, in tort law cases, firms are disproportionately likely to be defendants and thus to favor pro-defendant rules while plaintiff's lawyers are likely to prefer liability-expanding rules.[177] In other cases, for example, one involving a car accident between two private parties, neither party anticipates being a repeat player, and thus each is primarily concerned with the particular case outcome. In still other cases, anticipated repeat players appear on one side of the law and not the other.

Rubin argues that at least to some extent the outcome in a case will reflect the resources that parties invest in the case. Repeat players will generally be more willing to invest in creating a beneficial precedent than non-repeat players. Rubin envisions three paradigmatic cases. In the first, both parties are interested in the precedent and are thus willing to invest accordingly, with a resulting tendency toward efficiency. Rubin explains:

> If rules are inefficient, there will be an incentive for the party held liable to force litigation; if rules are efficient, there will be no such incentive. Thus, efficient rules will be maintained, and inefficient rules litigated until overturned.[178]

In the second, only one party has an interest in the precedent itself (as distinguished from the case outcome). Rubin argues:

> [T]here will be pressure for precedents to evolve in favor of that party which does have a stake in future cases, whether or not this is the

---

175. Portions of this discussion are based upon STEARNS, *supra* note 60, at 779–84.

176. Paul H. Rubin, *Why Is the Common Law Efficient?*, 6 J. LEGAL STUD. 51, 53 (1977) [hereinafter *Why is the Common Law Efficient?*]. For other works on this issue, see Martin J. Bailey & Paul H. Rubin, *A Positive Theory of Legal Change*, 14 INT'L REV. L. & ECON. 467, 476 (1994); Paul H. Rubin, *Common Law and Statute Law*, 11 J. LEGAL STUD. 205 (1982); Paul H. Rubin et al., *Litigation Versus Legislation: Forum Shopping by Rent Seekers*, 107 PUB. CHOICE 295 (2001); Paul H. Rubin & Martin J. Bailey, *The Role of Lawyers in Changing the Law*, 23 J. LEGAL STUD. 807 (1994). *See also* GORDON TULLOCK, TRIALS ON TRIAL: THE PURE THEORY OF LEGAL PROCEDURE 197–206 (1980).

177. What rules are defense lawyers likely to favor? Are their incentives to seek liability-reducing rules symmetrical or asymmetrical with those of plaintiff's lawyers? *See* Todd J. Zywicki & Jeremy Kidd, Public Choice and Tort Reform (forthcoming 2010).

178. *See* Rubin, *Why Is the Common Law Efficient, supra* note 176, at 53.

efficient solution. This is because a party with a stake in future decision[s] will find it worthwhile to litigate as long as liability rests with him; conversely, a party with no stake in future decisions will not find litigation worthwhile.[179]

Finally, in the third, neither party has an interest in the precedent. Rubin suggests that the result is a tendency toward random drift in the law, meaning that the current rule generally will persist, regardless of concerns for efficiency.

Rubin maintains that in the formative period of the common law the conditions for the evolution of efficient precedent prevailed. During the nineteenth century (and presumably before) both common law and statutory rule making were dominated by individual interests acting independently, rather than by organized interests acting collectively. As a result, the parties to the dispute generally had equal stakes in case outcomes. Moreover, legal relations might have been more reciprocal in nature because prior to large-scale industrial enterprises, legal interactions were largely between private individuals who were unlikely to systematically be either plaintiffs or defendants. Under conditions of reciprocity, there was a tendency to support efficient (and fair) rules rather than those that systematically favor one side. Rubin argues that over time this symmetry broke down and that several identifiable areas of law came to be dominated by repeat players who invested in securing law that favors their interests. Rubin argues that this characterized law for manufacturers in the nineteenth century and, in recent decades, certain bodies of tort law that are driven, disproportionately he claims, by plaintiffs' tort lawyers who have been able to organize to litigate strategically to promote preferred tort doctrine.[180] As a result, Rubin claims, the common law has tended to deviate from its traditional orientation toward efficiency in these areas.[181]

Professor George Priest has responded to Rubin's analysis with a model that rests neither on judicial predilection nor on precedent capture as the dominant force moving the common law toward efficiency.[182] Priest suggests an ingenious mechanism that rests solely on the incentives respecting the individual case ultimately presented for review in a common law court. Priest posits that inefficient common law rules provide the potential for greater gains from displacement than do efficient common law rules. This difference in potential gains arises because efficient rules are already welfare maximizing, while inefficient rules are welfare reducing. (At best, displacing an efficient rule with an inefficient rule produces distributed consequences, and at worst it also produces a welfare loss.) As a result, potential litigants themselves will generally perceive greater opportunities for gain from the litigation process when they are disadvan-

---

179. *Id.* at 55.

180. Rubin & Bailey, *supra* note 176, at 814–17.

181. Paul H. Rubin, *Public Choice and Tort Reform*, 124 PUB. CHOICE 223 (2005).

182. *See* George L. Priest, *The Common Law Process and the Selection of Efficient Rules*, 6 J. LEGAL STUD. 65 (1977).

taged by an inefficient, rather than by an efficient, common law rule. In this analysis, even if the judges themselves were indifferent to the efficiency of the common law, the aggregation of potential litigants would have a stronger incentive to litigate more cases challenging inefficient than efficient common law rules. Thus in a regime in which the judges simply flipped a coin to resolve each case, the law of large numbers would gradually, but inexorably, move the common law in the overall direction of efficiency.

Priest explains that even if an individual judge or small group of judges holds a preference for announcing inefficient common law rules, their ability to move common law doctrine in their preferred direction will succeed only if relatively few jurists hold such a view. We can express Priest's seeming counterintuition as an illustration of the fallacy of composition.[183] If a high percentage of jurists issue decisions in contravention of efficiency considerations, then under Priest's model, this creates many opportunities for gains through the litigation process to bring cases that seek to supplant inefficient with efficient common law rules. The process then moves the common law back in the direction of efficiency. Only if relatively few jurists move the common law away from efficiency, such that the aberrational results are not quickly identified as such, do the then smaller subset of inefficient common law rules have a substantial likelihood of staying in place for extended periods of time.

In later works, Priest has offered arguments suggesting a movement away from common law efficiency, for example, in such areas as tort doctrine.[184] Priest attributes this transformation to an intellectual revolution among judges who have come to adopt modern redistributive goals for tort law and who have imposed those ideological views on the law.[185] Has Rubin or Priest succeeded in constructing a model that avoids the difficulty with resting the claim of common law efficiency on a judicial predilection for efficient common law rulings? Why or why not? What assumptions about judicial rationality drive the Rubin and Priest models? Has Priest successfully constructed a model that does not embed an assumption about personal judicial motivations?

3. Supply Side Redux: Judicial Competition and Common Law Efficiency

Todd Zywicki has supplemented the models developed by Rubin and Priest with a supply-side analysis that explains what he characterizes as

---

183. *See supra* chapter 3, section II.A.

184. *See* George L. Priest, *Products Liability Law and the Accident Rate, in* LIABILITY: PERSPECTIVES AND POLICIES 184 (Robert E. Litan & Clifford Winston eds., 1988); George L. Priest, *The Modern Expansion of Tort Liability: Its Sources, Its Effects, and Its Reform*, J. ECON. PERSP., Summer 1991, at 31.

185. *See* George L. Priest, *Puzzles of the Tort Crisis*, 48 OHIO ST. L.J. 497 (1987); George L. Priest, *The Current Insurance Crisis and Modern Tort Law*, 96 YALE L.J. 1521 (1987); George L. Priest, *The Invention of Enterprise Liability: A Critical History of the Intellectual Foundations of Modern Tort Law*, 14 J. LEGAL STUD. 461 (1985).

the rise and fall of efficiency in the common law.[186] In particular, Zywicki notes that during the formative centuries of the English common law system, England had a competitive or "polycentric" legal order. Unlike current legal systems, during the Middle Ages multiple courts with overlapping jurisdictions existed side-by-side throughout England. These courts included ecclesiastical (church) courts, law merchant courts, local courts, the Chancery court, and three different common law courts, the King's Bench, the Court of Common Pleas, and the Exchequer Courts. For most legal matters a litigant could bring her case in several different courts. For instance, church courts had jurisdiction over all matters related to testamentary succession, but if the deceased owed a debt at the time of his death this suggested the possibility of jurisdiction in other courts as well.

Judges were paid in part from the litigant filing fees, thus providing competitive incentives respecting the scope of jurisdiction and expansion of judicial dockets.[187] As Adam Smith, writing in the eighteenth century, observed:

> The present admirable constitution of the courts of justice in England was, perhaps, originally in a great measure, formed by this emulation, which anciently took place between their respective judges; each judge endeavouring to give, in his own court, the speediest and most effectual remedy, which the law would admit, for every sort of injustice.[188]

Smith also noted that requiring judges to compete for fees motivated them to work harder and more efficiently, thereby removing incentives for judges to shirk or to indulge their personal preferences.[189] Zywicki claims that this form of judicial competition motivated by litigant incentives to engage in beneficial forum-shopping helped to drive the early common law toward efficiency. He further claims that in the United States, a similar, albeit somewhat attenuated system, arose under the regime of *Swift v. Tyson*,[190] which permitted the development of competing systems of law as between state and federal courts, a regime that was superseded by the *Erie* doctrine.[191]

In a recent article, Daniel Klerman has challenged some of these conclusions. Klerman argues that because early common law courts allowed plaintiffs to select the forum, interjurisdictional competition spurred the development of pro-plaintiff rules. Klerman rests this conclu-

186. *See* Zywicki, *supra* note 86, at 1581–1621.

187. 1 WILLIAM HOLDSWORTH, A HISTORY OF ENGLISH LAW 252–55 (A.L. Goodhart & H.G. Hanbury eds., 7th ed. rev. 1956); 2 ADAM SMITH, AN INQUIRY INTO THE NATURE AND CAUSES OF THE WEALTH OF NATIONS 241 (Edwin Cannan ed., Univ. of Chicago Press 1967) (5th ed. 1789).

188. 2 SMITH, *supra* note 187, at 241–42.

189. *Id.* at 241 ("Public services are never better performed than when their reward comes only in consequence of their being performed, and is proportioned to the diligence employed in performing them.").

190. 41 U.S. 1 (1842).

191. Erie R.R. v. Tompkins, 304 U.S. 64 (1938).

sion on the fact that in early common law courts, judicial compensation was based upon fees, thus furthering a pro-plaintiff bias. Klerman acknowledges that to some extent this bias was constrained by Chancery courts to which disputes could be removed.[192] Klerman further observes that this pro-plaintiff bias began to change as a result of statutes enacted in 1799 and 1825 that shifted judges to a salary-based compensation system, stripping them of their right to collect fees from litigants. Klerman claims that this reform led to the adoption of rules less favorable to plaintiffs.

How does Zywicki's analysis of law merchant courts affect Klerman's analysis of common law courts? Zywicki instead claims that competing jurisdiction among courts produced a more efficient set of common law rules. Is it possible to identify mechanisms that would push courts of overlapping jurisdiction in the direction of a pro-plaintiff bias, on the one hand, or toward efficiency, on the other? Consider the following argument. If plaintiffs have complete control over where to file suits, then the then-existing competitive regime would produce an incentive toward developing pro-plaintiff rules as this would increase the size of dockets along with corresponding fees. Alternatively, if more efficient common law rules create social welfare gains that can be shared as between plaintiffs and those with whom they contract or otherwise engage in repeat business, then plaintiffs would have a rational incentive to bargain for the selection of more efficient courts ex ante and share in any resulting gains. Which of these accounts seems more plausible and why?

Consider also the following observation by legal historian Thomas Scrutton: "If you read the [common] law reports of the seventeenth century you will be struck with one very remarkable fact; either Englishmen of that day did not engage in commerce, or they appear not to have been litigious people in commercial matters, each of which alternatives appears improbable."[193] According to Scrutton and other historians, most commercial disputes were heard outside the common law courts, and were instead heard in law merchant courts. Does this help to answer the preceding question? Why or why not?

Zywicki has shown that Lord Mansfield's incorporation of law merchant principles and practices into the common law during the mid-nineteenth century established many of the efficiency-enhancing rules for which he claims the common law became known. Zywicki further explains that the polycentric legal order in which the common law emerged as a result of judicial competition, spurred in part by the judges' own financial incentives, produced an additional beneficial effect. The regime allowed

---

192. Daniel Klerman, *Jurisdictional Competition and the Evolution of the Common Law*, 74 U. CHI. L. REV. 1179 (2007).

193. Thomas Edward Scrutton, *General Survey of the History of the Law Merchant*, 3 SELECT ESSAYS IN ANGLO-AMERICAN LEGAL HISTORY 7, 7 (Ass'n of American Law Schools ed., 1909). In some situations these were the "Staple Courts," which decided disputes that arose among traders in markets for various staple goods, such as wool and cotton. *See* Bernard Edward Spencer Brodhurst, *The Merchants of the Staple*, in 3 SELECT ESSAYS, *supra*, at 16–17; *see also* A.T. CARTER, A HISTORY OF ENGLISH LEGAL INSTITUTIONS 241–71 (1902).

dissatisfied parties to opt out of disadvantageous legal regimes and into preferable ones. For instance, merchants rarely resorted to common law courts, opting instead for law merchant courts, thus limiting the reach of sometimes archaic common law rules in commercial transactions.[194] Zywicki explains that a necessary coercive element in facilitating rent-seeking litigation was absent as a result of the power of potentially burdened parties to exit in favor of preferential courts.[195] He further maintains that this regime reduced incentives to invest in procuring inefficient precedents. Zywicki argues that this historical analysis bolsters Rubin's intuition that during its early formative period, the common law tended toward efficiency.

Zywicki attributes the subsequent tendency toward inefficient common law rules in some areas to the demise of competing courts in the United States and England. He further claims that the reduced ability of litigants to choose their court or to exit inefficient courts raised the agency costs associated with judicial decision making. Zywicki contends that his thesis is also consistent with Priest's claim that there has arisen a fundamental philosophical transformation of the judiciary. Under a system without competing courts, Zywicki claims, judges have a much greater ability to infuse ideology into their opinions.

Do you find Zywicki's alternative supply side account of common law efficiency persuasive? Is it consistent with the insights of Rubin and Priest? While Zywicki focuses on the *Erie* doctrine's effect on limiting federal-state judicial competition, what about the role of state-state competition? How does this affect the efficiency of common law in the United States? Are there reasons the elimination of federal-state competition is more or less important than state-state competition in facilitating efficient common law?[196] Why? How might Klerman respond to this analysis? Which model do you find more persuasive? Why?

4. Interest Group Theory and the Judiciary

As the foregoing discussion suggests, interest groups have the potential to influence both the judiciary and legislatures, although the nature of

---

194. *See* CARTER, *supra* note 193, at 261.

195. The analysis here anticipates some of the arguments that will be made in chapter 8 regarding of federalism and jurisdictional competition.

196. Legal commentators have long observed that early federal diversity jurisdiction was at least in part a social welfare program benefitting business going to more distant locations that reduced the risks associated with being subject to unpredictable or even hostile state laws. For relevant discussions, see William Howard Taft, *Possible and Needed Reforms in the Administration of Justice in the Federal Courts*, 45 ANN. REP. A.B.A. 250, 259 (1922) (observing that "[n]o single element in our governmental system has done so much to secure capital for the legitimate development of enterprises throughout the West and South as the existence of federal courts there, with a jurisdiction to hear diverse citizenship cases."); William L. Marbury, *Why Should We Limit Federal Diversity Jurisdiction?*, 46 A.B.A. J. 379, 380 (1960) (noting the "value to our present-day economy in a system which guarantees to the citizen who moves beyond the borders of his own community the protecting mantle of the federal judiciary.... [E]nterprise is definitely encouraged by the fact that the federal courts are available under such circumstances."); Robert J. Pushaw, Jr., *Article III's Case/Controversy Distinction and the Dual Functions of Federal Courts*, 69 NOTRE DAME L. REV. 447, 507 (1994) (citing numerous Framers and Ratifiers, as well as secondary sources, in support of this historical account). Does this account lend support to arguments for preferring to avoid state-state or federal-state competition? Why?

such influence might differ from institution to institution. In his article, *Does Interest Group Theory Justify More Intrusive Judicial Review?*,[197] Elhauge claims that judicial processes are subject to the same sorts of interest-group pressures as are legislatures. In particular, those groups seeking to change the law through litigation (as in Rubin's model of legal evolution) will confront many of the same collective action problems as groups seeking change (or to prevent change) through the legislative process. Discrete well-organized groups, for instance, will tend to be more effective in organizing strategic litigation in much the same manner that they will in organizing for effective lobbying. Well-organized groups may also be able to bring about settlements that prevent "bad" cases from establishing undesirable precedents,[198] or seek to influence judicial appointments or elections.[199]

This analysis suggests that it might not be enough for a group to be a repeat player to effect legal change. If the group members are heterogeneous, dispersed, or otherwise difficult to organize, they might be unable to monitor contributions effectively to ensure sufficient resources to bring about doctrinal change. Paul Rubin and Martin Bailey have noted that one reason trial lawyers have been effective in changing tort law in recent decades has been their considerable ability to organize and to engage in strategic litigation through organizations such as the American Association for Justice (formerly the Association of Trial Lawyers of America).[200]

Thomas Merrill has argued that although it is true that interest groups influence both judges and legislatures, the pattern of influence is not identical and, most notably, the demand curve for legal change differs in these two contexts.[201] Merrill claims that in general, interest groups seeking to lobby the legislature probably have to spend substantially more money to gain influence than do those seeking to effect legal change judicially. Specifically, he claims that the marginal return on each dollar invested in legislative lobbying is likely to decline much more slowly than for investments in litigation. Simply put, politicians always need more money for reelection. By contrast, Merrill claims that the marginal return from increased financial investments in litigation will likely fall off very rapidly.[202] Thus, Merrill argues, even if some groups are likely to outspend

---

197. Einer R. Elhauge, *Does Interest Group Theory Justify More Intrusive Judicial Review?*, 101 YALE L.J. 31 (1991).

198. For instance, in the case of *Taxman v. Board of Education*, 91 F.3d 1547 (3d Cir. 1996), which involved allegations that a school board had engaged in illegal "reverse discrimination," civil rights groups raised approximately $300,000 to fund a settlement that would moot the case before the Supreme Court ruled. Lederman, *supra* note 67, at 244–45.

199. *See* Rubin, *Public Choice and Tort Reform*, *supra* note 181, at 232.

200. *See* Rubin & Bailey, *supra* note 176, at 814–17.

201. *See* Thomas W. Merrill, *Does Public Choice Theory Justify Judicial Activism After All?*, 21 HARV. J.L. & PUB. POL'Y 219 (1997) [hereinafter Merrill, *Judicial Activism*]; Thomas W. Merrill, *Institutional Choice and Political Faith*, 22 LAW & SOC. INQUIRY 959 (1997).

202. Merrill, *Judicial Activism*, *supra* note 201, at 227–28. Merrill suggests that this may also explain why those who seek legal change through the courts often favor constitutionalizing large areas of law: "constitutional decisions are more difficult for legislatures to trump than are nonconstitutional decisions." *Id.* at 229 n.14.

in absolute terms, the *relative* difference in terms of the influence is likely to be much smaller in adjudication than in legislative lobbying.

Adam Pritchard and Todd Zywicki have argued that in addition to the difference in the demand function that Merrill identifies, there might also be a difference in the relevant supply curves.[203] The authors begin with the public choice premise that legislators generally seek election and reelection. In contrast, the judicial utility function is more elusive. None-theless, an important component appears to include the opportunity for judges to infuse their legal policy preferences in the cases that they decide. The authors further claim that judges are likely motivated by the desire for status and prestige. In the case of judges, the authors posit that status is substantially derived from perceptions of practicing lawyers and com-mentators in the academy and media. Thus, if lawyers and legal commen-tators have any sort of consistent ideological preferences, judges may tend to issue opinions that reflect those views.

Pritchard and Zywicki also suggest that judges might be biased in the direction of trying to enhance judicial power by absorbing a broad range of social issues under their jurisdictional umbrella. Moreover, the authors note, judges might not be entirely insulated from interest group pressures. Judges are obviously less susceptible than legislatures to influence pro-duced by various forms of financial contribution. Instead, interest groups "appeal to judges' interest in status, power, and ideological voting, rather than pecuniary gains or political support."[204] Interest group tools include strategic litigation, filing amicus briefs in pending cases, or organizing judicial rallies. Those seeking judicial influence also might write scholarly or popular articles. To the extent that the judicial ideology resembles that of journalists and professors, the authors contend, these approaches might influence judicial attitudes. Thus, while legislators are likely to be more responsive to those groups that can offer electoral and financial support, judges might be more receptive to those groups whose expressed views find reflection in the opinions they produce.

One implication of Pritchard and Zywicki's model is that it suggests that different interest groups will have a comparative advantage in pursuing their competing interests in different forums and will rationally allocate their resources and efforts to influence policy accordingly. The analysis thus implicates the demand function of interest group litigants and the supply functions of judges and legislators.

Does the preceding analysis help to explain which groups seek legal change and through which forum? Does it provide any insight as to the apparent contentiousness of judicial confirmation battles in recent years? Can you identify mechanisms that would reduce such interest group influence? If so, have such measures been resisted? Why?

---

203. A.C. Pritchard & Todd J. Zywicki, *Finding the Constitution: An Economic Analysis of Tradition's Role in Constitutional Interpretation*, 77 N.C. L. REV. 409 (1999).

204. *Id.* at 499.

5. The Common Law as a Rent–Seeking System

Scholars have explored the implications of public choice theory for evaluating the relative merits of the adversarial process within common law systems and the inquisitorial process within civil law systems. Gordon Tullock argues that the adversarial feature of common law adjudication is fundamentally a rent-seeking, or rent-dissipating, system.[205] As applied to a civil lawsuit, for example, Tullock assumes that the parties are exclusively concerned with the distributional consequences determined by which party prevails. Tullock posits that the parties within adversarial systems can increase their likelihood of prevailing by investing additional financial resources, thus transforming the litigation process into something akin to a rent-seeking game. Tullock likens the resulting litigation to an arms race in which each party has an incentive to expend increasing amounts with the risk that the overall process might dissipate the entire value of the dispute through lawyers' fees and other costs.

Tullock assumes that within each dispute one side's claim is consistent with revealing the truth to the factfinder, while the other side's expenditures primarily obstruct discovery of the truth. He further assumes that the most important normative criterion for comparing the adversarial and inquisitorial adjudicatory processes is the joint minimization of administrative and error costs (i.e., the highest level of accuracy at the lowest possible cost). Tullock contends that expenditures that obstruct the search for truth—or that would not arise but for the other side's tactical obfuscation of the truth—provide no social benefit. Within the inquisitorial system, the judges rather than the parties generally control the expenditure of resources in the quest for truth. Because inquisitorial judges internalize most of the costs of the litigation process, Tullock posits that they therefore lack incentives to expend resources in a manner that obstructs the quest for outcomes consistent with the truth. Tullock concludes that as compared with the adversarial systems, inquisitorial systems eliminate, or at least significantly reduce, incentives for rent dissipation. From a social perspective, Tullock maintains not only that the adversarial system is more expensive than the inquisitorial system, but also that the increased expense is unjustified given that as compared with the common law system the inquisitorial system produces more accurate judgments at lower cost.

Is Tullock correct that adversarial litigation is most meaningfully characterized in terms of rent seeking?[206] Is he correct that inquisitorial judges, who serve as bureaucratic civil servants, are immune from rent-seeking pressures that might result in expenditures other than in the pursuit of truth? If Tullock is concerned that parties have private incentives to dissipate resources in the adversary system, might judges in the

---

205. GORDON TULLOCK, THE CASE AGAINST THE COMMON LAW (1997); Gordon Tullock, *Technology: The Anglo–Saxons Versus the Rest of the World, in* 9 THE SELECTED WORKS OF GORDON TULLOCK 291–308 (Charles K. Rowley ed., 2005).

206. *See* Todd J. Zywicki, *Spontaneous Order and the Common Law: Gordon Tullock's Critique*, 135 PUB. CHOICE 35–53 (2008).

inquisitorial system, by contrast, have private incentives to "shirk" by under-investing in the pursuit of the truth?[207] Does Tullock's analysis overlook other important normative criteria that potentially conflict with the pursuit of truth, for example the quest for justice? Which system is preferable if one is concerned about bias by decision makers? Which is superior if one is concerned about the relative wealth of parties and their access to quality counsel?

Even limiting the analysis to the question of truth, what does truth mean in the context of common law adjudication? To what extent is truth contingent upon specified, and often evolving, legal obligations? While some cases center on narrow truth-based inquiries—for example, did Albert go through a red light, thus causing the collision with Bart?—complex civil litigation more generally presents competing claims to the truth, the normative validity of which turns on conflicting accounts of governing legal rules. Common law adjudication often presents two (or more) plausible, yet contested, accounts of the truth. Does Tullock's analysis of the relative merits of the two legal systems account for the positive lawmaking function of common law courts, as compared with civil courts, that emerges from the process of resolving such legal disputes? Is it possible to assess the relative merits of adversarial and inquisitorial processes without further considering the lawmaking relationship between courts and legislatures within nations whose judiciaries operate as civil or common law systems? How do the answers to these questions affect Tullock's broader claim about the relative merits of the two adjudicatory systems? Which system do you find more attractive and why? Is it possible that neither system is inherently superior to the other but that the choice presents tradeoffs of both competing normative criteria and "fit" within overall lawmaking systems, including the respective role of the courts and legislatures? Is it also possible that the choice depends upon, among other factors, the complexity of the cases under review?

II. CASE ILLUSTRATIONS

In this part, we consider the implications of several models of judicial behavior set out in this chapter for three high profile Supreme Court decisions: *Bush v. Gore*,[208] *Adarand Constructors, Inc. v. Pena*,[209] and *Gonzales v. Carhart*.[210] The first two cases involve equal protection doctrine. Beyond that surface similarity, however, these opinions apply equal protection in disparate contexts and with substantially different precedential implications. They also hold potentially divergent implications for the nature and role of judicial strategy in the context of Supreme Court decision making. The third case involves partial birth abortion, although the part of the opinion that we are concerned with involves abortion more generally.

---

207. Recall the discussion of the motivations of bureaucratic actors from chapter 6.
208. 531 U.S. 98 (2000).
209. 515 U.S. 200 (1995).
210. 550 U.S. 124 (2007).

These cases present complex issues and analyses, and our focus is limited to specific aspects that invite the possibility of elements of strategy among the deciding justices. We will present a summary of the background cases as needed to focus attention on targeted issues within or across the relevant opinions. We begin with the 2000 decision, *Bush v. Gore*, a case that is far less influential as a matter of equal protection doctrine than it was in determining the outcome of the 2000 presidential election in favor of Republican nominee George W. Bush over Democratic nominee Al Gore.[211] We then consider the 1995 decision, *Adarand Constructors, Inc. v. Pena*, a case that remains a centerpiece of modern equal protection jurisprudence, especially in the sensitive area of race and benign race-based preference. Finally, we present a very brief discussion of, and reproduce a concurring opinion from, *Gonzales v. Carhart*, a recent abortion case that upheld a federal ban on partial birth abortion just seven years following a contrary decision involving a similar state law restriction in *Stenberg v. Carhart*.[212]

As you read the discussions of the cases that follow, it will be helpful to bear the following questions in mind: Do these cases support or undermine the assumption that Supreme Court Justices vote sincerely or strategically? Do these cases help to identify judicial practices that inhibit strategic judicial decision making, whether or not those structures succeeded in doing so in the cases themselves? Do these cases support or detract from the Attitudinal Model? More generally, do these cases—or at least the features of the cases that are the focus of the presentations that follow—represent norms of judicial behavior on the Supreme Court, or exceptions to those norms, and why? Do they likely capture judicial behavior on other appellate courts? Why or why not? Do they support or undermine any preceding social choice model, and if so, which one?

A. BUSH v. GORE[213]

In *Bush v. Gore*,[214] the Supreme Court intervened for the second time in the controversial 2000 presidential election and the first time played a decisive role in choosing the President of the United States. The discussion that follows will establish a time line that will help to explain the relationship between the two cases, to assess the controlling case issues, to evaluate the various opinions in *Bush v. Gore*, and to construct a social choice account of that decision. The factual background and the case opinions are complex. After summarizing the key events, we present a graphic time line in Figure 7.A.1 that helps to frame the discussion that follows. We then review the opinions, consider a social choice analysis of

---

211. The analysis is based on STEARNS, *supra* note 96, at 315–23 (Afterword on *Bush v. Gore*). For a more detailed presentation, see Michael Abramowicz & Maxwell L. Stearns, *Beyond Counting Votes: The Political Economy of* Bush v. Gore, 54 VAND. L. REV. 1849 (2001).

212. 530 U.S. 914 (2000).

213. Portions of the discussion that follow are based upon Abramowicz & Stearns, *supra* note 211; MAXWELL L. STEARNS, CONSTITUTIONAL PROCESS: A SOCIAL CHOICE ANALYSIS OF SUPREME COURT DECISION MAKING 315–23 (paperback ed. 2002) (*Afterword* on Bush v. Gore).

214. 531 U.S. 98 (2000).

the case, and set out several questions that connect *Bush v. Gore* to the various models developed throughout this chapter.

1. The *Bush v. Gore* Timeline

Following the historically close November 7, 2000 election, it was clear that the assignment of the twenty-five Electoral College seats from Florida would control whether Al Gore or George Bush would become President. Bush led the Florida election by a mere 1784 votes, less than one half of one percent of the ballots cast. Under Florida law, a result within that margin produced an automatic machine recount.

In Florida, along with other states, the post-election period was divided into two phases. The protest period allowed challenges before Secretary of State Katherine Harris to alleged voting improprieties prior to the official certification of Electoral Votes. The contest period allowed time for a judicial challenge to the actual certification prior to sending the slate of electors to the Electoral College.[215] The timing of these two phases was zero sum for those states, like Florida, that sought the benefit of the so-called safe harbor provision of 3 U.S.C. § 5.[216] That statute, enacted in the aftermath of the contested Tilden–Hayes Election of 1876, provided that any slate of electors submitted six days prior to the meeting of the Electoral College that was selected in a manner consistent with state law in effect prior to the election is presumed conclusive. The original protest period in Florida ran from November 7, 2000 through November 14, 2000, and the original contest period ran from November 14, 2000 until December 12, 2000.

On November 14, 2000, Katherine Harris announced that Bush remained in the lead by the narrower margin of three hundred votes. The first Supreme Court decision followed a decision of the Florida Supreme Court issued on November 21, 2000. In *Palm Beach Canvassing Board v. Harris*,[217] the Florida Supreme Court had determined that to accommodate the manual recounts needed to resolve the alleged voting improprieties raised by Gore in his protest, it was necessary to extend the protest period from November 14 through November 26, 2000, with the effect of correspondingly shortening the contest period. The United States Supreme Court granted certiorari and heard oral argument on December 1, issuing a unanimous remand to the Florida Supreme Court in *Bush v. Palm Beach County Canvassing Board*,[218] on December 4. The *Palm Beach County Canvassing Board* remand inquired whether the Florida Supreme Court decision to extend Florida's statutory protest period at the expense of the statutory contest period was based upon an application of the relevant state statute or some other source of law, most notably the state constitution's requirement of equal protection. This question was

---

215. *See* FLA. STAT. ANN. § 102.166 (2000) (protest phase); *id.* § 102.168 (contest phase).

216. 3 U.S.C. § 5 (2000).

217. 772 So. 2d 1220 (Fla. 2000).

218. 531 U.S. 70 (2000).

important in assessing whether Florida Supreme Court's revised state election procedure had been implemented consistently with Article II of the U.S. Constitution. Article II confers upon state legislatures the power to make laws governing the state's selection of Electors to the Electoral College for the President and Vice President of the United States. By the time the Supreme Court decision in *Palm Beach County Canvassing Board* was issued, however, that question was essentially moot. Even under the extended protest period, Katherine Harris declared Bush the winner. The *Palm Beach County Canvassing Board* Court nonetheless issued a minimalist and unanimous decision that appeared to allow it to remain above the partisan fray while providing a check against a potentially problematical state court intervention into a presidential election that might have run afoul of Article II.

After Katherine Harris certified George W. Bush the winner of Florida's twenty-five electoral votes on November 26, 2000, Al Gore, along with other affected voters, contested the election outcome by filing four legal challenges. *Bush v. Gore* grew out of one of those challenges, filed on November 27, 2000, in Leon County seeking a manual recount of undervotes.[219] Undervotes are ballots that failed to properly register a vote for a President and Vice President and thus were not counted toward the final election result. Gore appealed an order by the Leon County Circuit Court denying his request to the Florida Supreme Court. While Gore had only requested manual recounts of undervotes in specified counties, the Florida Supreme Court instead ordered a recount of undervotes in all counties throughout the state in which such a recount had not yet taken place, and it did so subject to an intent-of-the-voter standard.

Immediately after the recount order, George W. Bush successfully petitioned the United States Supreme Court for certiorari and for a stay.[220] In addition to claiming that the Florida court ruling ran afoul of a federal statute that provides a safe harbor if the electors were certified by December 12, 2000,[221] Bush raised two constitutional challenges. First, he argued that Article II expressly grants the power to state legislatures to establish by statute the rules governing elections for the selection of electors of the president and vice president and that the Florida Supreme Court order, by altering the state legislated election process, had violated Article II. Second, he claimed that because the order failed to provide a mechanism with which to ensure that the recount would be consistently applied within and across counties throughout the state, and instead applied the problematic intent-of-the-voter standard, it violated the Fourteenth Amendment Equal Protection and Due Process Clauses.

The Supreme Court granted certiorari and stayed the recount, which was scheduled to begin on December 9, 2000. Following oral argument on December 11, 2000, the Supreme Court issued its ruling on December 12,

---

219.   531 U.S. at 101.

220.   531 U.S. 1048 (2000).

221.   531 U.S. at 103.

the final day of the certification period and six days prior to the scheduled meeting of the Electors. Table 7.A.1 summarizes the time line for the events leading up to *Bush v. Gore*.

In contrast with *Palm Beach County Canvassing Board*, the *Bush v. Gore* Court was badly fractured, producing a complex set of opinions. After some initial media confusion, it became clear that the opinions left no room for a recount, thus producing a victory for Bush. *Bush v. Gore* overturned the Florida Supreme Court's mandated statewide recount of undervotes in a *per curiam* opinion commanding the support of five Justices. The *per curiam* Supreme Court held that the Florida Supreme Court order had violated equal protection by failing to ensure a set of consistent standards for the operation of the recount and that the close timing required to satisfy the safe harbor provision of 3 U.S.C. § 5 prevented a timely cure. Because there was no possibility of conducting the recount in a manner consistent with equal protection standards, the Court effectively mandated that the Secretary of State's previously certified slate for Republican nominee, George W. Bush, remained final.

Table 7.A.1. *Bush v. Gore* Timeline (2000)

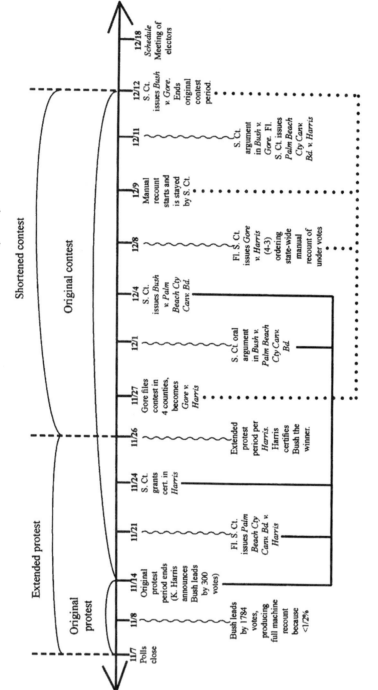

2. The *Bush v. Gore* Opinions

The *Bush v. Gore* Court divided into four major camps. The *per curiam* opinion, which found an equal protection violation, was joined by Chief Justice Rehnquist and Justices Kennedy, O'Connor, Scalia, and Thomas. In theory, the identified equal protection problem resulting from a lack of a uniform set of recount standards could have been cured on remand with a Florida Supreme Court order setting out more specific standards, and perhaps also including ballots other than just those classified as undervotes. The *per curiam* opinion effectively foreclosed that possibility, however. Because the date for certification was upon the Court (the opinion itself was issued on December 12, 2000, the same date as was required for the benefit of the safe harbor provision) and because one day earlier, in response to the *Palm Beach County Canvassing Board* remand, the Florida Supreme Court clarified that the state intended to benefit from the federal safe harbor provision,[222] the *per curiam* authors determined that timing considerations prevented a recount.

Chief Justice Rehnquist, joined by Justices Scalia and Thomas, who joined the *Bush v. Gore per curiam* opinion, also produced a separate concurrence. The concurring opinion rested on Article II, concluding that the Florida recount order was inconsistent with the delegation to the state legislature to set the rules governing the selection of electors for the President and Vice President. Justice Souter filed a separate dissent. Justice Breyer joined Justice Souter's dissent in its entirety and produced his own dissent. Together, Souter and Breyer found support for an equal protection violation but determined that the problem could be cured with a clearer standard and by allowing the Florida Supreme Court to determine whether to risk sacrificing the benefit of the safe harbor to allow additional time for a recount. Justices Stevens and Ginsburg joined Souter's dissent except with respect to the portion that expressed partial support for the *per curiam*'s equal protection analysis. Ginsburg and Breyer filed separate dissents in which they found no violation of either equal protection or of Article II.

The *per curiam* reasoned as follows:

> Upon due consideration of the difficulties identified to this point, it is obvious that the recount cannot be conducted in compliance with the requirements of equal protection and due process without substantial additional work. It would require not only the adoption (after opportunity for argument) of adequate statewide standards for determining what is a legal vote, and practicable procedures to implement them, but also orderly judicial review of any disputed matters that might arise. In addition, the Secretary [of State] has advised that the recount of only a portion of the ballots requires that the vote tabulation equipment be used to screen out undervotes, a function for which the machines were not designed. If a recount of overvotes were also required, perhaps even a second screening would be necessary. Use of the equipment for this purpose, and any new software developed for it, would have to be evaluated for accuracy by the Secretary [of State], as required by Fla. Stat. Ann. § 101.015 (Supp. 2001).

---

222. *See* Palm Beach County Canvassing Bd. v. Harris, 772 So. 2d 1273 (2000).

The Supreme Court of Florida has said that the legislature intended the State's electors to "participat[e] fully in the federal electoral process," as provided in 3 U.S.C. § 5. 772 So.2d, at 1289; see also *Palm Beach Canvassing Bd.* v. *Harris*, 772 So.2d 1220, 1237 (Fla. 2000). That statute, in turn, requires that any controversy or contest that is designed to lead to a conclusive selection of electors be completed by December 12. That date is upon us, and there is no recount procedure in place under the State Supreme Court's order that comports with minimal constitutional standards. Because it is evident that any recount seeking to meet the December 12 date will be unconstitutional for the reasons we have discussed, we reverse the judgment of the Supreme Court of Florida ordering a recount to proceed.[223]

The separate concurrence began by stating "We join the per curiam opinion."[224] The concurring Justices then offered an alternative analysis that rested on Article II. The opinion explained:

In Florida, the legislature has chosen to hold statewide elections to appoint the State's 25 electors. Importantly, the legislature has delegated the authority to run the elections and to oversee election disputes to the Secretary of State (Secretary), Fla. Stat. Ann. § 97.012(1) (Supp. 2001), and to state circuit courts, §§ 102.168(1), 102.168(8). Isolated sections of the code may well admit of more than one interpretation, but the general coherence of the legislative scheme may not be altered by judicial interpretation so as to wholly change the statutorily provided apportionment of responsibility among these various bodies. In any election but a Presidential election, the Florida Supreme Court can give as little or as much deference to Florida's executives as it chooses, so far as Article II is concerned, and this Court will have no cause to question the court's actions. But, with respect to a Presidential election, the court must be both mindful of the legislature's role under Article II in choosing the manner of appointing electors and deferential to those bodies expressly empowered by the legislature to carry out its constitutional mandate.[225]

Two dissenting Justices, Souter and Breyer, conceded the possibility of an equal protection problem, but contended that the problem could be cured even if doing so delayed the schedule for submitting Florida's slate of electors. As Justice Breyer explained:

Nonetheless, there is no justification for the majority's remedy, which is simply to reverse the lower court and halt the recount entirely. An appropriate remedy would be, instead, to remand this case with instructions that, even at this late date, would permit the Florida Supreme Court to require recounting *all* undercounted votes in Florida, including those from Broward, Volusia, Palm Beach, and

---

223.   531 U.S. at 110.

224.   *Id.* at 111 (Rehnquist, C.J., Scalia, J., and Thomas, J., concurring).

225.   *Id.* at 113–14.

Miami–Dade Counties, whether or not previously recounted prior to the end of the protest period, and to do so in accordance with a single uniform substandard.[226]

Justice Stevens, joined by Justice Ginsburg, altogether rejected the majority's equal protection analysis:

> Admittedly, the use of differing substandards for determining voter intent in different counties employing similar voting systems may raise serious concerns. Those concerns are alleviated—if not eliminated—by the fact that a single impartial magistrate will ultimately adjudicate all objections arising from the recount process. Of course, as a general matter, "[t]he interpretation of constitutional principles must not be too literal. We must remember that the machinery of government would not work if it were not allowed a little play in its joints." If it were otherwise, Florida's decision to leave to each county the determination of what balloting system to employ—despite enormous differences in accuracy—might run afoul of equal protection. So, too, might the similar decisions of the vast majority of state legislatures to delegate to local authorities certain decisions with respect to voting systems and ballot design.
>
> Even assuming that aspects of the remedial scheme might ultimately be found to violate the Equal Protection Clause, I could not subscribe to the majority's disposition of the case. As the majority explicitly holds, once a state legislature determines to select electors through a popular vote, the right to have one's vote counted is of constitutional stature. As the majority further acknowledges, Florida law holds that all ballots that reveal the intent of the voter constitute valid votes. Recognizing these principles, the majority nonetheless orders the termination of the contest proceeding before all such votes have been tabulated. Under their own reasoning, the appropriate course of action would be to remand to allow more specific procedures for implementing the legislature's uniform general standard to be established.[227]

In his separate dissent, Stevens criticized the Court's remarkable intervention:

> What must underlie petitioners' entire federal assault on the Florida election procedures is an unstated lack of confidence in the impartiality and capacity of the state judges who would make the critical decisions if the vote count were to proceed. Otherwise, their position is wholly without merit. The endorsement of that position by the majority of this Court can only lend credence to the most cynical appraisal of the work of judges throughout the land. It is confidence in the men and women who administer the judicial system that is the true backbone of the rule of law. Time will one day heal the wound to

---

226. *Id.* at 146 (Breyer, J., dissenting).

227. *Id.* at 126–27 (Stevens, J., dissenting) (quoting Bain Peanut Co. of Tex. v. Pinson, 282 U.S. 499, 501 (1931) (Holmes, J.) (alteration in original)) (footnote omitted)).

that confidence that will be inflicted by today's decision. One thing, however, is certain. Although we may never know with complete certainty the identity of the winner of this year's Presidential election, the identity of the loser is perfectly clear. It is the Nation's confidence in the judge as an impartial guardian of the rule of law.[228]

3. A Social Choice Analysis of Bush v. Gore

Professors Michael Abramowicz and Maxwell Stearns have analyzed the *Bush v. Gore* case using social choice analysis. The authors claim that the combined opinions exposed a series of fault lines that not only split the five Justice conservative majority from a four Justice liberal dissent, but that also divided the conservative majority itself over two potentially conflicting rationales.

Abramowicz and Stearns argue that beneath the surface of the apparent controlling majority in *Bush v. Gore* rested a likely set of divisions on how to define and resolve controlling case issues that threatened to destabilize the Court's ruling, or at least the appearance of consensus supporting the doctrinal justification for ending the Florida recount. These divisions were of potentially sufficient magnitude and importance that had the Justices voted consistently with what appears to have represented their initial preferred positions—or ideal points—the result might well have been to decide the first Supreme Court case controlling the outcome of a presidential election with a set of opinions that revealed the basis for cyclical preferences, thus calling into question the stability—and legitimacy—of the Court's opinion.

The authors identify a possible underlying cycle, but claim that the case is more significant in demonstrating significant limitations on the power of Justices to vote strategically. In effect, the authors contend that *Bush v. Gore* represents the exception proving (or at least supporting) the rule that Supreme Court decision-making processes substantially limit the incentives of the Justices to vote other than sincerely in resolving logically controlling case issues. The authors claim that based upon some reasonable assumptions, it plausible to demonstrate that at least one group of Justices, those who joined a separate concurring opinion, pursued what can be described as a strategic course.

The authors begin by noting that the *per curiam* opinion provided some hints that while a majority of five supported the equal protection rationale, not all did so enthusiastically. Beyond the opening sentence of the separate concurrence, which read "We join the per curiam opinion,"[229] the concurring Justices ignored equal protection in their separate opinion, resting on Article II. In addition, the *per curiam* itself contained the following prominent, and unusual, disclaimer: "Our consideration is limited to the present circumstances, for the problem of equal protection in

228. *Id.* at 128–29.
229. *Id.* at 111 (Rehnquist, C.J., Scalia, J., and Thomas, J., concurring).

election processes generally presents many complexities.''[230] In effect, the *per curiam* immediately disclaimed the case's own precedential significance beyond the facts of *Bush v. Gore.* Finally, the authors observe that many commentators also noted the apparent doctrinal inversion in which the conservative majority, which with the limited exception of affirmative action has almost uniformly rejected an expansive equal protection analysis, applied equal protection over the objection of their liberal colleagues, who generally took just the opposite approach.[231]

The *per curiam*'s equal protection analysis was sufficiently problematic on its own terms that in the aftermath of the decision, almost all conservative commentators seeking to support the outcome preferred to defend the holding based upon the concurrence's alternative Article II analysis.[232] If the Supreme Court had instead rested its analysis on Article II, and if the Florida Supreme Court order of a statewide manual recount violated the constitutional grant of authority to the state legislature, then there would have been nothing to cure upon remand and no need to worry that December 12, 2000, a date fixed by the safe harbor provision of 3 U.S.C. § 5, was already upon the Court.

Based upon this analysis, Abramowicz and Stearns claim that under the most plausible scenario for strategic voting in *Bush v. Gore*, the resulting strategy did not change the case outcome. Instead, it provided the heightened appearance of support for the same outcome that would have been achieved had all Justices instead voted sincerely.

The analysis proceeds in two steps. First the authors consider the implications of casting the Justices' preferences along a single normative dimension, such that a consensus position (or Condorcet winner) emerges. They then relax this assumption and consider the implications of their more nuanced presentation for the decision's more peculiar features.

Table 7.A.2 provides the first stylized breakdown of the various opinions in *Bush v. Gore.* The table presents the opinions along a normative issue dimension that evaluates the breadth or narrowness of the Supreme Court's power to scrutinize state court decisions that interfere with presidential elections. In this analysis, Chief Justice Rehnquist, joined by Justices Scalia and Thomas, the three Justices who at the time of *Bush v. Gore* were generally considered the most reliable conservatives on the Supreme Court, provided the broadest bases for overturning the Florida Supreme Court. These justices rested their analysis both on equal protection (indicated by their decision to join the *per curiam*) and on Article II (set out in the separate opinion). The *per curiam* opinion, also joined by the more moderate conservatives, Justices O'Connor and Kennedy, relied solely upon equal protection and found a violation based upon the subjective recount standard and the decision to limit the recount order

---

230. *Id.* at 109 (per curiam).

231. Abramowicz & Stearns, *supra* note 211, at 1867–73.

232. One notable exception: Nelson Lund, *The Unbearable Rightness of* Bush v. Gore, 23 CARDOZO L. REV. 1219 (2002).

only to undervotes. As stated previously, the *per curiam* also determined that the equal protection defect could not be cured without running afoul of the state's decision to benefit from the federal safe harbor provision. The leftmost dissenting Justices—those immediately to the right of the bolded vertical line separating those who voted consistently with the case outcome from those in dissent—in Table 7:A.2, Justices Souter and Breyer, agreed with the *per curiam* authors that the manual recount order presented a potential equal protection problem. In their view, however, any equal protection defect had the potential to be cured through a corrective order on remand. Finally, the rightmost dissenting Justices, Stevens and Ginsburg, concluded that there was neither a violation of Article II nor equal protection.

Table 7.A.2. A Unidimensional Social Choice Model of Bush v. Gore

(A) Rehnquist, Scalia, Thomas (concurring)	(B) O'Connor, Kennedy (per curiam)	(C) Souter, Breyer (dissenting)	(D) Stevens, Ginsburg (dissenting)
Florida Supreme Court decision violates Article II and equal protection	Florida Supreme Court decisions violates equal protection only; Florida Supreme Court's expressed desire to receive benefit of safe harbor prevents timely remand for corrective remedy satisfying equal protection	Florida Supreme Court decision violates equal protection only; safe harbor provision is not mandatory, thus permitting timely remand for corrective remedy satisfying equal protection	Florida Supreme Court decision does not violate Article II or equal protection
Broad Mandate to correct state judicial intervention in elections ←———→ Narrow Mandate to correct state judicial intervention in elections			

Table 7.A.2 presents a stylized account of the various opinions through which Abramowicz and Stearns preliminarily identify the nature and limits of any strategic interaction among the Justices in resolving *Bush v. Gore* based on the assumption that the concurring Justices had not elected to join the *per curiam* opinion. The analysis treats the case as the functional equivalent of a fractured panel case in which the opinions can be cast along a single issue dimension.

In this analysis, the concurring Justices provide two independent bases for overturning the Florida Supreme Court decision, one grounded in Article II and the other in equal protection. The analysis further assumes that while Justices O'Connor and Kennedy favored a judgment for Bush, they were disinclined to issue a ruling that rested on overturning a state court construction of state law, specifically one that construed the state statute to benefit from the safe harbor even at the expense of failing to remedy a meritorious challenge to voting irregularities. As a result, they were disinclined to support the concurring Justices' Article II analysis but were willing to accept a basis for overruling that was at least not inconsistent with the Florida court's prior interpretation of Florida law, which construed the state election law to permit such a remedial order. The analysis further assumes that Justices O'Connor and Kennedy were unwilling to join the liberal Breyer/Souter opinions that would have invited the possibility of a further recount, which, based upon available information at the time of decision, created the possibility of a victory for Gore. By necessary implication, O'Connor and Kennedy would also not have been willing to go farther, as did Stevens and Ginsburg, and find against any constitutional defect in the Florida court ruling.

In this scenario, if Justices O'Connor and Kennedy were seeking to produce a judgment overruling the Florida Supreme Court decision without resting that decision on Article II, then the positions of the remaining Justices provided these centrist jurists with little room to maneuver. They were bounded on the left by the concurring jurists' Article II analysis, and they were bounded on the right by an equal protection analysis that admitted of a potential cure upon remand. Only by grounding their opinion in the much criticized equal protection analysis, but finding that the factual peculiarities associated with the timing of the decision were such as to preclude a true remand, could they produce the desired narrowest-grounds result. While the *per curiam* analysis has been roundly criticized, even by those who favor the result, applying these assumptions, the opinion nonetheless appears to represent a stable outcome. And yet this analysis leaves some of the most anomalous features of *Bush v. Gore* unexplained, including why the concurring Justices joined in what became the *per curiam* opinion. Abramowicz and Stearns claim that the most obvious answer—to ensure a majority as needed to produce a governing precedent—is refuted by the limiting language disclaiming any pretense of meaningful precedential status. Thus, while the analysis might explain why Justices O'Connor and Kennedy found the equal protection analysis attractive, it does not explain why the concurring Justices also found that analysis appealing. The authors claim that this is problematic given the concurring Justices' general predisposition against expansive equal protection analysis especially in the area of voting rights and given that they could have achieved the same judgment by resting exclusively on Article II.

By relaxing the assumptions needed to create a unidimensional presentation of *Bush v. Gore*, Abramowicz and Stearns are able to evaluate the implications of a more nuanced presentation. While the prior analysis assumed that Chief Justice Rehnquist and Justices Scalia and Thomas sincerely held their views on Article II and on equal protection, and considered the options available to Justices O'Connor and Kennedy on the assumption that they sought to produce a result for Bush, in this analysis, the authors instead assume that Chief Justice Rehnquist and Justices Scalia and Thomas signed on to the *per curiam* analysis on the basis of potential strategic considerations.

The authors defend this intuition as follows. First, beyond the opening sentence in which the concurring Justices nominally join the *per curiam* opinion, the concurring opinion rested entirely upon Article II. Second, as stated above, in the context of voting rights, the concurring Justices generally embraced a conservative equal protection jurisprudence that appears to be in some tension with the *per curiam* analysis. And finally, the *per curiam* opinion itself provides a fact-specific disclaimer that might be the product of a compromise between Justices O'Connor and Kennedy and their more conservative concurring brethren on the equal protection issue. By suggesting that the concurring Justices did not embrace the equal protection analysis on the merits but instead joined for strategic reasons, the authors offer a set of intriguing relationships between and among the various opinions shown in Table 7.A.3.

Based upon the foregoing assumptions, Table 7.A.3 depicts the initial positions, or ideal points, of the various camps in *Bush v. Gore*. In this analysis, the concurring Justices embraced only the Article II analysis and Justices O'Connor and Kennedy embraced only the equal protection analysis grounds for reversing the Florida Supreme Court. Within the dissent box, the names Souter and Breyer appear in italics to reflect the fact that while they preferred to affirm, they did find an equal protection problem, albeit one that they determined could be cured on remand. Unlike table 7.A.2, table 7.A.3 presents the issues in *Bush v. Gore* along two dimensions, with asymmetrical preferences.[233] Thus, one majority— the *per curiam* Justices (excluding the concurring Justices who joined only for strategic reasons) and the dissenters—determined that the Florida Supreme Court decision could not be reversed on the basis of a violation of Article II. Another majority—the concurring Justices and the dissenters (totaling five if we include Souter and Breyer)—determined that the Florida Supreme Court could not be reversed on the basis of a violation of equal protection. Presumably, all nine deciding Justices agreed that absent a violation of either Article II or equal protection, there was no basis upon which to reverse the Florida Supreme Court. And yet, a third majority—those in concurrence plus O'Connor and Kennedy—voted to reverse and (nominally) to remand.

---

233. For a more detailed analysis of dimensionality and symmetry, see book website chapter 3 appendix A and cites therein.

Table 7.A.3. Bush v. Gore in Two Dimensions with Asymmetrical Preferences

	Florida Supreme Court ruling should be reversed on the basis of equal protection	Florida Supreme Court ruling should not be reversed on the basis of equal protection
Florida Supreme Court ruling should be reversed on the basis of Article II		(A) Rehnquist, Scalia, Thomas
Florida Supreme Court ruling should not be reversed on the basis of Article II	(C) O'Connor, Kennedy	(B) *Souter, Breyer*, Stevens, Ginsburg

The authors maintain that this more nuanced presentation casts a stronger light on the nature and limits of any strategic accommodation that might have arisen in *Bush v. Gore*. Even if every camp ruled strictly in accordance with its ideal point, under outcome voting the result would have been to reverse the Florida Supreme Court, thus favoring Bush. This holds even though separate and overlapping majorities prefer resolving each of the two identified dispositive issues in a manner that favors Gore.

Abramowicz and Stearns claim that if their underlying assumptions hold, the analysis reveals the exceedingly narrow possibilities for strategic behavior in *Bush v. Gore*. The analysis reveals that outcome voting inhibits not only strategic issue identification but also strategic voting on the resolution of issues the Justices have ultimately identified as controlling. Thus, in an issue-voting regime, the result of this case would have been for Gore, given that separate (hypothetically controlling) majorities would have found no violation either of equal protection or of Article II. In this regime, the Rehnquist camp would have been motivated to join in the equal protection analysis not to create precedent on that point of law, but rather to create an outcome for Bush. The outcome-voting regime makes that strategy unnecessary. By instead sticking to their respective ideal points and engaging in no strategic voting, under the outcome-voting regime, the Rehnquist and O'Connor camps formed a majority (albeit a split one) producing their favored outcome for Bush.

In fact, the authors conclude, the Rehnquist camp might have acquiesced in the *per curiam* opinion's equal protection analysis even though doing so might not have represented that camp's ideal point. But the decision to do so did not alter the judgment of the Court. The authors' social choice analysis provides an alternative instrumental justification for this limited form of strategic behavior, one motivated by political rather than doctrinal concerns. Abramowicz and Stearns contend that it is one thing to decide a case controlling the choice of President by a one-vote margin. It is quite another to control the outcome of a presidential election by one vote through a set of published opinions that reveal separate majority resolutions of each controlling issue in a manner that favors the candidate who lost. While *Bush v. Gore* reveals the limits on the power of individual Justices to vote strategically, it also explains why in the context of multidimensional and asymmetrical preferences the concurring Justices likely joined the *per curiam* opinion even if we assume less than sincere support. They did so, the authors claim, to create the appearance of a united front in resolving a case that would inevitably be subject to intense, perhaps unprecedented, media and public scrutiny.

DISCUSSION QUESTIONS

1. Does the attitudinal model provide an adequate account of *Bush v. Gore*? What does the social choice account add to an attitudinal analysis of the case? Can the attitudinal model account for the potential strategic judicial behavior described in the preceding analysis? Why or why not?

2. Is there any theory of precedent discussed in chapter 7 that can explain the attitude toward precedent articulated in *Bush v. Gore*, namely, that the case was not intended to have precedential effect? What, if anything, does the Court's declaration to that effect in *Bush v. Gore* say about that case or about judicial precedent more generally? Why do we not see Justices more regularly limiting the precedential scope of their opinions?

3. How, if at all, might the outcome and analysis of *Bush v. Gore* change under the approaches offered by Rogers, Post and Salop, Kornhauser and Sager, and Nash? Would any of these authors' alternative voting protocols have produced a more preferable outcome in the case? Why or why not?

4. Does the application of outcome voting in *Bush v. Gore* help to produce an outcome that legitimates the decision as the term legitimacy is used in chapter 3? Why or why not? Would an alternative voting protocol have affected the decision's legitimacy? Do you think the case is legitimate? Why or why not?

B. ADARAND v. PENA[234]

The next case illustrates yet another dimension of Supreme Court strategy, this time in a case that created an enormously influential precedent affecting race-based set-asides and the standard of review for evaluating them under equal protection doctrine. This case was decided against the backdrop of a series of equal protection cases involving race-based preferences. After briefly summarizing those cases, we will highlight the particular features of *Adarand* that invite questions concerning the potential role of strategic decision making.

The analysis begins with a longstanding debate among members of the Supreme Court concerning whether to apply the traditional strict scrutiny standard in cases that involve race when the purpose for using race is to benefit that affected minority group. Justice Brennan, joined by other liberal members of the Court, long took the position that while the use of race requires a more exacting standard than rational basis scrutiny, under which most racial classifications would survive judicial challenge, because the use of race in these cases is benign, it is not appropriate to employ strict scrutiny, the position advanced by Chief Justice Rehnquist and other conservatives on the Court, under which virtually all classifica-

---

234. Portions of this discussion are adapted from Stearns, *supra* note 124.

tions based upon race are likely to fail. In *Fullilove v. Klutznick*,[235] Justice Brennan, writing for a plurality of four, sustained a federal racial set-aside program in a case involving a minority preference program in the context of construction contracting, applying the intermediate scrutiny standard. That standard, associated most notably with sex- or gender-based classifications, requires an important governmental interest and means that substantially further that interest. In *City of Richmond v. J.A. Croson Co.*,[236] a majority rejected the application of the *Fullilove* standard to a program adopted by the City of Richmond, Virginia, that was primarily intended to mirror the federal program sustained under intermediate scrutiny. *Croson* instead applied strict scrutiny, holding that the states (and by extension municipalities) had less power over matters of race than did Congress, which was expressly given enforcement power under § 5 of the Fourteenth Amendment.

In *Metro Broadcasting, Inc. v. FCC*,[237] Justice Brennan finally succeeded in securing majority support for the application of intermediate scrutiny in the context of a racial preference for broadcast licensing as implemented by the Federal Communications Commission ("FCC"). In sustaining the FCC order under the intermediate scrutiny test, the *Metro Broadcasting* Court succeeded in distinguishing *Croson* and affording precedential status to the intermediate scrutiny test previously announced in the *Fullilove* plurality decision, at least for federal benign racial classifications.

Against this background, the Supreme Court once more confronted the question of what standard to apply in the context of race-based set-asides in the landmark 1995 decision, *Adarand Constructors, Inc. v. Pena*.[238] In *Adarand*, the Central Federal Lands Highway Division ("CFLHD"), part of the United States Department of Transportation ("DOT"), included a federal racial set-aside incentive for highway contracting. Adarand had submitted a lower bid than the successful bidder Gonzales, a covered minority under the incentive scheme. The general contractor stated that but for the incentive program, he would have accepted Adarand's lower bid.

While Justice O'Connor wrote a majority opinion for the *Adarand* Court, the decision nonetheless contained an important anomaly. In this instance, the relevant text *precedes* the formal majority opinion. The reporter's entry reads as follows:

> O'Connor, J., announced the judgment of the Court and delivered an opinion with respect to Parts I, II, III–A, III–B, III–D, and IV, which was for the Court except insofar as it might be inconsistent with the views expressed in the concurrence of Scalia, J., and an opinion with respect to Part III–C. Parts I, II, III–A, III–B, III–D, and IV of that

---

235. 448 U.S. 448 (1980).

236. 488 U.S. 469 (1989).

237. 497 U.S. 547 (1990).

238. 515 U.S. 200 (1995).

opinion were joined by Rehnquist, C.J., and Kennedy and Thomas, JJ., and by Scalia, J., to the extent heretofore indicated; and Part III–C was joined by Kennedy, J. Scalia, J., and Thomas, J., filed opinions concurring in part and concurring in the judgment. Stevens, J., filed a dissenting opinion, in which Ginsburg, J., joined. Souter, J., filed a dissenting opinion, in which Ginsburg and Breyer, JJ., joined. Ginsburg, J., filed a dissenting opinion, in which Breyer, J., joined.[239]

The *Adarand* Court produced a total of five separate opinions. These included Justice O'Connor's opinion, in part for a majority and in part for herself and Justice Kennedy; Justice Scalia's partial concurrence and partial concurrence in the judgment; and three dissents, authored by Justices Stevens, Souter, and Ginsburg. In its simplest form, the opinion represents a five-to-four split on the question whether to apply strict or intermediate scrutiny to this racial preference, with the conservative members of the Court applying strict scrutiny and thus striking the challenged program down. As in *Bush v. Gore*, however, beneath this surface-level agreement rested a set of fault lines that involved considerable disagreement not only between the majority and dissent but also among members of the apparent members of the majority coalition. Also, as in *Bush v. Gore*, an interesting question arises why at least one member of that coalition joined despite apparently significant differences between the two relevant ideal points.

The primary question in *Adarand* centered on the standard of review for assessing a benign race-based classification. In her opinion for the Court, Justice O'Connor reviewed the earlier history and then stated:

> A year [after *Croson*, a case applying strict scrutiny to a municipal race-based set-aside], however, the Court took a surprising turn. *Metro Broadcasting, Inc.* v. *FCC* involved a Fifth Amendment challenge to two race-based policies of the Federal Communications Commission (FCC). In *Metro Broadcasting*, the Court repudiated the long-held notion that "it would be unthinkable that the same Constitution would impose a lesser duty on the Federal Government" than it does on a State to afford equal protection of the laws. It did so by holding that "benign" federal racial classifications need only satisfy intermediate scrutiny, even though *Croson* had recently concluded that such classifications enacted by a State must satisfy strict scrutiny. "[B]enign" federal racial classifications, the Court said, "—even if those measures are not 'remedial' in the sense of being designed to compensate victims of past governmental or societal discrimination—are constitutionally permissible to the extent that they serve *important* governmental objectives within the power of Congress and are *substantially related* to achievement of those objectives." The Court did not explain how to tell whether a racial classification should be deemed "benign," other than to express "confiden[ce] that an 'exami-

---

239. 515 U.S. at 202–03 (internal citations omitted).

nation of the legislative scheme and its history' will separate benign measures from other types of racial classifications."

Applying this test, the Court first noted that the FCC policies at issue did not serve as a remedy for past discrimination. Proceeding on the assumption that the policies were nonetheless "benign," it concluded that they served the "important governmental objective" of "enhancing broadcast diversity," and that they were "substantially related" to that objective. It therefore upheld the policies.

By adopting intermediate scrutiny as the standard of review for congressionally mandated "benign" racial classifications, *Metro Broadcasting* departed from prior cases in two significant respects. First, it turned its back on *Croson's* explanation of why strict scrutiny of all governmental racial classifications is essential:

> Absent searching judicial inquiry into the justification for such race based measures, there is simply no way of determining what classifications are 'benign' or 'remedial' and what classifications are in fact motivated by illegitimate notions of racial inferiority or simple racial politics. Indeed, the purpose of strict scrutiny is to 'smoke out' illegitimate uses of race by assuring that the legislative body is pursuing a goal important enough to warrant use of a highly suspect tool. The test also ensures that the means chosen 'fit' this compelling goal so closely that there is little or no possibility that the motive for the classification was illegitimate racial prejudice or stereotype.

We adhere to that view today, despite the surface appeal of holding "benign" racial classifications to a lower standard, because "it may not always be clear that a so called preference is in fact benign." "[M]ore than good motives should be required when government seeks to allocate its resources by way of an explicit racial classification system."

Second, *Metro Broadcasting* squarely rejected one of the three propositions established by the Court's earlier equal protection cases, namely, congruence between the standards applicable to federal and state racial classifications, and in so doing also undermined the other two—skepticism of all racial classifications and consistency of treatment irrespective of the race of the burdened or benefited group. Under *Metro Broadcasting*, certain racial classifications ("benign" ones enacted by the Federal Government) should be treated less skeptically than others; and the race of the benefited group is critical to the determination of which standard of review to apply. *Metro Broadcasting* was thus a significant departure from much of what had come before it.

The three propositions undermined by *Metro Broadcasting* all derive from the basic principle that the Fifth and Fourteenth Amendments to the Constitution protect *persons*, not *groups*. It follows from that principle that all governmental action based on race—a *group* classification long recognized as "in most circumstances irrelevant and therefore prohibited,"—should be subjected to detailed judicial inquiry to ensure that the *personal* right to equal protection of the laws has not been infringed. These ideas have long been central to this Court's understanding of equal protection, and holding "benign" state and federal racial classifications to different standards does not square with them. "[A] free people whose institutions are founded upon the doctrine of equality," should tolerate no retreat from the principle that government may treat people differently because of their race only for the most compelling reasons. Accordingly, we hold today that all racial classifications, imposed by whatever federal, state, or local governmental actor, must be analyzed by a reviewing court under strict scrutiny. In other words, such classifications are constitutional only if they are narrowly tailored measures that further compelling governmental interests. To the extent that *Metro Broadcasting* is inconsistent with that holding, it is overruled.[240]

In part III.D of her opinion for the Court, Justice O'Connor responded to concerns that by raising the standard to strict scrutiny, the result would be to imperil any potentially benign use of race. Specifically, Justice O'Connor raised the possibility that even under the chosen standard, some challenged statutes might survive. O'Connor explained:

> Finally, we wish to dispel the notion that strict scrutiny is "strict in theory, but fatal in fact." The unhappy persistence of both the practice and the lingering effects of racial discrimination against minority groups in this country is an unfortunate reality, and government is not disqualified from acting in response to it. As recently as 1987, for example, every Justice of this Court agreed that the Alabama Department of Public Safety's "pervasive, systematic, and obstinate discriminatory conduct" justified a narrowly tailored race-based remedy. When race-based action is necessary to further a compelling interest, such action is within constitutional constraints if it satisfies the "narrow tailoring" test this Court has set out in previous cases.[241]

Justice Scalia produced a short concurring opinion, which we reproduce in full:

> I join the opinion of the Court, except Part III–C, and except insofar as it may be inconsistent with the following: In my view, government can never have a "compelling interest" in discriminating on the basis of race in order to "make up" for past racial discrimination in the opposite direction. Individuals who have been wronged by unlawful racial discrimination should be made whole; but under our Constitution there can be no such thing as either a creditor or a debtor race. That concept is alien to the Constitution's focus upon the individual, see Amdt. 14, § 1 ("[N]or shall any State ... deny *to any person*" the equal protection of the laws) (emphasis added), and its

---

240. *Id.* at 225–27 (citations omitted).

241. *Id.* at 237 (citations omitted).

rejection of dispositions based on race, see Amdt. 15, § 1 (prohibiting abridgment of the right to vote "on account of race"), or based on blood, see Art. III, § 3 ("[N]o Attainder of Treason shall work Corruption of Blood"); Art. I, § 9 ("No Title of Nobility shall be granted by the United States"). To pursue the concept of racial entitlement—even for the most admirable and benign of purposes—is to reinforce and preserve for future mischief the way of thinking that produced race slavery, race privilege and race hatred. In the eyes of government, we are just one race here. It is American.

It is unlikely, if not impossible, that the challenged program would survive under this understanding of strict scrutiny, but I am content to leave that to be decided on remand.[242]

The dissenters rejected the application of strict scrutiny altogether. Justice Souter provided the most detailed analysis on this issue:

> The result in *Fullilove* was controlled by the plurality for whom Chief Justice Burger spoke in announcing the judgment. Although his opinion did not adopt any label for the standard it applied, and although it was later seen as calling for less than strict scrutiny, none other than Justice Powell joined the plurality opinion as comporting with his own view that a strict scrutiny standard should be applied to all injurious race-based classifications.... Chief Justice Burger's non-categorical approach is probably best seen not as more lenient than strict scrutiny but as reflecting his conviction that the treble-tiered scrutiny structure merely embroidered on a single standard of reasonableness whenever an equal protection challenge required a balancing of justification against probable harm. Indeed, the Court's very recognition today that strict scrutiny can be compatible with the survival of a classification so reviewed demonstrates that our concepts of equal protection enjoy a greater elasticity than the standard categories might suggest.

> In assessing the degree to which today's holding portends a departure from past practice, it is also worth noting that nothing in today's opinion implies any view of Congress's § 5 power and the deference due its exercise that differs from the views expressed by the *Fullilove* plurality. The Court simply notes the observation in *Croson* "that the Court's 'treatment of an exercise of congressional power in *Fullilove* cannot be dispositive here,' because *Croson*'s facts did not implicate Congress's broad power under § 5 of the Fourteenth Amendment," and explains that there is disagreement among today's majority about the extent of the § 5 power....

> Finally, I should say that I do not understand that today's decision will necessarily have any effect on the resolution of an issue that was just as pertinent under *Fullilove*'s unlabeled standard as it is under the standard of strict scrutiny now adopted by the Court. The

---

242. *Id.* at 239 (Scalia, J., concurring in part and concurring in the judgment) (citations omitted).

Court has long accepted the view that constitutional authority to remedy past discrimination is not limited to the power to forbid its continuation, but extends to eliminating those effects that would otherwise persist and skew the operation of public systems even in the absence of current intent to practice any discrimination.... Indeed, a majority of the Court today reiterates that there are circumstances in which Government may, consistently with the Constitution, adopt programs aimed at remedying the effects of past invidious discrimination.

. . .

Surely the transition from the *Fullilove* plurality view (in which Justice Powell joined) to today's strict scrutiny (which will presumably be applied as Justice Powell employed it) does not signal a change in the standard by which the burden of a remedial racial preference is to be judged as reasonable or not at any given time. If in the District Court Adarand had chosen to press a challenge to the reasonableness of the burden of these statutes, more than a decade after *Fullilove* had examined such a burden, I doubt that the claim would have fared any differently from the way it will now be treated on remand from this Court.[243]

As you review these opinions, consider why Justice Scalia, who expressly rejected Justice O'Connor's strict scrutiny analysis as not being "strict in theory, but fatal in fact," nonetheless joined this portion of her opinion, and did so subject the caveat that "In my view, government can never have a 'compelling interest' in discriminating on the basis of race in order to 'make up' for past racial discrimination in the opposite direction."[244] In Scalia's analysis, therefore, strict scrutiny in race cases is always fatal since there is never a sufficiently compelling governmental interest to justify the use of race. And yet, Justice Scalia did join part III.D of O'Connor's opinion, subject to the unusual caveat described above, which created the possibility that strict scrutiny might be less than fatal.

DISCUSSION QUESTIONS

1. In a more ordinary course of events, we might instead have expected Justice Scalia to issue a concurrence in the judgment. This would have allowed him to vote consistently with the outcome—striking down the federal race-based preference—while also explaining that the application of strict scrutiny should invariably be fatal to such laws. Can you explain why, instead, Scalia elected to join the O'Connor opinion even though he disagreed on the fundamental question whether strict scrutiny is fatal? Is *Metro Broadcasting* relevant in answering this question? Why or why not?

---

243. *Id.* at 267–71 (Souter, J., dissenting) (citations and footnote omitted).

244. *Id.* at 239 (Scalia, J. concurring).

2. What motivated the differing views on whether strict scrutiny should or not should not be fatal? Is *Grutter v. Bollinger*[245] the Supreme Court decision that sustained the affirmative action program at the University of Michigan Law School, relevant in answering this question? Why or why not? If you think that *Grutter* is relevant, do you also think that anticipating this future case makes Scalia's position strategic? Does it make O'Connor's inclusion of a caveat—strict in theory is not fatal in fact—strategic? Can both positions be strategic? Why or why not?

3. Is *Adarand* consistent or in tension with the attitudinal model? While that model can certainly account for the 5-to-4 conservative majority, can it also account for the Justice Scalia's decision to join the majority opinion, rather than to write a concurrence in the judgment based upon his preferred view that strict scrutiny should be fatal in fact? Why or why not?

C. GONZALES v. CARHART

Before closing, it is worth briefly discussing one final case, *Gonzales v. Carhart*,[246] which upheld a federal Partial–Birth Abortion Ban Act. Just seven years earlier, in *Stenberg v. Carhart*,[247] the Supreme Court struck down Nebraska's partial birth abortion ban on the ground that it lacked an exception for the mother's health. The *Gonzales* Court reached a contrary conclusion even though that statute also lacked such a health exception, based upon Congressional findings that such a health exception was not necessary. While the constitutional issues surrounding this issue are interesting in their own right, for our purposes, the more notable point is the breakdown of the Justices and the separate opinion of Justice Thomas. Justice Kennedy wrote for a majority of five to uphold the federal ban. The majority also included Chief Justice Roberts and Justices Scalia, Thomas, and Alito. Justice Thomas filed separate concurrence that Justice Scalia also joined. Justice Ginsburg wrote a dissent, joined by Justices Stevens, Souter, and Breyer.

Justice Thomas's concurrence was short and we reproduce it in full:

> I join the Court's opinion because it accurately applies current jurisprudence, including *Planned Parenthood of Southeastern Pa. v. Casey*. I write separately to reiterate my view that the Court's abortion jurisprudence, including *Casey* and *Roe* v. *Wade*, has no basis in the Constitution. I also note that whether the Partial–Birth Abortion Ban Act of 2003 constitutes a permissible exercise of Congress' power under the Commerce Clause is not before the Court. The parties did not raise or brief that issue; it is outside the question presented; and the lower courts did not address it.[248]

---

245. Grutter v. Bollinger, 539 U.S. 306 (2003).

246. 550 U.S. 124 (2007).

247. 530 U.S. 914 (2000).

248. 550 U.S. at 168–69 (Thomas, J., concurring).

DISCUSSION QUESTIONS

1.   Justice Kennedy formed part of the jointly authored plurality opinion in *Planned Parenthood v. Casey*,[249] which in 1992 revised the 1973 framework set out in *Roe v. Wade*,[250] but which declined to overturn *Roe*'s "essential holding." The *Casey* revision included abandoning the trimester framework and stating that *Roe* had given inadequate weight to the state's interest in the potentiality of human life represented in the fetus. Based upon *Casey*, it appears likely that Justice Kennedy disagrees with Thomas on the merits of overturning *Roe*. That is certainly less obvious, however, for Chief Justice Roberts and Justice Alito. If, in fact, these two relatively new members of the Court agree with the merits of the assertion that *Roe* should not be retained, why did they nonetheless decline to join Justice Thomas's *Gonzales* dissent? Can we infer from their decision not to join that they disagree on the merits? If they agree but did not join, was this decision "strategic"? Why or why not? Are decisions not to join separate opinions, concurrences or dissents, different from decisions not to join controlling opinions? If so, how? Do the models set out in this chapter help to answer this question? Why or why not?

2.   Does the attitudinal model provide insight into the voting patterns in *Gonzales* and the Court's treatment of precedent? Easterbrook argues that when confronted with a case in which following precedent would lead judges to a non-preferred result, the Court prefers to sacrifice transitivity (treating like cases similarly) rather than range (ruling consistently with member selections over all options). Stearns argues that Supreme Court voting rules sacrifice range, but promote adherence to independence. Which view more accurately describes the outcomes and positions of various Justices in *Gonzales* and other abortion cases?

---

249.   505 U.S. 833 (1992).

250.   410 U.S. 113 (1973).

CHAPTER 8

CONSTITUTIONS

■ ■ ■

I. INTRODUCTION

Each of the preceding chapters in this part applied public choice to specific governmental institutions: legislatures, the executive branch (including and agencies), and the judiciary. This final set of institutional applications explores the implications of public choice for constitutional design and implementation. Constitutions are themselves institutions that result from a series of collective decision-making processes and in turn motivate other forms of collective action. These include initial drafting, pre-adoption modifications, debates over ratification, voting on ratification, amendments, and implementation and interpretation by various organs of government. Among the primary objectives of constitutions is to establish the legitimate foundations of governmental powers,[1] to allocate those powers among the specific organs of government that the constitution creates or recognizes,[2] and to provide a road map for the development of positive law and policy, including instructions for constitutional change.

Constitutions perform these complex functions in a variety of ways. First, as a *horizontal* matter, constitutions determine within a given level of government, for example, national or state, which institutional bodies possess particular powers. This sometimes includes the power of a given branch of government to establish its internal decision-making procedures. In the United States, this implicates such decision-making processes as bicameralism, presentment, and even constitutional judicial review. Second, as a *vertical* matter, constitutions divide powers among different levels of government: national, state, or local. This analysis implicates

---

1. Within the United States, this constitutional feature takes a different form in the federal and state contexts. Whereas state constitutions operate on a plenary powers model in which, most notably, legislative power is presumed unless restricted by the state or federal constitutions, the federal Constitution demands a specific or implied delegation of power, usually taken from the preexisting collective powers of the states, as a precondition to its exercise, and also includes express limitations on federal governmental powers. *See, e.g.*, Gibbons v. Ogden, 22 U.S. (9 Wheat.) 1, 233–34 (1824) (Johnson, J., concurring); Maxwell L. Stearns, *The Misguided Renaissance of Social Choice*, 103 YALE L.J. 1219, 1258 (1994).

2. The United States Constitution, for example, does not create state governments, but recognizes their pre-existing powers. *See, e.g.*, U.S. CONST. amend. X ("The powers not delegated to the United States by the Constitution, nor prohibited by it to the States, are reserved to the States respectively, or to the people.").

questions of federalism and the scope of federal and state governmental powers. Although the precise terminology for these levels of decision-making authority varies among nations, western democracies generally operate in a manner that includes some important similar structural characteristics. Third, constitutions typically set out enumerated protections of individual liberties. In the United States, this takes expression, most notably, in the Bill of Rights. The enumerated powers are generally not exhaustive, and through various interpretive mechanisms, including most notably judicial review, constitutions also provide a means for recognizing unenumerated rights. Finally, constitutions generally establish mechanisms for internal change, taking the form of amending provisions. In this chapter, we are primarily concerned with structural constitutionalism, rather than with the jurisprudential question concerning the proper set or sets of methodologies for constitutional judicial review.

In *Federalist No. 51*, James Madison described a fundamental problem that confronts constitutional architects:

> It may be a reflection on human nature that such devices [taking the form of various structural limitations on governmental institutions] should be necessary to control the abuses of government. But what is government itself but the greatest of all reflections on human nature? If men were angels, no government would be necessary. If angels were to govern men, neither external nor internal controls on government would be necessary. In framing a government which is to be administered by men over men, the great difficulty lies in this: you must first enable the government to control the governed; and in the next place oblige it to control itself. A dependence on the people is, no doubt, the primary control on the government; but experience has taught mankind the necessity of auxiliary precautions.[3]

As Madison observes, the government must be made strong enough "to control the governed," for example by protecting property rights, enforcing contracts, preventing crime, and securing national defense. At the same time, however, once the government is created with the necessary powers to promote the general welfare and to preserve the social order, it becomes necessary to restrain the government itself from unduly infringing on individual liberty. Madison's "auxiliary precautions" can be understood as an effort by the Framers of the United States Constitution to strike an appropriate balance that simultaneously ensures that the government is sufficiently strong to secure the legitimate ends of governance but not so strong as to threaten individual liberty.

As in our analysis of other institutions, we do not suggest that public choice, or economic analysis generally, provides the sole or dominant method of understanding the institutions under review. We do believe, however, that public choice helps to explain several important features about constitutional structure and decision making that remain anomalous when viewed exclusively with traditional methodologies. As you read

---

3. THE FEDERALIST No. 51, at 322 (James Madison) (Clinton Rossiter ed., 1961).

the following materials, consider the extent to which those concerns expressed by public choice theorists about developing appropriate mechanisms that limit opportunities for rent seeking by special interests and that avoid excessive agency costs by governmental actors help to frame the various tradeoffs that confront constitutional architects and those operating within constitutional systems.

II. CONSTITUTIONS THROUGH A PUBLIC CHOICE LENS

A. PURPOSES OF CONSTITUTIONS

We begin by recasting Madison's concerns expressed in *Federalist No. 51* with the tools of economics to emphasize those tradeoffs that public choice helps to assess.[4] The analysis focuses on two important aspects of constitutional design: first, pre-commitment strategies that limit governmental powers and that channel decision making through specified procedures, and second, mechanisms that reduce agency costs by limiting opportunities for government officials to benefit from pursuing objectives that depart from those for whom they are expected to serve and for whose benefit they derive their power.

First, constitutions can be understood as pre-commitment devices that specify that the government will only exercise powers that are properly delegated and in a particular manner that follows procedures specified in advance. Such procedures include, for example, rules for enacting legislation, rules for ratifying treaties, rules for impeachment, rules that limit police and prosecutorial authority, preconditions to the exercise of governmental powers, rules governing amendment, and judicial review to ensure compliance with the constitution's commands. For example, the United States Constitution demands both federal and state compliance with the Bill of Rights and also demands state compliance with the protections set out in the Reconstruction Amendments. To what extent do these or other constitutional limitations on the exercise of governmental powers limit the ability of special interests (or borrowing Madison's framing in *Federalist No. 10*—majoritarian factions), from capturing the legislature or other governmental organs and from using such powers to pursue private, rather than public, ends? To what extent do the same mechanisms have the contrary (and perhaps unintended) consequence of providing special interests with opportunities to use legislative or adjudicatory processes to their advantage?

Second, constitutions seek to mitigate the problem of agency costs. As seen in chapter 1, agency costs arise when government actors pursue their

---

4. For an accessible introduction that distinguishes the economic approach to constitutions from alternative perspectives, see James M. Buchanan, *The Constitutional Way of Thinking*, 10 Sup. Ct. Econ. Rev. 143 (2003). *See also* A.C. Pritchard & Todd J. Zywicki, *Finding the Constitution: An Economic Analysis of Tradition's Role in Constitutional Interpretation*, 77 N.C. L. Rev. 409 (1999) (defining "efficiency" purposes of constitutions as creating enforceable supermajoritarian precommitments and reducing agency costs by governmental actors).

own objectives at the expense of those for whom they have been entrusted with delegated powers. Judicial independence, for example, has the potential to reduce agency costs by limiting political pressures on judges to not enforce sometimes unpopular constitutional pre-commitments that limit the immediately desired exercise of governmental powers. Alternatively, however, the very same political insulation might provide judges with the opportunity to pursue their own private objectives, including leisure or case decisions that infuse ideological predilections or attitudes (as discussed in chapter 7).

B. THE CALCULUS OF CONSENT: LOGICAL FOUNDATIONS OF CONSTITUTIONAL DEMOCRACY

In the pioneering work *The Calculus of Consent: Logical Foundations of Constitutional Democracy*,[5] James Buchanan and Gordon Tullock provided an early public choice analysis that studied various aspects of constitutional design.[6] Most notably, the authors focused on the tradeoff between protecting against interest group capture on the one hand and limiting agency costs on the other. This work is particularly notable for applying frequently abstract and theoretical public choice intuitions to the specific context of the United States Constitution. Buchanan and Tullock also introduced a novel analytical approach. In thinking about constitutions, legal thinkers often begin by positing the *ends* of government and then deducing those constitutional rules that will bring about those ends. Buchanan and Tullock, in contrast, first considered the *means* that individuals would agree to use in setting up a constitution for self-governance and then relied upon such means to deduce agreeable ends.

1. Stages of Constitutional Decision Making

Buchanan and Tullock rely upon an exchange model of politics as the fundamental underpinning in understanding constitutional design. A foundational aspect of their analysis involves distinguishing two periods in governmental decision making: first, the "constitutional" stage, and second, the "post-constitutional" or positive law stage.[7] The constitutional

---

5. JAMES M. BUCHANAN & GORDON TULLOCK, THE CALCULUS OF CONSENT: LOGICAL FOUNDATIONS OF CONSTITUTIONAL DEMOCRACY (1962).

6. The analysis of Buchanan and Tullock rests in part on the philosophical foundation of "social contract" theory. For a historically grounded model of the emergence of constitutional rights premised on public choice insights, see Ejan Mackaay, *The Emergence of Constitutional Rights*, 8 CONST. POL. ECON. 15 (1997).

7. While Buchanan and Tullock imagine these stages as forming a chronological sequence, a more nuanced understanding recognizes that constitutional interpretation informs constitutional framing (stage 1) by refining foundational rules that affect those mechanisms governing the creation of positive law (stage 2). This process continues *even though* constitutional interpretation operates contemporaneously with positive law decision making in stage 2. For an analysis that posits a risk of unifying these stages and of entrenching power elites at one stage to form a preferred constitution in a later stage, see Tom Ginsburg, *Public Choice and Constitutional Design*, *in* ELGAR HANDBOOK IN PUBLIC CHOICE AND PUBLIC LAW (Daniel Farber & Anne Joseph O'Connell eds., forthcoming 2009), *manuscript available at* http://ssrn.com/abstract=1334318.

stage establishes the rules for how decisions will be made at the post-constitutional stage. For instance, the constitutional stage of analysis determines whether the legislature will take unicameral or bicameral form, whether the head of state will be selected through a Parliamentary (legislatively determined) or Presidential (electorally determined) system, and which substantive regulatory areas will be controlled at the national or state and local levels. Although refinements will continue through such means as practical accommodations, judicial decision making, or even amendment, in general, once the governmental structure is constituted, ordinary, or positive, lawmaking begins in the post-constitutional stage.

Buchanan and Tullock argue that for some issues, it is likely easier to achieve consensus during the constitutional stage, because at this point individuals are considering general rules intended to govern post-constitutional interactions. In the post-constitutional stage, individuals will be aware of their place in society and thus are apt to be concerned about how proposed policies will likely benefit or harm them. At the constitutional stage, in contrast, policy issues are presented at a higher level of generality. Thus, at the stage of constitutional formation, there is likely to be greater agreement on fair and neutral rules.[8] The authors liken the selection of constitutional rules to the adoption of rules at the outset of playing a game, where none of the players can anticipate which specific rules might benefit him or her during a particular round of play. As a result, as compared with rulemaking in the post-constitutional stage, this reduces conflicts of interest that will inevitably arise. As Buchanan and Tullock observe:

> This is not to suggest that he will act contrary to his own interest; but the individual will not find it advantageous to vote for rules that may promote sectional, class, or group interests because, by presupposition, he is unable to predict the role that he will be playing in the actual collective decision-making process at any particular time in the future. He cannot predict with any degree of certainty whether he is more likely to be in a winning or a losing coalition on any specific issue. Therefore, he will assume that occasionally he will be in one group and occasionally in the other. His own self-interest will lead him to choose rules that will maximize the utility of an individual in a series of collective decisions with his own preferences on the separate issues being more or less randomly distributed.[9]

Are Buchanan and Tullock correct in their assumption that at the constitutional stage of inquiry individuals will be largely unable to anticipate what the likely impact of the rules will be on their individual circumstances? If this is true at the initial constitutional stage, will it also be true of any subsequent amendments to the constitution? Bear these questions in mind as you read the discussion of the constitutional amendments at the end of this chapter.

---

8.   *See* BUCHANAN & TULLOCK, *supra* note 5, at 78.

9.   *Id.*

2. Normative Foundations of Constitutional Decision-Making Rules: The Primacy of Unanimity

In the context of collective decision making, Buchanan and Tullock posit that unanimity holds conceptual primacy. Like Pareto superiority, its counterpart in the private sphere, as a theoretical matter unanimity appears to avoid the problem of "externalities."[10] As a consequence, this decision-making rule uniquely ensures that collective action will be accomplished in a manner that ensures the probability of furthering social welfare.[11]

To appreciate the authors' argument, let us briefly return to the context of private exchange. In assessing whether a given exchange is welfare enhancing, meaning that it produces wealth, thus providing a net benefit to society, it is insufficient to rest upon the claimed benefits to the actual parties to a given exchange. We must also consider any external costs (or benefits) to third parties. For example, while A might employ B to provide a service on mutually beneficial terms, in performing the contract terms, B might cause pollution to C's detriment. Because A and B consent to the transaction, we can infer from their revealed preferences that both are thereby better off. (Recall that Pareto superiority demands at a minimum that at least one party is better off and neither party is worse off.) Unless A and B compensate C for any resulting externality, however, we cannot know if the transaction is welfare enhancing or, instead, if it produces negative social costs. If those suffering externalities are fully compensated and thus voluntarily consent to the transaction, then we can infer that exchange improves overall social welfare by making at least one party better off and leaving no others any worse off. In contrast, if the potential gains to A and B are insufficient to compensate C, then going forward with the transaction will reduce social welfare overall.

Although the Pareto criterion represents a normatively appealing measure of improved social welfare, it also poses intractable difficulties in implementation. The difficulties include identifying and bargaining with all individuals who might suffer from a given collective action. In addition, to ensure the optimal allocation of resources (meaning not only that individual transactions are Pareto superior, but also that all such transactions take place with the overall result of Pareto optimality), it is not sufficient to avoid *negative* externalities. It becomes necessary to identify and seek contributions from persons who benefit from *positive* externalities. Given the insuperable practical hurdles associated with locating and compensating potential losers (or seeking contributions from potential winners) from collective action, economists typically substitute Kaldor

---

10. As we will later see, this assertion creates potential difficulty in the context of constitutional choice. *See infra* p. 519–20.

11. Assuming no mistakes, the unanimity rule would invariably enhance social welfare, but as with any rule, it remains possible that individuals will erroneously proceed with transactions that prove mistaken, and thus welfare reducing.

Hicks efficiency as an acceptable, albeit imperfect, proxy for unanimity.[12] Under the Kaldor Hicks criterion, collective decisions are defined as efficient when the social gains are sufficiently large to compensate against losses even though the actual compensation is never realized.

As the following example illustrates, collective decision making raises social welfare concerns parallel to those that arise in the context of market exchange. Assume that A and B wish to build a road costing $60, allowing each to benefit by an amount of $25, but providing C no benefit.[13] Assume that A and B vote to fund the road by imposing a tax on all three constituents in equal amounts of $20. If A and B can force C to share this tax burden equally, C will suffer a net loss of $20.[14] Under a regime that demands the unanimous consent of all participants, in contrast, C would simply veto the project. In this example, under a unanimity rule, only if A and B gained sufficient social surplus from building the road to compensate C for the resulting tax burden would the project proceed. In fact, however, the total social benefit of the project, $50, is lower than the total social cost of $60. Only by imposing a negative external cost on C of $20, effectively forcing a non-beneficiary of the road to subsidize it, do A and B perceive a net gain of $10 (contributing $40 in taxes toward the road but receiving a combined benefit worth $50).[15]

Buchanan and Tullock argue that in the context of collective choice, unanimity serves the same function as does Pareto superiority in private exchange because it forces the necessary side payments from winners to losers that ensure that resulting transactions improve social welfare.[16] In an important passage, Buchanan and Tullock explain that while welfare economists have traditionally focused on private exchange externalities as a normative justification for market regulation, the political process itself is susceptible of generating its own externalities:

> [I]t is especially surprising that the discussion about externality in the literature of welfare economics has been centered on the external costs expected to result from *private* action of individuals or firms. To our knowledge little or nothing has been said about the *external* costs imposed on the individual by *collective* action. Yet the existence of such external costs is inherent in the operation of any collective decision-making rule other than that of unanimity. Indeed, the essence of the collective-choice process under majority voting rules is the fact that the minority of voters are forced to accede to actions which they cannot prevent and for which they cannot claim compensation for [resulting damages]. Note that this is precisely the definition previously given for externality.

---

12. RICHARD A. POSNER, ECONOMIC ANALYSIS OF LAW § 1.2, at 13 (6th ed. 2003).

13. In this illustration, A, B and C can represent individuals or, more plausibly, neighborhoods within a particular city.

14. *See supra* chapter 3, section II.E.

15. For a discussion of the related concept of forced riding, see *supra* chapter 1, section II.E.

16. BUCHANAN & TULLOCK, *supra* note 5, at 92.

> [T]he rule of unanimity makes collective decision-making volun-
> tary in [the] sense [that potentially disadvantaged persons possess
> effective veto power]. Therefore, in the absence of costs of organizing
> decision-making, voluntary arrangements would tend to be worked
> out which would effectively remove all relevant externalities. Collec-
> tivization, insofar as this is taken to imply some coercion, would never
> be chosen by the rational individual. As previously emphasized, the
> individual will choose collectivization only because of its relatively
> greater efficiency in the organization of decision-making. The exis-
> tence of external costs (or the existence of any externality) creates
> opportunities for mutually advantageous "trades" or "bargains" to be
> made among individuals affected and also profit possibilities for
> individuals who are acute enough to recognize such situations. Fur-
> thermore, if we disregard the costs of making the required arrange-
> ments, voluntary action would more or less automatically take place
> that would be sufficient to "internalize" all [externalities], that is, to
> reduce expected external costs to zero. As implied earlier, all ordinary
> market exchange is, in a real sense, directed toward this end. More-
> over, if there were no costs of organizing such exchanges, we could
> expect marketlike arrangements to expand to the point where all
> conceivable relevant externalities would be eliminated.[17]

Buchanan and Tullock treat two different costs as externalities: first,
those costs posed by activities that arise from adverse, or downstream,
effects on third parties, and second, the tax burdens imposed on those
forced to fund projects that provide them (as with *C* in our road hypothetical) with no corresponding benefit. Thus Buchanan and Tullock state:

> The private operation of the neighborhood plant with the smoking
> chimney may impose external costs on the individual by soiling his
> laundry, but this cost is no more external to the individual's own
> private calculus than the tax cost imposed on him unwillingly in order
> to finance the provision of public services to his fellow citizen in
> another area.[18]

Whatever difficulties the *Pareto* criterion poses for private market
exchange are exacerbated in the context of collective decision making. We
can frame the difficulty in terms of two kinds of transactions costs. First,
a unanimity standard for collective action would pose considerable costs
associated with identifying and negotiating with everyone who potentially
suffers adverse consequences from a proposed collective decision. Second,
unanimity invites a separate problem of strategic bargaining. By affording

---

17. *Id.* at 89–90.

18. *Id.* at 65–66. The authors further suggest that when collective action is not constrained by
institutions such as private property, government externalities might loom larger than private
market externalities. One way to frame the Buchanan and Tullock analysis is to distinguish
between "political" externalities (those identified by Buchanan and Tullock as created by
collective action, which includes what we have previously introduced as "forced riding") and
"economic" externalities (those created by private market actors). *See* Todd J. Zywicki, *Environmental Externalities and Political Externalities: The Political Economy of Environmental Regulation and Reform,* 73 TUL. L. REV. 845 (1999).

each individual full veto power over any proposed collective choice, unanimity would invite strategic behavior in which rational individuals would seek to secure a disproportionate share of the surplus resulting from welfare-enhancing collective action—perhaps even a complete bargaining breakdown—*whether or not* that action adversely affects them.[19]

DISCUSSION QUESTIONS

To what extent does the road hypothetical require assuming a single period of play? Would anticipating multiple rounds of play reduce the likelihood that *A* and *B*, who want the road, would support the welfare reducing result of spending $60 for a project with a social value of $50 by placing *C*, who receives no benefit, in the position of a forced rider?[20] Why or why not?

Consider the argument that the Buchanan and Tullock analysis of the unanimity baseline as a precondition to collective action implicitly limits social welfare considerations to payoffs and losses among private market participants. How, if at all, might the analysis change if the authors were to extend the sphere of inquiry to include the potential payoffs or losses among legislators? Do such cases as *Lochner v. New York*,[21] recognizing a right of economic substantive due process, on the one hand, and *West Coast Hotel Co. v. Parrish*,[22] applying rational basis scrutiny to economic regulations of working conditions, on the other, demonstrate the inevitability at some point within a constitutional democracy of choosing whether to adhere to the unanimity norm in either the market or the legislative spheres?[23] If so, does public choice analysis provide the framework for choosing which normative baseline to apply? Why or why not?

C. SPECIFIC FEATURES OF CONSTITUTIONAL DESIGN

In the analysis of Buchanan and Tullock, unanimity holds a privileged analytical position in assessing the efficiency of collective choice. But as

---

19. Some evidence from experimental economics indicates that the strategic bargaining problem might not be as important in practice as in theory and that the threat of strategic bargaining does not increase as group size increases and may actually fall. *See* DENNIS C. MUELLER, PUBLIC CHOICE III, at 73 (2003) (citing the experimental results of Vernon L. Smith and specifically the results of Elizabeth Hoffman & Matthew L. Spitzer, *Experimental Tests of the Coase Theorem with Large Bargaining Groups*, 15 J. LEGAL STUD. 149, 151 (1986), for the finding that " 'efficiency improved with larger groups' "). While one might object to the baseline problem associated with the use of "disproportionate" in the text, the problem is avoided when you consider that strategic bargaining introduces the threat of aggregate compensatory claims that exceed 100% of the value of the proposed government action. Should this occur, then without regard to who is claiming disproportionate entitlement, it is clear that someone clearly is.

20. For a related discussion, see *supra* chapter 3, section II.F (discussing vote-trading hypothetical) and chapter 5, section II.B.4 (same).

21.   198 U.S. 45 (1905).

22.   300 U.S. 379 (1937).

23. For a related discussion, see *supra* chapter 3, section III.B (discussing the tradeoff between honoring the unanimity norm in the market and legislative spheres). For a discussion demonstrating the possibility that in a direct democracy in which Coasian assumptions apply, unanimous consent to democratic action has the potential to produce the same results as private market unanimity since winners and losers could be fully compensated in both spheres, see James M. Buchanan, *The Coase Theorem and the Theory of the State*, 13 NAT. RESOURCES J. 579, 583–84 (1973).

previously noted, unanimity, like Pareto efficiency, proves unworkable in practice. With respect to the Pareto standard for private action, because of the insuperable practical hurdles associated with locating and compensating potential losers (or seeking contributions from potential winners) from collective action, economists use Kaldor Hicks efficiency as an alternative measure for assessing the efficiency of a given action.

Buchanan and Tullock claim that once we abandon the unanimity benchmark, no obvious normatively superior decision-making rule emerges. Each alternative presents its own set of conceptual difficulties. Buchanan and Tullock approach the choice of imperfect alternatives to unanimity by focusing on two problems that are inherent in collective choice—"external costs" and "decision costs"—and then propose that the optimal decision-making rule minimizes the sum of these costs.[24]

The "External–Costs Function" describes "for the single individual with respect to a single activity, the costs that he expects to endure as a result of the actions of others [as a function of] the number of individuals who are required to agree before a final political decision is taken for the group."[25] As noted above, collective decision-making can impose externalities where certain individuals are forced to bear greater costs than benefits from a particular collective decision. As a result, the expected *external* costs of a given collective decision (measured in present value terms) will be downward-sloping as the number of individuals needed to secure agreement increases. Thus, where the consent of only one or a few are needed for collective action, the expected external costs for all citizens in the polity will be relatively high, whereas if the consent of many members is needed, then expected external costs will be relatively low.

The "Decision–Making–Costs" function is the private costs that each member of the group must incur to participate in making a decision. As an initial matter, these costs include those private costs required to simply inform oneself about the decision to be made and to make up one's mind concerning, for example, such matters as whether to support a higher level of government expenditures or lower taxes. But such costs also include the time and effort to secure agreement with other members of the group. The costs of securing agreement take two forms. First, they include the costs of negotiation among the parties to reach agreement. As the size of the relevant group increases, thereby increasing the number of people who must consent, the negotiation costs of reaching agreement also rises. Second, such costs include the costs of dealing with strategic hold-outs. As the percentage of the group needed to reach agreement rises, so too do incentives and opportunities for strategic hold outs. Buchanan and Tullock explain:

24. Portions of the discussion that follow are adapted from MAXWELL L. STEARNS, PUBLIC CHOICE AND PUBLIC LAW: READINGS AND COMMENTARY 409–17 (1997).

25. BUCHANAN & TULLOCK, *supra* note 5, at 64.

Thus our bargaining-cost function operates in two ranges: in the lower reaches it represents mainly the problems of making up an agreed bargain among a group of people, any one of whom can readily be replaced. Here, as a consequence, there is little incentive to invest resources in strategic bargaining. Near unanimity, investments in strategic bargaining are apt to be great, and the expected costs very high.[26]

With respect to the decision-making costs function, therefore, the costs of reaching agreement will increase at an increasing rate as the number of individuals required to agree to a proposed collective action increases.

The cost functions are depicted on the graph below:[27]

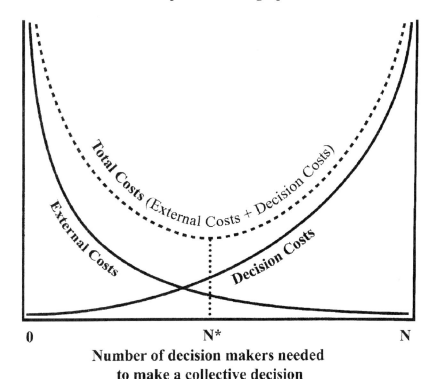

**Number of decision makers needed
to make a collective decision**

N* = Total costs minimized

Figure 8:1

Buchanan and Tullock argue that decision makers would choose the decision-making rule that minimizes the sum of external and decision-making costs.[28]

---

26. *Id.* at 69.

27. STEARNS, *supra* note 24, at 410.

28. The cost-minimization point might be to be to the left or right of the intersection of the two separate cost curves depending upon their slopes.

D. LIMITATIONS TO THE BUCHANAN AND TULLOCK DECISION-MAKING MODEL

Buchanan and Tullock's model of collective decision making describes a particular sort of direct democracy. Most political decisions, however, are made by representative government, not direct democracy. In *Federalist No. 10*, James Madison famously demonstrated that direct democracy is impractical because of the excessive decision costs associated with direct public participation and is normatively problematic because it conduces to the "violence of factions." As a result, Madison argued, representative democracy is not only a necessary expedient that reduces decision-making costs but also an important means through which to reduce the probability of an important category of problematic laws. For Madison, two principal devices helped to control the violence of factions: (1) the removal of the government in a large republic from local prejudices; and (2) the division of Congress into two chambers. Not surprisingly, each of these solutions raises its own problems as well.

1. Representative Democracy

Madison argued first for the superiority of representative democracy to direct democracy:

> The two great points of difference between a democracy and a republic are: first, the delegation of the government. . . .

> The effect of the first difference is, on the one hand, to refine and enlarge the public views by passing them through the medium of a chosen body of citizens, whose wisdom may best discern the true interest of their country and whose patriotism and love of justice will be least likely to sacrifice it to temporary or partial considerations. Under such a regulation it may well happen that the public voice, pronounced by the representatives of the people, will be more consonant to the public good than if pronounced by the people themselves, convened for the purpose. On the other hand, the effect may be inverted. Men of factious tempers, of local prejudices, or of sinister designs, may, by intrigue, by corruption, or by other means, first obtain the suffrages, and then betray the interests of the people.[29]

Madison further analyzed the optimal size of government as follows:

> In the first place it is to be remarked that however small the republic may be the representatives must be raised to a certain number in order to guard against the cabals of a few; and that however large it may be they must be limited to a certain number in order to guard against the confusion of a multitude. Hence, the number of representatives in the two cases not being in proportion to that of the constituents, and being proportionally greatest in the small republic, it follows that if the proportion of fit characters be not

---

29. THE FEDERALIST NO. 10 (James Madison), *supra* note 3, at 82.

less in the large than in the small republic, the former will present a greater option, and consequently a greater probability of a fit choice.

. . . .

. . . Extend the sphere and you take in a greater variety of parties and interests; you make it less probable that a majority of the whole will have a common motive to invade the rights of other citizens; or if such a common motive exists, it will be more difficult for all who feel it to discover their own strength and to act in unison with each other. Besides other impediments, it may be remarked that, where there is a consciousness of unjust or dishonorable purposes, communication is always checked by distrust in proportion to the number whose concurrence is necessary.[30]

Madison thus considers representative democracy, with large districts that combine multiple interests, superior to direct democracy in frustrating majority factions and promoting public-benefiting legislation.

At the same time, representative government raises a new problem of agency costs by elected representatives whose preferences or self interests potentially diverge from those of their constituencies. Madison acknowledges the potential for disloyal agents, "Men of factious tempers, of local prejudices, or of sinister designs, may, by intrigue, by corruption, or by other means, first obtain the suffrages, and then betray the interests, of the people." Agency costs represent the divergence between the preferences of the voter, or principal, and the policy chosen by the legislator, or agent. Agency costs are separate from those costs imposed by majorities on minorities. Recall that Madison posited that the latter costs will be reduced by representative government. Agency costs are those costs imposed by government officials on the public at large when legislators pursue personal interests rather than the public interest. Thus, agency costs are an inevitable feature of representative government. If all voters participated in the creation of public policy, as in the idealized New England town meeting, agency costs would be reduced to zero, although other costs would still remain.

There is thus an inherent tradeoff between direct and representative democracy: reducing decision costs raises agency costs, and the reverse also holds. Reducing agency costs raises decision-making costs by requiring greater public participation and less delegation of authority to elected officials. Similarly, reducing the size of the constituency of elected officials will tend to reduce agency costs by making constituent monitoring more effective. As district sizes are reduced, however, the size of the legislature must increase. Enlarging the size of the legislature reduces the likelihood of a sharp divergence between the views of those who govern and the views of those whom they represent (agency costs) but, at the same time, increases the costs of reaching a collective decision (decision costs). Conversely, reducing the size of the legislature makes collective decisions easier to reach (reducing decision costs) but increases the risk that the

---

30. *Id.* at 82–83.

enacted policies will diverge from those that the electorate prefers (increasing agency costs).

E. BICAMERALISM

Madison's second protection against majority faction is bicameralism, which requires that legislation pass through two Houses rather than one, thereby slowing its pace and raising the effective level of consent for legislative action. In explaining the need to divide the legislature into two chambers, Madison stated:

> In republican government, the legislative authority necessarily predominates. The remedy for this inconveniency is to divide the legislature into different branches; and to render them, by different modes of election and different principles of action, as little connected with each other as the nature of their common functions and their common dependence on the society will admit.[31]

Consistent with Madison's insights, Buchanan and Tullock show that public choice helps to explain the normative foundations for bicameralism, a prevalent feature among western democracies.[32] To explain bicameralism, the authors distinguished two categories of legislative proposals, one involving equal preference intensities among the electorate and the other involving varying preference intensities. As shown in chapter 2,[33] logrolling has the potential to enhance welfare when participants (or those they represent) hold varying intensities of preferences. In this sense, logrolling is comparable to the logic of voluntary market exchange: It is only because "people place different *marginal* valuations on *scarce* goods"[34] that trade occurs at all. If everyone placed the same marginal valuation on all goods then there would be no reason to expend the effort of trading. With equal intensities, those harmed cannot induce those benefiting to trade.[35] Buchanan and Tullock demonstrate that with equal preference intensities,

---

31. THE FEDERALIST No. 51 (James Madison), *supra* note 3, at 322.

32. BUCHANAN & TULLOCK, *supra* note 5, at 233.

33. For a related discussion, see *supra* chapter 1, section III.B.; *see also supra* chapter 2, section III.B.

34. ARMEN ALCHIAN & WILLIAM R. ALLEN, EXCHANGE & PRODUCTION: COMPETITION, COORDINATION, & CONTROL 45 (3d ed. 1983).

35. This insight is by no means limited to legislative vote trading. Of the two principle mediums for creating wealth in private markets, production and exchange, the latter rests upon disparate intensities of preference. Professors Alchian and Allen explain:

> Trade is commonly believed to occur because people have too much of some goods—that is, they supposedly have a **surplus** of those goods. But this is not so. Trade goes on all the time, but virtually never do we think we have "too much" of things. In fact, trade occurs because participants find it mutually attractive, because people place different *marginal* valuations on *scarce* goods. If my marginal personal value of something you own exceeds your marginal personal value, we would both find it attractive to engage in a sale of some of that good to me, at a price below my marginal personal value and above yours.

Id. Stated differently, exchange creates wealth to the extent that the participants procure surpluses, and those surpluses arise only if the participants' intensities of preference are not uniform for the goods or services that are subject to exchange. The same holds true in legislative markets for vote trading.

the requisite consensus level among the electorate to create public policy through the legislature is roughly the same in both a bicameral and unicameral legislature.[36] In the more common case, however, in which intensities are not uniform, Buchanan and Tullock demonstrate that bicameralism substantially—and favorably—alters the calculus of consent.

1. The Theory of Minimum Winning Coalitions Revisited

The analysis returns us once again to William Riker's theory of minimum winning coalitions.[37] Buchanan and Tullock demonstrate that if we assume enacting legislation is a zero-sum game in which side payments are permitted,[38] then just over one-half of the voters within each district would be a successful voting coalition in electing a representative from that district. In addition, just over one-half of the representatives in the legislature as a whole would be a successful coalition in enacting legislation. The result is that just over one-half of the voters in just over one-half the districts could effectively control legislative policy in a unicameral legislature. In a unicameral legislature with simple majority rule, therefore, just over 1/4 of the population has the potential to become a successful governing coalition, with the result of high external costs. Buchanan and Tullock posit that at the stage of constitutional formation, a rational populace is likely to adopt either of two devices to increase the size of successful electoral coalitions. The electorate could implement supermajority rule with a unicameral legislature or, alternatively, it could implement simple majority rule in a bicameral legislature.[39] The authors then demonstrate that simple majority rule with a bicameral legislature— assuming differing electoral requirements within each chamber[40]—raises the size of successful electoral coalitions from just over 1/4 to just over 7/16.[41] The latter figure, while still less than half the population, more closely accords with traditional understandings of majority rule.

To achieve the same consensus requirement in a unicameral legislature, we would need to impose a 7/8 supermajority voting requirement. That alternative, however, would substantially raise the decisional costs of legislation by allowing legislative minorities of 1/8 of the legislature to block legislation. Moreover, applying the above analysis, a voting minority of 1/16 in the population at large could block legislation by electing 1/8 of the legislature. Thus, although supermajority rules reduce external costs, they dramatically increase decision-making costs. In the bicameral legisla-

---

36. BUCHANAN & TULLOCK, *supra* note 5, at 243.

37. *See supra* chapter 2, section III.B.

38. WILLIAM H. RIKER, THE THEORY OF POLITICAL COALITIONS 32 (1962) (positing that "[i]n n-person, zero-sum games, where side-payments are permitted, where players are rational, and where they have perfect information, only minimum winning coalitions occur" (emphasis omitted)).

39. *See* BUCHANAN & TULLOCK, *supra* note 5, at 242.

40. The electoral composition will differ, for example, if in the Senate, each member is elected on a state-wide basis and in the House, each member is elected on a smaller district-wide basis. The consensus requirement is broadened because no majority within each House answers to precisely the same electorate.

41. *See* BUCHANAN & TULLOCK, *supra* note 5, at 244.

ture, the requisite consensus is raised without affording such a narrow minority within a single chamber—or within the population at large—effective veto power. With simple majority rule in a bicameral legislature (assuming no other impediments to the passage of legislation), blocking legislation requires the consent of a majority within one of the two chambers, each elected from the population as a whole. Based upon this analysis, Buchanan and Tullock posit that bicameralism is preferable to unicameralism because while both mechanisms reduce external costs, bicameralism does so with a smaller marginal increase in decision-making costs.

For bicameralism to be effective in raising the effective level of support for a decision, it is necessary that the members of the two houses respond to different constituencies. The value of bicameralism is diminished to the extent that the constituencies, and hence preferences, of the two houses of a bicameral legislature are similar. With similarly composed constituencies it becomes possible to replicate the same winning coalition in both houses of the legislature. Distinct constituencies improve the functioning of bicameralism by enhancing effective electoral support for resulting legislation. Two other prominent constitutional features significantly affect the calculus of consent. While bicameralism raises the consensus threshold to just under 1/2 of the population, the presidential veto, discussed more fully below,[42] raises the effective size of minimum winning coalitions to just over 1/2. If we assume that the President represents the entire electorate, then the veto power, at least in theory, affords a simple majority of the population at large with the power to block legislation.[43] In addition, constitutional judicial review further raises the requisite consensus level for certain categories of legislation in which simple majority rule in a bicameral legislature (and the potential capture by 7/16 of the electorate) has the potential to produce significant adverse consequences for affected minorities or with respect to certain fundamental rights.

2. Levmore's Alternative Account of Bicameralism[44]

Now consider Professor Saul Levmore's response to the foregoing Buchanan and Tullock thesis. Levmore questions whether the congressional model of bicameralism provides a good testing ground for the Buchanan and Tullock thesis given that there is considerable overlap among the relevant constituencies in both the Senate and House of Representatives. Within the Senate, the two senators from each state answer to the same electorate and as an extreme case, members of both the House and Senate elected in Wyoming answer to the very same statewide electorate. In fact, Levmore suggests, one would achieve more diversity in Congress by simply dividing each state in half and having the

---

42. *See infra* p. 526.

43. BUCHANAN & TULLOCK, *supra* note 5, at 248.

44. Portions of the discussion that follow are adapted from STEARNS, *supra* note 24, at 414–16.

separate halves of each state choose one Senator, so long as Senate districts were drawn differently from House districts.[45]

Levmore suggests that a better explanation for bicameralism is that it increases the size of the governing electoral coalition while allowing what he terms "strong-Condorcet winners," meaning those Condorcet winners that will prevail in each house on a given issue on matters of national legislative policy, to survive. In addition, Levmore suggests that bicameralism raises costs to agenda setters in each house given that for any bill to pass it must be approved in both houses in the same form.[46] While 26% of the electorate might govern in a bicameral regime, this does not mean that the same minority coalition will remain a stable governing coalition. Instead, with defections and newly formed coalitions, the effective governing coalition might give rise to something that closely resembles an empty core bargaining game, as coalitions are repeatedly made and broken.[47]

Levmore's larger insight is that solving the consensus problem in a unicameral legislature would require a stringent supermajority rule. The Condorcet criterion is of course grounded in the majoritarian norm,[48] and thus the difficulty with a supermajority voting rule is that it thwarts rather than furthers the legislature's ability to ensure that strong Condorcet winners prevail in the legislative process.

How might Buchanan and Tullock respond? Which explanation do you find more persuasive? Why? To what extent is the historical development of bicameralism in the United States consistent or in tension with the models developed by Buchanan and Tullock, on the one hand, and by Levmore, on the other?

3. Bicameralism in Historical Perspective: The Seventeenth Amendment

The theory of bicameralism highlights one frequently overlooked component of the United States Senate as created in the original Constitution. Prior to the enactment of the Seventeenth Amendment in 1913, United States Senators were elected indirectly by state legislatures. In contrast, members of the House of Representatives were always elected directly by the people based on geographic districting. A primary motivation for this arrangement was to place the House and Senate on the basis of different constituencies, in order to slow the process of legislation and to raise the level of consensus necessary for congressional action. As Madison observed in *Federalist No. 51*:

---

45. Saul Levmore, *Bicameralism: When Are Two Decisions Better Than One?*, 12 INT'L REV. L. & ECON. 145, 154 (1992). For instance, if we imagine House districts being drawn horizontally across a state, Senate districts could be drawn vertically so as to maximize the diversity between the two Houses.

46. *Id.* at 147–49, 155–59. Levmore acknowledges that the conference committee, which carries messages between the chambers to a substantial extent, might mitigate this benefit. *Id.* at 148–49.

47. *See id.* at 151–53. *See also supra* chapter 3, section II.C.

48. For a discussion of the Condorcet criterion, see *supra* chapter 3, section II.C.

But it is not possible to give to each department an equal power of self-defense. In republican government, the legislative authority necessarily predominates. The remedy for this inconveniency is to divide the legislature into different branches; and to render them, by different modes of election and different principles of action, as little connected with each other as the nature of their common functions and their common dependence on the society will admit.[49]

Madison further maintained that relying upon different constituencies would limit factional (or interest group) manipulation of the legislative process:

Another advantage accruing from this ingredient in the constitution of the Senate is the additional impediment it must prove against improper acts of legislation. No law or resolution can now be passed without the concurrence, first, of a majority of the people, and then of a majority of the States. It must be acknowledged that this complicated check on legislation may in some instances be injurious as well as beneficial; and that the peculiar defense which it involves in favor of the smaller States would be more rational if any interests common to them and distinct from those of the other States would otherwise be exposed to peculiar danger. But as the larger States will always be able, by their power over the supplies, to defeat unreasonable exertions of this prerogative of the lesser States, and as the facility and excess of law-making seem to be the diseases to which our governments are most liable, it is not impossible that this part of the Constitution may be more convenient in practice than it appears to many in contemplation.[50]

Passage of the Seventeenth Amendment in 1913 reduced the "diversity of constituencies" between the House of Representatives and the Senate by placing both houses on more similar constituency bases. One apparent effect of this has been to decrease the costs of federal legislation and thereby increase its volume. To what extent has the reduction in bicameralism corroborated Madison's intuition concerning the importance of dividing Congress and rendering each house accountable to different constituencies as a means of reducing the overall scope of legislation that is "injurious as well as beneficial"?

Todd Zywicki argues that by the overall effect of the Seventeenth Amendment might in fact have been biased in favor of increasing eroding the original bicameral protection of different electoral accountability between the houses, the ratio of special-interest to general-interest legislation.[51] Zywicki argues that this result was a foreseeable and perhaps even intended consequence of the amendment.

---

49. THE FEDERALIST No. 51 (James Madison), *supra* note 3, at 322.

50. THE FEDERALIST No. 62 (James Madison), *supra* note 3, at 378.

51. *See* Todd J. Zywicki, *Beyond the Shell and Husk of History: The History of the Seventeenth Amendment and Its Implications for Current Reform Proposals*, 45 CLEV. ST. L. REV. 165 (1997); Todd J. Zywicki, *Senators and Special Interests: A Public Choice Analysis of the Seventeenth Amendment*, 73 OR. L. REV. 1007 (1994).

Zywicki also argues that the history of the Seventeenth Amendment illustrates the theory of "Baptists and Bootleggers" described in chapter 2. On the one hand, the amendment was motivated by the "good government" progressive movement, which was largely premised upon an ideology of spreading democratic forms of governance, and which associated the then-existing system with corruption taking the form of alleged bribes that were claimed to influence the selection of particular Senators. On the other hand, the amendment also received support from the less high-minded desire of special interests that hoped to gain influence over federal legislation and of urban political machines to exert greater influence over electoral politics. Assuming the accuracy of this historical account, to what extent does it suggest that twentieth century growth of the federal government was not merely foreseeable, but possibly intended? If so, does public choice theory provide a basis for explaining the result? Can you identify any methods of determining whether in fact the Seventeenth Amendment has caused an increase in special-interest legislation or in the ratio of special to general interest legislation? Is it possible to isolate other factors contributing to the increase in national legislation as compared with the Seventeenth Amendment? If so, how?

F. SUPERMAJORITY RULES

1. Supermajority Rules in the U.S. Constitution

Despite concerns about the efficacy of supermajority rules, the United States Constitution nonetheless includes several specific provisions that demand higher levels of consensus than simple majorities. As an illustration, consider the Constitution's amendment provision, set out in Article V, which provides that proposed amendments will become effective only upon the consent of 2/3 of the United States House of Representatives and Senate as well as 3/4 of the states.[52] Article V imposes greater consensus restrictions on certain possible amendments, including a provision that "no State, without its Consent, shall be deprived of its equal Suffrage in the Senate."[53] The approval of two-thirds of the Senate is required for treaty ratification.[54] While an executive officer can be impeached by a mere majority of the House of Representatives, a minimum of two-thirds consent in the Senate is required for conviction.[55] In addition, to override a presidential veto, a two-thirds vote is required in each House of Congress.[56]

2. Fundamental Rights as Effectively Restoring Constitutional Unanimity

A corollary to Buchanan and Tullock's analysis of the optimal level of agreement necessary to take collective action is that failure to attain the

---

52. U.S. Const. art. V.

53. *Id.*

54. *Id.* art. II, § 2, cl. 2.

55. *Id.* art. I, § 3, cl. 6.

56. *Id.* art. I, § 7, cl. 3.

required level of agreement results in collective *inaction*. One predictable implication of this observation is that citizens will remove from the public sector those decisions where rational individuals are not willing to permit collective decisions to be made except at a very high level of consent, a level that might be unattainable in practice.[57]

Consider the role of fundamental rights analysis in effectively restoring a rule of unanimity over specified subject areas. Some rights or interests are viewed as so important to the individual that the fear of external costs looms large even in a regime characterized by bicameralism. Many of the provisions of the Bill of Rights reflect this intuition. Consider, for instance, the First Amendment's prohibition on the establishment of religion, at least as it has been interpreted by the Supreme Court.[58] It would be theoretically plausible to permit the establishment of an official government-sponsored church. Indeed, established religions are quite common in many other countries. The historical record suggests that this was possibly contemplated at the state level by the Framers of the Bill of Rights.[59] In America today, however, few individuals would consent to the establishment of a particular state-sponsored religion except at extraordinarily high levels of consent, approaching unanimity. Attaining such a high level of agreement is practically impossible, however, although it is possible that a lower level of consensus might be obtainable for generic expressions of belief in a universal deity as is reflected, for example, in the motto "In God We Trust" on coinage or in the general consensus that the inclusion of "one nation under God" in the Pledge of Allegiance does not offend the Establishment Clause.[60] The Constitution's prohibition on the establishment of religion effectively relegates questions of conscience to the sphere of private, non-collective action.

Another area in which constitutions might provide an effective unanimity check on the political process involves rights of the criminally accused. Ordinary political processes might systematically undervalue the rights of the accused in criminal proceedings because most citizens and legislators might be more prone to take the perspective of a potential crime victim rather than the perspective of a suspect or defendant.[61] This concern about systematic political failure might explain why criminal procedure is a particular focus of constitutional design and precommitments against majoritarian incursions.[62]

---

57. Thus, Professor Ginsburg has noted that protecting rights through constitutions reduces the stakes of politics by putting certain important substantive issues off-limits to the political process. *See* Ginsburg, *supra* note 7, at 23–24.

58. *See, e.g.,* Edwards v. Aguillard, 482 U.S. 578 (1987) (invalidating Louisiana's "Creationism Act" under the Establishment Clause).

59. For leading works, see PHILIP A. HAMBURGER, SEPARATION OF CHURCH AND STATE (2005); LEONARD LEVY, THE ESTABLISHMENT CLAUSE: RELIGION AND THE FIRST AMENDMENT (1994).

60. As an example of a suit, dismissed for want of standing, that claimed otherwise, see Elk Grove Unified Sch. Dist. v. Newdow, 542 U.S. 1, 4–5 (2004) (denying standing to raise Establishment Clause challenge to inclusion of "under God" in the Pledge of Allegiance).

61. *Cf.* Craig S. Lerner, *Legislators as the "American Criminal Class": Why Congress (Sometimes) Protects the Rights of Defendants*, 2004 U. ILL. L. REV. 599.

62. Professor Craig Lerner, in contrast, has observed that with respect to white collar crime, the analysis might be different. Lerner claims that a sufficient number of elected officials at one

Other constitutional protections can also be explained as limitations on the power of groups to impose undue external costs on certain individuals. For instance, the requirement that "just compensation" be paid for any taking of private property might reflect the intuition that individuals are generally unwilling to permit collective decision making that transforms private lands to public use, unless the burdened party is appropriately compensated.[63] This insight, that individuals are in some contexts unlikely to agree to collective action except at very high levels of consent, can be extended to include intimate questions of internal family decision making, certain familial relationships (including spousal privilege), and the choice of where to live and raise a family. As Buchanan has observed, one advantage of providing a sphere of individual liberty and market exchange is that it permits individuals to take actions that permit them to move from lower to higher levels of social welfare, and thereby increase overall social welfare, without requiring the agreement of others.[64]

3. Normative Arguments Concerning Supermajority Rules

Building on the analysis of Buchanan and Tullock, John McGinnis and Michael Rappaport have proposed a general positive and normative theory of supermajority rules under the Constitution.[65] McGinnis and Rappaport argue that the Buchanan and Tullock model fails to account for the opportunity cost of the foregone social benefits resulting from the operation of supermajority rules in blocking harmful legislation and for the costs associated with having many different voting rules governing different collective decisions. McGinnis and Rappaport refer to the former as "substitution costs" and to the latter as "administrative costs." "Substitution costs" are defined as those costs that arise when those blocked by a supermajority rule in one legislative arena try to achieve similar results in another arena governed by a less inclusive rule. Administrative costs are "the costs of identifying and applying the correct rule governing the legislative action and the costs from mistakenly applying the wrong rule."[66] For example, if a given end can be achieved either through taxation or regulation, and spending laws are subject to a supermajority rule but regulatory laws are not, interest groups will try to gain by regulation what they are unable to gain by appropriation.

---

time or another might themselves be criminal defendants or be friends with elected officials accused of crimes; in turn, they will seek to ensure protections of rights specifically in the white collar criminal context more so than in other criminal law contexts. *Id.* at 628.

63. *See* Armstrong v. United States, 364 U.S. 40, 49 (1960) ("The Fifth Amendment's guarantee that private property shall not be taken for a public use without just compensation was designed to bar Government from forcing some people alone to bear public burdens which, in all fairness and justice, should be borne by the public as a whole.").

64. *See* James M. Buchanan, *Social Choice, Democracy, and Free Markets*, 62 J. POL. ECON. 114, 121–22 (1954).

65. *See* John O. McGinnis & Michael B. Rappaport, *Majority and Supermajority Rules: Three Views of the Capitol*, 85 TEX. L. REV. 1115 (2007). While the authors present several independent arguments to justify supermajority rules, we focus here only on the argument that builds on the Buchanan and Tullock analysis.

66. *Id.* at 1126.

McGinnis and Rappaport argue that supermajority voting rules will be efficient where we are primarily concerned about special interests trying to enact legislation but inefficient where special interests will be seeking to block legislation. The authors thus advance the following normative proposal concerning such rules:

> On these assumptions, one possible solution is to apply supermajority rule to regulatory legislation and majority rule to deregulatory legislation. This strategy has the advantage of applying the voting rule most appropriate to the array of special interests.... [T]he possible disadvantage is an increase in administrative costs.[67]

Do you find their analysis persuasive? Is it feasible to determine what is or is not a "special interest" for purposes of determining when a supermajority rule might apply? Can you identify problems with implementing such a proposal? More generally, what are the costs of increasing the range of regulatory policies subject to supermajority rule? To what extent is social choice analysis, and specifically the implications of the Condorcet criterion in evaluating voting rules, helpful in answering this question? To what extent does this proposal reflect Elhauge's observation that public choice proposals often rest upon implicit premises concerning the appropriate extent of interest group involvement in political processes? What normative baseline are McGinnis and Rappaport applying?

4. General Questions and Comments

Using Buchanan and Tullock's analysis, can you explain why the Framers of the Constitution thought it might be appropriate to require a supermajority vote in some of these situations and majority vote in others? How does the choice of voting rule change based upon whether the decision is being made by one body acting independently or whether it requires the agreement of more than one body? For instance, treaty approval requires 2/3 support only in the U.S. Senate. Why would the Constitution require unicameralism with a supermajority rule in that context rather than bicameralism with simple majority rule? Does the economic analysis of constitutions provide a compelling explanation?

Consider also the question of whether the Senate should permit filibusters of judicial nominations for which cloture could be invoked only by a supermajority of sixty votes, thus raising the consensus threshold from 50% to 60%. Should it make a difference in determining the optimal voting rule whether both the President and the Senate are controlled by the same party? Consider the following argument. Appointment of judges potentially imposes external costs on those who disagree with the selection, especially for those judges who are more "extreme" than most. When the President and a majority of the Senate are controlled by the same party, the likelihood that judicial nominations will be more "extreme," or that a larger number of extreme judges will be nominated (as compared to when they are controlled by different parties), increases. This suggests

---

67. *Id.* at 1139.

that the external costs imposed on the minority party and its constituents might be higher when the President and Senate are controlled by the same party, which in turn might suggest the propriety of requiring a higher degree of consensus for decision making. Is there a rejoinder to this analysis? If you were empowered to amend the Constitution, would you impose differential consensus requirements for judicial nominees based upon whether the President and Senate are of the same party? Why or why not? Might the general need for unanimous consent to a jury verdict explain the right of litigants to exercise peremptory challenges as a measure to remove jurors who might be perceived as "outliers" and thus who might tend to obstruct a unanimous agreement?

G.   EXIT AS AN ALTERNATIVE TO UNANIMITY

As an alternative to demanding very high levels of consensus in order to reduce the risk of external costs, individuals can elect to *exit* the group, thereby protecting themselves from being bound by a disadvantageous collective decision. The right of exit implicates federalism, which we explore more fully below. For current purposes, however, note that the possibility of exit enables an individual to effectively truncate the tail of the distribution concerning the Buchanan and Tullock external cost function. Those who occupy the tail end of this distribution for particular regulatory activity, including for example those who strongly oppose (or support) the death penalty, abortion regulations, or laws governing same sex unions, have the ability to locate to other jurisdictions whose laws better match their views on these issues. The converse is also true. The exit of those in the tail of the distribution on divisive issues increases the homogeneity of preferences among those who remain, thus reducing the slope of the decision costs curve and improving the prospects for collective agreement.

Consider in this context Justice Scalia's partial dissenting opinion in *Planned Parenthood of Southeastern Pennsylvania v. Casey*,[68] in which he argued that highly contentious constitutional issues are more divisive on a national scale, where persons are likely to embrace very different belief systems, than at a more local level, where similarities in socioeconomic status, education, and religious views provide for a greater commonality of philosophical views. Scalia maintained that *Roe v. Wade*,[69] which identified a fundamental right to abortion, effectively undercut the possibility of such state level resolutions that he claimed would have provided most people with more satisfying results:

> Profound disagreement existed among our citizens over the issue—as it does over other issues, such as the death penalty—but that disagreement was being worked out at the state level. As with many other issues, the division of sentiment within each State was not as closely balanced as it was among the population of the Nation as a

---

68.   505 U.S. 833 (1992).

69.   410 U.S. 113 (1973).

whole, meaning not only that more people would be satisfied with the results of state-by-state resolution, but also that those results would be more stable.[70]

Does Scalia's observation that there is likely a higher degree of agreement on controversial social issues, such as abortion and the death penalty, at the state and local level as opposed to the national level appear sound? Whether or not it is empirically correct, is variance of preference on constitutional issues an appropriate basis for resting the final choice at the state level? Remember the argument about fundamental rights as effectively restoring a rule of unanimity. By labeling abortion a fundamental right, did the *Roe v. Wade* Court effectively categorize abortion as an area in which women seeking to terminate unwanted pregnancies would not agree to allow anything less than unanimity as a precondition to restrictions on this claimed right, at least at certain stages of the pregnancy? Is Scalia's analysis more consistent with an exit model and the fundamental rights analysis more consistent with a unanimity model? If so, can the two approaches be reconciled? How? If not, how does one choose which model is more appropriate to the issue of abortion, or for that matter, any claimed constitutional right? In an earlier constitutional period, the Supreme Court applied a fundamental rights analysis to protect "liberty of contract." In *Lochner v. New York*, as in *Roe v. Wade*, the Court thus limited the permissible range of majoritarian decision making within political processes. To what extent are the situations similar or different from a public choice perspective? Is the use of the "exit" option of federalism to protect individual rights in one situation more compelling than in the other? Why or why not?

H. A COMMENT ON COALITION FORMATION IN PARLIAMENTARY VERSUS PRESIDENTIAL VOTING REGIMES

Another important variable that affects coalition building in passing legislation involves the selection of the head of state.[71] Among the most important distinctions between the United States and parliamentary systems involves how the head of state is chosen. While voters in the United States select the President (albeit subject to the peculiarity of the Electoral College) through a direct election process, in parliamentary regimes, a successful legislative coalition elects the head of state who then forms the government.

In the parliamentary regime, a market for relatively small parties emerges as these parties hope to become tipping points in the formation of successful governing coalitions. In a parliament of sixty persons with three

---

70. *Planned Parenthood*, 505 U.S. at 995 (Scalia, J., concurring in the judgment in part and dissenting in part).

71. The analysis also relates to the discussion in the next section involving the role of the President in the formation of substantive legislative policy. *See infra* p. 527.

parties, *A*, *B*, *C*, of equal size, we might imagine that any of the following three coalitions of forty would form: *AB*, *BC*, or *CA*. But following the theory of minimum winning coalitions, we know that each of these coalitions is overweighted. If we start with *AB*, a subgroup comprising seventeen members of *C*—which we will refer to as *C'*—it can splinter off and propose to *B* that forming a new *BC'* coalition will improve the payoffs to the new members. The overall benefit of being in the governing coalition is now divided by thirty-seven, rather than by forty. Applying Riker's theory, this too is overweighted, and so we might imagine a subgroup of *A*, *A'*, with sixteen members splinting off and proposing to *B'* yet another iteration, with a now smaller governing coalition *C'A'* thirty-three members. With each round of forming, breaking, and reforming coalitions, newer and smaller parties will form that allow for a mix of strategies in the creation of governing coalitions.

In a regime that takes this form of bargaining, we might imagine that much of the bargaining over policy occurs at the stage of forming the governing coalition. How might this differ from the nature of coalition building over legislation in the United States Congress? Which system appears more likely to be conducive to special-interest politicking? Which is more likely conducive to providing public interest legislation? Why? How might one resolve these questions empirically?

As one interesting example, consider the Israeli Knesset. Studies have shown that while the majority coalitions vary, successful coalitions invariably include within them a group of minority religious parties. One consequence is to ensure a continuation of exemption from military service for ultra-orthodox Jews.[72] Does social choice analysis help to explain why in the United States, in contrast, the religious right has generally formed a coalition with the Republican Party? How does the difference between forming coalitions during the primary stage prior to elections in the United States versus in the post-election stage in the Knesset affect the formation of public policy affecting minority religious groups? More generally, is either a parliamentary or direct electoral system less likely to be subject to interest group influence? Or are the two systems equally subject to it but in different ways?

III. EXECUTIVE POWERS

A. EXECUTIVE VETO AS "TRICAMERALISM"

While a formal constitutional analysis would suggest that the President is empowered to execute laws created by Congress, the United States Constitution carves out a large role for the President in the enactment of congressional policy. Article I, § 7 provides that for a bill to become law, it must pass both Houses of Congress in identical form and be presented to the President, who then has the power to sign the bill into law or exercise his veto power.

---

72. *See* NORMAN SCHOFIELD & ITAI SENED, MULTIPARTY DEMOCRACY: ELECTIONS AND LEGISLATIVE POLITICS 92–95 (2006).

As an initial approximation we can model the President's veto power as essentially creating a "tricameral" legislature by placing the President in the position of "third house," whose approval is required for proposed legislation to become law. The analogy is of course imperfect in that unlike the two Houses of Congress, the President is presented with a binary choice to accept or to veto proposed bills. Nonetheless, applying the Buchanan and Tullock framework, the presidential veto certainly enhances the diversity of constituencies required to enact legislation. Whereas members of the House of Representatives represent geographic districts and Senators represent states as a whole (and originally represented state legislatures), the President represents the entire nation. At the same time, requiring consent of a third House raises decision-making costs.

At one level, the veto might suggest an additional safeguard against interest group driven, or otherwise undesirable, legislation. Alternatively, it might be viewed as a means to ensure that only those legislative bargains that meet the approval of a majority of the voters ultimately become law, thus increasing the effective size of governing coalitions.[73] If so, the veto helps control the external costs that are posed when discrete minority groups succeed through coalition formation in imposing external costs in resulting legislative packages. On the other hand, it is possible that the President might also be responsive to well-organized interest groups, although perhaps different interest groups than those influencing Congress, in which case the system might exacerbate special-interest influence over lawmaking.[74]

In *Federalist No. 73*, Alexander Hamilton argues that the veto will help frustrate majority faction and special-interest influence on legislation.[75] Hamilton claims:

> [I]t furnishes an additional security against the enaction of improper laws. It establishes a salutary check upon the legislative body, calculated to guard the community against the effects of faction, precipitancy, or of any impulse unfriendly to the public good, which may happen to influence a majority of that body.
>
> The propriety of a negative has, upon some occasions, been combated by an observation that it was not to be presumed a single man would possess more virtue and wisdom than a number of men; and that unless this presumption should be entertained, it would be improper to give the executive magistrate any species of control over the legislative body.
>
> But this observation, when examined, will appear rather specious than solid. The propriety of the thing does not turn upon the

---

73. *See* W. Mark Crain & Robert D. Tollison, *The Executive Branch in the Interest–Group Theory of Government*, 8 J. LEGAL STUD. 555, 556–57 (1979).

74. Peter H. Aranson, Ernest Gellhorn & Glen O. Robinson, *A Theory of Legislative Delegation*, 68 CORNELL L. REV. 1, 41 (1982).

75. We do not discuss here Hamilton's separate argument that the veto is necessary for the Executive to prevent encroachments on his power by the legislature.

supposition of superior wisdom or virtue in the executive, but upon the supposition that the legislature will not be infallible; that the love of power may sometimes betray it into a disposition to encroach upon the rights of other members of the government; that a spirit of faction may sometimes pervert its deliberations; that impressions of the moment may sometimes hurry it into measures which itself, on maturer reflection, would condemn. The primary inducement to conferring the power in question upon the executive is to enable him to defend himself; the secondary one is to increase the chances in favor of the community against the passing of bad laws, through haste, inadvertence, or design. The oftener the measure is brought under examination, the greater the diversity in the situations of those who are to examine it, the less must be the danger of those errors which flow from want of due deliberation, or of those missteps which proceed from the contagion of some common passion or interest. It is far less probable that culpable views of any kind should infect all the parts of the government at the same moment and in relation to the same object than that they should by turns govern and mislead every one of them.[76]

Hamilton further observes that the effect of this tricameral system is to frustrate the enactment of good laws as well as bad, but that by raising the effective level of consent for the proposed legislation, the veto will disproportionately block bad laws rather than good:

It may perhaps be said that the power of preventing bad laws includes that of preventing good ones; and may be used to the one purpose as well as to the other. But this objection will have little weight with those who can properly estimate the mischiefs of that inconstancy and mutability in the laws, which form the greatest blemish in the character and genius of our governments. They will consider every institution calculated to restrain the excess of lawmaking, and to keep things in the same state in which they happen to be at any given period as much more likely to do good than harm; because it is favorable to greater stability in the system of legislation. The injury which may possibly be done by defeating a few good laws will be amply compensated by the advantage of preventing a number of bad ones.

. . . .

It is evident that there would be greater danger of his not using his power when necessary, than of his using it too often, or too much. . . .[77]

The United States Constitution, however, creates a qualified veto rather than an absolute veto. Congress has the power to override the President's veto with a two-thirds vote of both Houses. In this analysis, the Constitution essentially creates two different paths to the enactment

---

76. THE FEDERALIST No. 73 (Alexander Hamilton), *supra* note 3, at 443.

77. *Id.* at 443–45.

of legislation: either approval by a tricameral process with simple majorities in both Houses of Congress or approval by a supermajority vote in a bicameral process.

B. THE EXECUTIVE VETO IN PRACTICE

Working in the interest group tradition, Professors Mark Crain and Robert Tollison have argued that the veto does in fact exacerbate interest group influence by giving such groups an additional bite at the legislative apple and thus allowing them to make interest group bargains more durable.[78] Recall from chapter 2 that in the basic interest group model of government, politicians act as "brokers" among interest groups who help facilitate bargains that are then embedded in resulting legislation. Building on this intuition, Crain and Tollison argue that "the veto power raises the costs of reneging on previous legislative contracts, and as such we expect to observe more vetoes in cases where attempts are being made to renege or to alter substantively previous legislative contracts with special interests."[79] Specifically, Crain and Tollison maintain that the veto provides a tool through which the President can prevent future sessions of Congress from reneging on prior bargains made to special-interest groups.

The authors predict that there will be more vetoes where there are *larger* majorities in the legislature than where legislative majorities are narrow, even when the legislature is controlled by the same party as that of the President. This is because larger majorities, who are more secure politically and thus less dependent upon particular special interests, will be better positioned to repeal prior interest group bargains and strike new ones. Crain and Tollison argue that if the traditional model were correct— i.e., that the veto serves to frustrate special-interest legislation—vetoes will be more likely where majorities are narrower, and thus when legislation is more likely to contain payoffs to special interests and less likely to reflect the majority will.

Examining American state-level data, Crain and Tollison find that vetoes are most common where legislative consensus is high, rather than low, such as where a single party holds a supermajority in the legislature, thereby contradicting Hamilton's argument. Vetoes are also less common where legislative turnover is low (and thus when legislative tenure is high), which they interpret as providing alternative means for ensuring the durability of interest group legislative bargains. In contrast, party correspondence between the executive and legislative branches makes no difference in the exercise of veto power, which they interpret as further contradicting Hamilton's account.

Do you find the Crain and Tollison theory persuasive? Can you reconcile this theory with the Buchanan and Tullock analysis that the veto is designed to raise the calculus of consent? If so, how? If not, why not?

---

78. Crain & Tollison, *supra* note 73, at 557.

79. *Id.*

C. EXECUTIVE VETO AND LEGISLATIVE BARGAINING[80]

While the President's veto power is formally binary—he must accept or reject bills in their entirety—it is mistaken to assume that this gives the President no role in the course of legislative bargaining. The President's veto power gives him substantial bargaining leverage during the process of legislative drafting. Studies of the item veto have centered on the nature of bargaining between the President and Congress, and offer important insights not only into the proposed modification of the veto, but also into its present use as a means of inter-branch bargaining.[81]

The item veto would provide the President with the power to excise specific items contained in larger bills approved by both Houses of Congress. Item veto advocates claim that this power would allow the President to respond effectively to what they regard as strategic congressional behavior that takes the form of bundling special-interest items in otherwise desired legislation and forcing a binary choice upon the President to accept or reject the overall package. In theory, the item veto would allow the President instead to strike the special-interest riders while retaining the larger pieces of public interest legislation to which those riders are attached.

Professor Glen Robinson analogizes the relationship between Congress and the President respecting the veto power to a "bilateral monopoly," in which the President buys the legislation that Congress sells.[82] Without the item veto, Congress has substantial leverage because the President is given a binary choice respecting each bill such that vetoing a bill to defeat a special-interest item it contains is rarely a politically palatable choice. The item veto would provide the President additional power, and as a result, would raise costs to Congress of enacting private interest legislation.

Robinson does not contend that the item veto will pose intractable problems for congressional bargaining and offers hypothetical inter-branch bargains in which Congress either threatens to hold larger, public interest bills hostage unless the President commits not to separately veto attached special-interest legislation, or in a less certain case, in which Congress disaggregates the package, forcing the President to approve the

---

80. This discussion draws upon Maxwell L. Stearns, *The Public Choice Case Against the Item Veto*, 49 WASH. & LEE L. REV. 385 (1992), and Glen O. Robinson, *Public Choice Speculations on the Item Veto*, 74 VA. L. REV. 403 (1988).

81. The item veto exists in some form in forty-three states. *See, e.g.*, Carl E. Klarner & Andrew Karch, *Why Do Governors Issue Vetoes? The Impact of Individual and Institutional Influences*, 61 POL. RES. Q. 574, 578 (2008). The line-item veto originated in the Constitution of the Confederate States of America, and in 1876, the first legislative proposal for presidential item veto authority was introduced and has been introduced into Congress more than 150 times since then. *See, e.g.*, John R. Carter & David Schap, *Line–Item Veto: Where Is Thy Sting?*, J. ECON. PERSP., Spring 1990, at 103, 103–04; Roger H. Wells, *The Item Veto and State Budget Reform*, 18 AM. POL. SCI. REV. 782, 782 (1924).

82. *See* Robinson, *supra* note 80, at 410–12.

special-interest legislation separately as a condition of forwarding the desired public interest bill.[83] Robinson also envisions the possibility that the President might threaten to veto a desired item to secure, for example, the support by the Senate Armed Services Committee Chair on a desired defense initiative, but cautions that the "[t]he President's threat is only as menacing as his bargaining position allows."[84]

Robinson concludes that by demanding that Congress pursue such complex bargaining strategies, the item veto raises the cost to the procurement of special-interest legislation. As a result, Robinson claims, the item veto is likely to have an overall positive effect, albeit perhaps a modest one, in favorably altering the ratio of special to general interest legislation.

Maxwell Stearns has offered an alternative and more skeptical public choice analysis of the item veto, which returns us to the dynamic variation of the Wilson–Hayes legislative bargaining model presented in chapter 5.[85] Recall that the Wilson–Hayes matrix can be recast to introduce two kinds of bargains, substantive bargaining and length bargaining, each with the effect of increasing the likelihood that desired general interest legislation will pass.[86] While bill sponsors can be expected to engage in both forms of bargaining, they will do so only to a point, as each form reduces the value of the bill to its sponsor as compared with its original proposed form (corresponding to the sponsor's ideal point). These forms of bargaining allow the bill sponsor to navigate the bill through the various negative legislative checkpoints as needed to secure a successful legislative coalition, which in Congress is generally well above minimum winning size.[87] Through substantive bargaining, the sponsor seeks to buy support by compromising the bill's terms (thus departing from her ideal policy position) to appease those interests most likely adversely affected by the bill in its original form. While such bargaining will increase the size of the legislative coalition, it is likely to prove insufficient for passage, or at least the sponsor might be unwilling to weaken the bill sufficiently to gain the necessary support for passage. To gain additional needed support, the bill sponsor can also negotiate adding special-interest riders that benefit vote sellers, which adds overall deadweight to the bill (albeit without affecting the bill's substance).

Stearns recasts the debate over the item veto as follows: Those supporting the item veto contend that the proposal would allow Congress to continue substantive bargaining, which falls within the Madisonian tradition of imposing barriers to factional legislative violence, but would limit length bargaining, which only produces undesirable special-interest legislation. It would do so, advocates claim, by either allowing the President to excise resulting bargains or by limiting the incentives to secure

---

83. *Id.* at 417–19 (illustrating with two negotiations over grants to smokestack industries as a precondition to passing air pollution regulation).

84. *Id.* at 418.

85. *See supra* chapter 5, section I.B.

86. *See supra* chapter 5, section I.D.2 (illustrating with environmental legislation).

87. *See supra* chapter 2, section III.B; *see* RIKER, *supra* note 38, at 32–46.

special-interest items in the first place. In this analysis, the item veto would allow the President to excise special-interest legislation but would have little or no effect on legislative policy.

Relying upon interest group theory, Stearns demonstrates that if members of Congress and the President behave rationally, the item veto is instead likely to have the opposite effect, namely allowing the President to influence the direction of legislative policy, while tying the President's hands respecting the most egregious special-interest legislation. The analysis rests on the observation that the President has greater control in selecting which bills to support than with whom he must bargain in Congress (who controls the various veto gates or negative legislative checkpoints) to get those bills passed. Rather than diminishing length bargaining, Stearns demonstrates that the item veto will simply change the locus of such bargaining to the President or his allies in Congress. The President will offer commitments to decline to exercise the item veto as needed to ensure that his preferred legislation gains the necessary support for passage. Because the President cannot control with whom he must bargain in Congress to secure passage, however, those in control of the various negative legislative checkpoints will serve as brokers for the most valuable special-interest legislation, which will provide the basis for the most valuable reciprocal commitments by those who directly benefit from the resulting special-interest legislation.

Stearns concludes that the overall effect of the item veto is ultimately not captured by the overall amount of general interest or special-interest legislation, but rather by the effect of the item veto on who controls the overall direction of legislative policy. Empirical studies generally have corroborated Stearns's hypothesis that, as used at the state level, the item veto has been used more to affect policy than to excise special-interest legislation.[88]

Which model of the item veto do you find more persuasive? How does the analysis of the item veto inform the Buchanan and Tullock analysis of the actual veto as a consensus raising measure? How does it inform the Crain and Tollison analysis of the actual veto as a special-interest bargain preservation device? Do you believe that the item veto is a sound policy? Why or why not? Do you think that the answer to this policy question is the same at the state and federal levels? Why or why not?

IV. THE JUDICIARY

A. THE ROLE OF JUDICIAL REVIEW AND THE INDEPENDENT JUDICIARY

As with bicameralism and the executive veto, the establishment of an independent judiciary is typically justified on the basis of its institutional

---

88. For studies that are consistent with the Stearns hypothesis, see Carter & Schap, *supra* note 81, at 112 (summarizing studies and concluding that "[t]he empirical studies to date ... provide little or no evidence that total spending, budget outcomes, or executive power are substantially affected in general by item-veto authority"); Douglas Holtz–Eakin, *The Line Item Veto and Public Sector Budgets: Evidence from the States*, 36 J. PUB. ECON. 269, 291 (1988) (concluding that "long-run budgetary behavior is not significantly affected by the power of an item veto [but that] in particular political circumstances the item veto may permit increased control over the budget").

ability to frustrate special-interest factions and to enforce individual rights against majoritarian factions. As Alexander Hamilton states in *Federalist No. 78*:

> This independence of the judges is equally requisite to guard the Constitution and the rights of individuals from the effects of those ill humors which the arts of designing men, or the influence of particular conjunctures, sometimes disseminate among the people themselves, and which, though they speedily give place to better information, and more deliberate reflection, have a tendency, in the meantime, to occasion dangerous innovations in the government, and serious oppressions of the minor party in the community. [Although the people have the right to government grounded in their consent] yet it is not to be inferred from this principle that the representatives of the people, whenever a momentary inclination happens to lay hold of a majority of their constituents incompatible with the provisions in the existing Constitution would, on that account, be justifiable in a violation of those provisions; or that the courts would be under a greater obligation to connive at infractions in this shape than when they had proceeded wholly from the cabals of the representative body. Until the people have, by some solemn and authoritative act, annulled or changed the established form, it is binding upon themselves collectively, as well as individually; and no presumption, or even knowledge of their sentiments, can warrant their representatives in a departure from it prior to such an act. But it is easy to see that it would require an uncommon portion of fortitude in the judges to do their duty as faithful guardians of the Constitution, where legislative invasions of it had been instigated by the major voice of the community.[89]

Scholars working in the public choice tradition have modeled the role of the independent judiciary similarly to that described by Hamilton. A.C. Pritchard and Todd Zywicki, for instance, argue that judicial review furthers the goals of precommitment and reduction of agency costs. As they define the terms, "Precommitment allows a super-majority to put certain actions beyond the power of government in order to preclude potentially rash actions by future majority coalitions that are inconsistent with society's long-term interest."[90] By placing the authority to enforce these constitutional precommitments in an independent body, society can "bind itself to the mast" to limit the choices of future majorities. Following Buchanan and Tullock, Pritchard and Zywicki note that, ideally, constitutional rights would be amendable only by unanimous vote, for the reasons described above. As previously discussed, however, the unanimity

---

89. THE FEDERALIST No. 78 (Alexander Hamilton), *supra* note 3, at 469–70. In addition, as discussed in chapter 5, Hamilton advanced the view that beyond policing unconstitutional laws, the independent judiciary could interpret statutes to further public interest goals, thus making special-interest payoffs from enacted statutes more difficult to secure. For a discussion, see IV.A.

90. Pritchard & Zywicki, *supra* note 4, at 446–47.

standard is impracticable, thus leading to the adoption of supermajority precommitments as a proxy for unanimity.

Recall that agency costs arise when public officials risk pursuing their own personal interests rather than the interests of their principals, namely their constituents. Pritchard and Zywicki summarize the forms that these agency costs might take:

> Actors in all three branches of government may impose agency costs on the citizenry (the "principal"): legislators, who will garner votes and money by extracting wealth from the public at large and transferring that wealth to concentrated interest groups; enforcement authorities, who may exploit a lack of monitoring by legislatures and voters to act in their own interests; and judges, who may use their positions and independence to impose their personal policy preferences on society and to increase their status.[91]

Pritchard and Zywicki describe as "constitutionally efficient" those policies that reduce agency costs or that are supported by a high degree of consensus, for example, as indicated by supermajorities, thus rendering them fit to be the subject of a precommitment. Judicial review in this model works to enforce precommitments and to limit agency costs. At the same time, however, the authors acknowledge that creating an independent judiciary potentially creates new and enhanced agency costs with respect to the judiciary itself if the judges, for instance, use their powers inappropriately to define new rights subject to precommitment that lack the necessary grounding in supermajority support.

Does public choice theory justify an independent judiciary that plays such a precommitment role in interpreting the Constitution? Consider, for instance, that the President has only a qualified veto of legislation that can be overridden by two-thirds vote in both Houses of Congress. In contrast, Article V of the Constitution is highly cumbersome and as discussed below is subject to several of the previously discussed agency costs problems, thus making the threat of constitutional amendment an extremely weak check on judicial agency costs. Is the amending process a sufficient check against unpopular Supreme Court decisions that interpret the Constitution?

Over the years, there have been several legislative proposals to allow Congress, by a supermajority vote, to overturn unpopular Supreme Court rulings.[92] Leaving aside the constitutional questions of such a practice, would this proposal be wise or unwise from the perspective of public choice theory? Would it make a difference as to the degree of consensus that would be required by Congress to do so, such as requiring two-thirds or some other supermajority support for the congressional override?

---

91. *Id.* at 447–48.

92. For one example, see Congressional Accountability for Judicial Activism Act, H.R. 3920, 108th Cong. (2004), introduced by Representative Lewis (R. Kan.), which would have permitted Congress to overrule Supreme Court decisions striking down acts of Congress on constitutional grounds. *See also* ROBERT BORK, COERCING VIRTUE: THE WORLDWIDE RULE OF JUDGES 80 (2003) (discussing related proposal).

B. THE INDEPENDENT JUDICIARY IN PRACTICE

In an important study of the federal judiciary,[93] William Landes and Richard Posner claimed that judicial independence is likely to prolong the durability of special-interest bargains secured in the legislature.[94] As compared with elected judges who are more likely to be responsive to the sitting legislature when construing statutes, Article III judges who are politically insulated are freer to interpret statutes with reference to the "intent of the enacting legislature."[95] As a result, the authors claim, to the extent that such legislation included bargains among interest groups to secure the deal, the independent judiciary is more likely than a dependent judiciary to seek evidence of, and to ensure and prolong the payoffs from, the resulting bargain. The result is to extend the reach of legislation beyond the life of the enacting legislature, thus increasing the expected value of the resulting economic rents.

Some scholars have criticized the Landes and Posner thesis on various normative grounds. Jonathan Macey has argued that, to the contrary, it is the role of the judiciary to minimize or avoid interest group payoffs.[96] Einer Elhauge maintains that political satisfaction is optimized when the judiciary resolves statutory ambiguities with reference to contemporary enactable preferences rather than with reference to those of prorogued legislative sessions.[97] Donald Boudreaux and Adam Pritchard argue that if in fact judicial independence prolongs the duration of interest group bargains, then given the higher present value of (and thus the cost of procuring) the resulting interest groups payoffs, the effect would be to inhibit, rather than encourage, legislative bargaining.[98] Instead, Boudreaux and Pritchard maintain, the purpose of judicial independence is to operate against the enforcement of legislative bargains.

Robert Tollison has claimed a partial corroboration of the Landes and Posner thesis. Extending the logic of their analysis, Tollison posits that if judicial independence prolongs the life of ordinary legislation, the frequency of state constitutional amending should be negatively correlated with the degree of judicial independence.[99] In states that have dependent

---

93. William M. Landes & Richard A. Posner, *The Independent Judiciary in an Interest–Group Perspective*, 18 J.L. & ECON. 875 (1975).

94. Recall from chapter 2 that increasing the durability of legislation increases the present value of economic rents to be transferred under the legislation and thereby increases the amount that interest groups are willing to pay to legislatures to secure the legislation.

95. Landes & Posner, *supra* note 93, at 883.

96. Jonathan R. Macey, *Promoting Public–Regarding Legislation Through Statutory Interpretation: An Interest Group Model*, 86 COLUM. L. REV. 223 (1986).

97. EINER ELHAUGE, STATUTORY DEFAULT RULES 9–10 (2008).

98. *See* Donald J. Boudreaux & A.C. Pritchard, *Reassessing the Role of the Independent Judiciary in Enforcing Interest–Group Bargains*, 5 CONST. POL. ECON. 1, 9–11 (1994).

99. *See* Robert D. Tollison, *Public Choice and Legislation*, 74 VA. L. REV. 339, 347 (1988); *see also* Gary M. Anderson, William F. Shughart II & Robert D. Tollison, *On the Incentives of Judges to Enforce Legislative Wealth Transfers*, 32 J.L. & ECON. 215, 220–27 (1989) (demonstrating that judges with a higher degree of independence—as measured by enforcement of original contracts—

judiciaries there is a greater benefit from state constitutional amending since this more difficult procedure is necessary to extend the life of the proposal as compared with states that have independent judiciaries, which are more solicitous of the views of the enacting legislature. Tollison claims support for his thesis in his empirical study of state constitutions.

While the Landes and Posner analysis has been criticized, to what extent do the criticisms fail to properly capture the underlying normative implications of the thesis? Consider the following argument. Assuming that the independent judiciary has the claimed effect of prolonging the life of special-interest bargains, it does not do so for the sake of interest group payoffs themselves. Rather, given the difficulty of securing federal legislation, including special-interest payoffs secured in the course of legislative bargaining,[100] the promise of an extended payoff from successful legislative procurements increases the motivation of interest groups to participate in legislative bargaining. The overall goal for the system, of course, is not to provide payoffs to special interests for their own sake. Instead, motivating active participation by special interests is the necessary grease that facilitates the passage of desired *general interest* legislation. In this analysis, by prolonging the life of special-interest legislation, the independent judiciary helps to motivate active political participation by interest groups as needed to facilitate the passage of desired general interest legislation.

To what extent does this suggested normative justification for judicial independence, which is consistent with the Landes and Posner thesis, run parallel to the normative argument for declining to adopt the item veto?[101] Both arguments presume that existing constitutional mechanisms (the independent judiciary and the actual presidential veto) can be viewed as benefiting special interests, but that the overriding normative justification for conferring the benefit is to encourage desired public interest legislation. In the context of the independent judiciary, do you find this argument persuasive? Why or why not?

V. FEDERALISM

Public choice theory also has important implications for the study of federalism, meaning the division of power between two or more levels of government. While it is common to view federalism as operating within nations, the increasing interdependency of the global economy has invited the development of new governance institutions with federalism-style structures operating internationally. Interdependencies created by the

---

receive higher salaries); *but see* Jonathan R. Macey, *Transactions Costs and the Normative Elements of the Public Choice Model: An Application to Constitutional Theory*, 74 Va. L. Rev. 471, 496–97 (1988) (criticizing Anderson, Shughart and Tollison thesis on the ground that, ironically, compensatory reward for enforcing original agreements demonstrates dependence on the sitting legislature).

100. *See supra* chapter 5, section I.B.2.

101. *See supra* at pp. 527–28 (describing Stearns's public choice analysis of item veto).

challenges of global trade, terrorism, environmental impacts, and migration have all contributed to the growth of such novel governance regimes. Many matters previously governed at the national or sub-national level are increasingly subject to the jurisdiction of regional, international, or global entities. Such institutions as the European Union, World Trade Organization, and United Nations, which did not exist a century or in some cases even decades ago, are now taking an increasingly large role with respect to a broad domain of human activity. This invites the challenge of knitting together diverse national economic, political, and cultural practices into novel governance structures and of allocating decision-making authority among spheres of government in a manner that sometimes challenges traditional notions of sovereignty but that also implicates the theoretical foundations of federalism.

Whether the challenges of federalism are old (such as the knitting together of the United States into a nation in the late Eighteenth Century) or new (such as constructing a global environmental policy), the underlying analytical structure—and the underlying challenges—remains the same: What is the appropriate level of governance for particular regulatory powers and should such power be exclusive or shared with other levels of government? The overarching goal as a normative matter should be to allocate primary governance where it can be exercised most effectively.

Accomplishing this objective requires balancing two offsetting policy goals, each of which gives rise to a distinct model of federalism. The first model presents federalism in static form. As a formal matter, how does the federalism regime "assign" or "match" a given power to the appropriate level of governance? The second model focuses on the dynamic relationships that emerge after the formal assignment process is complete. As a dynamic matter, how does "competitive federalism" affect the allocation of power among different jurisdictions within a given level of government, including how jurisdictions vie for citizens and tax revenues?

In theory, jurisdictional authority should be neither over nor under-inclusive with respect to the problem for which power has been assigned. Because political jurisdictions are constrained by geographic, historical, cultural, and strategic considerations, to name a few, they do not operate within a robust competitive environment. Instead, they tend by nature to be "lumpy." As a result, there is rarely if ever a perfect match that renders the organ or level of governance to which power is assigned perfectly suited to the underlying problems for which the assignment was made.[102]

A. STATIC FEDERALISM: THE MATCHING PROBLEM

We begin with the "assignment problem" or the "matching problem" and the related problem of localized spillovers or externalities. Solving this

---

102. Once again, it is helpful to remember the nirvana fallacy. The issue is not whether an assignment is perfect, but rather whether it is better than available alternatives. *See supra* chapter 3, section I.F.2.

problem requires a balancing of the problems of "free riding" and "forced riding."[103] Consider the following stylized example, which considers the proper level of governance as it affects bodies of water internal to a state, running through contiguous states, or abutting both contiguous and noncontiguous states.

The Commonwealth of Virginia contains or adjoins three different types of bodies of water: (1) lakes that are entirely self-contained within the state; (2) rivers that flow from points in Virginia to points in, or through, neighboring states; and (3) the Atlantic Ocean, which abuts not only Virginia and other states along the eastern shore, but also Canada and Mexico, along with countries on altogether different continents. Assume for purposes of illustration that the full impact (including any environmental impacts) respecting each body of water is limited to those states or nations that have direct physical contact with it and there are no other inter-jurisdictional spillover effects.

Based upon this premise, the formal theory of federalism suggests that the assigned regulatory powers respecting each of these three types of bodies of water will vary according to the governance level that represents the best fit based strictly upon the geographical consideration of physical contact with the relevant body of water. If, for example, an assignment is under-inclusive—giving Virginia exclusive regulatory powers respecting a river that also runs through North Carolina—this raises the risk that the regulators will fail to give adequate consideration to the concerns of affected interests of the neighboring state. For example, the governing body might permit Virginians to dump waste in a manner that adversely affects out-of-state downstream users.

The matching problem can also result from an over-inclusive assignment of decision-making authority. In the case of the lake contained within Virginia, for example, consider whether residents of North Carolina or Maryland would have the proper incentives regarding its usage if afforded regulatory power. One might, for example, imagine residents of North Carolina—who may be competing for tourism dollars—seeking to restrict the use of the lake in Virginia in connection with a resort.

Todd Zywicki has presented empirical support to establish that politicians in industrial northern states have historically exerted pressure to enact federal environmental regulations that operate to the economic detriment of states in the developing regions elsewhere in the United States as a means of protecting unionized manufacturing jobs from competition in the sunbelt.[104] Is this an example of failing to match regulatory powers with affected interests? Why or why not? Does the example illustrate the Buchanan and Tullock thesis that externalities

---

103. For discussions of these terms, see *supra* chapter 1, section II.E.

104. *See* Zywicki, *supra* note 18, at 866–68.

include not only activities that impose costs on non-beneficiaries of private activity but also on those who must make forced contributions to public activity benefiting others? How would you resolve the problem of regulation affecting the Atlantic Ocean, which touches upon multiple nations and continents? How is your answer affected by claims that global climate change resulting from, among other sources, mobile-sourced carbon emissions, threatens hurricanes and other environmental harms at a greater rate in countries that are not the primary contributors?[105]

B. DYNAMIC FEDERALISM: JURISDICTIONAL COMPETITION

One model of competitive federalism suggests that states compete to attract residents and resources and that rational individuals acting like consumers will select those jurisdictions that best match their preferences for publicly provided goods and taxes.[106] Under this model, public goods will be efficiently provided according to voter preferences where "(1) people and resources are mobile; (2) the number of jurisdictions is large; (3) jurisdictions are free to select any set of laws they desire; and (4) there are no spillovers" onto other jurisdictions.[107] Although the Tiebout model was designed to study mechanisms for providing an optimal mix of taxes and provisions of public goods, it can be extended to assess mechanisms that facilitate an optimal match of individual preferences respecting governmental policies in general, including preferences on social policies such as the death penalty, same-sex marriage, or abortion regulation.[108] On the other hand, individuals choose where to live based upon numerous variables other than public goods provisions and shared values. These typically include employment opportunities and family connections. While the Tiebout model predicts some degree of competition at the margin among political jurisdictions, as a practical matter, most people are inframarginal with respect to the decision where to live. If this is true, to what extent does it suggest that states have power to impose regulatory burdens on those who choose to live in a given jurisdiction for reasons unrelated to governmental policies? Economists, for example, have identified the concept of certain "agglomeration economies" associated with the

105. *See, e.g.,* Andrew C. Revkin, *Poor Nations to Bear Brunt as World Warms,* N.Y. TIMES, Apr. 1, 2007, http://www.nytimes.com/2007/04/01/science/earth/01climate.html (noting implications of Intergovernmental Panel on Climate Change report finding that poor countries, who have traditionally not been the largest polluters, are likely to bear most of the burden of climate change and be less capable of dealing with its effects.).

106. This has been attributed to Charles Tiebout and is often referred to as the "Tiebout model." *See* Charles M. Tiebout, *A Pure Theory of Local Expenditures,* 64 J. POL. ECON. 416 (1956), *reprinted in* 1 ECONOMICS OF FEDERALISM 5 (Bruce H. Kobayashi & Larry E. Ribstein eds., 2007). Tiebout's approach was to some extent anticipated in Friedrich A. Hayek, *The Economic Conditions of Interstate Federalism,* NEW COMMONWEALTH Q., Sept. 1939, at 131, *reprinted in* FRIEDRICH A. HAYEK, INDIVIDUALISM AND ECONOMIC ORDER 255 (1948); F.A. HAYEK, THE CONSTITUTION OF LIBERTY (1960).

107. Bruce H. Kobayashi & Larry E. Ribstein, *Introduction* to 1 ECONOMICS OF FEDERALISM, *supra* note 106, at xi. This is an idealized model of perfect competition among jurisdictions. Slight deviations from the conditions described would reduce the efficiency of inter-jurisdictional competition at the margin but would not entirely undermine the model.

108. Tiebout himself recognized that the principle extended to non-economic variables as well, such as the desire "to associate with 'nice' people." Tiebout, *supra* note 106, at 418 n.12.

clustering of firms in a particular industry in a given metropolitan area, such as the financial industry in New York City.[109] To what extent are the limitations of interstate competition affected, for example, by the location of business, ameliorated by the relatively greater competition among municipalities (as compared to states) for residents?[110]

A second model of competitive federalism focuses on the power of individuals to "exit" one jurisdiction and relocate to another.[111] The "exit" model is closely related to the Tiebout model, but rather than focusing on the ability of consumers to move into those jurisdictions that offer their preferred mix of policies, it instead focuses on the role of exit as a means of checking state governmental powers to tax and regulate. The massive migration of African–Americans from the American South to northern cities to escape institutionalized discrimination during the Jim Crow era provides an example of the use of "exit" rights under federalism.

The institutional structure of federalism also interacts with other constitutional institutions. The opportunity for exit rights under federalism, for example, helps to explain the seeming anomaly that Congress and state legislatures tend toward bicameralism, while local legislative bodies tend toward unicameralism.[112] Saul Levmore suggests that jurisdictional competition at the county and municipal level, which is more robust than at the state and federal levels, is more effective at disciplining regulatory waste. To be clear, this does not mean that governments do not engage in policies that some might consider unwise or wasteful; rather, consistent with the Tiebout model of jurisdictional competition, there is likely a better match between local provision of goods and services and the wants of the electorate than at the state or federal level. In addition, empirical studies have found that where local governments exceed a certain minimum size and face some degree of competition from surrounding municipalities, governmental spending tends to be proportionally smaller, suggesting that jurisdictional competition promotes a more efficient provision of public goods and services.[113] These insights are further supported by an argument generally attributed to Albert Hirschman, who suggested that if individuals are unable to exit a particular locality's jurisdiction, they still can more effectively exert a meaningful electoral "voice" at local than at higher levels of governance.[114]

---

109. *See* David Schleicher, Why Are There Cities? Local Government Law and the Economics of Agglomeration 64–65 (April 2009) (unpublished manuscript), *available at* https://docushare.gmu.edu/dsweb/Get/Document-34141/Schleicher.docx.

110. Tax incentives on commuting costs could potentially affect municipal exit. For an examination of tax policy and commuting expenses, see Tsilly Dagan, *Commuting*, 26 VA. TAX REV. 185 (2006).

111. *See* Richard A. Epstein, *Exit Rights Under Federalism*, LAW & CONTEMP. PROBS., Winter 1992, at 147.

112. Levmore, *supra* note 45, at 159–62.

113. Robert P. Inman & Daniel L. Rubinfeld, *The Political Economy of Federalism*, *in* PERSPECTIVES ON PUBLIC CHOICE 73, 80–86 (Dennis C. Mueller ed., 1997).

114. ALBERT O. HIRSCHMAN, EXIT, VOICE, AND LOYALTY: RESPONSES TO DECLINE IN FIRMS, ORGANIZATIONS, AND STATES (1970).

The ability of adversely affected parties to exit a given jurisdiction places a substantially greater constraint on the power of winning coalitions to impose external costs on political "losers." The threat, and even the actuality, of exit permits those most likely to be harmed by regulatory waste to truncate the external costs function (in the Buchanan and Tullock model), and the enhanced power of voice at the local level further checks against potentially excessive agency costs. Levmore thus suggests that the combined strategies of exit, per Tiebout, and voice, per Hirschman, thus operate as an effective substitute for either a supermajority requirement in a unicameral legislature or for bicameralism.[115]

1. A Comment on Exit and Choice of Law

Another approach to the relationship between federalism and exit is suggested by recent research on the question of contractual choice of law. Some scholars have argued that legal systems optimize preferences when they permit contractual choice of law subject to certain limits.[116] This allows contracting parties in a given jurisdiction to select an alternative jurisdiction's legal regime without requiring that either party demonstrate a traditionally required nexus to the governing law's jurisdiction. In short, this would allow parties a widespread ability to exit a jurisdiction's law without actually physically exiting the jurisdiction itself. While these proposals appear to involve private rather than constitutional law, in fact, they have significant implications for state sovereignty and federalism and for the relative efficacy of exit versus voice in affecting the direction of legal policy for contracting parties. Consider the following analysis.

Given the information costs associated with contracting out of a particular jurisdiction's legal regime, proposals to allow or to broaden contractual choice of law are most likely to benefit relatively wealthy and sophisticated actors. The choice of law argument presents the following choice: We can either allow jurisdictions to continue to "capture" those individuals and businesses who would most benefit from contractual choice of law or allow such persons and firms to effectively exit through the low cost means of contract (low cost because the parties need to physically relocate to gain the benefit of another jurisdiction's laws). The capture regime raises two potential costs: (1) the welfare reduction associ-

---

115. Levmore also inquires why juries are unicameral bodies of twelve, rather than, say, bicameral bodies of six. Levmore, *supra* note 45, at 145–46. Can you think of advantages or disadvantages to each of these regimes? If you were a criminal defendant, which would you prefer and why? If you were a prosecutor, which would you prefer and why? Does the choice of unicameralism favor one side over the other? For a social choice analysis of juries, see Edward P. Schwartz & Warren F. Schwartz, *Deciding Who Decides Who Dies: Capital Punishment as a Social Choice Problem*, 1 LEGAL THEORY 113 (1995); Edward P. Schwartz & Warren F. Schwartz, *Decisionmaking by Juries Under Unanimity and Supermajority Voting Rules*, 80 GEO. L.J. 775 (1992).

116. For a recent analysis, see ERIN A. O'HARA & LARRY E. RIBSTEIN, THE LAW MARKET (2009). The authors review the literature on contractual choice of law, discuss various contexts in which broadening access to choice of law might be beneficial, and suggest a legal rule to facilitate broader choice of law. The authors suggest two limits in their proposed choice of law regime: (1) those contracting for another jurisdiction's choice of law must take that jurisdiction's law in its entirety for the specific contract, rather than picking and choosing among various jurisdictions' laws; and (2) state jurisdictions can prevent parties from engaging in contractual choice of law by designating certain contract rules as super-mandatory. *See id.* at 218–22.

ated with insisting that parties operate against a set of background rules that they prefer to avoid; and (2) in cases in which this becomes unduly costly, the possibility that some of the disadvantaged parties might eventually physically exit to gain the benefit of another jurisdiction's law. Conversely, the capture regime carries the benefit of encouraging those who are most likely to be effective in doing so to work toward liberalizing the legal regime that they find immediately disadvantageous, rather than allowing them by contract away from the jurisdiction's law with the effect of truncating the decision cost curve for those who remain affected by the problematic law.

Does this fairly characterize the contractual choice of law debate? If so, which way does the analysis cut? Why? Is this yet another area in which traditional law and economics analysis and public choice analysis pull in different directions? Do you favor allowing parties to contract out of their jurisdiction's law? Why or why not?

C. THE FRANCHISE THEORY OF FEDERALISM[117]

In a provocative study of federal deference to local regulation, Jonathan Macey advanced what he terms the "franchise theory of federalism."[118] Macey explains:

> In an ordinary business franchise, the owner of a product, service, or technology, rather than market its own goods, often will choose to sell another firm the rights to market them under a franchise arrangement. Under certain circumstances firms find it in their interests to employ this sort of contractual arrangement. [We can identify] three general situations in which Congress [by analogy to franchisors] will "franchise" the right to regulate in a particular area to the states [by analogy to franchisees]: (1) when a particular state has developed a body of regulation that comprises a valuable capital asset and federal regulation would dissipate the value of that asset; (2) when the political-support-maximizing outcome varies markedly from area to area due to the existence of spatial monopolies, variegated local political optima, and variations in voter preferences across regions; and (3) where Congress can avoid potentially damaging political opposition from special-interest groups by putting the responsibility for a particularly controversial issue on state and local governments.[119]

Macey's franchise theory of federalism suggests that even with no constitutional or societal rule requiring that members of Congress defer to local decision makers, rational members of Congress would still sometimes find such deference in its best interest. In this analysis, federalism is not a

---

117. Portions of the discussions that follow are adapted from STEARNS, *supra* note 24, at 895–96.

118. *See* Jonathan R. Macey, *Federal Deference to Local Regulators and the Economic Theory of Regulation: Toward a Public–Choice Explanation of Federalism*, 76 VA. L. REV. 265, 268 (1990).

119. *Id.* at 268–69 (footnote omitted).

doctrine with independent political content but rather is a handy label that politicians attach to outcomes that they reach for independent reasons. Among the forces that Macey contends conduce to local, rather than national, decision-making in those instances when the Constitution permits regulation at either level, are the following: (1) the desire to appease constituents with intense and competing preferences on given issues that are more likely to be consistent within, than across, specific geographic regions; (2) the desire to allow local legislators to claim credit with their constituents for political victories; and (3) the desire to protect or reward investments that produce local political capital. Allowing local regulation enables politicians at the local level (those who create the political benefit) and at the national level (those who facilitated the local provision of that benefit) to claim credit with their constituents for the favorable results that are achieved. This model resembles the public choice account of agency delegation, which suggests that decisions to defer to agencies (like decisions to defer to state or local governmental units) provide a benefit to members of Congress because if the other decision-making unit performs well they can take the credit, and when it performs poorly, they can seize a new political opportunity for correction (and once accomplished, still take credit).[120]

Perhaps the most interesting illustration of the franchise theory involves allowing states to continue to regulate corporate chartering. Building upon the work of Professor Roberta Romano, who explained the persistence of Delaware's dominance of corporate chartering, Macey explains the mutual benefit to federal and state politicians from this regime. In her famous study of Delaware corporate law,[121] Roberta Romano offered the provocative thesis that Delaware's longstanding dominance in corporate law chartering does not result from the superiority of Delaware's substantive law—laws that virtually any other state could quickly replicate[122]—but rather from the state's unique ability to issue an effective bond. Summarizing Romano's thesis, Macey explains:

> Delaware is a small state. It obtains an extremely high proportion of its budget (sixteen percent) from franchise taxes on corporate chartering. Delaware relies on these revenues more than other states because for other states, revenues from corporate chartering represent only a small portion of their total budget. In other words, the high percentage of Delaware's budget that is derived from chartering revenues represents a credible (bonded) promise that the state will not renege on its earlier promise to respond in consistent ways to new phenomena. Delaware has been able to retain its dominance because it is able to offer a reliable promise that its corporation law will remain highly attractive to managers in the future. Competing states are unable to

---

120. For a related discussion, *see supra* chapter 2, section III.A.

121. *See* Roberta Romano, *Law as a Product: Some Pieces of the Incorporation Puzzle*, 1 J.L. ECON. & ORG. 225 (1985).

122. Macey, *supra* note 118, at 277.

match Delaware's promise of future performance because they cannot offer the same credible bond.[123]

Macey's franchise theory extends the Romano thesis to account for the general practice of federal lawmakers facilitating this corporate chartering, thus allowing Delaware, a tiny state, to assume a place of national prominence in this specialized area of law. The overall arrangement benefits both federal lawmakers (who benefit from facilitating successful local lawmaking) and state lawmakers (who get credit for providing managers valuable opportunities to incorporate in a state whose law remains predictable).

Professor Mark Roe has refined the model of Delaware's dominance in corporate law as the outcome of a complex interaction between Delaware and the national government.[124] Because of its prominence, Delaware essentially makes corporate law for the entire country, a task that typically would be thought to be allocated to the federal government. In fact, the federal government could at any time preempt all or much of the field of corporate law. Through its authority over the regulation of the sale of securities, Congress has in fact made major incursions from time to time on the scope of Delaware's authority.

Roe explains that Delaware typically has the opportunity to move first in creating new law governing corporations. Where managers and investors agree on the shape of the law, Delaware's primacy is generally assured. Even if these constituencies have an incentive to create lopsided laws in their favor, they restrain themselves from going too far out of a fear that Congress will intervene to strike a different balance. Where Delaware law breaks down, however, such as in a flurry of corporate scandals, Congress risks implicit public blame and is then more likely to intervene and displace Delaware law.

Roe analogizes the relationship between Delaware and the federal government to that between Congress and regulatory agencies (as described in Chapter 6). Congress will de facto delegate to Delaware so long as the benefits to Congress of "delegating" exceed the costs of relinquishing control over national, corporate legal policy. Where, however, the costs become large—such as in high-profile corporate scandals that create a media and public outcry for federal action, Congress will intervene. Roe argues that this dynamic is recently illustrated in the enactment of the Sarbanes–Oxley law, which was enacted in response to perceived failures in Delaware's regulation of corporate law. Sarbanes–Oxley provides federal rules for several areas of corporate governance that traditionally were governed by state law, including new disclosure rules designed to increase transparency, to provide stricter limits on conflicts of interest, and to provide stiffer criminal penalties for corporate malfeasance.[125]

---

123. *Id.* at 278 (footnotes omitted).

124. Mark J. Roe, *Delaware's Politics*, 118 HARV. L. REV. 2491 (2005).

125. *See id.* at 2521–22, 2528–29.

D. APPLICATION OF CONSTITUTIONAL FEDERALISM TO LEGAL DOCTRINE

The preceding discussion of federalism has implications for understanding several constitutional law doctrines. Here we briefly examine two doctrines: the "anti-commandeering" doctrine and the dormant Commerce Clause doctrine.

1. The Anti–Commandeering Doctrine[126]

An interesting contrast case for Macey's franchise theory of federalism involves the anti-commandeering doctrine. In *New York v. United States*,[127] the Supreme Court struck down a statute that effectively required states to legislate on Congress's behalf. The Court held that under Article I, § 8 of the United States Constitution, or alternatively under the Tenth Amendment (which Justice O'Connor described in her majority opinion for the *New York* Court as "mirror images" of each other), Congress lacks the power to commandeer the states.

The *New York* Court struck down the take title provisions of the Low–Level Radioactive Waste Policy Amendments Act of 1985.[128] Under the challenged law, states were required over a period of years to meet a series of progressive deadlines for self-sufficiency with respect to disposing of low-level radioactive waste. The controversial take title provision required that states failing to become self-sufficient by the specified deadlines, either by joining a regional pact with other states or by placing a waste disposal facility in state, take title of low-level radioactive waste generated in their borders or compensate producers of such waste for their failure to do so. New York, which challenged the provision, was the only state that had failed to comply with the statute's deadlines for self-sufficiency, and thus was the only state subject to the take title provision's draconian sanctions.

In striking down the challenged provision and holding that neither Article I, § 8 nor the Tenth Amendment permit Congress to commandeer states into legislating on its behalf, Justice O'Connor underscored yet another dimension of federalism, one closely tied to the economic theory of delegation. O'Connor explained:

> [W]here the Federal Government compels States to regulate, the accountability of both state and federal officials is diminished. If the citizens of New York, for example, do not consider that making provision for the disposal of radioactive waste is in their best interest, they may elect state officials who share their view. That view can always be pre-empted under the Supremacy Clause if it is contrary to

---

126. Portions of the discussions that follow are adapted from STEARNS, *supra* note 24, at 896–97.

127. 505 U.S. 144 (1992).

128. Pub. L. No. 99–240, 99 Stat. 1842.

the national view, but in such a case it is the Federal Government that makes the decision in full view of the public, and it will be federal officials that suffer the consequences if the decision turns out to be detrimental or unpopular. But where the Federal Government directs the States to regulate, it may be state officials who will bear the brunt of public disapproval, while the federal officials who devised the regulatory program may remain insulated from the electoral ramifications of their decision. Accountability is thus diminished when, due to federal coercion, elected state officials cannot regulate in accordance with the views of the local electorate in matters not pre-empted by federal regulation.[129]

In this analysis, the same credit-taking/blame-shifting that public choice theorists have associated with agency delegations also comes into play with congressional commandeering of state legislatures. If the regulatory program succeeds, members of Congress and of the state legislature can each take credit for its success. If the regulatory program fails, members of Congress can blame their state counterparts for creating the unsatisfactory result, and state legislatures can blame Congress for requiring them to regulate in the first instance. Do you find this analysis persuasive? Why or why not? Do you believe that the Supreme Court decided the *New York* case correctly? Why or why not? To what extent is your answer informed by public choice? How would you analyze this case under Macey's franchise theory of federalism?

2. The Dormant Commerce Clause Doctrine

While the prior discussions focused on the benefits of federalism, either as a matter of policy or as a matter of political accountability, the Supreme Court's dormant Commerce Clause doctrine is helpful in considering some of the resulting costs. In a game theoretical study of the dormant Commerce Clause doctrine,[130] Maxwell Stearns has demonstrated that under some circumstances individual states can obstruct benign pro-commerce regimes. Stearns's larger analysis rests on combining the prisoners' dilemma game and the multiple Nash equilibrium coordination game to explain the dormant Commerce Clause and related doctrines. For our immediate purposes, the critical analysis involves the multiple Nash equilibrium game.[131] The analysis reveals the conditions under which individual states have the capacity, and sometimes the tendency, to interfere with political union in a manner that justifies federal intervention, even when Congress has declined to reach the underlying issue by statute.

---

129. *New York*, 505 U.S. at 168–69.

130. *See* Maxwell L. Stearns, *A Beautiful Mend: A Game Theoretical Analysis of the Dormant Commerce Clause Doctrine*, 45 WM. & MARY L. REV. 1 (2003). For earlier works studying the problem of interstate coordination in promoting multistate commercial activity, see RICHARD A. EPSTEIN, BARGAINING WITH THE STATE 127–44 (1993); Dan L. Burk, *Federalism in Cyberspace*, 28 CONN. L. REV. 1095 (1996); and Saul Levmore, *Interstate Exploitation and Judicial Intervention*, 69 VA. L. REV. 563 (1983).

131. *See supra* chapter 4, section II.A.

To illustrate, imagine first a desired regulatory policy that will allow trucking vehicles to travel through states as needed to ensure the cost effective delivery of goods. As seen in the presentation of *Bibb v. Navajo Freight Lines, Inc.*,[132] when most or all states agree upon a common truck feature—in this instance, straight mudflaps—a single state, like Illinois, can disrupt the flow of commerce by instead insisting upon curved mudflaps. If we assume that neither policy is superior as a safety measure, then this rule implicates the multiple Nash equilibrium bargaining game. Either coordinated result—all straight or all curved mudflaps (or permitting either mudflap)—provides participating states a high payoff. Conversely, when a single state selects a contrary rule, the result is a mixed strategy equilibrium that limits the ability of the states to facilitate commerce in a cost effective manner. In this analysis, the election by Illinois of a contrary rule implies that it sought to reduce its share of the cost of facilitating interstate commerce, a result in tension with the constitutional objective of promoting national union.[133]

Do you find this explanation of *Bibb* persuasive? How does it relate to the franchise theory of federalism? How does it relate to the preceding analysis of the anti-commandeering doctrine? Can you explain why Congress tends not to interfere with Supreme Court decisions under the dormant Commerce Clause doctrine even though it is blackletter law that Congress has the authority to reverse them by ordinary legislation? Does public choice help in answering this question?[134]

E. PRESERVING FEDERALISM

Once federalism is established, the next issue becomes its preservation. After society agrees on a set of constitutional rules that further the general welfare, some may find it in their interest to deviate from those rules to advance other objectives, including those related to ideology. This concern might be particularly acute in the context of federalism. One immediate difficulty with the establishment of vertical federalism is the issue of jurisdictional supremacy. Under a typical system of federalism, as in the United States, the federal government holds a "trump" over state and local governments when acting within its sphere of authority. This can create a centrifugal force toward greater centralization of political power as decision makers have an incentive to push toward greater preemption of local activities. This pressure might arise from either interest groups or political actors who see a benefit from raising the level of political jurisdiction at which a given decision is made.

---

132. 359 U.S. 520 (1959). *See supra* chapter 4, section II.A..

133. For a similar account of *Kassel v. Consolidated Freightways*, 450 U.S. 662 (1981), see Stearns, *supra* note 130, at 49–55, 130–33.

134. For an analysis claiming that dormant Commerce Clause rulings should be mandatory and thus not subject to overruling by Congress, see Norman R. Williams, *Why Congress May Not "Overrule" the Dormant Commerce Clause*, 53 UCLA L. Rev. 153 (2005). For a contrary analysis using game theory to explain the default nature of dormant Commerce Clause rulings, see Maxwell L. Stearns, *The New Commerce Clause Doctrine in Game Theoretical Perspective*, 60 Vand. L. Rev. 1, 48 n.211 (2007).

Consider agriculture price subsidies as an example. Because agricultural products are sold in national and international markets, efforts to subsidize the price of certain crops (such as corn) will be largely ineffective if done on a state-by-state basis. Iowa, for instance, could not effectively unilaterally raise the market price of corn above the prevailing market price because its corn farmers would be undersold by farmers in other states. As a result, effective agriculture subsidies must operate at a national level.[135] In such situations, the elevation of decision-making authority to a higher jurisdiction acts as sort of a cartel enforcement mechanism to protect the favored interest from competition. How can constitutions be designed to preserve the structure of constitutional federalism (or other constitutional limitations) given the incentives to depart from structure?

To what extent does the preceding analysis suggest that while the United States Constitution establishes a regime of federalism, the ultimate protections for preserving federalism are political? Consider for example the following passage from Justice Blackmun's majority opinion in *Garcia v. San Antonio Metropolitan Transit Authority*,[136] a case overruling *National League of Cities v. Usery*.[137] In *National League of Cities*, the Court had relied upon a "traditional governmental functions" test to invalidate congressional power to apply the Fair Labor Standards Act's minimum wage and overtime provisions to state employees. In contrast, the *Garcia* Court sustained the application of such provisions to municipal employees, declaring the traditional governmental functions test as "unworkable." Writing for the *Garcia* majority, Justice Blackmun explained:

> [The States retain their sovereign powers only] to the extent that the Constitution has not divested them of their original powers and transferred those powers to the Federal Government....
>
>   . . . .
>
> ... [T]he principal means chosen by the Framers to ensure the role of States in the federal system lies in the structure of the Federal Government itself....
>
> ... State sovereign interests, then, are more properly protected by procedural safeguards inherent in the structure of the federal system than by judicially created limitations on federal power.[138]

In his separate opinion, Justice Powell referred to the "rise of numerous special interest groups that engage in sophisticated lobbying, and make substantial campaign contributions to some Members of Congress."[139] He added, "These groups are thought to have significant influence in the shaping and enactment of certain types of legislation. Contrary

---

135. For a consistent analysis explaining *Wickard v. Filburn*, 317 U.S. 111 (1942), as a proper result under the Commerce Clause, see Stearns, *supra* note 134.

136. 469 U.S. 528 (1985).

137. 426 U.S. 833 (1976).

138. *Garcia*, 469 U.S. at 549–50, 552.

139. *Id.* at 575 n.18 (Powell, J., dissenting).

to the Court's view, a 'political process' that functions in this way is unlikely to safeguard the sovereign rights of States and localities."[140]

Finally, Justice O'Connor, who later drafted the majority opinion in *New York v. United States*, responded in her *Garcia* dissent as follows:

> The central issue of federalism ... is whether any realm *is* left open to the States by the Constitution—whether any area remains in which a State may act free of federal interference. "The issue ... is whether the federal system has any *legal* substance, any core of constitutional right that courts will enforce." The true "essence" of federalism is that the States *as States* have legitimate interests which the National Government is bound to respect even though its laws are supreme....
>
>   . . . .
>
> ... With the abandonment of *National League of Cities*, all that stands between the remaining essentials of state sovereignty and Congress is the latter's underdeveloped capacity for self-restraint.[141]

Which if any of these views of federalism—those of Blackmun, Powell, or O'Connor—finds stronger support in the theory of public choice? Why? O'Connor suggests the possibility that absent judicial protection of federalism, Congress inevitably tends in the direction of increasing federal control over areas that were traditionally subject to state and local regulation. If this is true, is it owing to the problem of special interests that Powell recognizes in his opinion? How would Macey analyze *Garcia* under the franchise theory of federalism? How would Roe analyze this case? Notice that the analyses of Macey and Roe are consistent with the claim that special interests might prefer in some instances to retain regulatory powers at the state or local levels. Is this insight inconsistent with O'Connor's analysis? With Powell's? Which analysis is more persuasive? Why?

In the context of separation of powers, Madison believed that in the pursuit of self interest, each branch would jealously safeguard against unjust encroachments by another branch. This insight can be extended to the institutional context of federalism. Consider the following passage from *Federalist No. 51*:

> But the great security against a gradual concentration of the several powers in the same department consists in giving to those who administer each department the necessary constitutional means and personal motives to resist encroachments of the others.... Ambition must be made to counteract ambition. *The interest of the man must be connected with the constitutional rights of the place.*[142]

Professor Barry Weingast has recently relied upon this intuition to describe "self-enforcing federalism," meaning a scheme where all actors

---

140. *Id.*

141. *Id.* at 580–81, 588 (O'Connor, J., dissenting) (citation omitted).

142. THE FEDERALIST No. 51 (James Madison), *supra* note 3, at 321–22 (emphasis added).

find it in their individual self interest to adhere to the constitutional rules, thereby stabilizing the overall constitutional order.[143] Although Weingast's primary emphasis is on the preservation of democracy from transgression by political leaders,[144] to what extent does the same logic apply to the preservation of federalism against incursions by the central government? Do members of Congress or of state legislatures have a sufficient incentive to preserve the constitutional structure of federalism if acting on that principle would be contrary to the demands of their constituents? Are the "interest[s] of the man . . . connected with the constitutional rights of the place"[145] when it comes to a principled commitment to federalism? Have changes in the processes through which Senators are selected as a result of the Seventeenth Amendment compromised the ability of self interest to preserve federalism as a core value in the United States constitutional scheme?

Consider the following argument. In the original United States Constitution, state legislatures elected each state's United States Senators.[146] As Madison wrote, the appointment of Senators by the state legislatures would "giv[e] to the State governments such an agency in the formation of the federal government as must secure the authority of the former. . . ."[147] Todd Zywicki has argued that the Seventeenth Amendment, which replaced this scheme with direct election, effectively removed this protection of federalism from ordinary political processes operating at the level of Congress. Zywicki maintains that when state legislatures were the natural constituency of U.S. Senators, Senators rationally acted to advance the interests of their principals, the state legislators who elected them, by protecting state governments from incursion by the federal government. This arrangement, Zywicki maintains, embodied Madison's insight that the "interests of the man" should be "connected with the constitutional rights of the place." With respect to a wide range of fiscal and regulatory matters, Zywicki argues that this arrangement safeguarded state interests throughout most of the nineteenth century, thus limiting rent-seeking at the federal level that resulted in imposing significant costs upon states. During the nineteenth century, the federal government remained relative-

---

143. *See* Barry R. Weingast, *The Constitutional Dilemma of Economic Liberty*, J. Econ. Persp., Summer 2005, at 89, 102–05. The concept of self-enforcing constitutional rules can be found in James Madison's writings as well as those of the Nineteenth Century Swedish economist Knut Wicksell. *See* Richard E. Wagner & James D. Gwartney, *Public Choice and Constitutional Order*, *in* Public Choice and Constitutional Economics 29, 44–49 (James D. Gwartney & Richard E. Wagner eds., 1988). John C. Calhoun's proposal that a "concurrent majority" be required for certain important political decisions is also grounded in the idea of self-enforcing constitutionalism. *See* John C. Calhoun, A Disquisition on Government and a Discourse on the Constitution and Government of the United States (Richard K. Cralle ed., Charleston, Walker & James 1851).

144. *See* Barry R. Weingast, *The Economic Role of Political Institutions: Market–Preserving Federalism and Economic Development*, 11 J.L. Econ. & Org. 1 (1995).

145. The Federalist No. 54 (James Madison), *supra* note 3, at 322.

146. *See supra* note 51 and accompanying text.

147. The Federalist No. 62 (James Madison), *supra* note 3, at 377. Hamilton referred to this provision of election of U.S. Senators by state legislatures as the "absolute safeguard" to the states to preserve their authority from federal incursion. The Federalist No. 59 (Alexander Hamilton), *supra* note 3, at 364.

ly limited in scope and tended to focus its regulatory powers on those areas most obviously within its delegated spheres of authority, including the military and interstate transportation, such as building canals and roads. Even though the federal government naturally expanded in size during periods of crisis such as wars, Zywicki observes that it generally restored itself to a more modest size when the crisis abated, and correspondingly, state governments then reasserted the scope of their regulatory powers to earlier levels. Zywicki further claims that state legislators generally retained control over many of the issues that implicated special-interest politics, thus allowing state level politicians to reap the rewards of interacting with interest groups.

Consistent with the exit theory of federalism, Zywicki concludes that the practice of engaging in special-interest politics at the state level might have been social welfare maximizing by reducing the overall level of rent-seeking activity as compared with a regime of increased centralization of regulatory powers that he claims followed with the adoption of the Seventeenth Amendment. By contrast, Zywicki claims, under the present regime, the interests of the Senators are much closer to those of the members of the House of Representatives, and thus Senators have no institutional incentive to protect the authority of the states or to preserve the constitutional principle of federalism.

Do you find this analysis persuasive? Can you identify other mechanisms beside direct political responsiveness resulting from methods for choosing senators prior to the Seventeenth Amendment that could motivate federal political sensitivity to the concerns of states? If so, what are they, and how might they be implemented? If not, what does that suggest about the proper role of federal judicial power in enforcing federalism? To the extent that Macey is correct that federalism is ultimately a function of the political interests of federal actors, is this necessarily a bad result? Why or why not?

F. DIRECT DEMOCRACY

An important issue of constitutional economics that overlaps with federalism is the practice of direct democracy at the state level.[148] First appearing in 1898 in South Dakota, direct democracy is now commonplace at the state and local levels.[149] Twenty-seven states provide for the state-wide initiative, popular referendum, or both, although such activity has generally been concentrated in about a half-dozen states.[150] A legislative referendum for state constitutional amendments is required in every state

---

148. For a recent overview and analysis, see Elizabeth Garrett, *Direct Democracy and Public Choice, in* ELGAR HANDBOOK IN PUBLIC CHOICE AND PUBLIC LAW (Daniel Farber & Anne Joseph O'Connell eds., forthcoming 2009), *manuscript available at* http://ssrn.com/abstract=1217608.

149. *Id.* at 1–2.

150. *Id.* at 2.

except Delaware. Moreover, about half of the nation's cities also provide for some form of direct democracy.[151]

A commonly expressed justification for direct democracy is to overcome the previously mentioned problem of agency costs between elected officials and the public. The difficulty is attributed to the ability of well-organized special interests to influence the legislative process and thus to produce outcomes contrary to the will of the majority. Direct democracy is seen as a means for the public to "polic[e] their wayward legislative agents"[152] and to reassert majoritarian policy preferences against special-interest generated political outcomes. This result may be brought about in two ways: a direct effect of voters overriding the decisions of elected officials and an indirect effect of inducing elected officials to adopt policies closer to those preferred by the median electoral voter under the threat of being reversed by the voters in a referendum.[153]

Empirical evidence indicates that direct democracy promotes alignment of governmental policy with the preferences of the median electoral voter, especially in two types of areas: (1) where agency costs of elected officials are high, and (2) on highly-contested social issues.[154] This outcome requires that certain basic criteria be met including, most notably, sufficient turnout to ensure that voting preferences are meaningfully representative of the electorate as a whole.[155] Where concerns about agency costs and interest group influence are high, such as on issues of taxation and spending, direct democracy therefore has the potential to constrain the decisions of elected officials. Thus, for instance, states with the initiative process are more likely to adopt institutional reforms that impose tax and expenditure limits on the government and to require supermajority vote for tax increases. States with the initiative also tend to fund particular governmental services through greater reliance on user fees rather than broad-based taxes that facilitate wealth redistribution. Thus referenda operate as a check against certain progressive, or redistributive, tax policies. Taxing and spending, along with the salaries of senior executive officials, are generally lower overall in states with than those without the initiative.[156]

---

151. *Id.*

152. *Id.*

153. John G. Matsusaka, *Direct Democracy Works*, J. ECON. PERSP., Spring 2005, at 185, 192; Elisabeth R. Gerber, *Legislative Response to the Threat of Popular Initiatives*, 40 AM. J. POL. SCI. 99 (1996).

154. JOHN G. MATSUSAKA, FOR THE MANY OR THE FEW: THE INITIATIVE, PUBLIC POLICY, AND AMERICAN DEMOCRACY (2004). *See* Garrett, *supra* note 148, at 4. For an article that reaches a contrary conclusion, namely that initiatives might produce results that the public disfavors relative to the status quo as a result of proposals that are piecemeal components over larger issues of public policy and for which electoral preferences cycle; that are based upon incomplete information, for example, with respect to how enacted measures will be financed; and that are motivated by nonpolicy goals such as turning out voters to affect elections rather than to enact the specific initiative, which the authors label crypto-initiatives, see Thad Kousser & Mathew D. McCubbins, *Social Choice, Crypto-Initiatives, and Policymaking by Direct Democracy* 78 S. CAL. L. REV. 949 (2004–05). For an empirical analysis of some of claims set out in the Kousser and McCubbins article, see Matsusaka, *supra*, at 202.

155. *See* Garrett, *supra* note 148, at 4.

156. Matsusaka, *supra* note 154, at 195–96.

Access to the initiative process has been especially crucial in the enactment of term limits, an issue on which agency costs arising from legislator self-interest are likely to be high: "[Twenty-two] of 24 initiative states adopted term limits for their congressmen or state legislatures, compared to two of 26 noninitiative states."[157] Professor Ilya Somin has found that states with the initiative have been more likely to adopt laws that place strong limits on the power of the government to take private property for public development following of the Supreme Court decision, *Kelo v. City of New London*,[158] another issue on which agency costs and special interest activity might be high, whereas he claim that non-initiative states have adopted largely symbolic reforms.[159] Direct democracy also appears to be an effective way for grassroots citizen groups to end-run traditional political processes in which well-funded and sophisticated interest groups tend to hold a comparative advantage in influencing policy.[160] John Matsusaka claims empirical support for a correlation between direct democracy institutions (including its use in Switzerland) and various measures of governance quality, such as the efficient provision of governmental services.[161] Some scholars argue that direct democracy is effective in enacting laws that manifest community values, such as those related to the death penalty, parental consent for abortions, same-sex marriage, and prohibitions against employment discrimination.[162]

Direct democracy might also be useful in resolving issues that rely on the aggregation of dispersed public information, reflecting the insights of the Condorcet Jury Theorem, as compared with issues for which the resolution requires technical expertise and thus that tend to be reserved to legislatures.[163] Consider, however, whether the enactment of public policy is a context in which the assumptions that underlie the Condorcet Jury Theorem apply. The theorem is premised on an assumption that the question being asked actually admit of a correct answer, such as the number of beans in jar. Are the sorts of questions posed by referenda the types of questions that the Condorcet Jury theorem can usefully answer? Conversely, is it possible that the successful passage of multiple referenda over differing jurisdictions informs the efficacy of a particular substantive approach to a question of public policy, and that this has the effect of at least partly restoring the theorem's underlying intuitions?

---

157. *Id.* at 195.

158. 545 U.S. 469 (2005).

159. Ilya Somin, *The Limits of Backlash: Assessing the Political Response to* Kelo, 93 MINN. L. REV. 2100 (2009).

160. ELISABETH R. GERBER, THE POPULIST PARADOX: INTEREST GROUP INFLUENCE AND THE PROMISE OF DIRECT LEGISLATION (1999).

161. *See* Matsusaka, *supra* note 152, at 201 (summarizing studies).

162. *See id.* at 195 (summarizing studies).

163. For a discussion of the Condorcet Jury Theorem and its underlying assumptions, see *supra* chapter 7, section I.E.

Direct democracy facilitates a closer matching of policies to preferences of the median electoral voter by disaggregating political issues into more discrete choices. Elizabeth Garrett, for example, explains that political candidates hold views that represent " 'bundles' of issues, so a voter might decide to support a candidate because, on balance, her positions more closely track the voter's preferences even though the lawmaker's position on a particular issue is far from the voter's."[164] The initiative process, in contrast, enables citizens to separate out these bundles into discrete policy choices and invites an up or down vote on each separate issue. Some authors contend that this process produces a closer match between citizen preferences and policy outcomes.[165] Some critics of direct democracy argue that the outcomes of direct democracy are *too* majoritarian in that they may be a vehicle for majority tyranny and thus allowing laws that are discriminatory against unpopular minorities to pass.[166]

While the ability to unbundle issues appears to promote democracy— as defined by majority rule—it does not necessarily promote socially efficient results, at least once strength of preferences is taken into account. Consider the argument that legislative packaging is the primary means through which legislators and their constituents express cardinal preference for or against, rather than mere ordinal rankings over, proposed legislative alternatives.[167] To what extent are representative, democratic processes structured to provide those most likely affected by proposed legislation the means with which to express the intensity of their support or opposition? Consider in this regard, the passage from *Federalist No. 10* quoted earlier in this chapter, especially Madison's claim that representative democracy serves to "refine and enlarge the public views"[168]

Although Madison's primary point was that a larger representative republic was superior to smaller direct democracies for avoiding the vice of factions, consider also whether the processes used to "refine and enlarge the public views" has the added benefit of allowing those most affected by the passage of laws to express cardinal preferences rather than merely registering their views through a binary voting process. In this analysis, representative democracy, unlike direct democracy, might provide a means through which those most affected by a particular proposal to demonstrate the importance of that measure *to them*.

One potential risk that initiatives pose is that although the outcomes of the initiative process might reflect the preferences of the general electorate's median voter, it might not reflect preferred public policy when

---

164. Garrett, *supra* note 148, at 5.

165. Timothy Besley & Stephen Coate, *Issue Unbundling via Citizens' Initiatives* (Nat'l Bureau of Econ. Research, Working Paper No. 8036, 2000); ROBERT D. COOTER, THE STRATEGIC CONSTITUTION 143–48 (2000).

166. For empirical studies testing such claims, see Todd Donovan & Shaun Bowler, *Direct Democracy and Minority Rights: An Extension*, 42 AM. J. POL. SCI. 1020 (1998); Zoltan L. Hajnal, Elisabeth R. Gerber & Hugh Louch, *Minorities and Direct Legislation: Evidence from California Ballot Proposition Elections*, 64 J. POL. 154 (2002).

167. For a general discussion of cardinal versus ordinal preferences, see *supra* chapter 3.

168. THE FEDERALIST NO. 10 (James Madison), *supra* note 3, at 82.

the aggregation of voters' *strength* of preferences is taken into account.[169] The initiative process thus risks allowing a broad but weakly interested majority to outvote a minority that is intensely affected by the outcome. In ordinary legislature processes, strength of preferences may be reflected through such processes as logrolling or a variety of mechanisms, financial or otherwise, for expressing support for or opposition to particular candidates or for positions that they seek to advance or oppose. In this analysis, it is the packaging of legislation into bundles and the process of allowing negotiation in the legislature itself that furthers the interests of particular groups—including minority groups—who may fare less well when issues of particular concern to them are disaggregated through the referendum process.

Consider as one example reliance upon state-wide referenda to end the use of race in the context of affirmative action within various state jurisdictions.[170] Is this consistent with arguments supportive of direct democracy that it reduces agency costs and aligns preferences with those of the median voter or with the concerns about the effects of unbundling on the interests of minority groups? Why?

VI. CONSTITUTIONAL AMENDMENT

While constitutional architects seek to embed durable values into the constitutions they craft,[171] they also are concerned about the danger of obsolescence. Invariably, constitutions include amending provisions.[172] These include provisions that seek to strike the appropriate balance in promoting appropriate electoral accountability (reducing agency costs) and ensuring proper functioning (reducing decision or external costs). Whether or not constitutions are ever truly drafted behind a veil of ignorance, the process of amending certainly takes place with affected persons well aware of their respective positions in society. Not surprisingly, therefore, the process of constitutional amendment necessarily embraces many of the same interest group and agency cost dynamics that characterize ordinary legislative processes.

Building upon these assumptions, Donald Boudreaux and Adam Pritchard have proposed a public choice model of the constitutional amendment process.[173] Their analysis suggests the irony that interest

---

169. *See supra* chapter 3, section I.A (explaining that majority rule fails to account for strength of preference).

170. *See, e.g.*, Robert J. Delahunty, *"Constitutional Justice" or "Constitutional Peace"? The Supreme Court and Affirmative Action*, 65 WASH. & LEE L. REV. 11, 46 n.156 (2008) (concluding that "[w]hen some affirmative action policies have been put to the voters, they have been resoundingly *rejected*").

171. *See* William A. Niskanen, *Conditions Affecting the Survival of Constitutional Rules*, CONST. POL. ECON., Mar. 1990, at 53.

172. For a formal model of the optimal decision-making rule for constitutional amendments, see Thomas F. Schaller, *Consent for Change: Article V and the Constitutional Amendment Process*, 8 CONST. POL. ECON. 195 (1997).

173. Donald J. Boudreaux & A.C. Pritchard, *Rewriting the Constitution: An Economic Analysis of the Constitutional Amendment Process*, 62 FORDHAM L. REV. 111 (1993).

groups that are sufficiently powerful to be the object of constitutional constraint are likely also to be best poised to exert sufficient influence to amend the very constitutions that constrain them. The authors observe that an interest group seeking favorable governmental action can pursue this result through either of two means, ordinary legislation or a constitutional amendment. A constitutional amendment is more costly to secure because amending demands a greater number of successful successive supermajority coalitions. For that very reason, however, constitutional amendments are more durable once procured.[174] As a result, interest groups will pursue a constitutional amendment where the benefits of enhanced durability exceed the marginal costs of amending as compared with legislating.

Boudreaux and Pritchard claim that the incentives of interest groups to pursue a constitutional amendment rather than ordinary legislation is a function of two variables, first, "maintenance costs," and second, the strength and timing of opposition. Maintenance costs are "the costs an interest group incurs over time in order to continue to lobby effectively for privileges conferred by the government."[175] The authors posit that "interest groups with high maintenance costs have a greater demand for constitutional protection of their privileges than do groups with low maintenance costs."[176]

The authors cast this theory as an intertemporal or dynamic extension of Mancur Olson's theory of collective action.[177] While Olson focused primarily on the costs associated with initial organization, Boudreaux and Pritchard focus on the costs of maintaining group organization over time and on the rational response of other interest groups likely to be affected by such maintenance costs. For instance, an interest group that expects to become larger and more diffuse over time might fear a risk of a future decline in political influence as its organization and maintenance costs predictably rise. Such a group will rationally find more value in the possibility of a constitutional amendment than a group that predicts a continued similar composition over time and thus no discernible change in its ability to exert beneficial political influence in the future. As examples, the authors suggest that such ideologically motivated interest groups such as advocates for temperance in the early Twentieth Century might have anticipated higher maintenance costs over time than groups characterized by narrowly defined self interest, including labor unions or industry trade groups. As a result, the authors predict that interest groups that coalesce around ideological goals will be more likely to lobby for a constitutional amendment, whereas interest groups defined around a particular set of financial concerns might find legislative lobbying more cost effective.

---

174. Recall that the present value of the stream of economic rents to be transferred through a given law will be a function of both the value transferred each period as well as the expected durability of the law. *See supra* chapter 2, section II.C.2.

175. *See* Boudreaux & Pritchard, *supra* note 173, at 118.

176. *Id.*

177. For a discussion of Olson's theory, see *supra* chapter 2, section II.C.

The authors contend that a second factor affecting the choice between pursuing an amendment and pursuing legislation is the expectation over time of well organized political opposition. Presently weak opposition that is expected to grow might make it more attractive to pursue a constitutional amendment. Conversely, when future opposition is expected to be weak, interest groups will prefer investing in the legislative process.

Do you find the Boudreaux and Pritchard model persuasive? To what extent does it help to explain specific amendments to the United States Constitution? Does it help to explain the enactment of the Bill of Rights? Does it help to explain unsuccessful efforts to pursue amendments to secure an item veto, a balanced budget, or term limits? Why or why not? The authors also observe that although the Constitution has been amended to limit presidential terms, proposals to limit congressional terms have failed. They attribute this result to the fact that the President has no role under Article V in the amending process. Do you find this argument persuasive? Why or why not?

Mark Crain and Robert Tollison have also argued that interest groups will seek a constitutional amendment where it is an efficient way to increase the expected durability of a desired policy.[178] The authors claim that where other governmental mechanisms, including case decisions by an independent judiciary, prolong the durability of a legislatively procured benefit (and therefore the expected value to the interest group), this will temper demand for pursuing more costly constitutional amendments, a prediction that they corroborate empirically.

Subsequent studies found further consistent evidence that constitutional amendments are more common when other means for increasing the expected duration of interest group bargains are weaker.[179] For example, states with less independent judiciaries are likely to have longer and more active amending of their state constitutions, indicating a substitution between the two mechanisms for increasing durability. The relatively small number of amendments to the federal constitution might therefore reflect the effectiveness of the federal judiciary in securing interest group deals, consistent with the Landes and Posner analysis.[180]

An alternative account for the infrequency of federal constitutional amendments focuses on the role of the Supreme Court in effectively amending the Constitution. In this account, the infrequency of amendments is not due to the ability of interest groups to secure long term deals in legislation enforced by the independent judiciary, but rather it is due to the ability of interest groups to secure changes to the Constitution through judicial interpretation in independent courts. Perhaps the best

---

178. W. Mark Crain & Robert D. Tollison, *Constitutional Change in an Interest–Group Perspective*, 8 J. LEGAL STUD. 165 (1979).

179. Gary M. Anderson, Delores T. Martin, William F. Shughart II & Robert D. Tollison, *Behind the Veil: The Political Economy of Constitutional Change, in* PREDICTING POLITICS: ESSAYS IN EMPIRICAL PUBLIC CHOICE 89 (W. Mark Crain & Robert D. Tollison eds., 1990). Other structures such as the executive veto would presumably be relevant as well.

180. *See supra* pp. 532–33.

recent illustration is from Justice Ginsburg's explanation that the Equal Rights Amendment, which failed ratification, proved unnecessary since the Supreme Court itself basically accomplished the same result doctrinally through its gender-based equal protection jurisprudence.[181] In turn, interest groups would be expected to pursue in any given case the strategy—formal amendment versus judicial interpretation—that provides the greatest likelihood of success.[182] Can you reconcile these two accounts? If not, which is more persuasive? Why?

Adam Pritchard and Todd Zywicki have further drawn on public choice insights to inform the process of informal amendment through the judicial construction of constitutional provisions. The authors focus specifically on the use of tradition to inform constitutional interpretation.[183] In theory, they argue, tradition can be a valuable source of constitutional change. The authors maintain that properly understood, the development of tradition is a consensual, bottom-up process for developing new, widely shared supermajoritarian norms that can subsequently serve as a basis for new constitutional precommitments. Moreover, because of the spontaneous, consensual roots of tradition, it is resistant to interest group manipulation.

In fact, the authors claim, the Supreme Court has long looked to tradition as a source of constitutional values. But Pritchard and Zywicki criticize the sources of tradition used in practice by the Supreme Court. They focus on the two dominant approaches: first, that of Justice Scalia, which looks to the tradition of state regulation of a given activity as a source of tradition, and second, that of Justice Souter, which relies upon constitutional common law as developed by the Supreme Court.

The authors reject Scalia's approach on the ground that it allows state legislatures, which are subject to interest group pressures, to inform the permissible scope of constitutional limits on the scope of their own exercise of regulatory powers. In addition, they note, Scalia's approach would create a one-way "ratchet" in terms of limiting recognized constitutional rights since any example of a contrary state law would be a datum against recognizing the claimed constitutional tradition. Pritchard and Zywicki also reject Souter's approach because it merely substitutes different agency costs (by judges rather than legislators) and different special interests (those with a comparative advantage in litigation rather than in legislation). Moreover, the authors claim that rather than producing new norms through a decentralized, consensus-building process shaped by feedback, the articulation of new rules by the Supreme Court is a highly centralized process made by a handful of Justices with minimal feedback from the populace.

---

181. *See, e.g.,* Jeffrey Rosen, *The New Look of Liberalism on the Court,* N.Y. TIMES, Oct. 5, 1997, § 6 (Magazine), at 60 (discussing speech by Justice Ginsburg in which she stated: "There is no practical difference between what has evolved and the E.R.A.," and that "I would still like it as a symbol to see the E.R.A. in the Constitution for my granddaughter.").

182. *See* Pritchard & Zywicki, *supra* note 90.

183. *Id.*

Pritchard and Zywicki tentatively propose an alternative judicial "finding" model of tradition. In this model, the best source for identifying tradition returns the Justices to state constitutions, which are a bottom up source arising through a sufficiently complex set of processes so as to avoid the most obvious manifestations of interest group influence. The authors suggest, for example, that if three-quarters of the states came to recognize a new constitutional right (such as a right to privacy) or a new constitutional remedy (such as the exclusionary rule), the Supreme Court could claim that these rights have a root source in a legitimate American set of constitutional traditions.

Do you find this analysis persuasive? Does it set too high a standard for articulating constitutional rights? Why or why not? Does it set too low a standard? To what extent is it consistent with the framework set out by Buchanan and Tullock? Does this approach avoid the difficulties associated with formal amending under Article V? Why or why not?

VII. APPLICATIONS

In this section we present two cases, *INS v. Chadha*,[184] and *Romer v. Evans*.[185] Consider the extent to which the approaches that the separate Justices take in the various opinions and the outcomes in each of these two cases reflect insights from the materials in this chapter or the preceding chapters in this volume.

A. INS v. CHADHA

INS v. Chadha addressed the constitutionality of the "one-House veto," a procedure through which Congress, after delegating decision-making authority to an agency, retains the power to reverse an agency policy by unilateral action of one House of Congress, notwithstanding the requirements of bicameralism and presentment in the Constitution. This summary procedure allows Congress to retain a modicum of control by reducing the burdens of checking agency decision-making. As you will see, the Court invalidated the one-House veto, and in later cases extended this holding to the context of two House vetoes. More notably, in the three main opinions that we discuss, the majority opinion written by Chief Justice Burger, a concurrence by Justice Powell, and a dissent by Justice White,[186] each Justice takes a different view of the and propriety of the one-House veto and its relationship more generally to the function of agency delegation and separation of powers.

Chadha was an East Indian born in Kenya who held a British passport. He came to the United States in 1966 on a nonimmigrant

---

184.   462 U.S. 919 (1983).

185.   517 U.S. 620 (1996).

186.   Then–Associate Justice Rehnquist also produced a dissent, which we do not include in the discussion below. INS v. Chadha, 462 U.S. 919, 1013 (1983) (Rehnquist, J., dissenting).

student visa that expired in 1972. The following year, the District Director of the Immigration and Naturalization Service ordered that Chadha "show cause" why he should not be deported. Chadha applied for a suspension of deportation, which the immigration judge granted on the ground that Chadha had satisfied the statutory criteria, including most notably the "extreme hardship"[187] requirement. The Attorney General then transmitted the immigration judge's order to Congress as a recommendation to suspend deportation, which Congress had the power to accept or to override via the so-called one-House veto of either the House or Senate. If one House executed the one-House veto, the Attorney General was then required to carry out the deportation order. Based upon a review of 340 suspension cases, Representative Eilberg, the Chairman of the Judiciary Subcommittee on Immigration, Citizenship, and International Law, successfully introduced a resolution that ultimately won the approval of the House of Representatives. It reversed the suspension order for six aliens, including Chadha, who had overstayed their visas but who the immigration judge had determined met the eligibility requirements for suspending their deportation, " 'particularly as it relates to hardship.' "[188] Chief Justice Burger, writing for the Court, explained:

> The resolution was passed without debate or recorded vote. Since the House action was pursuant to § 244(c)(2), the resolution was not treated as an Art. I legislative act; it was not submitted to the Senate or presented to the President for his action.[189]

Chadha challenged the constitutionality of the proceedings under which he was ordered to be deported.

For the *Chadha* majority, the issue turned entirely on the constitutionality of the one-House veto, a procedure that the Court implicitly conceded had the benefit of allowing Congress to reduce the cost of monitoring agency action. Burger explained:

> [T]he fact that a given law or procedure is efficient, convenient, and useful in facilitating functions of government, standing alone, will not save it if it is contrary to the Constitution. Convenience and efficiency are not the primary objectives—or the hallmarks—of democratic government and our inquiry is sharpened rather than blunted by the fact that congressional veto provisions are appearing with increasing frequency in statutes which delegate authority to executive and independent agencies. . . .[190]

Burger then responded to an argument raised by Justice White in dissent, defending the one-House veto on grounds of administrative practicality:

---

187. The law required him to demonstrate that "he had resided continuously in the United States for over seven years, was of good moral character, and would suffer 'extreme hardship' if deported." *Id.* at 924 (majority opinion).

188. *Id.* at 926.

189. *Id.* at 927–28 (footnote omitted).

190. *Id.* at 944.

JUSTICE WHITE undertakes to make a case for the proposition that the one-House veto is a useful "political invention," and we need not challenge that assertion.... But policy arguments supporting even useful "political inventions" are subject to the demands of the Constitution which defines powers and, with respect to this subject, sets out just how those powers are to be exercised.[191]

The Court then turned to the questions of bicameralism and presentment raised by the one-House veto:

The Presentment Clauses

The records of the Constitutional Convention reveal that the requirement that all legislation be presented to the President before becoming law was uniformly accepted by the Framers. Presentment to the President and the Presidential veto were considered so imperative that the draftsmen took special pains to assure that these requirements could not be circumvented. During the final debate on Art. I, § 7, cl. 2, James Madison expressed concern that it might easily be evaded by the simple expedient of calling a proposed law a "resolution" or "vote" rather than a "bill." As a consequence, Art. I, § 7, cl. 3, was added.

The decision to provide the President with a limited and qualified power to nullify proposed legislation by veto was based on the profound conviction of the Framers that the powers conferred on Congress were the powers to be most carefully circumscribed. It is beyond doubt that lawmaking was a power to be shared by both Houses and the President....

. . . .

The President's role in the lawmaking process also reflects the Framers' careful efforts to check whatever propensity a particular Congress might have to enact oppressive, improvident, or ill-considered measures. The President's veto role in the legislative process was described later during public debate on ratification:

> "It establishes a salutary check upon the legislative body, calculated to guard the community against the effects of faction, precipitancy, or of any impulse unfriendly to the public good which may happen to influence a majority of that body.
>
> "... The primary inducement to conferring the power in question upon the Executive is, to enable him to defend himself; the secondary one is to increase the chances in favor of the community against the passing of bad laws, through haste, inadvertence, or design."

The Court also has observed that the Presentment Clauses serve the important purpose of assuring that a "national" perspective is grafted on the legislative process:

---

191. *Id.* at 945 (citation omitted).

"The President is a representative of the people just as the members of the Senate and of the House are, and it may be, at some times, on some subjects, that the President elected by all the people is rather more representative of them all than are the members of either body of the Legislature whose constituencies are local and not countrywide...."[192]

Chief Justice Burger further considered the implications of the one-House veto for the constitutional requirement of bicameralism:

By providing that no law could take effect without the concurrence of the prescribed majority of the Members of both Houses, the Framers reemphasized their belief ... that legislation should not be enacted unless it has been carefully and fully considered by the Nation's elected officials....

[After reviewing the views of several Framers on bicameralism, Burger stated:]

These observations are consistent with what many of the Framers expressed, none more cogently than Madison in pointing up the need to divide and disperse power in order to protect liberty:

"In republican government, the legislative authority necessarily predominates. The remedy for this inconveniency is to divide the legislature into different branches; and to render them, by different modes of election and different principles of action, as little connected with each other as the nature of their common functions and their common dependence on the society will admit."[193]

Burger then summarized the combined effect of bicameralism and presentment as follows:

We see therefore that the Framers were acutely conscious that the bicameral requirement and the Presentment Clauses would serve essential constitutional functions. The President's participation in the legislative process was to protect the Executive Branch from Congress and to protect the whole people from improvident laws. The division of the Congress into two distinctive bodies assures that the legislative power would be exercised only after opportunity for full study and debate in separate settings. The President's unilateral veto power, in turn, was limited by the power of two-thirds of both Houses of Congress to overrule a veto thereby precluding final arbitrary action of one person. It emerges clearly that the prescription for legislative action in Art. I, §§ 1, 7, represents the Framers' decision that the legislative power of the Federal government be exercised in accord with a single, finely wrought and exhaustively considered, procedure.[194]

192. *Id.* at 946–48 (citations and footnote omitted).

193. *Id.* at 948–50 (citations omitted).

194. *Id.* at 951 (citation omitted).

Burger then considered whether the one-House veto was "legislative" in nature and therefore subject to the requirements of bicameralism and presentment. Burger explained that while the spheres of legislative, executive, and judicial functions are not hermetically sealed, and while the Constitution itself identifies specific circumstances when a single House of Congress can act, the requirements of bicameralism and presentment apply to those actions that are " 'legislative in ... character and effect."[195] Burger explained:

> Examination of the action taken here by one House pursuant to § 244(c)(2) reveals that it was essentially legislative in purpose and effect. In purporting to exercise power defined in Art. I, § 8, cl. 4, to "establish an uniform Rule of Naturalization," the House took action that had the purpose and effect of altering the legal rights, duties, and relations of persons, including the Attorney General, Executive Branch officials and Chadha, all outside the Legislative Branch. Section 244(c)(2) purports to authorize one House of Congress to require the Attorney General to deport an individual alien whose deportation otherwise would be canceled under § 244. The one-House veto operated in these cases to overrule the Attorney General and mandate Chadha's deportation; absent the House action, Chadha would remain in the United States. Congress has *acted* and its action has altered Chadha's status.
>
> The legislative character of the one-House veto in these cases is confirmed by the character of the congressional action it supplants. Neither the House of Representatives nor the Senate contends that, absent the veto provision in § 244(c)(2), either of them, or both of them acting together, could effectively require the Attorney General to deport an alien once the Attorney General, in the exercise of legislatively delegated authority, had determined the alien should remain in the United States. Without the challenged provision in § 244(c)(2), this could have been achieved, if at all, only by legislation requiring deportation....
>
> The nature of the decision implemented by the one-House veto in these cases further manifests its legislative character. After long experience with the clumsy, time-consuming private bill procedure, Congress made a deliberate choice to delegate to the Executive Branch, and specifically to the Attorney General, the authority to allow deportable aliens to remain in this country in certain specified circumstances. It is not disputed that this choice to delegate authority is precisely the kind of decision that can be implemented only in accordance with the procedures set out in Art. I. Disagreement with the Attorney General's decision on Chadha's deportation—that is, Congress' decision to deport Chadha—no less than Congress' original choice to delegate to the Attorney General the authority to make that decision, involves determinations of policy that Congress can imple-

---

195. *Id.* at 952.

ment in only one way; bicameral passage followed by presentment to the President. . . .

Finally, we see that when the Framers intended to authorize either House of Congress to act alone and outside of its prescribed bicameral legislative role, they narrowly and precisely defined the procedure for such action. There are four provisions in the Constitution, explicit and unambiguous, by which one House may act alone with the unreviewable force of law, not subject to the President's veto [including initiating (by the House of Representatives) and trying (by the Senate) impeachments, the Senate's power of advice and consent for Presidential appointments, and the Senate's power to ratify treaties.]

Clearly, when the Draftsmen sought to confer special powers on one House, independent of the other House, or of the President, they did so in explicit, unambiguous terms. . . .

. . . .

The veto authorized by § 244(c)(2) doubtless has been in many respects a convenient shortcut; the "sharing" with the Executive by Congress of its authority over aliens in this manner is, on its face, an appealing compromise. In purely practical terms, it is obviously easier for action to be taken by one House without submission to the President; but it is crystal clear from the records of the Convention, contemporaneous writings and debates, that the Framers ranked other values higher than efficiency. . . .

The choices we discern as having been made in the Constitutional Convention impose burdens on governmental processes that often seem clumsy, inefficient, even unworkable, but those hard choices were consciously made by men who had lived under a form of government that permitted arbitrary governmental acts to go unchecked. There is no support in the Constitution or decisions of this Court for the proposition that the cumbersomeness and delays often encountered in complying with explicit constitutional standards may be avoided, either by the Congress or by the President. With all the obvious flaws of delay, untidiness, and potential for abuse, we have not yet found a better way to preserve freedom than by making the exercise of power subject to the carefully crafted restraints spelled out in the Constitution.[196]

Burger concluded that "the congressional veto provision in § 244(c)(2) is severable from the Act and that it is unconstitutional."[197]

In a concurrence in the judgment, Justice Powell took a very different view concerning the nature of the actions that the one-House veto represents:

---

196. *Id.* at 952–55, 958–59 (citation and footnotes omitted).

197. *Id.* at 959.

On its face, the House's action appears clearly adjudicatory. The House did not enact a general rule; rather, it made its own determination that six specific persons did not comply with certain statutory criteria. It thus undertook the type of decision that traditionally has been left to other branches.... Where, as here, Congress has exercised a power "that cannot possibly be regarded as merely in aid of the legislative function of Congress," the decisions of this Court have held that Congress impermissibly assumed a function that the Constitution entrusted to another branch.

The impropriety of the House's assumption of this function is confirmed by the fact that its action raises the very danger the Framers sought to avoid—the exercise of unchecked power. In deciding whether Chadha deserves to be deported, Congress is not subject to any internal constraints that prevent it from arbitrarily depriving him of the right to remain in this country. Unlike the judiciary or an administrative agency, Congress is not bound by established substantive rules. Nor is it subject to the procedural safeguards, such as the right to counsel and a hearing before an impartial tribunal, that are present when a court or an agency adjudicates individual rights. The only effective constraint on Congress' power is political, but Congress is most accountable politically when it prescribes rules of general applicability. When it decides rights of specific persons, those rights are subject to "the tyranny of a shifting majority."[198]

Responding to this argument, Chief Justice Burger observed:

JUSTICE POWELL'S position is that the one-House veto in this case is a *judicial* act and therefore unconstitutional as beyond the authority vested in Congress by the Constitution.... But the attempted analogy between judicial action and the one-House veto is less than perfect. Federal courts do not enjoy a roving mandate to correct alleged excesses of administrative agencies; we are limited by Art. III to hearing cases and controversies and no justiciable case or controversy was presented by the Attorney General's decision to allow Chadha to remain in this country.... Thus, JUSTICE POWELL'S statement that the one-House veto in this case is "clearly adjudicatory" simply is not supported by his accompanying assertion that the House has "assumed a function ordinarily [entrusted] to the federal courts." We are satisfied that the one-House veto is legislative in purpose and effect and subject to the procedures set out in Art. I.[199]

Writing in dissent, Justice White focused on what he regarded as the administrative benefits of the one-House veto. White began by noting the broad reach of the Court's ruling:

Today the Court not only invalidates § 244(c)(2) of the Immigration and Nationality Act, but also sounds the death knell for nearly 200 other statutory provisions in which Congress has reserved a

198. *Id.* at 964–66 (Powell, J., concurring) (citations and footnotes omitted).

199. *Id.* at 957 n.22 (majority opinion) (citations omitted).

"legislative veto." For this reason, the Court's decision is of surpassing importance. And it is for this reason that the Court would have been well advised to decide the cases, if possible, on the narrower grounds of separation of powers, leaving for full consideration the constitutionality of other congressional review statutes operating on such varied matters as war powers and agency rulemaking, some of which concern the independent regulatory agencies.

The prominence of the legislative veto mechanism in our contemporary political system and its importance to Congress can hardly be overstated. It has become a central means by which Congress secures the accountability of executive and independent agencies. Without the legislative veto, Congress is faced with a Hobson's choice: either to refrain from delegating the necessary authority, leaving itself with a hopeless task of writing laws with the requisite specificity to cover endless special circumstances across the entire policy landscape, or in the alternative, to abdicate its law-making function to the Executive Branch and independent agencies. To choose the former leaves major national problems unresolved; to opt for the latter risks unaccountable policymaking by those not elected to fill that role.... The device is known in every field of governmental concern: reorganization, budgets, foreign affairs, war powers, and regulation of trade, safety, energy, the environment, and the economy.[200]

Justice White linked the increased use of the one-House veto to the growth of the administrative state:

The legislative veto developed initially in response to the problems of reorganizing the sprawling Government structure created in response to the Depression. The Reorganization Acts established the chief model for the legislative veto. When President Hoover requested authority to reorganize the government in 1929, he coupled his request that the "Congress be willing to delegate its authority over the problem (subject to defined principles) to the Executive" with a proposal for legislative review. He proposed that the Executive "should act upon approval of a joint committee of Congress or with the reservation of power of revision by Congress within some limited period adequate for its consideration." Congress followed President Hoover's suggestion and authorized reorganization subject to legislative review. Although the reorganization authority reenacted in 1933 did not contain a legislative veto provision, the provision returned during the Roosevelt administration and has since been renewed numerous times. Over the years, the provision was used extensively. Presidents submitted 115 Reorganization Plans to Congress of which 23 were disapproved by Congress pursuant to legislative veto provisions.

. . . .

---

200. *Id.* at 967–68 (White, J., dissenting) (footnote omitted).

Over the quarter century following World War II, Presidents continued to accept legislative vetoes by one or both Houses as constitutional, while regularly denouncing provisions by which congressional Committees reviewed Executive activity . . . . .

. . . .

Even this brief review suffices to demonstrate that the legislative veto is more than "efficient, convenient, and useful." It is an important if not indispensable political invention that allows the President and Congress to resolve major constitutional and policy differences, assures the accountability of independent regulatory agencies, and preserves Congress' control over lawmaking. Perhaps there are other means of accommodation and accountability, but the increasing reliance of Congress upon the legislative veto suggests that the alternatives . . . are not entirely satisfactory.[201]

Turning to the constitutional issue, White explained:

The Constitution does not directly authorize or prohibit the legislative veto. Thus, our task should be to determine whether the legislative veto is consistent with the purposes of Art. I and the principles of separation of powers which are reflected in that Article and throughout the Constitution. We should not find the lack of a specific constitutional authorization for the legislative veto surprising, and I would not infer disapproval of the mechanism from its absence. From the summer of 1787 to the present the Government of the United States has become an endeavor far beyond the contemplation of the Framers. Only within the last half century has the complexity and size of the Federal Government's responsibilities grown so greatly that the Congress must rely on the legislative veto as the most effective if not the only means to insure its role as the Nation's lawmakers. But the wisdom of the Framers was to anticipate that the Nation would grow and new problems of governance would require different solutions. Accordingly, our Federal Government was intentionally chartered with the flexibility to respond to contemporary needs without losing sight of fundamental democratic principles. . . .

. . . In my view, neither Art. I of the Constitution nor the doctrine of separation of powers is violated by this mechanism by which our elected Representatives preserve their voice in the governance of the Nation.[202]

Justice White further explained how, as a practical matter, the interests of the President and both Houses are preserved in the one-House veto regime:

The President's approval is found in the Attorney General's action in recommending to Congress that the deportation order for a given alien be suspended. The House and the Senate indicate their approval

201. *Id.* at 968–69, 972–73 (citations omitted).

202. *Id.* at 977–79 (footnote omitted).

of the Executive's action by not passing a resolution of disapproval within the statutory period. Thus, a change in the legal status quo— the deportability of the alien—is consummated only with the approval of each of the three relevant actors. The disagreement of any one of the three maintains the alien's pre-existing status: the Executive may choose not to recommend suspension; the House and Senate may each veto the recommendation. The effect on the rights and obligations of the affected individuals and upon the legislative system is precisely the same as if a private bill were introduced but failed to receive the necessary approval. "The President and the two Houses enjoy exactly the same say in what the law is to be as would have been true for each without the presence of the one-House veto, and nothing in the law is changed absent the concurrence of the President and a majority in each House."

. . . .

Thus understood, § 244(c)(2) fully effectuates the purposes of the bicameralism and presentation requirements. . . .[203]

Turning to the question of separation of powers, White explained:

[T]he history of the separation-of-powers doctrine is also a history of accommodation and practicality. Apprehensions of an overly power-ful branch have not led to undue prophylactic measures that handicap the effective working of the National Government as a whole. The Constitution does not contemplate total separation of the three branches of Government. "[A] hermetic sealing off of the three branches of Government from one another would preclude the estab-lishment of a Nation capable of governing itself effectively."

Our decisions reflect this judgment. . . .[204]

Justice White concluded:

I regret the destructive scope of the Court's holding. . . . Today's decision strikes down in one fell swoop provisions in more laws enacted by Congress than the Court has cumulatively invalidated in its history. I fear it will now be more difficult "to insur[e] that the fundamental policy decisions in our society will be made not by an appointed official but by the body immediately responsible to the people." I must dissent.[205]

DISCUSSION QUESTIONS

1. In the case of Mr. Chadha, what is the actual harm that arises from the deviation from formal bicameralism and presentment? Applying the insights of public choice theory, is it possible that as a constitutional matter we might want to categorically permit or disallow the one-House veto even if the benefits and costs are not readily apparent in a given case?

---

203. *Id.* at 994–96.

204. *Id.* at 999 (citations and footnote omitted).

205. *Id.* at 1002–03 (citation omitted).

2. In his dissent, Justice White writes, "But the history of the separation of powers doctrine is also a history of accommodation and practicality." White is referring to a long line of cases that includes most notably the *Youngstown Sheet & Tube Co. v. Sawyer (Steel Seizure)*, 343 U.S. 579 (1952), in which Justices Black and Frankfurter debated in separate opinions the role of longstanding political accommodations between the President and Congress in informing constitutional separation of powers. So viewed, to what extent does this sort of accommodation inform our understanding of the external costs and decision costs in the Buchanan and Tullock framework? For example, does the prevalence of the one House veto suggest that the decision costs of passing full blown legislation to check against agency activity are too high? If so, is this a relevant factor in assessing the constitutionality of the one-House veto? Why or why not?

3. Chief Justice Burger's opinion, in marked contrast with that of Justice White, reflects a rigid separation of powers formalism that refuses to permit action by a single House other than in the circumstances precisely identified in the Constitution itself. Do the materials in this chapter suggest support for constitutional formalism in this context? Consider the argument that the one-House veto is not constitutionally problematic because contrary to Chief Justice Burger's argument, the underlying law that created it went through the "finely wrought and exhaustively considered, procedure" set out in Article I, § 7. In this analysis, because the statute creating the one-House veto was enacted by constitutional means, the vehicle it created to check against agency action lies outside the scope of Article I, § 7. Conversely, one might argue, given the high costs of securing constitutionally established lawmaking procedures, it is important to insist upon rigid adherence to formalism. Which of these arguments is more persuasive? Which finds stronger support in public choice? Why?

4. Justice Powell views Congress's action as akin to judicial decision-making. Chief Justice Burger replies by claiming that unlike Congress, a court does not have a "roving mandate to correct alleged excesses of administrative agencies; we are limited by Art. III to hearing cases and controversies." Does this argument undermine or strengthen Powell's position that the one-House veto is unconstitutional? Why? Does the analysis help to inform the understanding developed in this chapter and elsewhere in this book concerning the differences between adjudicatory and legislative lawmaking? Why or why not?

5. In chapter 6, we examined the question of delegation by Congress to agencies from the perspective of public choice theory. Based upon your review of *Chadha*, how does that analysis relate to the question of the propriety of the one-House veto?

B. ROMER v. EVANS

In *Romer v. Evans*,[206] the Supreme Court addressed the constitutionality of Colorado Amendment 2, a 1992 statewide referendum affecting access by gays, lesbians, and other sexual minorities to various protections under state and municipal law. Prior to adopting the amendment, several

---

206. 517 U.S. 620 (1996).

Colorado municipalities had "banned discrimination in many transactions and activities, including housing, employment, education, public accommodations, and health and welfare services"[207] on a variety of bases including sexual orientation. Amendment 2 effectively repealed these ordinances by proclaiming that no state or municipal law shall give protected status on the basis of sexual orientation.

The amendment, which Justice Kennedy writing for the *Romer* majority reproduced in its entirety, provides as follows:

> No Protected Status Based on Homosexual, Lesbian or Bisexual Orientation. Neither the State of Colorado, through any of its branches or departments, nor any of its agencies, political subdivisions, municipalities or school districts, shall enact, adopt or enforce any statute, regulation, ordinance or policy whereby homosexual, lesbian or bisexual orientation, conduct, practices or relationships shall constitute or otherwise be the basis of or entitle any person or class of persons to have or claim any minority status, quota preferences, protected status or claim of discrimination. This Section of the Constitution shall be in all respects self-executing.[208]

Justice Kennedy began his opinion by explaining how the amendment does more than simply repeal specific protections on the basis of "homosexual, lesbian or bisexual orientation, conduct, practices or relationships." Kennedy explained:

> Yet Amendment 2, in explicit terms, does more than repeal or rescind these provisions. It prohibits all legislative, executive or judicial action at any level of state or local government designed to protect the named class, a class we shall refer to as homosexual persons or gays and lesbians. . . .[209]

While Justice Kennedy agreed with the Colorado Supreme Court that the amendment violated the Constitution, he disagreed that the relevant test was strict scrutiny. Justice Kennedy began his analysis by considering the argument the state advanced in support of the amendment:

> The State's principal argument in defense of Amendment 2 is that it puts gays and lesbians in the same position as all other persons. So, the State says, the measure does no more than deny homosexuals special rights. This reading of the amendment's language is implausible. We rely not upon our own interpretation of the amendment but upon the authoritative construction of Colorado's Supreme Court. The state court, deeming it unnecessary to determine the full extent of the amendment's reach, found it invalid even on a modest reading of its implications. The critical discussion of the amendment, set out in *Evans I*, is as follows:

---

207.   *Id.* at 624.

208.   *Id.* (quoting Colorado Amendment 2).

209.   *Id.*

> "The immediate objective of Amendment 2 is, at a minimum, to repeal existing statutes, regulations, ordinances, and policies of state and local entities that barred discrimination based on sexual orientation. . . .

Sweeping and comprehensive is the change in legal status effected by this law. So much is evident from the ordinances the Colorado Supreme Court declared would be void by operation of Amendment 2. Homosexuals, by state decree, are put in a solitary class with respect to transactions and relations in both the private and governmental spheres. The amendment withdraws from homosexuals, but no others, specific legal protection from the injuries caused by discrimination, and it forbids reinstatement of these laws and policies.

The change Amendment 2 works in the legal status of gays and lesbians in the private sphere is far reaching, both on its own terms and when considered in light of the structure and operation of modern antidiscrimination laws. That structure is well illustrated by contemporary statutes and ordinances prohibiting discrimination by providers of public accommodations. "At common law, innkeepers, smiths, and others who 'made profession of a public employment,' were prohibited from refusing, without good reason, to serve a customer." The duty was a general one and did not specify protection for particular groups. The common-law rules, however, proved insufficient in many instances, and it was settled early that the Fourteenth Amendment did not give Congress a general power to prohibit discrimination in public accommodations. In consequence, most States have chosen to counter discrimination by enacting detailed statutory schemes.[210]

After explaining that "Colorado's state and municipal laws"[211] specify a broader class of covered businesses than was customary under the common law, Kennedy described the class of persons "within [the] ambit of [the laws'] protection," as follows:[212]

> Enumeration [of groups of persons] is the essential device used to make the duty not to discriminate concrete and to provide guidance for those who must comply. In following this approach, Colorado's state and local governments have not limited antidiscrimination laws to groups that have so far been given the protection of heightened equal protection scrutiny under our cases. Rather, they set forth an extensive catalog of traits which cannot be the basis for discrimination, including age, military status, marital status, pregnancy, parenthood, custody of a minor child, political affiliation, physical or mental disability of an individual or of his or her associates—and, in recent times, sexual orientation.

---

210. *Id.* at 626–28 (citations omitted).

211. *Id.* at 628.

212. *Id.*

Amendment 2 bars homosexuals from securing protection against the injuries that these public-accommodations laws address. That in itself is a severe consequence, but there is more. Amendment 2, in addition, nullifies specific legal protections for this targeted class in all transactions in housing, sale of real estate, insurance, health and welfare services, private education, and employment.

Not confined to the private sphere, Amendment 2 also operates to repeal and forbid all laws or policies providing specific protection for gays or lesbians from discrimination by every level of Colorado government. . . .

. . . .

. . . [E]ven if, as we doubt, homosexuals could find some safe harbor in laws of general application, we cannot accept the view that Amendment 2's prohibition on specific legal protections does no more than deprive homosexuals of special rights. To the contrary, the amendment imposes a special disability upon those persons alone. Homosexuals are forbidden the safeguards that others enjoy or may seek without constraint. They can obtain specific protection against discrimination only by enlisting the citizenry of Colorado to amend the State Constitution or perhaps, on the State's view, by trying to pass helpful laws of general applicability. This is so no matter how local or discrete the harm, no matter how public and widespread the injury. We find nothing special in the protections Amendment 2 withholds. These are protections taken for granted by most people either because they already have them or do not need them; these are protections against exclusion from an almost limitless number of transactions and endeavors that constitute ordinary civic life in a free society.[213]

After describing the reach of Amendment 2, Justice Kennedy explained why it violates the Constitution even under rational basis scrutiny:

The Fourteenth Amendment's promise that no person shall be denied the equal protection of the laws must coexist with the practical necessity that most legislation classifies for one purpose or another, with resulting disadvantage to various groups or persons. We have attempted to reconcile the principle with the reality by stating that, if a law neither burdens a fundamental right nor targets a suspect class, we will uphold the legislative classification so long as it bears a rational relation to some legitimate end.

Amendment 2 fails, indeed defies, even this conventional inquiry. First, the amendment has the peculiar property of imposing a broad and undifferentiated disability on a single named group, an exceptional and, as we shall explain, invalid form of legislation. Second, its sheer breadth is so discontinuous with the reasons offered for it that

---

213. *Id.* at 628–29, 631 (citations omitted).

the amendment seems inexplicable by anything but animus toward the class it affects; it lacks a rational relationship to legitimate state interests.

. . . By requiring that the classification bear a rational relationship to an independent and legitimate legislative end, we ensure that classifications are not drawn for the purpose of disadvantaging the group burdened by the law.

Amendment 2 confounds this normal process of judicial review. It is at once too narrow and too broad. It identifies persons by a single trait and then denies them protection across the board. The resulting disqualification of a class of persons from the right to seek specific protection from the law is unprecedented in our jurisprudence. The absence of precedent for Amendment 2 is itself instructive. . . .

It is not within our constitutional tradition to enact laws of this sort. . . . A law declaring that in general it shall be more difficult for one group of citizens than for all others to seek aid from the government is itself a denial of equal protection of the laws in the most literal sense. . . .

 . . . .

A . . . related point is that laws of the kind now before us raise the inevitable inference that the disadvantage imposed is born of animosity toward the class of persons affected. "[I]f the constitutional conception of 'equal protection of the laws' means anything, it must at the very least mean that a bare . . . desire to harm a politically unpopular group cannot constitute a *legitimate* governmental interest." . . . Amendment 2, however, in making a general announcement that gays and lesbians shall not have any particular protections from the law, inflicts on them immediate, continuing, and real injuries that outrun and belie any legitimate justifications that may be claimed for it. We conclude that, in addition to the far-reaching deficiencies of Amendment 2 that we have noted, the principles it offends, in another sense, are conventional and venerable; a law must bear a rational relationship to a legitimate governmental purpose, and Amendment 2 does not.

 . . . .

. . . Amendment 2 violates the Equal Protection Clause, and the judgment of the Supreme Court of Colorado is affirmed.[214]

Justice Scalia, with whom the Chief Justice and Justice Thomas joined, dissented:

The Court has mistaken a Kulturkampf for a fit of spite. The constitutional amendment before us here is not the manifestation of a " 'bare . . . desire to harm' " homosexuals, but is rather a modest attempt by seemingly tolerant Coloradans to preserve traditional

---

214. *Id.* at 631–36 (citations omitted).

sexual mores against the efforts of a politically powerful minority to revise those mores through use of the laws. That objective, and the means chosen to achieve it, are not only unimpeachable under any constitutional doctrine hitherto pronounced (hence the opinion's heavy reliance upon principles of righteousness rather than judicial holdings); they have been specifically approved by the Congress of the United States and by this Court.

In holding that homosexuality cannot be singled out for disfavorable treatment, the Court contradicts a decision, unchallenged here, pronounced only 10 years ago, and places the prestige of this institution behind the proposition that opposition to homosexuality is as reprehensible as racial or religious bias. Whether it is or not is *precisely* the cultural debate that gave rise to the Colorado constitutional amendment (and to the preferential laws against which the amendment was directed). Since the Constitution of the United States says nothing about this subject, it is left to be resolved by normal democratic means, including the democratic adoption of provisions in state constitutions. This Court has no business imposing upon all Americans the resolution favored by the elite class from which the Members of this institution are selected, pronouncing that "animosity" toward homosexuality, is evil. I vigorously dissent.[215]

Justice Scalia began his equal protection analysis by claiming that "[t]he amendment prohibits *special treatment* of homosexuals, and nothing more."[216] Scalia explained:

[The Amendment] would not affect, for example, a requirement of state law that pensions be paid to all retiring state employees with a certain length of service; homosexual employees, as well as others, would be entitled to that benefit. But it would [for example] prevent the State or any municipality from making death-benefit payments to the "life partner" of a homosexual when it does not make such payments to the long-time roommate of a nonhomosexual employee. . . .

. . . .

. . . The only denial of equal treatment it contends homosexuals have suffered is this: They may not obtain *preferential* treatment without amending the State Constitution. That is to say, the principle underlying the Court's opinion is that one who is accorded equal treatment under the laws, but cannot as readily as others obtain *preferential* treatment under the laws, has been denied equal protection of the laws. If merely stating this alleged "equal protection" violation does not suffice to refute it, our constitutional jurisprudence has achieved terminal silliness.[217]

215. *Id.* at 636 (Scalia, J., dissenting) (citations omitted).

216. *Id.* at 638.

217. *Id.* at 638–39.

Justice Scalia then set out an analysis that turns on the nature of lawmaking in a multilevel democracy:

> The central thesis of the Court's reasoning is that any group is denied equal protection when, to obtain advantage (or, presumably, to avoid disadvantage), it must have recourse to a more general and hence more difficult level of political decisionmaking than others. The world has never heard of such a principle, which is why the Court's opinion is so long on emotive utterance and so short on relevant legal citation. And it seems to me most unlikely that any multilevel democracy can function under such a principle. For *whenever* a disadvantage is imposed, or conferral of a benefit is prohibited, at one of the higher levels of democratic decisionmaking (*i.e.*, by the state legislature rather than local government, or by the people at large in the state constitution rather than the legislature), the affected group has (under this theory) been denied equal protection.... [T]he Court's theory is unheard of.
>
> ... The Court's entire novel theory rests upon the proposition that there is something *special*—something that cannot be justified by normal "rational basis" analysis—in making a disadvantaged group (or a nonpreferred group) resort to a higher decisionmaking level. That proposition finds no support in law or logic.[218]

Justice Scalia then described what he viewed as a rational justification for the enacted law:

> I turn next to whether there was a legitimate rational basis for the substance of the constitutional amendment—for the prohibition of special protection for homosexuals. It is unsurprising that the Court avoids discussion of this question, since the answer is so obviously yes. The case most relevant to the issue before us today is not even mentioned in the Court's opinion: In *Bowers* v. *Hardwick*, we held that the Constitution does not prohibit what virtually all States had done from the founding of the Republic until very recent years— making homosexual conduct a crime.... If it is constitutionally permissible for a State to make homosexual conduct criminal, surely it is constitutionally permissible for a State to enact other laws merely *disfavoring* homosexual conduct.... And *a fortiori* it is constitutionally permissible for a State to adopt a provision *not even* disfavoring homosexual conduct, but merely prohibiting all levels of state government from bestowing *special protections* upon homosexual conduct....
>
> ... If it is rational to criminalize the conduct, surely it is rational to deny special favor and protection to those with a self-avowed tendency or desire to engage in the conduct....[219]

---

218. *Id.* at 639–40.

219. *Id.* at 640–42 (citation and footnote omitted).

Justice Scalia then described why he regarded the amendment as a reasonable exercise of regulatory power:

First, as to its eminent reasonableness. The Court's opinion contains grim, disapproving hints that Coloradans have been guilty of "animus" or "animosity" toward homosexuality, as though that has been established as un-American. Of course it is our moral heritage that one should not hate any human being or class of human beings. But I had thought that one could consider certain conduct reprehensible—murder, for example, or polygamy, or cruelty to animals—and could exhibit even "animus" toward such conduct. Surely that is the only sort of "animus" at issue here: moral disapproval of homosexual conduct, the same sort of moral disapproval that produced the centuries-old criminal laws that we held constitutional in *Bowers*. The Colorado amendment does not, to speak entirely precisely, prohibit giving favored status to people who are *homosexuals*; they can be favored for many reasons—for example, because they are senior citizens or members of racial minorities. But it prohibits giving them favored status *because of their homosexual conduct*—that is, it prohibits favored status for *homosexuality*.

But though Coloradans are, as I say, *entitled* to be hostile toward homosexual conduct, the fact is that the degree of hostility reflected by Amendment 2 is the smallest conceivable. . . . Colorado not only is one of the 25 States that have repealed their antisodomy laws, but was among the first to do so. But the society that eliminates criminal punishment for homosexual acts does not necessarily abandon the view that homosexuality is morally wrong and socially harmful; often, abolition simply reflects the view that enforcement of such criminal laws involves unseemly intrusion into the intimate lives of citizens.

There is a problem, however, which arises when criminal sanction of homosexuality is eliminated but moral and social disapprobation of homosexuality is meant to be retained. The Court cannot be unaware of that problem; it is evident in many cities of the country, and occasionally bubbles to the surface of the news, in heated political disputes over such matters as the introduction into local schools of books teaching that homosexuality is an optional and fully acceptable "alternative life style." The problem (a problem, that is, for those who wish to retain social disapprobation of homosexuality) is that, because those who engage in homosexual conduct tend to reside in disproportionate numbers in certain communities, and, of course, care about homosexual-rights issues much more ardently than the public at large, they possess political power much greater than their numbers, both locally and statewide. Quite understandably, they devote this political power to achieving not merely a grudging social toleration, but full social acceptance, of homosexuality.

By the time Coloradans were asked to vote on Amendment 2, their exposure to homosexuals' quest for social endorsement was not limited to newspaper accounts of happenings in places such as New York, Los Angeles, San Francisco, and Key West. Three Colorado cities—Aspen, Boulder, and Denver—had enacted ordinances that listed "sexual orientation" as an impermissible ground for discrimination, equating the moral disapproval of homosexual conduct with racial and religious bigotry. The phenomenon had even appeared statewide: The Governor of Colorado had signed an executive order pronouncing that "in the State of Colorado we recognize the diversity in our pluralistic society and strive to bring an end to discrimination in any form," and directing state agency-heads to "ensure non-discrimination" in hiring and promotion based on, among other things, "sexual orientation." I do not mean to be critical of these legislative successes; homosexuals are as entitled to use the legal system for reinforcement of their moral sentiments as is the rest of society. But they are subject to being countered by lawful, democratic countermeasures as well.

> That is where Amendment 2 came in. It sought to counter both the geographic concentration and the disproportionate political power of homosexuals by (1) resolving the controversy at the statewide level, and (2) making the election a single-issue contest for both sides. It put directly, to all the citizens of the State, the question: Should homosexuality be given special protection? They answered no. The Court today asserts that this most democratic of procedures is unconstitutional. Lacking any cases to establish that facially absurd proposition, it simply asserts that it *must* be unconstitutional, because it has never happened before.[220]

Justice Scalia then responded to Justice Kennedy's argument that included in the " '[c]onstitution's guarantee of equal protection is the principle that government and each of its parts remain open on impartial terms to all who seek its assistance.' "[221]

> [This proposition] is proved false every time a state law prohibiting or disfavoring certain conduct is passed, because such a law prevents the adversely affected group . . . from changing the policy thus established in "each of [the] parts" of the State. . . .
>
> . . . The Constitutions of the States of Arizona, Idaho, New Mexico, Oklahoma, and Utah *to this day* contain provisions stating that polygamy is "forever prohibited." Polygamists, and those who have a polygamous "orientation," have been "singled out" by these provisions for much more severe treatment than merely denial of favored status; and that treatment can only be changed by achieving amendment of the state constitutions. The Court's disposition today suggests that these provisions are unconstitutional, and that polygamy must be permitted in these States on a state-legislated, or perhaps

---

220. *Id.* at 644–47 (citations omitted).

221. *Id.* at 647.

even local-option, basis—unless, of course, polygamists for some reason have fewer constitutional rights than homosexuals.

. . . .

Has the Court concluded that the perceived social harm of polygamy is a "legitimate concern of government," and the perceived social harm of homosexuality is not?

I strongly suspect that the answer to the last question is yes, which leads me to the last point I wish to make: . . . The Court's stern disapproval of "animosity" towards homosexuality might be compared with what an earlier Court (including the revered Justices Harlan and Bradley) said in *Murphy* v. *Ramsey*, rejecting a constitutional challenge to a United States statute that denied the franchise in federal territories to those who engaged in polygamous cohabitation:

> "[C]ertainly no legislation can be supposed more wholesome and necessary in the founding of a free, self-governing commonwealth, fit to take rank as one of the co-ordinate States of the Union, than that which seeks to establish it on the basis of the idea of the family, as consisting in and springing from the union for life of one man and one woman in the holy estate of matrimony; the sure foundation of all that is stable and noble in our civilization; the best guaranty of that reverent morality which is the source of all beneficent progress in social and political improvement."

I would not myself indulge in such official praise for heterosexual monogamy, because I think it no business of the courts (as opposed to the political branches) to take sides in this culture war.

But the Court today has done so, not only by inventing a novel and extravagant constitutional doctrine to take the victory away from traditional forces, but even by verbally disparaging as bigotry adherence to traditional attitudes. To suggest, for example, that this constitutional amendment springs from nothing more than " 'a bare . . . desire to harm a politically unpopular group,' " is nothing short of insulting. (It is also nothing short of preposterous to call "politically unpopular" a group which enjoys enormous influence in American media and politics, and which, as the trial court here noted, though composing no more than 4% of the population had the support of 46% of the voters on Amendment 2.)

When the Court takes sides in the culture wars, it tends to be with the knights rather than the villeins—and more specifically with the Templars, reflecting the views and values of the lawyer class from which the Court's Members are drawn. How that class feels about homosexuality will be evident to anyone who wishes to interview job applicants at virtually any of the Nation's law schools. The interviewer may refuse to offer a job because the applicant is a Republican; because he is an adulterer; because he went to the wrong prep school or belongs to the wrong country club; because he eats snails; because he is a womanizer; because she wears real-animal fur; or even because he hates the Chicago Cubs. But if the interviewer should wish not to be an associate or partner of an applicant because he disapproves of the applicant's homosexuality, *then* he will have violated the pledge which the Association of American Law Schools requires all its member schools to exact from job interviewers: "assurance of the employer's willingness" to hire homosexuals. This law-school view of what "prejudices" must be stamped out may be contrasted with the more plebeian attitudes that apparently still prevail in the United States Congress, which has been unresponsive to repeated attempts to extend to homosexuals the protections of federal civil rights laws.

Today's opinion has no foundation in American constitutional law, and barely pretends to. The people of Colorado have adopted an entirely reasonable provision which does not even disfavor homosexuals in any substantive sense, but merely denies them preferential treatment. Amendment 2 is designed to prevent piecemeal deterioration of the sexual morality favored by a majority of Coloradans, and is not only an appropriate means to that legitimate end, but a means that Americans have employed before. Striking it down is an act, not of judicial judgment, but of political will. I dissent.[222]

DISCUSSION QUESTIONS

1. Compare the ruling and logic in *Romer v. Evans* with the Court's holding in *Powers v. Harris*, discussed in chapter 5. Both cases purport to apply the same level of scrutiny to the law in question, rational basis, and yet they achieve seemingly contrary results in terms of actual deference afforded to the state lawmakers. Can you identify reasons for this seeming divergence in the application of this judicial standard? To what extent is public choice helpful in answering that question?

2. Writing for the *Romer* majority, Justice Kennedy suggests that there is a preferred level at which the relevant political decisions concerning antidiscrimination policies in various settings should be made, and in this case it is local rather than state. Writing in dissent, Justice Scalia observes that, traditionally, higher levels of governmental authority retain the power to trump lower levels of governmental authority when their regulatory authority is concurrent. Does public choice provide any guidance as to the preferred level at which such policies should be made? Does Madison's "size" principle say anything about this question? Does Tiebout's exit model? Does Levmore's analysis explaining why local governments tend toward unicameralism, while state and federal governments tend toward bicameralism? Does it matter that the challenged law was not secured through ordinary legislation, but rather through a statewide referendum? Why or why not?

3. *Romer* also raises an important issue concerning how to identify operative constitutional baselines. The majority frames Amendment 2 as

222. *Id.* at 647–48, 651–53 (citations omitted).

manifesting hostility toward gays and lesbians by denying them the benefit of statutory protections afforded others. In contrast, the dissent frames the amendment as denying the same group special treatment. Can either framing be said to be "correct"? Can this question be answered without first answering whether gays and lesbians are a suspect or quasi suspect class? Can you identify reasons why Justice Kennedy did not resolve this preliminary issue? Is it possible to know whether this is an example of majority vindication or minority suppression? To what extent, if any, does public choice help in answering these questions?

4.   The majority opinion in *Romer* suggests that gays and lesbians might be uniquely subject to political animus or bias because of traditional societal hostility. Justice Scalia's dissent, in contrast, claims that this group holds disproportionate political influence due to such factors as geographic concentration, and group cohesion. In other words, the majority suggests that the political process may be prone to a political market failure at the state level that disproportionately disadvantages gays and lesbians, thus requiring federal judicial correction, while the dissent suggests a political market failure at the local level disproportionately benefiting gays and lesbians, thus justifying statewide correction in the form of a referendum. Is it possible to know which of the two claimed (and opposite) forms of political market failure better characterizes the underlying facts? Why or why not?

5.   Justice Scalia states: "[Amendment 2] sought to counter both the geographic concentration and the disproportionate political power of homosexuals by (1) resolving the controversy at the statewide level, and (2) making the election a single-issue contest for both sides. It put directly, to all the citizens of the State, the question: Should homosexuality be given special protection?" Consider this argument in light of the discussion of referenda. Does Amendment 2 relate to subject matter that is well suited to the referendum process? Is this an area in which it is normatively preferable to locate the preference of the median electoral voter or instead to allow those most affected by the proposed law to register their intensities of preference? Are the public choice tools developed in this chapter and more broadly in this book helpful in answering this question? Why or why not?

6.   Justice Scalia notes that Colorado was one of twenty-five states (at that time) that had repealed prior laws criminalizing homosexual behavior. Does that observation shed any light on the question of whether the *Romer* majority properly relied upon an animus analysis in striking the Colorado initiative down under rational basis scrutiny? Why or why not?

7.   After *Romer*, in 2003, the Supreme Court struck down *Bowers v. Hardwick*, in the case of *Lawrence v. Texas*, 539 U.S. 558 (2003). Justice Scalia relies upon *Bowers* in his dissenting opinion in *Romer* as reflecting social norms consistent with Amendment 2. Does the rejection by the Supreme Court of *Bowers* affect the analysis? If so, how?

*

INDEX

References are to Pages

___

A

Abortion. *See also* Husband and wife
    Generally, 442–446
    Constitutional design, 521–522
    Dimensionality, 132–133, 337
    Median voter theorem, 98–99
    Parliamentary rules, dimensionality and symmetry, 132–133
    Partial-birth abortion, 475–476, 497–498
    Presidential elections, dimensionality and turnout, 337
    Voting, rationality of, 22
Abramowicz, Michael
    Bush–Gore, election in 2000, 484–490
Absolute priority rule
    Bankruptcy, 166
Ackerman, Bruce
    Individual rationality, assumption of, 8–9
    Interest groups, special protection of minorities, 86–87
Administrative agencies. *See also* Agriculture and farms; Banks and banking; Environmental protection; Food stamps; New Deal
    Generally, 324–327
    For specific agencies, *see* names of specific agencies throughout this index
    Autonomy of agencies, motivations for bureaucratic action, 346–349
    Characteristics of agency behavior, 358–367
    Characteristics of bureaucratic action, 340–358
    Chevron deference. Judicial deference to agency interpretation of statutes, below
    Civil service system, 325, 357
    Constitutional design
        one-house veto of administrative action, 556–566
        purpose, 501–502
    Control by Congress as motive for bureaucratic action, 349–356
    Control by Congress of delegated legislative authority, 367–370
    Costs, response by executive branch to, 366–367
    Delegation of legislative authority, 258, 367–376
    Enactable preferences, Chevron deference, 287

Administrative agencies. *See also* Agriculture and farms; Banks and banking; Environmental protection; Food stamps; New Deal—Cont'd
    Expansion of agencies, motivations for bureaucratic action, 342–346
    False positives and false negatives, systematic bias in decision-making, 358–361
    Foreign poultry inspection rules, Chevron deference, 297–298, 299–314
    Independent *vs.* executive agencies, 324–327
    Judicial deference to agency interpretation of statutes
        generally, 328, 376–405
        Chevron deference
            generally, 383–391
            enactable preferences, statutory construction, 287
            foreign poultry inspection rules, 297–298, 299–314
            presidential elections, regulatory policy as affected by two-staged election, 338–340
        enactable preferences, Chevron deference, 287
        foreign poultry inspection rules, Chevron deference, 297–298, 299–314
        presidential elections, regulatory policy as affected by two-staged election, 338–340
        self interest of agency, deference to, 391–405
        Skidmore deference, 380, 385–390
    Marginality and cost externalization, 361–363
    Presidential elections, regulatory policy as affected by two-staged election, 338–340
    Public monitoring, motivations for bureaucratic action, 356–358
    Response by Congress to agency drift, 371–376
    Rulemaking, judicial review of agency action, 380–383
    Selection bias and commitment to regulatory mission, 363–366
    Self interest of agency, judicial deference to, 391–405
    Skidmore deference, 380, 385–390
    Systematic bias in decision-making, 358–361

References are to Pages

C

O

Z

Zywicki, Todd
  Administrative agencies
    judicial deference to agency determination of jurisdiction, 404
    selection bias and commitment to regulatory mission, 365
  Bankruptcy legislation and cycling, 163–164
  Bicameralism and Seventeenth Amendment, 516–517
  Common law courts, efficiency of, 465, 468–471, 473
  Constitutional design
    amendments, 555–556
    bicameralism and Seventeenth Amendment, 516–517

Zywicki—Cont'd
  Constitutional design—Cont'd
    federalism, 547–548
    judicial review and independent judiciary, 530–531
  Economic regulation theory, eminent domain and holdouts, 65–66
  Federalism, 547–548
  Federalism, matching problem, 535–536
  Judicial deference to agency determination of jurisdiction, 404
  New London urban restoration project, eminent domain and holdouts, 222
  Selection bias and commitment to regulatory mission, 365
  Stare decisis, interest groups, 431–433

†